Second Edition-2024

SYSTEMATIC APPROACH TO

GST

CA. S K Mishra

M.Com (Gold Medalist),
LL.B, MBA, FCA, FCMA

7/22, Ansari Road, Darya Ganj, New Delhi
Tel.: +91-11-4077 5252, 2327 3880
E-mail: orders@atlanticbooks.com
Web: www.atlanticbooks.com

Published by Atlantic Publishers & Distributors (P) Ltd 2024

First Edition, 2017
Second Edition, 2024

Disclaimer

- The author and the publisher have taken every effort to the maximum of their skill, expertise and knowledge to provide correct material in the book. Even then if some mistakes persist in the content of the book, the publisher does not take responsibility for the same. The publisher shall have no liability to any person or entity with respect to any loss or damage caused, or alleged to have been caused directly or indirectly, by the information contained in this book.
- The author has fully tried to follow the copyright law. However, if any work is found to be similar, it is unintentional and the same should not be used as defamatory or to file legal suit against the author.
- If the readers find any mistakes, we shall be grateful to them for pointing out those to us so that these can be corrected in the next edition.
- All disputes are subject to the jurisdiction of Delhi courts only.

Printed & bound in India by Atlantic Print Services

Foreword

Introduction of Goods and Services Tax (GST) in 2017 was not merely a tax reform. It was a complete overhaul of the pre-existing indirect tax regime. The journey with Goods and Services Tax (GST) that India Inc. embarked on six years back is finally turning into a successful tax regime. Considering the current taxation structure, it would not be inappropriate to conclude that the key objectives with which the GST was introduced, i.e., unifying the entire nation as a single market, are being achieved.

Since it was a new tax regime, taxpayers, tax professionals and tax authorities had to face various challenges in the implementation and compliance with the provisions of the GST laws. However, with the coordinated efforts of lawmakers, executives, judiciary, and other stakeholders, it can be seen that GST has begun to settle.

Like any other fiscal statute, compliances are the backbone for the implementation; therefore, it is of utmost importance that such compliances are undertaken in an appropriate manner.

The updated 2nd edition of the book title "**Systematic Approach to GST**" authored by CA. S K Mishra, has been written in a very lucid & simple language with a perspective to enable the taxpayers, GST practitioner & other stakeholders to ensure proper compliance with applicable provision of GST laws. I, congratulate CA. S K Mishra for bringing out this publication.

I am confident that the updated edition of the book will be extremely useful for the students of professional courses such as CA/CMA/CS, finance professionals, GST practitioners and other stakeholders as well.

Place: Faridabad

(R P Goyal)
Director (Finance)
NHPC Ltd

Preface to Second Edition

Goods & Services Tax (GST), India's biggest indirect tax reform since independence has turn six years on 30th June 2023. The Indian GST system is still in the making. The GST council is continuously reviewing the situation & making course correction. The GST council has so far met 52 times & the last meeting was held on 7th October 2023 at New Delhi. Tax rate structure has also been revised over the time to improve market competitiveness. Maximum revenue to the extent of around 65% of net GST collection comes from the 18% slab. The 28% slab fetches around 16% of revenue, while approx. 10% of GST collection comes from the 5% rate slab. In a major step, the highest 28% GST rate slab was substantially pruned to only about 50 tariff headings in November 2017, from 224 tariff headings. Thereafter, it is mostly luxury items or sin goods such as tobacco products, motor vehicles, yachts, air conditioners, personal use aircrafts, etc. that remain in this rate slab.

Prior to the launch of unified tax system as GST, Indian indirect tax regime was highly fragmented. Centre and States were separately taxing goods and services. The Centre was empowered to tax goods at the production or manufacturing stage, whereas the States had the power to tax goods at distribution stage. The Centre was also empowered to levy tax on services. The States were precluded from taxing services.

The Constitution (101st Amendment) Act, 2016 paved the way for implementation of GST in India. Article 246A (intra-state supply) & Article 269A (inter-state supply) of the 101st Constitution Amendment Act, 2016 are the enabling provisions for levy of GST in India. In view of the federal structure of our country, India has adopted a "Dual GST" model. Centre and States both have been empowered to levy GST on every supply of goods or services or both (*unless otherwise exempted or kept outside the ambit of GST*), which takes place within a State or Union Territory. Article 246A confers simultaneous power to the Union & State legislature to legislate upon the GST. In respect of inter-state supply of goods or services or both, the Central Government alone has been empowered to levy IGST.

GST has transformed the entire landscape of how business is transacted in the country. GST has not only created a uniform market in India but also has eliminated cascading effect of taxes, and allows seamless & cross utilization of input tax credit. Further, the entire process of GST is completely online, i.e. from filing application for registration to return filing, payment of taxes, refund claim, e-invoicing, e-way bill, cancellation of registration, assessment & proceedings, etc. E-invoicing has been introduced to automate tax-filing processes for taxpayers.

The GST Regime has created an enabling environment for the Micro, Small and Medium Enterprise (MSME) to grow. Many relaxation & exemptions have been provided to small entrepreneur in GST. Special measures for MSMEs provided ease of compliances through Composition Scheme, QRMP Scheme, optional annual return and waiver of annual reconciliation statement. The threshold limit of registration for supplier of goods have been kept at ₹40 lakhs. Small businesses with aggregate annual turnover up to ₹1.5 crores can opt for Composition scheme & pay GST at fixed rate on their turnover without filing return on monthly basis. The benefits of composition scheme have been extended to service provider also by making amendment in the Act. The amendment made by Finance Act, 2023 has also allowed composition scheme dealer to sell goods through e-commerce platform. Compliance burden on MSMEs has reduced significantly with the option of availing the QRMP (Quarterly Return with Monthly Payment) scheme by the taxpayers having aggregate annual turnover up to ₹5 crore. The requirement of mandatory audit of accounts by a CA/CMA which was provided in Sec 35(5) of CGST Act, 2017 has been omitted by Finance Act, 2021 thereby giving huge relief to the registered person.

The prime objective of any tax reform is simplified tax administration, minimal compliance/documentations, reduction in tax evasion, improvement in ease of doing business & increased tax revenue for the govt. The government is relentlessly trying to simplify GST laws for better tax compliance & a non-intrusive tax system. Various administrative and policy based interventions have resulted in higher compliance by the taxpayers. A number of significant developments/changes has taken place in the GST Acts/Rules since its implementation. E-way bill for inter-state movement of goods, TDS/TCS provision, blocking of E-Way bill for non-filers of GST Return, E-Invoicing for registered person having turnover more than ₹5 crores (B2B supply) & invoicing matching facilities for availing ITC has been introduced to check tax evasion.

GST is indeed a complex subject. It requires organized study constantly over a period of time to gain effective understanding & command over the subject. All efforts have been made to make the language simple & the provisions of GST law have been explained in a very lucid manner.

We hope the updated second edition of this book will be quite helpful for the reader to gain conceptual clarity on the subject.

Comments, suggestions and criticisms from the readers relating to the present work are most welcome. The readers may write to us at gstresolve@gmail.com.

Place: New Delhi

(CA. S K Mishra)
Author

Preface to First Edition

Goods & Services Tax (GST) is a comprehensive tax on supply of goods or services or both. It is one of the major tax reforms since independence in the area of indirect taxation. The reform that took more than a decade of mutual co-operation, continuous discussion and intense debate between Central and State Governments about implementation methodology, has been finally implemented with effect from 1st July 2017, subsuming almost all indirect taxes levied at the Central and State levels.

GST has been introduced with the objective to mitigate the cascading effect of taxes by allowing seamless credit across goods and services, facilitate free flow of goods and services across India and boosting tax revenue from better compliance and widening the tax base. A remarkable feature of GST implementation is that all the States in India came together with the Centre to form a unique federal body called GST Council, which is entrusted with the objective of recommending policies and procedural matters in the formation and implementation of GST legislation.

The Constitution (101st Amendment) Act, 2016 paved the way for implementation of GST in India. In view of the federal structure of our country, India has adopted a "Dual GST" model. Centre and States both have been empowered to levy GST on every supply of goods or services or both (unless otherwise exempted or kept outside the ambit of GST), which takes place within a State or Union Territory. In respect of inter-state supply of goods or services or both, the Central Government alone has been empowered to levy IGST.

Since it is a new tax regime, taxpayers, GST practitioner and finance professional may face various challenges in the implementation and compliance with the provisions of the GST laws. In order to ease GST compliance, the present edition of the book have been written in a very lucid language supported with relevant rules, notifications etc. & legal jargon have been kept to the minimum in order to facilitate understanding of the various provision of GST laws. The book cover procedural aspects like registration, refund, return, invoice, input tax credit etc. An attempt have been made to cover all important provision of GST laws at one place and is intended to give general guidance to all stakeholders and also help them in resolving issues that they may face during the course of their compliances under GST.

We hope, the 1st edition of the book will be quite helpful for the taxpayer, finance professionals & other stake holders in a hassle free compliance of GST laws.

Comments, suggestions and criticisms from the readers relating to the present work are most welcome.

Place: New Delhi

(CA. S K Mishra)
Author

GST Compliance Calendar

Taxpayer Type	Return/FORM	Return filing frequency	Due Date	Remarks
Aggregate Turnover > ₹5 Crores	GSTR 1	Monthly	11th of following month	Return of outward supply
Aggregate Turnover < ₹5 Crores	GSTR 1	Monthly	11th of following month	Return of outward supply
Aggregate Turnover < ₹5 Crores	GSTR 1 IFF (QRMP Scheme)	Monthly	13th of following month	Return of outward supply
Aggregate Turnover > ₹5 Crores	GSTR 3B	Monthly	20th of following month	
Aggregate Turnover < ₹5 Crores	GSTR 3B	Monthly	20th of following month	
Aggregate Turnover up to ₹5 Crores	GSTR 3B	Quarterly	22nd of month following the end of Quarter	Chhattisgarh, Madhya Pradesh, Gujarat, Maharashtra, Karnataka, Goa, Kerala, Tamil Nadu, Telangana, Andhra Pradesh, Daman & Diu and Dadra & Nagar Haveli, Puducherry, Andaman and Nicobar Islands, Lakshadweep
Aggregate Turnover up to ₹5 Crores	GSTR 3B	Quarterly	24th of month following the end of Quarter	Himachal Pradesh, Punjab, Uttarakhand, Haryana, Rajasthan, Uttar Pradesh, Bihar, Sikkim, Arunachal Pradesh, Nagaland, Manipur, Mizoram, Tripura, Meghalaya, Assam, West Bengal, Jharkhand, Odisha, Jammu and Kashmir, Ladakh, Chandigarh, Delhi
Non Resident Tax payer	GSTR 5	Monthly	13th of following month	
OIDAR Service Provider	GSTR 5A	Monthly	20th of following month	
Input Service Distributors	GSTR 6	Monthly	13th of following month	

TDS Deductor (U/s 51)	GSTR 7	Monthly	10th of following month	Govt Deptt, PSU, Local authority etc
TCS Collector (U/s 52)	GSTR 8	Monthly	10th of following month	E Commerce Operator
Annual Return	GSTR 9	Annually	31st December following the end of relevant financial year	Registered person having aggregate turnover more than ₹2 Crores
Annual Return	GSTR 9C	Annually	31st December following the end of relevant financial year	Registered person having aggregate turnover more than ₹5 Crores
Final Return	GSTR 10	Once	Within 3 months of cancellation of Registration	Registered person whose registration has been cancelled or surrendered
UIN holders	GSTR 11	Monthly	28th of following month	
QRMP Scheme Tax Payers	PMT 06	Monthly	25th of following month	Challan for payment of taxes, interest, penalties under GST

Major Policy Initiatives at a Glance (Post Roll-out of GST in July 2017)

Sl. No.	Subject matter	Implementation date
1	Time of supply de-linked with receipt of advance in case of supply of goods	October 2017
2	Supply of services through e-commerce operator without mandatory registration up to specified threshold	November 2017
3	Increase in limit of composition scheme for supplier of goods – up to ₹1.5 crore (₹75 lakh for certain States)	April 2019
4	Composition scheme for service providers – Sec 10(2A)	April 2019
5	Interest on Net Cash Liability	Retrospectively w.e.f. 1st July, 2017
6	Nationwide e-Way bill system for inter-State movement of goods	01st April, 2018
7	TDS provision under GST	October 2018
8	Increase in threshold limit for registration of supplier of goods up to ₹40 lakh (₹20 lakh in certain States)	April 2019
8	Composition Scheme for supplier of services	April 2019
9	Blocking of generation of e-way bill for supply of goods, when the supplier has defaulted in furnishing of GST returns	August 2021
10	Transfer of funds from one head to another in Electronic Cash Ledger	April 2020
11	Filing of NIL return by SMS	June 2020
12	Aadhar linked registration	August 2020
13	Auto drafted input tax credit statement in FORM GSTR-2B	August 2020
14	E-invoicing for B2B supplies for registered person having turnover of ₹500 crores or more (reduced to ₹10 Crores in graded manner)	October 2020
15	Editing facilities in GSTR-3B	December 2020
16	QR based B2C Invoices	December 2020
17	Linkage of GSTR-1/GSTR-2B with GSTR-3B	December 2020
18	Quarterly Return Monthly Payment (QRMP) Scheme	January 2021
19	Maximum late fee on late filing of Nil GSTR-1/GSTR-3B caped at ₹500	June 2021
20	Automatic revocation of suspension of registration upon filing of pending return	July 2022
21	Refund of unutilized Input Tax Credit on account of Export of Electricity	July 2022
22	Omission of Mandatory audit of accounts by a practicing CA/CMA under Sec 35(5) of CGST Act by Finance Act 2021	August 2021

23	Self-certified Reconciliation Statement (GSTR 9C) for taxpayers having aggregate annual turnover of more than ₹5 crore	August 2021 (For Reconciliation Statement for the FY 2020-21 onwards)
24	Reduced frequency of filing ITC -04 in respect of goods sent to job worker (a) turnover above ₹5 Crores–once in six months (b) turnover up to ₹5 Crores – Annually (Notification No. 35/2021-Central Tax dated 24.09.2021)	October 2021
25	Reporting of ITC availment, reversal and Ineligible ITC in Table 4 of GSTR 3B	September 2022
26	Transfer of balance in electronic cash ledger (ECL) from one GSTIN to other GSTIN of same legal entity (distinct person) through GST PMT-09	October 2022
27	Do away with the concept of claiming input tax credit on a provisional basis	October 2022
28	Minimum threshold limit of tax amount for lunching prosecution raised to ₹2 Crores from ₹1 Crores	Amended by Finance Act 2023
29	E-commerce operator shall be liable to pay penalty if inter-state supply of goods & services is allowed to in-eligible person	Amended by Finance Act 2023
30	Maximum time period allowed for filing GST return (GSTR-1/GSTR-3B & GSTR-9) restricted to three years	Amended by Finance Act 2023
31	ITC not available in respect of GST paid on goods or services procured which are used for CSR activities	Amended by Finance Act 2023
32	Composition scheme dealer allowed to supply goods through e-commerce portal	Amended by Finance Act 2023
33	De-criminalize certain offences specified under clause (g), (j) and (k) of section 132(1) of CGST Act, 2017	Amended by Finance Act 2023
34	Reduction in fee for late filing of Annual Return (GSTR-9) by registered person having aggregate turnover up to ₹20 Crores	49th GST Council meeting -18th Feb 2023
35	Time limit for making an application for revocation of cancellation of registration increased from 30 days to 90 days	49th GST Council meeting -18th Feb 2023
36	Time period for filing of return by non-filers for enabling deemed withdrawal of best judgment assessment order increased from 30 days to 60 days	49th GST Council meeting -18th Feb 2023
37	Threshold limit for issuing E-Invoicing reduced from ₹10 Crores to ₹5 Crores	1st August 2023
38	Registered person with aggregate turnover upto ₹2 Crores in the FY 2022-23 have been exempted from filing Annual Return in GSTR 9 for the said financial year, Vide Notification No.32/2023–CT Dated 31-07-2023	July 2023
39	Actionable claims supplied in Casinos, Horse racing and Online gaming taxable at the rate of 28% on full face value, irrespective of whether the activities are a game of skill or chance	51st GST Council meeting -2nd August 2023
40	Waive off the requirement of mandatory registration under section 24(ix) of CGST Act for person supplying goods through ECOs, subject to certain conditions	1st October 2023
41	Supply of all goods & services by Indian Railways taxable under forward charge (N. No. 14/2023–CT (R) Dated 19-10-2023)	20th October 2023
42	Services provided to a Governmental Authority by way of water supply, public health, sanitation and conservancy, solid waste management and slum improvement and upgradation have been exempted from levy of GST. (N. No. 13/2023–CT (R) Dated 19-10-2023)	20th October 2023

Contents

Arrangement of Sections The Central Goods & Services Tax Act, 2017

The Integrated Goods & Services Tax Act, 2017

The Goods & Services Tax (Compensation to States) Act, 2017

Section	Description
1	Short title, extent and commencement
2	Definitions
3	Projected growth rate
4	Base year
5	Base year revenue
6	Projected revenue for any year
7	Calculation and release of compensation
8	Levy & collection of Cess
9	Returns, payments and refunds
10	Crediting proceeds of Cess to Fund
11	Other provisions relating to Cess
12	Power to make rules
13	Laying of rules before Parliament
14	Power to remove difficulties
8(2)	Compensation Cess Rate Schedule

The Central Goods & Services Rules, 2017

Chapter	Description	Rule
1	Chapter I: Preliminary	1-2
2	Chapter II: Composition Levy	2-6
3	Chapter III: Registration	8-26
4	Chapter IV: Determination of Value of Supply	27-35
5	Chapter V: Input Tax Credit	36-45
6	Chapter VI: Tax Invoice, Credit & Debit Notes	46-55A
7	Chapter VII: Accounts & Records	56-58
8	Chapter VIII: Returns	59-84
9	Chapter IX: Payment of Tax	85-88A
10	Chapter X: Refund	89-97A
11	Chapter XI: Assessment & Audit	98-102
12	Chapter XII: Advance Ruling	103-107A
13	Chapter XIII: Appeals & Revision	108-116
14	Chapter XIV: Transitional Provision	117-121
15	Chapter XV: Anti-Profiteering	122-137
16	Chapter XVI: E Way Rules	138-138E
17	Chapter XVII: Inspection, Search & Seizure	139-141
18	Chapter XVIII: Demands & Recovery	142-161
19	Chapter XIX: Offences & Penalties	162

Articles of Constitutions of India

Article No.	Description
1(1)	India is Union of States
148	C&AG Audit
243G	Functions entrusted to Panchayat
243W	Functions entrusted to Municipality
245	Bifurcation of Power between Union & States
246A	Concurrent power to Union & States to levy GST
248	Residual powers with Parliament
265	Taxation Powers-Limitations under Constitution
268 to 271	Distribution of Revenue between Union & States
269A	IGST for inter-state supply
269A(1)	Apportionment of IGST between Union & States
269A(2)	Powers to determine place of supply & interstate supply
279A	Council of GST
286	Restriction on power of taxation
301 to 303	Inter-state Trade & commerce—No restrictions
366(12)	Definitions of "goods"
366(12A)	Definitions of "GST"
366(26A)	Definitions of "service"
366(29A)	Deemed sale of goods under Constitution

Chapter 1

Basic Concepts

1.1 PREAMBLE

The Central Goods and Services Tax Act, 2017 (CGST Act) is an Act to make a provision for levy and collection of tax on intra-State supply of goods or services or both by the Central Government and for matters connected therewith or incidental thereto.

1.2 EXTENT AND COMMENCEMENT

The CGST Act, 2017 extends to the whole of India including the state of Jammu & Kashmir. The appointed day is 1st July 2017 for whole of India except the state of J&K. The appointed day for the State of Jammu and Kashmir is 8th July 2017. The introduction of Jammu & Kashmir Reorganization Act, 2019 has led to the bifurcation of State of Jammu & Kashmir into two Union Territories, namely the Union Territory of Jammu & Kashmir & the Union Territory of Ladakh. The Re-organization is effective from 31st October 2019.

1.3 INTRODUCTION TO GST

Goods and Services Tax (GST) is a comprehensive, multi-stage, destination-based indirect tax levied on the supply of goods and services. Comprehensive because it has subsumed almost all the indirect taxes barring few. Multi-staged, as it is imposed at every step in the supply chain, but is meant to be refunded to all parties in the supply chain other than the ultimate consumer. A destination-based tax, as it is collected from point of consumption and not point of origin like previous indirect tax regime (e.g. excise duty (ED) on manufacturer).

The term "GST" has been defined in Article 366 (12A) of the Constitution of India as under: "Goods and services tax" means any tax on supply of goods, or services or both except taxes on the supply of the alcoholic liquor for human consumption.

As per Sec. 2(52) of CGST Act: "Goods" means every kind of movable property other than money and securities but includes actionable claim, growing crops, grass and things attached to or forming part of the land which are agreed to be severed before supply or under a contract of supply.

As per Sec. 2(102) of CGST Act: "Services" means anything other than goods, money and securities but includes activity relating to the use of money or its conversion by cash or by any other mode, from one form, currency or denomination, to another form, currency or denomination for which a separate consideration is charged.

Explanation: For the removal of doubts, it is hereby clarified that the expression "services" includes facilitating or arranging transactions in securities.

Broadly,

(a) all movable property other than money and securities is goods and

(b) anything other than goods, money and securities is defined as services.

So, money and securities have been excluded from the definition of goods as also services.

1.4 CONSTITUTIONAL PROVISION

India has a three-tier federal structure, comprising the Union Government, the State Governments and the Local Government. The power to levy taxes and duties is distributed among the three tiers of Governments, in accordance with the provisions of the Indian Constitution.

The Constitution of India is the supreme law of India. It consists of a Preamble, 25 parts containing 448 Articles and 12 Schedules.

Power to levy Goods & Services Tax (GST) has been conferred by Article 246A through the 101st Constitution Amendment Act, which was promulgated on 8th September 2016.

Article 246A: Power to make laws with respect to Goods and Services Tax:

Newly inserted Article 246A

(1) Notwithstanding anything contained in Articles 246 and 254, Parliament, and, subject to clause (2), the Legislature of every State, have power to make laws with respect to goods and services tax imposed by the Union or by such State.

(2) Parliament has exclusive power to make laws with respect to goods and services tax where the supply of goods, or of services, or both takes place in the course of inter-State trade or commerce.

Explanation: The provisions of this article, shall, in respect of goods and services tax referred to in clause (5) of Article 279A, take effect from the date recommended by the Goods and Services Tax Council.

1.5 POWER TO LEVY

Power to levy and collect taxes whether, direct or indirect emerges from the constitution of India. Article 265 of the Constitution provides that 'no tax shall be levied or collected except by Authority of Law'.

The Constitution includes three lists in the Seventh Schedule providing authority to the Central Government and the State Governments to levy and collect taxes on subjects stated in the lists.

Seventh Schedule to Article 246 of Constitution		
Union List (List I)	**State List (List II)**	**Concurrent List (List III)**
It contains the matters in respect of which the Parliament (Central Government has exclusive right to make laws).	It contains the matters in respect of which the State Governments has exclusive right to make laws.	It contains the matters in respect of which both the Central & State Governments have power to make laws.

Entries 82 to 97 of List I enumerate the subjects where the Central Government has power to levy taxes. Entries 45 to 63 of List II enumerate the subjects where the State Governments have the power to levy taxes. Parliament has a further power to make any law for any part of India not comprised in a State even if such matter is included in the State List.

Income tax is levied by virtue of Entry 82-Taxes on income other than agricultural income and customs duty vide Entry 83-Duties of Customs including export duties of the Union List.

Entry 92-C of List I (Service Tax) has been now deleted from Union list.

Entry 52 of List II (Entry tax for sale in state) has been now deleted from State list.

Entry 55 of List I (Advertisement) have been now deleted from State list.

Power to Levy Goods & Services Tax (GST) has been conferred by Article 246A of the Constitution, which was introduced by the Constitution (101st Amendment) Act 2016.

Article 268A has been repealed so as to subsumed Service tax within the ambit of GST.

Article 269 empowers the Parliament to make GST laws for inter-State trade/commerce.

Article 269A has been inserted which provides for goods and services tax on supplies in the course of inter-State trade or commerce which shall be levied and collected by the Government of India.

Article 270 provides for distribution of GST collected by the Union between the Union & the State.

Article 271 has been amended which restricts power of the Parliament to levy surcharge under GST. In effect, surcharge cannot be imposed on goods and services which are subject to tax under Article 246A.

Article 279A provides for constitution of GST council.

1.6 GST ACTS & RULES

The CGST Act came into operation on 01.07.2017, the date appointed by the Central Government. Certain provisions were came into force w.e.f. 22.06.2017 and the remaining provisions from 1st July 2017 as notified by the Central Government. Hence, appointed day for the CGST Act, IGST, UTGST Acts, SGST Acts is 1st July 2017.

The appointed day for the State of Jammu and Kashmir is 8th July 2017.

The Jammu & Kashmir Reorganization Act, 2019 which became effective from 31st October 2019 has led to the bifurcation of State of Jammu & Kashmir into two Union Territories namely the Union Territory of Jammu & Kashmir & the Union Territory of Ladakh.

Sl No.	GST Acts	Number of Sections	Number of Schedules
1.	The Central Goods & Services Tax Act, 2017	174	3
2.	The Integrated Goods & Services Tax Act, 2017	25	-
3.	The Union Territory Goods & Services Tax Act, 2017	26	-
4.	The Goods & Services Tax (Compensation to States) Act, 2017	14	1

Though each State & Union territories of India have their own GST Act, all the provisions in these Acts are identical with Central Goods & Services tax Act (CGST Act).

1.7 RATE OF GST

The CGST/SGST & IGST Acts do not provide for GST rate structure. Rates under GST shall be as may be notified by the Government on the recommendations of the GST Council.

As per Section 9 of CGST Act, rate of CGST will be as notified by Central/State Government. The CGST rate shall not exceed 20%. Similar provision is there in SGST Act of each state. Thus, total GST rate for intra-state supplies will not exceed 40%.

As per Section 5 of IGST Act, rate of IGST will be as notified by Central Government. The IGST rate shall not exceed 40%.

Compensation Cess u/s 8 of the Goods & Services Tax (Compensation to States) Act, 2017 is levied on certain specified luxury and demerit goods, like tobacco and tobacco products, pan masala, aerated water, motor vehicles, etc.

The maximum rate of GST prescribed under different Acts are as under:

Act	Authority to notify GST rate	Maximum rate of GST
CGST Act	Central Government	20% u/s 9
SGST Act	Concern State Government	20% u/s 9
UTGST Act	Central Government	20% u/s 7
IGST Act	Central Government	40% u/s 5

(a) CGST & IGST Rate Schedule of Goods

The Central Government vide Notification No. 01/2017-Central Tax (Rate), dt. 28-06-2017 and Notification No. 01/2017-Integrated Tax (Rate), dt. 28-06-2017 has notified CGST and IGST rates for intra-State and inter-State supplies of goods categorized into following six schedules which is effective from 1st July 2017.

Schedule	Rate of CGST	Rate of IGST
I	2.5%	5%
II	6%	12%
III	9%	18%
IV	14%	28%
V	1.5%	3%
VI	0.125%	0.25%

Equivalent rate of SGST/UTGST similar to that of CGST shall also be levied. Rate of IGST is approximately the sum total of CGST and SGST/UTGST. The rate of tax so notified will apply on the value of supply as determined under Section 15.

In addition to above, GST Compensation Cess over the peak rate of 28%, may also be levy on certain luxury and demerit goods like Motor Vehicles, Yacht, Aircraft, Coal, Lignite, Cigarettes, Pan Masala, Tobacco etc. under Section 8 of the Goods and Services Tax (Compensation to States) Cess Act, 2017.

(b) GST Rate Schedule for Services

The GST Council has broadly approved the GST rates for services at Nil, 5%, 12%, 18% and 28%. The Central Government vide Notification No. 12/2017-Central Tax (Rate) dated 28.06.2017 has notified the list of services which attract Nil rate of GST (i.e. exempted services).

1.8 INDIRECT TAXES SUBSUMED & NOT SUBSUMED INTO GST

The GST law has subsumed almost all previous indirect taxes that were levied on production/sale of goods or provision of services by either Central or State Government. Subsuming of large number of indirect taxes and other levies will now allow free flow of larger pool of tax credits at both Central and State level.

(A) State Taxes

Taxes subsumed	Taxes NOT subsumed
Value added tax (VAT)/State Sales Tax	State excise duty on alcoholic liquor for human consumption
Entry tax	Stamp duty
Octroi	Motor Vehicle tax
Purchase Tax	Sales tax on five petroleum products such as Crude oil, Petrol, diesel, Natural Gas, ATF
Luxury tax	Electricity duty
Taxes on Betting, Gambling & Lottery	Entertainment Tax levied by local authority
State Surcharge & Cess	Professional Tax (Tax on employment)

(B) Central Taxes

Taxes subsumed	Taxes NOT subsumed
Central Excise Duty (CENVAT)	Basic Customs Duty
Additional Duties of Excise	Tax on Securities
Excise on Medicinal and Toiletries Preparation Act	
Additional Customs Duty (CVD)–equal to central excise on like goods manufactured in India	
Special Additional Duty of Customs (SAD)–Supposed to be equal to CST which was earlier 4%. Not changed in spite of drop in CST rate to 2%.	
Central Sales Tax (CST)	
Surcharge & Cess	
Service Tax	

Notes

1. CVD and SAD are customs duties charged on import of goods but in lieu of excise duty and VAT respectively.
2. Amongst Customs duties, only CVD and SAD have been subsumed into GST, but basic customs duty has not been subsumed into GST.

Chapter 2

Definitions

The various terms under GST has been defined in Section 2 of the Central Goods & Services Tax (CGST) Act, 2017 as under:

(1) "actionable claim" shall have the same meaning as assigned to it in section 3 of the Transfer of Property Act, 1882;

(2) "address of delivery" means the address of the recipient of goods or services or both indicated on the tax invoice issued by a registered person for delivery of such goods or services or both;

(3) "address on record" means the address of the recipient as available in the records of the supplier;

(4) "adjudicating authority" means any authority, appointed or authorised to pass any order or decision under this Act, but does not include the Central Board of Indirect Taxes and Customs, the Revisional Authority, the Authority for Advance Ruling, the Appellate Authority for Advance Ruling [the Appellate Authority, the Appellate Tribunal and the Authority referred to in sub-section (2) of section 171];

(5) "agent" means a person, including a factor, broker, commission agent, *arhatia*, *del credere* agent, an auctioneer or any other mercantile agent, by whatever name called, who carries on the business of supply or receipt of goods or services or both on behalf of another;

(6) "aggregate turnover" means the aggregate value of all taxable supplies (excluding the value of inward supplies on which tax is payable by a person on reverse charge basis), exempt supplies, exports of goods or services or both and inter-State supplies of persons having the same Permanent Account Number, to be computed on all India basis but excludes central tax, State tax, Union territory tax, integrated tax and cess;

(7) "agriculturist" means an individual or a Hindu Undivided Family who undertakes cultivation of land:

(a) by own labour, or

(b) by the labour of family, or

(c) by servants on wages payable in cash or kind or by hired labour under personal supervision or the personal supervision of any member of the family;

(8) "Appellate Authority" means an authority appointed or authorised to hear appeals as referred to in section 107;

(9) "Appellate Tribunal" means the Goods and Services Tax Appellate Tribunal constituted under section 109;

(10) "appointed day" means the date on which the provisions of this Act shall come into force;

(11) "assessment" means determination of tax liability under this Act and includes self-assessment, re-assessment, provisional assessment, summary assessment and best judgment assessment;

(12) "associated enterprises" shall have the same meaning as assigned to it in section 92A of the Income-tax Act, 1961;

(13) "audit" means the examination of records, returns and other documents maintained or furnished by the registered person under this Act or the rules made there under or under any other law for the time being in force to verify the correctness of turnover declared, taxes paid, refund claimed and input tax credit availed, and to assess his compliance with the provisions of this Act or the rules made thereunder;

(14) "authorised bank" shall mean a bank or a branch of a bank authorised by the Government to collect the tax or any other amount payable under this Act;

(15) "authorised representative" means the representative as referred to in section 116;

(16) "Board" means the Central Board of Indirect Taxes and Customs constituted under the Central Boards of Revenue Act, 1963;

(17) "business" includes:

(a) any trade, commerce, manufacture, profession, vocation, adventure, wager or any other similar activity, whether or not it is for a pecuniary benefit;

(b) any activity or transaction in connection with or incidental or ancillary to sub-clause (a);

(c) any activity or transaction in the nature of sub-clause (a), whether or not there is volume, frequency, continuity or regularity of such transaction;

(d) supply or acquisition of goods including capital goods and services in connection with commencement or closure of business;

(e) provision by a club, association, society, or any such body (for a subscription or any other consideration) of the facilities or benefits to its members;

(f) admission, for a consideration, of persons to any premises;

(g) services supplied by a person as the holder of an office which has been accepted by him in the course or furtherance of his trade, profession or vocation;

(h) activities of a race club including by way of totalisator or a license to book maker or activities of a licensed book maker in such club; and

(i) any activity or transaction undertaken by the Central Government, a State Government or any local authority in which they are engaged as public authorities;

(18) "business vertical" means a distinguishable component of an enterprise that is engaged in the supply of individual goods or services or a group of related goods or services which is subject to risks and returns that are different from those of the other business verticals.

Explanation: For the purposes of this clause, factors that should be considered in determining whether goods or services are related include:

(a) the nature of the goods or services;

(b) the nature of the production processes;

(c) the type or class of customers for the goods or services;

(d) the methods used to distribute the goods or supply of services; and

(e) the nature of regulatory environment (wherever applicable), including banking, insurance, or public utilities;

Note: This definition has been omitted in entirety as per CGST Amendment Act 2018;

(19) "capital goods" means goods, the value of which is capitalised in the books of account of the person claiming the input tax credit and which are used or intended to be used in the course or furtherance of business;

(20) "casual taxable person" means a person who occasionally undertakes transactions involving supply of goods or services or both in the course or furtherance of business, whether as principal, agent or in any other capacity, in a State or a Union territory where he has no fixed place of business;

(21) "central tax" means the central goods and services tax levied under section 9;

(22) "cess" shall have the same meaning as assigned to it in the Goods and Services Tax (Compensation to States) Act;

(23) "chartered accountant" means a chartered accountant as defined in clause (b) of sub-section (1) of section 2 of the Chartered Accountants Act, 1949;

(24) "Commissioner" means the Commissioner of central tax and includes the Principal Commissioner of central tax appointed under section 3 and the Commissioner of integrated tax appointed under the Integrated Goods and Services Tax Act;

(25) "Commissioner in the Board" means the Commissioner referred to in section 168;

(26) "common portal" means the common goods and services tax electronic portal referred to in section 146;

(27) "common working days" in respect of a State or Union territory shall mean such days in succession which are not declared as gazetted holidays by the Central Government or the concerned State or Union territory Government;

(28) "company secretary" means a company secretary as defined in clause (c) of sub-section (1) of section 2 of the Company Secretaries Act, 1980;

(29) "competent authority" means such authority as may be notified by the Government;

(30) "composite supply" means a supply made by a taxable person to a recipient consisting of two or more taxable supplies of goods or services or both, or any combination thereof, which are naturally bundled and supplied in conjunction with each other in the ordinary course of business, one of which is a principal supply;

Illustration: *Where goods are packed and transported with insurance, the supply of goods, packing materials, transport and insurance is a composite supply and supply of goods is a principal supply;*

(31) "consideration" in relation to the supply of goods or services or both includes:

(a) any payment made or to be made, whether in money or otherwise, in respect of, in response to, or for the inducement of, the supply of goods or services or both, whether by the recipient or by any other person but shall not include any subsidy given by the Central Government or a State Government;

(b) the monetary value of any act or forbearance, in respect of, in response to, or for the inducement of, the supply of goods or services or both, whether by the recipient or by any other person but shall not include any subsidy given by the Central Government or a State Government:

Provided that a deposit given in respect of the supply of goods or services or both shall not be considered as payment made for such supply unless the supplier applies such deposit as consideration for the said supply;

(32) "continuous supply of goods" means a supply of goods which is provided, or agreed to be provided, continuously or on recurrent basis, under a contract, whether or not by means of a wire, cable, pipeline or other conduit, and for which the supplier invoices the recipient on a regular or periodic basis and includes supply of such goods as the Government may, subject to such conditions, as it may, by notification, specify;

(33) "continuous supply of services" means a supply of services which is provided, or agreed to be provided, continuously or on recurrent basis, under a contract, for a period exceeding three months with periodic payment obligations and includes supply of such services as the Government may, subject to such conditions, as it may, by notification, specify;

(34) "conveyance" includes a vessel, an aircraft and a vehicle;

(35) "cost accountant" means a cost accountant as defined in clause (b) of sub-section (1) of section 2 of the Cost and Works Accountants Act, 1959;

(36) "Council" means the Goods and Services Tax Council established under article 279A of the Constitution;

(37) "credit note" means a document issued by a registered person under sub-section (1) of section 34;

(38) "debit note" means a document issued by a registered person under sub-section (3) of section 34;

(39) "deemed exports" means such supplies of goods as may be notified under section 147;

(40) "designated authority" means such authority as may be notified by the Board;

(41) "document" includes written or printed record of any sort and electronic record as defined in clause (t) of section 2 of the Information Technology Act, 2000;

(42) "drawback" in relation to any goods manufactured in India and exported, means the rebate of duty, tax or cess chargeable on any imported inputs or on any domestic inputs or input services used in the manufacture of such goods;

(43) "electronic cash ledger" means the electronic cash ledger referred to in sub-section (1) of section 49;

(44) "electronic commerce" means the supply of goods or services or both, including digital products over digital or electronic network;

(45) "electronic commerce operator" means any person who owns, operates or manages digital or electronic facility or platform for electronic commerce;

(46) "electronic credit ledger" means the electronic credit ledger referred to in sub-section (2) of section 49;

(47) "exempt supply" means supply of any goods or services or both which attracts *nil* rate of tax or which may be wholly exempt from tax under section 11, or under section 6 of the Integrated Goods and Services Tax Act, and includes non-taxable supply;

(48) "existing law" means any law, notification, order, rule or regulation relating to levy and collection of duty or tax on goods or services or both passed or made before the commencement of this Act by Parliament or any Authority or person having the power to make such law, notification, order, rule or regulation;

(49) "family" means:

(i) the spouse and children of the person, and

(ii) the parents, grandparents, brothers and sisters of the person if they are wholly or mainly dependent on the said person;

(50) "fixed establishment" means a place (other than the registered place of business) which is characterized by a sufficient degree of permanence and suitable structure in terms of human and technical resources to supply services, or to receive and use services for its own needs.

(51) "Fund" means the Consumer Welfare Fund established under section 57;

(52) "goods" means every kind of movable property other than money and securities but includes actionable claim, growing crops, grass and things attached to or forming part of the land which are agreed to be severed before supply or under a contract of supply;

(53) "Government" means the Central Government;

(54) "Goods and Services Tax (Compensation to States) Act" means the Goods and Services Tax (Compensation to States) Act, 2017;

(55) "goods and services tax practitioner" means any person who has been approved under section 48 to act as such practitioner;

(56) "India" means the territory of India as referred to in article 1 of the Constitution, its territorial waters, seabed and sub-soil underlying such waters, continental shelf, exclusive economic zone or any other maritime zone as referred to in the Territorial Waters, Continental Shelf, Exclusive Economic Zone and other Maritime Zones Act, 1976, and the air space above its territory and territorial waters;

(57) "Integrated Goods and Services Tax Act" means the Integrated Goods and Services Tax Act, 2017;

(58) "integrated tax" means the integrated goods and services tax levied under the Integrated Goods and Services Tax Act;

(59) "input" means any goods other than capital goods used or intended to be used by a supplier in the course or furtherance of business;

(60) "input service" means any service used or intended to be used by a supplier in the course or furtherance of business;

(61) "Input Service Distributor" means an office of the supplier of goods or services or both which receives tax invoices issued under section 31 towards the receipt of input services and issues a prescribed document for the purposes of distributing the credit of central tax, State tax, integrated tax or Union territory tax paid on the said services to a supplier of taxable goods or services or both having the same Permanent Account Number as that of the said office;

(62) "input tax" in relation to a registered person, means the central tax, State tax, integrated tax or Union territory tax charged on any supply of goods or services or both made to him and includes:

(a) the integrated goods and services tax charged on import of goods;

(b) the tax payable under the provisions of sub-sections (3) and (4) of section 9;

(c) the tax payable under the provisions of sub-sections (3) and (4) of section 5 of the Integrated Goods and Services Tax Act;

(d) the tax payable under the provisions of sub-sections (3) and (4) of section 9 of the respective State Goods and Services Tax Act; or

(e) the tax payable under the provisions of sub-sections (3) and (4) of section 7 of the Union Territory Goods and Services Tax Act, but does not include the tax paid under the composition levy;

(63) "input tax credit" means the credit of input tax;

(64) "intra-State supply of goods" shall have the same meaning as assigned to it in section 8 of the Integrated Goods and Services Tax Act;

(65) "intra-State supply of services" shall have the same meaning as assigned to it in section 8 of the Integrated Goods and Services Tax Act;

(66) "invoice" or "tax invoice" means the tax invoice referred to in section 31;

(67) "inward supply" in relation to a person, shall mean receipt of goods or services or both whether by purchase, acquisition or any other means with or without consideration;

(68) "job work" means any treatment or process undertaken by a person on goods belonging to another registered person and the expression "job worker" shall be construed accordingly;

(69) "local authority" means:

(a) a "Panchayat" as defined in clause (d) of Article 243 of the Constitution;

(b) a "Municipality" as defined in clause (e) of Article 243P of the Constitution;

(c) a Municipal Committee, a Zilla Parishad, a District Board, and any other authority legally entitled to, or entrusted by the Central Government or any State Government with the control or management of a municipal or local fund;

(d) a Cantonment Board as defined in section 3 of the Cantonments Act, 2006;

(e) a Regional Council or a District Council constituted under the Sixth Schedule to the Constitution;

(f) a Development Board constituted under Article 371 and article 371J of the Constitution; or

(g) a Regional Council constituted under Article 371A of the Constitution;

(70) "location of the recipient of services" means:

(a) where a supply is received at a place of business for which the registration has been obtained, the location of such place of business;

(b) where a supply is received at a place other than the place of business for which registration has been obtained (a fixed establishment elsewhere), the location of such fixed establishment;

(c) where a supply is received at more than one establishment, whether the place of business or fixed establishment, the location of the establishment most directly concerned with the receipt of the supply; and

(d) in absence of such places, the location of the usual place of residence of the recipient;

(71) "location of the supplier of services" means:

(a) where a supply is made from a place of business for which the registration has been obtained, the location of such place of business;

(b) where a supply is made from a place other than the place of business for which registration has been obtained (a fixed establishment elsewhere), the location of such fixed establishment;

(c) where a supply is made from more than one establishment, whether the place of business or fixed establishment, the location of the establishment most directly concerned with the provisions of the supply; and

(d) in absence of such places, the location of the usual place of residence of the supplier;

(72) "manufacture" means processing of raw material or inputs in any manner that results in emergence of a new product having a distinct name, character and use and the term "manufacturer" shall be construed accordingly;

(73) "market value" shall mean the full amount which a recipient of a supply is required to pay in order to obtain the goods or services or both of like kind and quality at or about the same time and at the same commercial level where the recipient and the supplier are not related;

(74) "mixed supply" means two or more individual supplies of goods or services, or any combination thereof, made in conjunction with each other by a taxable person for a single price where such supply does not constitute a composite supply.

Illustration: A supply of a package consisting of canned foods, sweets, chocolates, cakes, dry fruits, aerated drinks and fruit juices when supplied for a single price is a mixed supply. Each of these items can be supplied separately and is not dependent on any other. It shall not be a mixed supply if these items are supplied separately;

(75) "money" means the Indian legal tender or any foreign currency, cheque, promissory note, bill of exchange, letter of credit, draft, pay order, traveler cheque, money order, postal or electronic remittance or any other instrument recognized by the Reserve Bank of India when used as a consideration to settle an obligation or exchange with Indian legal tender of another denomination but shall not include any currency that is held for its numismatic value;

(76) "motor vehicle" shall have the same meaning as assigned to it in clause (28) of section 2 of the Motor Vehicles Act, 1988;

(77) "non-resident taxable person" means any person who occasionally undertakes transactions involving supply of goods or services or both, whether as principal or agent or in any other capacity, but who has no fixed place of business or residence in India;

(78) "non-taxable supply" means a supply of goods or services or both which is not leviable to tax under this Act or under the Integrated Goods and Services Tax Act;

(79) "non-taxable territory" means the territory which is outside the taxable territory;

(80) "notification" means a notification published in the Official Gazette and the expressions "notify" and "notified" shall be construed accordingly;

(81) "other territory" includes territories other than those comprising in a State and those referred to in sub-clauses (a) to (e) of clause (114);

(82) "output tax" in relation to a taxable person, means the tax chargeable under this Act on taxable supply of goods or services or both made by him or by his agent but excludes tax payable by him on reverse charge basis;

(83) "outward supply" in relation to a taxable person, means supply of goods or services or both, whether by sale, transfer, barter, exchange, license, rental, lease or disposal or any other mode, made or agreed to be made by such person in the course or furtherance of business;

(84) "person" includes:

(a) an individual;

(b) a Hindu Undivided Family;

(c) a company;

(d) a firm;

(e) a Limited Liability Partnership;

(f) an association of persons or a body of individuals, whether incorporated or not, in India or outside India;

(g) any corporation established by or under any Central Act, State Act or Provincial Act or a Government company as defined in clause (45) of section 2 of the Companies Act, 2013;

(h) any body corporate incorporated by or under the laws of a country outside India;

(i) a co-operative society registered under any law relating to co-operative societies;

(j) a local authority;

(k) Central Government or a State Government;

(l) society as defined under the Societies Registration Act, 1860;

(m) trust; and

(n) every artificial juridical person, not falling within any of the above;

(85) "place of business" includes:

(a) a place from where the business is ordinarily carried on, and includes a warehouse, a godown or any other place where a taxable person stores his goods, supplies or receives goods or services or both; or

(b) a place where a taxable person maintains his books of account; or

(c) a place where a taxable person is engaged in business through an agent, by whatever name called;

(86) "place of supply" means the place of supply as referred to in Chapter V of the Integrated Goods and Services Tax Act;

(87) "prescribed" means prescribed by rules made under this Act on the recommendations of the Council;

(88) "principal" means a person on whose behalf an agent carries on the business of supply or receipt of goods or services or both;

(89) "principal place of business" means the place of business specified as the principal place of business in the certificate of registration;

(90) "principal supply" means the supply of goods or services which constitutes the predominant element of a composite supply and to which any other supply forming part of that composite supply is ancillary;

(91) "proper officer" in relation to any function to be performed under this Act, means the Commissioner or the officer of the central tax who is assigned that function by the Commissioner in the Board;

(92) "quarter" shall mean a period comprising three consecutive calendar months, ending on the last day of March, June, September and December of a calendar year;

(93) "recipient" of supply of goods or services or both, means:

(a) where a consideration is payable for the supply of goods or services or both, the person who is liable to pay that consideration;

(b) where no consideration is payable for the supply of goods, the person to whom the goods are delivered or made available, or to whom possession or use of the goods is given or made available; and

(c) where no consideration is payable for the supply of a service, the person to whom the service is rendered, and any reference to a person to whom a supply is made shall be construed as a reference to the recipient of the supply and shall include an agent acting as such on behalf of the recipient in relation to the goods or services or both supplied;

(94) "registered person" means a person who is registered under section 25 but does not include a person having a Unique Identity Number;

(95) "regulations" means the regulations made by the Board under this Act on the recommendations of the Council;

(a) despatch of the goods for delivery by the supplier thereof or by any other person acting on behalf of such supplier; or

(b) collection of the goods by the recipient thereof or by any other person acting on behalf of such recipient;

(96) "removal" in relation to goods, means:

(a) despatch of the goods for delivery by the supplier thereof or by any other person acting on behalf of such supplier; or

(b) collection of the goods by the recipient thereof or by any other person acting on behalf of such recipient;

(97) "return" means any return prescribed or otherwise required to be furnished by or under this Act or the rules made there under;

(98) "reverse charge" means the liability to pay tax by the recipient of supply of goods or services or both instead of the supplier of such goods or services or both under sub-section (3) or sub-section (4) of section 9, or under sub-section (3) or sub-section (4) of section 5 of the Integrated Goods and Services Tax Act;

(99) "Revisional Authority" means an authority appointed or authorized for revision of decision or orders as referred to in section 108;

(100) "Schedule" means a Schedule appended to this Act;

(101) "securities" shall have the same meaning as assigned to it in clause (h) of section 2 of the Securities Contracts (Regulation) Act, 1956;

(102) "services" means anything other than goods, money and securities but includes activities relating to the use of money or its conversion by cash or by any other mode, from one form, currency or denomination, to another form, currency or denomination for which a separate consideration is charged;

Explanation: For the removal of doubts, it is hereby clarified that the expression "services" includes facilitating or arranging transactions in securities.

(103) "State" includes a Union territory with Legislature;

(104) "State tax" means the tax levied under any State Goods and Services Tax Act;

(105) "supplier" in relation to any goods or services or both, shall mean the person supplying the said goods or services or both and shall include an agent acting as such on behalf of such supplier in relation to the goods or services or both supplied;

(106) "tax period" means the period for which the return is required to be furnished;

(107) "taxable person" means a person who is registered or liable to be registered under section 22 or section 24;

(108) "taxable supply" means a supply of goods or services or both which is leviable to tax under this Act;

(109) "taxable territory" means the territory to which the provisions of this Act apply;

(110) "telecommunication service" means service of any description (including electronic mail, voice mail, data services, audio text services, video text services, radio paging and cellular mobile telephone services) which is made available to users by means of any transmission or reception of signs, signals, writing, images and sounds or intelligence of any nature, by wire, radio, visual or other electromagnetic means;

(111) "the State Goods and Services Tax Act" means the respective State Goods and Services Tax Act, 2017;

(112) "turnover in State" or "turnover in Union territory" means the aggregate value of all taxable supplies (excluding the value of inward supplies on which tax is payable by a person on reverse charge basis) and exempt supplies made within a State or Union territory by a taxable person, exports of goods or services or both and inter-State supplies of goods or services or both made from the State or Union territory by the said taxable person but excludes central tax, State tax, Union territory tax, integrated tax and cess;

(113) "usual place of residence" means:

(a) in case of an individual, the place where he ordinarily resides;

(b) in other cases, the place where the person is incorporated or otherwise legally constituted;

(114) "Union territory" means the territory of:

(a) the Andaman and Nicobar Islands;

(b) Lakshadweep;

(c) Dadra and Nagar Haveli and Daman and Diu;

(d) Ladakh;

(e) Chandigarh; and

(f) other territory.

Explanation.—For the purposes of this Act, each of the territories specified in sub-clauses (a) to (f) shall be considered to be a separate Union territory;

(115) "Union territory tax" means the Union territory goods and services tax levied under the Union Territory Goods and Services Tax Act;

(116) "Union Territory Goods and Services Tax Act" means the Union Territory Goods and Services Tax Act, 2017;

(117) "valid return" means a return furnished under sub-section (1) of section 39 on which self-assessed tax has been paid in full;

(118) "voucher" means an instrument where there is an obligation to accept it as consideration or part consideration for a supply of goods or services or both and where the goods or services or both to be supplied or the identities of their potential suppliers are either indicated on the instrument itself or in related documentation, including the terms and conditions of use of such instrument;

(119) "works contract" means a contract for building, construction, fabrication, completion, erection, installation, fitting out, improvement, modification, repair, maintenance, renovation, alteration or commissioning of any immovable property wherein transfer of property in goods (whether as goods or in some other form) is involved in the execution of such contract;

(120) words and expressions used and not defined in this Act but defined in the Integrated Goods and Services Tax Act, the Union Territory Goods and Services Tax Act and the Goods and Services Tax (Compensation to States) Act shall have the same meaning as assigned to them in those Acts;

(121) any reference in this Act to a law which is not in force in the State of Jammu and Kashmir, shall, in relation to that State be construed as a reference to the corresponding law, if any, in force in that State.

Chapter 3

Administration

Chapter II of the CGST Act, 2017 (Section 3 to 6) deals with provision relating to Appointment of Officers & their power.

3.1 OFFICERS UNDER CGST ACT (SEC 3)

The Government shall, by notification, appoint the following classes of officers for the for the efficient administration of the GST law, namely:

(a) Principal Chief Commissioners of Central Tax or Principal Directors General of Central Tax,
(b) Chief Commissioners of Central Tax or Directors General of Central Tax,
(c) Principal Commissioners of Central Tax or Principal Additional Directors General of Central Tax,
(d) Commissioners of Central Tax or Additional Directors General of Central Tax,
(e) Additional Commissioners of Central Tax or Additional Directors of Central Tax,
(f) Joint Commissioners of Central Tax or Joint Directors of Central Tax,
(g) Deputy Commissioners of Central Tax or Deputy Directors of Central Tax,
(h) Assistant Commissioners of Central Tax or Assistant Directors of Central Tax, and
(i) Any other class of officers it may deem fit:

Provided that the officers appointed under the Central Excise Act, 1944 shall be deemed to be the officers appointed under the provisions of this Act.

3.2 APPOINTMENT OF OFFICERS (SEC 4)

All statutory functions cannot be performed by executive officers. There is a necessity to appoint administrative staff to assist executive officers. The administrative staff make up the entire working team of administrative staff also called 'field formations'. The authority to appoint administrative staff is left to the Board—Central Board of Indirect Taxes & Customs.

(1) The Board may, in addition to the officers as may be notified by the Government under section 3, appoint such persons as it may think fit to be the officers under this Act.

(2) Without prejudice to the provisions of sub-section (1), the Board may, by order, authorize any officer referred to in clauses (a) to (h) of Section 3 to appoint officers of central tax below the rank of Assistant Commissioner of central tax for the administration of this Act.

3.3 POWERS OF OFFICERS (SEC 5)

(1) Subject to such conditions and limitations as the Board may impose, an officer of central tax may exercise the powers and discharge the duties conferred or imposed on him under this Act.

(2) An officer of central tax may exercise the powers and discharge the duties conferred or imposed under this Act on any other officer of central tax who is subordinate to him.

(3) The Commissioner may, subject to such conditions and limitations as may be specified in this behalf by him, delegate his powers to any other officer who is subordinate to him.

(4) Notwithstanding anything contained in this section, an Appellate Authority shall not exercise the powers and discharge the duties conferred or imposed on any other officer of central tax.

3.4 AUTHORIZATION OF OFFICERS OF STATE TAX OR UNION TERRITORY TAX AS PROPER OFFICER IN CERTAIN CIRCUMSTANCES (SEC 6)

Since India has adopted a "Dual GST" model, i.e. Centre & States/UT, both have been empowered to levy GST on same tax base across value chain. Therefore, it is necessary to develop a mechanism to avoid duplication of tax administration by officers of Central Tax and by officers of State/UT Tax.

For the purposes of administration of this act, it is permitted to authorize officers of State/UT Tax to simultaneously also be the officer of Central Tax. In order to establish non-overlapping of administrative power, it is provided that an officer in respect of central tax is required to duly exercise his authority even in respect of State/UT Tax where the executive action is in respect of the same taxing base and shall intimate the officer of State/UT Tax in respect of all his actions. Further, where administrative power has been invoked by the proper officer of the State/UT Tax in any proceeding, such action will preclude the officer of central tax from exercising any administrative power in respect of transactions covered by the said proceedings.

Any proceedings for rectification, appeal and revision, wherever applicable, of any order passed by an officer appointed under Central Act shall not lie before an officer appointed under the State Goods and Services Tax Act or the Union Territory Goods and Services Tax Act.

Relevant Circulars, Notifications and Clarifications

1. Notification No. 02/2017-Central Tax, dated 19.06.2017 notifying the jurisdiction of Central Tax Officers.
2. Notification No. 14/2017-Central Tax, dated 01.07.2017 issued to assign the jurisdiction and powers of various directorates.
3. Notification No. 39/2017-Central Tax, dated 13.10.2017 read with Notification No. 10/2018-Central Tax, dated 23.01.2018 issued to cross-empower State Tax officers for processing and granting of refunds.
4. Circular No. 3/3/2017 dated 05.07.2017 read with Circular No. 31/05/2018 dated 09.02.2018 issued to clarify the functions of the proper officers.
5. Circular No. 9/9/2017 dated 18.10.2017 issued regarding the officer authorized for enrollment of GST Practitioners.
6. Circular No. 31/5/2018-GST dated 9.02.2018, notifying proper officer under sections 73 & 74 of CGST Act.
7. Notification No. 79/2018-Central Tax, dated 31.12.2018 notifying the jurisdiction of Central Tax Officers & their sub-ordinates.
8. Notification No. 04/2019-Central Tax, dated 29.01.2019 define the jurisdiction of Joint Commissioner (Appeal).
9. Order No. 02/2019, dated 12.03.2019 appointment of common authority for the purpose of exercise of power under sections 73, 74, 75, 76.
10. Circular No. 05/2020-CT dated 13.01.2020, authorizing revisional authority.
11. Notification No. 01/2023-Central Tax, dated 04.01.2023 assign powers of Superintendent of central tax to Additional Assistant Directors in DGGI, DGGST & DG Audit.

Chapter 4

Supply Under GST

4.1 MEANING & SCOPE OF SUPPLY

The provisions relating to meaning and scope of supply are contained in Chapter III of the CGST Act, 2017 read with various schedules given under the said Act.

As per Section 7(1), the expression "supply" includes:

(a) all forms of supply of goods or services or both such as sale, transfer, barter, exchange, license, rental, lease or disposal made or agreed to be made for a consideration by a person in the course or furtherance of business;

(aa) the activities or transactions, by a person, other than an individual, to its members or constituents or vice-versa, for cash, deferred payment or other valuable consideration;

(b) import of services for a consideration whether or not in the course or furtherance of business; and

(c) the activities specified in Schedule I, made or agreed to be made without a consideration.

As per Section 7(1A), where certain activities or transactions constitute a supply in accordance with the provisions of sub-section (1), they shall be treated either as supply of goods or supply of services as referred to in Schedule II.

The modes of supply mentioned above in Section 7(1)(a) are only in the forms of examples and the list is not exhaustive. This is substantiated by the use of words '*such as*' in the definition.

The term, "supply" has been inclusively defined in the Act. The meaning and scope of supply under GST can be understood in terms of following six parameters, which can be adopted to characterize a transaction as supply:

1. Supply of goods or services. Supply of anything other than goods or services does not attract GST.
2. Supply should be made for a consideration (exception given in Schedule I).
3. Supply should be made in the course or furtherance of business.
4. Supply should be made by a taxable person.
5. Supply should be a taxable supply.
6. Supply should be made within the taxable territory.

While these six parameters describe the concept of supply, there are a few exceptions to the requirement of supply being made for a consideration and in the course or furtherance of business. Any transaction involving supply of goods or services without consideration is not a supply, barring few exceptions, in which a transaction is deemed to be a supply even without consideration. Further, import of services for a consideration, whether or not in the course or furtherance of business is treated as supply.

Section 7(2): The expression "supply" does not includes:

(a) activities or transactions specified in **Schedule III**; or

(b) such activities or transactions undertaken by the Central Government, a State Government or any local authority in which they are engaged as public authorities, as may be notified by the Government on the recommendations of the Council.

Section 7(3): The Government may, on the recommendations of the Council, specify, by notification, the transactions that are to be treated as:

(a) a supply of goods and not as a supply of services; or

(b) a supply of services and not as a supply of goods.

4.2 INTER/INTRA STATE SUPPLY

The location of the supplier and the place of supply determine whether a supply is treated as an Intra-State supply or an Inter-State supply. Determination of the nature of supply is essential to ascertain whether integrated tax (IGST) is to be paid or Central plus State tax (CGST+SGST) are to be paid.

Inter-State supply of goods means a supply of goods where the location of the supplier and place of supply are in different States or Union territories. Imports, supplies from and to SEZs are treated as deemed Inter-State supplies.

Intra-State supply of goods means supply of goods where the location of the supplier and the place of supply are in the same State or Union territory.

NATURE OF SUPPLY

Nature of Supply	Transactions covered
Intra-State Supply	Supply of goods within the State or Union Territory
	Supply of services within the State or Union Territory
Inter-state Supply	Supply of goods from one State or Union Territory to another State or Union Territory
	Supply of services from one State or Union Territory to another State or Union Territory
	Import of goods till they the cross customs frontier
	Import of services
	Export of goods or services
	Supply of goods/services to/by SEZ
	Supplies to international tourists
	Any other supply in the taxable territory which is not intra-State supply

4.3 TAXABLE SUPPLY [SECTION 2(108)]

A supply to attract GST, it must be taxable supply. Taxable supply has been broadly defined and means any supply of goods or services or both which, is leviable to tax under the Act. Exemptions may be provided to the specified goods or services or to a specified category of persons/entities making supply.

For a transaction to qualify as a taxable supply, following requirement should be fulfilled:

(1) The transaction must involve supply of either goods or services, or both of them.

(2) Such goods or services should not be specified under Schedule III (neither a supply of goods nor a supply of services).

(3) The transaction should fall within the meaning of 'supply' in terms of Section 7 of the CGST Act.

(4) The supply should be leviable to GST, i.e., it should not be covered within the meaning of 'non-taxable supply' as defined under Section 2(78), i.e., alcoholic liquor for human consumption. This implies that supplies enjoying a full exemption from tax by way of an exemption notification would also be treated as taxable supplies.

> Taxable supply [Sec 2(108) includes those supply of goods & services which are leviable to tax under GST, including supply exempted u/s 11. Nil rate means, supply is taxable (HSN/SAC code assigned) but it covers under 0% tax slab by means of notification. This may be brought under other tax slab, as & when GST council will decide.
>
> This means, supplies enjoying a full exemption from tax by way of an exemption notification would also be treated as taxable supplies.

4.4 WHAT IS CONSIDERATION

Consideration has specifically been defined in **Sec 2(31)** of the CGST Act, 2017. It can be in money or in kind. Any subsidy given by the Central Government or a State Government is not considered as consideration. It is immaterial whether the payment is made by the recipient or by any other person.

Further, when there is barter of goods or services, the same activity constitutes supply as well as a consideration. When a barber cuts hair in exchange for a painting, hair cut is a supply of services by the barber. It is a consideration for the painting received.

4.5 PAYMENT THAT ARE NOT TO BE TREATED AS CONSIDERATION

(1) **Donations:** Donations are given in kind, money or by way of services to charitable trust or relief fund for charity, humanitarian aid, or to benefit a cause. The recipient doesn't supply any goods or services or both in return.

The CBIC vide Circular No. 116/35/2019-GST dated 11th October 2019 has clarified that GST is not leviable on donation, where all the following three conditions are satisfied namely:

(a) The gift or donation is made to a charitable organization
(b) The payment has the character of gift or donation
(c) The purpose is philanthropic (i.e. it leads to no commercial gain) and not advertisement

(2) **Grant/Subsidy:** As per Section 2(31), Grant/subsidy given by Central/State Government is not a consideration in the hands of recipient of the grant.

(3) **Project/Research funding:** Businesses & government bodies may co-sponsors a research & development project by contributing funds to the project, the benefits of which will be not accrued to them. The amount contributed by the sponsors are based on cost of the project & not on the basis of any commercial benefits. The payment/funding will not be treated as consideration for supply.

(4) **Deposits:** As per Section 2(31), Deposit (whether refundable or not) given in respect of the supply of goods or services shall not be considered as payment made for the supply unless the supplier applies the deposit as consideration for the supply.

(5) **Sponsorship payment:** Payment made for sponsoring an event which does not involve any tangible or intangible benefits in return, either in terms of advertising, publicity or other economic benefits is not a consideration for supply.

(6) **Fines and penalty for violation of laws:** Fine or penalties paid to Govt. for violation of any statute, such as penalty for late filing of TDS/GST return, violation of traffic light, violation of pollution norms, late fee for delay in deposit of taxes or any statutory levies or fine/penalty paid for violation of any other laws is not a consideration for supply. Therefore, GST not applicable on the same (Ref Circular No. 178/10/2022-GST dated 3rd August 2022).

(7) **Cheque dishonor fine/penalty:** The fine or penalty that the supplier or a banker imposes, for dishonour of a cheque, is a penalty imposed not for tolerating the act or situation but a fine, or penalty imposed for not tolerating, penalizing and thereby deterring and discouraging such an act or situation. Therefore, cheque dishonor fine or penalty is not a consideration for any service and not taxable.

(8) **Liquidated damages or penalty for breach of contract [Circular No. 178/10/2022-GST dated 3rd August 2022]:** Where the amount paid as 'liquidated damages' is an amount paid only to compensate for injury, loss or damage suffered by the aggrieved party due to breach of the contract and there is no agreement, express or implied, by the aggrieved party receiving the liquidated damages, to refrain from or tolerate an act or to do anything for the party paying the liquidated damages, in such cases liquidated damages are mere a flow of money from the party who causes breach of the contract to the party who suffers loss or damage due to such breach.

Such payments do not constitute consideration for a supply and are not taxable. Examples of such cases are damages resulting from damage to property, negligence, piracy, unauthorized use of trade name, copyright, penalty stipulated in a contract for delayed execution of works or delayed supply of materials, etc.

(9) **Forfeiture of salary or payment of bond amount in the event of the employee leaving the employment before the minimum agreed period:** The provisions for forfeiture of salary or recovery of bond amount in the event of the employee leaving the employment before the minimum agreed period are incorporated in the employment contract to discourage non-serious candidates from taking up employment. The said amounts are recovered by the employer not as a consideration for tolerating the act of such premature quitting of employment but as penalties for dissuading the non-serious employees from taking up employment and to discourage and deter such a situation. Further, the employee does not get anything in return from the employer against payment of such amounts. Therefore, such amounts recovered by the employer are not taxable as consideration for the service of agreeing to tolerate an act or a situation.

(10) **Forfeiture of Earnest Money Deposit (EMD):** Forfeiture of earnest money from a successful bidder failing to act after winning the bid is a mere flow of money, as the buyer or the successful bidder does not get anything in return for such forfeiture of earnest money. Forfeiture of earnest money is in such cases is not a consideration for tolerating the breach of contract but as a compensation for the losses suffered and as a penalty for discouraging

the non-serious bidders. Such payments being merely flow of money are not a consideration for any supply and are not taxable.

(11) No Claim Bonus given by Insurance Company: As per practice prevailing in the insurance sector, the insurance companies deduct No Claim Bonus from the gross insurance premium amount, when no claim is made by the insured person during the previous insurance period(s).

There is no supply provided by the insured to the insurance company in form of agreeing to the obligation to refrain from the act of lodging insurance claim during the previous year(s)and No Claim Bonus cannot be considered as a consideration for any supply provided by the insured to the insurance company.

4.6 DEEMED SUPPLY [SECTION 7(1)(C) READ WITH SCHEDULE I]

There are exceptions to the requirement of 'consideration' as a pre-condition for a supply to be called a "supply" as per GST. As per **Schedule I,** to the CGST Act, 2017, activities as mentioned below shall be treated as supply even if made without consideration:

(1) Permanent transfer or disposal of business assets where input tax credit has been availed on such assets.

(2) Supply of goods or services or both between related persons or between distinct persons as specified in section 25, when made in the course or furtherance of business:

Provided that gift not exceeding ₹ 50,000 in value in a financial year by an employer to an employee shall not be treated as supply of goods or services or both.

(3) Supply of goods (a) by a principal to his agent where the agent undertakes to supply such goods on behalf of the principal; or (b) by an agent to his principal where the agent undertakes to receive such goods on behalf of the principal.

(4) Import of services by a person from a related person or from any of his other establishments outside India, in the course or furtherance of business.

4.7 TAXABILITY OF SUPPLY MADE BETWEEN RELATED PERSONS

Supplies between the related persons with consideration at arm's length price shall constitute as 'Supply' like any other transaction.

Whereas, the supply made between related persons for inadequate or no consideration is cover under Paragraph 2 of Schedule I of the CGST Act. Such transactions shall be treated as 'Supply' only if it happens in the course or furtherance of business.

Exception: Where an employer gifts his employee and the value of gift is less than ₹ 50,000. It is not consider as Supply.

Further, import of service by a person from a related person or establishment outside India (without consideration) but for furtherance of business, shall be considered as a supply.

Hence, import of services by entities which are not registered under GST (say, they are only making exempted supplies) but are otherwise engaged in business activities is taxed when received from a related person or from any of their establishments outside India.

The term "related person" has been defined in explanation to Section 15 as under:

(a) persons shall be deemed to be "related persons" if—

  (i) such persons are officers or directors of one another's businesses;

  (ii) such persons are legally authorized partners in business;

  (iii) such persons are employer and employee;

  (iv) any person directly or indirectly owns, controls or holds twenty-five per cent. Or more of the outstanding voting stock or shares of both of them;

  (v) one of them directly or indirectly controls the other;

  (vi) both of them are directly or indirectly controlled by a third person;

  (vii) together they directly or indirectly control a third person; or

  (viii) they are members of the same family;

(b) the term "person" also includes legal persons;

(c) persons who are associated in the business of one another in that one is the sole agent or sole distributor or sole concessionaire, howsoever described, of the other, shall be deemed to be related.

4.8 DISTINCT PERSONS [SPECIFIED UNDER SECTION 25 OF CGST ACT, 2017]

A person who has obtained/is required obtaining more than one registration, whether in one State/Union territory or more than one State/Union territory shall, in respect of each such registration, be treated as **distinct persons.**

Further, where a person who has obtained or is required to obtain registration in a State or Union territory in respect of an establishment, has an establishment in another State or Union territory, then such establishments shall be treated as **establishments of distinct persons.**

4.9 SUPPLY OF GOODS/SERVICES BETWEEN EMPLOYER & EMPLOYEE

By virtue of the definition of related person, employer and employee are related persons. However, services provided by an employee to the employer in the course of or in relation to his employment are not treated as supply of services [Schedule III of CGST Act].

Gift by employer to employee

Schedule I, appended to the CGST Act, 2017 provides that gifts not exceeding ₹ 50,000 in value in a financial year by an employer to an employee shall not be treated as supply of goods or services or both. However, gifts of value more than ₹ 50,000 made without consideration are subject to GST, when made in the course or furtherance of business.

The term 'gift' have not been define in the GST law. In common parlance, gift is made without consideration, is voluntary in nature and is made occasionally. The employee cannot demand it as a matter of right and cannot move a court of law for obtaining a gift.

Services by an employee to the employer in the course of or in relation to his employment are outside the scope of GST (neither supply of goods nor supply of services). Remuneration paid to Director of the company, which are not shown as salary or payment on which TDS has been deducted u/s 194-J of Income tax Act, 1961 is taxable under RCM u/s 9(3) of CGST Act in the hands of the company, i.e. service recipient [Refer Circular No. 140/10/2020-GST dated 10-06-2020].

Supply by the employer to the employee in terms of contractual agreement entered into between the employer and the employee, will not be subjected to GST as per Schedule III.

4.10 DIFFERENCE BETWEEN VARIOUS TYPES OF SUPPLIES UNDER GST

Nature of Supply	Description	Remarks
Zero-Rated supply	**Example:** Export & Supply to SEZ.	Zero-rated supply may be made against bond/ LUT or payment of IGST.
		Subsequently, GST paid on the output supplies as well as on the inputs or input services used in making said supply can be claim as refund by the supplier. Input Tax credit available. Refund of un-utilized ITC also available, except the goods are subject to export duty.
Nil-rated supply	Supply of goods and services that attract 0% GST. Nil-rated items are listed in Schedule 1 of GST rate schedule. **Example:** Salt, Unbranded Wheat/ flour/Rice, Meat, Fish, fresh fruits, Electrical Energy, Judicial/Non judicial stamp paper, Khadi Yarn, etc.	Outward supply attract 0% GST. Input Tax credit not available.

Nature of Supply	Description	Remarks
Exempt supply	Exempt Supply are notified under Sec 11 of CGST Act or Sec 6 of IGST Act, on which no GST is payable. **Example:** Goods notified Vide Notification No. 2/2017-Central Tax (Rate) dated 28th June 2017. Services such as transmission & distribution of electricity, renting of residential building for residential purposes to an un-registered person, etc.	No GST on outward supply. Input Tax credit not available. A registered person supplying exempted goods or services or both shall issue 'bill of supply' instead of tax invoice.
Non-GST supply or non-taxable supply	The supply of goods and services that does not come under the purview of GST while taxes under other statute such as Excise duty, VAT, etc. may be levied. **Example:** Crude Oil, Petrol, Diesel, ATF, Natural gas, Alcohol for human consumptions and transactions specified in Schedule III of the CGST Act.	No GST on outward supply. However, taxes under other statute such as Excise duty, VAT, etc. are levied. GST Invoice Rules not applicable. No question of ITC under GST, since the supply outside the scope of GST.

4.11 TAXABILITY OF COMPOSITE & MIXED SUPPLY [SECTION 8]

GST is payable on individual goods or services or both at the notified rates. The application of rates poses no problem if the supply is of individual goods or individual services, which is clearly identifiable and such goods or services are subject to a particular rate of tax.

However, in certain cases, supplies are not such simple and clearly identifiable supplies. Some of the supplies are a combination of goods or combination of services or combination of goods and services both and each individual component of such supplies may attract a different rate of tax.

In such a case, the rate of tax to be levied on such supplies may be a challenge. It is for this reason, that the GST Law identifies composite supplies, mixed supplies, and provides certainty in respect of tax treatment under GST for such supplies.

The term Composite supply has been define in Sec 2(30) as under:

> Composite supply means a supply made by a taxable person to a recipient consisting of two or more taxable supplies of goods or services or both, or any combination thereof, which are naturally bundled and supplied in conjunction with each other in the ordinary course of business, one of which is a principal supply.
>
> ***Illustration**: Where goods are packed and transported with insurance, the supply of goods, packing materials, transport and insurance is a composite supply and supply of goods is a principal supply.*

Section 8 of the CGST Act, 2017 lays down the provision relating to tax liability of composite or mixed supply in the following manner.

(a) **Composite Supply** comprising two or more supplies one of which, is a principal supply, shall be treated as supply of such principal supply.

(b) **Mixed Supply** comprising two or more supplies, shall be treated as supply of that particular supply which attracts the highest rate of tax.

Description	Composite Supply	Mixed Supply
Meaning	Comprising two or more taxable supplies of goods or services or any combination thereof, which are **naturally bundled**	Comprising two or more supplies of goods or services or any combination thereof, which are **not naturally bundled**
Rate of Tax	Rate of principal item will apply	Rate of item having highest rate will apply
Example	Charger supplied along with mobile phones	A gift pack comprising chocolates and sweets

The salient features of composite supply are as under:

(a) supply is made by a taxable person to a recipient,

(b) such supply comprises two or more supplies of goods and/or services or any combination thereof,

(c) such combination of two or more supplies of goods and/or services is naturally bundled,

(d) such naturally bundled goods and/or services is supplied in conjunction with each other in the ordinary course of business,

(e) out of the naturally bundled goods and/or services, one is a principal supply.

Principal supply: Section 2(90)

"Principal supply" means the supply of goods or services which constitutes the predominant element of a composite supply and to which any other supply forming part of that composite supply is ancillary.

Mixed Supply: It means two or more individual supplies of goods or services, which are not naturally bundled.

The salient features of mixed supply are given below:

(a) supply is made by a taxable person to a recipient

(b) supply is made for a single price

(c) it is a supply of two or more individual supplies of goods or services, or any combination thereof

(d) such supply is made in conjunction with each other

(e) the individual supplies are independent of each other and are not naturally bundled.

Mixed Supply is define in Section 2(74) as under:

"Mixed supply" means two or more individual supplies of goods or services, or any combination thereof, made in conjunction with each other by a taxable person for a single price where such supply does not constitute a composite supply.

Illustration. *A supply of a package consisting of canned foods, sweets, chocolates, cakes, dry fruits, aerated drinks and fruit juices when supplied for a single price is a mixed supply. Each of these items can be supplied separately and is not dependent on any other. It shall not be a mixed supply if these items are supplied separately.*

Bundle of Goods and Services: Bundle of Goods and Services means Mixture of Goods and Services, i.e. supply of Goods and Services simultaneously.

Whether services are bundled in the ordinary course of business would depend upon the normal or frequent practices followed in the area of business to which services relate. Such normal and frequent practices adopted in a business can be ascertained from several indicators some of which are listed below:

- Perception of the consumer or the service receiver
- Majority of service providers in a particular area of business provide similar bundle of services
- The nature of various services
- Advertised as a single package
- Single price
- different elements aren't available separately
- different elements are integral to one overall supply
- No straightjacket formula can be laid down to determine whether a service is naturally bundled in the ordinary course of business
- Each case has to be individually examined in the backdrop of several factors some of which are outlined above.

Further, Bundle is classified into two categories:

(i) Naturally Bundled: It means Goods and/or Services that does not change the essential character of Goods and/or Services being provided. For example, supply of Machinery (Goods) along with installation (Service) thereof at the customer site. This service is clearly said to be naturally bundled. In the said example, essential character of provision of Goods/or Services shall be Supply of Goods (Machinery) and not the installation service, which is regarded as only an ancillary service.

Example 1:

(1) Airfare inclusive of food being served on board, free insurance, and the use of airport lounge. In this case, the transport of passenger, constitutes the pre-dominant element of the composite supply, and is treated as the principal supply and all other supplies are ancillary.

(2) Supply of laptop with carry case.

(3) Repair of computer with requisite parts.

(4) Supply of health care services along with medicaments.

(5) Works contract as defined in Sec 2(119) of the CGST Act 2017 is a Composite supply. However, this has been treated as "supply of service" in Paragraph 6(a) of Schedule II of CGST Act. As such, GST rate of "works contract" services will apply for this.

(ii) Not Naturally Bundle: It means provision of Goods and/or Services, which are not naturally bundled: The following guiding principles could be adopted to determine whether a supply would be a composite supply or a mixed supply. However, every supply should be independently analyzed.

Description	Composite Supply	Mixed Supply
Naturally bundled	Yes	No
Supplied together	Yes	Yes
Can be supplied separately	No	Yes
One is predominant supply for recipient	Yes	No
Other supply is not 'aim in itself' of recipient	Yes	No
Each supply priced separately	No	No
All supplies are goods	Yes	Yes
All supplies are services	Yes	Yes
One supply is goods and other supply is services	Yes	Yes

(iii) In conjunction with each other: It means goods & services are supplied at the same event, same time and under same contract jointly or together for a single price.

Example:

(1) Accommodation with breakfast

(2) Supply of water purifier with first time installation

(3) Supply of DTH with installation

(4) Health care service with medicines, foods.

Query 1: What is the impact on taxability if the Principal Supply happens to be non-taxable supply or is exempt from tax under GST?

Ans. The query needs to be analyse in two parts:

(1) When the principal supply is non-taxable supply (i.e. Petrol, Diesel, Natural Gas, etc.)?

As per definition provided in Section 2(30), composite supply consist of two or more taxable supply. So, if the principal supply is non-taxable supply, it is not a composite supply under GST.

(2) When the principal supply is exempt supply?

If the principal supply happens to be exempt supply, it will be treated as exempt composite supply. For example, in case of healthcare services, medical treatment is provided alongwith medicines, foods etc. where medicines, foods are taxable under GST but medical treatment (principal supply) is exempted from GST.

[Refer Advance Ruling No. KAR ADRG 26/2018 dated 13-11-2018 in the matter of Columbia Asia Hospitals Private Limited (GST AAR Karnataka)]

4.12 SCHEDULE I, CGST ACT 2017

ACTIVITIES TO BE TREATED AS SUPPLY EVEN IF MADE WITHOUT CONSIDERATION

SCHEDULE I

[See Section 7]

Para No.	Heading	Nature of Activities
1.	Transfer/disposal of business assets	Permanent transfer or disposal of business assets where input tax credit (ITC) has been availed on such assets.
2.	Supply between related/ distinct person	Supply of goods or services or both between related persons or between distinct persons as specified in section 25, when made in the course or furtherance of business Provided that gifts not exceeding fifty thousand rupees in value in a financial year by an employer to an employee shall not be treated as supply of goods or services or both.
3.	Supply of goods between Principal & Agent	**Supply of goods** (a) by a principal to his agent where the agent undertakes to supply such goods on behalf of the principal; or (b) by an agent to his principal where the agent undertakes to receive such goods on behalf of the principal.
4.	Import of Service	Import of services by a person from a related person or from any of his other establishments outside India, in the course or furtherance of business.

1. Permanent transfer or disposal of business assets where input tax credit has been availed on such assets.

Normally, GST is not applicable on supply made without consideration. However, permanent transfer/disposal of **business assets** without consideration is one exception to this general principle.

"Permanent transfer" means transfer without any intention of receiving the goods back.

Goods sent on job work or goods sent for testing/certification will not qualify, as supply as there is no permanent transfer.

Donation of business assets or scrapping or disposal in any other manner would also qualify as 'supply', where input tax credit has been claimed.

GST is applicable only on sale of business assets and not on sale/transfer of personal assets such as land/ building or other movable or immovable assets.

Example 1: XYZ Limited has provided company car to its senior executive Mr. Rakesh for use in official purposes with the option to buy back the said car after five years at depreciated value. Will it attract GST? Will the answer be different if it is transferred to the executive free of cost after five years?

Answer: Employer & employee are related parties as per explanation appended to Sec 15 of CGST Act, 2017. Supply of goods or services or both between related, when made in the course or furtherance of business is taxable under GST even if made without consideration.

Query 1: Use of assets without transfer of rights is supply of service. Use of company car for official purposes is in the course of employment and not in the course or furtherance of business. As such, it will not cover under Para 2 of Schedule I. Hence, not a taxable supply under GST & GST liability will not arise. However, when the car is transfer to the employee at depreciated value, GST liability will arise. Employer shall be liable to pay GST on sale of car to employee.

Query 2: If the car is transfer to employee after five years without consideration, it will be consider as gift. As per proviso to Para 2 of Schedule I of CGST Act, 2017 gifts not exceeding fifty thousand rupees in value in a financial year by an employer to an employee shall not be treated as supply of goods or services or both.

If the value of car as per valuation Rule 28 will be more than ₹ 50,000, employer shall be liable to pay GST on said transaction.

Example 2: ABC is a partnership firm engaged in trading business having annual turnover of ₹ 60 lakhs and registered under Composition Scheme. It has provided a motor cycle of the firm costing ₹ 65000 to its employee free of cost. Will it attract GST?

Answer: A dealer under Composition Scheme cannot avail input tax credit (ITC). Transfer of business assets without consideration, where input tax credit has not been availed is not taxable. But in the instant case, since the value of gift exceed ₹ 50,000, gift to employee in excess of ₹ 50,000 per annum to an employee is taxable in the hands of Employer.

2. Supply of goods, services, or both between related persons or between distinct persons as specified in section 25, when made in the course or furtherance of business:

Provided that gifts not exceeding fifty thousand rupees in value in a financial year by an employer to an employee shall not be treated as supply of goods or services or both.

Related person includes employer & employee. Gift by an employer to an employee in excess of ₹ 50,000 in a financial year will be treated as "Supply of good or services or both" and it will attract GST.

Note: A person who is under influence of another person is called a related person like member of same family or subsidiary of a company. The term related person has been defined in explanation to Section 15.

Example 3: Suppose a partner of a CA firm represents his employee before Income tax authorities, in respect of notice served on his employee by IT Department, without charging any professional fee, it would constitute a taxable supply under GST and be subject to levy and collection of taxes.

In terms of Sec 25 of CGST Act, branches or division of a company/business entity will be treated as distinct person, if separate registration has been obtained for branch/business vertical, though it has only one Permanent Account Number (PAN).

Example 4: ITC Ltd. has its manufacturing unit in West Bengal and it has branches in different state of the country. Suppose there are excess stock in its branch office in Bihar and its branch office in Odisha is running out of stock. Will the transfer of stock from Bihar branch to Odisha branch without consideration is a taxable supply under GST?

Answer. If stock is transfer from Bihar to Odisha, it will treated as "Supply" between two distinct person, and separate registration is required for each state under GST. The stock transfer/branch transfer between distinct person, though belong to same entity, would be subject to levy and collection of GST.

3. Supply of goods

(a) by a principal to his agent where the agent undertakes to supply such goods on behalf of the principal; or

(b) by an agent to his principal where the agent undertakes to receive such goods on behalf of the principal.

Section 2(5) of the Act: "Agent means a person, including a factor, broker, commission agent, arhatia, del credere agent, an auctioneer or any other mercantile agent, by whatever name called, who carries on the business of supply or receipt of goods or services or both on behalf of another".

Section 2(88) of the Act: "Principal means a person on whose behalf an agent carries on the business of supply or receipt of goods or services or both".

Example 5: A company based in Lucknow employs an agent in Kanpur (UP). The principal send the goods to his Kanpur agent without consideration. Agent sell the goods on behalf of principal on commission basis. The agent may collect payments on behalf of the principal or the customer might make direct payment to the principal. Is it a supply?

Answer. There is no sale because agent does not receive any consideration from Principal. However, it will be treated as deemed supply as per Para 3(a) of Schedule I and GST is payable. The person paying GST can later claim input tax credit (ITC).

Similarly, supply of goods by an agent to his principal on commission basis, where the agent undertakes to receive/collect such goods on behalf of the principal is deemed as supply of goods.

Example 6: A company employ an agent in Mumbai on commission basis. The agent receive the goods from various vendor of Maharashtra and supply to the company, i.e. principal. Is it a supply under GST?

Answer. As per Para 3(a) of Schedule I, Supply of goods by an agent to his principal where the agent undertakes to receive such goods on behalf of the principal is deemed supply. Both agent and principal will be liable to pay GST jointly and severally.

4. Import of services by a person from a related person or from any of his other establishments outside India, in the course or furtherance of business.

Import of services by a person from a related person or from any of his other establishments outside India, for business purposes, will be treated as supply even if the import involves no consideration.

Example 7: Infotech Ltd., Bengaluru has a branch in Singapore. The Singapore unit provides service to its HO in Bengaluru, India without any consideration. Is it a supply under GST?

Ans. Import of Service by a company from any of his other establishments outside India without consideration, in the course or furtherance of business is a supply under GST as per Para 4 of Schedule I. Therefore, service received by Bengaluru branch of Infotech Ltd. from its Singapore branch will be treated as import of Service & shall be liable to GST under reverse charge (RCM) basis in India.

4.13 SCHEDULE II, CGST ACT 2017

Activities or Transactions to be Treated as a Supply of Goods or Supply of Services

The time of supply and place of supply provisions are different for goods & services. The GST Council has also prescribed different rates of GST for Supply of Goods & Supply of Services. As such, it is necessary to classify a transaction as to whether it is "Supply of Goods" or "Supply of services".

To avoid any confusion Schedule II of CGST Act 2017 has clearly specified certain activities or transactions, which is to be categorize as either supply of goods or supply of services.

(Activities or transactions to be treated as supply of Goods or supply of Services)

Para No.	Heading	Nature of Activities	To be Treated as Supply of Goods/ Services
1.	**Transfer**	(a) Transfer of the title in goods	Supply of goods
		(b) Transfer of right or share in goods (undivided) without the transfer of title thereof	Supply of services
		(c) Transfer of title in goods under an agreement that property in goods shall pass at a future date on payment (i.e. forward contract)	Supply of goods
2.	**Land & Building**	(a) Lease rent, tenancy, easement, license to occupy land	Supply of services
		(b) Lease or letting out of the building for business or commerce (building may be commercial, industrial or residential complex)	Supply of services
3.	**Treatment or Process**	Any treatment or process which is applied to another person's goods (for example, a job worker processing for a manufacturer)	Supply of services
4.	**Transfer of Business Assets/Goods**	(a) Transfer/disposal of any business assets by the owner or its direction, to any person, with or without consideration	Supply of goods
		(b) Transfer of business assets to any person for private use with or without consideration	Supply of services
		(c) If the owner ceases to be taxable person, than the business assets will be assumed to be supplied by him in the course of his business immediately before he ceases to be taxable person	Supply of goods
5.	**Supply of Service**	(a) Renting of Immovable Property (Except rented for residential purposes to an unregistered person)	Supply of services

Para No.	Heading	Nature of Activities	To be Treated as Supply of Goods/ Services
		(b) Construction of a building including a complex or building intended for sell to a buyer wholly or partly (if entire consideration received after issue of completion certificate, i.e. ready to move, it will not cover here)	Supply of services
		(c) Temporary transfer or permitting the use of any intellectual property rights (this covers allowing the use of trademark, copyright, design, patents, etc.)	Supply of services
		(d) Development, design, programming, upgradation, implementation of IT software	Supply of services
		(e) Agreeing to the obligation to refrain from an act, or to tolerate an act or a situation, or to do an act (this covers non-compete agreement, refraining from an act, agreeing/allowing an act against consideration, etc.)	Supply of services
		(f) Transfer of the right to use any goods for any purpose for a consideration	Supply of services
6.	**Composite Supply**	(a) Works contract, Section 2(119) (construction/ repair, maintenance of immovable property)	Supply of services
		(b) Supply by way of serving food and drink (except alcohol) in restaurant or outdoor catering	Supply of services
7.	**Supply of goods to members of society**	Supply of goods by any unincorporated association or body of persons to a members (for cash, deferred payment or other valuable consideration)	Supply of goods

4.14 SCHEDULE III, CGST ACT 2017: EXCLUSION FROM SUPPLY

Activities or Transactions, which shall be Treated neither as a "Supply of Goods" nor a "Supply of Services"

Schedule III to the CGST Act, 2017 spells out activities or transactions which shall be treated as neither "Supply of Goods" nor "Supply of Services" i.e. not within the meaning and scope of supply, as such not taxable under GST. This includes:

Para	Heading	Nature of Activities
1.	Employment	Services by an employee to the employer in the course of or in relation to his employment.
2.	Court/Tribunal	Services by any court or Tribunal established under any law for the time being in force.
3.	MP/MLA/ Constitutional Authority	(a) The functions performed by the Members of Parliament, Members of State Legislature, Members of Panchayats, Members of Municipalities and Members of other local authorities; (b) The duties performed by any person who holds any post in pursuance of the provisions of the Constitution in that capacity; or (c) The duties performed by any person as a Chairperson or a Member or a Director in a body established by the Central Government or a State Government or local authority and who is not deemed as an employee before the commencement of this clause.

Para	Heading	Nature of Activities
4.	Funeral	Services of funeral, burial, crematorium or mortuary including transportation of the deceased.
5.	Sale of land/ready to move building	Sale of land and, subject to clause (b) of paragraph 5 of Schedule II, sale of building.
6.	Actionable claim	Actionable claims, other than specified actionable claim.
7.	Supply from non-taxable territory to a non-taxable territory	Supply of goods from a place in the non-taxable territory to another place in the non-taxable territory without such goods entering into India.
8(a)	Supply of warehoused goods	Supply of warehoused goods to any person before clearance for home consumption.
8(b)	Supply by endorsement of documents	Supply of goods by the consignee to any other person, by endorsement of documents of title to the goods, after the goods have been dispatched from the port of origin located outside India but before clearance for home consumption.

Note: Sr Nos. 7 and 8 have been added as per CGST Amendment Act, 2018.

Explanation:

(1) For the purposes of Paragraph 2, the term "court" includes District Court, High Court and Supreme Court.

(2) For the purposes of paragraph 6, "Actionable Claim" means a claim to any debt, other than a debt secured by mortgage of immovable property or by hypothecation or pledge of moveable property, or to any beneficial interest in moveable property not in possession either actual or constructive, of the claimant, which the civil courts authorize as affording grounds of relief whether such debt or beneficial interest be existent, accruing or conditional or contingent (Sec 2(1) of the CGST Act, 2017 read with Section 3 of the Transfer of Property Act, 1882).

In simple terms: Actionable claim means a claim (enforceable right) in which amount is recoverable with the help of law on civil grounds.

Example of Actionable Claim

(1) The benefit of a contract giving an option to purchase the land
(2) Claim for arrears of rent
(3) Claim for rent to fall due in future
(4) An option to repurchase the properties sold
(5) Earnest money deposit (EMD) becoming repayable
(6) Dividend due on shares/stocks
(7) Amount due under a policy of life insurance
(8) Fixed deposit receipts.

4.15 GST ON CERTAIN SPECIFIED SUPPLY/TRANSACTIONS

(1) GST on Sale of Scrap Materials: The term "Scrap" has not been defined any where in the GST Laws. As such one can derive its meaning as per normal business or commerce parlance. As per business dictionary "scrap" means "waste that either has no economic value or only the value of its basic material content recoverable through recycling". In GST regime, in order to be taxable, the waste and scrap don't have to pass the test of "*manufacture*" or "*mechanical process*" *or* "*marketability*".

Scrap is a taxable supply under GST. The rate of GST on scrap depends upon nature of scrap and its HSN Code. For the purpose of determination of value of supply under GST, tax collected at source (TCS) under the provisions of the Income Tax Act, 1961 shall not be includible. TCS u/s 206(C)(1) of Income-Tax Act, 1961 should be collected on value inclusive of GST.

While taxability of waste and scrap is no longer contentious, finding proper HSN code is definitely a tedious task. The highest rate of GST for scraps material is 18%.

GST RATE CHART OF SCRAP MATERIALS

HSN Code	Description	GST Rate
3915	Plastic waste, parings or scrap	5%
4004	Rubber waste, parings or scrap	5%
4017 00 20	Hard rubber waste or scrap	5%
4401	Wood scrap	5%
4415	Packing cases, box, crates, drums	5%
4707	Paper waste or scrap	5%
7001	Cullet or other waste or scrap of glass	5%
2524	Asbestos waste	5%
7112	Waste and scrap of precious metal	3%
3006	Pharmaceutical waste (except contraceptives)	12%
3825	Municipal waste, sewage sludge, clinical waste	0%
2621	Slag & Ash waste	18%
7204	Vehicle scrap	18%
7204	MS Scrap of all types	18%
7204	Scrap US rail	18%
7404	Copper waste & scrap	18%
7408	Bronze waste & scrap	18%
7503	Nickel waste & scrap	18%
7602	Aluminum waste & scrap	18%
7902	Zinc waste & scrap	18%
8002	Tin waste & scrap	18%
8113	Cermet's and articles thereof waste and scrap	18%
84 or 85	E-waste	18%
8548	Waste and scrap of primary cells primary batteries and electric accumulators	18%

Notes

(a) E-waste means electrical and electronic equipment listed in Schedule I of the E-Waste (Management) Rules, 2016, published in the Gazette of India vide G.S.R. 338 (E) dated the 23rd March 2016, including the components, consumables, parts and spares which make these products operational.

(b) The HSN code for a large number of scraps materials has till now not yet been notified. If someone does not find appropriate HSN code of a scrap item, he may cover the same under residual Entry 453 of Schedule III of Notification No. 1/2017-Central Tax (Rate) dated 28th June 2017.

(c) The rate of GST on E-waste (Tariff item 84 or 85) has be increased from 5% to 18% with effect from 18th July 2022 Vide Notification No. 6/2022-Intergrated Tax (Rate) dated 13th July 2022.

(2) GST on sale of waste and scrap by Government departments: It is a taxable supply under GST. Waste and scrap sold by Government departments to a registered dealer is taxable under RCM, i.e. the buyer shall be liable to pay GST under RCM as per Notification No. 36/2017-Central Tax (Rate) dated 13.10.2017. However, if the waste and scrap sold by Government departments to an un-registered person, the respective Government departments (i.e. Central Government, State Government, Union territory or a local authority) shall be liable to get registered and pay GST thereon.

(3) GST on lease/rental transactions: A lease is a contractual arrangement between owner (lessor) and user (lessee) whereby one party, the lessor, grants the right to use a particular assets (such as a parcel of land, building, equipment, or machinery, etc.) for a specific period and under specified conditions to the other party, the lessee.

Leases are broadly classified into two categories:

1. Finance Lease: Finance lease is relatively for a longer period which is sufficient to amortize the capital invested by the lessor (owner) and leave some profit. It involves the transfer of all risk and rewards associated with the ownership of assets to the lessee but the title may or may not be transferred at the end of lease period.

2. Operating Lease/Service Lease/Maintenance Lease: Operating lease is relatively for a short period of time. The lease period is shorter than economic life of the assets. Operating lease require the lessor to maintain and service the leased assets.

As per Sec 7 of the CGST Act, 2017, the expression supply includes all forms of supply of goods or services or both such as sale, transfer, barter, exchange, licence, rental, lease or disposal made or agreed to be made for a consideration by a person in the course or furtherance of business.

GST does not differentiate between Finance & Operating leases. The time of supply of lease depends upon whether "transfer of title" involves in the lease transactions or not.

(a) If the lease agreement stipulates transfer of title : Supply of goods

(b) If the lease agreement does not stipulate transfer of title : Supply of services

As per Sl No. 2(a) of Schedule II of CGST Act, 2017 any lease, tenancy, easement, license to occupy land is a supply of services. However, as per Sl No. 5 of Schedule III, Sale of land is neither supply of goods nor services. GST paid on lease rent is eligible for ITC as it is not covered in the list of blocked credit u/s 17(5).

GST rates on lease transactions

Sl. No.	Description of Services	Rate of GST
01	Service by way of granting of long-term lease of (thirty years, or more) of industrial plots or plots for development of infrastructure for financial business, provided by the State Government Industrial Development Corporations or Undertakings or by any other entity having 20 per cent or more ownership of Central Government, State Government, Union territory to the industrial units or the developers in any industrial or financial business area.	Nil Rate Entry No. 41 of Exemption Notification No. 12/2017 dated 28.06.2017
02	Service by way of granting of long-term lease of thirty years, or more, on or after 01.04.2019, for construction of residential apartments by a promoter in a project, intended for sale to a buyer, wholly or partly, except where the entire consideration has been received after issuance of completion certificate, where required, by the competent authority or after its first occupation, whichever is earlier.	Nil Rate Entry No. 41-B of Exemption Notification No. 12/2017 dated 28.06.2017
03	Renting or leasing of agro machinery or vacant land with or without a structure incidental to its use for cultivation or agricultural produce.	Nil Rate Entry No. 54(d) of Exemption notification No. 12/2017 dated 28.06.2017
04	Long-term lease of land (30 years or more) by any person against consideration in the form of upfront amount (called as premium, salami, cost, price, development charges or by any other name) and/or periodic rent for construction of a project by a promoter.	18% Taxable under RCM under entry No. 5C
05	Renting/leasing of immovable property by the Central Government, State Government, Union territory or local authority to a registered person.	18% Taxable under RCM under entry No. 5A
06	Leasing/renting of vacant land by any person for commercial purpose (other than 1 to 5 above)	18% under forward charge

Sl. No.	Description of Services	Rate of GST
07	Renting/leasing of residential dwelling to a registered person by any person.	18% Taxable under RCM under entry No. 5AA (N.No. 04/2022-CT(R) dt. 13-07-2022)
08	Renting/leasing of residential dwelling to an un-registered person by a registered person for use as residence.	Exempted Entry No. 12 of Exemption notification No. 12/2017 dated 28.06.2017
09	Renting/leasing of any motor vehicle designed to carry passengers where the cost of fuel is included in the consideration charged from the service recipient, provided to a body corporate.	5% Taxable under RCM under entry No. 15 in the hands of body corporate
10	Renting/leasing of any motor vehicle designed to carry passengers where the cost of fuel is not included in the consideration charged from the service recipient.	18%
11	Renting of vehicles to state transport undertakings and local authorities.	Nil Entry No. 22 of Exemption notification No. 12/2017 dated 28.06.2017
12	Transfer of right to use any goods for any purpose (whether or not for a specified period).	Same rate of GST and compensation cess as applicable on supply of similar goods
13	Any transfer of right in goods or of undivided share in goods without the transfer of title thereof.	Same rate of GST and compensation cess as applicable on supply of similar goods
14	Leasing or rental services concerning construction machinery and equipment with or without operator [SAC 997313].	18%
15	Leasing or rental services concerning office machinery and equipment (except computers) with or without operator [SAC 997314].	18%
16	Leasing or rental services concerning computers with or without operators [SAC 997315].	18%
17	Leasing or rental services concerning televisions, radios, video cassette recorders, projectors, audio systems and related equipment and accessories (home entertainment equipment) [SAC 997321].	18%
18	Leasing or rental services concerning furniture and other household appliances [SAC 997323].	18%
19	Licensing services for the right to use computer software and databases. [SAC 997331].	18%
20	Licensing services for the right to use other intellectual property products and other resources N.E.C. [SAC 997339].	18%

Note: Please refer Exemption Notification No. 12/2017-Central Tax (Rate), dated 28-06-2017 and RCM Notification No. 13/2017-Central Tax (Rate), dated 28-06-2017 as amended from time to time.

(4) GST on Real Estate transaction: A real estate transaction is the process whereby rights in a unit of property (or designated real estate) is transferred between two or more parties, e.g. in case of conveyance one party being the seller(s) and the other being the buyer(s).

A "Residential Real Estate Project" means a "Real Estate Project" in which the carpet area of the commercial apartments is not more than 15% of the total carpet area of all the apartments in the project.

As per GST law, the activity of construction of complex, buildings, civil structures or part thereof is cover within the meaning and scope of works contracts services as defined in Sec 2(119) of CGST Act, 2017 and it is a supply of services.

As per Para 5 of Schedule III of CGST Act, 2017 sale of land & building (where the entire consideration has been received after issuance of completion certificate or after its first occupation, whichever is earlier) is neither supply of goods nor supply of services.

As per CBIC Circular No. 177/09/2022-TRU dated 3rd August 2022, land may be sold either as it is or after some development such as levelling, laying down of drainage lines, water lines, electricity lines, etc. It is clarified that sale of such developed land is also sale of land and is covered by Sr. No. 5 of Schedule III of the Central Goods and Services Tax Act, 2017 and accordingly does not attract GST.

As per Para 5(b) of Schedule II of CGST Act, 2017, construction of a complex, building, civil structure or a part thereof, including a complex or building intended for sale to a buyer, wholly or partly, except where the entire consideration has been received after issuance of completion certificate, where required, by the competent authority or after its first occupation, whichever is earlier is a supply of service. For levy of GST, there should be an underlying supply of goods or services, or both, for a consideration in the course or furtherance of business.

Therefore, GST is applicable only on under construction building, flat and apartment including commercial property (shops, godowns, offices, etc.) and not on sale or transfer of property after issuance of completion certificate or after its first occupation.

Rate of GST on Real Estate Transaction

Sl. No.	**Type of Property**	**Effective rate of GST (After 1/3rd deduction for value of land) Before 1st April 2019**	**Effective Rate of GST (After 1/3rd deduction for value of land) w.e.f. 1st April 2019 (Notification No. 03/2019 dated 29th March 2019.)**
1.	Residential Property (affordable housing scheme)	8% with ITC	1% without ITC on total consideration
2.	Residential Property (Non-affordable housing scheme)	12% with ITC	5% without ITC on total consideration
3.	Commercial properties (shops, godowns, offices etc.)	12% with ITC	5% without ITC on total consideration (constructions in RREP)
			12% with ITC on total consideration (constructions in REP)

Note: The rates given above is after one-third deduction for the value of land.

(A) Conditions for new tax rate:

(a) Input tax credit shall not be available.

(b) 80% of inputs and input services shall be purchased from registered persons. On shortfall of purchases from 80%, tax shall be paid by the builder under RCM.

(c) Services by way of grant of development rights, long-term lease of land (against upfront payment in the form of premiums, 'salami', development charges, etc.) or FSI (including additional FSI), electricity, high-speed diesel, motor spirit and natural gas will not form a part of the value of procurements for the purpose of 80% procurement condition as given above.

(d) Developers are liable to pay tax at the rate of 18% on a shortfall in the value of procurements, except in the case of cement and capital goods, wherein tax is liable to be paid at the applicable rate as per the tariff. Any tax paid under reverse charge on input and input services will be deemed to have been procured from registered persons.

(e) Procurements from registered and unregistered persons shall be maintain project-wise and should be reported with the shortfall, along with the tax payment, by 30 June of the following financial year. However, tax on cement received from unregistered persons is to be paid in the month in which the cement is received. Input tax credit that has not been availed needs to be reported every month by reporting it as ineligible credit in GSTR-3B.

(B) Valuation of Supply: The value of construction services provided by developers in lieu of development rights or FSI shall be deemed equal to the total amount charged for similar apartments in the project from independent buyers other than landowners nearest to the date of transfer of such development rights or FSI, less the value of land.

For landowners, the value of supply of services by way of transfer of development rights or FSI by a person in lieu of residential or commercial apartments will be deemed to be equal to the value of similar apartments charged from independent buyers nearest to the date of transfer of development rights or FSI.

Where the landowner transfer his share of flats under JDA, while the property is under construction, he is required to pay GST on said transfer.

(C) Taxability of Joint Development Agreement (JDA): Under a JDA, the landowner enters an agreement (registered or unregistered) with a developer to develop a project, along with a power of attorney providing the developer with rights such as right to develop, rights to obtain necessary approvals and create a charge on land, etc.

In lieu of such development rights, the landowner is compensated in one of the following ways:

(i) Fixed consideration
(ii) Fixed built-up area
(iii) Percentage of total realization

The role of the landowner is typically restricted to providing the developer with development rights and the landowner does not generally participate in construction or development of property.

The key tax implications relating to this are discussed below:

Typically, in a JDA, there are two underlying transactions—transfer of development rights by the landowner in lieu of construction services and supply of construction services by the developer in lieu of development rights. Taxability of both these transactions has been specified under GST law, which is summarized below:

(a) Landowner: For the landowner, the activity of lease, tenancy, easement and license to occupy land is deemed to be supply of services according to Schedule II. Therefore, the activity of transfer of development rights can be categorized as transfer of right or license in land to the developer, which is qualify as supply of services and subject to GST @ 18%.

(b) Developer: For the developer, the construction of a complex, building, civil structure or a part thereof is a supply of services and attract GST at the rate of 1.5% or 7.5% (based on the type of project) on the total value, along with one-third deduction towards the value of land [Vide notification no. 03/2019-Central Tax (Rate) dated 29th March 2019].

Point of taxation: The time of supply for both kinds of transactions, i.e. transfer of development rights by the landowner to the developer against consideration in the form of construction services and by the developer against consideration in the form of development right is governed by Notification No. 4/2018 dated 25 January 2018. In terms of said notification, the point of taxation under GST will arise at the time when the developer transfers the possession or the right in the constructed property to the landowner by entering a deed of conveyance or instrument such as an allotment letter.

However, if the arrangement is in the form of revenue share or immediate cash payment, then the time of supply shall be the date of signing of the JDA.

(D) Definition/clarification issued by TRU, Govt of India dated 7th May 2019

(1) Affordable housing: A residential house/flat of carpet area of up to 90 sqm in non-metropolitan cities/towns and 60 sqm in metropolitan cities having value up to ₹ 45 lacs (both for metropolitan and non-metropolitan cities). Metropolitan Cities are Bengaluru, Chennai, Delhi NCR (limited to Delhi, Noida, Greater Noida, Ghaziabad, Gurgaon, and Faridabad), Hyderabad, Kolkata and Mumbai (whole of MMR).

(2) Ongoing Projects: A project which meets the following conditions shall be considered as an ongoing project.

(i) Commencement certificate for the project, where required, has been issued by the competent authority on or before 31st March 2019, and it is certified by a registered architect, chartered engineer or a licensed surveyor that construction of the project has started (i.e. earthwork for site preparation for the project has been completed and excavation for foundation has started) on or before 31st March 2019.

(ii) Where commencement certificate in respect of the project, is not required to be issued by the competent authority, it is to be certified by any of the authorities specified in (i) above that, construction of the project has started on or before the 31st March 2019.

(iii) Completion certificate has not been issued or first occupation of the project has not taken place on or before the 31st March 2019.

(iv) Apartments of the project have been, partly or wholly, booked on or before 31st March 2019.

At least some apartments in the project should have been booked prior to 1st April 2019. At least one instalment should have been received from the flat buyer and should be credited to the bank account of the promoter.

(3) RREP (Residential Real Estate Projects): A "Residential Real Estate Project" means a "Real Estate Project" in which the carpet area of the commercial apartments is not more than 15% of the total carpet area of all the apartments in the project.

(4) Commencement certificate: "Commencement certificate" means the commencement certificate or the building permit or the construction permit, by whatever name called issued by the competent authority to allow or permit the promoter to begin development works on an immovable property, as per the sanctioned plan.

(5) What is the criteria to be used by an architect, a chartered engineer or a licensed surveyor for certifying that construction of the project has started by 31st March 2019: Construction of a project shall be considered to have been started on or before 31st March 2019, if the earthwork for site preparation for the project has been completed, and excavation for foundation has started on or before the 31st March 2019.

(6) What shall be the classification of and rate of tax applicable to works contract service provided by a contractor to a developer or promoter under the new dispensation effective from 01-04-2019 for

(i) New project after 1.4.2019 and ongoing projects where option has been exercised for new rate and

(ii) Ongoing projects where option has not been exercised for new rate?

The rate of tax applicable on the work contract service provided by a contractor to a promoter for construction of a real estate project shall be 12% or 18% depending upon whether such work contract service is provided for construction of affordable residential apartments or residential apartments other than affordable residential apartments. Rate of tax applicable on such work contract service provided by a contractor to a promoter on construction of commercial apartments shall be 18% (irrespective of option exercised by developer-promoter). The relevant entries of the notification are at items (iv), (v), (va) and (vi) against sl. no. 3 of the table in Notification No. 11/2017-Cenral Tax (rate) dated 28-06-2017 prescribing rate of 12% for works contract services of construction of affordable apartments/apartments being constructed under schemes specified therein. In case of works contract services for construction of other apartments, rate of 18% as prescribed in item (xii) against sl. no. 3 of the table in Notification No. 11/2017-Cenral Tax (rate) dated 28-06-2017 shall be applicable.

(7) Can a developer take deduction of actual value of Land involved in sale of unit instead of taking deduction of deemed value of Land as per Paragraph 2 to Notification No. 11/2017-CTR?

No. Valuation mechanism prescribed in paragraph 2 of the notification No. 11/2017-CT (R) dated 28.06.2017 clearly prescribes one-third abatement towards value of land.

(8) Land owner being an individual is not engaged in the business of land relating activities and thus whether the transfer of development rights by an individual to a promoter is liable for GST and whether the same will fall within the scope of "Supply" as defined in Section 7 of CGST/SGST Act, 2017?

The term business has been assigned a very wide meaning in the CGST Act and it includes any trade, commerce, manufacture, profession, vacation, adventure, or any other similar activity whether or not it is for a pecuniary benefit irrespective of the volume, frequency, continuity or regularity of such activity or transaction. Therefore, the activity of transfer of development rights by a landowner, whether an individual or not, to a promoter is a supply of service subject to GST.

(9) Can a buyer excise option to pay tax at new or old rate in respect of balance instalments after April 2019 in respect of flat/apartment booked prior to 1st April 2019 and paid some instalments with 12% GST?

The buyer cannot exercise option to pay tax at the new or old rates. It is the builder, who has to exercise the option to pay tax on construction of apartment.

(5) GST on Guarantee fee paid for Corporate guarantee provided for securing Debt: A corporate guarantee is a guarantee given by the corporate to cover exposure of some other related entity to their bank. The corporate guarantee is only for the limited purpose of securing loans to its subsidiaries. Corporate guarantees are issue in order to safeguard the financial health of their associate enterprises and to provide it support. When a holding/ parent company gives guarantees of repayment of a loan granted to one of its subsidiaries, if the subsidiary defaults on the loan, the guarantor who agreed, guarantees that the loan will be repaid. Corporate guarantees are provided without any security of underlying assets.

By guaranteeing credit facility, the guarantor primarily assists the borrower in availing credit facility, therefore it is a supply of service.

Guarantee fee paid towards guaranteeing debt of a subsidiary company is a financial service. Corporate guarantee is a surety given to the lender bank. If in future, the borrower fails to pay the due amount owed to those lenders, the Corporate guarantor will pay to those lenders.

As per Sl No. 34A of Notification No. 12/2017-Central Tax (Rate) dated 28.06.2017, Services supplied by Central Government, State Government, Union territory to their undertakings or Public Sector Undertakings (PSUs) by way of guaranteeing the loans taken by such undertakings or PSUs from the banking companies and financial institutions, is exempted under GST.

Corporate guarantee provided by any entity other than by Govt. is a taxable supply under GST.

This service is taxable under ' Services Auxiliary to financial services' attracting GST @ 18% [SAC 997159].

(6) GST on works contract: A works contract is a "composite supply" involving supply of both goods & services. Composite supply relating to immovable property only treated as "works contract" under GST law. As per Para 6(a) of Schedule II to the CGST Act, 2017, works contract as defined in section 2(119) of the CGST Act, 2017 shall be treated as supply of service. So, any composite supply which is movable in nature is not covered under "works contract" in GST regime. It is pertinent to mention that all "works contracts" are composite supply but all composite supplies are not "works contract".

As per Section 2(119) of the CGST Act, 2017 "works contract" means a contract for:

- building, construction,
- fabrication,
- completion, erection, installation,
- fitting out,
- improvement, modification,
- repair, maintenance, renovation,
- alteration or commissioning

of any immovable property wherein transfer of property in goods (whether as goods or in some other form) is involved in the execution of such contract."

Rate of GST on works contract service

The rate of GST for Works Contract service have been prescribed in serial number 3 of Notification No. 11/2017-CT (Rate) dated 28.06.2017 as amended from time to time. The latest amendment in rate of GST for works contract services has been made Vide N.N. 03/2022-CT(R) dt. 13-07-2022 w.e.f. 18th July 2022.

The concessional rate of GST @12% applicable on works contract services (e.g. canal, dam, irrigation work, road, bridge, tunnel, etc.) covered under Sl. No. 3 (iii) and (iv) introduced vide N.N. 20/2017-CT(R) dt. 22-08-2017, provided to Central Govt, State Govt, Union Territory and local authority has been withdrawn Vide N.N. 03/2022-CT(R) dt. 13-07-2022 w.e.f. 18th July 2022.

Sl. No.	Description of Services	Rate of GST (CGST+SGST)	Remarks
(i)	Construction of affordable residential apartments by a promoter in a Residential Real Estate Project (herein after referred to as RREP) which commences on or after 1st April 2019 or in an ongoing RREP in respect of which the promoter has not exercised option to pay central tax on construction of apartments at the rates as specified for item (ie) or (if) below, as the case may be, in the manner prescribed therein, intended for sale to a buyer, wholly or partly, except where the entire consideration has been received after issuance of completion certificate, where required, by the competent authority or after its first occupation, whichever is earlier.	1.5%	Amended Vide Notification No. 03/2019-Central Tax (Rate) dated 29.03.2019 (Provisions of paragraph 2 of this notification shall apply for valuation of this service)

Sl. No.	Description of Services	Rate of GST (CGST+SGST)	Remarks
(ia)	Construction of residential apartments other than affordable residential apartments by a promoter in an RREP which commences on or after 1st April 2019 or in an ongoing RREP in respect of which the promoter has not exercised option to pay central tax on construction of apartments at the rates as specified for item (ie) or (if) below, as the case may be, in the manner prescribed therein, intended for sale to a buyer, wholly or partly, except where the entire consideration has been received after issuance of completion certificate, where required, by the competent authority or after its first occupation, whichever is earlier.	7.5%	-do-
(ib)	Construction of commercial apartments (shops, offices, godowns, etc.) by a promoter in an RREP which commences on or after 1st April 2019 or in an ongoing RREP in respect of which the promoter has not exercised option to pay central tax on construction of apartments at the rates as specified for item (ie) or (if) below, as the case may be, in the manner prescribed therein, intended for sale to a buyer, wholly or partly, except where the entire consideration has been received after issuance of completion certificate, where required, by the competent authority or after its first occupation, whichever is earlier.	7.5%	-do-
(ic)	Construction of affordable residential apartments by a promoter in a Real Estate Project (herein after referred to as REP) other than RREP, which commences on or 0.75 3 after 1st April 2019 or in an ongoing REP other than RREP in respect of which the promoter has not exercised option to pay central tax on construction of apartments at the rates as specified for item (ie) or (if) below, as the case may be, in the manner prescribed therein, intended for sale to a buyer, wholly or partly, except where the entire consideration has been received after issuance of completion certificate, where required, by the competent authority or after its first occupation, whichever is earlier.	1.5%	-do-
(id)	Construction of residential apartments other than affordable residential apartments by a promoter in a REP other than a RREP which commences on or after 1st April 2019 or in an ongoing REP other than RREP in respect of which the promoter has not exercised option to pay central tax on construction of apartments at the rates as specified for item (ie) or (if) below, as the case may be, in the manner prescribed therein, intended for sale to a buyer, wholly or partly, except where the entire consideration has been received after issuance of completion certificate, where required, by the competent authority or after its first occupation, whichever is earlier.	7.5%	-do-

Sl. No.	Description of Services	Rate of GST (CGST+SGST)	Remarks
(ie)	Construction of an apartment in an ongoing project under any of the schemes specified in sub-item (b), sub-item (c), sub-item (d), sub-item (da) and sub-item (db) of item (iv); sub-item (b), sub-item (c), sub-item (d) and sub-item (da) of item (v); and sub-item (c) of item (vi), against serial number 3 of the Table, in respect of which the promoter has exercised option to pay central tax on construction of apartments at the rates as specified for this item.	12%	-do-
(if)	(i) Construction of a complex, building, civil structure or a part thereof, including, commercial apartments (shops, offices, godowns, etc.) by a promoter in a REP other than RREP. (ii) Residential apartments in an ongoing project, other than affordable residential apartments, in respect of which the promoter has exercised option to pay central tax on construction of apartments at the rates as specified for this item in the manner prescribed herein, but excluding supply by way of services specified at items (i), (ia), (ib), (ic), (id) and (ie) above intended for sale to a buyer, wholly or partly, except where the entire consideration has been received after issuance of completion certificate, where required, by the competent authority or after its first occupation, whichever is earlier.	18%	-do-
(ii)	Omitted		This entry omitted Vide N.No. 03/2019-CT(R) dt. 29-03-2019 w.e.f. 1st April 2019
(iii)	Omitted		This entry omitted Vide N.No. 03/2022-CT(R) dt. 13-07-2022 w.e.f. 18th July 2022
(iv)	Omitted		This entry omitted Vide N.No. 03/2022-CT(R) dt. 13-07-2022 w.e.f. 18th July 2022
(v)	Omitted		This entry omitted Vide N.No. 03/2022-CT(R) dt. 13-07-2022 w.e.f. 18th July 2022
(va)	Omitted		This entry omitted Vide N.No. 03/2022-CT(R) dt. 13-07-2022 w.e.f. 18th July 2022
(vi)	Omitted		This entry omitted Vide N.No. 03/2022-CT(R) dt. 13-07-2022 w.e.f. 18th July 2022

Sl. No.	Description of Services	Rate of GST (CGST+SGST)	Remarks
(vii)	Composite supply of works contract as defined in clause (119) of section 2 of the Central Goods and Services Tax Act, 2017, involving predominantly earth work (that is, constituting more than 75% of the value of the works contract) provided to the Central Government, State Government, Union territory, local authority, a Governmental Authority or a Government Entity.	5%	Provided that where the services are supplied to a Government Entity, they should have been procured by the said entity in relation to a work entrusted to it by the Central Government, State Government, Union territory or local authority, as the case may be.
(viii)	Composite supply of works contract as defined in clause (119) of section 2 of the Central Goods and Services Tax Act, 2017 and associated services, in respect of offshore works contract relating to oil and gas exploration and production (E&P) in the offshore area beyond 12 nautical miles from the nearest point of the appropriate base line.	12%	
(ix)	Omitted	12%	This entry omitted Vide N.No. 03/2022-CT(R) dt. 13-07-2022 w.e.f. 18th July 2022
(x)	Composite supply of works contract as defined in clause (119) of section 2 of the Central Goods and Services Tax Act, 2017 provided by a sub-contractor to the main contractor providing services specified in item (vii) above to the Central Government, State Government, Union territory or a local authority.	12% (Increased from 5% to 12% Vide N.No. 03/2022-CT(R) dt. 13-07-2022 w.e.f. 18th July 2022)	Provided that where the services are supplied to a Government Entity, they should have been procured by the said entity in relation to a work entrusted to it by the Central Government, State Government, Union territory or local authority, as the case may be.
(xi)	Services by way of housekeeping, such as plumbing, carpentering, etc. where the person supplying such service through electronic commerce operator is not liable for registration under sub-section (1) of section 22 of the Central Goods and Services Tax Act, 2017.	5%	Provided that credit of input tax charged on goods and services has not been taken.
(xii)	Construction services other than (vii), (viii) above.	18%	Amended Vide N.No. 03/2022-CT(R) dt. 13-07-2022 w.e.f. 18th July 2022

Please refer Chapter 28 on works contract provision for detailed discussion.

(7) GST on interest, penalty, delayed charges collected from customer against supply of goods and services: CBIC Vide Circular No. 102/21/2019-GST dated 28th June 2019 has clarified that penal interest charged on delayed payment for supply of goods and services will be included in the value of supply and will stand liable for GST. Whereas penal interest charged on the delayed payment of loan repayment will be exempt under GST.

The above circular can be analysed as under:

(1) Penal charges in case of delayed payment of instalment of supply of goods and services shall be included in the value of supply as per section 15(2) (d) of the CGST Act. The same shall be liable to tax under GST.

(2) Penal charges in case of delayed payment of instalment of a loan is money to money transaction will be included in the value of supply as per section 15(2) (d) of the CGST Act. The same shall be exempt through serial no. 27 of the notification No. 12/2017-Central Tax (Rate) dated 28th June 2017. Therefore, penal charges in this case shall not be taxable under GST.

(8) Implication of GST on Liquidated damages/Penalty/Notice period pay/Bond money: [Circular No. 178/10/2022-GST dated 3rd August 2022]: As per Para 5(e) of Schedule II to the CGST Act, 2017 the activity of 'agreeing to the obligation to refrain from an act, or to tolerate an act or a situation, or to do an act' is a supply of service.

The CBIC has clarified that amount received in lieu of liquidated damages/Penalty/Notice period pay/Bond money for breach of contract is not a consideration for supply of any goods or services.

'Liquidated damages' is an amount paid only to compensate for injury, loss or damage suffered by the aggrieved party due to breach of the contract and there is no agreement, express or implied, by the aggrieved party receiving the liquidated damages, to refrain from or tolerate an act or to do anything for the party paying the liquidated damages, in such cases liquidated damages are mere a flow of money from the party who causes breach of the contract to the party who suffers loss or damage due to such breach. Such payments do not constitute consideration for a supply and are not taxable.

The forfeiture of salary or payment of bond money recovered by the employer from employee in the event of the employee leaving the employment before the minimum agreed period is not a consideration for tolerating the act of such premature quitting of employment but as penalties for dissuading the non-serious employees from taking up employment and to discourage and deter such a situation. Further, the employee does not get anything in return from the employer against payment of such amounts. Therefore, such amounts recovered by the employer are not taxable as consideration for the service of agreeing to tolerate an act or a situation.

(9) GST on Solar EPC contract: The rate of GST shall be regulated as per explanation provided against Sl. No. 234 of Notification No. 24/2018-Central Tax (Rate) dated 31st December 2018, read with entry at Sl. No. 38 of the notification No. 11/2017-Central Tax (Rate), dated 28th June 2017.

Notification No. 8/2021-Central Tax (Rate) dated 30th September 2021 [Ref Circular No. 163/19/2021-GST dated 6th October 2021, Para 13].

The value of supply of goods shall be deemed as 70% of the gross consideration charged for all such supplies, and the remaining 30% of the gross consideration charged shall be deemed as value of the said taxable service.

Tax Rate:

(1) Goods: Seventy percent (70%) of the gross consideration charged shall be taxable @12% under HSN code 8504/8507/85414011 and 85322990 (5% up to 30th Sept. 2021 and 12% from 1st October 2021, Entry No. 201A).

(2) Services: Thirty percent (30%) of the gross consideration charged shall be taxable @18% under SAC code 9954 and 998335.

(10) GST on insurance claim received: The term "Actionable Claim" has been defined in Section 3 of the Transfer of Property Act, 1882. In the *Union of India* vs. *Sarada Mills* (1972) case, the Hon'ble Supreme Court held that the actionable claim would include a right to recover insurance money. Hence, an insurance claim received on account of damage to capital assets/stocks is an actionable claim. As per Para 6 of Schedule III to the CGST Act, actionable claims other than lottery, betting, and gambling are treated as "neither supply of goods nor supply of services". Hence, GST not applicable on insurance claim received against loss/damaged to insured assets.

(11) Penalty imposed for violation of laws: Penalties imposed for violation of laws is not a consideration charged by Government or a Local Authority for tolerating violation of laws. Laws are not framed for tolerating their violation. They stipulate penalty not for tolerating violation but for not tolerating, penalizing and deterring such violations. There is no agreement between the Government and the violator specifying that violation would be allowed or permitted against payment of fine or penalty. There cannot be such an agreement as violation of law is never a lawful object or consideration. Hence, penalty recovered by Govt. for violation of laws is not a consideration against supply of any services. Thus, not taxable under GST.

(12) GST implications on mobilization advances and Advance against supply of goods: As a common practice in the execution of large works contracts or turnkey project, mobilization advances provision is kept in the contract agreement to facilitate the contractor to make payment against mobilization of man, material and other resources required for timely take off of the project and easy procurement of equipment, etc. The advance is normally interest bearing and secured against Bank Guarantee submitted by the contractor.

The said advance amount is later adjusted/recovered in a phased manner from the running account (RA Bill) payable to the contractor upon execution of scheduled quantity as provided in Letter of Award (LOA). Therefore, mobilization advance is basically a secured refundable advance in the nature of deposit and the same is neither part of the contract price nor form part of revenue of the contractor.

For any advances to be taxable, under GST regime, it must be in the nature of consideration against a taxable supply.

Under the GST regime, 'deposit' has been excluded from the scope of consideration via the Proviso to Section 2(31) of the CGST Act, 2017. It has been expressly provided that it would not form part of consideration, unless applied as such for the supply.

The service tax appellate tribunal, Mumbai branch in its order No. A/85800/2020 dated 23-07-2020 in the matter of *M/s. Gammon India Limited* vs. *Commissioner of Service Tax–V* has also opined that mobilization advance is not an advance towards the provision of taxable service.

Therefore, mobilization advance is not a consideration for supply of any taxable goods or services, hence not liable to GST.

GST implications on Advance against supply of goods

Generally, GST is imposed on a supplier of goods and service at the time of receipt of payment. However, in some cases, an advance payment is first made by the recipient of the goods or/and service or both to the supplier.

When a payment is made ahead of its actual schedule such payment is termed as advance payment, such as making the payment for the goods or service before the receipt of goods or service. In addition to this, sometimes the supplier of the goods and service requires an advance payment as a safeguard against non-payment, or to cover its costs for supplying a product or rendering of a service.

As per Notification no. 66/2017 dated 15.11.2017, no GST is required to be paid on advances received against supply of goods. This exemption applies to all suppliers of goods who have not opted for composition scheme. The time of supply would arise only at the time of issuance of the invoice and the tax liability needs to be discharged only at that time. However, suppliers of services are required to pay GST at the time of receipt of advances.

Treatment of Advance received against supply of goods in GSTR

In GST Return, details of the amount received as the advance are required to be mentioned in Sr. No. 11A of the GSTR–1. This will reflect the figure of the advance money received in the tax period for which invoice has not been issued.

(13) **GST implication on employer-employee transactions:** Transactions between employer and employee are cover under related parties transactions as per explanations appended to Section 15 of CGST Act, 2017. Schedule I and Schedule III of CGST Act, 2017, govern the taxability of such transaction.

Companies might allow employees to purchase asset of the company like laptop, vehicles, official furniture, etc. after certain period of use in their business at depreciated value or at a nominal cost. In some cases, an organization allow the employee to use company asset for personal purposes. Permanent transfer of business assets is supply of goods while free use of company assets by employee for personal use which are not in the nature of perquisites or cost to company, is supply of services. The employer shall be liable to pay GST in both the cases under forward charge on transaction value, irrespective of whether consideration involved or not.

Schedule I of CGST Act, 2017 covers transactions which are treated as supply, even if consideration not involved.

Schedule III of CGST Act, 2017 covers transactions that is treated as neither supply of goods nor supply of services.

Schedule of CGST Act	**Description**
Para 1: Schedule I (Supply, even if consideration not involved)	Permanent transfer or disposal of business assets where input tax credit has been availed on such assets. "Permanent transfer" means transfer without any intention of receiving the goods back.
Para 2: Schedule I (Supply, even if consideration not involved)	Supply of goods or services or both between related persons or between distinct persons as specified in section 25, when made in the course or furtherance of business: Provided that gifts not exceeding fifty thousand rupees in value in a financial year by an employer to an employee shall not be treated as supply of goods or services or both.

Para 1: Schedule III (Neither supply of goods nor supply of services)	Services by an employee to the employer in the course of or in relation to his employment.

As per Para 2 of Schedule I of CGST Act, 2017, the employer will have to pay taxes on supply of goods or services to employee when made in the course or furtherance of business, irrespective of whether the credit is availed on such assets or not and even if consideration is not involved.

Supply	Taxability	Remarks
Gift by employer (Festival gifts/New year gifts, etc.)	Exempted up to ₹ 50,000 per employee per year	Para 2: Schedule I
Services provided by an employee to the employer in the course or in relation to his employment (Services provided as per contractual agreement between employer & employee)	Neither supply of goods nor supply of services	Para 1: Schedule III
Use of company asset by employee for personal purposes	Supply of services Taxable service in the hands of employer even if provided without consideration	Para 2: Schedule I
Sale/Transfer/disposal of business assets by employer to employee with/without consideration (e.g. laptop, car, furniture, mobile, etc.)	Taxable supply (goods) in the hands of employer	Para 2: Schedule I
Sale/Transfer/disposal of business assets by employer to employee without consideration on which ITC availed (e.g. laptop, car, furniture, mobile, etc.)	Taxable supply (goods) in the hands of employer (because employer employee are related person as per explanation appended to Section 15)	Para 1: Schedule I Valuation Rule 28 will apply
Employee of parent company providing services to subsidiary/associates company	Supply of services Taxable service in the hands of employer. (Parent company shall be liable to pay GST on services provided to Subsidiary/associates company)	Since subsidiary/associates company are separate legal entity having different PAN/ GSTIN, this transaction will not covered within the meaning & scope of distinct person
Service provided by Director to a company (If Director's remuneration is treated by the company in its books as professional services & not salary)	Supply of services Taxable service in the hands of the company under RCM u/s 9(3)	Para 2: Schedule I [Refer Circular No. 140/10/2020-GST dated 10-06-2020]
Reimbursement of bills or allowance (TA/Conveyance/Medical bill/Telephone bill/Membership fee, etc.	Not a taxable supply under GST, if provided as per terms of employment	

GST on perquisites provided by companies to its employees

(CBIC Press release dated 10th July 2017)

(1) Services by an employee to an employer in the course of employment are outside the scope of GST.

(2) Any supply by the employer to the employee in terms of a contractual agreement between the employer and the employee will not be subject to GST.

(3) If membership of a club or health and fitness center is provided free of charge to all the employees by the employer, the same will not be subject to GST, if GST is paid when procured by the employer.

(4) Similarly, when free housing is provided to the employees in terms of the contract between the employer and the employee and is part and parcel of the cost-to-company, it would not be subject to GST.

> **Any activity for the comfort, convenience and welfare of employee cannot be treated as having been done in the course or furtherance of business. This has been held by the Hon'ble Bombay High Court (Nagpur bench), in its order dated 11.10.2010, in the matter of *Central Excise, Nagpur* vs. *M/s Manikgarh Cement* [2010(20) S.T.R.456 (Bom)].**
> The guesthouse service provided by employer to employee as well as non-employee cannot be treated as an activity in the course or furtherance of its business. Hence, tax paid on inward supply of goods & services for maintenance of guesthouse are not eligible for ITC [Order No. 02-03/ODISHA-AAAR/2018-19 dated 21.01.2019].

(14) Taxability of 'No Claim Bonus' offered by insurance companies: Circular No. 186/18/2022-GST dated 27.12.2022: There is no supply provided by the insured to the insurance company in form of agreeing to the obligation to refrain from the act of lodging insurance claim during the previous year(s) and No Claim Bonus cannot be considered as a consideration for any supply provided by the insured to the insurance company.

No Claim Bonus (NCB) is a permissible deduction under Section 15(3)(a) of the CGST Act, 2017 for the purpose of calculation of value of supply of the insurance services provided by the insurance company to the insured. Accordingly, where the deduction on account of NCB is provided in the invoice issued by the insurer to the insured, GST shall be leviable on actual insurance premium amount, payable by the policyholders to the insurer, after deduction of No Claim Bonus mentioned on the invoice.

(15) Applicability of GST on monthly subscription/contribution charged by a RWA (Resident Welfare Association)/Housing Society: Circular no. 109/28/2019-GST dated 22nd July 2019: Supply of service by a RWA (unincorporated body or a non-profit entity registered under any law) to its own members by way of reimbursement of charges or share of contribution up to an amount of ₹ 7500 per month per member for providing services and goods for the common use of its members in a housing society or a residential complex are exempt from GST.

If aggregate turnover of an RWA does not exceed ₹ 20 lakh in a financial year, it shall not be required to take registration and pay GST even if the amount of maintenance charges exceeds ₹ 7500 per month per member. RWA shall be required to pay GST on monthly subscription/contribution charged from its members, only if such subscription is more than ₹ 7500 per month per member and the annual aggregate turnover of RWA by way of supplying of services and goods is also ₹ 20 lakhs or more.

> Prior to 25th January 2018, the exemption was available if the charges or share of contribution did not exceed ₹ 5000 per month per member. The limit was increased to ₹ 7500 per month per member with effect from 25th January 2018 [Refer clause (c) of Sl. No. 77 to the notification No. 12/2018-Central Tax (Rate) dated 28.06.2018].

Exemption of ₹ 7500 is available to a member for each apartment. If a member own two residential apartment in a housing society, exemption of ₹ 7500 is available in respect of each apartment.

In case, the charges exceed ₹ 7500 per month per member per apartment, the entire amount is taxable. For example, if the maintenance charges are ₹ 9000 per month per member, GST @18% shall be payable on the entire amount of ₹ 9000 and not on ₹ 1500 [₹ 9000–₹ 7500].

RWAs are entitled to take ITC of GST paid by them on capital goods (generators, water pumps, lawn furniture etc.), goods (taps, pipes, other sanitary/hardware fillings, etc.) and input services such as repair and maintenance services.

(16) GST on Renting of vehicles to State Transport Undertakings and Local Authorities: The expression "giving on hire" in Sl. No. 22 of the Notification No. 12/2017-CT (Rate) includes renting of vehicles. Accordingly, services where the said vehicles are rented or given on hire to State Transport Undertakings or Local Authorities are eligible for the said exemption, irrespective of whether such vehicles are run on routes, timings as decided by the State Transport Undertakings or Local Authorities and under effective control of State Transport Undertakings or Local Authorities which determines the rules of operation or plying of vehicles or not.

(17) GST on health care services: Health care services means the treatment provided in recognized system of medicine. As per Section 2(h) of Clinical establishments Act, 2010, "recognized system of medicine" means Allopathy, Yoga, Naturopathy, Ayurveda, Homeopathy, Siddha and Unani system of medicines or any other system of medicine as recognized by the central government.

Supply of health care services has been exempted from levy of GST Vide Notification No. 12/2017-Central Tax (Rate) dated 28.06.2017 as under:

Sl No.	Description of Services	Tax Rate
46	Services by a veterinary clinic in relation to health care of animals or birds.	Nil
73	Services provided by the cord blood banks by way of preservation of stem cells or any other service in relation to such preservation.	Nil Taxable w.e.f. 18th July 2022 Vide N.No. 04/2022-CT(R) dt. 13-07-2022
74	Services by way of (a) health care services by a clinical establishment, an authorized medical practitioner or paramedics "Provided that nothing in this entry shall apply to the services provided by a clinical establishment by way of providing room [other than Intensive Care Unit (ICU)/Critical Care Unit (CCU)/Intensive Cardiac Care Unit (ICCU)/ Neo natal Intensive Care Unit (NICU)] having room charges exceeding ₹ 5000 per day to a person receiving health care services." (Inserted Vide N.No. 04/2022-CT(R) dt. 13-07-2022 w.e.f. 18th July 2022) (b) services provided by way of transportation of a patient in an ambulance, other than those specified in (a) above.	Nil

Notes:

(1) Room rent in hospital provided to a person receiving health care services is exempted up to ₹ 5000 per day.

(2) Room rent is fully exempted from levy of GST in respect of Intensive Care Unit (ICU)/Critical Care Unit (CCU)/Intensive Cardiac Care Unit (ICCU)/Neo natal Intensive Care Unit (NICU) irrespective of amount charged.

(3) CBIC vide Circular No. 32/06/2018-GST dated 12.02.2018 has clarified on the taxability of nursing, food supplies to the inpatients, etc. as under:

Description of services	Taxability
Services provided by senior doctors/consultants/technicians hired by the hospitals, whether employees or not, are healthcare services	Exempted
Food supplied to the in-patients as advised by the doctor/nutritionists is a part of composite supply of healthcare	Exempted
Food by a hospital to patients (not admitted) or their attendants or visitors	Taxable
Nursing care, infrastructure facilities, paramedic care, emergency services, checking of temperature, weight, blood pressure, etc.	Exempted

Notification No. 03/2022-Central Tax (Rate) New Delhi, the 13th July 2022.

Chapter heading	Description of services	Rate of GST (CGST+ SGST)	Remarks
9996	Services provided by a clinical establishment by way of providing room [other than Intensive Care Unit (ICU)/Critical Care Unit (CCU)/Intensive Cardiac Care Unit (ICCU)/Neo natal Intensive Care Unit (NICU)] having room charges exceeding ₹ 5000 per day to a person receiving health care services	5%	The credit of input tax charged on goods and services used in supplying the service has not been taken
9994	Services by way of treatment or disposal of biomedical waste or the processes incidental thereto by a common bio-medical waste treatment facility to a clinical establishment	12%	

The various terms used in health care services has been defined in the footnote of Notification No. 12/2017-Central Tax (R) dated 28.06.2017 as under:

(k) "authorized medical practitioner" means a medical practitioner registered with any of the councils of the recognized system of medicines established or recognized by law in India and includes a medical professional having the requisite qualification to practice in any recognized system of medicines in India as per any law for the time being in force.

(s) "clinical establishment" means a hospital, nursing home, clinic, sanatorium or any other institution by, whatever name called, that offers services or facilities requiring diagnosis or treatment or care for illness, injury, deformity, abnormality or pregnancy in any recognized system of medicines in India, or a place established as an independent entity or a part of an establishment to carry out diagnostic or investigative services of diseases.

(zg) "health care services" means any service by way of diagnosis or treatment or care for illness, injury, deformity, abnormality or pregnancy in any recognized system of medicines in India and includes services by way of transportation of the patient to and from a clinical establishment, but does not include hair transplant or cosmetic or plastic surgery, except when undertaken to restore or to reconstruct anatomy or functions of body affected due to congenital defects, developmental abnormalities, injury or trauma.

(18) Taxability of share capital held in subsidiary company by the holding/parent company: Circular No. 196/08/2023-GST dated 17th July 2023: Securities are considered neither goods nor services in terms of definition of goods under section 2(52) of CGST Act and the definition of services under section 2 (102). Further, securities include 'shares' as per definition of securities under clause (h) of section 2 of Securities Contracts (Regulation) Act, 1956.

This implies that the securities held by the holding company in the subsidiary company are neither goods nor services. Further, purchase or sale of shares or securities, in itself is neither a supply of goods nor a supply of services. For a transaction/activity to be treated as supply of services, there must be a supply as defined under section 7 of CGST Act.

It cannot be said that a service is being provided by the holding company to the subsidiary company, solely on the basis that there is a SAC entry '997171' in the scheme of classification of services mentioning; "the services provided by holding companies, i.e. holding securities of (or other equity interests in) companies and enterprises for the purpose of owning a controlling interest.", unless there is a supply of services by the holding company to the subsidiary company in accordance with section 7 of CGST Act.

Therefore, the activity of holding of shares of subsidiary company by the holding company per se cannot be treated as a supply of services by a holding company to the said subsidiary company and cannot be taxed under GST.

(19) Taxability of Services provided by/to educational institutions: [Ref Entry No. 66 of exemption Notification No. 12/2017-Central Tax (Rate) dated 28.06.2017]: "Education" is not defined in the CGST Act but as per Apex Court decision in *Loka Shikshana Trust* vs. *CIT*, education is process of training and developing knowledge, skill and character of students by normal schooling.

Education Services are classified in heading 9992 (as per Notification No. 11/2017-Central Tax (Rate)) and are further sub-divided into six groups (as per the Annexure to the said notification) comprising Pre-primary, primary, secondary, higher, specialised and other educational and support services

Following services are exempted from levy of GST [Ref Entry 66]

Services provided:

(a) by an educational institution to its students, faculty and staff;

(aa) by an educational institution by way of conduct of entrance examination against consideration in the form of entrance fee;

(b) to an educational institution, by way of,—

  (i) transportation of students, faculty and staff;

  (ii) catering, including any mid-day meals scheme sponsored by the Central Government, State Government or Union territory;

  (iii) security or cleaning or house-keeping services performed in such educational institution;

  (iv) services relating to admission to, or conduct of examination by, such institution;

  (v) supply of online educational journals or periodicals:

Provided that nothing contained in sub-items (i), (ii) and (iii) of item (b) shall apply to an educational institution other than an institution providing services by way of pre-school education and education up to higher secondary school or equivalent:

Provided further that nothing contained in sub-item (v) of item (b) shall apply to an institution providing services by way of,

(i) pre-school education and education up to higher secondary school or equivalent; or

(ii) education as a part of an approved vocational education course.

Education Services are under forward charge. Therefore, GST shall be paid by the supplier of services.

(20) GST on Reimbursement of Expenses: The term 'reimbursement' has not been defined in the Income-tax Act, 1961 (IT Act). It is also not defined in the Central Goods and Service Tax Act, 2017, although references of the term can be found within the concept of a 'pure agent'.

According to the dictionary meanings, reimbursement can be considered repayment of what has already been spent or incurred. Therefore, it should not be considered as a reward or compensation for a service rendered. The determinative factor to be considered is the obligation of a party to bear expenses. A reimbursement will be subject to GST if it is a consideration for supply of goods or services.

Reimbursement of expenses can be classified as under:

(1) Reimbursement of Expenses in form of incidental expenses and

(2) Reimbursement of Expenses in form of expenses paid by Supplier as a Pure Agent.

GST is applicable on Reimbursement of Expenses in form of Incidental Expenses and no GST shall be applicable on Reimbursement of Expenses in form of expenses paid by Supplier as a Pure Agent, as per Rule 33 of CGST Rules 2017.

Section 15(2(c)) of CGST Act, 2017 provides that value of taxable supply shall include incidental expenses like packing and forwarding charges, transportation charges, home delivery charges etc. charged by the supplier to the recipient whether incur "at the time of" or "before" supply of goods or services.

However, all types of reimbursement of incidental expenses are not subject to GST. The reimbursement of expenses are actually not towards the service rendered but they are only towards other expenditure incurred on behalf of the client by the service provider. The applicability of GST depends upon terms of contract and nature of reimbursement. Hence, the same need to be analyse carefully.

For example, if in a letter of award/appointment letter it is specifically mentioned that reimbursement of travelling, fooding and hotel bills etc. shall be reimbursed to the consultant or service provider on actual cost basis without any mark-up/profit and the consultant raises separate bill for reimbursement of said out of pocket expenses, GST shall not be applicable on such reimbursement of expenses.

The following case laws may be relied upon:

Sl No.	Citation	Gist
1.	*Rolex Logistics Pvt. Limited* vs. *CST, Bangalore* 2008 (CESTAT-Bang.)	Held, demand of service tax on reimbursements of expenses not sustainable.
2.	*Scott Wilson Kirkpatric* (I) Pvt. Ltd. vs. *CST, Bangalore* 2007 (5) STR 118 (Tri-Bang.)	Held, reimbursements of expenses are not subject to service tax.
3.	*B.S. Refrigeration Ltd.* vs. *CST, Bangalore* 2006 (1) STR 103(Tri.-bang.)	Held, demand of service tax on entire amount reimbursed not sustainable.
4.	*Glaxo Smithkline Pharmaceuticals Ltd.* vs. *CCE, Mumbai*-IV	Held, service tax not leviable on expenses recovered.

A supplier may be known as a 'pure agent' when he enters a contract with the recipient in order to incur expenditure or costs in the course of, and in addition to supply of goods or services to the recipient on his or her own account. In view of the fact that the supplies are procured on behalf of the recipient, the pure agent should not hold a title or use such supplies for his or her own interests and should only recoup from the recipient the actual amount incurred (i.e., without any mark-up).

In order to qualify as a pure agent, the supplier has the obligation to substantiate that:

(a) the supplies procured are in addition to supplies made on his or her own account to the recipient,

(b) the payment is made to the vendor as an agent of the recipient,

(c) payment is indicated separately on the invoice issued by the supplier.

(d) he does not use the goods or services so procured for his own interest, and

(e) there is no profit or mark –up charged on reimbursement claimed from recipient.

Example of Pure Agent

1. ROC fee paid by a professional on behalf of the client and collected subsequently.
2. Expenses incurred by Clearing and Forwarding agent and reimbursed by principal such as freight, godown charges.
3. Income tax, GST or any other statutory dues paid to the government on behalf of the client and collected subsequently.

TDS on reimbursement: The Central Board of Direct Taxes (CBDT) has issued Circular No. (FAQ no. 30) to clarify situations where tax will be deducted on the gross amount. The said Circular clarifies that for contractual and Fee for Technical Service (FTS) payments, reimbursements cannot be deducted out of the bill amount for deduction of TDS.

However, the Tribunals:

(a) *ITO* vs. *Dr. Willmar Schwabe India (P) Ltd.* (Delhi Tribunal);
(b) *ACIT* vs. *Premier Marine Foods* (Cochin Tribunal);
(c) *DCIT* vs. *Choice Sanitaryware Industries* (Rajkot Tribunal),

have held that this circular is only applicable in a situation where a single invoice is raised for the gross amount (i.e., inclusive of reimbursements), and where two separate invoices are raised, one for service fees and the other for reimbursement of expenses, for instance, out-of-pocket expenses—tax should be deducted on service fees only.

However, for the purpose of deduction of GST (TDS), reimbursement of expenses shall also be included in the values of supply, if GST invoice is raised by the supplier against supply of such goods or services.

(21) Applicability of GST on BOCW Cess: In case of works contract which are covered within the definition of "Building & other construction work" as per Section 2(1)(d) of the BOCW Act, BOCW Cess @1% on value of work is loaded. What will be the transaction value for the purpose of levy of GST, i.e. the value of supply arrived after including BOCW Cess or excluding BOCW Cess?

Section 15 (2) of CGST Act, 2017 says that the value of supply shall include:

(a) any taxes, duties, cesses, fees and charges levied under any law other than GST Act.
(b) any amount that the supplier is liable to pay but incurred by recipient and not included while deciding sole consideration of supply.
(c) any incidental expenses charged by supplier at the time of, or before delivery of goods or supply of services.
(d) interest or late fee or penalty for delayed payment of consideration.
(e) subsidies directly linked to the price—excluding subsidies provided by the Central Government and State Government.

Therefore, the value of supply arrived after including BOCW Cess shall be transaction value for the purpose of levy of GST. It means GST to be paid on BOCW Cess also, though it is a statutory dues.

(22) Taxability of services provided by Head Office (HO) of an organisation to branch office (BO) in another State (both being distinct persons)

Circular 199/11/2023-GST dt. 17.07.2023

(a) HO has an option to distribute ITC in respect of common input services procured from a third party by following ISD mechanism or by issuing tax invoice under section 31 of CGST Act to the concerned BOs and the BOs can then avail ITC on such common ITC subject to the provisions of sections 16 and 17 of CGST Act. However, the distribution of ITC in respect a common input services procured from a third party can be made by the HO to a BO through ISD mechanism only if:

(i) it gets itself registered mandatorily as an ISD in accordance with section 24(viii) of the CGST Act, and
(ii) the said input services are attributable to the said BO or have actually been provided to the said BO, and

(b) Whether the cost of all components including salary cost of HO employees involved in providing the said services has to be included in the computation of value of services provided by HO to BOs when full input tax credit is available to the BOs?

In respect of internally generated services provided by the HO to BOs, the value declared in the invoice by HO shall be deemed to be the open market value of such services, in terms of second proviso to rule 28 of CGST

Rules, irrespective of the fact whether cost of any particular component of such services, like employee cost etc., has been included or not in the value of the services in the invoice.

(i) Value of supply of internally generated services provided by HO to BOs in cases where HO is not issuing tax invoice, but full input tax credit is available to the concerned BO. In such cases, the value of services may be deemed to be declared as Nil by HO to BO and may be deemed as open market value in terms of second proviso to rule 28 of CGST Rules.

(ii) Value of internally generated services where HO is issuing tax invoice to the BOs and full input tax credit is not available to the concerned BO. In respect of internally generated services provided by the HO to BO but full ITC is not available to the BO, the cost of salary of employees of the HO, involved in providing services to BOs is not mandatorily required to be included while computing the taxable value of supply of services.

(23) **Applicability of GST on Carbon Credit:** Carbon credits are generated through a process that involves quantifying, verifying, and certifying the reduction or removal of greenhouse gas emissions.

Whether Carbon Credits are goods or services for levying GST?

Carbon Credits were declared as goods under the Securities Contracts (Regulation) Act, 1956. The National Commodity & Derivative Exchange Limited (NCDEX) vide the Circular No. NCDEX/ TRADING-035/2008/080 dated April 7, 2008, notified the launch of future/forwards contract pertaining to Carbon Credit.

Carbon Credits, are alike Priority Sector Lending Certificates (PSLCs) and Renewable Energy Certificates (RECs).

CBIC Vide Circular No. 34/8/2018-GST dated 01.03.2018 and Circular No. 46/20/2018-GST dated 06.06.2018, has clarified the applicability of GST on PSLCs and RECs.

RECs, PSLCs etc. are classified under heading 4907 and attract GST @18% w.e.f. 1st October 2021 Vide N. No. 8/2021-Central Tax (Rate) dated 30.09.2021.

Chapter 5

Charge of Tax

5.1 LEVY AND COLLECTION OF GST

Article 246A (intra-state supply) and Article 269A (inter-state supply) of the 101st Constitution Amendment Act, 2016 is the enabling provision for levy of GST in India, which came into operation w.e.f. 16th Sept. 2016.

The charging section is a must in any tax law for levy and collection of tax. Before imposing any tax, it must be ensured that the transaction falls within the ambit of the taxable event and that the person on whom the tax is so imposed, also covered within the scope and ambit of the charging section. Taxable event under GST is "Supply". **CGST and SGST/UTGST** are levied on all **intra-State supplies** of goods and/or services while **IGST** is levied on all **inter-State supplies** of goods and/or services.

Section 9 is the charging section of the CGST Act, 2017 while Section 5 is the charging section of the IGST Act, 2017.

Every supply will be liable to tax, if it is covered within the meaning and scope of supply u/s 7(1), unless otherwise exempted by way of notification. The nature of tax would depend upon the nature of supply, viz., inter-State supplies will be liable to IGST and intra-State supplies will be liable to CGST and SGST (UTGST).

Section 9 is the charging section of the CGST Act, 2017, it provides that:

(1) All intra-State supplies of goods or services or both (except on the supply of alcoholic liquor for human consumption), is liable to Central tax (CGST), on the value determined under section 15 and at such rates, not exceeding twenty per cent, or as may be notified by the Government on the recommendations of the GST Council.

(2) The central tax on the supply of petroleum crude, high-speed diesel, motor spirit (commonly known as petrol), natural gas and aviation turbine fuel shall be levied with effect from such date as may be notified by the Government on the recommendations of the Council.

(3) The Government may, on the recommendations of the Council, by notification, specify categories of supply of goods or services or both, the tax on which shall be paid on reverse charge basis by the recipient of such goods or services or both and all the provisions of this Act shall apply to such recipient as if he is the person liable for paying the tax in relation to the supply of such goods or services or both.

(4) The central tax in respect of the supply of taxable goods or services or both by a supplier, who is not registered, to a registered person shall be paid by such person on reverse charge basis as the recipient and all the provisions of this Act shall apply to such recipient as if he is the person liable for paying the tax in relation to the supply of such goods or services or both.

Thus, a registered person would be required to pay GST on all supplies received by it from un-registered persons. This is applicable to both, goods as well as, services.

From 1st July 2017 to 12th October 2017, the RCM provision u/s 9(4) of CGST Act/u/s 5(4) of IGST was in force. It means, a registered person was liable to pay GST on all inward taxable supplies received by it from un-registered persons.

The above RCM provision was suspended till 30.09.2019 vide Notification No. 22/2018-Central Tax (Rate) dated 6th August 2018 & Notification No. 23/2018-Integrated Tax (Rate)dated 6th August 2018. This was rescinded vide Notification No. 01/2019-Central Tax (Rate), dated 29-01-2019 w.e.f. 1st Feb 2019 due to CGST amendment Act 2018 coming into operation.

CGST amendment Act 2018, which came into operation w.e.f. 1st Feb. 2019 has amended the RCM provision u/s 9(4) of CGST Act/u/s 5(4) of IGST Act. Now only specified classes of registered person shall be liable to pay tax under RCM in case of supply of specified categories of goods or services or both received from an unregistered supplier as notified by Govt.

Provision of Section 9(4) has been amended vide CGST Amendment Act, 2018 as under:

9(4) The Government may, on the recommendations of the Council, by notification, specify a class of registered persons who shall, in respect of supply of specified categories of goods or services or both received from an unregistered supplier, pay the tax on reverse charge basis as the recipient of such supply of goods or services or both.

(5) Where any supply of services is effected through e-commerce operators (commonly known as services provided by aggregators), the law provides that the Central/State Government may on the recommendation of the Council specify (notify) that the e-commerce operator will be liable to discharge the tax on such supplies. It is important to note that, in such supplies, the e-commerce operator is neither the actual supplier of service/s nor does he actually receive the services. The actual supplier of services is a third party who provides such services to the customer through e-commerce operator. Instead of levying tax on such actual supplier, the law has imposed levy on e-commerce operator. Therefore, this is an exception to the general provision of levy of tax:

Provided further that where an electronic commerce operator does not have a physical presence in the taxable territory and also, he does not have a representative in the said territory, such electronic commerce operator shall appoint a person in the taxable territory for the purpose of paying tax and such person shall be liable to pay tax.

Analysis: The levy of tax on supply of goods and/or services can be grouped under four categories:

Section	Taxability
Section 9 (1)	In the hands of the supplier (No GST on the supply of alcoholic liquor for human consumption)—under forward charge
Section 9(2)	GST on supply of petroleum crude, high speed diesel, motor spirit (commonly known as petrol), natural gas and aviation turbine fuel (ATF) shall be levied from such date as may be notified by the Government on the recommendations of the GST Council
Section 9 (3)/9(4)	In the hands of the recipient of goods, services or both under reverse charge mechanism—RCM
Section 9(5)	In case of specified services, in the hands of electronic commerce operator

5.2 REVERSE CHARGE MECHANISM (RCM) UNDER GST [SECTION 9(3)/9(4)]

Generally, the person effecting taxable supplies is liable to pay taxes. However, in case of imports and supply of certain goods or services as may be notified by the Government on the recommendations of the GST Council, the tax shall be paid by the recipient of such goods or services, which is called payment under reverse charge.

The terms "reverse charge" means liability to pay tax by the recipient instead of the supplier of goods or services or both. Reverse charge applies to both goods & services.

As per Sec 2(98) of the CGST Act, 2017 "reverse charge" means the liability to pay tax by the recipient of supply of goods or services or both instead of the supplier of such goods or services or both under sub-section (3) or sub-section (4) of section 9 of CGST Act, or under sub-section (3) or sub-section (4) of section 5 of the IGST Act, 2017.

It is mandatory for a person to obtain registration under GST who are liable to pay tax under reverse charge mechanism (RCM), irrespective of turnover and whether supplying taxable goods or service or not. Persons who are not engaged in any business activities will not be required to obtain registration and pay tax under reverse charge mechanism.

The scheme of partial reverse charge or joint charge, prevailing under the previous Service tax regime not available in GST regime.

Key Aspects of RCM Provision

Sl No.	RCM Provision
1.	A supply would be subjected to tax under RCM in the hands of the recipient only if it is a notified supply u/s 9(3) of CGST Act or Section 5(3) of IGST Act.
2.	List of goods covered under Section 9(3) are notified under Notification No. 4/2017-Central Tax (Rate) and services are notified under Notification No. 13/2017-Central Tax (Rate), as amended from time to time.
3.	In case of supplies received from unregistered persons, it is taxable under RCM in the hands of registered person u/s 9(4) of CGST Act, only in respect of (a) 'class of registered persons' and (b) 'categories of goods or services' as notified under Notification No. 07/2019-Central Tax (Rate) dated 29-03-2019 (w.e.f. 1st April 2019).
4.	All taxpayers required to pay tax under reverse charge have to mandatorily obtain registration and the threshold exemption is not applicable on them.
5.	No partial reverse charge will be applicable under GST. 100% tax will be paid by the recipient if reverse charge mechanism applies.
6.	Payment of taxes under Reverse Charge has to be made in cash and cannot be made by utilizing Input Tax Credit.

Discharge of RCM Tax Liability

Reverse charge tax liability is to be paid by cash by debiting electronic cash ledger and cannot be discharge by utilizing input tax credit (ITC). However, GST paid on goods or services under reverse charge mechanism is available as ITC to the registered person provided that such goods or services are used or will be used for business or furtherance of business.

A supplier cannot take Input Tax Credit of GST paid on goods or services used to make supplies on which the recipient is liable to pay tax under reverse charge.

Input tax credit includes tax paid on reverse charge basis. Once tax is paid under Section 9(3) of CGST Act (or 5(3) of IGST Act), character of the payment remains GST and by operation of law, be treated as 'input tax'.

Incidence of Reverse Charge

(1) Supply of notified goods or services or both [Sec 9(3) of CGST Act/5(3) of IGST Act]

(2) Supply of notified goods & services by an un-registered person to specified categories of registered persons [Sec 9(4) of CGST Act/5(4) of IGST Act].

5.3 SUPPLIES LIABLE TO TAX UNDER REVERSE CHARGE

There are two types of reverse charge scenario provided in GST Law:

(1) Reverse charge u/s 9(3) of CGST Act, 2017 and u/s 5(3) of IGST Act, 2017: Certain goods & services has been notified by the Central Government through notification on the recommendation of GST council, on which tax shall be payable by the specified category of recipient of such goods or services under RCM.

Goods notified u/s 9(3) of CGST Act, 2017 and u/s 5(3) of IGST Act, 2017
(1) Notification No. 4/2017-Central Tax (Rate) dated 28th June 2017
(2) Notification No. 36/2017-Central Tax (Rate) dated 13th October 2017
(3) Notification No. 43/2017-Central Tax (Rate) dated 14th November 2017
(4) Notification No. 11/2018-Central Tax (Rate) dated 28th May 2018

Services notified u/s 9(3) of CGST Act, 2017 and u/s 5(3) of IGST Act, 2017
Notifications under CGST Act (1) Notification No. 13/2017-Central Tax(Rate) dated 28th June 2017 (2) Notification No. 33/2017-Central Tax(Rate) dated 13th Oct. 2017 (3) Notification No. 03/2018-Central Tax (Rate) dated 25th Jan. 2018 (4) Notification No. 15/2018-Central Tax (Rate) dated 26th Jul. 2018 (5) Notification No. 29/2018-Central Tax (Rate) dated 31st Dec. 2018 (6) Notification No. 22/2019-Central Tax (Rate) dated 30th Sept. 2019 (7) Notification No. 29/2019-Central Tax (Rate) dated 31st Dec. 2019 (8) Notification No. 05/2022-Central Tax (Rate) dated 13th July 2022 Notifications under IGST Act (1) Notification No. 10/2017-**Integrated Tax (Rate)** dated 28th June 2017 (2) Notification No. 34/2017-**Integrated Tax (Rate)** dated 13th June 2017 (3) Notification No. 03/2018-**Integrated Tax (Rate)**dated 25th Jan. 2018 (4) Notification No. 16/2018-**Integrated Tax (Rate)**dated 26th July 2018 (5) Notification No. 30/2018-**Integrated Tax (Rate)** dated 31st Dec. 2018 (6) Notification No. 21/2019-**Integrated Tax (Rate)** dated 30th Sept. 2019

In case the recipient of notified goods and/or services covered u/s 9(3)/5(3) is an un-registered person, he is required to obtain registration under GST, irrespective of turnover and whether supplying taxable goods or services or not.

(2) Reverse charge u/s 9(4) of CGST Act, 2017 and u/s 5(4) of IGST Act, 2017: Supply of taxable goods and/or services or both by an un-registered supplier to a registered person is taxable under reverse charge u/s 9(4) of CGST Act, 2017 and u/s 5(4) of IGST Act, 2017 in the hands of the recipient (if registered).

Particulars	From 1st July 2017 to 12th October 2017	From 13th October 2017 to 31st Jan 2019
Supply of taxable goods and/or services or both by an un-registered supplier to registered person	Taxable in the hands of Registered person	Not taxable (Neither in the hands of supplier nor in the hands of recipient)

CGST amendment Act, 2018, which came into operation w.e.f. 1st Feb 2019 has amended the RCM provision u/s 9(4) of CGST Act. Now only specified classes of registered person shall be liable to pay tax under RCM in respect of supply of specified categories of goods or services or both received from un-registered person.

Therefore, wherever a supply is covered under RCM, all other provisions of the CGST Act, 2017 and IGST Act, 2017 as applicable, will apply to the recipient of such goods and/or services, as if the recipient is the "supplier" and liable to pay tax in relation to supply of such goods and/or services.

List of items covered under RCM u/s 9(4) of CGST Act, 2017 and u/s 5(4) of IGST Act, 2017
Relevant Notifications Notification No. 07/2019-Central Tax (Rate) dated 29-03-2019 (w.e.f. 1st April 2019) Notification No. 07/2019-Integrated Tax (Rate) dated 29th March 2019 (w.e.f. 1st April 2019)

As per Sec 31(3) of the CGST Act, 2017 in respect of goods or services or both received by a registered person from the supplier who is not registered shall issue an invoice on the date of receipt of goods or services or both and a payment voucher at the time of making payment to the un-registered supplier.

As per Sec 31 of CGST Act, 2017 read with rule 46 of the CGST Rule, 2017, every tax invoice has to mention whether the tax in respect of supply on the invoice is payable on reverse charge basis.

Difference between Section 9(3) and 9(4)

Government has notified a list of goods and services along with the type of recipient who shall be liable to pay tax on those supplies covered under reverse charge as per section 9(3). If the goods or the services are not listed or the recipient is not notified, then provision of reverse charge does not apply.

For example, tax in respect of services of advocate availed by a business entity is payable on reverse charge basis. If the recipient is a religious trust, who availed services of an advocate, which is not a business entity, reverse charge provision will not applicable.

Whereas, as per section 9(4), every inward supply received by a registered person from an unregistered person is liable for payment of tax on reverse charge basis by such recipient. ***(This provision was applicable from 1st July 2017 to 12th October 2017 and was kept in abeyance from 13th October 2017 till CGST Amendment Action 2018 came into operation i.e. up to 31st Jan 2019).***

With effect from 1st Feb 2019, only "specified classes of registered person" shall be liable to pay tax under RCM u/s 9(4), in respect of supply of "specified categories of goods or services or both" received from un-registered person.

The CBIC vide Notification No. 07/2019-Central Tax (Rate) dated 29-03-2019 has notified certain classes of registered person who shall be liable to pay GST under reverse charge u/s 9(4) of CGST Act, 2017 on procurement of certain notified goods/services from un-registered person.

Taxable Event under Reverse Charge

Reverse charge is applicable when there is a supply and the time of supply is to be determined as per the provision of section 12 or 13 of the CGST Act. **Reverse charge is applicable at the time of advance even though actual supply is yet to take place.** Rule 52 provides for the issuance of a Payment Voucher in cases where tax is to be paid on reverse charge basis.

Implication of Goods return on which GST paid under RCM

Refer Circular no. 137/07/2020-GST dated 13th April 2020

There is no provision in CGST Act or Rules regarding reversal of tax paid. The recipient who has paid the tax may apply for refund under section 54 of the CGST Act of GST paid on such advances by filing FORM GST RFD-01 under the category "Refund of excess payment of tax" and shall not issue credit note or revised invoice for which there is no provision.

Tax on Import of Goods or Services or Both

In terms of Section 7 of the IGST Act, 2017, import of goods or services or both shall be treated to be a supply in the course of inter-state trade or commerce. Accordingly, tax under the provisions of IGST Act shall apply on import of goods or services or both.

GST on ocean freight to be paid by importer under Reverse Charge Mechanism (RCM).

5.4 GOODS COVERED UNDER REVERSE CHARGE

Notification No. 4/2017-Central Tax (Rate) dated 28-06-2017

Following goods are notified u/s 9(3) of CGST Act and u/s 5(3) of IGST Act, 2017

Sl. No.	Description of supply of goods	Supplier of goods	Recipient of goods
1.	Cashew nuts (not shelled or peeled)	Agriculturist	Any registered person
2.	Bidi Wrapper leaves (tendu)	Agriculturist	Any registered person
3.	Tobacco leaves	Agriculturist	Any registered person
4.	Silk yarn	Any person who manufactures silk yarn from raw silk or silk worm cocoons for supply of silk yarn	Any registered person
4A.	Raw Cotton	Agriculturist	Any registered person
5.	Supply of Lottery	State Government, Union Territory or any local authority	Lottery distributor or selling agent
6.	Used vehicles, seized and confiscated goods, old and used goods, waste and scrap	Central/State Government, Union territory or a local authority	Any registered person
7.	Priority Sector Lending Certificate	Any registered person	Any registered person

5.5 SERVICES COVERED UNDER REVERSE CHARGE

Notification No. 13/2017-Central Tax (Rate) dated 28-06-2017

Following Services are notified u/s 9(3) of CGST Act and u/s 5(3) of IGST Act, 2017

Sl. No.	Category of supply of services	Supplier of Service	Recipient of Service
1.	Supply of services by a **Goods Transport Agency (GTA)**, in respect of transportation of goods by road: Provided that nothing contained in this entry shall apply where, (i) the supplier has taken registration under the CGST Act, 2017 and exercised the option to pay tax on the services of GTA in relation to transport of goods supplied by him under forward charge; and (ii) the supplier has issued a tax invoice to the recipient charging Central Tax at the applicable rates and has made a declaration as prescribed in Annexure III on such invoice issued by him."; (Ref N.No. 05/2022-CT(R) dt. 13.07.2022.	Goods Transport Agency (GTA)	(a) any factory registered under or governed by the Factories Act, 1948; or (b) any society registered under the Societies Registration Action 1860 or under any other law for the time being in force in any part of India; or (c) any co-operative society established by or under any law; or (d) any person registered under the CGST Act or the IGST Act or the SGST Act or the UTGST Act; or (e) any Body corporate established, by or under any law; or (f) any partnership firm whether registered or not under any law including association of persons; or (g) any casual taxable Person: Provided that nothing contained in this entry shall apply to services provided by a goods transport agency, by way of transport of goods in a goods carriage by road, to,— (a) a Department or Establishment of the Central Government or State Government or Union territory; or (b) local authority; or (c) Governmental agencies, which has taken registration under the Central Goods and Services Tax Act, 2017 (12 of 2017) only for the purpose of deducting tax under section 51 and not for making a taxable supply of goods or services.
2.	Services provided by an individual advocate including a senior advocate or firm of advocates by way of legal services, directly or indirectly.	An individual advocate including a senior advocate or firm of advocates.	Any business entity located in the taxable territory.
3.	Services supplied by an arbitral tribunal to a business entity.	An arbitral tribunal	Any business entity located in the taxable territory.
4.	Services provided by way of **sponsorship** to any Body corporate or partnership firm.	Any person	Any body corporate or partnership firm located in the taxable territory.

5.	Services supplied by the Central Government, State Government, Union territory or local authority to a business entity excluding,— (1) renting of immovable property, and (2) services specified below: (i) services by the Department of Posts by way of speed post, express parcel post, life insurance, and agency services provided to a person other than Central Government, State Government or Union territory or local authority; (ii) services in relation to an aircraft or a vessel, inside or outside the precincts of a port or an airport; (iii) transport of goods or passengers.	Central Government, (excluding the Ministry of Railways) State Government, Union territory or local authority.	Any business entity located in the taxable territory.
5A.	Services supplied by the Central Government, State Government, Union territory or local authority by way of renting of immovable property to a person registered under the Central Goods and Services Tax Act, 2017 (12 of 2017).	Central Government, (excluding the Ministry of Railways) State Government, Union territory or local authority.	Any person registered under the Central Goods and Services Tax Act, 2017.
5AA.	Service by way of renting of residential dwelling to a registered person.	Any person	Any registered person
5B.	Services supplied by any person by way of transfer of development rights or Floor Space Index (FSI) (including additional FSI) for construction of a project by a promoter.	Any person	Promoter
5C.	Long-term lease of land (30 years or more) by any person against consideration in the form of upfront amount (called as premium, salami, cost, price, development charges or by any other name) and/or periodic rent for construction of a project by a promoter.	Any person	Promoter
6.	**Services supplied by a director** of a company/body corporate to the said company/body corporate.	A director of a company or a body corporate.	The company or a body corporate located in the taxable territory.
7.	**Services supplied by an insurance agent** to any person carrying on insurance business.	An insurance agent	Any person carrying on insurance business, located in the taxable territory.
8.	**Services supplied by a recovery agent** to a banking company or a financial institution or a non-banking financial company.	A recovery agent	A banking company or a financial institution or a non banking financial company, located in the taxable territory.
9.	Supply of **services by an author, music composer, photographer, artist** or the like by way of transfer or permitting the use or enjoyment of a copyright covered under section 13(1)(a) of the Copyright Act, 1957 relating to original literary, dramatic, musical or artistic works **to a publisher, music company, producer** or the like.	Author or music composer, photographer, artist, or the like.	Publisher, music company, producer or the like, located in the taxable territory. (Upto 30th Sept. 2019)

9.	Supply of services by a music composer, photographer, artist or the like by way of transfer or permitting the use or enjoyment of a copyright covered under clause (a) of sub-section (1) of section 13 of the Copyright Act, 1957 relating to original dramatic, musical or artistic works to a music company, producer or the like.	Music composer, photographer, artist, or the like.	Music company, producer or the like, located in the taxable territory. (w.e.f. 1st October 2019, Vide Notification No. 22/2019-Central Tax (Rate), dated 30.09.2019.
9A.	Supply of services by an author by way of transfer or permitting the use or enjoyment of a copyright covered under clause (a) of sub-section (1) of section 13 of the Copyright Act, 1957 relating to original literary works to a publisher.	Author	Publisher located in the taxable territory: Provided that nothing contained in this entry shall apply where, (i) the author has taken registration under the Central Goods and Services Tax Act, 2017 (12 of 2017), and filed a declaration, in the form at Annexure I, within the time limit prescribed therein, with the jurisdictional CGST or SGST commissioner, as the case may be, that he exercises the option to pay central tax on the service specified in column (2), under forward charge in accordance with Section 9 (1) of the Central Goods and Service Tax Act, 2017 under forward charge, and to comply with all the provisions of Central Goods and Service Tax Act, 2017 (12 of 2017) as they apply to a person liable for paying the tax in relation to the supply of any goods or services or both and that he shall not withdraw the said option within a period of 1 year from the date of exercising such option; (ii) the author makes a declaration, as prescribed in Annexure II on the invoice issued by him in Form GST Inv-I to the publisher.
10.	Supply of service by the members of overseeing committee to Reserve Bank of India.	Members of the Overseeing Committee constituted by the Reserve Bank of India.	Reserve Bank of India
11.	Services supplied by individual Direct Selling Agents (DSAs) other than a body corporate, partnership or limited liability partnership firm to bank or non-banking financial company (NBFCs).	Individual Direct Selling Agents (DSAs) other than a body corporate, partnership or limited liability partnership firm.	A banking company or a non-banking financial company, located in the taxable territory.
12.	Services provided by business facilitator (BF) to a banking company.	Business facilitator (BF)	A banking company, located in the taxable territory.

13.	Services provided by an agent of business correspondent (BC) to business correspondent (BC).	An agent of business correspondent (BC).	A business correspondent, located in the taxable territory.
14.	Security services (services provided by way of supply of security personnel) provided to a registered person: Provided that nothing contained in this entry shall apply to, (i)(a) a Department or Establishment of the Central Government or State Government or Union territory; or (b) local authority; or (c) Governmental agencies; which has taken registration under the Central Goods and Services Tax Act, 2017 (12 of 2017) only for the purpose of deducting tax under section 51 of the said Act and not for making a taxable supply of goods or services; or (ii) a registered person paying tax under section 10 of the said Act.	Any person other than a body corporate.	A registered person, located in the taxable territory.
15.	Services provided by way of renting of any motor vehicle designed to carry passengers where the cost of fuel is included in the consideration charged from the service recipient provided to a body corporate.	Any person, other than a body corporate who supplies the services to a body corporate and does not issue an invoice charging central tax at the rate of 6% to the service recipient.	Any body corporate located in the taxable territory.
16.	Services of lending of securities under Securities Lending Scheme, 1997 ("Scheme") of Securities and Exchange Board of India ("SEBI"), as amended.	Lender, i.e. a person who deposits the securities registered in his name or in the name of any other person duly authorized on his behalf with an approved intermediary for the purpose of lending under the Scheme of SEBI.	Borrower, i.e. a person who borrows the securities under the Scheme through an approved intermediary of SEBI.

Effective date of applicability of above RCM provisions are as under:

Serial No.	Effective date
Serial No. 1 to 9	w.e.f. 1st July 2017
Serial No. 5A	w.e.f. 25th January 2018
Serial No. 10	w.e.f. 13th October 2017
Serial No. 11	w.e.f. 27th July 2018
Serial No. 12, 13 & 14	w.e.f. 1st Jan. 2019
Serial No. 5B, 5C	w.e.f. 1st April 2019
Serial No. 9A, 15 & 16	w.e.f. 1st October 2019
Serial No. 5AA	w.e.f. 18th July 2022

In addition to above services, following two additional services has been notified by the Central Government vide Notification No. 10/2017-Integrated Tax (Rate) dated 28-06-2017 wherein whole of the tax shall be payable by the recipient on services u/s 5(3) of IGST Act, 2017 on Reverse charge basis.

Sl No.	Category of supply of services	Supplier of Service	Recipient of Service
1.	Any service supplied by any person who is located in a non-taxable territory to any person other than non-taxable online recipient.	Any person located in a non-taxable territory.	Any person located in the taxable territory other than non-taxable online recipient.
2.	Services supplied by a person located in non-taxable territory by way of transportation of goods by a vessel from a place outside India up to the Customs Station of clearance in India.	A person located in a non-taxable territory.	Importer, as defined in Sec 2(26) of the Customs Act, 1962, located in the taxable territory.

Clarification issued by CBIC on applicability of RCM on renting of Motor Vehicle

Refer: (a) Notification No. 29/2019-Central Tax (Rate) dated 31.12.2019

(b) Circular No. 130/49/2019-GST dated 31-12-2019.

When any service is placed under RCM, the supplier shall not charge any tax from the service recipient as this is the settled procedure in law under RCM.

Prior to 30-09-2019, any supplier including body corporates, providing 'Renting of Motor Vehicle services', where the cost of fuel forms part of the consideration received, were eligible to pay GST under either of the following options:

(1) 5% GST (i.e. 2.5% CGST and SGST each or 5% IGST) with restriction on availment of input tax credit i.e. ITC available in same line of business or

(2) 12% GST with no restriction of ITC.

The aforesaid services were taxable under forward charge prior to 1st October 2019 and service providers were eligible to opt for any of the above options for payment of GST. Also, on provision of such services, there was no GST liability under reverse charge mechanism up to 30-09-2019.

Entry No. 15, services provided by way of "renting of any motor vehicle designed to carry passengers where the cost of fuel is included in the consideration" has been brought under the ambit of RCM Vide *Notification No. 22/2019-Central Tax (Rate) dated 30th Sept. 2019 (Effective from 01-10-2019).*

Circular No. 130/49/2019-GST dated 31-12-2019

RCM shall be applicable on the service by way of renting of any motor vehicle designed to carry passengers where the cost of fuel is included in the consideration charged from the service recipient only if the supplier fulfils all the following conditions:

(a) is other than a body corporate;

(b) does not issue an invoice charging GST @12% (6% CGST + 6% SGST) from the service recipient; and

(c) supplies the service to a body corporate.

If all the conditions referred here in above are satisfied, the liability of payment of GST @ 5% has been casted upon the body corporates under RCM, as a recipient of such services.

The above provision can be summarized as under:

Sl. No.	Supplier of Service	Recipient of Service	Rate of Tax	Applicability of RCM
1.	Body corporate (Registered)	Body Corporate	5%/12%	No
2.	Body corporate (Un-Registered)	Body Corporate	–	No
3.	Non-Body corporate (Registered)	Body Corporate	12% (Ref Note a)	No
4.	Non-Body corporate (Registered)	Body Corporate	5% (Ref Note b)/Nil	Yes
5.	Non-Body corporate (Un-Registered)	Body Corporate	–	Yes
6.	Non-Body corporate (Registered)—If cost of fuel not included in hire charges	Body Corporate	18%	No

Notes:

(a) Where the supplier of the service charges GST @ 12% from the service recipient, the service recipient shall not be liable to pay GST under RCM.

(b) A service provider who is a non-body corporate, may opt to pay GST @ 5% under forward charge on services provided to non-body corporate but can not charge 5% GST on service provided to body corporate, since body corporate is liable to pay GST @ 5% under RCM.

(c) When any service is placed under RCM, the supplier shall not charge any tax from the service recipient as this is the settled procedure in law under RCM.

RCM Provision u/s 9(4)

With effect from 1st Feb. 2019, the charging provision u/s 9(4) has been amended and Government has been empowered to notify specific classes of registered person who shall be liable to pay tax under Reverse charge on supply received on specified class of goods & services from un-registered person.

List of goods or services covered under RCM u/s 9(4) of CGST Act, 2017

In exercise of the powers conferred by section 9(4) of the Central Goods and Services Tax Act, 2017, the Central Government, on the recommendations of the GST Council, has notified that the registered person specified in column (3) of the table below, shall in respect of supply of goods or services or both specified in column (2) of the table below, received from an unregistered supplier shall pay tax on reverse charge basis as recipient of such goods or services or both.

Notification No. 07/2019-Central Tax (Rate) dated 29-03-2019 (w.e.f. 1st April 2019)

Sl No.	Category of supply of goods and services	Recipient of goods and services
1.	Supply of such goods and services or both [other than services by way of grant of development rights, long-term lease of land (against upfront payment in the form of premium, salami, development charges, etc.) or FSI (including additional FSI)] which constitute the shortfall from the minimum value of goods or services or both required to be purchased by a promoter for construction of project, in a financial year (or part of the financial year till the date of issuance of completion certificate or first occupation, whichever is earlier) as prescribed in notification No. 11/2017-Central Tax (Rate), dated 28th June 2017, at items (i), (ia), (ib), (ic) and (id) against serial number 3 in the table, published in Gazette of India vide G.S.R. No. 690, dated 28th June 2017, as amended.	Promoter
2.	Cement falling in chapter heading 2523 in the first schedule to the Customs Tariff Act, 1975 (51 of 1975).	Promoter
3.	Capital goods falling under any chapter in the first schedule to the Customs Tariff Act, 1975 (51 of 1975) supplied to a promoter for construction of a project on which tax is payable or paid at the rate prescribed for items (i), (ia), (ib), (ic) and (id) against serial number 3 in the table, in notification No. 11/2017-Central Tax (Rate), dated 28th June, 2017, published in Gazette of India vide G.S.R. No. 690, dated 28th June, 2017, as amended.	Promoter

Explanation: For the purpose of this notification,

(i) the term "promoter" shall have the same meaning as assigned to it in clause (zk) of section 2 of the Real Estate (Regulation and Development) Act, 2016 (16 of 2016);

(ii) "project" shall mean a Real Estate Project (REP) or a Residential Real Estate Project (RREP);

(iii) the term "Real Estate Project (REP)"shall have the same meaning as assigned to it in in clause (zn) of section 2 of the Real Estate (Regulation and Development) Act, 2016 (16 of 2016);

(iv) "Residential Real Estate Project (RREP)"shall mean a REP in which the carpet area of the commercial apartments is not more than 15 per cent of the total carpet area of all the apartments in the REP.

(v) the term "floor space index (FSI)" shall mean the ratio of a building's total floor area (gross floor area) to the size of the piece of land upon which it is built.

Note: All houses which meet the definition of affordable houses as decided by GSTC (area 60 sqm in metros/90 sqm in non-metros and value up to ₹ 45 lakhs) are affordable house.

Purchase from un-registered person by developer/builder opting for concessional rate of GST

The GST Council in the 34th meeting held on 19th March 2019 has taken following decision regarding GST rate on real estate sector.

The new tax rates of 1% (on construction of affordable) and 5% (on other than affordable houses) shall be available subject to following conditions.

(a) Input tax credit shall not be available,

(b) 80% of inputs and input services (other than capital goods, TDR/JDA, FSI, long-term lease (premiums)) shall be purchased from registered persons. On shortfall of purchases from 80%, tax shall be paid by the builder on RCM basis as under:

Particulars	Rate of GST
Cement	28%
Other input/input services	18%

(c) The developer/builder shall be liable to GST under Reverse Charge Mechanism on receipt of development rights.

5.6 SERVICES TAXABLE IN THE HANDS OF ELECTRONIC COMMERCE OPERATOR (ECOM) [SEC. 9(5)]

E-Commerce operators display products as well as services on their web portal, which are actually supplied by some other person to the consumer. The consumers buy such goods/services through these portals. On placing the order for a particular product/service, the actual supplier supplies the selected product/service to the consumer. The price/consideration for the product/service is collected by the E-Commerce operator from the consumer and passed on to the actual supplier after deduction of their commission.

Central Government Vide Notification No. 17/2017-Central Tax (Rate) dated 28.06.2017 & Notification No. 23/2017-Central Tax (Rate) dated 22.08.2017 has notified the following categories of services, when supplied through E-Commerce operator, tax thereon shall be payable by E-Commerce operator, though they are neither supplier nor recipient of goods or services.

(a) services by way of transportation of passengers by a radio-taxi, motor cab, maxi cab and motor cycle;

(b) services by way of providing accommodation in hotels, inns, guest houses, clubs, campsites or other commercial places meant for residential or lodging purposes, except where the person supplying such services through electronic commerce operator is liable for registration under section 22(1) of the CGST Act;

(c) Service by way of housekeeping such as plumbing, carpentering, etc. except where the person supplying such services through E-Com operator is liable for registration under Section 22(1) of CGST Act, 2017.

Meaning of Various Terms
(i) Radio taxi: means a taxi including a radio cab, by whatever name called, which is in two-way radio communication with a central control office and is enabled for tracking using Global Positioning System (GPS) or General Packet Radio Service (GPRS).
(ii) Maxi cab/Motor cab/Motor cycle: shall have the same meanings as assigned to them respectively in clauses (22), (25) and (26) of section 2 of the Motor Vehicles Act, 1988. As per Motor Vehicles Act, 1988, **Maxi cab:** means any motor vehicle constructed or adapted to carry more than six passengers, but not more than 12 passengers, excluding the driver, for hire or reward. **Motor cab:** means any motor vehicle constructed or adapted to carry not more than six passengers excluding the driver for hire or reward. **Motor car:** means any motor vehicle other than a transport vehicle, omnibus, road-roller, tractor, motor cycle or invalid carriage.

Chapter 6

Composition Levy

6.1 MEANING OF COMPOSITION LEVY [SECTION 10]

Composition levy is an alternative method of levy of tax designed for small taxpayers. It is a very simple, hassle-free compliance scheme for small taxpayers whose aggregate turnover in the previous financial year does not exceed ₹ 1.5 crores (₹ 75 lakhs for special category States). It is a voluntary and optional scheme.

However, upon opting for this scheme, the registered person cannot issue tax invoice under GST law and can neither collect GST from his customers nor can claim Input Tax credit (ITC) on his purchases. Such taxpayer does not have to maintain elaborate accounts and no need to file monthly return of inward and outward supply.

The threshold limit of ₹ 1 crore has been revised to ₹ 1.5 crore vide Notification No. 14/2019-Central Tax dated 07.03.2019 which is effective from 1st April 2019. For special category states, the threshold limit shall be ₹ 75 lakhs.

> As per explanation in clause (iii) to Section 22 of the CGST (Amendment) Act, 2018, the expression "special category States" shall mean states specified in Article 279A(4)(g) of the Constitution, other than the State of Jammu and Kashmir, Arunachal Pradesh, Assam, Himachal Pradesh, Meghalaya, Sikkim and Uttarakhand. Therefore, w.e.f. 1st Feb. 2019, only Manipur, Mizoram, Nagaland and Tripura are covered under Special Category States for the limited purpose of GST provision.

SPECIAL CATEGORIES STATES

Particulars		States
Special category state as per Constitution	Special category state as per Section 22 of CGST Act	Manipur
		Mizoram
		Nagaland
		Tripura
	Others	Arunachal Pradesh
		Meghalaya
		Sikkim
		Uttarakhand
		Assam
		Himachal Pradesh
		Jammu & Kashmir

The objective of composition scheme is to bring simplicity and to reduce the compliance cost for the small taxpayers. Moreover, it is optional and the eligible person opting to pay tax under this scheme can pay tax at a prescribed percentage of his turnover every quarter, instead of paying tax at normal rate.

Suppliers opting for composition levy need not worry about the classification of their goods or services or both, the rate of GST applicable on the same, etc. They are not required to raise any tax invoice, but simply need to issue a Bill of Supply wherein no tax will be charged from the recipient.

Provisions related to composition levy have been provided under section 10 of the CGST Act, 2017 read with Rule 3 to Rule 7 (Chapter II) of the CGST Rules, 2017.

6.2 SALIENT FEATURES OF COMPOSITION SCHEME

(1) Restrictions on supply of goods, which are not liable for GST, such as petroleum products (Crude, Diesel, Petrol, ATF & Natural Gas), alcohol for human consumption, etc.

(2) Cannot make inter-state outward supply of goods/services. Supply to SEZ not possible, since it is inter-state supply.

(3) Cannot make supply through e-Commerce operator who is required to collect tax under Sec 52 (TCS). With effect from 01-10-2023, Composition scheme dealer can make intra-state supply through e-Commerce operator.

(4) Restrictions on manufacture of notified goods (Ice cream, Pan Masala, Tobacco product, Aerated water)

(5) Prohibited from collecting tax on outward supply. GST will have to be borne out of his own pocket.

(6) Not entitled to avail input tax credit (ITC).

(7) Not applicable to persons who are casual taxable person (CTP) or non-resident taxable person (NRTP).

(8) If any inward supply is covered under RCM, the composition dealer will have to pay tax at normal rate.

(9) Quarterly payment of Tax, annual filing of Return.

(10) Cannot issue tax invoice. Not permitted to collect GST. The composition dealer shall mention the words "Composition taxable person, not eligible to collect tax on supplies" at the top of the "bill of supply" issued by him.

(11) The taxable person opting composition scheme for services and mixed supplies shall mention the words at the top of the bill of supply, namely **"taxable person paying tax in terms of Notification No. 2/2019-Central Tax (Rate) dated 07.03.2019, not eligible to collect tax on supplies."**

(12) Composition scheme would become applicable for all the business verticals having separate registrations within the State and all other registrations outside the State, which are held by the person with same PAN.

(13) Intimation to pay tax under composition scheme shall be filed only once, not every year.

(14) Composition dealer must mentioned "composition taxable person" on every notice/signboard, at both principal & additional place(s) of business.

(15) The registered person opting composition scheme shall issue, instead of tax invoice, a bill of supply as referred to in section 31(3)© of the GST Act with particulars as prescribed in rule 49 of Central Goods and Services Tax Rules.

(16) Composition scheme is voluntary & optional. Once the scheme is opted, actual duty liability under normal procedure is not relevant.

Conditions applicable on a composition supplier:

Once a person has opted to pay tax under the composition scheme, the following conditions would stand attracted:

(i) Every notice or signboard in every registered place of business, displayed at a prominent place, shall carry the words "Composition taxable person";

(ii) Every bill of supply issued by the composition suppliers shall carry the declaration "Composition taxable person, not eligible to collect tax on supplies" on top of the bill;

(iii) **RCM on inward supplies:** The composition supplier shall be liable to make payment at the rate applicable on the supply in respect of every inward supply liable to tax under the reverse charge mechanism, under section 9(3)/9(4) of the CGST Act, regardless of the rate of tax that is applied on him on the outward supplies effected by him.

(iv) The composition taxpayer is prohibited from collecting any GST/Cess applicable on the outward supplies effected by him. Accordingly, the recipients of supply would also not be eligible to claim any credits where the inward supply is from a composition taxpayer;

(v) A composition supplier shall not be entitled to issue any tax invoice. However, to effect supplies of goods/ services the supplier will have to issue "Bill of Supply" without indicating any tax amount on it.

(vi) If a composition taxpayer switches over to become a regular taxpayer, he will be entitled to take input tax in respect of inputs held in stock (as inputs, contained in semi-finished or finished goods) on the day immediately preceding the date from which he becomes liable to pay tax under Section 9 (regular taxpayer).

(vii) In case of migration of old registration into registration under GST, option to avail composition scheme under GST Laws can be exercised only if the goods held in stock by such taxable person, on the appointed day have not been purchased in the course of inter-state trade or commerce or imported from a place outside India or received from his branch situated outside the State, or from his agent or principal outside the State.

6.3 ELIGIBILITY FOR GST COMPOSITION LEVY

Section 10(1): A taxable person may opt for composition scheme, whose 'aggregate turnover' across all States under the same PAN in the immediately preceding financial year did not exceed the threshold limit of ₹ 1.5 crore (₹ 75 lacs in case of Special Category States being Manipur, Mizoram, Nagaland and Tripura) and shall pay tax at the rate prescribed in Rule 7 of CGST Rules, 2017 in lieu of tax payable under section 9(1) of the CGST Act, 2017.

Section 10(2): The registered person shall be eligible to opt under Section 10(1), if:

(a) he is not engaged in the supply of services other than supplies referred to in clause (*b*) of paragraph 6 of Schedule II (i.e. Restaurant services);

(However, as per CGST Amendment Act 2018, a registered person other than Restaurant services provider *shall also be eligible to opt for composition levy, if they supply services of value not exceeding 10% of their turnover in the preceding financial year in a State/Union Territory or ₹ 5 lakhs, whichever is higher)*

(b) he is not engaged in making any supply of goods, which are not leviable to tax under this Act;

(c) he is not engaged in making any inter-State outward supplies;

(d) he is not engaged in making any supply of goods or services through an electronic commerce operator who is required to collect tax at source under Section 52; [Eligible to supply goods through ECOM as per amendment made by Finance Act, 2023]; and

(e) he is not a manufacturer of such goods as may be notified by the Government on the recommendations of the Council:

Provided that where more than one registered persons are having the same Permanent Account Number (issued under the Income-tax Act, 1961), the registered person shall not be eligible to opt for the scheme under Section 10(1) unless all such registered persons opt to pay tax under composition scheme.

> *As per CGST Amendment Act, 2018, a registered person opting for composition scheme is permitted to render services other than restaurant services as per second proviso to Sec 10(1) up to specified value. The specified value is 10% of Turnover in a State/UT in the preceding financial year or ₹ 5 lakhs whichever is higher.*

(f) he is neither a casual taxable person nor a non-resident taxable person.

6.3.1 Composition scheme for service providers—Section 10(2A)

Notification No. 02/2019-CT(Rate) dated 07-03-2019, amended by Notification no 9/2019-CT(Rate) dated 29-3-2019 has introduced a new composition scheme for registered person whose aggregate turnover in the preceding financial year was fifty lakh rupees or below and not engaged in making any inter-State outward supply. This scheme is applicable from 1st April 2019.

New scheme introduces a fixed tax rate of 6% with 3% CGST and 3% SGST. Independent service providers, as well as mixed suppliers of goods and services with an annual turnover of up to ₹ 50 lakhs in the preceding financial year can opt for this scheme.

6.3.2 Salient features [Sec 10(2A) read with Rule 5]

(a)	Eligibility	(i) Aggregate turnover during previous financial year did not exceed ₹ 50 lakhs. (ii) The person is not eligible for composition scheme under Sec 10(1). (iii) He is not engaged in making any supply of goods or services which are not leviable to tax under this Act; (iv) He is not engaged in making any inter-State outward supplies of goods or services; (v) He is not engaged in making any supply of goods or services through an electronic commerce operator who is required to collect tax at source under section 52 [Eligible to supply goods through ECOM as per amendment made by Finance Act, 2023];

		(vi) He is not a manufacturer of such goods or supplier of such services as may be notified by the Government on the recommendations of the Council [ice cream, pan masala, or tobacco, etc.]; and (vii) He is not a casual taxable person or a non-resident taxable person. **Note:** Where more than one registered person are having the same Permanent Account Number issued under the Income-tax Act, 1961, the registered person shall not be eligible to opt for the scheme under Sec 10(2A) unless all such registered persons opt to pay tax under this scheme.
(b)	Rate of Tax	As may be prescribed but not exceeding 6% (3% + 3%) of the turnover in the STATE or Union Territory.
(c)	Conditions & restrictions	The person exercising the option to pay tax under section 10 (2A) shall comply with the following conditions [Rule 5(1) of CGST Rules, 2017]: (a) Mention the words "composition taxable person" on every notice or signboard displayed at a prominent place at his principal place of business and at every additional place or places of business. (b) Mention the words "composition taxable person, not eligible to collect tax on supplies" at the top of the bill of supply issued by him. (c) Not entitled to any Input Tax Credit. (d) Not allowed to collect GST from customer. (e) Cannot show GST in their invoice.
(d)	Reverse charge tax liability	A Composition Dealer shall pay tax under Reverse Charge Mechanism u/s 9(3) or 9(4) on inward supply at applicable rate wherever applicable.
(e)	Procedure to opt for Composition scheme	The taxpayer shall electronically file an intimation in form GST CMP-02, duly signed or verified, on the Common Portal, prior to the commencement of the financial year for which the option to pay tax under composition scheme is exercised.
(f)	Return & Payment of Taxes	Quarterly payment of tax (FORM CMP 08) & Annual filing of Return (GSTR-4).

6.4 THRESHOLD LIMIT OF COMPOSITION LEVY [SECTION 10(1)]

A taxable person can opt for composition scheme, whose 'aggregate turnover' in the immediately preceding financial year does not exceed following amount:

Category of tax payer	Applicable up to 12th October 2017	Applicable with effect from 13th October 2017*	Applicable with effect from 1st April 2019
Registered person in States other than states mentioned below	₹ 75 lakhs	₹ 1 crore	₹ 1.5 crore**
Arunachal Pradesh, Assam, Manipur, Meghalaya, Mizoram, Nagaland, Sikkim, Tripura, Himachal Pradesh	₹ 50 lakhs	₹ 75 lakhs	₹ 75 lakhs
Uttarakhand	₹ 75 lakhs	₹ 100 lakhs	₹ 75 lakhs

* Vide Notification No. 46/2017-Central tax dated 13-10-2017.

** The turnover limit of ₹ 1 crore has been revised to ₹ 1.5 crores as per CGST Amendment Act 2018. **(Notification No. 10/2019-Central Tax dated 07.03.2019)**

> As per explanation in clause (iii) of Section 22 of the CGST (Amendment) Act 2018, the expression "special category States" shall mean states specified in Article 279A (4)(g) of the Constitution, other than the State of Jammu and Kashmir, Arunachal Pradesh, Assam, Himachal Pradesh, Meghalaya, Sikkim and Uttarakhand. Therefore, w.e.f. 1st Feb 2019, only Manipur, Mizoram, Nagaland and Tripura are covered under Special Category States for the limited purpose of GST provision.

6.4.1 Aggregate Turnover for Determining Eligibility to Opt Composition Scheme

Ref. Notification No. 01/2020-Central Tax dated 01-01-2020

(1) The expression "aggregate turnover" shall include the value of all supplies (taxable and exempt supply) made by a person from the 1st day of April of a financial year up to the date when he becomes liable for registration under this Act.

(2) The expression "aggregate turnover "shall not include the value of exempt supply of services provided by way of extending deposits, loans or advances in so far as the consideration is represented by way of interest or discount.

(3) The expression "aggregate turnover" excludes

(i) inward supplies effected by a person which are liable to tax under reverse charge mechanism; and

(ii) Various taxes under the GST law and Compensation cess

6.5 RATE OF TAX UNDER COMPOSITION LEVY [Rule 7]

The category of registered persons, eligible for composition levy under section 10, shall pay tax at following rates [Section 10(1)]:

(1) Notification No. 8/2017-Central Tax dated 27th June 2017

(2) Notification No. 01/2018-Central Tax dated 01st January 2018

(3) Notification No. 05/2019-Central Tax dated 29th January 2019

(4) Notification No. 02/2019-Central Tax (Rate) dated 7th March 2019

(5) Notification No. 50/2020-Central Tax dated 24th June 2020

Sl No.	Category of Registered Person	Rate of Tax (CGST+SGST) Up to 31-12-2017	Rate of Tax (CGST+SGST) w.e.f. 1st Jan 2018
1.	Manufacturers, other than manufacturers of such goods as may be notified by the Government (e.g. ice cream, pan masala, tobacco products, Aerated water, etc.)	2%	1%
2.	Suppliers making supplies referred to in clause (b) of paragraph 6 of Schedule II i.e. Restaurant Service (not serving Alcohol)	5%	5%
3.	Any other supplier eligible for composition levy under section 10(1) & 10(2) (Tax payable on turnover of taxable supplies of goods and services)	1%	1%
4.	Registered persons not eligible under the composition levy under sub-sections (1) and (2), but eligible to opt to pay tax under sub-section (2A), of section 10 i.e. Supplier of Services (or Mixed supplier) with aggregate turnover up to ₹ 50 lakhs	-	6% (w.e.f. 1st April 2019)

Notes:

(1) For traders (Sl. No. 3) under composition scheme, tax shall be payable on taxable supplies of goods. (Notification No. 01/2018-Central Tax dated 01.01.2018)

(2) The Central Government vide Notification No. 05/2019-Central Tax dated 29th January 2019 has substituted the rate of tax for suppliers other than (manufacturers and Restaurant service providers) under composition scheme. As per new rule 7, such person shall be liable for payment of tax @1% (CGST+SGST) on taxable supplies of goods & services.

(3) The Central Government vide Notification No. 02/2019-Central Tax (Rate) dated 7th March, 2019 has introduced a new composition scheme for Service provider (mixed supplier) whose "aggregate turnover" is up to ₹ 50 lakhs. Such person shall be liable for payment of tax @6% (CGST+SGST) on taxable supplies of goods & services. This notification is effective from 1st April 2019.

(4) Composition scheme dealer are restricted from manufacture of Aerated water w.e.f. 1st October 2019, 43/2019-Central Tax dated 30.09.2019.

(5) A person engaged in manufacture of goods notified under Section 10(2)(e) cannot opt for composition scheme u/s 10(2). However, law does not bar traders/suppliers of such goods to opt for composition scheme.

(6) A person engaged in manufacture of notified goods or supply of services (e.g. ice cream and other edible ice, whether or not containing cocoa, pan masala, all goods covered under chapter 24 (i.e. tobacco and manufactured tobacco substitutes), aerated water etc. as notified by the government on the recommendation of GST council) not eligible to opt for composition scheme u/s 10(2A). [Refer Notification No. 02/2019-Central Tax (Rate) dated 07-03-2019 & Notification No. 18/2019-Central Tax (Rate) dated 30-09-2019.]

(7) For the purposes of determining the tax payable by a person under section 10, the expression "turnover in State or turnover in Union territory "shall not include the value of following supplies, namely:
   (i) supplies from the first day of April of a financial year up to the date when such person becomes liable for registration under this Act; and
   (ii) exempt supply of services provided by way of extending deposits, loans or advances in so far as the consideration is represented by way of interest or discount.

(8) The tax rate will be applicable on the 'turnover in State' particular to a taxable person, which should be paid by him in the State in which he has obtained registration.

(9) Turnover in State includes 'all' taxable supplies which includes exempt supplies also.

6.6 FILING OF RETURN AND PAYMENT OF TAX

The persons paying tax under composition scheme are required to pay tax on quarterly basis and also required to file a quarterly return in FORM GSTR-4 by the 18th of the month following the end of the quarter instead of any statement of outward or inward supplies on monthly basis.

The proper officer may cancel the registration where the said person has not furnished returns for three consecutive tax periods. Registered person opting for composition levy have to file Annual Return in FORM GSTR-9A by 31st December, following the end of financial year.

As per the decision taken in 32nd GST council meeting, with effect from 1st April 2019, A composition scheme dealer shall be required to file only one annual return (GSTR-4) before 30th day of April following the end of such financial year but payment of tax to be made on quarterly basis [Refer Rule 62(1) (ii)].

Special Procedure for Furnishing of Return and Payment of Tax

The Central Government vide N. No. 21/2019-CT dated 23rd April 2019 has provided the special procedure to be followed by persons paying tax under the provisions of Section 10 or persons availing the benefit of Notification No. 02/2019-CT @ dated 7th March 2019, for furnishing of return and payment of tax which is explained as below:

(i) The said persons shall furnish a statement, every quarter or, as the case may be, part thereof containing the details of payment of self-assessed tax in FORM GST CMP-08 of the CGST Rules, 2017, until the 18th day of the month succeeding such quarter.

(ii) The said persons shall furnish a return for every financial year or, as the case may be, part thereof in FORM GSTR-4 of the CGST Rules, 2017, on or before the 30th day of April following the end of such financial year.

(iii) The registered persons paying tax by availing the benefit of the said notification, in respect of the period for which he has availed the said benefit, shall be deemed to have complied with the provisions of Section 37 and Section 39 of the said Act if they have furnished FORM GST CMP-08 and FORM GSTR4 as provided in para 1 and para 2 above.

Bill of Supply

A taxable person opting for the scheme has to issue bill of supply in prescribed manner, as he is not eligible to issue tax invoice under GST. He has to mention the words "composition taxable person, not eligible to collect tax on supplies" at the top of every bill of supply issued by him.

6.7 INTIMATION FOR OPTING COMPOSITION SCHEME [RULES 3 AND 4]

The procedure to opt for GST Composition scheme has been prescribed in Rules 3 and 4 of the CGST rules, 2017. A person who opts to pay tax under composition levy scheme shall electronically file intimation in prescribed form on the GST Common Portal [www.gst.gov.in].

Sl No.	Various Scenarios for opting the Scheme	How to Opt	Effective date for Composition
1.	The taxable person migrating to GST from previous regime	Can opt by filing FORM GST CMP-01 not later than 30 days or such further period as may be extended, from the Appointed date	Effective from Appointed date
2.	Person taking new registration under GST	Can opt at the time of obtaining registration in Part B of FORM GST REG-01	Effective form the date of registration
3.	A registered person under GST opting for composition scheme	May opt by filing FORM GST CMP-02 prior to commencement of FY for which option is exercised	Effective from the beginning of the financial year
4.	The taxable person migrating to GST from previous regime and Person taking new registration under GST (one time) but opting for Composition Scheme after the appointed date or his date of registration	By filing intimation in FORM GST CMP-02	Effective from the first day of the month immediately succeeding the month in which he files an intimation

Voluntary withdrawal from Composition scheme:

A person, even though still eligible for composition scheme, may opt out of the composition scheme by filing an application for withdrawal on which an order of withdrawal is required to be passed by the appropriate officer. It is clarified that in a case where the taxpayer has sought withdrawal from the composition scheme, the effective date shall be the date indicated by him in his intimation/application filed, but such date may not be prior to the commencement of the financial year in which such intimation/application for withdrawal is being filed.

6.8 APPLICABILITY OF COMPOSITION SCHEME

(1) **Applicable for "Supply" of all goods:** Composition scheme may be opted for by taxable persons, in respect of supply of any goods (without any reference to classification or type of goods). A taxable person **cannot** opt for payment of taxes under composition scheme, say for supply of one class of goods and opt for regular scheme of payment of taxes for supply of other classes of goods or services.

Exceptions: Suppliers who are engaged in making any supply of goods, which are not leviable to tax under CGST/SGST (UTGST) Act 2017, are not entitled to avail composition scheme. Hence, suppliers supplying alcoholic liquor for human consumption, petroleum crude, high speed diesel, motor spirit (petrol), natural gas and aviation turbine fuel (ATF), or making inter-state outward supply of goods on which tax is levied under IGST Act are apparently not eligible for composition scheme.

(2) **Restriction on Manufacturer:** Composition scheme is not applicable to the manufacturers of notified goods (i.e. goods that are notified by the Government on recommendations of the Council).

As per *Notification No. 08/2017-Central Tax dated 27.06.2017*, registered person who are engaged in manufacture of **ice cream** and other **edible ice**, whether or not containing cocoa (Chapter heading 21050000), **pan masala** (Chapter heading 21069020), all goods of Chapter 24, i.e. Tobacco and manufactured tobacco substitutes, **Aerated water** (Chapter heading 22021010) are not eligible to opt for Composition Scheme.

(3) **Composition scheme for services:** There are three categories of composition scheme available for service provider:

(1) Restaurant Service provider, other than serving alcoholic liquor for human consumption and having turnover limit of ₹ 1.5 crore/₹ 75 lakhs as the case may be (GST 5%).

(2) Manufacturer/trader opting composition scheme (permitted to provide service of value not exceeding 10% of turnover in a State or Union territory in the preceding financial year or ₹ 5 lakh, whichever is higher) (GST 1%).

(3) Supplier of Service (or Mixed suppliers) having annual turnover up to ₹ 50 lakhs (effective from 1st April 2019) (GST 6%).

As per CGST Amendment Act, 2018, a new proviso is being added to section 10(1) to provide that a person who opts to pay tax under composition scheme may supply services (other than restaurant services), of value not exceeding 10% of turnover in a State or Union territory in the preceding financial year or ₹ 5 lakh, whichever is higher.
The Central Government vide Notification No. 02/2019-Central Tax(Rate) dated 7th March 2019 has introduced a new composition scheme for Service provider (mixed supplier) whose "aggregate turnover" in the preceding FY is up to ₹ 50 lakhs. Such person shall be liable for payment of tax @6% (CGST+SGST) on taxable supplies of goods & services. This notification is effective from 1st April 2019.

6.9 VALIDITY AND WITHDRAWAL FROM COMPOSITION SCHEME

The option exercised by registered person to pay tax under composition scheme shall remain valid so long as he satisfies all the conditions. He may not file a fresh intimation every year and he may continue to pay tax under the said section subject to the provisions of the Act and these rules.

The option to pay tax under composition scheme lapses from the day on which his aggregate turnover during the financial year exceeds the specified limit or he ceases to satisfy any of the conditions of this Scheme. He is required to file an intimation for withdrawal from the scheme in FORM GST CMP-04 within seven days from the day on which the threshold limit has been crossed. A registered person paying tax under this scheme may also voluntarily opt out by filing FORM GST CMP-04.

After opting out of the scheme, he has to pay tax as normal taxpayer and issue tax invoice for every taxable supply made thereafter. Subsequently, he has to file a statement in FORM GST ITC-01 containing details of the stock of the inputs and inputs contained in semi-finished or finished goods held in stock by him on the date on which the option is withdrawn. The said statement has to be submitted on the common portal within 30 days from the date of withdrawal. He shall be entitled to take credit of input tax in respect of inputs held in stock, inputs contained in semi-finished or finished goods held in stock and on capital goods on the day immediately preceding the date from which he becomes liable to pay tax as normal taxpayer under section 9 of the CGST Act, 2017.

Action for wrongly opting Composition scheme or for contravention of any provision of the scheme

When the proper officer has reason to believe that the registered person has wrongly opted for the scheme or has contravened the provisions of the scheme, then he will seek a reply by issuing a show cause notice to such person in the FORM GST CMP-05. This notice is to be reply within 15 days of receipt of the same. Thereafter within 30 days of receipt of reply, officer has to issue an order in FORM GST CMP-07, either accepting the reply or denying the option to pay tax under the scheme.

If a taxable person has paid tax under the composition scheme though he was not eligible for the scheme then the person would be liable to penalty and the provisions of section 73 or 74 shall be applicable for determination of tax and penalty. He shall be liable to pay tax at normal rate plus penalty equal to such amount of tax.

Chapter 7

Exemption from GST

7.1 STATUTORY PROVISION

Section 11 of the CGST Act, 2017 confers powers on the Central Government to exempt either absolutely or conditionally goods or services or both of any specified description from whole or part of the central tax, on the recommendations of the GST Council. It also confers power on the Central Government to exempt from payment of tax any goods or services or both, by special order, on recommendation of the Council.

Power to grant exemption from IGST is covered under section 6 of the IGST Act, 2017.

Exemption under CGST Act	Deemed to exempt under SGST Act
	Deemed to exempt under UTGST Act
Exemption under IGST Act	No Auto Application of Exemption

Exemption is where tax is leviable but exempted from the payment of the tax.

Section 11(1) read as under:

Where the Government is satisfied that it is necessary in the public interest so to do, it may, on the recommendations of the Council, by notification, exempt generally, either absolutely or subject to such conditions as may be specified therein, goods or services or both of any specified description from the whole or any part of the tax leviable thereon with effect from such date as may be specified in such notification.

> **As per Section 2(47):** "exempt supply" means supply of any goods or services or both which attracts *nil* rate of tax or which may be wholly exempt from tax under section 11, or under section 6 of the Integrated Goods and Services Tax Act, and includes non-taxable supply.

Exempt supplies comprise the following three types of supplies:

(a) Supplies taxable at a 'NIL' rate of tax;
(b) Supplies that are wholly or partially exempted from CGST or IGST, by way of a notification;
(c) Non-taxable supplies as defined under Section 2(78)—supplies that are not taxable under the Act (viz. alcoholic liquor for human consumption).

The following aspects need to be noted:

(a) Zero-rated supplies such as exports would not be treated as supplies taxable at 'NIL' rate of tax;
(b) Input tax credit attributable to exempt supplies will not be available for utilization/setoff.

Non-taxable Supply

A transaction must be a 'supply' as defined under the GST law, to qualify as a non-taxable supply under the GST law.

Points to be noted:

(1) Stock transfers to unit within the State for which no separate registration is obtained, which does not qualify as a 'supply' as defined under Section 7 of the CGST Act, cannot be said to be a non-taxable supply.
(2) Transactions specified in Schedule III, which are treated as neither a supply of goods, nor a supply of services, would also not qualify as non-taxable supplies.

(3) Supplies that enjoy the benefit of being wholly exempted from taxes, nil-rated supplies and zero-rated supplies are also not covered under the umbrella of 'non-taxable supplies' given that the goods or services are in fact liable to tax, and such tax is exempted by virtue of an exemption notification, or the tax rate is nil.

(4) Only those supplies that are excluded from the scope of taxation under GST are covered by this definition, i.e., alcoholic liquor for human consumption.

Statutory Provision

Power to grant exemption from GST is covered in Section 11 of the CGST Act, 2017 and Section 6 of the IGST Act, 2017, subject to the following conditions:

(i) Exemption should be in public interest
(ii) By way of issue of notification
(iii) On recommendation of the Council
(iv) Absolute/conditional exemption may be for any goods and/or services
(v) Exemption by way of special order (and not notification) may be granted by citing the circumstances which are of exceptional nature.

Exemptions by Way of Notification

Purpose of notification	Supply of goods	Supply of services
Prescribing Rate of Tax	01/2017-Central Tax (Rate)	11/2017-Central Tax (Rate)
Granting exemption	02/2017-Central Tax (Rate) Amended vide Notification No. 28/2017, 35/2017, 42/2017, 7/2018, 19/2018, 19/2021, 13/2022-Central Tax (Rate)	12/2017-Central Tax (Rate) Amended vide Notification No. 21/2017, 25/2017, 32/2017 and 47/2017, 2/2018, 2/2019, 05/2020, 07/2021, 04/2022-Central Tax (Rate)

Notification No. 09/2017-Central Tax (Rate) dated 28.06.2017

Intra state "Supply" received by a deductor u/s 51 from unregistered person, who is otherwise not required to registered under GST, is exempted from payment of tax under Reverse charge basis.

Notification No. 10/2017-Central Tax (Rate) dated 28.06.2017

Intra State "Supply" received by a registered person from unregistered person, dealing in buying and selling of second hand goods and who pays the central tax on the value of outward supply is exempted from payment of tax under Reverse charge basis.

Notification No. 22/2018-Central Tax (Rate) dated 06.08.2018

Intra State supplies of goods or services or both received by a registered person from a supplier who is not registered is exempted from payment of whole of the tax leviable thereon under reverse charge u/s 9(4) of the CGST Act, 2017, till 31st Jan 2019.

Note:

It is pertinent to mention that the exemption would be in respect of goods or services or both, and not specifically for any classes of persons, e.g. an absolute exemption could be granted in respect of supply of Electricity. A conditional exemption could be supply of goods to canteen stores department.

1.	Services provided to the United Nations or a specified international organization is exempt by way of refund and Services provided to a foreign diplomatic mission or consular post in India or for personal use or for the use of the family members of diplomatic agents or career consular officers posed therein, is exempt by way of refund. *Notification-16/2017-Central Tax (Rate) dated 28th June 2017 & Notification* 13/2017-IGST (Rate), *28th June 2017.*
2.	Services by the Central Government or State Government or any local authority by way of any activity in relation to a function entrusted to a Panchayat under Article 243G of the Constitution is neither a supply of goods nor a supply of service as per Section 7(2). Notification-14/2017-Central Tax (Rate) dated 28th June 2017 and 16/2018 Central Tax (Rate) dated 26-07-2018.

3	Service by way of grant of alcoholic liquor licence, against consideration in the form of licence fee or application fee or by whatever name it is called is neither supply of goods nor supply of services. Notification-25/2019-Central Tax(Rate) dated 30th Sept 2019.

Example of Absolute Exemption

(1) Transmission or distribution of electricity by an electricity transmission or distribution utility.

(2) Services by way of renting of residential dwelling for use as residence, except to registered person.

(3) Services by a veterinary clinic in relation to health care of animals or birds.

Where an exemption in respect of goods and/or services has been granted absolutely, the registered person supplying such goods and/or services shall not collect tax on such goods and/or services.

Example of Conditional Exemption

(1) Services by a hotel, inn, guesthouse, club or campsite, by whatever name called, for residential or lodging purposes, having declared tariff of a unit of accommodation less than ₹ 1000 per day, till 17-08-2022.

(2) Supply of service by a RWA (unincorporated body or a nonprofit entity registered under any law) to its own members by way of reimbursement of charges or share of contribution up to an amount of ₹ 7500 per month per member in a housing society or a residential complex are exempt from GST.

Concessional rate of GST on intra-state supply of bricks subject to the condition that credit of input tax charged on goods or services used exclusively in supplying such goods has not been taken. [N.No. 02/2022-Central Tax(Rate) dated 31.03.2022.

Exemption by Special Order

As per section 11(2) of CGST Act and SGST Act, the Central Government and State Governments have power to grant exemptions provided the following conditions are fulfilled:

(1) Exemption should be in public interest

(2) Exemptions are by way of special order in each case and on the recommendations of GST council

(3) Order should mention the circumstances of exceptional nature.

Applicability of exemption notifications issued under CGST/IGST to SGST/UTGST and vice-versa

As per section 11(4) of SGST Act and section 8(4) of UTGST Act, any notification issued by the Central Government, on the recommendations of the Council, under section 11(1) or order issued section 11(2) of the CGST Act shall be deemed to be a notification or, as the case may be, an order issued under SGST/UTGST Act.

7.2 LIST OF EXEMPTION NOTIFICATIONS

Sl. No.	Notification No.	Particulars
1.	02/2017-Central Tax(Rate) dated 28.06.2017	Exempted supplies of around 149 items of goods in terms of Section 11(1) of the CGST Act, 2017, e.g. electricity, salt, fresh fruits, potato, tomato, onion, plastic bangles, passenger baggage, etc.
2.	Notification No. 03/2017-Central Tax(Rate) dated 28.06.2017	Goods specified in the List annexed required in connection with various kinds of petroleum operations undertaken are given concessional rate i.e. at the rate of 2.5% under CGST i.e. 5% IGST.
3.	Notification No. 07/2017-Central Tax(Rate) dated 28.06.2017	Exemption to supplies by CSD to Unit Run Canteens and supplies by CSD/Unit Run Canteens to authorized customers.
4.	Notification No. 18/2017-Integrated Tax(Rate) dated 05.07.2017	Exemption from IGST to SEZs on import of Services by a unit/ developer in an SEZ.
5.	Notification No. 08/2017-Central Tax(Rate) dated 28.06.2017 (As amended Vide Notification No. 38/2017-Central Tax (Rate) dated 13.10.2017	Exemption granted from levy of CGST under RCM on supplies received from unregistered persons.

Sl. No.	Notification No.	Particulars
6.	Notification No. 09/2017-Central Tax(Rate) dated 28.06.2017	Exemption granted to supplies to a TDS deductor by an unregistered supplier.
7.	Notification No. 10/2017-Central Tax (Rate) dated 28.06.2017	Exemption to supplies of second hand goods received by registered person dealing in buying and selling of second hand goods from unregistered person provided the dealer pays central tax on supply of such second-hand goods as per Valuation Rules.
8.	Notification No. 12/2017-Central Tax (Rate) dated 28.06.2017	Exemption to supply of 81 services under CGST Act.
9.	Notification No. 21/2017-Central Tax (Rate) dated 22.08.2017	Seeks to amend notification No. 12/2017-CT (R) to exempt services provided by Fair Price Shops to Government and those provided by and to FIFA for FIFA U-17. Also, to substitute RWCIS & PMFBY for MNAIS & NAIS, and insert explanation for LLP.
10.	Notification No. 25/2017-Central Tax (Rate) dated 21.09.2017	Seeks to amend notification No. 12/2017-CT (R) to exempt right to admission to the events authorize under FIFA U-17 World Cup 2017.
11.	Notification No. 26/2017-Central Tax (Rate) dated 21.09.2017	Exempts intra-state supply of heavy water and nuclear fuels by the Department of Atomic Energy to the Nuclear Power Corporation of India Ltd.
12.	Notification No. 30/2017-Central Tax (Rate) dated 29.09.2017	Exempting supply of services associated with transit cargo both to and from Nepal and Bhutan.
13.	Notification 32/2017-Central Tax (Rate) dated 13th October 2017	Exempting Service provided by GTA to un-registered person, other than to a factory, society, Co-operative Society, Body corporate, partnership firm.
14.	Notification No. 30/2017-Integrated Tax (Rate) dated 22nd September 2017	Exempts Interstate supply of Skimmed milk powder, or concentrated milk from payment of whole of IGST leviable thereon u/s 5 of the IGST Act.
15.	Notification No. 32/2017-Integrated Tax (Rate) dated 13th October 2017	Interstate supply of goods or services or both received by a registered person from any supplier, who is not registered is exempted from payment of whole of IGST leviable thereon u/s 5(4) of the IGST Act.
16.	Notification 2/2018-Central Tax (Rate) dated 25th January 2018	Amendment of exemption notification 12/2017-Central Tax (Rate) dated 28.06.2017 and addition of new services in the list of exempted services.
17.	Notification 7/2018-Central Tax (Rate) dated 25th January 2018	De-oiled rice bran, Cotton seed oil cake and parts for manufacture of hearing aids added to the list of goods exempted from GST.
18.	Notification 7/2018-Central Tax (Rate) dated 25th January 2018	De-oiled rice bran, Cotton seed oil cake and parts for manufacture of hearing aids added to the list of goods exempted from GST.
19.	Notification 14/2018-Central Tax (Rate) dated 26th July 2018	Services by old age home, NPS to its members, services by FSSAI, exempted from GST.
20.	Notification 28/2018-Central Tax (Rate) dated 31st Dec 2018	Service provided by GTA to Govt/local authority, Banking company to account holder of Pradhan Mantri Jan Dhan Yojana exempted from GST.
21.	Notification 13/2019-Central Tax (Rate) dated 31st July 2019	Hiring of Electric buses by local authorities exempted from GST.
22.	Notification 25/2019-Central Tax (Rate) dated 30th Sept 2019	Service by way of grant of alcoholic liquor licence, against consideration in the form of licence fee or application fee or by whatever name it is called, shall be treated neither as a supply of goods nor a supply of service.

7.3 GOODS EXEMPTED FROM GST

In excise of the power conferred under Section 11(1) of the CGST Act, 2017 and section 6(1) of the IGST Act, 2017, exemption has been given to Intra State Supplies and Inter State Supplies of Goods through notifications.

Example of Goods exempted from GST

Almost all raw food products which are not packed in any container, live animal, live tree & plants, animal & poultry feeds, fresh fruit, vegetables, egg, milk, unpacked paneer, unbranded natural honey, coconuts, salt, contraceptive, human blood, hearing aid, space craft, Indian National flag, Handloom, cotton used in Khadi yarn, coffee beans, unprocessed green tea leaves, judicial & non-judicial stamp papers, etc. are covered in the list of goods, exempt from Tax under GST.

Goods imported by unit/developer in SEZ exempt from IGST

SEZ is an area considered to be situated outside India, any supply to SEZ is at par export, and such supply attracts zero rate as zero-rated supply.

All goods imported by a unit/developer in the Special Economic Zone (SEZ) for authorized operations are exempt from the whole of the integrated tax leviable thereon under section 3(7) of the Customs Tariff Act, 1975 read with section 5 of the IGST Act, 2017 *[Notification No. 64/2017 Customs dated 05.07.2017].*

Any supply from SEZ Unit to DTA shall be treated as Imports and would be taxable under Reverse Charge Basis in the hand of the recipient.

As per section 2 (i) of Special Economic Zones Act, 2005, DTA (Domestic Tariff Area) means "the whole of India but does not include the area of the special economic zones".

7.4 SERVICES EXEMPTED FROM GST

In exercise of the powers conferred by section 11(1) of the Central Goods and Services Tax Act, 2017 & by virtue of section 6(1) of the IGST Act, 2017, the Central Government vide Notification No. 12/2017-Central Tax (Rate) dated 28.06.2017 and Notification No. 09/2017-Integrated Tax (Rate) dated 28.06.2017 and through subsequent notifications, has so far notified following broad category of Services which are exempt from Tax under GST.

LIST OF SERVICES EXEMPTED FROM GST

Notification No. 12/2017-Central Tax (Rate) dated 28.06.2017

Sl. No.	Description of Services
1.	Services by an entity registered under section 12AA of the Income-tax Act, 1961 (43 of 1961) by way of charitable activities.
2.	Services by way of transfer of a going concern, as a whole or an independent part thereof.
3.	Pure services (excluding works contract service or other composite supplies involving supply of any goods) provided to the Central Government, State Government or Union territory or local authority by way of any activity in relation to any function entrusted to a Panchayat under article 243G of the Constitution or in relation to any function entrusted to a Municipality under article 243W of the Constitution.
3A.	Composite supply of goods and services in which the value of supply of goods constitutes not more than 25 per cent of the value of the said composite supply provided to the Central Government, State Government or Union territory or local authority by way of any activity in relation to any function entrusted to a Panchayat under article 243G of the Constitution or in relation to any function entrusted to a Municipality under article 243W of the Constitution.
4.	Services by Central Government, State Government, Union territory, local authority or governmental authority by way of any activity in relation to any function entrusted to a municipality under article 243W of the Constitution.
5.	Services by a Central Government, State Government, Union territory, local authority or Governmental Authority by way of any activity in relation to any function entrusted to a Panchayat under article 243G of the Constitution.
6.	Services by the Central Government, State Government, Union territory or local authority excluding the following services— (a) services by the Department of Posts ~~by way of speed post, express parcel post, life insurance, and agency services provided to a person other than the Central Government, State Government, Union territory~~; (Omitted w.e.f. 18th July 2022 Vide N.No. 04/2022-CT(R) dt. 13-07-2022);

Sl. No.	Description of Services
	(b) services in relation to an aircraft or a vessel, inside or outside the precincts of a port or an airport; (c) transport of goods or passengers; or (d) any service, other than services covered under entries (a) to (c) above, provided to business entities.
7.	Services provided by the Central Government, State Government, Union territory or local authority to a business entity with an aggregate turnover of up to such amount in the preceding financial year as makes it eligible for exemption from registration under the Central Goods and Services Tax Act, 2017 (12 of 2017). **Explanation:** For the purposes of this entry, it is hereby clarified that the provisions of this entry shall not be applicable to (a) services (i) by the Department of Posts ~~by way of speed post, express parcel post, life insurance, and agency services provided to a person other than the Central Government, State Government, Union territory~~; (Omitted w.e.f. 18th July 2022 Vide N.No. 04/2022-CT(R) dt. 13-07-2022); (ii) in relation to an aircraft or a vessel, inside or outside the precincts of a port or an airport; (iii) of transport of goods or passengers; and (b) services by way of renting of an immovable property.
8.	Services provided by the Central Government, State Government, Union territory or local authority to another Central Government, State Government, Union territory or local authority: Provided that nothing contained in this entry shall apply to services (i) by the Department of Posts ~~by way of speed post, express parcel post, life insurance, and agency services provided to a person other than the Central Government, State Government, Union territory~~; (Omitted Vide N.No. 04/2022-CT(R) dt. 13-07-2022, w.e.f. 18th July 2022); (ii) in relation to an aircraft or a vessel, inside or outside the precincts of a port or an airport; (iii) of transport of goods or passengers.
9.	Services provided by Central Government, State Government, Union territory or a local authority where the consideration for such services does not exceed five thousand rupees: Provided that nothing contained in this entry shall apply to (i) services by the Department of Posts ~~by way of speed post, express parcel post, life insurance, and agency services provided to a person other than the Central Government, State Government, Union territory~~; (Omitted Vide N.No. 04/2022-CT(R) dt. 13-07-2022, w.e.f. 18th July 2022); (ii) services in relation to an aircraft or a vessel, inside or outside the precincts of a port or an airport; (iii) transport of goods or passengers: Provided further that in case where continuous supply of service, as defined in sub-section (33) of section 2 of the Central Goods and Services Tax Act, 2017, is provided by the Central Government, State Government, Union territory or a local authority, the exemption shall apply only where the consideration charged for such service does not exceed five thousand rupees in a financial year.
9A.	Services provided by and to Fédération Internationale de Football Association (FIFA) and its subsidiaries directly or indirectly related to any of the events under FIFA U-17 World Cup 2017 to be hosted in India.
9AA.	Services provided by and to Fédération Internationale de Football Association (FIFA) and its subsidiaries directly or indirectly related to any of the events under FIFA U-17 Women's World Cup 2020 to be hosted in India.
9AB.	Services provided by and to Asian Football Confederation (AFC) and its subsidiaries directly or indirectly related to any of the events under AFC Women's Asia Cup 2022 to be hosted in India.
9B.	Supply of services associated with transit cargo both to and from Nepal and Bhutan (landlocked countries).
9C.	Supply of service by a Government Entity to Central Government, State Government, Union territory, local authority or any person specified by Central Government, State Government, Union territory or local authority against consideration received from Central Government, State Government, Union territory or local authority, in the form of grants.
9D.	Services by an old age home run by Central Government, State Government or by an entity registered under section 12AA or 12AB of the Income-tax Act, 1961 (43 of 1961) to its residents (aged 60 years or more) against consideration upto twenty-five thousand rupees per month per member, provided that the consideration charged is inclusive of charges for boarding, lodging and maintenance.

Sl. No.	Description of Services
10.	Services provided by way of pure labour contracts of construction, erection, commissioning, installation, completion, fitting out, repair, maintenance, renovation, or alteration of a civil structure or any other original works pertaining to the beneficiary-led individual house construction or enhancement under the Housing for All (Urban) Mission or Pradhan Mantri Awas Yojana.
10A.	Services supplied by electricity distribution utilities by way of construction, erection, commissioning, or installation of infrastructure for extending electricity distribution network up to the tube well of the farmer or agriculturalist for agricultural use.
11.	Services by way of pure labour contracts of construction, erection, commissioning, or installation of original works pertaining to a single residential unit otherwise than as a part of a residential complex.
11A.	Service provided by Fair Price Shops to Central Government, State Government or Union territory by way of sale of food grains, kerosene, sugar, edible oil, etc. under Public Distribution System against consideration in the form of commission or margin.
11B.	~~Service provided by Fair Price Shops to State Governments or Union territories by way of sale of kerosene, sugar, edible oil, etc. under Public Distribution System (PDS) against consideration in the form of commission or margin.~~ (Omitted vide notification No. 47/2017-Central Tax (Rate) dt 14.11.2017)
12.	Services by way of renting of residential dwelling for use as residence *except where the residential dwelling is rented to a registered person* (w.e.f. 18th July 2022, Vide N.No. 04/2022-CT(R) dt. 13-07-2022) **Explanation:** For the purpose of exemption under this entry, this entry shall cover services by way of renting of residential dwelling to a registered person where, (i) the registered person is proprietor of a proprietorship concern and rents the residential dwelling in his personal capacity for use as his own residence; and (ii) such renting is on his own account and not that of the proprietorship concern. (w.e.f. 1st January 2023, Vide N.No. 15/2022-CT(R) dt. 30-12-2022)
13.	Services by a person by way of (a) conduct of any religious ceremony; (b) renting of precincts of a religious place meant for general public, owned or managed by an entity registered as a charitable or religious trust under section 12AA or 12AB of the Income Tax Act, 1961 (hereinafter referred to as the Income-tax Act) or a trust or an institution registered under sub-clause (v) of clause (23C) of section 10 of the Income-tax Act or a body or an authority covered under clause (23BBA) of section 10 of the said Income Tax Act: **Provided that nothing contained in entry (b) of this exemption shall apply to:** (i) renting of rooms where charges are one thousand rupees or more per day; (ii) renting of premises, community halls, kalyana mandapam or open area, and the like where charges are ten thousand rupees or more per day; (iii) renting of shops or other spaces for business or commerce where charges are ten thousand rupees or more per month.
14.	~~Services by a hotel, inn, guesthouse, club or campsite, by whatever name called, for residential or lodging purposes, having **value of supply** of a unit of accommodation below or equal to one thousand rupees per day or equivalent.~~ (This entry Omitted w.e.f. 18th July 2022 Vide N.No. 04/2022-CT(R) dt. 13-07-2022)
15.	Transport of passengers, with or without accompanied belongings, by: (a) air in economy class, embarking from or terminating in an airport located in the state of Arunachal Pradesh, Assam, Manipur, Meghalaya, Mizoram, Nagaland, Sikkim, or Tripura or at Bagdogra located in West Bengal; (b) non-air conditioned contract carriage other than radio taxi, for transportation of passengers, excluding tourism, conducted tour, charter or hire; or (c) stage carriage other than air-conditioned stage carriage: "Provided that nothing contained in items (b) and (c) above shall apply to services supplied through an electronic commerce operator, and notified under sub-section (5) of Section 9 of the Central Goods and Services Tax Act, 2017 (12 of 2017)."

Sl. No.	Description of Services
16.	Services provided to the Central Government, by way of transport of passengers with or without accompanied belongings, by air, embarking from or terminating at a regional connectivity scheme airport, against consideration in the form of viability gap funding: Provided that nothing contained in this entry shall apply on or after the expiry of a period of **three year** from the date of commencement of operations of the regional connectivity scheme airport as notified by the Ministry of Civil Aviation.
17.	Service of transportation of passengers, with or without accompanied belongings, by: (a) railways in a class other than: (i) first class; or (ii) an air-conditioned coach; (b) metro, monorail or tramway; (c) inland waterways; (d) public transport, other than predominantly for tourism purpose, in a vessel between places located in India; and (e) metered cabs or auto rickshaws (including e-rickshaws): "Provided that nothing contained in item (e) above shall apply to services supplied through an electronic commerce operator, and notified under sub-section (5) of Section 9 of the Central Goods and Services Tax Act, 2017 (12 of 2017)."
18.	Services by way of transportation of goods (a) by road except the services of— (i) a goods transportation agency; (ii) a courier agency; (b) by inland waterways.
19.	Services by way of transportation of goods by an aircraft from a place outside India up to the customs station of clearance in India.
19A.	Services by way of transportation of goods by an aircraft from customs station of clearance in India to a place outside India. (applicable till 30th Sept 2022)
19B.	Services by way of transportation of goods by a vessel from customs station of clearance in India to a place outside India. (applicable till 30th Sept 2022)
19C.	Satellite launch services ~~supplied by Indian Space Research Organisation, Antrix Corporation Limited or New Space India Limited.~~ (Omitted w.e.f. 27th July 2023 Vide N.No. 07/2023-CT(R) dt. 26-07-2023)
20.	Services by way of transportation by rail or a vessel from one place in India to another of the following goods: (a) relief materials meant for victims of natural or man-made disasters, calamities, accidents or mishap; (b) defence or military equipments; (c) newspaper or magazines registered with the Registrar of Newspapers; (d) railway equipments or materials; (Omitted w.e.f. 18th July 2022 Vide N.No. 04/2022-CT(R) dt. 13-07-2022) (e) agricultural produce; (f) milk, salt and food grain including flours, pulses and rice; and (g) organic manure.
21.	Services provided by a goods transport agency, by way of transport in a goods carriage of: (a) agricultural produce; ~~(b) goods, where consideration charged for the transportation of goods on a consignment transported in a single carriage does not exceed one thousand five hundred rupees;~~ ~~(c) goods, where consideration charged for transportation of all such goods for a single consignee does not exceed rupees seven hundred and fifty; (b & c, omitted w.e.f. 18th July 2022 Vide N.No. 04/2022-CT(R) dt. 13-07-2022)~~ (d) milk, salt and food grain including flour, pulses and rice; (e) organic manure; (f) newspaper or magazines registered with the Registrar of Newspapers; (g) relief materials meant for victims of natural or man-made disasters, calamities, accidents or mis-hap; or (h) defence or military equipments.

Sl. No.	Description of Services
21A.	Services provided by a goods transport agency to an unregistered person, including an unregistered casual taxable person, other than the following recipients, namely: (a) any factory registered under or governed by the Factories Act, 1948 (63 of 1948); or (b) any Society registered under the Societies Registration Act, 1860 (21 of 1860) or under any other law for the time being in force in any part of India; or (c) any Co-operative Society established by or under any law for the time being in force; or (d) any Body corporate established, by or under any law for the time being in force; or (e) any partnership firm whether registered or not under any law including association of persons; (f) any casual taxable person registered under the Central Goods and Services Tax Act or the Integrated Goods and Services Tax Act or the State Goods and Services Tax Act or the Union Territory Goods and Services Tax Act.
21B.	Services provided by a goods transport agency, by way of transport of goods in a goods carriage, to: (a) a Department or establishment of the Central Government or State Government or Union territory; or (b) local authority; or (c) Governmental agencies, which has taken registration under the Central Goods and Services Tax Act, 2017 (12 of 2017) only for the purpose of deducting tax under Section 51 and not for making a taxable supply of goods or services.
22.	Services by way of giving on hire: (a) to a state transport undertaking, a motor vehicle meant to carry more than twelve passengers; or (aa)to a local authority, an electrically operated vehicle meant to carry more than twelve passengers; or (b) to a goods transport agency, a means of transportation of goods; or (c) motor vehicle for transport of students, faculty and staff, to a person providing services of transportation of students, faculty and staff to an educational institution providing services by way of pre-school education and education up to higher secondary school or equivalent.
23.	Service by way of access to a road or a bridge on payment of toll charges.
23A.	~~Service by way of access to a road or a bridge on payment of annuity~~ (Omitted w.e.f. 1st January 2023 Vide N.No. 15/2022-CT(R) dt. 30-12-2022)
24.	Services by way of loading, unloading, packing, storage or warehousing of rice.
24A.	Services by way of warehousing of minor forest produce.
24B.	Services by way of storage or warehousing of cereals, pulses, fruits and vegetables. (Amended w.e.f. 18th July 2022 Vide N.No. 04/2022-CT(R) dt. 13-07-2022)
24C.	Services by the Department of Posts by way of post card, inland letter, book post and ordinary post (envelopes weighing less than 10 grams). (Inserted w.e.f. 18th July 2022 Vide N.No. 04/2022-CT(R) dt. 13-07-2022)
25.	Transmission or distribution of electricity by an electricity transmission or distribution utility.
26.	~~Services by the Reserve Bank of India.~~ (Omitted Vide N.No. 04/2022-CT(R) dt. 13-07-2022 w.e.f. 18th July 2022)
27.	Services by way of: (a) extending deposits, loans or advances in so far as the consideration is represented by way of interest or discount (other than interest involved in credit card services); (b) inter se sale or purchase of foreign currency amongst banks or authorized dealers of foreign exchange or amongst banks and such dealers.
27A.	Services provided by a banking company to Basic Saving Bank Deposit (BSBD) account holders under Pradhan Mantri Jan Dhan Yojana (PMJDY).
28.	Services of life insurance business provided by way of annuity under the National Pension System regulated by the Pension Fund Regulatory and Development Authority of India under the Pension Fund Regulatory and Development Authority Act, 2013 (23 of 2013).
29.	Services of life insurance business provided or agreed to be provided by the Army, Naval and Air Force Group Insurance Funds to members of the Army, Navy and Air Force, respectively, under the Group Insurance Schemes of the Central Government.
29A.	Services of life insurance provided or agreed to be provided by the Naval Group Insurance Fund to the personnel of Coast Guard under the Group Insurance Schemes of the Central Government.

Sl. No.	Description of Services
29B.	Services of life insurance provided or agreed to be provided by the Central Armed Police Forces (under Ministry of Home Affairs) Group Insurance Funds to their members under the Group Insurance Schemes of the concerned Central Armed Police Force.
30.	Services by the Employees' State Insurance Corporation to persons governed under the Employees' State Insurance Act, 1948 (34 of 1948).
31.	Services provided by the Employees Provident Fund Organisation to the persons governed under the Employees Provident Funds and the Miscellaneous Provisions Act, 1952 (19 of 1952).
31A.	Services by Coal Mines Provident Fund Organisation to persons governed by the Coal Mines Provident Fund and Miscellaneous Provisions Act, 1948 (46 of 1948).
31B.	Services by National Pension System (NPS) Trust to its members against consideration in the form of administrative fee.
32.	~~Services provided by the Insurance Regulatory and the Development Authority of India to insurers under the Insurance Regulatory and the Development Authority of India Act, 1999(41 of 1999).~~ (Omitted Vide N.No. 04/2022-CT(R) dt. 13-07-2022 w.e.f. 18th July 2022)
33.	~~Services provided by the Securities and Exchange Board of India set up under the Securities and Exchange Board of India Act, 1992 (15 of 1992) by way of protecting the interests of investors in securities and to promote the development of, and to regulate, the securities market.~~ (Omitted Vide N.No. 04/2022-CT(R) dt. 13-07-2022 w.e.f. 18th July 2022)
34.	Services by an acquiring bank, to any person in relation to settlement of an amount up to two thousand rupees in a single transaction transacted through credit card, debit card, charge card or other payment card service. **Explanation:** For the purposes of this entry, "acquiring bank" means any banking company, financial institution including non-banking financial company or any other person, who makes the payment to any person who accepts such card.
34A.	Services supplied by Central Government, State Government, Union territory to their undertakings or Public Sector Undertakings (PSUs) by way of guaranteeing the loans taken by such undertakings or PSUs from the banking companies & financial institutions.
35.	Services of general insurance business provided under following schemes: (a) Hut Insurance Scheme; (b) Cattle Insurance under Swarnajaynti Gram Swarozgar Yojna (earlier known as Integrated Rural Development Programme); (c) Scheme for Insurance of Tribals; (d) Janata Personal Accident Policy and Gramin Accident Policy; (e) Group Personal Accident Policy for Self-Employed Women; (f) Agricultural Pumpset and Failed Well Insurance; (g) premia collected on export credit insurance; (h) Restructured Weather Based Crop Insurance Scheme (RWCIS) approved by the Government of India and implemented by the Ministry of Agriculture; (i) Jan Arogya Bima Policy; (j) Pradhan Mantri Fasal BimaYojana (PMFBY) (k) Pilot Scheme on Seed Crop Insurance; (l) Central Sector Scheme on Cattle Insurance; (m) Universal Health Insurance Scheme; (n) Rashtriya Swasthya Bima Yojana; (o) Coconut Palm Insurance Scheme; (p) Pradhan Mantri Suraksha BimaYojna; (q) Niramaya Health Insurance Scheme implemented by the Trust constituted under the provisions of the National Trust for the Welfare of Persons with Autism, Cerebral Palsy, Mental Retardation and Multiple Disabilities Act, 1999 (44 of 1999); (r) Bangla Shasya Bima.

Sl. No.	Description of Services
36.	Services of life insurance business provided under following schemes (a) Janashree Bima Yojana; (b) Aam Aadmi Bima Yojana; (c) Life micro-insurance product as approved by the Insurance Regulatory and Development Authority, having maximum amount of cover of two lakhs rupees; (d) Varishtha Pension BimaYojana; (e) Pradhan Mantri Jeevan JyotiBimaYojana; (f) Pradhan Mantri Jan DhanYogana; (g) Pradhan Mantri Vaya Vandan Yojana.
36A.	Services by way of reinsurance of the insurance schemes specified in serial number 35 or 36 or 40.
37.	Services by way of collection of contribution under the Atal Pension Yojana.
38.	Services by way of collection of contribution under any pension scheme of the State Governments.
39.	Services by the following persons in respective capacities: (a) business facilitator or a business correspondent to a banking company with respect to accounts in its rural area branch; (b) any person as an intermediary to a business facilitator or a business correspondent with respect to services mentioned in entry (a); or (c) business facilitator or a business correspondent to an insurance company in a rural area.
39A.	Services by an intermediary of financial services located in a multi services SEZ with International Financial Services Centre (IFSC) status to a customer located outside India for international financial services in currencies other than Indian rupees (INR).
40.	Services provided to the Central Government, State Government, Union territory under any insurance scheme for which total premium is paid by the Central Government, State Government, Union territory.
41.	Upfront amount (called as premium, salami, cost, price, development charges or by any other name) payable in respect of service by way of granting of long-term lease of thirty years, or more) of industrial plots or plots for development of infrastructure for financial business, provided by the State Government Industrial Development Corporations or Undertakings or by any other entity having 20 per cent or more ownership of Central Government, State Government, Union territory to the industrial units or the developers in any industrial or financial business area. **Explanation:** For the purpose of this exemption, the Central Government, State Government or Union territory shall have 20 per cent or more ownership in the entity directly or through an entity which is wholly owned by the Central Government, State Government or Union territory.
41A.	Service by way of transfer of development rights (herein refer TDR) or Floor Space Index (FSI) (including additional FSI) on or after 1st April 2019 for construction of residential apartments by a promoter in a project, intended for sale to a buyer, wholly or partly, except where the entire consideration has been received after issuance of completion certificate, where required, by the competent authority or after its first occupation, whichever is earlier. The amount of GST exemption available for construction of residential apartments in the project under this notification shall be calculated as under: [GST payable on TDR or FSI (including additional FSI) or both for construction of the project] × (carpet area of the residential apartments in the project ÷ Total carpet area of the residential and commercial apartments in the project)
41B.	Upfront amount (called as premium, salami, cost, price, development charges or by any other name) payable in respect of service by way of granting of long-term lease of thirty years, or more, on or after 01.04.2019, for construction of residential apartments by a promoter in a project, intended for sale to a buyer, wholly or partly, except where the entire consideration has been received after issuance of completion certificate, where required, by the competent authority or after its first occupation, whichever is earlier. The amount of GST exemption available for construction of residential apartments in the project under this notification shall be calculated as under: [GST payable on upfront amount (called as premium, salami, cost, price, development charges or by any other name) payable for long term lease of land for construction of the project] × (carpet area of the residential apartments in the project ÷ Total carpet area of the residential and commercial apartments in the project)

Sl. No.	Description of Services
42.	Services provided by the Central Government, State Government, Union territory or local authority by way of allowing a business entity to operate as a telecom service provider or use radio frequency spectrum during the period prior to the 1st April, 2016, on payment of license fee or spectrum user charges, as the case may be.
43.	~~Services of leasing of assets (rolling stock assets including wagons, coaches, locos) by the Indian Railways Finance Corporation to Indian Railways.~~ (Omitted Vide N.No. 07/2021-CT(R) dt. 30-09-2021 w.e.f. 1st Oct 2021)
44.	Services provided by an incubate up to a total turnover of fifty lakh rupees in a financial year subject to the following conditions, namely: (a) the total turnover had not exceeded fifty lakh rupees during the preceding financial year; and (b) a period of three years has not elapsed from the date of entering into an agreement as an incubate.
45.	Services provided by (a) an arbitral tribunal to: (i) any person other than a business entity; or (ii) a business entity with an aggregate turnover up to such amount in the preceding financial year as makes it eligible for exemption from registration under the Central Goods and Services Tax Act, 2017 (12 of 2017); (iii) the Central Government, State Government, Union territory, local authority, Governmental Authority or Government Entity. (b) a partnership firm of advocates or an individual as an advocate other than a senior advocate, by way of legal services to: (i) an advocate or partnership firm of advocates providing legal services; (ii) any person other than a business entity; (iii) a business entity with an aggregate turnover up to such amount in the preceding financial year as makes it eligible for exemption from registration under the Central Goods and Services Tax Act, 2017 (12 of 2017); (iv) the Central Government, State Government, Union territory, local authority, Governmental Authority or Government Entity. (c) a senior advocate by way of legal services to (i) any person other than a business entity; (ii) a business entity with an aggregate turnover up to such amount in the preceding financial year as makes it eligible for exemption from registration under the Central Goods and Services Tax Act, 2017 (12 of 2017); (iii) the Central Government, State Government, Union territory, local authority, Governmental Authority or Government Entity.
46.	Services by a veterinary clinic in relation to health care of animals or birds.
47.	Services provided by the Central Government, State Government, Union territory or local authority by way of: (a) Registration required under any law for the time being in force; (b) testing, calibration, safety check or certification relating to protection or safety of workers, consumers or public at large, including fire license, required under any law for the time being in force.
47A.	~~Services by way of licensing, registration and analysis or testing of food samples supplied by the Food Safety and Standards Authority of India (FSSAI) to Food Business Operators.~~ (Omitted Vide N.No. 04/2022-CT(R) dt. 13-07-2022 w.e.f. 18th July 2022)
48.	Taxable services, provided or to be provided, by a Technology Business Incubator or a Science and Technology Entrepreneurship Park authorized by the National Science and Technology Entrepreneurship Development Board of the Department of Science and Technology, Government of India or bio-incubators authorized by the Biotechnology Industry Research Assistance Council, under the Department of Biotechnology, Government of India.
49.	Services by way of collecting or providing news by an independent journalist, Press Trust of India or United News of India.
50.	Services of public libraries by way of lending of books, publications or any other knowledge-enhancing content or material.

Sl. No.	Description of Services
51.	~~Services provided by the Goods and Services Tax Network to the Central Government or State Governments or Union territories for implementation of Goods and Services Tax.~~ (Omitted Vide N.No. 04/2022-CT(R) dt. 13-07-2022 w.e.f. 18th July 2022)
52.	Services by an organiser to any person in respect of a business exhibition held outside India.
52A.	Tour operator service, which is performed partly in India and partly outside India, supplied by a tour operator to a foreign tourist, to the extent of the value of the tour operator service which is performed outside India: Provided that value of the tour operator service performed outside India shall be such proportion of the total consideration charged for the entire tour which is equal to the proportion which the number of days for which the tour is performed outside India has to the total number of days comprising the tour, or 50% of the total consideration charged for the entire tour, whichever is less: Provided further that in making the above calculations, any duration of time equal to or exceeding 12 hours shall be considered as one full day and any duration of time less than 12 hours shall be taken as half a day. (Inserted Vide N.No. 04/2022-CT(R) dt. 13-07-2022 w.e.f. 18th July 2022)
53.	Services by way of sponsorship of sporting events organised: (a) by a national sports federation, or its affiliated federations, where the participating teams or individuals represent any district, State, zone or Country; (b) by Association of Indian Universities, Inter-University Sports Board, School Games Federation of India, All India Sports Council for the Deaf, Paralympic Committee of India or Special Olympics Bharat; (c) by the Central Civil Services Cultural and Sports Board; (d) as part of national games, by the Indian Olympic Association; or (e) under the Panchayat Yuva Kreeda Aur Khel Abhiyaan Scheme.
53A.	~~Services by way of fumigation in a warehouse of agricultural produce.~~ (Omitted Vide N.No. 04/2022-CT(R) dt. 13-07-2022 w.e.f. 18th July 2022)
54.	Services relating to cultivation of plants and rearing of all life forms of animals, except the rearing of horses, for food, fiber, fuel, raw material or other similar products or agricultural produce by way of— (a) agricultural operations directly related to production of any agricultural produce including cultivation, harvesting, threshing, plant protection or testing; (b) supply of farm labour; (c) processes carried out at an agricultural farm including tending, pruning, cutting, harvesting, drying, cleaning, trimming, sun drying, fumigating, curing, sorting, grading, cooling or bulk packaging and such like operations which do not alter the essential characteristics of agricultural produce but make it only marketable for the primary market; (d) renting or leasing of agro machinery or vacant land with or without a structure incidental to its use; (e) loading, unloading, packing, storage or warehousing of agricultural produce; (f) agricultural extension services; (g) services by any Agricultural Produce Marketing Committee or Board or services provided by a commission agent for sale or purchase of agricultural produce; (h) ~~services by way of fumigation in a warehouse of agricultural produce.~~ (Entry h, omitted Vide N.No. 04/2022-CT(R) dt. 13-07-2022 w.e.f. 18th July 2022)
55.	Carrying out an intermediate production process as job work in relation to cultivation of plants and rearing of all life forms of animals, except the rearing of horses, for food, fiber, fuel, raw material or other similar products or agricultural produce.
55A.	Services by way of artificial insemination of livestock (other than horses).
56.	~~Services by way of slaughtering of animals.~~ (Omitted Vide N.No. 04/2022-CT(R) dt. 13-07-2022 w.e.f. 18th July 2022)
57.	Services by way of pre-conditioning, pre-cooling, ripening, waxing, retail packing, labelling of fruits and vegetables which do not change or alter the essential characteristics of the said fruits or vegetables.
58.	Services provided by the National Centre for Cold Chain Development under the Ministry of Agriculture, Cooperation and Farmer's Welfare by way of cold chain knowledge dissemination.
59.	Services by a foreign diplomatic mission located in India.

Sl. No.	Description of Services
60.	Services by a specified organisation in respect of a religious pilgrimage facilitated by the Government of India, under bilateral arrangement.
61.	Services provided by the Central Government, State Government, Union territory or local authority by way of issuance of passport, visa, driving licence, birth certificate or death certificate.
61A.	Services by way of granting National Permit to a goods carriage to operate throughout India/contiguous States
62.	Services provided by the Central Government, State Government, Union territory or local authority by way of tolerating non-performance of a contract for which consideration in the form of fines or liquidated damages is payable to the Central Government, State Government, Union territory or local authority under such contract.
63.	Services provided by the Central Government, State Government, Union territory or local authority by way of assignment of right to use natural resources to an individual farmer for cultivation of plants and rearing of all life forms of animals, except the rearing of horses, for food, fibre, fuel, raw material or other similar products.
64.	Services provided by the Central Government, State Government, Union territory or local authority by way of assignment of right to use any natural resource where such right to use was assigned by the Central Government, State Government, Union territory or local authority before the 1st April, 2016: Provided that the exemption shall apply only to tax payable on one time charge payable, in full upfront or in installments, for assignment of right to use such natural resource.
65.	Services provided by the Central Government, State Government, Union territory by way of deputing officers after office hours or on holidays for inspection or container stuffing or such other duties in relation to import export cargo on payment of Merchant Overtime charges.
65A.	Services by way of providing information under the Right to Information Act, 2005 (22 of 2005).
65B.	Services supplied by a State Government to Excess Royalty Collection Contractor (ERCC) by way of assigning the right to collect royalty on behalf of the State Government on the mineral dispatched by the mining lease holders.
66.	Services provided: (a) by an educational institution to its students, faculty and staff; (aa) by an educational institution by way of conduct of entrance examination against consideration in the form of entrance fee (b) to an educational institution, by way of, (i) transportation of students, faculty and staff; (ii) catering, including any mid-day meals scheme sponsored by the Central Government, State Government or Union territory; (iii) security or cleaning or house-keeping services performed in such educational institution; (iv) services relating to admission to, or conduct of examination by, such institution; (v) supply of online educational journals or periodicals: Provided that nothing contained in sub-items (i), (ii) and (iii) of item (b) shall apply to an educational institution other than an institution providing services by way of pre-school education and education up to higher secondary school or equivalent: Provided further that nothing contained in sub-item (v) of item (b) shall apply to an institution providing services by way of, (i) pre-school education and education up to higher secondary school or equivalent; or (ii) education as a part of an approved vocational education course.
67.	~~Services provided by the Indian Institutes of Management, as per the guidelines of the Central Government, to their students, by way of the following educational programmes, except Executive Development Programme:~~ ~~(a) two-year full time Post Graduate Programmes in Management for the Post Graduate Diploma in Management, to which admissions are made on the basis of Common Admission Test (CAT) conducted by the Indian Institute of Management;~~ ~~(b) fellow programme in Management;~~ ~~(c) five-year integrated programme in Management~~ **Note: This entry has been deleted vide Notification 28/2018-Central Tax (Rate) dated 31st Dec. 2018.**

Sl. No.	Description of Services
68.	Services provided to an authorized sports body by (a) an individual as a player, referee, umpire, coach or team manager for participation in a sporting event authorize by a recognized sports body; (b) another authorized sports body.
69.	Any services provided by, (a) the National Skill Development Corporation set up by the Government of India; (b) a Sector Skill Council approved by the National Skill Development Corporation; (c) an assessment agency approved by the Sector Skill Council or the National Skill Development Corporation; (d) a training partner approved by the National Skill Development Corporation or the Sector Skill Council, in relation to (i) the National Skill Development Programme implemented by the National Skill Development Corporation; or (ii) a vocational skill development course under the National Skill Certification and Monetary Reward Scheme; or (iii) any other Scheme implemented by the National Skill Development Corporation.
70.	Services of assessing bodies authorize centrally by the Directorate General of Training, Ministry of Skill Development and Entrepreneurship by way of assessments under the Skill Development Initiative Scheme.
71.	Services provided by training providers (Project implementation agencies) under Deen Dayal Upadhyaya Grameen Kaushalya Yojana implemented by the Ministry of Rural Development, Government of India by way of offering skill or vocational training courses certified by the National Council for Vocational Training.
72.	Services provided to the Central Government, State Government, Union territory administration under any training programme for which 75% or more of the total expenditure is borne by the Central Government, State Government, Union territory administration.
73.	~~Services provided by the cord blood banks by way of preservation of stem cells or any other service in relation to such preservation.~~ (Omitted Vide N.No. 04/2022-CT(R) dt. 13-07-2022 w.e.f. 18th July 2022)
74.	Services by way of (a) health care services by a clinical establishment, an authorized medical practitioner or paramedics: "Provided that nothing in this entry shall apply to the services provided by a clinical establishment by way of providing room [other than Intensive Care Unit (ICU)/Critical Care Unit (CCU)/Intensive Cardiac Care Unit (ICCU)/Neo natal Intensive Care Unit (NICU)] having room charges exceeding ₹ 5000 per day to a person receiving health care services." (Inserted Vide N.No. 04/2022-CT(R) dt. 13-07-2022 w.e.f. 18th July 2022) (b) services provided by way of transportation of a patient in an ambulance, other than those specified in (a) above.
74A.	Services provided by rehabilitation professionals authorized under the Rehabilitation Council of India Act, 1992 (34 of 1992) by way of rehabilitation, therapy or counseling and such other activity as covered by the said Act at medical establishments, educational institutions, rehabilitation centers established by Central Government, State Government or Union territory or an entity registered under section 12AA or 12AB of the Income tax Act, 1961 (43 of 1961).
75.	~~Services provided by operators of the common bio-medical waste treatment facility to a clinical establishment by way of treatment or disposal of bio-medical waste or the processes incidental thereto.~~ (Omitted Vide N.No. 04/2022-CT(R) dt. 13-07-2022 w.e.f. 18th July 2022)
76.	Services by way of public conveniences such as provision of facilities of bathroom, washrooms, lavatories, urinal or toilets.
77.	Service by an unincorporated body or a non-profit entity registered under any law for the time being in force, to its own members by way of reimbursement of charges or share of contribution: (a) as a trade union; (b) for the provision of carrying out any activity which is exempt from the levy of Goods and service Tax; or (c) up to an amount of seven thousand five thousand rupees per month per member for sourcing of goods or services from a third person for the common use of its members in a housing society or a residential complex.

Sl. No.	Description of Services
77A.	Services provided by an unincorporated body or a non-profit entity registered under any law for the time being in force, engaged in: (i) activities relating to the welfare of industrial or agricultural labour or farmers; or (ii) promotion of trade, commerce, industry, agriculture, art, science, literature, culture, sports, education, social welfare, charitable activities and protection of environment, to its own members against consideration in the form of membership fee upto an amount of one thousand rupees (₹ 1000) per member per year.
78.	Services by an artist by way of a performance in folk or classical art forms of (a) music, or (b) dance, or (c) theatre, if the consideration charged for such performance is not more than one lakh and fifty thousand rupees: Provided that the exemption shall not apply to service provided by such artist as a brand ambassador.
79.	Services by way of admission to a museum, national park, wildlife sanctuary, tiger reserve or zoo.
79A.	Services by way of admission to a protected monument so declared under the Ancient Monuments and Archaeological Sites and Remains Act, 1958 (24 of 1958) or any of the State Acts, for the time being in force.
80.	Services by way of training or coaching in (a) recreational activities relating to arts or culture, or (b) sports by charitable entities registered under section 12AA or 12AB of the Income-tax Act. (Amended Vide N.No. 04/2022-CT(R) dt. 13-07-2022 w.e.f. 18th July 2022)
81.	Services by way of right to admission to: (a) circus, dance, or theatrical performance including drama or ballet; (b) award function, concert, pageant, musical performance or any sporting event other than a organised sporting event; (c) organised sporting event; (d) planetarium, where the consideration for right to admission to the events or places as referred to in items (a), (b), (c) or (d) above is not more than ₹ 500 per person.
82.	Services by way of right to admission to the events organised under FIFA U-17 World Cup 2017.
82A.	Services by way of right to admission to the events organised under FIFA U-17 Women's World Cup 2020. [whenever rescheduled]
82B.	Services by way of right to admission to the events organised under AFC Women's Asia Cup 2022.

In addition to above following exemptions are notified under IGST Act:

1.	Services received from a provider of service located in a non-taxable territory by: (a) the Central Government, State Government, Union territory, a local authority, a governmental authority or an individual in relation to any purpose other than commerce, industry or any other authority or an individual in relation to any purpose other than commerce, industry or any other business or profession; (b) an entity registered under section 12AA of the Income-tax Act, 1961 (43 of 1961) for the purposes of providing charitable activities; or (c) a person located in a non-taxable territory: Provided that the exemption shall not apply to: (i) online information and database access or retrieval services received by persons specified in entry (a) or entry (b); or (ii) services by way of transportation of goods by a vessel from a place outside India up to the customs station of clearance in India received by persons specified in the entry.
2.	Services received by the Reserve Bank of India, from outside India in relation to management of foreign exchange reserves.
3.	Services provided by a tour operator to a foreign tourist in relation to a tour conducted wholly outside India.
4.	Supply of services having place of supply in Nepal or Bhutan, against payment in Indian Rupees.

Definitions: For the purposes of this notification

(1) "approved vocational education course" means:

(i) a course run by an industrial training institute or an industrial training centre affiliated to the National Council for Vocational Training or State Council for Vocational Training offering courses in designated trades notified under the Apprentices Act, 1961 (52 of 1961); or

(ii) a Modular Employable Skill Course, approved by the National Council of Vocational Training, run by a person registered with the Directorate General of Training, Ministry of Skill Development and Entrepreneurship.

(2) "charitable activities" means activities relating to:

(i) public health by way of,

(A) care or counselling of

(I) terminally ill persons or persons with severe physical or mental disability;

(II) persons afflicted with HIV or AIDS;

(III) persons addicted to a dependence-forming substance such as narcotics drugs or alcohol; or

(B) public awareness of preventive health, family planning or prevention of HIV infection;

(ii) advancement of religion, spirituality or yoga;

(iii) advancement of educational programmes or skill development relating to,

(A) abandoned, orphaned or homeless children;

(B) physically or mentally abused and traumatized persons;

(C) prisoners; or

(D) persons over the age of 65 years residing in a rural area;

(iv) preservation of environment including watershed, forests and wildlife;

(3) "educational institution" means an institution providing services by way of,

(i) pre-school education and education up to higher secondary school or equivalent;

(ii) education as a part of a curriculum for obtaining a qualification recognized by any law for the time being in force;

(iii) education as a part of an approved vocational education course.

(4) "e-rickshaw" means a special purpose battery powered vehicle of power not exceeding 4000 watts, having three wheels for carrying goods or passengers, as the case may be, for hire or reward, manufactured, constructed or adapted, equipped and maintained in accordance with such specifications, as may be prescribed in this behalf.

(5) "Government Entity" means an authority or a board or any other body including a society, trust, corporation,

(i) set up by an Act of Parliament or State Legislature; or

(ii) established by any Government, with 90 per cent or more participation by way of equity or control, to carry out a function entrusted by the Central Government, State Government, Union Territory or a local authority.

(6) "health care services" means any service by way of diagnosis or treatment or care for illness, injury, deformity, abnormality or pregnancy in any recognized system of medicines in India and includes services by way of transportation of the patient to and from a clinical establishment, but does not include hair transplant or cosmetic or plastic surgery, except when undertaken to restore or to reconstruct anatomy or functions of body affected due to congenital defects, developmental abnormalities, injury or trauma.

(7) "original works" means all new constructions; (i) all types of additions and alterations to abandoned or damaged structures on land that are required to make them workable; (ii) erection, commissioning or installation of plant, machinery or equipment or structures, whether pre-fabricated or otherwise.

(8) "residential complex" means any complex comprising of a building or buildings, having more than one single residential unit.

(9) The functions entrusted to a municipality under the Twelfth Schedule to Article 243W of the Constitution are as under:

(a) Urban planning including town planning.

(b) Regulation of land-use and construction of buildings.

(c) Planning for economic and social development.

(d) Roads and bridges.

(e) Water supply for domestic, industrial and commercial purposes.
(f) Public health, sanitation conservancy and solid waste management.
(g) Fire services.
(h) Urban forestry, protection of the environment and promotion of ecological aspects.
(i) Safeguarding the interests of weaker sections of society, including the handicapped and mentally retarded.
(j) Slum improvement and upgradation.
(k) Urban poverty alleviation.
(l) Provision of urban amenities and facilities such as parks, gardens, playgrounds.
(m) Promotion of cultural, educational and aesthetic aspects.
(n) Burials and burial grounds; cremations, cremation grounds; and electric crematoriums.
(o) Cattle pounds; prevention of cruelty to animals.
(p) Vital statistics including registration of births and deaths.
(q) Public amenities including street lighting, parking lots, bus stops and public conveniences.
(r) Regulation of slaughter houses and tanneries.

(10) The functions entrusted to a Panchayat under the Eleventh Schedule to Article 243G of the Constitution are as under:

(i) Agriculture, including agricultural extension.
(ii) Land improvement, implementation of land reforms, land consolidation and soil conservation. (iii) Minor irrigation, water management and watershed development.
(iv) Animal husbandry, dairying and poultry.
(v) Fisheries.
(vi) Social forestry and farm forestry.
(vii) Minor forest produce.
(viii) Small scale industries, including food processing industries.
(ix) Khadi, village and cottage industries.
(x) Rural housing.
(xi) Drinking water.
(xii) Fuel and fodder.
(xiii) Roads, culverts, bridges, ferries, waterways and other means of communication.
(xiv) Rural electrification, including distribution of electricity.
(xv) Non-conventional energy sources.
(xvi) Poverty alleviation programme.
(xvii) Education, including primary and secondary schools.
(xviii) Technical training and vocational education.
(xix) Adult and non-formal education.
(xx) Libraries.
(xxi) Cultural activities.
(xxii) Markets and fairs.
(xxiii) Health and sanitation, including hospitals, primary health centres and dispensaries.
(xxiv) Family welfare.
(xxv) Women and child development.
(xxvi) Social welfare, including welfare of the handicapped and mentally retarded.
(xxvii) Welfare of the weaker sections, and in particular, of the Scheduled Castes and the Scheduled Tribes.
(xxviii) Public distribution system.
(xxix) Maintenance of community assets.

Chapter 8

Time of Supply

8.1 INTRODUCTION

Taxable supply means a supply of goods and/or services, which is chargeable to tax. Supply holds the key to the incidence of GST, but it is the 'time of supply' that dictates the occasion when this incidence will come to rest. It is important to note that "time of supply" is not a fact to be inquired by the taxable person but one that is to be admitted as the time of supply appointed by the will of legislature as declared in the sections 12, 13 and 14 of the Central GST Act, 2017 (CGST Act) and by virtue of Section 20 of the Integrated GST Act, 2017 (IGST Act).

In order to calculate and discharge tax liability, it is important to know the date when the tax liability arises, i.e. the date on which the charging event has occurred. In GST law, it is known as Time of Supply. Liability to pay tax arises at the time of supply. The concept of time of supply is relevant only when one or more aspects of a transaction, i.e. date of provisioning of service, date of invoice and date of payment fall into two different tax periods.

The GST law has provided separate provisions to determine the time of supply of goods and time of supply of services.

Point of time is when supplier receives the payment or date of receipt of payment. The phrase "the date on which supplier receives the payment" or "the date of receipt of payment" means the date on which payment is entered in his books of accounts or the date on which the payment is credited to his bank account, whichever is earlier.

Events like issuing of invoices, receipt of payment, provision of service, receipt of services in books of account need to be analyzed to determine the time of supply when the tax on supply is payable under forward charge.

When the tax on supply is payable under reverse charge, events like date of receipt of goods, date of making payment etc. need to be analyzed to determine the time of supply.

Section	Provision
12	Time of supply of goods
13	Time of supply of services
14	Time of supply when there is change in Rate of Tax

8.2 TIME OF ISSUE OF INVOICE

(a) Goods: Section 31(1): Where supply involves movement of goods: An invoice for supply of goods needs to be issued before or at the time of removal of goods for supply to the recipient.

Other cases: An invoice needs to be issued before or at the time of delivery of goods or while making goods available to the recipient.

(1) In case of continuous supply of goods, the invoice should be issued **before** or **at the time** of issuance of periodical statement/receipt of periodical payment (Section 31(4)).

(2) In case of goods sent or taken on approval for sale or return, invoice should be issued before or at the time of supply or six months from the date of removal, whichever is earlier (Section 31(7)).

Case	Last date of issue of Invoice
When supply involves movement of goods (goods dispatch to customer)	Time of removal of goods (Time of sending goods to recipient)
Other cases (goods taken from shop)	At the time of delivery of goods to recipient (customer)

(b) Services: Section 31(2): An invoice for supply of services needs to be issued before or after the provision of services but **not later than thirty days** from the date of provision of services.

In case of supply of services, invoice to be issued

(a) Within 30 days of providing services

(b) In case of Banks/NBFC within 45 days

As per Notification No. 45/2017-Central Tax dated 13.10.2017, Banks/NBFC may issue invoice or any other document at the end of the month.

(c) Supply of capital goods/inputs to the job-worker: The provisions relating to job-work provides for supply of capital goods/inputs to the job-worker without payment of tax (section 143). The intention of the law is not to tax capital goods/inputs sent to job-worker as supply since in such an arrangement the goods are received back by the principal. However, if such goods are not received back within three years and one year respectively, it would qualify as supply by way of operation of deeming fiction provided under section 143(2) and section 143(3). In such a scenario, the date of sending the goods to the job-worker would be deemed to be the date when the goods were sent to the job-worker originally.

In this regard, the Central Government has issued Circular No. 38/12/2018 dated 26.03.2018 wherein it is clarified that the principal should issue an invoice on expiry of three years/one year and should declare such supplies in the return filed for the month in which the time period of three years/one year is expired.

8.3 TIME OF SUPPLY OF GOODS [SECTION 12]

Section 12 of CGST Act, 2017 stipulate the provisions relating to determination of time of supply of goods.

Section	Provision
12(1)	Liability to pay tax on goods arises at the time of supply
12(2)	Time of supply of Goods covered under forward charge
12(3)	Time of supply of Goods covered under reverse charge
12(4)	Time of supply of Vouchers that can be used to pay for goods
12(5)	Residual cases (where not possible to determine time of supply as per Section 12(2), 12(3) or 12(4) above)
12(6)	Addition to value of supply by way of interest or late fee or penalty for delayed payment of consideration

Section 12 must be read in conjunction with Section 31, which prescribes the date on which Tax invoice for supply of goods/services should be issued.

Time of supply of goods covered under forward charge (Default Rule) [Section 12(2)]

Earliest of the following two events:

Event 1	Date of issue of an invoice by the supplier (or the last date on which the supplier is legally bound to issue the invoice u/s 31)
Event 2	Date on which the supplier receives the payment

Notes:

(1) **Composition dealer:** Time of supply is earliest of Event 1 or Event 2.

(2) **Taxable person other than Composition dealer:** GST not payable on advance received against future supply of goods.

Period	Taxability of consideration received in Advance against future supply of goods	
	Aggregate Turnover less than ₹ 1.5 crores	Aggregate Turnover more than ₹ 1.5 crores
01-07-2017 to 12-10-2017	Taxable	Taxable
13-10-2017 to 15-11-2017	Not taxable	Taxable
15-11-2017 & onwards	Not taxable	Not taxable

Example 1: M/s Ratan Lal Trading Company, a registered supplier, is liable to pay GST under forward charge. Determine the time of supply from following information furnished.

(a) Goods supplied 13-10-2018
(b) Invoice issued on 15-10-2018
(c) Payment received on 09-10-2018

Ans. As per Section 12 of CGST Act, 2017 time of supply of goods, tax on which shall be payable under forward charge is earliest of the following dates:

Date of supply of goods :13-10-2018

Invoice issued :15-10-2018

Therefore, time of supply of goods will be 13-10-2018.

Note: In case of supply of goods, invoice is required to be issued before or at time of supply of goods. **Advance payment** received on 09-10-2018 for future supply of goods will not attract GST. Please refer *Notification 66/2017-Central Tax, dated 15th November 2017.*

Notification 40/2017-Central Tax, dated 13th October 2017

Person having aggregate turnover of less than ₹ 1.5 crores (other than composition scheme) during the previous FY/current year, shall pay GST on the outward supply of **goods** at the time of supply of goods and not at the time of receipt of advance payment from customer.

Notification 66/2017-Central Tax, dated 15th November 2017

All suppliers of **goods** who have not opted for composition scheme, has been exempted from paying GST on Advances received for future supply. GST payable at the time of supply of goods.

Note: Composition supplier is not required to pay any tax on advance received, as the same does not form part of taxable supply and also does not form part of the turnover. They are required to pay GST at prescribed rate on aggregate turnover on quarterly basis.

Meaning of "Date of receipt of payment"

"Date of receipt of payment" in the above situation refers to the date on which the payment is recorded in the books of account of the entity (supplier of goods) that receives the payment, or the date on which the payment is credited to the entity's bank account, whichever is earlier.

Goods sent or taken on approval for sale or return basis

Certain goods are sent to the recipient without supplying/selling the same at its outset. These goods can be examined or tested by the recipient as to whether his requirements are fulfilled. The recipient can either approve the said supply or return the said goods. If the goods are returned, no supply will be deemed to have taken place. If the goods are approved by the supplier, then it will amount to a supply. The last date of issuance of invoice in such cases as per Section 31(7) of the CGST Act 2017 has been given as earlier of:

(a) Before or at the time of supply
(b) Six months from the date of removal

Here, time of supply refers to the time when the confirmation is given by the recipient that he is willing to accept the goods. The last date of issuance of invoice in such cases will be the confirmation of acceptance subject to the fact that this acceptance should not take place after six months from the date of removal. If the approval does not come within the period of six months/comes after the period of six months from the date of removal, then the last date of invoice arises on the date when this period of six months from the date of removal expires.

Time of supply of goods—Reverse charge [Section 12(3)]

Event 1	Date of receipt of goods
Event 2	Date of payment as entered in the books of accounts of the recipient (or the date on which the payment is debited in his bank account, whichever is earlier)
Event 3	Date immediately following 30 days from the date of issue of invoice (any other legal document in lieu of invoice) by the supplier
Time of Supply	Event 1, Event 2 or Event 3, whichever is earlier.

Note: Where, it is not possible to determine the time of supply in aforesaid manner, then the time of supply is the date of entry of the transaction in the books of accounts of the recipient of supply.

Exception: Date of receipt of payment shall be the date on which the payment is accounted in the books of the supplier or the date reflected in the bank account of the supplier, whichever is earlier.

Example 2: Mr. Govind, an agriculturist supplied raw cotton worth ₹ 10 lakhs to M/s Century Cotton Mills Ltd., Mumbai a taxable person under GST. Determine time of supply from following information:

Date	Event
2nd Feb 2019	Mr. Govind raised bill on M/s Century Cotton Mills Ltd.
15th Feb 2019	M/s Century Cotton Mills Ltd. received the goods
6th Mar 2019	M/s Century Cotton Mills Ltd. makes the payment to Mr. Govind

Ans. Supply of Raw cotton by Agriculturist to a taxable person is covered under Reverse Charge. Therefore, 15th Feb. 2019 will be time of supply being earliest of date of receipt of goods, date of payment and date immediately following 30 days from the date of issue of invoice or any other legal document in lieu of invoice by the supplier.

Time of supply—Vouchers [Section 12(4)]

Vouchers are commonly used for transaction in the Indian economy. It is an instruments, which can be exchanges as payment for goods or services of the designated value.

A voucher has been defined in Section 2(118) of the CGST Act as an instrument where there is an obligation to accept it as consideration or part consideration for a supply of goods or services or both, and where the goods or services or both to be supplied or the identities of their potential suppliers are either indicated on the instrument itself or in related documentation, including the terms and conditions of use of such instrument.

A shopkeeper may issue vouchers for a specific supply, i.e. supply which is identifiable at the time of issuance of voucher. In trade parlance, these are known as single purpose vouchers. For example, vouchers for pressure cookers or television or for spa or haircut.

Similarly, a voucher can be a general-purpose voucher which can be used for multiple purposes. For example, a ₹ 1000 voucher issued by Shopper's Stop store can be used for buying any product or service at any Shopper's Stop store.

The time of supply is different in case of single purpose voucher and in the case of general purpose voucher.

Event	Time of Supply
If the supply is identifiable at the time of issue of Voucher	Date of issue of voucher
Other cases	Date of redemption of the voucher

Example 3: Sodexo coupon were sold to a company on 5th Feb 2019 for being distributed among its employee. The coupon has a validity period of three months and can be used against purchase of food items from selected stores. The employee uses them in various stores for purchase of various food items on various dates throughout its validity. What is the time of supply of coupons?

Ans. The coupon can be used for purchase of variety of food items which attract different rate of GST. The supply cannot be identified at the time of purchase of coupons. Therefore, time of supply of coupon will be date of their redemption.

Time of supply of goods (Residual provisions) [Section 12(5)]

In case it is not possible to determine the time of supply of goods under Sec 12(2), 12(3) or 12(4) above, the time of supply shall be determined as follows:

Event	Time of Supply
Where periodical return has to be filed	Due date of filing of return
Other cases	Date of payment of tax

Time of Supply—Enhancement in value [Section 12(6)]

Section 12(6) prescribes that time of supply in case of addition in value by way of interest/late fee/penalty for delayed payment of consideration for goods.

Time of supply related to an addition in the value of supply by way of interest, late fee or penalty for delayed payment of any consideration shall be the date on which supplier receives such addition in value.

Example 4: A supplier receives consideration in the month of September 2019, instead of due date of July 2019 for goods supplied. For such delay he is eligible to receive an interest amount of ₹ 1000 as per terms of supply and the said amount is received on 15.12.2019. The time of supply of such amount (₹ 1000) will be 15.12.2019, i.e. the date on which it is received by the supplier and tax liability on this is to be discharged by 20.01.2020, in case of normal registered person.

Time of supply—Continuous supply of goods

In terms of section 2(32) of the CGST Act, 2017, 'continuous supply of goods' means a supply of goods which is provided, or agreed to be provided, continuously or on recurrent basis, under a contract, whether or not by means of a wire, cable, pipeline or other conduit, and for which the supplier invoices the recipient on a regular or periodic basis and includes supply of such goods as the Government may, subject to such conditions, as it may, by notification, specify.

Due date for issuance of invoice in terms of section 31(4) involving successive statement of accounts (SOA) or successive payments is:

- Before/at the time of issue of each SOA or
- Before/at the time of receipt such successive payment.

Accordingly, the time of continuous supply of goods, in terms of section 12 shall be earliest of the following:

(a) Date of issue of invoice; or
(b) Due date of issue of invoice.

Time of supply of Goods—Supplied through e-commerce entities

The CGST Act, 2017 does not provide separate provisions for ascertaining time of supply of goods through/by e-commerce entities. Accordingly, the same provisions as to time of supply of goods will be applicable whether a supplier makes supply through e-commerce entity or the e-commerce entity himself makes the supply.

8.4 TIME OF SUPPLY OF SERVICES [SECTION 13]

Section 13 of CGST Act, 2017 stipulate the provisions relating to determination of time of supply of services.

Section	Provision
13(1)	Liability to pay tax on services arises at the time of supply
13(2)	Time of supply of Services covered under forward charge
13(3)	Time of supply of Services covered under reverse charge
13(4)	Time of supply of Vouchers that can be used to pay for Services
13(5)	Residual cases (where not possible to determine time of supply as per Sec 13(2), 13(3) or 13(4) above)
13(6)	Addition to value of supply by way of interest or late fee or penalty for delayed payment of consideration

Section 13 must be read in conjunction with section 31(2) read with rule 47 of CGST Rules, which prescribes the date on which Tax invoice for supply of goods/services should be issued.

Time limit for issuance of invoice for supply of services

- The tax invoice needs to be issued either before the provision of service or within 30 days (45 days in case of insurance companies/banking companies/financial institutions/NBFCs) from the date of supply of services.
- In case of cessation of supply of services before completion of supply, the invoice (to the extent of the supply made before such cessation) should be issued at the time when the supply ceases.
- In case of continuous supply of services, the invoice should be issued either
  (i) on/before the due date of payment or
  (ii) before/at the time when the supplier of service receives the payment or
  (iii) on/before the date of completion of the milestone event when the payment is linked to completion of an event.
- In case of insurance companies/banking companies/financial institutions including NBFCs/telecom companies/notified supplier of services making taxable supplies between distinct persons as specified in

section 25, invoice may be issued before or at the time of recording such supply in the books of account or before the expiry of the quarter during which the supply was made.

- As per Notification No. 45/2017-Central Tax dt 13.10.2017, where the supplier of taxable service is an insurer or a banking company or a financial institution, including a non-banking financial company, the said supplier may issue a tax invoice or any other document in lieu thereof, by whatever name called for the supply of services made during a month at the end of the month.

Time of supply of services—Forward charge (Default Rule) [Section 13(2)]

Supply of services on which supplier is liable to pay GST, time of supply will be earlier of the dates arrived by following two methods:

(a) Date of issue of invoice or the date of receipt of payment whichever is earlier (If the invoice is issued within the legally prescribed period under section 31(2) of the CGST Act)

(b) Date of provision of services or the date of receipt of payment, whichever is earlier (If the invoice is not issued within the legally prescribed period under section 31(2) of the CGST Act)

In case the aforesaid two provisions do not apply, time of supply of services will be the date on which the recipient shows the receipt of services in his books of account.

Time of supply of services depends upon whether invoice is issued within prescribed time or not.

Situations	Time of Supply of Service
Invoice is issued within prescribed time	Time of supply of service is earlier of (a) Date of invoice, (b) Date of receipt of payment
Invoice is not issued within prescribed time	Time of supply of service is earlier of (a) Date of providing service, (b) Date of receipt of payment
Other cases (where invoice not to be issued)	Time of supply is Date of receipt of service in the books of account of recipient

As per explanation (i) to Section 13(2), the supply of goods or services shall be deemed to have been made to the extent it is covered by the invoice or by the payment, as the case may be.

Option in case of Advance received up to ₹ 1000

Although tax is payable on any advance received for a supply of services (not applicable for goods), however for the convenience of trade, it is provided that if a supplier of taxable services receives an amount up to ₹ 1000 in excess of the amount indicated on the tax invoice, then the supplier has an option to take the date of issue of invoice in respect of such supply at the time of supply.

For example, if a supplier of service has received an amount of ₹ 1500 against an invoice of ₹ 1100 on 25.07.2018 and the date of invoice of next supply to the said recipient is 14.08.2018, then he has an option to treat the time of supply w.r.t. ₹ 400 either as 25.07.2018 or 14.08.2018.

Example 5: Mr X, a practising CA provided Professional service to M/s ABC Ltd. for ₹ 60,000as under:

Date	Event
10-04-2019	An Advance of ₹ 20,000 received from M/s ABC Ltd.
13-04-2019	Consultancy service was provided by Mr X
16-05-2019	Mr X received balance amount of ₹ 40,000

What will be the Time of supply if Mr X issues Invoice on (a) 14-04-2019 or (b) 15-05-2019?

Answer:

(a) If Invoice issued on 14-04-2019: In the given case, the invoice is issued on 14.04.2019, which is within 30 days of the supply of services, i.e. within the prescribed period. Therefore, for ₹ 20,000, the time of supply will be 10.04.2019 which is the date of receipt of advance payment. For the balance amount, time of supply will be 14.04.2019 which is earlier of 14.04.2019 (date of invoice) and 16.05.2019 (date of receipt of payment).

(b) If Invoice issued on 15-05-2019: Here, invoice is issued on 15.05.2019, which is not issued within the prescribed time period of 30 days of supply of service. Therefore, for ₹ 20,000, the time of supply will be 10.04.2019, which is the date of receipt of advance payment. For the balance amount, time of supply will be 13.04.2019 which is earlier of 13.04.2019 (date of providing service) and 16.05.2019 (date of receipt of payment).

Time of supply of life insurance services

Insurance policies are contracts for indemnifying any loss suffered by the policyholder. The policyholder is required to pay a premium at the time of inception of the policy. Renewal premiums are required to be paid on periodical basis during the tenure of the policy.

Nature of Policy	Time of Supply
New Policy	At the time of issuance of the policy
Renewal of Policy	The time of issuance of renewal notice for insurance premium
Other charges including ULIP charges	At the time of levy or recovery of the charges from the policyholder

Time of supply—Continuous supply of service

As per Section 2(33) of the CGST Act, 2017, continuous supply of services means a supply of services which is provided or agreed to be provided continuously or on recurrent basis under a contract for a period exceeding three months with periodic payment obligations and includes supply of services as the Government may subject to such conditions as it may by notification specify.

This means that there are three important conditions to be satisfied in order to be a continuous supply of services:

(a) The services should be provided continuously or on recurrent basis
(b) The contract period should be exceeding three months
(c) The payment obligations should be periodical

For example an annual maintenance contract (AMC), cleaning/sweeping/up keeping manpower contract, security service, construction contract, etc. may be considered as continuous supply of services if the aforesaid conditions are satisfied.

The date of issuance of invoice in respect of continuous supply of services has been given under Section 31(5) of the CGST Act, 2017 as follows:

Due date of payment	Date of invoice
Ascertainable from the contract	On or before the due date of payment (as per the contract terms)
Not ascertainable from the contract	Before or at the time of receipt of the payment\
Linked to completion of an event	On or before the date of completion of that event

Therefore, the time of continuous supply of service, in terms of Section 13 shall be earliest of the following:

(a) Date of issue of invoice; or
(b) Due date of issue of invoice; or
(c) Date on which payment is entered in books of accounts of the supplier; or
(d) Date on which payment is credited to the bank account.

As per section 31(6) of the CGST Act, 2017, in case where the supply of services ceases under a contract before the completion of the supply, the invoice shall be issued at the time when the supply ceases and such invoice shall be issued to the extent of the supply made before such cessation.

Example: Mr. Narayan Thakur (a contractor) enter into an agreement with M/s NHPC Ltd. for providing R&M work (cleaning/sweeping work) for a period of five months. He furnishes following information:

(a) Date of commencement of providing services 01-10-2019
(b) Date of completion of service 28-02-2020
(c) Date of receipt of payment by contractor 30-03-2020

Determine the time of issue of invoice as per the provisions of CGST Act, 2017 in the following circumstances:

(1) If no due date of payment is agreed upon between the two parties
(2) If payment is linked to completion of service
(3) If, NHPC Ltd. has to make payment on 25-03-2020 as per contract between them.

Ans. (1) Where the due date of payment is not ascertainable from the contract, the invoice shall be issued before or at the time when the supplier of service receives the payment.

Thus, in the given case the invoice should be issued on or before 30-03-2020.

(2) If payment is linked to the completion of an event, the invoice should be issued on or before the date of completion of that event.

Since in the given case payment is linked to the completion of service, invoice should be issued on or before 28-02-2020 (date of completion of service).

(3) Where the due date of payment is ascertainable from the contract, the invoice should be issued on or before the date of payment.

If M/s NHPC Ltd. has to make payment on 25-03-2020 as per contract, then invoice should be issued on or before 25.03.2020.

Time of supply of services—Reverse charge [Section 13(3)]

Earliest of the following dates:

(a) Date of payment as entered in the books of account of the recipient or the date on which the payment is debited in his bank account, whichever is earlier.

(b) Date immediately following 60 days from the date of issue of invoice or any other legal document in lieu of invoice by the supplier.

However, if it is not possible to determine the time of supply in aforesaid manner, then the **time of supply is the date of entry of the transaction in the books of accounts of the recipient** of supply.

Time of Supply in case of Reverse Charge Mechanism (RCM)

Goods	Services
It is earlier of (a) Date of Payment (b) 30 days from issue of Invoice (c) Date of receipt of goods	It is earlier of (a) Date of Payment (b) 60 days from issue of Invoice

Example 1: Determine the time of supply of following services assuming GST is payable on reverse charge.

Sl No.	Date of issue of invoice by supplier	Date of payment by recipient
1.	15th Jan 2019	10th Mar 2019
2.	8th Jan 2019	15th Mar 2019

Answer:

In case of Sl No. 1, time of supply will be 10th March 2019

In case of Sl No. 2, time of supply will be 8th March 2019

Example 2: Mr. A.R. Rehman, a famous music composer received ₹ 50 lakhs on 25th January 2019 from T Series Music Company Ltd. for music programme held on 31st December 2018 on New Year occasion. Mr. Rehman raised invoice on 10th January 2019. What will be the time of supply?

Ans. The service provided by a music composer to music company is a notified service cover under Reverse charge u/s 9(3) of CGST Act, 2017.

Therefore, time of supply of service covered under RCM will be earliest of the following

(1) Date of payment (i.e. 25th January 2019) or

(2) Date immediately following 60 days from the date of issue of invoice (i.e. 11th Mar. 2019)

Thus, time of supply of service is 25th Jan 2019.

Example 3: Mr. Gopal Sharma, a Senior Advocate of Delhi raised a bill of ₹ 10,000 on NTPC Ltd., Faridabad on 30th March 2022, in respect of a legal hearing appeared on behalf of the company on 25th Feb. 2022. Payment was released by the company on 15th April 2022.

(a) What is time of supply for above service?

(b) Who & when will deposit GST in the instant case?

Ans: Legal service provided by an Advocate to a Body Corporate is a notified service, covered under RCM u/s 9(3).

In case of service covered under RCM, time of supply shall be earliest of the following:

(1) Date of payment (i.e. 15th April 2022) or

(2) Date immediately following 60 days from the date of issue of invoice (i.e. 30th May 2022)

Thus, time of supply of service is 15th April 2022. Here NTPC Ltd. will deposit GST under RCM by 20th May 2022.

Import of Services between Associated Enterprises

Time of supply shall be earliest of the following:

- Date of entry in the books of account of the recipient or
- The date of payment.

Time of supply of vouchers that can be used to pay for services [Section 13(4)]

The time of supply of vouchers that are exchangeable for services shall be determined as under:

(i) **if the supply is identifiable:** Date of issue of the voucher

(ii) **in other cases:** Date of redemption of the voucher.

Time of supply of services—Residual cases [Section 13(5)]

If the situation is not covered by any of the provisions discussed above, the time of supply is fixed, in the following manner:

(a) Date on which periodical return for the period is required to be filed, or

(b) In any other case, date on which GST is paid

Time of supply, when there is enhancement of value on account of interest/late fee/penalty, etc. for delayed payment of consideration [Section 13(6)]

Section 13(6) prescribes that time of supply in case of addition in value by way of interest/late fee/penalty for delayed payment of consideration for a service is the date on which the supplier receives such addition in value.

8.5 TIME OF SUPPLY (GOODS AND SERVICES) WHEN THERE IS CHANGE IN RATE OF TAX [SECTION 14]

In case of change in rate of tax, determination of rate of tax depends upon following three events:

(i) date of supply of goods or services

(ii) date of issue of invoice

(iii) date of receipt of payment

If any two of the above events occur before the change of rate, the time of supply is before the change of rate or vice versa. Using this principle, time of supply, in case of change in rate of tax, can be determined as under:

(1) Supply is completed before the change in rate of tax

Invoice issued before the date of change in tax rate	Payment received before the date of change in tax rate	Time of supply	Applicable rate of tax
No	No	Earliest of the date of invoice or payment	New rate of tax
Yes	No	Date of issue of invoice	Old tax rate
No	Yes	Date of receipt of payment	Old tax rate

(2) Supply is completed after the change in rate of tax

Invoice issued before the date of change in tax rate	Payment received before the date of change in tax rate	Time of supply	Applicable rate of tax
Yes	Yes	Earliest of the date of invoice or payment	Old tax rate
Yes	No	Date of receipt of payment	New rate of tax
No	Yes	Date of issue of invoice	New rate of tax

Clubbing the above two scenario, time of supply can be analyzed as under, when there is change in rate of tax.

Sl No.	Supplied	Invoice issued	Payment received	Time of supply is earliest of the date of		Section
1.	Before change	After change	After change	Receipt of payment	Issue of invoice	14(a)(i)
2.		Before change	After change	–	Issue of invoice	14(a)(ii)
3.		After change	Before change	Receipt of payment	–	14(a)(iii)
1.	After change	Before change	After change	Receipt of payment	–	14(b)(i)
2.		Before change	Before change	Receipt of payment	Issue of invoice	14(b)(ii)
3.		After change	Before change	-	Issue of invoice	14(b)(iii)

Example 4: M/s XYZ Ltd. placed supply order for 10 Nos. 32″ LED TV to M/s Audio Vision, Bhubaneswar on 15th December 2018, which attract 28% GST. The Govt reduced the rate of 32″ LED TV to 18% vide notification dated 26th Dec 2018 based on recommendation of 31st GST Council meeting. The firm supplied the LED TV to XYZ Ltd. on 28th Dec 2018, bearing invoice dated 20th Dec 2018. Payment was made to supplier on 31st Dec 2018. What is the time of supply?

Ans. Here, date of supply of goods & date of payment falls after change in rate of tax, but invoice has been raised prior to change in rate of tax. Therefore, time of supply will be date of receipt of payment. Rate of GST applicable for the supply is 18%.

Date of receipt of payment in case of change in rate of tax

Normally, the date of receipt of payment is the date of credit in the bank account of the recipient of payment or the date on which the payment is entered into his books of account, whichever is earlier. However, in cases of change in rate of tax, the date of receipt of payment is the date of credit in the bank account if such credit is after four working days from the date of change in rate of tax.

Chapter 9

Value of Supply

9.1 INTRODUCTION

Every fiscal statue makes provision for the determination of value, where tax is payable on ad-valorem basis. In GST also, tax is payable on ad-valorem basis, i.e. percentage on value of the supply of goods or services.

Since GST is levied as a percentage of the value of supply, whether of goods or of services, it becomes important to know how to arrive at the value on which tax is to be paid.

GST is payable

(i) on supply of goods and/or services for a consideration in the course of or furtherance of business;

(ii) on certain supplies made without a consideration as specified in Schedule I to the CGST Act, 2017.

Determination of the value on which GST would be levied has been described in Chapter IV of CGST Act, 2017. Section 15 of the CGST Act and Determination of Value of Supply, CGST Rules, 2017 contain provisions related to valuation of supply of goods or services made in different circumstances and to different persons. Section 15 of the CGST Act provides common provisions for determining the value of goods and services. Provisions of value of supply under CGST Act have also been made applicable to IGST Act vide section 20 of the IGST Act, 2017.

9.2 VALUE OF TAXABLE SUPPLY [SECTION 15]

The Value of Supply of goods or services or both shall be the Transaction Value.

Transaction value is the basis for valuation for supply of goods and/or services under GST regime. For the purpose of levy of GST, first we have to determine the transaction value. Transaction value, i.e. price actually paid or payable, provided the supplier & the recipient are not related and price is the sole consideration. In most of the cases of regular normal trade, the invoice value will be the taxable value. However, to determine value of certain specific transactions, Determination of Value of Supply rules have been prescribed in CGST Rules, 2017 [Rule 27 to Rule 35].

Section 15 of the CGST Act, 2017 applies to both goods and services supplied for purposes of valuation of the taxable supply. The valuation method provided in this section applies to UTGST, SGST, CGST and IGST. Valuation must be as provided exclusively in this section.

'Transaction value' has not been defined but is provided in the section itself as the 'price'.

Price is consideration in money terms. Value, as stated earlier, is price that would be prevalent under controlled conditions. These conditions being:

- Transaction having a price
- Between persons not related
- And that price being the sole consideration

"Transaction value" is the price actually paid or payable for the said supply of goods and/or services or both where the supplier and the recipient of the supply are not related and the price is the sole consideration for the supply.

This is subject to dual conditions: Section 15(1)

- Supplier & Recipient are not related;
- Price is the sole consideration for the supply

Meaning of "Price is not the sole consideration"

Under the GST law, consideration can be in "money or otherwise", and also includes the monetary value of an act or forbearance, in relation to a supply. Consideration may also flow from any person other than the recipient. In cases, where the money received in respect of the supply is not the sole consideration, the "price is not the sole consideration". For example, buyer of capital goods discharges the loan of seller, goods purchased on exchange offer, etc.

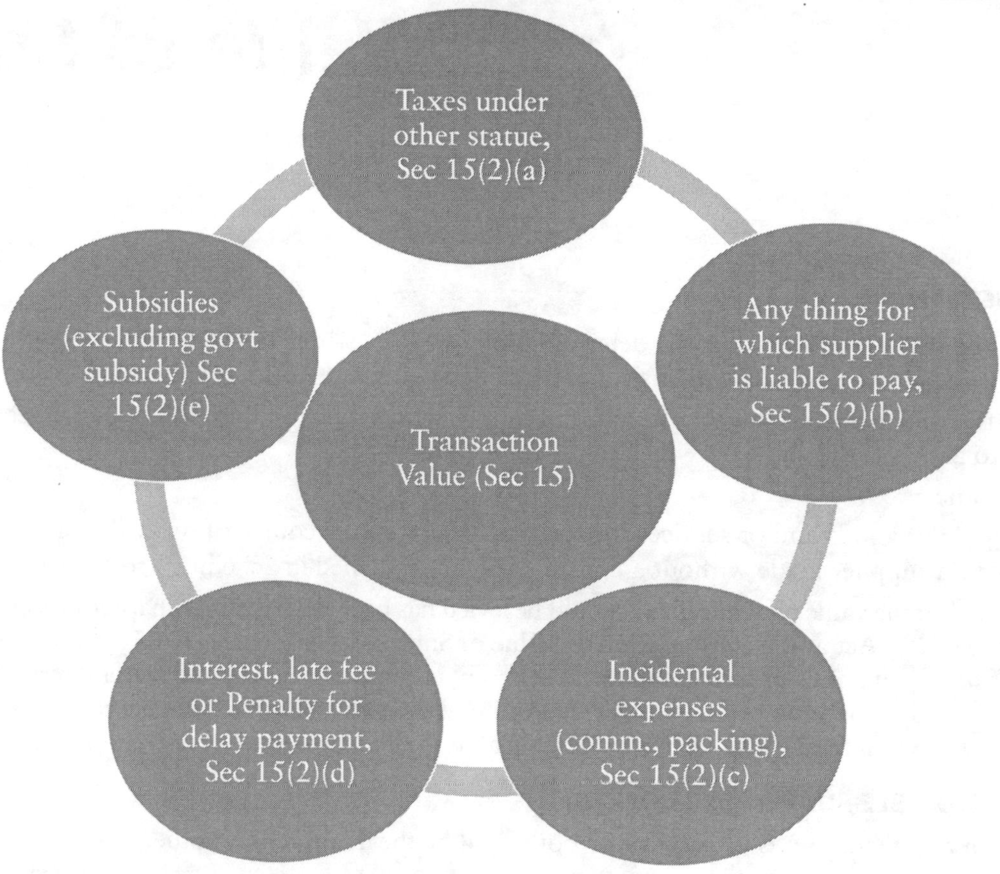

9.2.1 Inclusions in the Transaction Value [Section 15(2)]

The value of supply under GST shall include:

(1) Any taxes, duties, cess, fees and charges levied under any act, except GST. GST Compensation cess will be excluded if charged separately by the supplier.
(2) Any amount that the supplier is liable to pay which has been incurred by the recipient and is not included in the price.
(3) The value will include all **incidental expenses** in relation to sale such as packing, forwarding, insurance, transportation cost (in case of FOR, if borne by supplier) commission, etc.
(4) Interest/late fee/penalty for delayed payment of consideration.
(5) Subsidies linked to supply (except Government subsidies).

The transaction value shall include the following:

Section 15(2)(a)	Taxes & duties under any other law	Any taxes, duties, cess, fees and charges levied under any law other than CGST Act/IGST Act, if charged separately by the supplier to the recipient.
Section 15(2)(b)	Any amount for which supplier is liable to pay	Any amount that the supplier is liable to pay in relation to such supply but which has been incurred by the recipient of the supply and not included in the price actually paid or payable for the goods and/or services.
Section 15(2)(c)	Incidental expenses	Packing, forwarding, transit insurance, loading, weightment charges transportation cost, certification, installation, testing, etc.

Section 15(2)(d)	Interest/late fee/penalty for delayed payment	Interest/late fee/penalty received by supplier from customer for delayed payment will also form part of transaction value.
Section 15(2)(e)	Non-Govt subsidy	Any amount received from person/entity other than Govt to keep the price of goods or services low shall be added to value of supply to arrive at transaction value.

TCS on goods, levied under Income Tax Act, 1961 shall not form part of value of Supply

Section 15(2)(a) of the CGST Act specifies that the value of supply shall include "any taxes, duties, cess, fees and charges" levied under any law for the time being in force other than this Act, the SGST Act, the UTGST Act and the GST (Compensation to States) Act, if charged separately by the supplier.

The CBDT has clarified that Tax collection at source (TCS) is not a tax on goods but an interim levy on the possible "income" arising from the sale of goods by the buyer and to be adjusted against the final income-tax liability of the buyer.

CBIC Vide Circular *No. 76/50/2018-GST dated 7th March 2019* has clarified that for the purpose of determination of value of supply under GST, Tax collected at source (TCS) under the provisions of the Income Tax Act, 1961 would not be includible as it is an interim levy not having the character of tax.

Example 1: As per Rent contract, if the tenant is required to deposit taxes levied by the local body as per actual directly with the authority. Such tax will form part of consideration for the supply of renting services.

Example 2: Levy of Entertainment tax has not been subsumed in the GST. Therefore, right to levy is still available with local authority and consequently it appears that any entertainment tax charged by the local authority will form part of transaction value.

Example 3: Expenses incurred by the tenant on account of repair & maintenance of the house such as plumbing work, painting work, etc. which has been reimbursed by the land lord will form part of transaction value for the purpose of levy of GST.

Example 4: Mr. X has placed an order with Mr. Y for supply of stationery items, with a condition to deliver the goods at the premises of Mr. X. The supplier Mr. Y packed the goods and booked with a transporter. The lorry receipt shows that Mr. X. will pay freight.

Here in lieu of Mr. Y, payment is being made by Mr. X. Therefore, such payment will form part of transaction value of product. Thus, in a contract, the obligation undertaken by the supplier for making supply of goods needs to be determined. All the expenses in respect of such obligation must be incurred by the supplier. But here the supplier was under obligation for which receiver has made the payment and therefore, the payment in connection with the supply, i.e. transportation will form part of transaction value.

Example 5: West Bengal Govt entered into an agreement with HCL Technologies for supply of Laptop to students enroll in Govt colleges. As per the agreement, HCL Technologies shall supply Laptop to student @₹ 5000, whose market price is ₹ 15,000. Govt of West Bengal will give subsidy of ₹ 10,000 per laptop supplied to HCL Tech. What is the taxable value for the purpose of levy of GST? Will your answer be different, if the subsidy was provided by ITC Ltd. under CSR scheme?

Here, the taxable value shall be ₹ 5000 laptop, since Govt subsidy does not form part of transaction value. In case ITC Ltd. provides subsidy, transaction value shall be ₹ 15,000 per laptop, since it is non-Govt subsidy.

Example 6: Calculate the value of supply on which GST shall be levied M/s XYZ Ltd., a company registered under GST, sold Timber scrap of ₹ 2 lakhs (excluding Tax) to Mr. A, who is also a registered person under GST. The company collected TCS@2.5% from the buyer i.e. Mr. A as per the provision of Income Tax Act, 1961. Rate of GST on timber scrap is 5%. Compute the value of supply & GST, which shall be levied on such sale of scrap.

Ans. GST on sale of scrap shall be computed as under:

Particulars	Amount (₹)
Amount before Tax	2,00,000
TCS@2.5%	5,000
Amount collected from buyer (excluding GST)	2, 05,000

Particulars	Amount (₹)
Value of supply for the purpose of levy of GST	2,00,000
GST @ 5% on ₹ 2 lakhs	10,000
Total Amount to be collected from buyer (including GST)	**2, 15,000**

Note: As clarified by CBDT, TCS is not a tax. Therefore, it will not cover within the ambit of Section 15(2) of CGST, Act. Therefore, transaction value for the purpose of levy of GST shall not include TCS levied under the provision of Section 206 of Income Tax Act, 1961.

Example 7: M/s Technico (India) Pvt Ltd., Kolkata sold a machine to M/s ABB Ltd. It has furnished following particulars in this regard:

Sl No.	Particulars	Amount(₹)
1.	Price of the machine (excluding taxes and incidental charges)	8,00,000
2.	Machine was subject to third party inspection (inspection charges have been directly paid by ABB Ltd. to the inspecting agency)	50,000
3.	Freight charges for delivery of the machine (as per terms of contract, it was suppliers responsibility to deliver machine at buyer premises)	80,000
4.	Subsidy received by M/s Technico (India) Pvt. Ltd. from Govt of India under Make in India promotion scheme	30,000
5.	Discount of 2% is offered to M/s ABB Ltd. on the price charged for machine & recorded in the Invoice	–

Note: Items given in Sl No. 2 to 5 have not been considered in the price mentioned at Sl. No. 1.

Determine the value of taxable supply made by M/s Technico (India) Pvt. Ltd. to M/s ABB Ltd.

Ans. Computation of value of taxable supply made by M/s Technico (India) Pvt Ltd.

Particulars	Amount (₹)
Price of the machine (less Govt Subsidy of ₹ 30,000)	7,70,000
Add. Third party inspection charges (Any amount for which supplier is liable to pay but paid by recipient, includible in taxable value)	50,000
Add. Freight charges for delivery of machine (Liability of supplier)	80,000
TOTAL	9,00,000
Less: Discount @ 2% on the price charged for machine (i.e. on ₹ 8,00,000)	16,000
Value of Taxable Supply	8,84,000

9.2.2 Exclusion from Transaction Value [Section 15(3)]

Discounts like trade discount, quantity discount, etc. are part of the normal trade and commerce. Therefore, pre-supply discounts, i.e. discounts recorded in the invoice have been allowed to be excluded while determining the taxable value.

Discounts provided after the supply can also be excluded while determining the taxable value, provided two conditions are met, namely:

(a) discount is established in terms of a pre-supply agreement between the supplier & the recipient and such discount is linked to relevant invoices

(b) input tax credit attributable to the discounts is reversed by the recipient.

The value of supply shall not include discount, provided:

- It is allowed before supply
- It is allowed after supply provided that it is established in agreement linked to specific supplies and corresponding credit is reversed by recipient.

Example 8: Hindustan Unilever announces turnover discount every year in the month of December for its distributors based on turnover achieved during the previous financial year. Distributors who achieved turnover of more than ₹ 100 crores during the previous FY are given 1% discount on incremental turnover over and above ₹ 100 crores. Mr. X, a distributors achieved a turnover of ₹ 130 crores during previous FY Compute the value of supply for the purpose of GST.

Since these discounts were not known at the time of supply and it is not linked to any particular invoice, it will not be deducted from the total value of supply of ₹ 130 crores.

9.3 TREATMENT OF TRADE/CASH DISCOUNTS

Offering trade and cash discounts is a built-in promotional scheme of almost every entity. Companies generally offer trade discounts to increase sales, while cash discounts are given to recover payments speedily.

GST doesn't differentiate between trade and cash discounts. Rather, GST segregates the discounts allowed into two categories:

(1) those given before or at the time of supply
(2) those given after the time of supply

(1) If a discount has been allowed before or at the time of supply, and it has been mentioned in the invoice separately, it will not be added in the value of supply.

(2) If discount is allowed **after the supply,** it may or may not be added in the value of the supply, depending on the following factors:

(a) whether the discount can be linked directly to the relevant invoice of supply,
(b) whether the discount has been allowed as per the terms already agreed upon before or at the time of supply, or
(c) whether the input tax credit related to the amount of the discount allowed has been reversed by the recipient of the supply.

Example 9: A company offers a 2% discount on the sale of goods worth ₹ 1000. If the company mentions the discount amount (i.e. ₹ 20) separately in the invoice, the value of the taxable supply will be ₹ 980 (1000–20).

Example 10: A company has a policy of allowing a cash discount of 1% if a customer pays a particular invoice within 30 days. If the company sells goods worth ₹ 1000 to a customer and the customer pays the invoice within 30 days to avail the discount, the discount amount will not be added to the value of taxable supply.

Example 11: A company has supplied goods worth ₹ 1000 to a customer and the customer didn't pay the amount. The company does not have a policy of offering cash discounts to customers at the time of payment. If this company now offers the customer 10% discount in order to encourage the customer to clear all his debts, but the discount was not agreed before or at the time of supply, and cannot be linked to a particular invoice, this discount will be added in the value of the taxable supply.

Example 12: ABC Ltd., a registered supplier of Kolkata has supplied goods to Ratan Enterprise, Patna and Mahesh Traders, Siliguri during the month of May 2023 as per details furnished hereunder:

Sl. No.	Particulars	Ratan Enterprise, Patna (₹)	Mahesh Traders, Siliguri (₹)
1.	Price of goods supplied (excluding GST)	50,000	60,000
2.	Transportation charges	3,000	3,500
3.	Packing & forwarding	1,500	1,500
4.	Weightment charges	500	600
5.	Cash discount for prompt payment (recorded in invoice)	–	400

The goods attract GST @ 18%. Compute value of taxable supply and GST liability.

Ans. Computation of GST liability

Sl. No.	Particulars	Ratan Enterprise, Patna (₹)	Mahesh Traders, Siliguri (₹)
1.	Price of goods (excluding GST)	50,000	60,000
2.	Add: Transportation charges	3,000	3,500
3.	Add: Packing & forwarding	1,500	1,500
4.	Add: Weightment charges	500	600
5.	Less: Cash Discount for prompt payment (recorded in invoice)	–	400
	Value of Taxable Supply	55,000	65,200
	IGST @18%	9,900	–
	CGST @9%	–	5868
	SGST @9%	–	5868

Note: Incidental charges such as transportation charges, packing & forwarding & weightment charges, etc. charged by supplier to recipient will be included in the value of supply. Since discount is known at the time of supply, it is deductible from the value of supply as per Section 15 to arrive at taxable value for the purpose of levy of GST.

Example 13: M/s Tridev Enterprise has agreed to supply goods to consumer's premises. Goods valued ₹ 60,000 are taxable at 18% IGST as it is an inter-state supply. It also pays freight and transit insurance of ₹ 8,000. GTA is a registered entity and has charged GST (6% CGST and 6% SGST) under forward charges.

(a) Compute the value of supply including IGST.

(b) What will be the invoice value of supply including IGST, if the supply was under ex-factory basis instead of door delivery basis?

Ans. Computation of Invoice value of Supply

(a) When the supplier agrees to supply the goods at customer's premises (i.e. freight & transit insurance paid by supplier)

Particulars	Amount (₹)
Value of goods supplied	60,000
Add. Freight & transit insurance (since the supplier has agreed to delivered the goods at the customer premises and to pay for freight & insurance, the contract of supply becomes a composite supply, the principal supply being the supply of goods)	8,000
Total	68,000
Add. IGST @18%	12,240
Invoice value of Supply	80,240

(b) When the supplier agrees to supply the goods on ex-factory basis, i.e. the buyer pays the freight & transit insurance

Particulars	Amount (₹)
Value of goods supplied	60,000
Add. IGST @18%	10,800
Invoice value of Supply	70,800

Note: When the contract is ex-factory, freight & transit insurance is the responsibility of buyer and does not form part of taxable value of supply.

9.4 DETERMINATION OF VALUE OF SUPPLY (VALUATION RULES)

Value of Taxable Supply

Section 15 (1): The value of a supply of goods or services or both shall be the transaction value, which is the price actually paid or payable for the said supply of goods or services or both where the supplier and the recipient of the supply are not related and the price is the sole consideration for the supply.

Section 15 (4): Where the value of the supply of goods or services or both cannot be determined under section 15(1), the same shall be determined in such manner as may be prescribed.

> As per Para 2 of Schedule I of CGST, Act 2017, Supply of goods or services or both between related persons or between distinct persons as specified in section 25, when made in the course or furtherance of business shall be treated as supply even if made without consideration.
>
> Therefore, in case of transaction between related persons or distinct persons value of supply shall be determine as per valuation rules.

Valuation Rule 27 to Rule 35 of CGST Rules, 2017 prescribe the manner of valuation of supply.

Related Person

As per explanations given in Section 15 of CGST Act, 2017

(a) persons shall be deemed to be "related persons" if:
   (i) such persons are officers or directors of one another's businesses;
   (ii) such persons are legally recognised partners in business;
   (iii) such persons are employer and employee;
   (iv) any person directly or indirectly owns, controls or holds twenty-five per cent. or more of the outstanding voting stock or shares of both of them;
   (v) one of them directly or indirectly controls the other;
   (vi) both of them are directly or indirectly controlled by a third person;
   (vii) together they directly or indirectly control a third person; or
   (viii) they are members of the same family.

(b) the term "person" also includes legal persons.

(c) persons who are associated in the business of one another in that one is the sole agent or sole distributor or sole concessionaire, howsoever described, of the other, shall be deemed to be related.

As per Section 15(4), if the transaction value cannot be determined as per Section 15(1), reference to CGST Rules related to valuation is permitted.

Hence, recourse to the Valuation Rules is permitted only in the following circumstances:

- Supplies not covered by section 7(1)(a), i.e. price is not the sole consideration
- Supplies covered by section 7(1)(a) but between related persons
- Supplies covered by section 7(1)(a) and not adjusted for aspects provided by section 15(2).

Government is free to notify tariff values in specific cases to determine the tax payable on such cases. This would prevail over the valuation provided for in section 15(1).

Valuation Rules are prescribed in Rules 27 to 35 under Chapter IV of the Central Goods & Services Tax Rules, 2017.

Valuation Rules

Rule	Description
Rule-27	Value of supply of goods or services where consideration is not wholly in money
Rule-28	Value of supply of goods or services or both between distinct or related persons, other than through an agent
Rule-29	Value of supply of goods made or received through an agent
Rule-30	Value of supply of goods or services or both based on cost
Rule-31	Residual method for determination of value of supply of goods or services or both
Rule-31A	Value of supply in case of lottery, betting, gambling and horse racing

Rule	Description
Rule-32	Determination of value in respect of certain supplies
Rule-33	Value of supply of services in case of pure agent
Rule-34	Rate of exchange of currency, other than Indian rupees, for determination of value
Rule-35	Value of supply inclusive of integrated tax, Central tax, State tax, Union territory tax

Rule 27: Taxable value when consideration is not solely in money: Where consideration for a supply is not solely in money, taxable value has to be determined as prescribed in the rules. In such cases, following values have to be taken sequentially to determine the taxable value:

(i) Open Market Value of such supply.

(ii) Total money value of the supply, i.e. monetary consideration plus money value of the non-monetary consideration

(iii) Value of supply of like kind and quality

(iv) Value of supply based on cost, i.e. cost of supply plus 10% mark-up

(v) Value of supply determined by using reasonable means consistent with principles & general provisions of GST law. (Best Judgment method)

Open Market Value means the full value of money excluding taxes under GST laws, payable by a person to obtain such supply at the time when supply being valued is made, provided such supply is between unrelated persons and price is the sole consideration for such supply.

Supply of like kind & quality means any other supply made under similar circumstances, is same or closely resembles in respect of characteristics, quality, quantity, functionality, reputation to the supply being valued.

Illustration:

(1) Where a new phone is supplied for ₹ 20000 along with the exchange of an old phone and if the price of the new phone without exchange is ₹ 24000, the open market value of the new phone is ₹ 24000.

(2) Where a laptop is supplied for ₹ 40000 along with a barter of printer that is manufactured by the recipient and the value of the printer known at the time of supply is ₹ 4000 but the open market value of the laptop is not known, the value of the supply of laptop is ₹ 44,000.

(3) M/s Tridev Enterprise Pvt. Ltd. is a supplier of "Crompton" electric motor & registered under GST. The company supplied electric motor to Mr. Ashok for consideration of ₹ 3,54,000 (inclusive of GST @ 18%). Mr. Ashok also gave his old motor, which was not in working conditions against said supply, whose value was ₹ 20,000 (excluding GST).

M/s Tridev Enterprise has supplied similar electric motor to another customer, Mr. Rajesh at a price of ₹ 3,75,240 (inclusive of GST @ 18%).

(a) Determine the value of goods supplied by M/s Tridev Enterprise Pvt. Ltd. to Mr. Ashok as per the provision of CGST Act.

(b) What will be the value of supply, if the price at which motor sold to Mr. Rajesh is not available at the time of supply to Mr. Ashok?

Answer

(a) In the given case, price is not the sole consideration for the supply. Apart from monetary consideration, the buyer has given some material to the supplier. Hence, the value of supply cannot be determined based on the transaction value in terms of Section 15(1) of the CGST Act.

Here the value will be determined with the help of Rule 27 of the CGST Rule, 2017.

Open market value of a supply means the full value in money, excluding the applicable GST, where the supplier and the recipient are not related and the price is the sole consideration, to obtain such supply at the same time when the supply being valued is made.

Therefore, in the given case, the open market value of the goods supplied is ₹ 3,18,000 (3,75,240* 100/118) and is therefore the value of such goods.

(b) Rule 27 provides that, if open market value of the supply is not known, the value of the supply will be the consideration in money plus the money equivalent to the non-monetary, if such amount is known at the time of supply.

Therefore, the value in the given case will be ₹ 3,20,000 (3,54,000*100/118 plus 20,000).

Rule 28: Value of supply between distinct and related persons (excluding Agents): A person who is under influence of another person is called a related person like members of the same family or subsidiaries of a group company, etc. The term "related persons" has been defined in explanation to Section 15 of CGST Act, 2017. As relation may influence the price between two related persons, therefore special valuation rule has been framed to arrive at the taxable value of transactions between related persons.

In such cases, following values have to be taken sequentially to determine the taxable value:

(i) Open Market Value
(ii) Value of supply of like kind and quality.
(iii) Value of supply based on cost, i.e. cost of supply plus 10% mark-up.
(iv) Value of supply determined by using reasonable means consistent with principles & general provisions of GST law. (Best Judgment method)

However, if the recipient is eligible for full input tax credit, the invoice value will be accepted as taxable value. It has also been provided that where the goods being supplied are intended for further supply as such be the recipient, the value shall, at the option of the supplier, be an amount equivalent to 90% of the price charged for the supply of goods of like kind and quality by the recipient to his unrelated customer.

Rule 29: Value of supply of goods made or received through an agent

(a) Open market value of goods being supplied, or, at the option of the supplier, 90% of the price charged for the supply of goods of like kind and quality by the recipient to his unrelated customer.

Illustration: Where a principal supplies groundnut to his agent and the agent is supplying groundnuts of like kind and quality in subsequent supplies at a price of ₹ 5000 per quintal on the day of supply. Another independent supplier is supplying groundnuts of like kind and quality to the said agent at the price of ₹ 4550 per quintal. The value of the supply made by the principal shall be ₹ 4550 per quintal or where he exercises the option the value shall be 90% of the ₹ 5000 i.e. is ₹ 4500 per quintal.

(b) In case value cannot be determined under (a) then following values have to be taken sequentially to determine the taxable value:

(i) Value of supply based on cost, i.e. cost of supply plus 10% mark-up
(ii) Value of supply determined by using reasonable means consistent with principles & general provisions of GST law. (Best Judgment method)

Rule 30: Value of supply of goods or services or both based on cost: Where the value of a supply of goods or services or both is not determinable by any of the preceding rules, the value shall be 110% of the cost of production or manufacture or cost of acquisition of such goods or cost of provision of such services.

Rule 31: Residual method for determination of value of supply of goods or services or both: Where the value of supply of goods or services or both cannot be determined under Rules 27 to 30, the same shall be determined using reasonable means consistent with the principles and general provisions of Section 15 and these rules, provided that in case of supply of services, the supplier may opt for this rule, disregarding Rule 30.

Rule 31A: Value of supply in case of lottery, betting, gambling and horse racing: 'Lottery ticket', is actionable claim and is classified as 'Goods' under GST. However, an actionable claim is specifically covered under the negative list-Schedule III of the CGST Act, keeping it outside the scope of GST except sale of Lottery tickets.

Hence, the sale of lottery tickets would be considered to be supply of taxable goods and will attract GST.

Sl No.	Type of Lottery	Value of Supply
1.	Lottery Run by State Government	Higher of: 100/128* of the face value of ticket or 100/128 of the prices as notified in the official gazette.
2.	Lottery Authorized by State Government	Higher of: 100/128 of the face value of ticket or 100/128 of the prices as notified in the official gazette.
3.	Actionable claim in the form of chance to win in betting gambling or horse racing in a Race Club	100% of the face value of the bet or the amount paid into the totalizator.

******Note:*** Lottery run by State Government will attract 28% GST w.e.f. 1st March 2020, as per decision taken in 38th GST Council meeting. Notification No. 1/2020-Central Tax (Rate) dated 21st Feb. 2020. Prior to this, it was 12%.

Explanation: For the purposes of this sub-rule, the expressions:

(a) lottery run by State Governments means a lottery not allowed to be sold in any State other than the organizing State.

(b) lottery authorized by State Governments means a lottery, which is authorized to be sold in State(s) other than the authorized State also.

(c) The value of supply of actionable claim in the form of chance to win in betting, gambling or horseracing in a race club shall be 100% of the face value of the bet or the amount paid into the totalizator.

Rule 31B: Value of supply in case of Online Gaming including online money gaming: Value of supply of online gaming, including supply of actionable claims involved in online money gaming, shall be the total amount paid or payable to or deposited with the supplier by way of money or money's worth, including virtual digital assets, by or on behalf of the player.

Further, any amount returned or refunded by the supplier to the player for any reasons whatsoever, including player not using the amount paid or deposited with the supplier for participating in any event, shall not be deductible from the value of supply of online money gaming.

Rule 31C: Rule 31B: Value of supply in case of Online Gaming including online money gaming: Value of supply of actionable claims in casino shall be the total amount paid or payable by or on behalf of the player for:

(i) purchase of the tokens, chips, coins or tickets, by whatever name called, for use in casino; or

(ii) participating in any event, including game, scheme, competition or any other activity or process, in the casino, in cases where the token, chips, coins or tickets, by whatever name called, are not required.

Further, any amount returned or refunded by the casino to the player on return of token, coins, chips, or tickets, as the case may be, or otherwise, shall not be deductible from the value of the supply of actionable claims in casino.

For the purpose of above rules 31B and 31C, any amount received by the player by winning any event, including game, scheme, competition or any other activity or process, which is used for playing by the said player in a further event without withdrawing, shall not be considered as the amount paid to or deposited with the supplier by or on behalf of the said player.

Rule 32: Determination of value in respect of few specific supplies: This rule provides the valuation method for five specific supplies & also optional. The supplies prescribed in this rule need not to be valued by sequentially following rules 27 to 31.

(a) Purchase or sale of foreign currency including money changing

(b) Booking of tickets for air travel by an air travel agent

(c) Life insurance business

(d) Value of supply of Second hand goods

(e) Value of redeemable vouchers/stamps/coupons/tokens

The special provisions related to determination of above supplies are as below:

(a) Purchase or sale of foreign currency including money changing

Case 1: Transaction where one of the currencies exchanged is Indian Rupees: Taxable value is difference between buying rate or selling rate of currency and RBI reference rate for that currency at the time of exchange multiplied by total units of foreign currency.

However, if RBI reference rate for a currency is not available then taxable value is 1% of the gross amount of Indian Rupees provided/received by the person changing the money.

Case 2: Transaction where neither of the currencies exchanged is Indian Rupees

Option 1: Taxable value will be 1% of the lesser of the two amounts the person changing the money would have received by converting (at RBI reference rate) any of the two currencies in Indian Rupees.

Option 2: The person supplying the services may also exercise the following option to ascertain the taxable value. However, once opted, he cannot withdraw it during the remaining part of the financial year.

Sl No.	Currency exchange	Value of supply
1.	Up to ₹ 1 lakhs	1% of gross amount or ₹ 250 whichever is higher
2	Exceeding ₹ 1 lakh & up to ₹ 10 lakhs	₹ 1,000 + 0.50% of (Gross amount of currency exchange—₹ 1 lakhs)
3	Exceeding ₹ 10 lakhs	₹ 5,500 + 0.10% of (Gross amount of currency exchange—₹ 10 lakhs) or ₹ 60,000 whichever is lower

Notes:

(1) Inter se sale or purchase of foreign currency amongst banks or authorized dealers of foreign exchange or amongst banks and such dealers is an exempted supply of service as per Sl. No. 27 of Notification No. 12/2017-Central Tax (Rate) dated 28.06.2017.

(2) Forex transactions involving outward remittances out of EEFC balances or crediting to EEFC account GST need not be collected.

Example 1: Mr. Rohit converted USD 100 into ₹ 8200 @₹ 82/USD on 22nd Feb 2023 through Western Union Money exchanger. RBI reference rate on 22nd Feb 2023 was ₹ 83/USD. Compute the value of supply on which GST shall be levied.

Answer: Taxable Value = (83-82)*100= ₹ 100 on which GST shall be levied @18%.

Example 2: Mr. Brajesh converted USD 2000 into GBP 1585 on 22nd Dec 2023 through Western Union Money exchanger. RBI reference rate at that time for USD was ₹ 83/USD and for GBP was ₹ 99/GBP. Compute the value of taxable supply for the purpose of levy of GST.

Answer: In the given case, value of taxable supply will be 1% of the lesser of the two amounts the person changing the money would have received by converting into Indian rupees.

(a) USD converted into INR = 2000*83= ₹ 1,66,000

(b) GBP converted into INR = 1585*93= ₹ 1,47,405

Value of taxable supply = 1% of ₹ 1,47,405 = ₹ 1474

Note: He can also exercise 2nd option.

Example 3: Mr Abhisek, a money changer, exchanged USD 10,000 to Indian rupees through RBI @₹ 69/USD on 2nd January 2019. Compute value of taxable supply as per rule 32(2)(b) of CGST rules?

As per rule 32(2)(b) of CGST Rules, 2017 the value in relation to the supply of foreign currency, including money changing is deemed to be:

(i) Up to ₹ 1 lakhs, 1% of gross amount subject to a minimum of ₹ 250

(ii) For amount exceeding ₹ 1 lakh & upto ₹ 10 lakhs, ₹ 1,000 + 0.50% of (Gross amount of currency exchange—₹ 1 lakhs)

Therefore, the value of supply shall be computed as under:

Particulars	Amount(₹)
Value of Currency exchanged in INR	₹ 6,90,000 (USD 10,000@₹ 69)
Up to ₹ 1 lakh	₹ 1000
Above ₹ 1 lakh	₹ 2950 (@0.50% on ₹ 5,90,000)
Value of supply	₹ 3950

(b) Booking of tickets for air travel by an air travel agent

Sl No.	Nature of Travel	Value of Supply
1.	Domestic travel	5% of basic fare
2.	International travel	10% of basic fare

The expression 'basic fare' means that part of the air fare on which commission is normally paid to the air travel agent by the Airlines.

(c) Life insurance business.

Sl No.	Nature of Policy	Value of supply
1.	Policy has dual benefits of risk coverage and investment	Gross premium charged *less* amount allocated for investments or savings (if intimated to the policy holder at the time of collection of premium)
2.	Single premium annuity policy	10% of premium
3.	Other cases	25% of premium charged from the policy holder in the first year and 12.5% of premium charged for subsequent years.
4.	Only risk coverage (e.g. Term insurance)	Entire premium

(d) Value of supply of second hand goods: The expression "supply" as per Section 7(1) of CGST Act, 2017 includes sale, lease, and disposal. Therefore, sale/disposal of old or used vehicle by a registered dealer for a consideration is in the course or furtherance of business and hence it will qualify to be a supply. Therefore, GST shall be applicable.

As per Rule 32(5) of the CGST Rules, 2017, where a taxable supply is provided by a person dealing in buying and selling of second hand goods, i.e. used goods as such or after such minor processing which does not change the nature of the goods and where no input tax credit has been availed on the purchase of such goods, the value of supply shall be the difference between the selling price and the purchase price and where the value of such supply is negative, it shall be ignored. If input tax credit is availed, then such supply will be governed by normal GST valuation.

Margin Scheme

Normally, GST is charged on the transaction value of the goods. However, in respect of second hand goods/ car, a person dealing is such goods may be allowed to pay tax on the margin.

(i) in case of a registered person who has claimed depreciation under Section 32 of the Income Tax Act, 1961 (43 of 1961) on the said goods, the value that represents the margin of the supplier shall be the difference between the consideration received for supply of such goods and the depreciated value of such goods on the date of supply, and where the margin of such supply is negative, it shall be ignored; and

(ii) in any other case, the value that represents the margin of supplier shall be, the difference between the selling price and the purchase price and where such margin is negative, it shall be ignored.

The purpose of the scheme is to avoid double taxation as the goods, having once borne the incidence of tax, re-enter the supply and the economic supply chain.

Rate of GST on Supply of Old/Used Vehicles

Notification No. 8/2018-Central Tax (Rate) dated 25-01-2018

Sl No.	Chapter Heading	Description of Goods	GST Rates (CGST+SGST)
01	8703	Old & used petrol, LPG or CNG driven motor vehicle having engine capacity >=1200CC and length of >=4000 mm	18%
02	8703	Old & used diesel driven motor vehicle having engine capacity >=1500CC and length of 4000 mm	18%
03	8703	Old & used motor vehicle of engine capacity >1500CC (SUVs & UVs)	18%
04	87	Old & used motor vehicle other than covered in Sl Nos. 1 to 3	12%

Notes:

The above notification shall not apply, if the supplier of such goods has availed input tax credit as defined in clause (63) of section 2 of the Central Goods and Services Tax Act, 2017, CENVAT as defined in CENVAT Credit Rules, 2004 or the input tax credit of Value Added Tax or any other taxes paid, on such goods.

GST Compensation Cess shall not be applicable by virtue of Notification No. **1/2018 Compensation Cess** (Rate) dated 25th January 2018.

Central Government Vide Notification No. 37/2017 dated 13th October 2017 has notified that sale of second hand motor vehicle would be chargeable to tax@65% of rate applicable for original vehicle of same type, provided the supplier had purchased the said vehicle prior to 1st July 2017.

Valuation of old & used vehicle for the purpose of levy of GST

Notification No. 8/2018-Central Tax (Rate) dated 25-01-2018: GST shall be calculated on value of Margin of Supply in the following manner:

(i) **If depreciation under Income-tax Act availed:** In case of a registered person who has claimed depreciation under section 32 of the Income Tax Act, 1961 on the said goods, the value that represents the margin of the supplier shall be the difference between the consideration received for supply of such goods and the depreciated value of such goods as per IT Act, on the date of supply. Where the margin of supply is negative, it shall be ignore.

(ii) **In other cases:** The value that represents the margin of supplier shall be, the difference between the selling price and the purchase price and where such margin is negative, it shall be ignored.

Sale of used/seized vehicles supplied by Government

CBIC Vide **Circular No. 76/50/2018-GST dated 31-12-2018 has clarified** that intra-State and inter-State supply of used vehicles, seized and confiscated goods, old and used goods, waste and scrap made by the Central Government, State Government, Union territory or a local authority is a taxable supply under GST.

In case of used vehicles, supplied by Central Government, State Government, Union territory or a local authority to a registered person, the registered buyer shall be liable to pay GST under reverse charge (**Notification No. 36/2017-CT (Rate) dated 13-10-2017**).

In case of sale of used vehicles supplied by Government to a un-registered person, respective department of Central Government, State Government, Union territory or a local authority should obtain GST registration and pay GST thereon under forward charge.

Example: M/s True Value Car (P) Ltd., Delhi a registered person under GST deals in sale/purchase of used or second hand cars. During the month of October 2019, the company effected following intrastate transactions.

Particulars	Purchase Price (₹)	Sale Price (₹)
Honda Jazz	2,20,000	2,60,000
Maruti Dzire	2,60,000	3,30,000
Bolero	3,80,000	3,60,000
Hyundai I20	2,60,000	3,40,000

The Company had purchased Hyundai car from another Car dealer who had charged GST of ₹ 36,000. Accordingly, M/s True Value Car (P) Ltd. wish to avail ITC on the same. Determine GST liability of the company assuming rate of GST @ 18%.

Solution: In case of sale of old & used car, GST is payable on Margin (difference between sale price & purchase price). Where margin is negative, it shall be ignored. However, if ITC is availed, GST payable on transaction value (not on margin). In the present case, since the company wish to avail ITC on Hyundai car, GST payable on ₹ 3,40,000. So the Net tax liability shall be ₹ 45,000.

Value of supply of goods repossessed from a defaulting borrower

In the event of default in repayment of loan, normally the goods/assets are repossessed by the lender. In such cases, the value of supply in the hands on lender shall be calculated as under:

If the defaulting borrower is un-registered	If the defaulting borrower is Registered
Purchase price in the hands of such borrower reduced by 5% for every quarter or part thereof, between the date of purchase and the date of disposal by the person making such repossession.	The repossessing lender agency will discharge GST at the supply value without any reduction from actual/ notional purchase value.

(e) **Value of redeemable vouchers/stamps/coupons/tokens:** The value of a token, or a voucher, or a coupon, or a stamp (other than postage stamp) which is redeemable against a supply of goods or services or both shall be equal to the money value of the goods or services or both redeemable against such token, voucher, coupon, or stamp.

(f) **Value of services provided by notified service provider [Rule 32(7)]:** Value of taxable services provided by such class of service providers as may be notified by the Government on the recommendations of the Council as referred to in paragraph 2 of Schedule I between distinct persons as referred to in Section 25, where input tax credit is available, shall be deemed to be NIL.

Rule 33: Value of supply of services in case of a pure agent: A pure agent is one who, while making a supply to the recipient, also receives and incurs expenditure on some other supply on behalf of the recipient and claims reimbursement (as actual, without adding it to the value of his own supply) for such supplies from the recipient of the main supply. While the relationship between them (provider of service and recipient of service) in respect of the main service is on a principal-to-principal basis, the relationship between them in respect of other ancillary services is that of a pure agent.

As per the explanations appended to Rule 33 of the CGST Rules, 2017, the term "pure agent" means a person who:

(a) enters into a contractual agreement with the recipient of supply to act as his pure agent to incur expenditure or costs in the course of supply of goods or services or both;
(b) neither intends to hold nor holds any title to the goods or services or both so procured or supplied as pure agent of the recipient of supply;
(c) does not use for his own interest such goods or services so procured; and
(d) receives only the actual amount incurred to procure such goods or services in addition to the amount received for supply he provides on his own account.

The important thing to note is that a pure agent does not use the goods or services so procured for his own interest and this fact has to be determined from the terms of the contract.

The valuation rules provide that expenditure incurred as pure agent, will be excluded from the value of supply, and thus also from aggregate turnover, only & only if all the following conditions are satisfied, namely:

(i) the supplier acts as a pure agent of the recipient of the supply, when he makes the payment to the third party after authorization by such recipient;
(ii) the payment made by the pure agent on behalf of the recipient of supply has been separately indicated in the invoice issued by the pure agent to the recipient of service; and
(iii) the supplies procured by the pure agent from the third party as a pure agent of the recipient of supply are in addition to the services he supplies on his own account.

Some examples of pure agent are:

1. Port fees, port charges, custom duty, dock dues, transport charges etc. paid by Customs Broker on behalf of owner of goods.
2. Expenses incurred by C&F agent and reimbursed by principal such as freight, godown charges.
3. ROC filing fee paid by CA/CS on behalf of client for company formation.

Illustration 1: Mr. A of Kolkata approaches M/s XYZ & Associates, Chartered Accountants for incorporation of a Pvt. Ltd. Company. The professional fee for the said service was ₹ 25,000. Mr. A also authorizes the CA firm to incur all the expenditure on his behalf and deposit the entire fee with the Registrar of Companies (ROC), which he will reimburse the CA firm subsequently on production of fee receipts at actual.

M/s XYZ & Associates raised bill of ₹ 2,25,000 on Mr. A which includes fee of ₹ 2 lakhs paid to the ROC and ₹ 25,000 towards professional charges for rendering services, shown separately in the invoice. What is the value of supply for the purpose of levy of GST?

Solution: The fees charged by the Registrar of Companies for the registration of company is compulsorily levied on Mr. A. M/s XYZ & Associates is merely acting as a pure agent in the payment of those fees. Therefore, recovery of such expenses by M/s XYZ & Associates is a reimbursement and not part of the value of supply made to Mr. A. The taxable value in the instant case shall be ₹ 25,000 only, on which GST shall be levied.

Illustration 2: A Customs Broker issues an invoice for reimbursement of a few expenses and for consideration towards agency service rendered to an importer. The amounts charged by the Customs Broker are as below:

Component of Invoice	Amount (₹)
Agency fee	25,000
Travelling expenses & Hotel Bill	20,000
Customs Duty	75,000
Dock dues	5,000

Compute the value of supply on which GST shall be levied.

Solution: Agency fee and travelling/hotel expenses shall be added for determining the value of supply for the purpose of levy of GST whereas docks dues and the Customs Duty shall not be added to the value provided the conditions of pure agent are satisfied.

Illustration 3: Rural Electricity Corporation, New Delhi signed a MOU with NBCC Limited for undertaking a project for construction of PCC Road, Community halls and other social utility structures in Bihar under CSR Project. NBCC in turns execute the said works through contractors on open competitive bidding process. As per the terms of agreement, REC made advance payment of ₹ 9 crores to NBCC Ltd. prior to commencement of work, being cost of awarded value which is deposited in a separate bank account. Expenditure is meet out of the same. The agreement stipulates that, any surplus fund is refunded back to REC and in the event of actual cost exceeds, additional cost is reimbursed to NBCC Ltd. NBCC is also eligible to receive 8% of actual cost of the project as 'Agency Fee'. Actual cost incurred for the project was ₹ 10 crores & Agency fee paid to NBCC was ₹ 80 lakhs.

What is the GST implication & value of supply for the purpose of levy of GST?

Solution: The intention of the agreement is to engage NBCC Ltd. in the capacity of pure agent to incur expenditure on behalf of REC Ltd. and not to hold the title to goods and services procured in relation to this project nor does NBCC intends to use such goods or services for his own interest. Therefore, NBCC fulfills the criteria laid down for 'pure agent' in Rule 33 of Central Goods and Services Tax Rules, 2017.

As per the GST Act, such service shall be covered under SAC code 998339, i.e. project management services for construction projects, attracting GST rate at the rate 18%.

Value of supply for the purpose of levy of GST shall be ₹ 80 lakhs (8% of actual cost of the project).

Rule 34: Rate of exchange of currency, other than Indian rupees, for determination of value

Goods: Rate of exchange notified by CBIC under section 14 of the Customs Act, 1962 for the date of time of supply of such goods in terms of Section 12 of the CGST Act.

Services: Rate of exchange determined as per the GAAP for the date of time of supply of such services in terms of Section 13 of the CGST Act.

Rule 35: Value of supply inclusive of Integrated tax, Central tax, State tax, Union territory tax

In terms of Rule 35, where the value of supply is inclusive of GST, the tax amount shall be determined in the following manner,

Tax amount = (Value inclusive of taxes × GST tax rate in %)/(100 + sum of GST tax rates in %)

For example: If the value inclusive of tax is ₹ 100 and applicable GST tax rate is 18% then,

Tax amount = (100 × 18)/(100+18)= 1800/118=₹ 15.25.

Chapter 10

Input Tax Credit

10.1 WHAT IS INPUT TAX CREDIT

Un-interrupted and seamless chain of input tax credit (herein after referred to as, "ITC") is one of the key features of Goods and Services Tax. ITC is a mechanism to avoid cascading of taxes. Cascading of taxes, in simple language, is 'tax on tax'. Under the earlier system of taxation, credit of taxes being levied by Central Government was not available as set-off for payment of taxes levied by State Governments, and vice versa.

One of the most important features of the GST system is that the entire supply chain would be subject to GST to be levied by Central and State Government concurrently. As the tax charged by the Central or the State Governments would be part of the same tax regime, the credit of tax paid at every stage would be available as set-off for payment of tax at every subsequent stage.

Input tax in relation to a registered person, means the CGST, SGST, IGST or UTGST paid on purchase of goods or services or both (including tax paid under RCM). Input Tax Credit means claiming the credit of the GST paid on purchase of goods and services, which are used, for the furtherance of business.

Input tax credit in respect of GST compensation cess paid on inward supply of goods and services, shall be utilised only towards payment of cess on outward supply of goods and services leviable under section 8 of GST (Compensation to States) Act, 2017.

Input: Section 2(59)

Input means:

- any goods
- other than capital goods
- used or intended to be used by a supplier
- in the course or furtherance of business.

Input tax: Section 2(62)

Input tax in relation to a registered person, means the central tax, State tax, integrated tax or Union territory tax charged on any supply of goods or services or both *made to him* and includes:

(a) the integrated goods and services tax charged on import of goods;

(b) the tax payable under the provisions of sub-sections (3) and (4) of section 9;

(c) the tax payable under the provisions of sub-sections (3) and (4) of section 5 of the IGST Act;

(d) the tax payable under the provisions of sub-section (3) and sub-section (4) of section 9 of the respective State Goods and Services Tax Act; or

(e) the tax payable under the provisions of sub-section (3) and sub-section (4) of section 7 of the Union Territory Goods and Services Tax Act, but does not include the tax paid under the composition levy.

Input tax credit: Section 2(63)

"input tax credit" means credit of 'input tax' as defined in sub-section (62) of section 2.

Input tax credit includes tax paid on reverse charge basis. Once tax is paid under section 9(3) of CGST Act (or 5(3) of IGST Act), character of the payment remains GST and by operation of law, be treated as 'input tax'.

10.2 STATUTORY PROVISION

Chapter V of the CGST Act [Sections 16 to 21] & Chapter V: Input Tax Credit of the CGST Rules [Rules 36-45] prescribes the provisions relating to ITC. State GST laws also prescribe identical provisions in relation to ITC.

Provisions of ITC under CGST Act have also been made applicable to IGST Acts vide section 20 of the IGST Act, 2017.

Input Tax Credit (ITC) of GST Compensation Cess

As per proviso to section 11(2) of GST Compensation Cess Act, 2017 input tax credit in respect of cess on supply of goods and services leviable under section 8, shall be utilised only towards payment of said cess on supply of goods and services leviable under the said section.

The various provisions of Input tax credits are covered in following sections of Central Goods & Services Tax (CGST) Act, 2017.

Section 16	Eligibility and conditions for taking input tax credit
Section 17	Apportionment of credit and blocked credits
Section 18	Availability of credit in special circumstances
Section 19	Taking input tax credit in respect of inputs and capital goods sent for job work
Section 20	Manner of distribution of credit by Input Service Distributor
Section 21	Manner of recovery of credit distributed in excess
Section 42	Matching, reversal and reclaim of input tax credit (Omitted w.e.f. 1st October 2022 Vide N.No. 18/22-CT dated 28.09.2022)
Section 43	Matching, reversal and reclaim of reduction in output tax liability (Omitted w.e.f. 1st October 2022 Vide N.No. 18/22-CT dated 28.09.2022)
Section 43A	Procedure for furnishing return and availing input tax credit (Omitted w.e.f. 1st October 2022 Vide N.No. 18/22-CT dated 28.09.2022)

Relevant provision of CGST Rules, 2017.

Rule 36	Documentary requirements and conditions for claiming input tax credit
Rule 37	Reversal of input tax credit in the case of non-payment of consideration
Rule 37A	Reversal of input tax credit in the case of non-payment of tax by the supplier and re-availment thereof
Rule 38	Claim of credit by a banking company or a financial institution
Rule 39	Procedure for distribution of input tax credit by Input Service Distributor
Rule 40	Manner of claiming credit in special circumstances.
Rule 41	Transfer of credit on sale, merger, amalgamation, lease or transfer of a business
Rule 41A	Transfer of credit on obtaining separate registration for multiple places of business within a State or Union territory
Rule 42	Manner of determination of input tax credit in respect of inputs or input services and reversal thereof
Rule 43	Manner of determination of input tax credit in respect of capital goods and reversal thereof in certain cases
Rule 44	Manner of reversal of credit under special circumstances
Rule 44A	Manner of reversal of credit of Additional duty of Customs in respect of Gold dore bar.

10.3 ELIGIBILITY & CONDITIONS FOR TAKING INPUT TAX CREDIT [SECTION 16]

10.3.1 Eligibility for taking input tax credit (ITC): Section 16(1): Every registered taxable person (other than composition scheme dealer) shall be entitled to take credit of input tax charged on any supply of goods or services or both to him, which are used or intended to be used in the course, or furtherance of his business and the said amount shall be credited to the electronic credit ledger of such person.

Eligibility & Conditions for availing ITC

(1)	Must be a registered person under GST.
(2)	The goods or services or both should have been used or intended to be used in the course of or furtherance of his business.
(3)	Must be in possession of Tax invoice/debit note issued by registered supplier.
(4)	Must have received the goods or services or both.
(5)	Tax charges on such supply has been actually paid by the supplier to the Govt either through cash or through utilization of input tax credit admissible.
(6)	GST return should have filed by the supplier under Section 37 and details have been communicated to the recipient of such invoice or debit note.
(7)	The details of input tax credit in respect of the said supply communicated to such registered person under section 38 has not been restricted.
(8)	The recipient should have furnish return under section 39.
(9)	Where goods against an invoice are received in lots/installments, the recipient shall be entitled to take credit only upon receipt of last lot/installment.
(10)	The amount towards value of supply & tax there on should be paid within 180 days of date of issue of invoice.
(11)	The benefits of depreciation under IT Act, 1961 on GST component of capital goods/P&M should not have claimed.
(12)	Maximum time limit to avail ITC is earliest of (a) 30th November following the end of financial year to which such invoice or debit note pertain or (b) furnishing of the relevant Annual Return.

10.3.2 Conditions for availing input tax credit (ITC) [Section 16(2)]: The registered person will be entitled to avail input tax credit only if all the following four conditions are satisfied:

(a) he is in possession of an original tax invoice or debit note issued by a supplier registered under this Act, or such other tax paying documents (i.e. documents issued by ISD or bill of entry under customs Act) as may be prescribed.

(a) he has received the goods or services or both.

(ba) the details of input tax credit in respect of the said supply communicated to such registered person under section 38 has not been restricted.

Explanation: For the purposes of this clause, it shall be deemed that the registered person has received the goods or, as the case may be, services:

(i) where the goods are delivered by the supplier to a recipient or any other person on the direction of such registered person, whether acting as an agent or otherwise, before or during movement of goods, either by way of transfer of documents of title to goods or otherwise;

(ii) where the services are provided by the supplier to any person on the direction of and on account of such registered person.

(b) Subject to the provision of section 41, the tax charged in respect of such supply has been actually been paid either in cash or through utilization of ITC to the account of the appropriate Government; and

(c) he has furnished the return under section 39:

Provided that where the goods against an invoice are received in lots or installments, the registered taxable person shall be entitled to take credit upon receipt of the last lot or installment:

Provided where a recipient of services fails to pay the supplier within 180 days of issue of invoice, the amount availed by recipient as ITC, shall be paid with interest thereon. Interest will be paid @ 18% from the date of availing credit till the date when the payment is made to the supplier.

However, once the amount is paid the supplier, the recipient will be entitled to avail the credit again. In case part payment has been made, proportionate credit would be allowed.

Exceptions: This condition of payment of value of supply plus tax within 180 days does not apply in the following situations:

(a) Supplies on which tax is payable under reverse charge
(b) Deemed supplies without consideration
(c) Additions made to the value of supplies on account of suppliers liability, in relation to such supplies being incurred by the recipient of the supply.

Under situations (b) & (c) above, the value of supply is deemed to have been paid.

Rule 36: Documentary Requirement

(1) The input tax credit shall be availed by a registered person, including the Input Service Distributor, on the basis of any of the following documents.

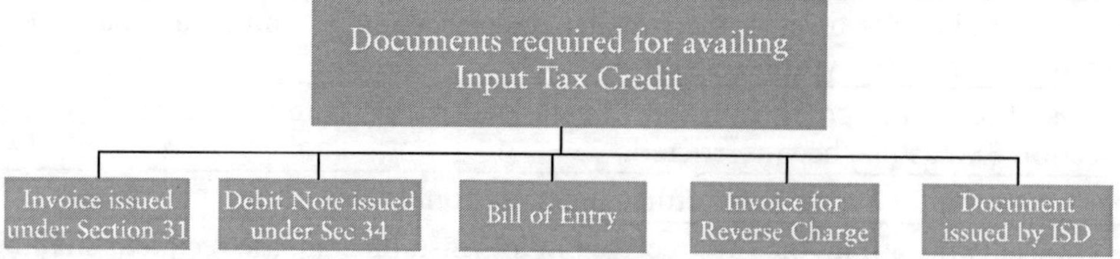

(2) Input tax credit shall be availed by a registered person only if all the applicable particulars as specified in the provisions of Chapter VI are contained in the above documents:
Provided that if the said document does not contain all the specified particulars but contains the details of the amount of tax charged, description of goods or services, total value of supply of goods or services or both, GSTIN of the supplier and recipient and place of supply in case of inter-State supply, input tax credit may be availed by such registered person.

(3) No input tax credit shall be availed by a registered person in respect of any tax that has been paid in pursuance of any order where any demand has been confirmed on account of any fraud, willful misstatement or suppression of facts.

(4) No input tax credit shall be availed by a registered person in respect of invoices or debit notes the details of which are required to be furnished under section 37(1) unless:

(a) the details of such invoices or debit notes have been furnished by the supplier in the statement of outward supplies in FORM GSTR-1 or using the invoice furnishing facility; and

(b) the details of input tax credit in respect of such invoices or debit notes have been communicated to the registered person in FORM GSTR-2B under rule 60 (7).

Example: Mr. X entered into a contract with M/s ABC Ltd. for supply of 1 MT Cement for ₹ 76,800 inclusive of GST of ₹ 16,800) in the month of Feb 2019. M/s ABC Ltd. raised the tax invoice on Mr. X for full amount in Feb 2019 but Cement was delivered in three (3) lots in the month of Feb, March & April 2019.

Though Mr. X paid full amount along with tax in Feb 2019, he can take ITC on the same only on receipt of last installments in the month of April 2019.

10.4 RESTRICTIONS ON AVAILMENT OF ITC

ITC was initially allowed to be availed on provisional basis based on documents such as Tax invoice, Debit note, bill of entry, etc.

Rule 36(4) was amended w.e.f. 9th Oct 2019 vide Circular No. 49/2019-Central Tax dated 09.10.2019, where restrictions on claiming ITC on provisional basis was imposed (availed during period 9th Oct. 2019 to 31st Dec. 2019).

As per said rule, Input tax credit to be availed by a registered person in respect of invoices or debit notes, the details of which have not been uploaded by the suppliers under section 37(1), shall not exceed 20% [10 per cent w.e.f. 01.01.2020] of the eligible credit available in respect of invoices or debit notes the details of which have been uploaded by the suppliers under section 37(1).

The taxpayer may have to ascertain the same from his auto populated FORM GSTR 2A as available on the due date of filing of FORM GSTR-1 under section 37(1).

The said restriction was further curtailed to 10% w.e.f. 01.01.2020 and to 5% w.e.f. 01.01.2021.

Rule 36(4) was amended further w.e.f. 1st January 2022 as under: No input tax credit shall be availed by a registered person in respect of invoices or debit notes the details of which are required to be furnished under Section 37(1) unless:

(a) the details of such invoices or debit notes have been furnished by the supplier in the statement of outward supplies in FORM GSTR-1 or using the invoice furnishing facility; and

(b) the details of such invoices or debit notes have been communicated to the registered person in FORM GSTR-2B under rule 60 (7).

> **Notification No. 18/2022-Central Tax dated 28.09.2022:** The CGST Amendment Act, 2022 which is effective from 1st October 2022, has inserted a New clause (ba) to Section 16(2) to allow ITC only if the details of input tax credit in respect of the said supply communicated to the recipient under Section 38 has not been restricted.
>
> So, GSTR-2B (Part A & Part B) is now the document for determining ITC eligibility and ineligibility.

Sections 42, 43, and 43A of the CGST Act are being omitted so as to do away with:

- The concept of "claim" of eligible input tax credit on a "provisional" basis and subsequent matching, reversal and reclaim of such credit.
- Concept of matching, reversal and reclaim of reduction in output tax liability.
- Two-way communication in return filing.

If depreciation claimed on tax component, ITC not allowed [Section 16(3)]

Where the registered person has claimed depreciation on the tax component of the cost of capital goods and plant and machinery under the provisions of the Income-tax Act, 1961, the input tax credit on the said tax component shall not be allowed.

10.5 TIME LIMIT FOR AVAILING INPUT TAX CREDIT (ITC) [Section 16(4)]

A registered person shall not be entitled to take input tax credit in respect of any invoice or debit note for supply of goods or services or both after 30th November following the end of financial year (FY) to which invoice pertains or date of filing of relevant annual return, whichever is earlier.

Example: Last date of availing ITC of Invoice received in FY 2022-23 is earlier of:

(a) 30th November 2023

(b) Filing Annual Return of FY 2022-23

> **Notification No. 18/2022-Central Tax dated 28.09.2022**
> The CGST Amendment Act, 2022 which is effective from 1st October 2022 has amended Section 16 (4) as under. The word *"due date of furnishing of the return under section 39 for the month of September"* has been substituted with *"30th November"*.

Notes:

(1) The time limit u/s 16(4) does not apply to claim for re-availing of credit that has been reversed earlier.

(2) In case of person covered under Section 18(1) (a), (b), (c) and (d), the time limit to avail ITC is one year from the date of issue of tax invoice relating to such supply.

Example 1: Mr. X of Patna, a registered person under GST purchased material worth ₹ 50,000 against a tax invoice NO.TI/105/2021-22 dated 3rd March 2022 from Mr. Y of Delhi, a registered person on which IGST of ₹ 9000 was paid. Mr. X filed the annual return (GSTR 9) of FY 2021-22 in Dec 2022. Therefore, the time limit of availing ITC on said purchase is 30th November 2022.

10.6 APPORTIONMENT OF CREDIT & BLOCKED CREDIT [SECTION 17]

ITC in the following cases to be allowed to the extent attributable to business purpose:

1. Where goods and/or services are used partly for the purpose of any business and partly for other purposes. [Sec 17(1)]
2. Where goods and/or services are used partly for effecting taxable supplies including zero-rated supplies and partly for effecting exempt supplies. [Section 17(2)]

ITC on the basis of usage in business

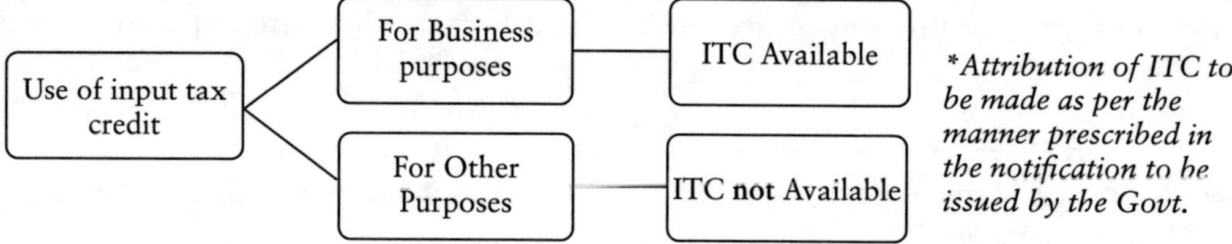

In both the above cases, full ITC on inward supply cannot be taken, only proportionate ITC is allowed.

Restriction of ITC [Section 17(1) and 17(2)]

ITC is restricted in proportion of the use of the goods and/or services:

(i) in the taxable and/or zero-rated part of the supply

(ii) for business purposes.

As per Section 17(3), the value of exempt supply shall be such, as may be prescribed, and shall include:

(a) Supply on which recipient is liable to pay tax on reverse charge basis

(b) Transaction in securities

(c) Sale of land and

(d) Sale of building (when entire consideration received after issuance of completion certificate).

> The expression "value of exempt supply" shall not include the value of activities or transactions specified in Schedule III, except those specified in paragraph 5 of the said Schedule.

When input tax credit available/not available

<table>
<tr><th>Section</th><th>Use of input goods/services by registered person</th><th>Input tax credit available/not available</th></tr>
<tr><td rowspan="2">17(1)</td><td>Used for business purposes</td><td>ITC available</td></tr>
<tr><td>Used for other purposes</td><td>ITC not available</td></tr>
<tr><td rowspan="5">17(2)/17(3)</td><td>Used for taxable supplies</td><td rowspan="3">ITC available</td></tr>
<tr><td>Used for zero-rated supplies (Export/supply to SEZ)</td></tr>
<tr><td>Used for activities/transaction specified in Schedule III(except for sale of land & building (para 5) and supply of warehouse goods to any person before clearance for home consumption (para 8)) (As per CGST amendment Act 2018/2023)</td></tr>
<tr><td>Used for non-taxable supplies (i.e. alcoholic liquor for human consumption, petroleum products such as Crude, ATF, Diesel, Petrol etc.)</td><td rowspan="2">ITC not available
ITC attributable to such supplies need to be reversed.</td></tr>
<tr><td>Used for exempt/nil rated supplies (exempt supplies shall cover supplies charged to tax under RCM, transaction in securities, sale of land & building after issue of completion of certificate, etc.)
Here exempt supplies excludes supply of service having place of supply in Nepal or Bhutan against payment in INR, supply of service by way of accepting deposit, extending loans or advances where consideration is either interest or discounts except by Banking/financial/NBFC.
Value of land & building shall be taken as adopted for paying stamp duty.
Value of securities shall be taken as 1% of the sale value of such security.</td></tr>
</table>

Example: Mr. X is a registered dealer under GST, whose main business is dealing in petrol/diesel. He is also providing some taxable services under same registration. Whether Input tax credit (ITC) of GST paid on consumables purchased for providing services will be available?

Ans. Input tax credit of GST paid on procurement of goods or services, which are used in the course, or furtherance of business would be available. If person were engaged in supply of taxable as well as non-taxable goods or services, then credit of input taxes would be available proportionately as per Section 17 of CGST Act. However, input used exclusively for supply of taxable goods or services would be available in full if it is identified at invoice level.

10.6.1 Apportionment of Credit by Banking and Financial Institution [Section 17(4)]: A banking or financial institution shall avail input tax credit in following manner:

(1) It will avail every month an amount calculated in accordance with Section 17(2).

(2) It will avail every month, an amount equal to fifty per cent of the eligible input tax credit on inputs, capital goods and input services in that month and the rest shall lapse.

(3) The option once exercised shall not be withdrawn during the remaining part of the financial year.

(4) The restriction of fifty per cent shall not apply to the tax paid on supplies made by one registered person to another registered person having the same Permanent Account Number (PAN).

10.6.2 Methodology for Apportionment of ITC [Rule 42 of the CGST Rules, 2017]: The input tax credit in respect of inputs or input services, which attract the provisions of Sec 17(1) or 17(2) shall be attributed to the purposes of business or for effecting taxable supplies and reversal of ineligible credit shall be made in the manner provided in Rule 42 of the CGST Rules 2017.

Particulars	Reference
Total input tax on input goods/services	T
Input tax attributable to inputs intended to be used exclusively for non-business purposes	T1
Input tax attributable exclusively for making exempt supplies	T2
Input tax pertaining to ineligible items (Section 17(5)-Blocked credit)	T3
Input tax credit credited to Electronic credit ledger C1 = T–(T1+T2+T3)	C1

Particulars	Reference
Input tax credit attributable to inputs intended to be used exclusively for effecting taxable supplies (including zero-rated supplies)	T4
Common credit (C1–T4) (input tax credit left after adjustment of above)	C2
Aggregate value of exempt supplies made during the tax period	E
Total turnover in the state of the registered person during the tax period	F
Input tax credit attributable towards exempt supplies (E/F × C2)	D1
ITC attributable to non-business purposes (5% of C-2)	D2
Eligible common credit (C2–D1 +D2)	C3
Total ITC eligible (T4 + C3)	G

Notes:

(1) T1, T2, T3, T4 shall be determined by the registered person at invoice level.

(2) If turnover of tax period not available, then last tax period for which turnover available should be considered.

(3) The value of exempt supplies & total turnover shall exclude amount of any duties or tax levied under central excise/VAT on tobacco, crude oil, ATF, Natural Gas, Petrol, diesel, Alcoholic liquor for human consumption.

(4) Compute C3 separately for ITC of IGST, CGST, SGST/UTGST.

(5) Protocol for utilization of ITC should be followed as provided in Section 49A of CGST Act.

Methodology for apportionment of Credits of Capital goods and reversal thereof (Rule, 43 of the CGST Rules 2017)

If capital goods are acquired by a registered person for used or intended to be used exclusively for effecting supplies other than exempted supplies but including zero-rated supplies, he can avail ITC on whole amount. However, if the capital goods are used for non-business purposes or for the purpose of making exempt supplies, reversal of credit is required. The mode of reversal is given in Rule 43 of CGST rules.

Particulars	Reference
Input tax credit on capital goods used exclusively for non-business purposes	T1
Input tax credit on capital goods used exclusively for effecting exempt supplies	T2
Input tax credit on capital goods used exclusively for taxable supplies	T3
Input tax credit on capital goods (whose residual life remain in beginning of tax period)	Tr
Aggregate value of exempt supplies made during the tax period	E
Total turnover of the registered person during the tax period	F
Common credit attributable to exempt supplies (E/F × Tr)	Te

10.6.3 Blocked-Credits [Section 17(5)]: ITC of tax paid on almost every inputs and input services used for supply of taxable goods or services or both is allowed under GST except on list of items provided below:

List of Blocked Credits

Sl No.	Particulars
a	Motor vehicles for transportation of persons having approved seating capacity of not more than thirteen persons (including the driver), except when they are used for making the following taxable supplies, namely: (A) further supply of such motor vehicles; or (B) transportation of passengers; or (C) imparting training on driving such motor vehicles
aa	Vessels and aircraft except when they are used: (i) for making the following taxable supplies, namely: (A) further supply of such vessels or aircraft; or (B) transportation of passengers; or (C) imparting training on navigating such vessels; or (D) imparting training on flying such aircraft (ii) for transportation of goods

Sl No.	Particulars
ab	Services of general insurance, servicing, repair and maintenance in so far as they relate to motor vehicles, vessels or aircraft referred to in clause (a) or clause (aa) above: *Provided that the input tax credit in respect of such services shall be available:* (i) where the motor vehicles, vessels or aircraft referred to in clause (a) or clause (aa) are used for the purposes specified therein; (ii) where received by a taxable person engaged (I) in the manufacture of such motor vehicles, vessels or aircraft; or (II) in the supply of general insurance services in respect of such motor vehicles, vessels or aircraft insured by him.
b	The following supply of goods or services or both provided in relation to: (i) food and beverages, outdoor catering, beauty treatment, health services, cosmetic and plastic surgery, leasing, renting or hiring of motor vehicles, vessels or aircraft referred to in clause (a) or clause (aa) except when used for the purposes specified therein, life insurance and health insurance: Provided that the input tax credit in respect of such goods or services or both shall be available where an inward supply of such goods or services or both is used by a registered person for making an outward taxable supply of the same category of goods or services or both or as an element of a taxable composite or mixed supply; (ii) membership of a club, health and fitness centre; and (iii) travel benefits extended to employees on vacation such as leave or home travel concession: Provided that the input tax credit in respect of such goods or services or both shall be available, where it is obligatory for an employer to provide the same to its employees under any law for the time being in force.
c	Works contract services when supplied for construction of an immovable property (other than plant and machinery) except where it is an input service for further supply of works contract service (e.g. a contractor receiving works contract services from sub-contractor, which is to be further supplied to client, i.e. contractee is eligible for ITC).
d	Goods or services or both received by a taxable person for construction of an immovable property (other than plant or machinery) on his own account including when such goods or services or both are used in the course or furtherance of business.
	Explanation: For the purposes of clauses (c) and (d), the expression “construction” includes re-construction, renovation, additions or alterations or repairs, to the extent of capitalization, to the said immovable property.
e	Goods and/or services on which tax has been paid under Section 10 (composition scheme).
f	Inward supplies received by a non-resident taxable person except on goods imported by him.
fa	Goods or services or both received by a taxable person, which are used or intended to be used for activities relating to his obligations under corporate social responsibility (CSR) referred to in section 135 of the Companies Act, 2013.
g	Goods or services or both used for personal consumption.
h	Goods lost, stolen, destroyed, written off or disposed of by way of gift or free samples and
i	Any tax paid under Section 74, 129 & 130 (i.e. on account of fraud, suppression, mis-declaration, etc.)
	The expression “plant and machinery” means apparatus, equipment, and machinery fixed to earth by foundation or structural support that are used for making outward supply of goods or services or both and includes such foundation and structural supports but excludes: (i) land, building or any other civil structures; (ii) telecommunication towers; and (iii) pipelines laid outside the factory premises.

10.6.4 Restrictions and availability of ITC on goods & services

Nature of Supply	Blocked credit/denial of ITC	Allowable ITC
ITC on purchase of motor vehicle with seating capacity up to thirteen persons (including the driver)	If used by the company for official use of its employee	If used by a company for renting out purposes for transportation of passengers

Nature of Supply	Blocked credit/denial of ITC	Allowable ITC
ITC on purchase of Vessels & Aircraft	If used by a company for official use of its CEO/Top management	If used by a Aviation school for training purpose
ITC on general insurance of motor car	If motor car used for official purpose	If motor car used for renting purpose
ITC on membership fee paid for club, health and fitness centre	If it is not obligatory for an employer to provide to its employees under any law	Where it is obligatory for an employer to provide the same to its employees under any law
ITC on works contract services (other than P&M)	When received for own use as a consumer	When received for further supply to a client
ITC on inputs, input service & capital goods used in relation to free sample.	When distributed as free sample	When supplied under "Buy one get one offer" or "buy more, save more" offer

10.7 CREDIT IN SPECIAL CIRCUMSTANCES (SECTION 18)

Entitlement of ITC at the time of Registration/Voluntary registration/switching over to normal scheme from composition [Section 18(1) and 18(2)].

(1) Availability of ITC [Section 18(1)]

(a) A person who has applied for registration within 30 days of becoming liable for registration is entitled to ITC of input tax in respect of goods held in stock (inputs, semi-finished or finished goods) on the day immediately preceding the date from which he becomes liable to pay tax.

Example 1: A person becomes liable to pay tax on 1st August 2019 and has obtained registration on 15th August 2019. Such person is eligible for input tax credit on inputs held in stock as on 31st July 2019.

> ITC of input tax in respect of only inputs (not capital goods) on the day immediately preceding the date from which he becomes liable to pay tax is allowed when a person get registration for the first time.

(b) A person who has taken voluntary registration under section 23(3) of the CGST Act, 2017 is entitled to ITC of input tax in respect of goods held in stock (inputs as such and inputs contained in semi-finished or finished goods) on the day, immediately preceding the date of registration.

Example 2: Mr. X applies for voluntary registration on 5th June 2019 and obtained registration on 22nd June 2019. Mr. X is eligible for input tax credit on inputs held in stock as on 21st June 2019.

(c) A person switching over to normal scheme from composition scheme under Section 10 is entitled to ITC in respect of goods held in stock (inputs as such and inputs contained in semi-finished or finished goods) and capital goods on the day immediately preceding the date from which he becomes liable to pay tax as normal taxpayer.

Example 3: Mr. Y, a registered person was paying tax under composition rate up to 30th July 2019. However, w.e.f. 31st July 2019, Mr. Y becomes liable to pay tax under regular scheme. Mr. is eligible for input tax credit on inputs held in stock as on closure of business hours on 30th July 2019.

(d) Where an exempt supplier of goods or services or both by a registered person become taxable, the person making such supplies shall be entitled to take ITC in respect of goods held in stock (inputs as such and inputs contained in semi-finished or finished goods) relatable to exempt supplies. He shall also be entitled to take credit on capital goods used exclusively for such exempt supply, subject to reductions for the earlier usage as prescribed in the rules.

(2) Time limit for availing ITC [Section 18(2)]: ITC, in respect of cases mentioned in Section 18(1), is to be availed within one year from the date of issue of tax invoice by the supplier.

(3) Availability of ITC in case of change in constitution on account of sale, merger, demerger, amalgamation, lease or transfer of the business [Section 18(3)]: In case of change of constitution of a registered person on account of sale, merger, demerger, death of proprietor, etc., with the specific provision for transfer of liabilities, the said registered person shall be allowed to transfer the input tax credit, which remains unutilized in his electronic credit ledger to such sold, merged, demerged, amalgamated, leased or transferred business.

The manner of transfer of ITC is provided in Rule 41 of CGST Rule

A registered person shall, in the event of sale, merger, de-merger, amalgamation, lease or transfer or change in the ownership of business for any reason, furnish the details of sale, merger, de-merger, amalgamation, lease or transfer of business, in FORM GST ITC-02, electronically on the common portal along with a request for transfer of unutilized input tax credit lying in his electronic credit ledger to the transferee.

In the case of demerger, the input tax credit shall be apportioned in the ratio of the value of assets of the new units as specified in the demerger scheme.

The transferor shall also submit a copy of a certificate issued by a practicing chartered accountant or cost accountant certifying that the sale, merger, de-merger, amalgamation, lease or transfer of business has been done with a specific provision or the transfer of liabilities.

The transferee shall, on the common portal, accept the details so furnished by the transferor and, upon such acceptance, the un-utilized credit specified in FORM GST ITC-02 shall be credited to his electronic credit ledger.

(4) Availability of ITC in case of switching over from normal scheme to composition scheme or taxable supply become exempt supply [Section 18(4)]: A person switching over from normal scheme to composition scheme under section 10 or where a taxable supply become exempt, the ITC availed in respect of goods held in stock (inputs as such and inputs contained in semi-finished or finished goods) as well as capital goods will have to be paid.

Rule 44 mandates credit reversal when a registered person switches from regular scheme to composition scheme or goods and services supplied by him become wholly exempt, pay an amount by debiting electronic cash ledger/credit ledger, equivalent to input tax credit of:

(a) Inputs held in stock
(b) Inputs contained in semi-finished or finished goods held in stock and
(c) Capital goods

on the day immediately preceding the date of such switch over. Balance of input tax credit lying in the electronic credit ledger, after payment of the above said amount shall lapse.

(5) ITC in case of sale of capital goods or plant and machinery [Section 18(6)]: In case of supply of capital goods or plant and machinery, on which ITC is taken, an amount equivalent to ITC availed minus the reduction as prescribed in rules (5% for every quarter or part thereof) shall have to be paid. In case the tax on transaction value of the supply is more, the same would have to be paid.

10.8 INPUT TAX CREDIT ON GOODS SENT FOR JOB WORK [SECTION 19]

Job work means undertaking any treatment or process by a person on the goods belonging to another registered taxable person. The person who is treating or processing the goods belonging to other person is called "job worker" and the person to whom the goods belongs is called "Principal".

(1) Entitlement of credit on inputs: The principal can take credit of input tax on inputs sent to job-worker subject to fulfillment of the following conditions:

(a) The inputs, after completion of job-work, are received back by the principal within one year of their being sent out.
(b) In case of direct supply, the period of one year shall be reckoned from the date the job worker receives such inputs.
(c) The credit of inputs can be taken even if inputs are sent directly to job-worker's premises without bringing it to principal's place of business.
(d) If the inputs are not received back within one year, it shall be deemed that such inputs had been supplied by principal to the job worker on the day when the said inputs were sent out.

(2) Entitlement to credit on capital goods: The principal can take credit of input tax on capital goods sent to job-worker subject to the fulfillment of the following conditions:

(a) The capital goods, after completion of job-work, are received back by him within three years of their being sent out.
(b) The principal can take credit of capital goods even if such capital goods are sent directly to job-worker's place without bringing to principal's place of business.
(c) If the capital goods are not received back within three years, it shall be deemed that such capital goods had been supplied by principal to the job worker on the day when the said capital goods were sent out.

(d) Procedures listed in respect of inputs under Rule 45 of the Input Tax Credit Rules will apply to capital goods also.

Rule 45 of ITC Rules provides the following:

(i) The principal shall issue a challan for transfer of inputs to the job-worker including where they are sent directly (to maintain paper trail of transaction).

(ii) Challan issued by principal to the job worker shall contain all details as required in respect of an invoice in Rule 55 (of Invoice Rules). Reference may be made to Chapter VII relating to Tax Invoice, credit & debit notes for the particulars to be included in the document & for detailed description.

(iii) All challans issued in respect of inputs sent to job-worker and those received back are to be reported in GSTR-1.

(iv) In case of non-receipt of the inputs within the time prescribed, the challan issued will be deemed to be invoice for the implied supply of inputs.

10.9 MANNER OF DISTRIBUTION OF CREDIT BY INPUT SERVICE DISTRIBUTORS (ISD) [SECTION 20]

As per Section 2(61), "Input Service Distributor" means an office of the supplier of goods or services or both which receives tax invoices issued under section 31 towards the receipt of input services and issues a prescribed document for the purposes of distributing the credit of central tax, State tax, integrated tax or Union territory tax paid on the said services to a supplier of taxable goods or services or both having the same Permanent Account Number as that of the said office.

There are certain common expenditure incurred by a business/company for all the units across the country having same PAN but different GSTIN. The common expenditure is distributed among all the consuming units proportionately. SD mechanism enable proportionate distribution of credit of input services amongst all the consuming units. An ISD cannot accept any invoice on which tax is to be discharged under Reverse Charge Mechanism. This is because the ISD mechanism is only to facilitate distribution of credit of taxes paid. The ISD itself cannot discharge any tax liability & remit tax to Government account. If ISD wants to receive supply falls under RCM, then in that case ISD has to separately register as normal taxpayer.

It is pertinent to note that ISD mechanism is meant only for distributing the credit on common invoices pertaining to INPUT SERVICES and not goods (inputs or capital goods). Separate registration as ISD is mandatory and there is no threshold limit for registration. A company may have multiple ISD registration like for marketing division, security division, facility management division (FMD), etc. An ISD is required to file monthly return GSTR 6 within 13 days after the end of the month. An ISD is not required to file Annual return.

Inter-branch supply of services should not be misinterpreted as a distribution by ISD. It is pertinent to mention that ISD cannot be an office that does any supply of its own but must be one that merely collects invoice for services and issues prescribed document for its distribution.

The procedure for distribution of input tax credit by ISD has been prescribed in Section 20 of CGST Act, 2017 read with rule 39 of CGST Rule, 2017. Input tax credit (of services) is distributed to supplier of goods or services or both of the same entity having same PAN.

Procedural aspect of distribution of credit by ISD

(1) The input tax credit available for distribution in a month shall be distributed in the same month and the details thereof shall be furnished in FORM GSTR 6.

(2) The Input Service Distributor shall issue an ISD invoice, as prescribed in rule 54(1), clearly indicating in such invoice that it is issued only for distribution of input tax credit to each of the recipient of credit.

(3) Credit distributed should not exceed the credit available for distribution.

(4) Tax paid on input services used by a particular location (registered as supplier), is to be distributed only to that location.

(5) Credit of tax paid on input service used by more than one location who are operational is to be distributed to all of them based on the pro rata basis of turnover of each location in a State to aggregate turnover of all such locations who have used such services.

(6) Both ineligible & eligible ITC are distributed separately.

(7) ITC of CGST, SGST/UTGST and IGST are distributed separately.

(8) The Input Service Distributor shall issue an ISD credit note for reduction in credit.

Example: M/s A Ltd. as an ISD has input service credit of ₹ 25 lakhs used by more than one locations, to be distributed among recipients locations X, Y and Z. The turnover of X, Y & Z in the preceding financial year, is

₹ 5 crores, ₹ 3 crores and ₹ 2 crores respectively. The credit of ₹ 5 lakhs pertain to input service received only by Z. Distribute the ITC available with the Input Service Distributors.

Ans. The credit attributable to X, Y, Z are as follows:

Particulars	Amount (₹)
Total credit available for distribution	₹ 25 lakhs
Credit of service used only by Z location	₹ 5 lakhs
Common Credit available for distribution for all units	₹ 20 lakhs
Credit distributable to X 5 crores/10 crores * 20 lakhs	₹ 10 lakhs
Credit distributable to Y 3 crores/10 crores * 20 lakhs	₹ 6 lakhs
Credit distributable to Z 2 crores/10 crores * 20 lakhs = 4 lakhs Credit directly attributable to Z = 5 lakhs	₹ 9 lakhs

10.10 RECOVERY OF CREDIT DISTRIBUTED IN EXCESS (SECTION 21)

The CGST Act clearly lays down that credit distribution is not 'to self', that is, a registered taxable person cannot distribute credit to himself. Each registered person being a distinct person u/s 25, must distribute to another registered taxable person but having the same PAN to whom the credit is most accurately attributable.

Excess credit distributed to one or more recipient of credit in contravention of ISD provision under Section 20 is recoverable from the recipient (not from ISD) of such credit along with Interest as per the provision contained in Section 73 or 74.

10.11 ORDER OF UTILISATION OF ITC

ITC credited to electronic credit ledger can be utilized for payment of output tax liability.

Input tax credit (ITC) of CGST and SGST/UTGST will be available throughout the supply chain, but cross utilization of credit of CGST and SGST/UTGST will not be possible.

In terms of Section 49(5) set off of IGST, CGST & SGST can be done in following chronological order:

The protocol to avail and utilize the credit of taxes are as follows (until 31 Jan 2019):

CREDIT OF	TO BE UTILISED FIRST FOR	MAY BE UTILISED FURTHER FOR PAYMENT OF
CGST	CGST	IGST
SGST/UTGST	SGST/UTGST	IGST
IGST	IGST	CGST, then SGST/UTGST

Section 49 A and Section 49 B was inserted vide CGST Amendment Act, 2018 which provides for utilization of ITC as follows:

CREDIT OF	TO BE UTILISED FIRST FOR	MAY BE UTILISED FURTHER FOR PAYMENT OF
IGST	IGST	CGST/SGST/UTGST (in any order)
CGST	CGST	IGST
SGST/UTGST	SGST/UTGST	IGST

Rule 88A, order of utilization of Input Tax Credit

(Inserted vide N.No. 16/2019-Central Tax dated 29th March 2019)

The Central Government vide Circular No. 98/17/2019-GST dated 23rd April 2019 has clarified regarding the manner of utilization of ITC.

Available ITC of account of IGST will first be utilized for payment of IGST & the order of utilization of IGST against CGST/SGST can be in any order.

Example: A taxable person has following output tax liability & un-utilized ITC during a month. Compute the net tax payable during the month after utilizing ITC.

Particulars	IGST	CGST	SGST
Output tax liability	100	100	100
Available ITC	200	50	50

Up to 31st March 2019

Particulars	IGST	CGST	SGST
ITC utilized	100	50	50
Balance ITC	100	-	-
Unpaid output liability	-	50	50
Utilization of IGST	(100)	50	50
Balance ITC	-	-	-
Net liability to be paid by cash	-	-	-

After 1st April 2019

Particulars	IGST	CGST	SGST
ITC utilized	100	100	-
Balance ITC	-	50	50
Unpaid output liability		-	50
Utilization of ITC	-	-	-
Balance ITC	-	50	-
Net liability to be paid by cash	-	-	50

Credit of	To be adjusted with
IGST	(1) IGST
	(2) CGST
	(3) SGST/UTGST
CGST	(4) CGST
	(5) IGST
SGST/UTGST	(6) SGST/UTGST
	(7) IGST

Notes:

(1) RCM tax liability can be discharge only through payment by cash and not by adjusting against input tax credit available. However, the ITC can be utilized against output tax liability.

(2) GST is payable on advance payment received even if supply of services are not completed but ITC can be availed only upon receipt of such services by the recipient.

(3) No ITC on goods lost, stolen, destroyed or disposed by way of gift or free sample.

(4) The time limit to pay value of supply with taxes is 180 days to avail ITC.

Manner of calculating interest on delayed payment of tax [Rule 88B]

Notification No. 14/2022-Central Tax dated 05.07.2022

(1) In case, where the supplies made during a tax period are declared by the registered person in the return for the said period and the said return is furnished after the due date in accordance with provisions of section 39, except where such return is furnished after commencement of any proceedings under section 73 or section 74 in respect of the said period, the interest on tax payable in respect of such supplies shall be calculated on the portion of tax which is paid by debiting the electronic cash ledger, for the period of delay in filing the said return beyond the due date, at such rate as may be notified under section 50 (1).

(2) In all other cases, where interest is payable in accordance with section 50 (1), the interest shall be calculated on the amount of tax which remains unpaid, for the period starting from the date on which such tax was due to be paid till the date such tax is paid, at such rate as may be notified under section 50 (1).

(3) In case, where interest is payable on the amount of input tax credit wrongly availed and utilized in accordance with section 50(3), the interest shall be calculated on the amount of input tax credit wrongly availed and utilized, for the period starting from the date of utilization of such wrongly availed input tax credit till the date of reversal of such credit or payment of tax in respect of such amount, at such rate as may be notified under said sub-section of section 50 (3).

Chapter 11

Registration

11.1 STATUTORY PROVISION

In any tax system, registration is the most fundamental requirement for identification of taxpayers ensuring tax compliance in the economy. Registration of any business entity under the GST Law implies obtaining a unique number from the concerned tax authorities for the purpose of collecting tax on behalf of the government and to avail Input Tax Credit for the taxes on his inward supplies. Without registration, a person can neither collect tax from his customers nor claim any input Tax Credit of tax paid by him.

The registration under GST is PAN based and State specific. Every taxable person (subject to threshold limit) is required to obtain a PAN-based registration in each of such State or Union territory from where he effects taxable supply. Registration under GST is not tax specific, which means there is single registration for all the taxes i.e. CGST, SGST/UTGST, IGST and Cess.

Sections 22 to 30 in Chapter VI of the Central Goods and Services Tax Act, 2017 contain the provisions governing registration. In addition, Chapter-III of CGST Rules, 2017 contains the procedural aspect associated with registration. State GST laws also prescribe identical provisions in relation to Registration.

Provisions of registration under CGST Act have also been made applicable to IGST Act vide section 20 of the IGST Act, 2017.

Section 22 prescribes certain conditions, subject to fulfillment of which, registration must be obtained. However, Section 24 enlists certain categories of persons who shall compulsorily obtain the registration, whether or not the conditions prescribed under Section 22 are triggered in such cases.

Section	Description
Section 22	Person liable for Registration
Section 23	Person not liable for Registration
Section 24	Compulsory Registration
Section 25	Procedure of Registration

In GST registration, the supplier is allotted an unique 15-digit alphanumeric number called "GSTIN" (GST Identification Number) begin with state code, and a certificate of registration incorporating therein GSTIN is made available to the applicant on the GSTN common portal. A business entity having more than one place of business/office in a State may obtain separate registration for each of its office or place of business. It is pertinent to mention that registration is required 'in' the State 'from which' taxable supplies are made.

For the purposes of obtaining registration, it is important to identify the 'origin' of supply even though GST is a 'destination' based tax. Tax goes to the destination State but registration is required in the origin-State. In case of "works contract" service, which is immovable in nature, place of supply is where the immovable property is located. Place of Supply (as determined from IGST Act) provides the 'destination' and this is not relevant for registration. The location of Supplier is relevant for registration.

Every person requiring registration under GST is required to make an online application in the GST common portal i.e. www.gst.gov.in in FORM GST REG-01 within 30 days of becoming liable for registration. There is no fee or any charges for registration. In case of failure to obtain registration a penalty of ₹ 10,000 or the amount of tax involved, whichever is greater shall be imposed u/s Section 122(1).

In case a person wants to make inter-state outward supply of goods (except handicraft goods/goods sent for job work), registration under GST is mandatory irrespective of turnover. In case of inter-state outward supply of services, registration is required only if, the aggregate turnover exceeds threshold limit of ₹ 20 lakhs/10 lakhs, depending upon normal state or special category state.

However, if a person is exclusively engaged in supply of exempted goods or services/exclusively engaged in supply of goods or services which are covered under RCM (i.e. recipient is liable to pay tax), registration under GST not required, irrespective of turnover.

11.2 THRESHOLD LIMIT FOR REGISTRATION UNDER GST

The threshold limit applicable for registration varies depending on the following factors:

(1) States/Union Territories from where the supply is taking place.

(2) Supply undertaken by the supplier i.e. whether exclusively supplier of goods or supplier of both goods and services or exclusively supplier of services.

Types of Supply	Threshold limit for Registration (₹)
Intra/Interstate supply of services	20 lakhs/10 lakhs as the case may be
Inter-state outward supply of goods	Nil (except handicraft goods/goods sent for job work). It means registration mandatory irrespective of turnover.
Intra state supply of goods & services	20 lakhs/10 lakhs as the case may be
Exclusively engaged in supply of goods	40 lakhs*

*Notification No. 10/2019-Central Tax dated 07.03.2019 (w.e.f. 1st April 2019).

For Special category of states, i.e. Manipur, Mizoram, Nagaland & Tripura, the threshold limit for registration is ₹ 10 lakhs.

Type of supplier	Intra-state supply		Inter-state Supply (Aggregate turnover in a FY)
	Up to 31st March 2019 (Aggregate turnover in a FY)	w.e.f. 1st April 2019 (Aggregate turnover in a FY)	
Supplier of Services	20 lakhs	20 lakhs	20 lakhs
Supplier of goods (exclusively engaged in the business of supply of goods, not even any small or exempted service provided)	20 lakhs	40 lakhs*	Nil
Mixed supply (Goods plus Services)	20 lakhs/10 lakhs as the case may be	20 lakhs/10 lakhs as the case may be	Nil

For some specified category of person such as CTP, NRTP, ISD, TDS/TCS deductor, etc. there are no threshold limit.

Notes:

(1) Registration under GST mandatory for a normal taxpayer, if the "aggregate turnover" on all India basis against single PAN exceeds above threshold limit in a financial year.

(2) The threshold limit is ₹ 10 lakh (in place of ₹ 20 lakhs) for taxable person who conduct business in Special Category States as specified in Article 279A(4)(g) of the Constitution, other than the State of Jammu and Kashmir, Arunachal Pradesh, Assam, Himachal Pradesh, Meghalaya, Sikkim and Uttarakhand.

(3) With the amendment in explanation (iii) to Sec 22, as per CGST (Amendment) Act, 2018 which came into operation w.e.f. 1st Feb 2019, only Manipur, Mizoram, Nagaland and Tripura are covered under Special Category States for the limited purpose of GST provision, for whom threshold limit of registration is ₹ 10 lakhs.

(4) As per notification No. 10/2019-Central Tax, dated 07.03.2019, with effect from 1st April 2019, person who is exclusively engaged in supply of goods & whose aggregate turnover in the FY does not exceed ₹ 40 lakhs are exempted from the requirement of registration except for following:

<table>
<tr><th colspan="2">Particulars</th><th>States</th><th>Threshold limit of registration (who are exclusively engaged in supply of taxable goods) (Amount)</th></tr>
<tr><td colspan="2" rowspan="2">State other than Special category states
Telangana</td><td>Puducherry</td><td>₹ 20 lakhs</td></tr>
<tr><td>₹ 20 lakhs</td><td></td></tr>
<tr><td rowspan="11">Special category state as per Constitution</td><td rowspan="4">Special category state as per Sec 22 of CGST Act</td><td>Manipur</td><td>₹ 10 lakhs</td></tr>
<tr><td>Mizoram</td><td>₹ 10 lakhs</td></tr>
<tr><td>Nagaland</td><td>₹ 10 lakhs</td></tr>
<tr><td>Tripura</td><td>₹ 10 lakhs</td></tr>
<tr><td rowspan="7">Others</td><td>Arunachal Pradesh</td><td>₹ 20 lakhs</td></tr>
<tr><td>Meghalaya</td><td>₹ 20 lakhs</td></tr>
<tr><td>Sikkim</td><td>₹ 20 lakhs</td></tr>
<tr><td>Uttarakhand</td><td>₹ 20 lakhs</td></tr>
<tr><td>Assam</td><td>₹ 40 lakhs</td></tr>
<tr><td>Himachal Pradesh</td><td>₹ 40 lakhs</td></tr>
<tr><td>Jammu & Kashmir</td><td>₹ 40 lakhs</td></tr>
</table>

(5) Person making inter-state supply of goods (except handicraft goods).

(6) A person who supplies on behalf of some other taxable person (i.e. an Agent of some Principal), E-commerce operators who are notified as liable for GST payment under Section 9(5) of the CGST Act, Input Service Distributors (ISD), Casual Taxable Person (CTP), NRTP & person liable to pay GST under Reverse Charge (RCM) u/s 9(3) of CGST Act or u/s 5(3) of IGST Act, registration is mandatory & there are no threshold exemption limit.

(7) Persons engaged only in making taxable supplies where total tax is liable to be paid by the recipient on reverse charge basis are not required to be registered under GST irrespective of turnover.

(8) Casual taxable person making taxable supplies of handicraft goods is not required to obtained registration (Notification No. 38/2017-Central Tax dated 13.10.2017).

(9) Persons effecting inter-State taxable supplies of handicraft goods are exempted from registration where the aggregate value of supplies on pan-India basis does not exceed 20 lakh in a year (10 lakh for Special Category States) w.e.f. 14.09.2017. *Notification No. 8/2017-Integrated Tax dated 14.09.2017.*

(10) In case of supplier where the consideration with respect to supplies made on electronic commerce is not collected by the electronic commerce operator, then in such case, such supplier will be eligible to claim the threshold benefit for registration.

(11) Supply of goods by a registered job-worker, after completion of job work, shall be treated as the supply of goods by the "principal" referred to in section 143. The value of such goods shall not be included in the aggregate turnover of the registered job worker.

(12) Persons who are required to deduct tax at source u/s 51 or collect tax u/s 52 need mandatory registration without threshold exemption, in addition to normal registration u/s 22.

(13) Charitable organizations engaged exclusively in charitable activities are exempted from obtaining registration irrespective of turnover.

(14) Once registration is taken, the assesse shall mandatorily require to collect and pay tax to the government irrespective of turnover.

11.3 NEED AND ADVANTAGES OF REGISTRATION

Registration will confer the following advantages to a taxable person:

(a) legally recognized as supplier of goods or services.

(b) legally authorized to collect taxes from his customers and pass on the credit of the taxes paid on the goods or services supplied to the purchasers/recipients.

(c) can claim Input Tax Credit of taxes paid and can utilize the same for payment of taxes due on outward supply of goods or services.

(d) seamless flow of Input Tax Credit from suppliers to recipients at the national level.

(e) permitted to make interstate supply of goods.

11.4 FORMAT OF GSTIN

Registration Type	Digit														
	1	2	3	4	5	6	7	8	9	10	11	12	13	14	15
Regular Registration	State Code		PAN										No of Registration in the state	Code for Regular Registration	Check Digit
Example	0	2	A	A	A	C	N	0	1	4	9	C	1-9 or A to Z	Z	1-9 or A to Z

Nature of Registration

- The registration under GST is PAN based and State specific.
- One GSTIN (Goods & Services Tax Identification Number) per state against one PAN (Multiple registration can also be taken as per CGST Amendment Act, 2018 w.e.f. 1st Feb 2019).
- It is 15-digit alphanumeric code begin with state code.
- First two digits—State Code-Next 10 characters-PAN-next two digits-entity codes—the last digit is check sum random character.
- Registration under GST is not tax specific, which means there is single registration for all the taxes, i.e. CGST, SGST/UTGST, IGST and Cess.
- A business entity having its branches in multiple States will require separate registration in each such state.
- A person having multiple places of business in a State or Union territory may be granted a separate registration for each such place of business, subject to such conditions as may be prescribed. [GST (Amendment) Act, 2018]
- Where an entity is having more than one branch in a state, it requires single registration in that state. In such case one place/branch to be declared as principal place of business and other branches as additional place of business.
- However, a business entity having separate business verticals (as defined in section 2 (18) of the CGST Act, 2017) in a state may obtain separate registration for each of its business verticals.
- GST Amendment Act, 2018 applicable from 1st day of February 2019 as per Notification No. 02/2019-Central Tax dated 29th January 2019. The concept of business vertical is gone. A taxable person may obtain separate registration for each unit/office in a state.
- Registration certificate under GST is not transferrable. In case of change in constitution/PAN of the taxable person, fresh registration under GST required.

11.5 PERSONS LIABLE FOR REGISTRATION (SECTION 22)

(1) Every supplier effecting the taxable supplies shall be liable to be registered under the Act "in" the State "from which" he makes a taxable supply of Goods or Services or both if turnover exceeds threshold limit.

Registration is not required 'in' the State 'to' which taxable supplies are made, even though GST is a destination-based tax.

Registration is required if the "**aggregate turnover**" of a taxable person in a financial year exceeds ₹ 20 lakhs. This threshold limit is ₹ 10 lakhs, if a taxable person conducts his business in any of the special category states as specified in Article 279A(4)(g) of the Constitution of India, other than the State of Jammu and Kashmir, Arunachal Pradesh, Assam, Himachal Pradesh, Meghalaya, Sikkim and Uttarakhand.

[Provided further that the Government may, at the request of a special category State and on the recommendations of the Council, enhance the aggregate turnover referred to in the first proviso from ten lakh rupees to such amount, not exceeding twenty lakh rupees and subject to such conditions and limitations, as may be so notified.]

(2) Every person who, on the day immediately preceding the appointed day, is registered or holds a license under an earlier law, such as Excise/VAT/Service Tax etc. shall be liable to be registered under this Act with effect from the appointed day.

(3) Where a business carried on by a taxable person registered under this Act is transferred, whether on account of succession or otherwise, to another person as a going concern, the transferee or the successor, as the case may be, shall be liable to be registered with effect from the date of such transfer or succession.

(4) In a case of transfer pursuant to sanction of a scheme or an arrangement for amalgamation or, as the case may be, demerger of two or more companies pursuant to an order of a High Court/Tribunal, the transferee shall be liable for fresh registration under GST with effect from the date on which the Registrar of Companies issues a certificate of incorporation.

The expression "aggregate turnover" shall include all supplies (taxable/exempt/export of goods/services/ interstate supplies) made by the taxable person, whether on his own account or made on behalf of all his principals.

Exemption from Registration not applicable to specified Job workers

The Central Government vide N No. 02/2019-IT dated 29th January 2019 has provided that the job workers who are involved in making supply of services in relation to Live poultry i.e. fowls of the species Gallus domesticus, ducks, geese, turkeys and guinea fowls are compulsorily required to take registration.

11.6 PERSONS NOT LIABLE FOR REGISTRATION (SECTION 23)

(1) (a) Person who is supplying ONLY exempt goods and/or service and not liable to tax or wholly exempt from tax under this Act or under the Integrated Goods and Services Tax Act.

(b) Agriculturist for supply out of agricultural land.

The main criterion to remain out of the purview of registration is to exclusively engage in the supply of exempted goods or services or both. The term exclusive indicates engaging in only those supplies, which are exempted. If a supplier is supplying both exempted and non-exempted goods and/or services, then this provision is not applicable and he is required to take registration under Section 22.

As per Section 2 (7) agriculturist means an individual or HUF who undertakes cultivation of land:

(a) By own labour or

(b) By the labour of family, or

(c) By servants on wages payable in cash or kind or by hired labour under personal supervision or the personal supervision of any member of the family.

Thus, an agriculturist is not liable for registration only to the extent of supply of produce out of cultivation of land. If an agriculturist undertakes supplies, which are not linked to the cultivation of land, he will fall within the provisions of Section 22 and may have to take registration in respect of such supplies, if the "aggregate turnover" exceed threshold limit.

(2) Persons making inter-state supplies of "taxable services" and having an "aggregate turnover" less than threshold limit.

(3) Person engaged in making taxable supplies, GST on which is payable by the recipient under Reverse charge.

If a person is engaged only is making taxable supply of goods or services, GST on which is liable to be paid on reverse charge basis by the recipient, registration is not required (even if aggregate turnover is more than the threshold limit of ₹ 20 lakh/₹ 10 lakh).

(4) A job worker (with turnover less than ₹ 20 lakhs/₹ 10 lakhs as the case may be) has been exempted from registration, who are making inter-State taxable supply of job work service to a registered person as long as the goods move under the cover of an e-way bill, irrespective of the value of the consignment.

(5) Persons making supplies of services, other than supplies specified under section 9(5) of the CGST Act through an electronic commerce operator who is required to collect tax at source under section 52 and having an aggregate turnover, to be computed on all India basis, not exceeding threshold limit. (N.N. 65/2017-Central Tax dated 15th Nov 2017)

(6) Person who is engaged exclusively in intra-state supply of goods and whose aggregate turnover in the financial year does not exceed ₹ 40 lakhs (w.e.f. 1st April 2019), registration not mandatory.

Notification No. 10/2019-Central Tax dated 07.03.2019
(w.e.f. 1st April 2019)

Any person, who is engaged in exclusive supply of goods and whose aggregate turnover in the financial year does not exceed ₹ 40 lakhs, except:

(a) persons required to take compulsory registration under section 24 of CGST Act;

(b) persons engaged in making supplies of specified goods (ice cream, pan masala, tobacco product, aerated water);

(c) persons engaged in making intra-State supplies in the States of Arunachal Pradesh, Manipur, Meghalaya, Mizoram, Nagaland, Puducherry, Sikkim, Telangana, Tripura, Uttarakhand; and

(d) persons who have opted for voluntary registration under section 25(3) of CGST Act & who intend to continue with their registration under the said Act.

11.7 COMPULSORY REGISTRATION IN CERTAIN CASES [SECTION 24]

Generally, the liability to register under GST arises when a person is a supplier within the meaning of the term, and also his "aggregate turnover" in the financial year is above the exemption threshold of ₹ 20 lakh/₹ 10 lakhs as the case may be.

However, the GST law enlists certain categories of suppliers who are required to get compulsory registration irrespective of their turnover, i.e. even if it is below the threshold exemption.

The following categories of taxable persons shall get registered compulsorily under GST.

(i) persons making inter-State taxable supply of goods other than notified goods.
(ii) casual taxable persons making taxable supply;
(iii) persons who are required to pay tax under reverse charge;
(iv) persons who are required to pay tax under section 9(5) (Electronic commerce operator);
(v) non-resident taxable persons making taxable supply;
(vi) persons who are required to deduct tax under section 51 (Tax Deduction at Source);
(vii) persons who supply goods or services or both on behalf of other registered taxable persons whether as an agent or otherwise;
(viii) input service distributor (ISD);
(ix) persons who supply goods, other than supplies specified under section 9(5), through such electronic commerce operator who is required to collect tax at source under section 52 [w.e.f. 1st October 2023, persons whose aggregate turnover does not exceeds threshold limit are allowed to make intra-state supply of goods through E-COM operator based on PAN based enrolment number, Ref Cir 34/2023 dated 31st July 2023];
(x) every electronic commerce operator who required to collect tax at source u/s 52;
(xi) every person supplying online information and database access or retrieval services from a place outside India to a person in India, other than a registered taxable person;
(xii) The Central Government vide Notification No. 02/2019-Integrated Tax dated 29th January 2019 has notified that the job workers who are involved in making supply of services in relation to live poultry i.e. fowls of the species Gallus domesticus, ducks, geese, turkeys and guinea fowls are compulsorily required to take registration;
(xiii) Every person having a unit in a Special Economic Zone or being a Special Economic Zone developer or supplying goods/services to SEZ or exporter; and
(xiv) such other person or class of persons as may be notified by the Central Government or a State Government on the recommendations of the Council.

In respect of supplies by some notified agencies of United Nations Organizations, multinational financial institutions and other organizations, a unique identification number (UIN) is issued.

Mr. X is engaged in wholesale & retail trading of medicines in the state of Maharashtra. His aggregate turnover during the FY 2019-20 is ₹ 9 lakhs intra-state supply & ₹ 1 lakhs inter-state supply. Is he required to obtained registration under GST?

Answer. Person making inter-state taxable supply of goods is required to obtain registration under GST compulsorily, irrespective of the quantum of aggregate turnover.

Exemption from Registration
Notification No. 34/2023-Central Tax dated 31st July 2023, w.e.f. 1st October 2023
Persons making intra-state supply of goods through E-COM operators are exempted from registration under GST, if aggregate turnover is below threshold limit.

11.8 PROCEDURE OF REGISTRATION [SECTION 25]

Section 25 read with rule 8 to 26 of CGST Rules, 2017 provides a detailed road map on the procedural aspects of registration. Section 25(1) says that every person who is liable to be registered under Section 22 or Section 24 shall apply for registration within thirty days from the date he becomes liable for registration in every such State or Union territory in which he is so liable to be registered. Casual taxable person (CTP) or a non-resident taxable person (NRTP) shall have to obtain the registration at least five days prior to the commencement of business.

GST Registration Rules

Rules	Description
Rule 8	Application for registration
Rule 9	Verification of application and approval
Rule 10	Issue of Registration Certificate
Rule 11	Separate registration for multiple places of business within a State or a Union territory
Rule 12	Grant of registration to persons required to deduct tax at source or to collect tax at source
Rule 13	Grant of registration to non-resident taxable person
Rule 14	Grant of registration to a person supplying online information and data base access or retrieval services from a place outside India to a non-taxable online recipient
Rule 15	Extension in period of operation by casual taxable person and non-resident taxable person
Rule 16	Suo moto registration
Rule 17	Assignment of Unique Identity Number to certain special entities
Rule 18	Display of registration certificate and Goods and Services Tax Identification Number on the name board
Rule 19	Amendment of registration
Rule 20	Application for Cancellation of Registration
Rule 21	Registration to be cancelled in certain cases
Rule 21A	Suspension of registration
Rule 22	Cancellation of Registration
Rule 23	Revocation of cancellation of registration
Rule 24	Migration of persons registered under the existing law
Rule 25	Physical verification of business premises in certain cases
Rule 26	Method of authentication

A total of 31 forms/formats have been prescribed in the GST registration rules. For every process in the registration chain such as application for registration, acknowledgment, query, rejection, registration certificate, show cause notice for cancellation, reply, cancellation, amendment, field visit report, etc., there are standard formats. This will make the process uniform all over the country. The decision-making process will also be fast. Strict time lines have been stipulated for completion of different stages of registration process.

Procedure of Registration

Every person liable to get registered and person seeking voluntary registration shall, before applying for registration, declare his Permanent Account Number (PAN), mobile number, e-mail address, State/UT in **Part A** of FORM GST REG-01 on GST Common Portal www.gst.gov.in, either directly or through a Facilitation Centre notified by the Commissioner.

1. PAN, mobile number and email address are validated
2. PAN validated online from CBDT database

3. Mobile number and email verified through one-time password (OTP) sent to it
4. Aadhar Number of Authorized signatories

Temporary Reference Number (TRN) is generated and communicated to the applicant on the validated mobile number and e-mail address. Using TRN, applicant shall electronically submit application in **Part B** of application form, along with specified documents at the Common Portal. On submission of said application, an acknowledgement in the prescribed form shall be issued to the applicant electronically & the form shall be forwarded to the proper officer.

Documents required while filing application for registration under GST

Valid Email Valid Mobile No. PAN card of the Individual, HUF, Partnership firm, Company, AoP or other person Proof of constitution of business (except for Individual/Proprietorship & HUF) Proof of Authorized signatories (PAN card, Photo, Board resolution, authorization letter) Proof of Principal place of business (Property tax receipt/Electricity bill/Rent or lease agreement/Rent receipt/ legal ownership document) Proof of bank accounts details (First page of pass book/bank statement/cancelled cheque) Aadhar Number of Authorized signatories **Notes:** • Maximum file size for photograph allowed is 100 KB and File Type must be JPEG only. • Other documents should be of JPEG/PDF type having maximum size of 1 MB each.

Aadhar authentication while applying for registration under GST

[Section 25(6)(A), (B), (C), (D) read with Rules 8 and 9 of CGST Rules]

Notification No. 19/2020-Central Tax dated 23.03.2020

As per Rule 8(4A), the applicant shall, while submitting an application for registration under GST, with effect from 01.04.2020, undergo authentication of Aadhaar number for grant of registration

Exemption from Aadhar authentication

Notification No. 17/2020-Central Tax dated 23.03.2020

Aadhar authentication shall not apply to a person who is not a citizen of India or to a class of persons other than the following class of persons, namely:

(a) Individual;
(b) authorized signatory of all types;
(c) Managing and Authorized partner; and
(d) Karta of a Hindu undivided family.

Verification Procedures for Registration [Rule 9 of CGST Rules 2017]

Rule 9(1)	The application shall be forwarded to the proper officer who shall examine the **application and the accompanying documents**. If the same is found to be in order, approve the grant of registration to the applicant **within three working days** from the date of submission of application.
Proviso to Rule 9	In case, a person fails to undergo Aadhaar the registration shall be granted only after **physical verification of the principal place of business** in the presence of the said person, not later than sixty days from the date of application.
Rule 9(2)	If the application is found to be deficient or proper officer requires clarification, he may issue a notice to the applicant electronically in form GST REG-03, within three working days from the date of submission of application. The applicant shall furnish such clarification, information, or documents sought electronically, in form GST REG-04, **within seven working days** from the date of receipt of such notice.

Rule 9(3)	If the proper officer is satisfied with the clarification or documents furnished by the applicant, he may approve the **grant of registration to the applicant within seven working days,** from the date of receipt of such clarification or information or documents.
Rule 9(4)	If no reply is furnished by the applicant or where the proper officer is not satisfied with the clarification, information or documents furnished, he shall, *for reasons to be recorded in writing*, reject the application for registration under GST and inform the applicant electronically in form GST REG-05.
Rule 9(5)	Deemed registration—The application for grant of registration shall be deemed to have been approved, if the proper officer fails to take any action: (a) within three working days from the date of submission of application, or (b) within seven working days from the date of receipt of clarification, information or documents furnished by the applicant.

An individual should undergo authentication of Aadhar no. in order to be eligible for registration. However, if Aadhar no. is not assigned to any individual, he shall be offered alternate and viable means of identification in the manner specified in rule 9 [Notification No. 18/2020 dated 23-03-2020].

Effective Date of Registration [Rule 10]

Where an applicant submits application for registration	Effective date of registration is
within 30 days from the date he becomes liable to registration	the date on which he becomes liable to registration
after 30 days from the date he becomes liable to registration	date of grant of registration
when applied for voluntary registration	date of grant of registration

11.8.1 Statutory Provisions of Registration

(1) Every person who is liable to be registered under section 22 or section 24 shall apply for registration in every such State or Union territory in which he is so liable. An application in FORM GST REG-01 has to be submitted online through the GST common portal (GSTN) within thirty days from the date when liability to register arose, there are no fee.

(2) A person seeking registration under this Act shall be granted a single registration in a State or Union territory.

However, w.e.f. 1st Feb 2019, proviso to Section 25(2) read with Rule 11 provides that, any person having multiple places of business within a State or a Union territory may apply for separate registration for each such place of business *(multiple registrations allowed)*.

(3) A person, though not liable to be registered under Section 22, may get himself registered voluntarily, and once registered all the provisions of GST Act, shall apply to such person.

(4) A person who has obtained or is required to obtain more than one registration, whether in one State or Union territory or more than one State or Union territory shall, in respect of each such registration, be treated as distinct persons for the purposes of this Act.

(5) Where a person who has obtained or is required to obtain registration in a State or Union territory in respect of an establishment, has an establishment in another State or Union territory, then such establishments shall be treated as establishments of distinct persons for the purposes of this Act.

(6) Every person shall have a Permanent Account Number issued under the Income Tax Act, 1961 in order to be eligible for grant of registration. A person required to deduct tax under section 51 may have, in lieu of a PAN, a TAN issued under the Income Tax Act in order to be eligible for grant of registration.

(6A) Existing registered persons will have to get verified through Aadhaar number in a phase manner—inserted vide Finance (No. 2) Act, 2019 w.e.f. 01.01.2020.

(6B) In phase 1, Aadhaar number is made mandatory for fresh registration inserted vide Finance (No. 2) Act, 2019 w.e.f. 01.01.2020.

(6C) For other than an individual (partnership firm, company, trust, HUF, AOP, etc.) the authentication will be by verification of Aadhaar number of partner, director, trustee, authorized representative, managing committee member or Karta of HUF-inserted vide Finance (No. 2) Act, 2019 w.e.f. 01.01.2020. Notification No. 19/2020-Central Tax dated 23.03.2020 applicable w.e.f. 01.04.2020.

(7) The Casual Taxable Person (CTP) and Non-Resident Taxable Persons (NRTP) need to apply for registration at least five days prior to the commencement of the business. Registration is granted to them or period of operation is extended only after they make advance deposit of the estimated net tax liability.

(8) Where a person who is liable to be registered under this Act fails to obtain registration, the proper officer may proceed to register such person in such manner as may be prescribed.

The registration or the Unique Identity Number shall be granted or rejected after due verification in such manner and within such period as may be prescribed.

A certificate of registration shall be made available in GST common portal in FORM GST REG-06 showing the principal place of business and additional place or places of business with GSTIN (15 Alphanumeric characters).

11.8.2 Registration for United Nations or Consulate or Embassy

Any specialized agency of the United Nations Organization or any Multilateral Financial Institution and Organization notified under the United Nations (Privileges and Immunities) Act, 1947 (46 of 1947), Consulate or Embassy of foreign countries and any other person or class of persons as may be notified by the Commissioner, shall obtain a Unique Identity Number. The registration shall be for the purpose(s) notified, including seeking to claim refund of taxes paid by them, on the notified supplies of goods and/or services received by them. The supplier supplying to these organization is expected to mention the UID on the invoices and treat such supplies as business-to-business (B2B) supplies.

11.8.3 Deemed Registration [Section 26]

(1) **Issuance of Registration by Proper Authority:** The registration or Unique Identity Number (UID) is granted/issued with effective dates. The registration or UID is granted or rejected after due verification and within the time prescribed. A certificate of registration shall also be issued in prescribed form with effective date as may be prescribed. A registration or a UID shall be deemed to have been granted after the period prescribed (under rule 9) if no deficiency has been communicated to the applicant within that period. Also, the grant of registration or the Unique Identity Number under the CGST Act/SGST Act shall be deemed to be a grant of registration or the Unique Identity Number under the SGST/CGST Act, provided that the application for registration or the UID has not been rejected/no deficiency has been communicated to applicant by the proper officer under SGST/CGST Act within the time specified.

(2) **Rejection of Application for Registration:** The proper officer shall not reject the application for registration or the Unique Identification Number (UID) without giving a notice to show cause and without giving the person a reasonable opportunity of being heard. This implies that the decision to reject an application under this section shall be only after following the principles of Natural justice and after a due process of law by issuance of an order. It should also be noted that any rejection of application for registration or the Unique Identity Number under the CGST Act/SGST Act shall be deemed to be a rejection of application for registration under the SGST Act/CGST Act respectively as the case may be.

11.8.4 Goods and Services Tax (GST) Forms for Registration

Sr. No.	FORM Number	Description
1.	GST REG-01	Application for registration
2.	GST REG-02	Acknowledgement
3.	GST REG-03	Notice seeking additional information regarding Registration/Amendments/Cancellation
4.	GST REG-04	Furnishing clarification sought in GST
5.	GST REG-05	Order for rejection of application for Registration/Amendment/Cancellation/Revocation of Cancellation
6.	GST REG-06	Issued Registration Certificate
7.	GST REG-07	Application for Registration as TDS or TCS
8.	GST REG-08	Order for Cancellation of Application for Registration as TDS/TCS
9.	GST REG-09	Application for Registration by Non-Resident Taxable Person
10.	GST REG-10	Application for registration of person supplying online information and data base access or retrieval services from a place outside India to a person in India, other than a registered person

Sr. No.	FORM Number	Description
11.	GST REG-11	Application for extension in period of causal taxable person or nonresident taxable person
12.	GST REG-12	Temporary Suo Moto Registration
13.	GST REG-13	Grant of Unique Identity Number (UIN) to UN Bodies/Embassies/others Application Form
14.	GST REG-14	Application for Amendment in Registration Particulars (for all types of registered persons)
15.	GST REG-15	Amendment Order
16.	GST REG-16	Application for Cancellation of Registration
17.	GST REG-17	Show Cause Notice for Cancellation of Registration
18.	GST REG-18	Reply to Show Cause Notice issued for Cancellation of Registration
19.	GST REG-19	Order for Cancellation of Registration
20.	GST REG-20	Order for Dropping the proceedings for cancellation of registration
21.	GST REG-21	Application for Revocation of Cancellation of Registration
22.	GST REG-22	Order for revocation of cancellation of registration
23.	GST REG-23	Show Cause Notice for rejection of application for revocation of cancellation of registration
24.	GST REG-24	Reply to the notice for rejection of application for revocation of cancellation of registration
25.	GST REG-25	Provisional Registration Certificate
26.	GST REG-26	Application for Enrolment of Existing Taxpayer
27.	GST REG-27	Show Cause Notice for cancellation of provisional registration
28.	GST REG-28	Order of cancellation of provisional registration
29.	GST REG-29	Application for cancellation of provisional registration
30.	GST REG-30	Field Visit Report Form
31.	GST REG-31	Intimation of suspension and notice for cancellation of registration

11.8.5 Grant of Registration to Person Required to Deduct TDS/TCS [Rule 12]

Any person required to deduct tax in accordance with the provisions of section 51 or a person required to collect tax at source in accordance with the provisions of section 52 shall electronically submit an application, duly signed or verified through electronic verification code, in FORM GST REG-07 for the grant of registration through the common portal.

Even if a person is registered under Sec 22 or Sec 24 of CGST Act, 2017, separate registration as tax deductor/ tax collector is required under GST.

11.8.6 Grant of Registration to a Person Supplying OIDAR [Rule 14]

Any person supplying online information and database access or retrieval services from a place outside India to a non-taxable online recipient in India shall electronically submit an application for registration under GST, duly signed or verified through electronic verification code through GST common portal.

The supplier (or intermediary) of online information and database access or retrieval services (OIDAR) shall, for payment of integrated tax, take a single registration under the Simplified Registration Scheme in Form GST REG-10 & registration shall be granted in FORM GST REG-06. The supplier shall take registration at Principal Commissioner of Central Tax, Bengaluru West who has been the designated for grant registration in such cases vide Notification No. 2/2017-Integrated Tax dated 19 June 2017.

Physical verification of business premises in certain cases [Rule 25]

(1) Where the proper officer is satisfied that the physical verification of the place of business of a person is required after the grant of registration, he may get such verification of the place of business done and the verification report along with the other documents, including photographs, shall be uploaded in FORM GST REG-30 on the common portal within a period of fifteen working days following the date of such verification.

(2) Where the physical verification of the place of business of a person is required before the grant of registration in the circumstances specified in the proviso to sub-rule (1) of rule 9, the proper officer shall get such verification of the place of business done and the verification report along with the other documents, including photographs, shall be uploaded in FORM GST REG-30 on the common portal at least five working days prior to the completion of the time period specified in the said proviso.

11.8.7 Special Provision Relating to CTP & NRTP [Section 27]

Casual Taxable Person: Section 2(20): "Casual taxable person" means a person who occasionally undertakes transactions involving supply of goods or services or both in the course or furtherance of business, whether as principal, agent or in any other capacity, in a State/UT where he has no fixed place of business.

Non-Resident Taxable Person: Section 2(77): "Non-Resident taxable person" means any person who occasionally undertakes transactions involving supply of goods or services or both, whether as principal or agent or in any other capacity, but who has no fixed place of business or residence in India.

A Casual taxable person (CTP) is one who has a registered business in some State in India, but wants to effect supplies from some other State in which he is not having any fixed place of business. Such person needs to register in the State from where he seeks to supply as a Casual taxable person.

A Non-Resident taxable person (NRTP) is one who is a foreigner and occasionally wants to affect taxable supplies from any State in India, and for that he needs GST registration. GST law prescribes special procedure for registration, as also for extension of the operation period of such Casual or Non-Resident taxable persons.

(A) Both CTP and NRTP have to compulsorily get registered under GST irrespective of the threshold limit, at least five days prior to commencement of business.

(B) As per Section 25(6), every person must have a PAN to be eligible for registration.

While Income Tax PAN is the basis of GST registration, the registration to a non-resident taxable person (NRTP) is given on the basis of his valid passport (in case of individual) or the Tax Identification Number (TAN) issued by the respective country (if it is incorporated business entity).

NRTP has to submit a self-attested copy of his valid passport along with the application signed by his authorized signatory who is an Indian Resident having valid PAN. However, in case of a business entity incorporated or established outside India, the application for registration shall be submitted along with its tax identification number or unique number on the basis of which the entity is identified by the Government of that country or it's PAN, if available.

Application will be submitted by NRTP in **FORM GST REG-09**, whereas CTP will submit the application for registration in the normal form for application for registration i.e. **FORM GST REG-01** and the registration of CTP will be a PAN-based registration.

Validity of Registration: The certificate of registration issued to a "casual taxable person" or a "non-resident taxable person" shall be valid for a period specified in the application for registration or ninety days from the effective date of registration, whichever is earlier, extendable by proper officer for further period of maximum 90 days at the request of taxable person.

Advance deposit of tax: A casual taxable person or a non-resident taxable person while seeking registration shall make an advance deposit of tax in an amount equivalent to the estimated tax liability.

Where any extension of time is sought, such taxable person shall deposit an additional amount of tax equal to the estimated tax liability for the period for which the extension is sought.

Such advance deposit shall be credited to the electronic cash ledger of and utilized in the manner provided under section 44 (Payment of Tax, interest, penalty and other amounts) of the Act.

Since the nature of the activity carried out by a casual taxable person and non-resident taxable person are temporary as compared to a regular taxable person, additional safeguards have been placed to ensure that the registration is granted for a limited period and the tax liability is recovered in advance.

Registration is granted to a CTP or period of operation is extended only after they make advance deposit of the estimated net tax liability.

Casual taxable person (CTP)	Non-resident taxable person (NRTP)
Defined in Section 2(20) of the CGST Act, 2017	Defined in Section 2(77) of the CGST Act, 2017
Occasionally undertake transaction in supply of goods or services or both in a state or territory where he has no fixed place of business	A foreigner who occasionally undertake transaction in supply of goods or services or both, may or may not having a fixed place of business in India
Require PAN under Income Tax Act, 1961 for registration under GST	PAN not required for registration under GST
Same application form as normal taxable person for applying registration under GST (GST REG-01)	Separate application form for NRTP for applying registration under GST (GST REG-09)
Have to apply for registration at least five days in advance before making any supply	Have to apply for registration at least five days in advance before making any supply
Has to undertake transaction in the course or furtherance of business	Business test is absent in the definition
Has a fixed place of business in India	No fixed place of business or residence in India
Has to pay advance deposit of tax equivalent to the estimated Net tax liability	Has to pay advance deposit of tax equivalent to the estimated Net tax liability
Certificate of registration initially valid for maximum period of 90 days.	Certificate of registration initially valid for maximum period of 90 days.

11.8.8 Registration of "Corporate Debtor Under Insolvency and Bankruptcy Code, 2016 (31 of 2016)"

[Notification No. 11/2020-Central Tax, dated 21-03-2020]: Corporate debtors under the provisions of the Insolvency and Bankruptcy Code, 2016 (31 of 2016), undergoing the corporate insolvency resolution process and the management of whose affairs are being undertaken by interim resolution professionals (IRP) or resolution professionals (RP) shall, with effect from the date of appointment of IRP/RP, be treated as a distinct person of the corporate debtor, and shall be liable to take a new registration in each of the States or Union territories where the corporate debtor was registered earlier, within thirty days of the appointment of the IRP/RP:

Provided that in cases where the IRP/RP has been appointed prior to the date of this notification, he shall take registration within thirty days from the commencement of this notification, with effect from date of his appointment as IRP/RP.

Return: The said class of persons shall, after obtaining registration file the first return under section 40 of the said Act, from the date on which he becomes liable to registration till the date on which registration has been granted.

Input tax credit: (1) The said class of persons shall, in his first return, be eligible to avail input tax credit on invoices covering the supplies of goods or services or both, received since his appointment as IRP/RP but bearing the GSTIN of the erstwhile registered person, subject to the conditions of Chapter V of the said Act and the rules made thereunder, except the provisions of sub-section (4) of section 16 of the said Act and sub-rule (4) of rule 36 of the Central Goods and Service Tax Rules, 2017 (hereinafter referred to as the said rules).

(2) Registered persons who are receiving supplies from the said class of persons shall, for the period from the date of appointment of IRP/RP till the date of registration as required in this notification or thirty days from the date of this notification, whichever is earlier, be eligible to avail input tax credit on invoices issued using the GSTIN of the erstwhile registered person, subject to the conditions of Chapter V of the said Act and the rules made thereunder, except the provisions of sub-rule (4) of rule 36 of the said rules.

(3) Any amount deposited in the cash ledger by the IRP/RP, in the existing registration, from the date of appointment of IRP/RP to the date of registration in terms of this notification shall be available for refund to the erstwhile registration.

11.9 SUO MOTO REGISTRATION [Rule 16]

(1) Where, pursuant to any survey, enquiry, inspection, search or any other proceedings under the Act, the proper officer finds that a person liable to registration under the Act has failed to apply for such registration, such officer may register the said person on a temporary basis and issue an order in FORM GST REG-12.

(2) The registration granted under sub-rule (1) shall be effective from the date of such order granting registration.

(3) Every person to whom a temporary registration has been granted under sub-rule (1) shall, within a period of ninety days from the date of the grant of such registration, submit an application for registration in the form and manner provided in rule 8 or rule 12.

11.10 DISPLAY OF GSTIN ON NAME BOARD [Rule 18]

Every registered person shall display his

(1) Certificate of registration in a prominent location at his principal place of business and at every additional place or places of business.

(2) GSTIN on the name board exhibited at the entry of his principal place of business and at every additional place or places of business.

11.11 AMENDMENT OF CERTIFICATE OF REGISTRATION [SECTION 28 READ WITH RULE 19]

Where there is any change in any of the particulars furnished in the application for registration in FORM GST REG-01 or FORM GST REG-07 or FORM GST REG-09 or FORM GST REG-10 or for Unique Identity Number in FORM GST REG-13, either at the time of obtaining registration or Unique Identity Number or as amended from time to time, the registered person shall, within a period of fifteen days of such change, submit an application, duly signed or verified through electronic verification code, electronically in FORM GST REG-14, along with the documents relating to such change at the common portal, the certificate of registration shall stand amended upon submission of the application.

Where the change relates to:

(i) legal name of business;

(ii) address of the principal place of business or any additional place(s) of business; or

(iii) addition, deletion or retirement of partners or directors, Karta, Managing Committee, Board of Trustees, Chief Executive Officer or equivalent, responsible for the day-to-day affairs of the business, which does not warrant cancellation of registration under section 29.

The proper officer shall, after due verification, approve the amendment within a period of fifteen working days from the date of the receipt of the application in FORM GST REG-14 and issue an order in FORM GST REG-15 electronically and such amendment shall take effect from the date of the occurrence of the event warranting such amendment.

For other changes like the name of day-to-day functionaries, e-mail IDs, mobile numbers, etc. approval of the Proper Officer is not required, and the amendment can be affected by the taxable person on his own after online verification through the common portal.

Where a change in the constitution of any business results in change of PAN of a registered person, the said person shall apply for fresh registration. The reason for the same is that GSTIN is PAN based. Any change in PAN would warrant a new registration.

Application for Amendment of Registration cannot be filed for following reason:

(a) Change in PAN

(b) Change in constitution of business resulting in change of PAN

(c) Change in place of business from one state to another

In such cases, one need to apply for fresh registration.

11.12 CANCELLATION OR SUSPENSION OF REGISTRATION [SECTION 29]

The provisions relating to cancellation or suspension of registration and its revocation are contained in Sections 29 read with rules 20 to 23 of the CGST Rules, 2017.

The GST law provides for two scenarios where cancellation of registration can take place:

(1) When the taxable person no more requires it (voluntary cancellation).

(2) When the Proper Officer considers the registration liable for cancellation in view of certain specified defaults.

11.12.1 Voluntary Cancellation by Tax Payer [Section 29(1)]

The taxable person desirous of cancellation of registration shall submit the **FORM GST REG-16** on the common portal within 30 days of occurrence of the event warranting the cancellation. He will also declare in the application, the stock held on the date with effect from which he seeks cancellation. He will also work out and declare the quantum of dues of payments and credit reversal, and the particulars of payments made towards discharge of such liabilities.

If satisfied, the Proper Officer has to cancel the registration within 30 days from the date of application or the date of reply to notice (if issued, when rejection is concluded by the officer).

Voluntary cancellation by taxpayer (Rule 20 of the CGST Rules)

The taxpayer may voluntarily apply for cancellation of registration on following ground:

- Closure of business
- Below threshold for registration
- Transfer of business/merger/amalgamation
- Change of PAN/Change in the constitution of the business
- Non-commencement of business within the stipulated time period
- No tax liability post registration
- Death of proprietor

11.12.2 Suo Moto Cancellation [Section 29(2)]

Suo moto Cancellation, i.e. cancellation by proper officer in view of certain specified defaults.

The proper officer may cancel the registration of a person from such date, including any retrospective date, as he may deem fit, where:

(a) the registered taxable person has contravened such provisions of the Act or the rules made there under as may be prescribed; or

(b) a person paying tax under Composition Scheme has not furnished the return for a financial year beyond three months from the due date of furnishing the said return; or

(c) any taxable person (other than composition scheme) who has not furnished returns for such continuous tax period as may be prescribed; or

(d) any person who has taken voluntary registration and has not commenced business within six months from the date of registration; or

(e) where registration has been obtained by means of fraud, willful misstatement or suppression of facts.

11.12.3 Registration to be cancelled in certain cases [Rule 21]

The registration granted to a person is liable to be cancelled, if the said person:

(a) does not conduct any business from the declared place of business; or

(b) issues invoice or bill without supply of goods or services or both in violation of the provisions of this Act, or the rules made thereunder; or

(c) violates the provisions of section 171 of the Act or the rules made thereunder; or

(d) violates the provision of rule 10A; or

(e) avails input tax credit in violation of the provisions of section 16 of the Act or the rules made thereunder; or

(f) furnishes the details of outward supplies in FORM GSTR-1 under section 37 for one or more tax periods which is in excess of the outward supplies declared by him in his valid return under section 39 for the said tax periods; or

(g) violates the provision of rule 86B; or

(h) being a registered person required to file return under section 39(1) for each month or part thereof, has not furnished returns for a continuous period of six months; or

(i) being a registered person required to file return under proviso to section 39(1) for each quarter or part thereof, has not furnished returns for a continuous period of two tax periods.

The proper officer shall not cancel the registration without giving the person an opportunity of being heard. Where the proper officer has reasons to believe that the registration of a person is liable to be cancelled, he shall issue a notice to such person in FORM GST REG-17, requiring him to show cause, within a period of seven working days, as to why his registration shall not be cancelled.

11.12.4 Suspension of Registration [Rule 21A]

(1) Where a registered person has applied for cancellation of registration under rule 20, the registration shall be deemed to be suspended from the date of submission of the application or the date from which the cancellation is sought, whichever is later, pending the completion of proceedings for cancellation of registration under rule 22.

(2) Where the proper officer has reasons to believe that the registration of a person is liable to be cancelled under section 29 or under rule 21, he may, suspend the registration of such person with effect from a date to be determined by him, pending the completion of the proceedings for cancellation of registration under rule 22.

(2A) Where, a comparison of the returns furnished by a registered person under section 39 with

(a) the details of outward supplies furnished in FORM GSTR-1; or

(b) the details of inward supplies derived based on the details of outward supplies furnished by his suppliers in their FORM GSTR-1,

or such other analysis, as may be carried out on the recommendations of the Council, show that there are significant differences or anomalies indicating contravention of the provisions of the Act or the rules made thereunder, leading to cancellation of registration of the said person, his registration shall be suspended and the said person shall be intimated in FORM GST REG-31, electronically, on the common portal, or by sending a communication to his e-mail address provided at the time of registration or as amended from time to time, highlighting the said differences and anomalies and asking him to explain, within a period of thirty days, as to why his registration shall not be cancelled.

(3) A registered person, whose registration has been suspended under sub-rule (1) or sub-rule (2) or sub-rule (2A), shall not make any taxable supply during the period of suspension and shall not be required to furnish any return under section 39.

Explanation: For the purposes of this sub-rule, the expression "shall not make any taxable supply" shall mean that the registered person shall not issue a tax invoice and, accordingly, not charge tax on supplies made by him during the period of suspension.

(3A) A registered person, whose registration has been suspended under sub-rule (2) or sub-rule (2A), shall not be granted any refund under section 54, during the period of suspension of his registration.

(4) The suspension of registration under sub-rule (1) or sub-rule (2) or sub-rule (2A) shall be deemed to be revoked upon completion of the proceedings by the proper officer under rule 22 and such revocation shall be effective from the date on which the suspension had come into effect:

Provided that the suspension of registration under this rule may be revoked by the proper officer, anytime during the pendency of the proceedings for cancellation, if he deems fit:

Provided further that where the registration has been suspended under sub-rule (2A) for contravention of the provisions contained in clause (b) or clause (c) of section 29 (2) and the registration has not already been cancelled by the proper officer under rule 22, the suspension of registration shall be deemed to be revoked upon furnishing of all the pending returns.

(5) Where any order having the effect of revocation of suspension of registration has been passed, the provisions of section 31 (3) (a) and section 40 in respect of the supplies made during the period of suspension and the procedure specified therein shall apply.

Automatic revocation of suspended Registration

Insertion of second proviso in Rule 21A (4) (Automatic revocation): There will be automatic revocation of suspended GST registration upon furnishing of pending GST returns, if GST registration was suspended due to non-filing of GST returns for three consecutive tax periods by the composition taxpayer or a continuous period of six months by registered persons (other than composition taxpayer) subject to the condition that the registration has not been cancelled by the proper officer under rule 22.

Notification No. 14/2022-Central Tax dated 05.07.2022: Where suspension of registration was done by the system, for non-compliance in terms of clause (b) or clause (c) of sub-section (2) of Section 29, i.e. for continuous non-filing of specified number of returns, in such cases, once all the pending returns are filed on the portal by such taxpayers, the suspension of his GST registration will be automatically revoked by system without requiring taxpayer to make any application with the tax officer for the revocation of the suspension of the registration.

Cancellation does not discharge liability of taxpayer: The cancellation of registration shall not affect the liability of the taxable person to pay tax and other dues under the Act for any period prior to the date of cancellation whether or not such tax and other dues are determined before or after the date of cancellation. Where the registration is cancelled, the registered taxable person shall pay an amount equivalent to the credit of input tax in respect of inputs held in stock and inputs contained in semi-finished or finished goods held in stock on the day immediately preceding the date of such cancellation or the output tax payable on such goods, whichever is higher. The payment can be made by way of debit in the electronic credit or electronic cash ledger.

In case of capital goods, the taxable person shall pay an amount equal to the input tax credit taken on the said capital goods reduced by the prescribed percentage points or the tax on the transaction value of such capital goods [under sub-section (1) of section 15 (Value of Taxable Supply) of Act], whichever is higher. The amount payable under these provisions shall be calculated in accordance with generally accepted accounting principles.

Concurrent cancellation under all GST Acts: The cancellation of registration under State Goods and Services Tax Act or the Union Territory Goods and Services Tax Act shall be deemed to be a cancellation of registration under the Central Goods and Service Tax Act.

11.13 REVOCATION OF CANCELLATION OF REGISTRATION [SECTION 30]

The provisions relating to revocation are contained in section 30 read with rule 23 of the CGST Rules, 2017: In case where registration is cancelled suo-motu by the Proper Officer, the taxable person can apply in FORM GST REG-21 within 90 days of service of cancellation order, requesting the officer for revoking the cancellation ordered by him. Where the registered person fails to apply for such revocation within 90 days, the said time period may be extended by the Commissioner or an officer authorized by him in this behalf for a further period not exceeding 180 days. However, before applying, the person has to make good the defaults (by filing all pending returns, making payment of all dues and so) for which the registration was cancelled by the officer. If satisfied, the proper officer will revoke the cancellation earlier ordered by him.

However, if the officer concludes to reject the request for revocation of cancellation, he will first observe the principle of natural justice by way of issuing notice to the person and hearing him on the issue.

Chapter 12

Tax Invoice, Credit and Debit Notes

12.1 STATUTORY PROVISIONS

An invoice is a commercial instrument issued by a seller to a buyer. It identifies both the parties, and lists, describes, and quantifies the items sold/services provided, prices and discounts, if any, and the payment terms.

GST requires that an invoice, tax invoice or bill of supply to be issued on the occurrence of certain event or within a prescribed time. Therefore, an invoice, among others is required to be issued for every other form of supply such as sale, transfer, barter, exchange, license, rental, lease or disposal.

Invoice plays an important role in GST Regime. Since availing of input tax credit is based on the principle of Invoice matching, a registered person can avail Input tax credit only if, he is in possession of a tax invoice or a debit note. The Invoice of inwards supplies of the person claiming the credit (recipient) should match with that of outward supplies of the supplier(s) in GST Return.

The provisions relating to tax invoices, debit and credit notes are contained in Chapter VII—Tax Invoice, Credit and Debit Notes (Sections 31 to 34) of the CGST Act, 2017, as well as in Chapter VI: Tax Invoice, Credit and Debit Notes of Central Goods and Services (CGST) Rules, 2017. State GST laws also prescribe identical provisions in relation to Tax Invoice, Credit and Debit Notes.

Invoice Rules

Rule 46	Tax Invoice
Rule 46A	Invoice Cum Bill of Supply
Rule 47	Time limit for issuing Tax Invoice
Rule 48	Manner of issuing Tax Invoice
Rule 49	Bill of Supply
Rule 50	Receipt Voucher
Rule 51	Refund Voucher
Rule 52	Payment Voucher
Rule 53	Revised Tax Invoice, Credit & Debit Note
Rule 54	Tax Invoice in Special cases
Rule 55	Transportation of Goods without issue of Invoice

Sec 31	Tax Invoice
Sec 32	Prohibition of unauthorized collection of Tax
Sec 33	Amount of Tax to be indicated in Tax invoice and other documents
Sec 34	Credit & Debit Note

12.2 TAX INVOICE [SECTION 31]

Under the GST regime, an "invoice" or "tax invoice" means the tax invoice referred to in section 31 of the CGST Act, 2017. This section mandates the issuance of an invoice or a bill of supply for every supply of goods or services. It is not necessary that only a person supplying goods or services needs to issue an invoice. The GST law mandates that any registered person buying goods or services from an unregistered person, which are covered u/s 9(3)/9(4) of CGST Act needs to issue a payment voucher as well as a tax invoice.

> There is no format prescribed for the Tax Invoice. Only certain fields have been prescribed as mandatory fields. Further, invoices may be issued manually or electronically. Issuance of electronic invoices is not mandatory.
>
> *Ref Notification No. 05/2021-CT dt. 8th March 2021.*
>
> In case of B2B supply by a registered person whose aggregate turnover in a financial year exceeds ₹ 50 crore, he will issue E-Invoice as per Rule 48(4) w.e.f. 1st April 2021.
>
> *Ref Notification No. 01/2022-CT dt. 24th Feb 2022.*
>
> In case of B2B supply by a registered person whose aggregate turnover in a financial year exceeds ₹ 20 Crore, E-Invoice is mandatory w.e.f. 1st April 2022.
>
> Ref Notification No. 10/2023-CT dt. 10th May 2023.
>
> In case of B2B supply by a registered person whose aggregate turnover in a financial year exceeds ₹ 5 Crore, E-Invoice is mandatory w.e.f. 1st August 2023.
>
> *Notification No. 23/2021-Central Tax dated 01-06-2021*
>
> A government department or a local authority are exempted from the requirement of issue of e-invoice.

Any invoice or debit note issued in pursuance of any tax payable in accordance with the provisions of section 74 or section 129 or section 130 shall prominently contain the words "INPUT TAX CREDIT NOT ADMISSIBLE".

As per Rule 53, wherever any revised invoice will be issued, the word "revised Invoice" shall be indicated prominently on the Tax Invoice.

The type of invoice to be issued under GST depends upon type of supply & the category of registered person making the supply.

(1) **Tax Invoice:** For all type of taxable supply by a registered person (except by composition dealer)

(2) **Bill of Supply:** For Exempt supply + Supply by composition dealer

For both goods & services	It will be of same series (bill book)
For local & Central Sales	Same bill book
For exempted goods	Separate bill book

No specific format has been prescribed for **Tax invoice/bill of supply** under GST Invoice Rules. Only some field/information has been made mandatory. However, in case of B2B supply by a registered person whose aggregate turnover in a financial year exceeds ₹ 20 crore, he will issue E-Invoice as per schema approved by GST Council (w.e.f. 1st April 2022). The threshold limit for applicability E-Invoice has been further revised to ₹ 10 crore w.e.f. 1st October 2022 (Ref Notification No. 17/2022-Central Tax dated 01-08-2022).

For example, if a registered person is making outward taxable supply, then a tax invoice needs to be issued by such registered person. However, if a registered person is dealing only in exempted supplies or is availing the composition scheme (composition dealer), then such a registered person needs to issue a "bill of supply" in lieu of invoice. The invoice should contain description, quantity and value & such other prescribed particulars (in case of supply of goods), and the description and value & such other prescribed particulars (in case of supply of services).

12.3 BILL OF SUPPLY

It is an invoice in GST, which does not contain taxes. It is issued in following circumstances:

(1) Exempt supply

(2) Supply by composition dealer

> As per Rule 46A, where a registered person is supplying taxable as well as exempted goods or services or both to an unregistered person, a single "invoice-cum-bill of supply" may be issued for all such supplies.

As per Section 31(3) (b), an invoice or a bill of supply need not be issued if the value of the supply is less than ₹ 200, subject to following conditions.

(a) the recipient is not a registered person; and

(b) the recipient does not require such invoice.

However, in respect of such supplies the supplier shall issue a consolidated tax invoice for such supplies at the close of each day in respect of all such supplies.

Section 31A: Facility of digital payment to Specified Recipient/buyer of goods or services or both: The Government may, on the recommendations of the Council, prescribe a class of registered persons who shall provide prescribed modes of electronic payment to the recipient of supply of goods or services or both made by him and give option to such recipient to make payment accordingly, in such manner and subject to such conditions and restrictions, as may be prescribed.

12.4 SUPPLIER PERMITTED TO ISSUE ANY DOCUMENT OTHER THAN TAX INVOICE

(Proviso to section 31(2) read with rules 54 and 55)

The Commissioner, on the recommendations of the Council, is empowered to specify the class of persons rendering services who can:

- issue any other document which could be construed to be a tax invoice or
- when a tax invoice need not be issued.

Further, Government may, on the recommendations of the Council, by notification, specify the categories of goods or supplies in respect of which a tax invoice shall be issued, within such time and in such manner as may be prescribed.

Following suppliers may issue a tax invoice, but they are also permitted to issue any other document in lieu of tax invoice, by whatever name called:

- Insurer/Banking company/Financial institution, including NBFC
- Goods Transport Agency (GTA) supplying services in relation to transportation of goods by road in a goods carriage
- Supplier of passenger transportation service.

12.4.1 Importance of Tax Invoice Under GST

Under GST, a tax invoice is an important document. It not only evidences the supply of goods or services, but is also an essential document for the recipient to avail Input Tax Credit (ITC).

Tax invoices are to be issued under section 31 (1) of CGST Act 2017 for supply of goods & under section 31 (2) for supply of services, as per Rule 46 of Invoice Rules.

A registered person cannot avail Input Tax Credit unless he is in possession of a tax invoice or a debit note. GST is chargeable at the time of supply. Invoice is an important indicator of the time of supply. Broadly speaking, the time of supply of goods or services is the date of issuance of an invoice or receipt of payment, whichever is earlier.

The tax invoice is the primary document evidencing the supply and vital for availing Input Tax Credit.

12.4.2 Delivery Challan

Rule 55 of CGST Rule, 2017 specifies the cases where, goods may be removed on delivery challan and invoice may be issued after delivery. These are provided in the following table:

Nature of supply	Delivery Challan to be issued	Particulars of Delivery Challan
(1) Supply of liquid gas where the quantity at the time of removal from the place of business of the supplier is not known (2) Transportation of goods for job work (3) Transportation of goods for reasons other than by way of supply, or (4) Such other supplies as may be notified by the Government	Serially numbered not exceeding 16 characters in one or multiple series at the time of removal of goods for transportation	Date and number of the delivery challan
		Name, address and GSTIN of the consigner, if registered
		Name, address and GSTIN or UIN of the consignee, if registered
		HSN code and description of goods
		Quantity (provisional, where the exact quantity being supplied is not known)
		Taxable value
		Tax rate and tax amount: central tax, state tax, integrated tax, union territory tax or cess, where the transportation is for supply to the consignee Place of supply, in case of inter-state movement
		Signature

The delivery challan shall be prepared in TRIPLICATE, in case of supply of goods, in the following manner:

(a) Original for : Buyer
(b) Duplicate for : Transporter
(c) Triplicate for : Consignor

Declaration in E-way Bill: Where goods are being transported on a delivery challan in lieu of invoice, the same shall be declared in E-Way Bill.

Tax invoice to be issued after delivery of goods: Where the goods being transported are for the purpose of supply to the recipient but the tax invoice could not be issued at the time of removal of goods for the purpose of supply, the supplier shall issue a tax invoice after delivery of goods.

12.5 TIME OF ISSUE OF TAX INVOICE [SECTION 31]

The time for issuing an invoice would depend on the nature of supply, viz. whether it is a supply of goods or services.

(1) Supplier of taxable goods is required to issue a tax invoice, Section 31(1):

(a) Before or at the time of removal of the goods where the supply involves movement of goods; or
(b) Before or at the time of delivery of the goods to the recipient where the supply does not involve movement of goods.

Example: M/s Everest Industries, Delhi entered into an agreement with M/s Sintex Industries, Rajasthan for supply of PVC pipes on 15th January 2022. As per contract, the PVC pipes were to be delivered on 30th January 2022. Everest Industries removed the PVC pipes from its factory on 28th January 2022. Determine the date on which tax invoice must be issued by Everest Industries as per GST Laws.
Answer: 28th January 2022.

(2) Supplier of services is required to issue a tax invoice Section 31(2):

(a) Before provision of the services.
(b) After provision of the services but within a specified time.
(c) If the invoice is issued after the provision of service, it has to be done within the specified period of 30 days from the date of supply of service, as per invoice rules.

Where the supplier of services is an insurer or a banking company or a financial institution, including a non-banking financial company, the period within which the invoice or any document in lieu thereof is to be issued shall be forty-five (45) days from the date of supply of service.

(3) Invoice in case of continuous supply of goods, Section 31(4): In case of Continuous supply of goods, the invoice, i.e. tax invoice or bill of supply is required to be issued:

(a) when the statement or a running-claim is issued; or
(b) when payment is received, whichever is earlier.

(4) Invoice in case of continuous supply of services, Section 31(5): As per Section 2(33) "continuous supply of services" means a supply of services which is provided, or agreed to be provided, continuously or on recurrent basis, under a contract, for a period exceeding three months with periodic payment obligations and includes supply of such services as the Government may, subject to such conditions, as it may, by notification, specify;

In case of continuous supply of services, where:

(a) the due date of payment is **ascertainable** from the contract, the invoice shall be issued on or before the due date of payment.
(b) the due date of payment is **not ascertainable** from the contract, the invoice shall be issued before or at the time when the supplier of service receives the payment.
(c) the payment is linked to the completion of an event, the invoice shall be issued on or before the date of completion of that event.

(5) Issue of invoice in case, where supply of services ceases before the completion of supply, Section 31(6): In a case where the supply of services ceases under a contract before the completion of the supply, the invoice shall be issued at the time when the supply ceases and such invoice shall be issued to the extent of the supply made before such cessation.

(6) **Goods sent on sale or return basis, Section 31(7):** Where the goods being sent or taken on approval for sale or return are removed before the supply takes place, the invoice shall be issued:

- before or at the time of supply or
- six months from the date of removal,

whichever is earlier.

Tax invoice: In case of supply of goods

Supply of Taxable Goods	Time for Issue of Tax Invoice
Involves Movement of Goods	Before or at the time of removal
Does not involve movement of goods	Before or at the Time of Delivery or making available the Goods to the recipient
Continuous supply of Goods Successive Statement of accounts are involved	Before or At the time each statement is issued
Continuous supply of Goods Successive payments are involved	Before or At the time each payment is received
Goods sent on approval	Six months from the date of removal or approval to accept whichever is earlier

Tax invoice: In case of supply of service

Supply of Taxable Service	Time for Issue of Tax Invoice
General	Before or after provision of service but within 30 days from the date of supply
In case of Banks/Financial Institutions/NBFC/Insurance	Within 45 days of date supply of service May issue a consolidated tax invoice for the supply of services made during a month at the end of the month [Rule 54(2)]
Continuous supply of Services Due date for payment is ascertainable from the contract	On or before the due date for payment
Continuous supply of Services Due date for payment is not ascertainable from the contract	On or before the time supplier receives payment
Continuous supply of Services Payment linked to completion of an event	On or before the date of completion of event

12.5.1 Tax Invoice in Special Cases

(1) **Revised Invoice Section 31(3)(a):** A registered person may, within one month from the date of issuance of certificate of registration and in such manner as prescribed in the Invoice Rules, issue a revised invoice against the invoice already issued during the period beginning with the effective date of registration till the date of issuance of certificate of registration to him.

This provision is necessary, as a person who becomes liable for registration has to apply for registration within 30 days of becoming liable for registration. When such an application is made within the time period and registration is granted, the effective date of registration is the date on which the person became liable for registration. Thus, there would be a time lag between the date of grant of certificate of registration and the effective date of registration. For supplies made by such person during this intervening period, the law enables the issuance of a revised invoice, so that ITC can be availed by the recipient on such supplies.

(2) **Consolidated Revised Tax Invoices in certain cases [Rule (53)(2)]:** A registered person may issue a consolidated revised tax invoice in respect of all taxable supplies made to a recipient who is not registered under the GST Act, during the period starting from the effective date of registration till the date of the issuance of the certificate of registration.

However, in case of inter-State supplies, where the value of a supply does not exceed ₹ 2,50,000, a consolidated revised invoice may be issued separately in respect of all the recipients located in a State, who are not registered under the Act.

(3) Tax Invoice if value of supply < ₹ 200: Section 31(3)(b) read with fourth proviso to rule 46: A registered person may not issue a Tax Invoice if:

(i) Value of the goods/services/both supplied < ₹ 200;

(ii) the recipient is unregistered; and

(iii) the recipient does not require such invoice.

Instead, such registered person shall issue a **Consolidated Tax Invoice** for such supplies at the close of each day in respect of all such supplies.

(4) Bill of Supply: Section 31(3)(C) read with rule 49: A registered person supplying exempted goods or services or both or paying tax under composition levy shall issue a bill of supply instead of a tax invoice.

(5) Receipt Voucher: Section 31(3)(d) read with rule 50: Receipt of advance will require that a 'receipt voucher' be issued and not an invoice (of either kind).

As per Section 31(3)(d), a registered person upon receive of an advance payment with respect to any supply of goods or services or both, he has to issue a receipt voucher or any other document, containing such particulars as prescribed in the Invoice Rules, evidencing the receipt of such payment.

(6) Refund Voucher: Section 31(3)(e) read with rule 51: Where any such receipt voucher is issued, but subsequently no supply is made and no tax invoice is issued, the registered person who has received the advance payment can issue a refund voucher against such payment.

(7) Invoice in case of tax payable on Reverse charge or supply received from unregistered person, Section 31(3)(f) & (g) read with second proviso to rule 46 and rule 52: Recipient is liable to pay tax on reverse charge basis where he receives supply of such goods/services/both, which are notified for reverse charge purposes. Such supplies can be received from a registered or an unregistered supplier [Section 9(3)].

Further, a registered person is also liable to pay tax where taxable goods/services/both have been received from an unregistered supplier [Section 9(4)]. *This provision was suspended from 13th Oct 2017 to 31st Jan 2019.*

Central Government Vide Notification No. 01/2019-CT (Rate) dated 29th January 2019 has rescinded the said provision. GST Amendment Act, 2018 which came into operation w.e.f. 1st Feb 2019 has restrict the levy of tax on RCM u/s 9(4) on receipt of supplies of certain specified categories of goods or services or both by notified classes of registered persons from unregistered suppliers.

A registered person who is liable to pay tax under reverse charge [u/s 9(3)/9(4) of the CGST Act] shall issue an **Invoice** in respect of goods or services or both received by him from the supplier who is not registered on the date of receipt of goods or services or both. Thus, a recipient liable to pay tax by virtue of section 9(3) has to issue invoice only when supplies have been received from an unregistered supplier.

(8) Supplier permitted to issue any document other than tax invoice [Proviso to section 31(2) read with rules 54 and 55].

(a) Input Service distributors: Where the Input Service Distributor is an office of a banking company or a financial institution, including a non-banking financial company, a tax invoice shall include any document in lieu thereof, by whatever name called, whether or not serially numbered but containing the prescribed information.

(b) Insurance/Banking/Financial Companies/NBFC: Where the supplier of taxable service is an insurer or a banking company or a financial institution, including a non-banking financial company, the said supplier shall issue a tax invoice or any other document in lieu thereof, by whatever name called, whether or not serially numbered, and whether or not containing the address of the recipient of taxable service but containing other information as prescribed under rule 46 of Invoice Rules.

(c) Goods Transport Agency (GTA): Where the supplier of taxable service is a goods transport agency (GTA) supplying services in relation to transportation of goods by road in a goods carriage, the said supplier shall issue a tax invoice or any other document in lieu thereof, by whatever name called, containing the gross weight of the consignment, name of the consignor and the consignee, registration number of goods carriage in which the goods are transported, details of goods transported, details of place of origin and destination, GSTIN of the person liable for paying tax whether as consignor, consignee or goods transport agency, and also containing other information as prescribed under rule 46 of Invoice Rules.

(d) Passenger transportation service: Where the supplier of taxable service is supplying passenger transportation service, a tax invoice shall include ticket in any form, by whatever name called, whether or not serially numbered, and whether or not containing the address of the recipient of service but containing other information as prescribed under rule 46 of Invoice Rules.

(e) **Transportation of goods without an invoice:** In the following cases, it is permissible for the consignor to issue a delivery challan in lieu of invoice at the time of removal of goods:

(a) Supply of liquid gas where the quantity at the time of removal from the place of business of the supplier is not known
(b) Transportation of goods for job work
(c) Transportation of goods for reasons other than by way of supply
(d) Such other supplies as may be notified by the Board

Where goods are being transported on a delivery challan in lieu of invoice, the same shall be declared in FORM [WAYBILL].

Where the goods being transported are for the purpose of supply to the recipient but the tax invoice could not be issued at the time of removal of goods for the purpose of supply, the supplier shall issue a tax invoice after the delivery of goods.

Supplier of taxable service	**Document in lieu of the tax invoice**	
	Optional information	**Mandatory information**
Insurer/Banking company/Financial institution, including NBFC	Serial number Address of the recipient of taxable service	Other information as prescribed for a Tax Invoice, under rule 46
		Such document may be issued/made available, physically/electronically
Goods Transport Agency (GTA) supplying services in relation to transportation of goods by road in a goods carriage	None	Gross weight of the consignment
		Name of the consignor and the consignee
		Registration number of goods carriage in which the goods are transported
		Details of goods transported
		Details of place of origin and destination
		GSTIN of the person liable for paying tax whether as consignor, consignee or GTA
		Other information as prescribed for a tax invoice, under rule 46
Supplier of **passenger Transportation service**	Serial number Address of the recipient of taxable service	Other information as prescribed for a tax invoice, under rule 46
		Tax invoice shall include ticket in any form, by whatever name called

12.5.2 Contents of Tax Invoice [Section 31(1) and (2) read with rule 46]

There is no format prescribed for an invoice, however, Invoice rule 46, makes it mandatory for an invoice to have the following fields:

(a) Name, address and GSTIN of the supplier;
(b) A consecutive serial number, not exceeding sixteen characters, in one or multiple series, containing alphabets or numerals or special characters like hyphen or dash and slash symbolized as "-" and "/" respectively, and any combination thereof, unique for a financial year;
(c) Date of its issue;
(d) Name, address and GSTIN or UIN, if registered, of the recipient;
(e) Name and address of the recipient and the address of delivery, along with the name of State and its code, if such recipient is un-registered and where the value of taxable supply is fifty thousand rupees or more;
(f) Name and address of the recipient and the address of delivery, along with the name of the State and its code, if such recipient is un-registered and where the value of the taxable supply is less than fifty thousand rupees and the recipient requests that such details be recorded in the tax invoice;
(g) Harmonized System of Nomenclature code for goods or services;
(h) Description of goods or services;
(i) Quantity in case of goods and unit or Unique Quantity Code thereof;

(j) Total value of supply of goods or services or both;
(k) Taxable value of the supply of goods or services or both taking into account discount or abatement, if any;
(l) Rate of tax (central tax, State tax, integrated tax, Union territory tax or cess);
(m) Amount of tax charged in respect of taxable goods or services (central tax, State tax, integrated tax, Union territory tax or cess);
(n) Place of supply along with the name of the State, in the case of a supply in the course of inter-State trade or commerce;
(o) Address of delivery where the same is different from the place of supply;
(p) Whether the tax is payable on reverse charge basis; and
(q) Signature or digital signature of the supplier or his authorized representative:

Provided also that in case of export of goods or services, the invoice shall carry an endorsement "SUPPLY MEANT FOR EXPORT ON PAYMENT OF INTEGRATED TAX" or "SUPPLY MEANT FOR EXPORT UNDER BOND OR LETTER OF UNDERTAKING WITHOUT PAYMENT OF INTEGRATED TAX", as the case may be, and shall, in lieu of the details specified in clause (e), contain the following details:
(i) name and address of the recipient;
(ii) address of delivery; and
(iii) name of the country of destination.

Revised Tax Invoice and Credit or Debit Notes [Rule 53]

As per explanation to Section 31, the expression "tax invoice" shall include any revised invoice issued by the supplier in respect of a supply made earlier.

(1) A revised tax invoice referred to in Section 31 shall contain the following particulars, namely:
(a) the word "Revised Invoice", wherever applicable, indicated prominently;
(b) name, address and Goods and Services Tax Identification Number of the supplier;
(c) a consecutive serial number not exceeding sixteen characters, in one or multiple series, containing alphabets or numerals or special characters—hyphen or dash and slash symbolised as "-" and "/" respectively, and any combination thereof, unique for a financial year;
(d) date of issue of the document;
(e) name, address and Goods and Services Tax Identification Number or Unique Identity Number, if registered, of the recipient;
(f) name and address of the recipient and the address of delivery, along with the name of State and its code, if such recipient is un-registered;
(g) serial number and date of the corresponding tax invoice or, as the case may be, bill of supply; and
(h) signature or digital signature of the supplier or his authorized representative.

(2) A credit or debit note referred to in section 34 shall contain the following particulars, namely:
(a) name, address and Goods and Services Tax Identification Number of the supplier;
(b) nature of the document;
(c) a consecutive serial number not exceeding sixteen characters, in one or multiple series, containing alphabets or numerals or special characters—hyphen or dash and slash symbolized as "-" and "/" respectively, and any combination thereof, unique for a financial year;
(d) date of issue of the document;
(e) name, address and Goods and Services Tax Identification Number or Unique Identity Number, if registered, of the recipient;
(f) name and address of the recipient and the address of delivery, along with the name of State and its code, if such recipient is un-registered;
(g) serial number(s) and date(s) of the corresponding tax invoice(s) or, as the case may be, bill(s) of supply;
(h) value of taxable supply of goods or services, rate of tax and the amount of the tax credited or, as the case may be, debited to the recipient; and
(i) signature or digital signature of the supplier or his authorized representative.

(3) Every registered person who has been granted registration with effect from a date earlier than the date of issuance of certificate of registration to him, may issue revised tax invoices in respect of taxable supplies effected during the period starting from the effective date of registration till the date of the issuance of the certificate of registration:

Provided that the registered person may issue a consolidated revised tax invoice in respect of all taxable supplies made to a recipient who is not registered under the Act during such period:

Provided further that in the case of inter-State supplies, where the value of a supply does not exceed two lakh and fifty thousand rupees, a consolidated revised invoice may be issued separately in respect of all the recipients located in a State, who are not registered under the Act.

12.5.3 Manner of Issuing Invoice [Section 31(1) and (2) read with rule 48]

(1) **With respect to Supply of Goods:**

The Tax Invoice shall be prepared in Triplicate copy

(a) Original for Recipient
(b) Duplicate for Transporter
(c) Triplicate for Supplier

(2) **With Respect to supply of Services:**

The Tax invoice shall be prepared in Duplicate

(a) Original for Recipient
(b) Duplicate for Supplier

The serial number of invoices issued during a tax period shall be furnished electronically in FORM GSTR-1 [Details of outward Supplies of goods or services].

12.6 ELECTRONIC INVOICE (E-INVOICE) [RULE 48(4)]

The Central Government Vide **Notification No. 68/2019** dated 13th December 2019 has notified the CGST (Eighth Amendment) Rules, 2019 by inserting a new sub-rule (4) under Rule 48 of CGST Rules, which read as under:

"(4) *The invoice shall be prepared by such class of registered persons as may be notified by the Government, on the recommendations of the Council, by including such particulars contained in* ***FORM GST INV-1*** *after obtaining an Invoice Reference Number by uploading information contained therein on the Common Goods and Services Tax Electronic Portal in such manner and subject to such conditions and restrictions as may be specified*".

The schema of E-Invoice has been notified Vide Notification No. 60/2020-Central Tax dated 30th July 2020.

With effect from 1st October 2020, invoice generated by registered person whose turnover exceeds ₹ 500 crore in a financial year, from any accounting/billing/ERP system will not be valid unless the said invoice is registered in the Invoice Reporting Portal (IRP) & IRN is assigned.

Reporting of invoices on the IRP Portal A time limit of 30 days has been imposed for reporting of invoices including debit or credit note from the date of invoice, or as the case may be, date of issue debit or credit note on e-invoice portals for taxpayers with Aggregate Annual Turnover (AATO) greater than or equal to 100 crores. Hence, the taxpayers in this category will not be allowed to report invoices older than 30 days on the date of reporting. This validation shall come into effect from 1st Nov, 2023.

The Central Government vide Notification No. 01/2022-CT dt. 24th Feb. 2022 has revised the turnover limit to ₹ 20 crores for the purpose of generation of e-invoice. Hence, with effect from 1st April 2022 e-invoice shall be mandatory for a registered person for B2B supply whose turnover exceeds ₹ 20 crores in a financial year.

The turnover limit for the purpose of generation of e-invoice has been further reduced to ₹ 5 Crores with effect from 1st August 2023 vide Notification No. 10/2023-CT dt. 10th May 2023.

Notification No. 23/2021-Central Tax dated 01-06-2021

A government department or a local authority are exempted from the requirement of issue of e-invoice.

What is E-Invoice?

E-Invoice does not mean generation of invoice from a billing/accounting/ERP system in electronic/digital format or GST portal. Only those invoices which are reported to & generated from Invoice Reporting Portal (IRP) having Invoice Reference Number (IRN) is called e-invoice. The IRP will generate e-invoice, not invoice.

The Invoice will be generated by the registered person from its own ERP/Accounting/Billing system in specified format as per "schema" approved by the GST Council & generate JSON file & report/registered the same to IRP. After successful validation by IRP, it will assign an IRN and return back to supplier. The GST Council has given the responsibility to design the standard of e-invoice and update the same from time to time, to GSTN which is the custodian of Returns and invoices contained in the same.

Therefore, the e-invoice system consists of two important parts namely,

(a) Generation of invoice in a standard format as approved by GST council from the accounting/billing/ERP system used by the supplier and

(b) Reporting of invoice to an Invoice Reporting Portal (IRP).

The Invoice Reporting Portal (IRP) will validate two parameters i.e. correctness of GSTIN of both parties (i.e. supplier & buyer) & unique Invoice number. After validation, if it is found correct, a unique Invoice Reference Number (IRN) will be assigned to each invoice and digitally sign the e-invoice and also generate a QR code & return back to the supplier. If, validation is not successful, the IRP will generate error code.

An invoice will be treated as valid E-Invoice, only if it bears Invoice Reference Number (IRN) assigned by the Invoice Reporting Portal (IRP). IRN will be generated by IRP only. It is not required to be generated by the registered person. The IRN will be generated by using an algorithm of three parameters, viz: GSTIN of seller, invoice number of seller & financial year.

Type of documents are to be reported to GST System.

While the word invoice is used in the name of e-invoice, it covers other documents that will be required to be reported to IRP by the creator of the document:

(i) Invoice by Supplier

(ii) Credit Note by Supplier

(iii) Debit Note by Supplier

(iv) Any other document as required by law to be reported by the creator of the document

(v) Invoice issued for inward supply covered under RCM.

The invoice having no tax component is generally known as Bill of supply. Thus, challan and bill of supply are not required to obtain IRN.

For Whom E-invoicing applicable

As per ***Notification No.*** *61/2020-Central Tax dated 30th July 2020 (Amended Vide N.N. 70/2020-Central Tax dated 30th Sept 2020), E-Invoicing is applicable for following:*

(a) Registered person whose aggregate turnover in any preceding financial year from 2017-18 onwards exceeds ₹ 500 crore and

(b) Supply of Goods/Services or both to a Registered Person (B2B) or for exports.

As per **Notification No. 72/2019** dated 13th December 2019, **in case of B2C supply,** if the aggregate turnover of registered person in a financial year exceeds five hundred crore rupees, the invoice issued to un-registered person must bear Quick Response (QR) code:

Provided that where such registered person makes a Dynamic Quick Response (QR) code available to the recipient through a digital display, such B2C invoice issued by such registered person containing cross-reference of the payment using a Dynamic Quick Response (QR) code, shall be deemed to be having Quick Response (QR) code.

E-Invoicing is applicable in India from 1st October 2020 for B2B supply by registered person having aggregate turnover more than ₹ 500 crores in any preceding financial year from 2017-18 onwards. The threshold limit has been reduced in a graded manner over the years.

The Central Government vide Notification No. 10/2023-CT dt. 10th May 2023 has revised the threshold limit of aggregate turnover for applicability of e-invoicing for B2B supply from ₹ 10 crore to ₹ 5 crore. The said amendment is effective from 1st August 2023.

Sl. No.	Aggregate Turnover	Applicable Date	Notification No.
1.	More than ₹ 500 crores	01-10-2020	13/2020-Central Tax dated 21-03-2020 61/2020-Central Tax dated 30-07-2020 70/2020-Central Tax dated 30-09-2020
2.	More than ₹ 100 crores	01-01-2021	88/2020-Central Tax dated 10-11-2020

Sl. No.	Aggregate Turnover	Applicable Date	Notification No.
3.	More than ₹ 50 crores	01-04-2021	5/2021-Central Tax dated 08-03-2021
4.	More than ₹ 20 crores	01-04-2022	1/2022-Central Tax dated 24-02-2022
5.	More than ₹ 10 crores	01-10-2022	17/2022-Central Tax dated 01-08-2022
6.	More than ₹ 5 crores	01-08-2023	10/2023-Central Tax dated 10-05-2023

The Central Government vide Notification No. 10/2023-CT dt. 10th May 2023 has revised the threshold limit of aggregate turnover for applicability of e-invoicing for B2B supply from ₹ 10 crore to ₹ 5 crore. The said amendment is effective from 1st August 2023.

Non-applicability of E-Invoice [Refer Rule 54 (2), (3), (4), (4A)]

[Notification No. 13/2020-Central Tax dated 21st March 2020]

Following class of registered persons are exempted from the requirement of issuing e-invoices even if the aggregate turnover exceeds the specified limit:

Banking company	Passenger transportation service
Insurance company	Goods Transport Agency (GTA)
Financial institution	Special Economic Zone (SEZ)
Non-banking financial institution	Admission to Multiplex, movies, Cinematographic film

12.7 HSN/SAC CODE REQUIRED ON TAX INVOICE [RULE 46]

The primary purpose of the HSN code is the systematic classification of goods. Harmonized System of Nomenclature (HSN) Codes was developed by World Customs Organization (WCO) in 1986 as a standardized system that classifies goods all over the world. Services Accounting Code (SAC) is used for classification of services. SAC code begin with 99.

The CBIC may, on the recommendations of the Council, by notification, specify

(i) the number of digits of HSN code for goods or services, that a class of registered persons shall be required to mention, for such period as may be specified in the said notification

(ii) the class of registered persons that would not be required to mention the HSN code for goods or services, for such period as may be specified in the said notification.

Central Government vide *Notification No. 12/2017-Central Tax, dt. 28-06-2017,* has w.e.f. 1st July 2017 notified the following number of digits of Harmonized System of Nomenclature (HSN) Codes, which are required to be mentioned in a tax invoice issued by a registered person having prescribed annual turnover:

Sl No.	Annual Turnover in the preceding FY	Number of Digits of HSN Code
1.	Up to ₹ 1.5 crore	Nil
2.	More than ₹ 1.5 crore and up to ₹ 5 crores	2
3:	More than ₹ 5 crores	4

Revised requirement of declaring HSN for goods and SAC for services in invoices and in FORM GSTR-1 w.e.f. 01.04.2021 are as under (*Notification No. 78/2020-Central Tax, dt. 15-10-2020*):

(a) HSN/SAC at 6 digits for supplies of both goods and services for taxpayers with aggregate annual turnover above ₹ 5 crores;

(b) HSN/SAC at 4 digits for B2B supplies of both goods and services for taxpayers with aggregate annual turnover up to ₹ 5 crores;

(c) Government to have power to notify eight digit HSN on notified class of supplies by all taxpayers.

12.7.1 Contents of Bill of Supply [Rule 49]

If a registered person is dealing only in exempted supplies or is availing the composition scheme (composition dealer), then such a registered person needs to issue a "bill of supply" in lieu of invoice.

A bill of supply shall be issued by the supplier containing the following details:

(a) Name, address and GSTIN of the supplier
(b) A consecutive serial number, in one or multiple series, containing alphabets or numerals or special characters like hyphen or dash and slash symbolized as "-" and "/" respectively, and any combination thereof, unique for a financial year
(c) Date of its issue
(d) Name, address and GSTIN or UIN, if registered, of the recipient
(e) HSN Code of goods or Accounting Code for Services
(f) Description of goods or services or both
(g) Value of supply of goods or services or both taking into account discount or abatement, if any
(h) Signature or digital signature of the supplier or his authorized representative:

[Provided also that the signature or digital signature of the supplier or his authorized representative shall not be required in the case of issuance of an electronic bill of supply in accordance with the provisions of the Information Technology Act, 2000 (21 of 2000)].

12.7.2 Contents of Receipt Voucher [Rule 50]

A receipt voucher referred to in section 31(3) (d) shall contain the following particulars:

(a) name, address and GSTIN of the supplier;
(b) a consecutive serial number not exceeding sixteen characters, in one or multiple series, containing alphabets or numerals or special characters like hyphen or dash and slash symbolized as "-" and "/" respectively, and any combination thereof, unique for a financial year;
(c) date of its issue;
(d) name, address and GSTIN or UIN, if registered, of the recipient;
(e) description of goods or services;
(f) amount of advance taken;
(g) rate of tax (central tax, State tax, integrated tax, Union territory tax or cess);
(h) amount of tax charged in respect of taxable goods or services (central tax, State tax, integrated tax, Union territory tax or cess);
(i) place of supply along with the name of State and its code, in case of a supply in the course of inter-State trade or commerce;
(j) whether the tax is payable on reverse charge basis; and
(k) signature or digital signature of the supplier or his authorized representative:

Provided that where at the time of receipt of advance,

(i) the rate of tax is not determinable, the tax shall be paid at the rate of eighteen per cent;
(ii) the nature of supply is not determinable, the same shall be treated as inter-State supply.

12.7.3 Contents of Refund Voucher [Rule 51]

A refund voucher referred to in section 31(3) (e) shall contain the following particulars:

(a) name, address and GSTIN of the supplier;
(b) a consecutive serial number not exceeding sixteen characters, in one or multiple series, containing alphabets or numerals or special characters like hyphen or dash and slash symbolized as "-" and "/" respectively, and any combination thereof, unique for a financial year;
(c) date of its issue;
(d) name, address and GSTIN or UIN, if registered, of the recipient;
(e) number and date of receipt voucher issued in accordance with provisions of sub-rule 5;
(f) description of goods or services in respect of which refund is made;
(g) amount of refund made;
(h) rate of tax (central tax, State tax, integrated tax, Union territory tax or cess);
(i) amount of tax paid in respect of such goods or services (central tax, State tax, integrated tax, Union territory tax or cess);
(j) whether the tax is payable on reverse charge basis; and
(k) signature or digital signature of the supplier or his authorized representative.

12.7.4 Contents of Payment Voucher [Rule 52]

A payment voucher referred to in section 31(3)(g) shall contain the following particulars, namely:

(a) name, address and Goods and Services Tax Identification Number of the supplier if registered;

(b) a consecutive serial number not exceeding sixteen characters, in one or multiple series, containing alphabets or numerals or special characters hyphen or dash and slash symbolized as "-" and "/" respectively, and any combination thereof, unique for a financial year;

(c) date of its issue;

(d) name, address and Goods and Services Tax Identification Number of the recipient;

(e) description of goods or services;

(f) amount paid;

(g) rate of tax (central tax, State tax, integrated tax, Union territory tax or cess);

(h) amount of tax payable in respect of taxable goods or services (central tax, State tax, integrated tax, Union territory tax or cess);

(i) place of supply along with the name of State and its code, in case of a supply in the course of inter-State trade or commerce; and

(j) signature or digital signature of the supplier or his authorized representative.

Tax Invoice or bill of supply to accompany transport of goods [RULE 55A]

The person in charge of the conveyance shall carry a copy of the tax invoice or the bill of supply issued in accordance with the provisions of rules 46, 46A or 49 in a case where such person is not required to carry an e-way bill under these rules.

Key Points Regarding Tax Invoice

- The time period for issuance of invoice is different for goods and services.
- For goods, it is any time before or at its delivery and for services, it is within 30 days from the date of supply of services.
- Registered persons are free to design their own Tax Invoice Format.
- GST law requires that only certain fields are mandatory in the Tax Invoice.
- Taxpayers with annual turnover up to ₹ 1.5 crores need not to mention the HSN code of the goods in the invoices.
- Signature/digital signature of supplier/authorized representative on Electronic Tax Invoice not required.
- E-Invoice is mandatory in case of B2B supply for registered person having turnover more than ₹ 20 crores (w.e.f. 1st April 2022).

12.8 PROHIBITION OF UNAUTHORISED COLLECTION OF TAX [SECTION 32]

A registered person shall not collect tax except in accordance with the provisions of this Act or the rules made there under. Collection of tax is not a statutory right but a contractual right. Every taxable person (in case of forward charge) remains liable to deposit applicable tax to the Government. The law does not say that taxable person shall be liable only if it is received from recipient. Eligibility to claim credit also does not impose any implicit duty to reimburse the tax if the terms of offer are silent about tax.

This provision casts an obligation of each—unregistered person and registered taxable person with regard to collection of tax on supply:

- unregistered person is not to collect tax or any sum 'by way of' tax; and
- registered person is to collect tax only in the manner prescribed.

12.9 AMOUNT OF TAX TO BE INDICATED IN TAX INVOICE & OTHER DOCUMENTS [SECTION 33]

Where any supply is made for a consideration, every person who is liable to pay tax for such supply shall prominently indicate in all documents relating to assessment, tax invoice and other like documents, the amount of tax which shall form part of the price at which such supply is made.

This provision therefore holds that the price charged to be the 'cum tax' price of the supply. Tax included in the price is that actually assessed on the supply.

It means that if the supply price is ₹ 1680 which is inclusive of tax @12% then every document must state that "the price of ₹ 1680 includes, say IGST of ₹ 180" or alternatively say supply price is ₹ 1500 and IGST of ₹ 180 & total amount is ₹ 1680.

12.10 CREDIT AND DEBIT NOTES [SECTION 34]

The provision relating to issue of Credit/Debit Notes are contained in Section 34 of CGST Act, 2017 & Chapter VI of CGST Rules, 2017. Credit Notes/Debit Notes are to be issued with reference to a specific tax invoice for adjustment of tax liability. A single Credit Notes/Debit Notes can also be issued for multiple tax invoices *(As per CGST Amendment Act, 2018).*

Example: *Supplier "A" has raised tax invoice of ₹ 11, 200 on "B" in respect of goods sold which includes GST of ₹ 1200 calculated @12% on basic cost of ₹ 10,000. Subsequently, it was discovered that the actual value of goods sold was ₹ 9500 instead of ₹ 10,000 resulting in excess invoicing. To address this problem, supplier "A" will issue Credit note on "B", as it will result in reduction in value of goods as well as tax.*

In simple language, Credit Note is issued for decrease/reduction in tax liability while Debit Note is issued for increase in tax liability.

(A) Credit Note [Section 34(1)]

Where one or more tax invoices have been issued for supply of any goods or services or both and the taxable value or tax charged in that tax invoice is found to exceed the taxable value or tax payable in respect of such supply, or where the goods supplied are returned by the recipient, or where goods or services or both supplied are found to be deficient, the registered person, who has supplied such goods or services or both, may issue to the recipient one or more credit notes for supplies made in a financial year containing such particulars as may be prescribed.

A supplier of goods or services or both is mandatorily required to issue a tax invoice. However, during the course of trade or commerce, after the invoice has been issued there could be situations like:

(a) The supplier has erroneously declared a value, which is more than the actual value of the goods or services provided.
(b) The supplier has erroneously declared a higher tax rate than what is applicable for the kind of the goods or services or both supplied.
(c) The quantity received by the recipient is less than what has been declared in the tax invoice.
(d) The quality of the goods or services or both supplied is not to the satisfaction of the recipient thereby necessitating a partial or total reimbursement on the invoice value.
(e) Any other similar reasons.

In order to regularize these kinds of situations the supplier is allowed to issue what is called as credit note to the recipient. Once the credit note has been issued, the tax liability of the supplier will reduce.

A credit note is a convenient and legal method by which the value of the goods or services in the original tax invoice can be amended or revised. The issuance of the credit note will allow the supplier to **decrease his tax liability** in his returns.

Format: There is no prescribed format but credit note issued by a supplier must contain the following particulars, namely:

(a) name, address and Goods and Services Tax Identification Number of the supplier;
(b) nature of the document;
(c) a consecutive serial number not exceeding sixteen characters, in one or multiple series, containing alphabets or numerals or special characters hyphen or dash and slash symbolized as "-" and "/" respectively, and any combination thereof, unique for a financial year;
(d) date of issue;
(e) name, address and Goods and Services Tax Identification Number or Unique Identity Number, if registered, of the recipient;
(f) name and address of the recipient and the address of delivery, along with the name of State and its code, if such recipient is un-registered;
(g) serial number and date of the corresponding tax invoice or, as the case may be, bill of supply;

(h) value of taxable supply of goods or services, rate of tax and the amount of the tax credited to the recipient; and

(i) signature or digital signature of the supplier or his authorized representative.

When Credit Note to be issued

> A Credit note can be issued by a supplier only in the following circumstances:
> (a) The taxable value shown in the invoice exceeds the taxable value of the supply;
> (b) The tax charged in the invoice exceeds the tax payable on the supply;
> (c) The goods supplied are returned by the recipient;
> (d) The goods/services are found to be deficient.

Records: The records of the credit note have to be retained until the expiry of seventy-two months from the due date of furnishing of annual return for the year pertaining to such accounts and records. Where such accounts and documents are maintained manually, it should be kept at every related place of business mentioned in the certificate of registration and shall be accessible at every related place of business where such accounts and documents are maintained digitally.

Credit note cannot be issued if the incidence of tax and interest on such supply has been passed by taxpayer to any other person.

Time Limit for Declaration of Credit Note in Return [Section 34(2)]

Any registered person who issues a credit note in relation to a supply of goods or services or both shall declare the details of such credit note in the return for the month during which such credit note has been issued but not later than the thirtieth day of November following the end of the financial year in which such supply was made, or the date of furnishing of the relevant annual return, whichever is earlier, and the tax liability shall be adjusted in such manner as may be prescribed:

Provided that no reduction in output tax liability of the supplier shall be permitted, if the incidence of tax and interest on such supply has been passed on to any other person.

(B) Debit Note [Section 34(3)]

The issuance of a debit note or a supplementary invoice creates additional tax liability. The treatment of a debit note or a supplementary invoice would be identical to the treatment of a tax invoice as far as returns and payment are concerned.

> Where one or more tax invoices have been issued for supply of any goods or services or both and the taxable value or tax charged in that tax invoice is found to be less than the taxable value or tax payable in respect of such supply, the registered person, who has supplied such goods or services or both, shall issue to the recipient one or more debit notes for supplies made in a financial year containing such particulars as may be prescribed.

A supplier of goods or services or both is mandatorily required to issue a tax invoice. However, during the course of trade or commerce, after the invoice has been issued there could be situations like:

(1) The supplier has erroneously declared a value, which is less than the actual value of the goods, or services or both provided.

(2) The supplier has erroneously declared a lower tax rate than what is applicable for the kind of the goods or services or both supplied.

(3) The quantity received by the recipient is more than what has been declared in the tax invoice.

(4) Any other similar reasons.

When a tax invoice has been issued for supply of any goods or services or both and the taxable value or tax charged in that tax invoice is found to be less than the taxable value or tax payable in respect of such supply, the registered person, who has supplied such goods or services or both, shall issue to the recipient a debit note containing the prescribed particulars.

The debit note or a supplementary invoice is therefore a convenient and legal method by which the value of the goods or services in the original tax invoice can be enhanced.

Time Limit for Declaration of Debit Note in Return [Section 34(4)]

Any registered person who issues a debit note in relation to a supply of goods or services or both shall declare the details of such debit note in the return for the month during which such debit note has been issued and the tax liability shall be adjusted in such manner as may be prescribed.

Records: The records of the debit note or a supplementary invoice have to be retained until the expiry of seventy-two months from the due date of furnishing of annual return for the year pertaining to such accounts and records. Where such accounts and documents are maintained manually, it should be kept at every related place of business mentioned in the certificate of registration and shall be accessible at every related place of business where such accounts and documents are maintained digitally.

Format: There is no prescribed format but debit note issued by a supplier must contain some prescribed particulars, similar to that of tax invoice.

When Debit Note to be issued

A debit note should be issued by a supplier in the following circumstances:

(a) The taxable value shown in the invoice is lesser than the taxable value of the supply; or

(b) The tax charged in the invoice is less than the tax payable on the supply

Time Limit for Issue of Debit/Credit Note

Debit/credit note can be issued either during the same month or subsequent months subject to a maximum time limit of earliest of the following:

- 30th November, following the end of financial year or
- The last date of filing of the relevant annual return.

Chapter 13

Accounts and Records, E-Way Bill

13.1 STATUTORY PROVISIONS

Assessment in GST is mainly focused on self-assessment by the taxpayers themselves. Every taxpayer is required to self-assess the taxes payable and furnish a return for specified tax periods. The GST law has cast obligation on the taxpayer for keeping and maintaining "true & correct" accounts and records. Every registered person shall keep & maintain accounts and records at his principal place of business & where more than one place of business is specified in the certificate of registration the accounts relating to each place of business shall be kept at respective places of business concerned. Records can be maintained manually or in any electronic form.

As per Rule 56(7), every registered person shall keep the books of account at the principal place of business and books of account relating to additional place of business mentioned in his certificate of registration and such books of account shall include any electronic form of data stored on any electronic device.

Circular No. 23/23/2017-GST dated 21.12.2017 provides relaxation from maintenance of books of accounts relating to additional place of business by a principal or an auctioneer for the purpose of auction of tea, coffee, rubber, etc. subject to prescribed conditions.

The provisions relating to accounts & records required to be maintained under GST are contained in Secs 35 & 36 of CGST Act, 2017 read with Rules 56 to 58 of Chapter VII—Accounts & Records of CGST Rule, 2017 as stated hereunder:

CGST Act, 2017

Section	Description
35	Accounts and other records
36	Period of retention of accounts

CGST Rule, 2017

Rule	Description
56	Maintenance of accounts by registered persons
57	Generation and maintenance of electronic records
58	Records to be maintained by owner or operator of godown or warehouse and transporters

13.2 PERSON REQUIRED TO MAINTAIN ACCOUNTS & RECORDS [SECTION 35]

(1) Every registered person
(2) Every owner or operator of warehouse or godown or any other place used for storage of goods (whether registered or not)
(3) Every transporter (whether registered or not)
(4) Any class of taxable person notified by commissioner.

13.2.1 Accounts & Records Required to be Maintained [Section 35(1)]

A true & correct account of following is to be maintained:

(a) production or manufacture of goods;
(b) inward and outward supply of goods or services or both;

(c) stock of goods;
(d) input tax credit availed;
(e) output tax payable and paid; and
(f) such other particulars as may be prescribed.

In addition, Rule 56 also provide to keep and maintain records by

(1) every registered person a true & correct account of goods or services imported/exported or supplies attracting payment of tax on reverse charge along with the relevant documents, including invoices, bills of supply, delivery challans, credit notes, debit notes, receipt vouchers, payment vouchers, refund vouchers and e-way bills.

(2) every registered person, other than a person paying tax under section 10, shall maintain the accounts of stock in respect of goods received and supplied by him, and such accounts shall contain particulars of the opening balance, receipt, supply, goods lost, stolen, destroyed, written off or disposed of by way of gift or free sample and the balance of stock including raw materials, finished goods, scrap and wastage thereof.

(3) separate accounts of advances received, paid & adjustment made thereto.

As per Rule 56(5), every registered person shall keep the particulars of:

(a) names and complete addresses of suppliers from whom he has received the goods or services chargeable to tax under the Act;
(b) names and complete addresses of the persons to whom he has supplied goods or services, where required under the provisions of this Chapter;
(c) the complete address of the premises where goods are stored by him, including goods stored during transit along with the particulars of the stock stored therein.

13.2.2 Records not Required to be Maintained by Composition Dealer

As per Rule 56(2) & 56(4), a supplier opting composition scheme is not required to maintain following records:

(1) Stock of goods including raw materials, finished goods, scrap and wastage thereof, goods stolen, written off or disposed of by way of gift or free sample.

(2) Details of tax payable (including tax payable under RCM), tax collected and paid, input tax, input tax credit claimed, together with a register of tax invoice, credit notes, debit notes, delivery challan issued or received during any tax period.

13.2.3 Records to be Maintained by Different Category of Person

(1) Records to be maintained by Agent [Rule 56(11)]: Every agent shall maintain accounts depicting the:

(a) particulars of authorization received by him from each principal to receive or supply goods or services on behalf of such principal separately;
(b) particulars including description, value and quantity (wherever applicable) of goods or services received on behalf of every principal;
(c) particulars including description, value and quantity (wherever applicable) of goods or services supplied on behalf of every principal;
(d) details of accounts furnished to every principal; and
(e) tax paid on receipts or on supply of goods or services effected on behalf of every principal.

(2) Records to be maintained by Manufacturer [Rule 56(12)]: Every registered person manufacturing goods shall maintain monthly production accounts showing quantitative details of raw materials or services used in the manufacture and quantitative details of the goods so manufactured including the waste and by products thereof.

(3) Records to be maintained by supplier of Service [Rule 56(13)]: Every registered person supplying services shall maintain the accounts showing quantitative details of goods used in the provision of services, details of input services utilized and the services supplied.

(4) Accounts of works contract [Rule 56(14)]: Every registered person executing works contract shall keep separate accounts for works contract showing:

(a) the names and addresses of the persons on whose behalf the works contract is executed;
(b) description, value and quantity (wherever applicable) of goods or services received for the execution of works contract;
(c) description, value and quantity (wherever applicable) of goods or services utilized in the execution of works contract;

(d) the details of payment received in respect of each works contract; and

(e) the names and addresses of suppliers from whom he received goods or services.

(5) **Records to be maintained by custodian/clearing & forwarding agent [Rule 56(17)]:** Any person having custody over the goods in the capacity of a carrier or a clearing and forwarding agent for delivery or dispatch thereof to a recipient on behalf of any registered person shall maintain true and correct records in respect of such goods handled by him on behalf of such registered person and shall produce the details thereof as and when required by the proper officer.

(6) **Records to be maintained by owner or operator of godown or warehouse & transporter [Section 35(2) read with Rule 58]:** Every owner or operator of warehouse or godown or any other place used for storage of goods and every transporter, irrespective of whether he is a registered person or not, shall maintain records of the consigner, consignee and other relevant details of the goods in such manner as may be prescribed.

The transporters, owners or operators of godowns, if not already registered under the GST Act(s), shall submit the details regarding their business electronically on the Common Portal in FORM GST ENR-01. A unique enrolment number shall be generated and communicated to them.

Every person engaged in the business of transporting goods shall maintain records of goods transported, delivered and goods stored in transit by him and for each of his branches. Every owner or operator of a warehouse or godown shall maintain books of accounts, with respect to the period for which particular goods remain in the warehouse, including the particulars relating to dispatch, movement, receipt, and disposal of such goods.

The goods shall be stored in such manner that they can be identified item wise and owner wise and shall facilitate any physical verification or inspection, by the proper officer on demand.

13.2.4 Generation & Maintenance of Records [Rule 56(7), (8), (9) (15), (16), (18)]

Every registered person shall keep the books of account at the principal place of business and books of account relating to additional place of business mentioned in his certificate of registration and such books of account shall include any electronic form of data stored on any electronic device.

Any entry in registers, accounts and documents shall not be erased, effaced or overwritten, and all incorrect entries, otherwise than those of clerical nature, shall be scored out under attestation and thereafter the correct entry shall be recorded and where the registers and other documents are maintained electronically, a log of every entry edited or deleted shall be maintained.

Each volume of books of account maintained manually by the registered person shall be serially numbered.

The records prescribed in Section 35 read with Rule 56 may be maintained in electronic form and the record so maintained shall be authenticated by means of a digital signature. [Rule 56(15)]

The following requirements have been prescribed for maintenance of records in electronic form. [Rule 57]

(1) Proper electronic back up of records shall be maintained so that information can be restored within a reasonable period of time

(2) The registered person shall produce, on demand, the relevant records or documents, duly authenticated, in hard copy or in any electronically readable format

(3) The registered person, shall, on demand, provide the details of such files, passwords of such files and explanation for codes used, where necessary, for access and any other information which is required for such access along with a sample copy in print form of the information stored in such files.

13.3 AUDIT OF ACCOUNTS [SECTION 35(5)]

[Omitted by Finance Act, 2021 w.e.f. 01.08.2021 vide Notification No. 29/2021-C.T. dated 30th July, 2021]

Section 35 of the CGST Act, deals with the maintenance of books of accounts, documents and records. Section 35(5) read with Section 44(2) of the CGST Act and the corresponding Rule 80(3) of the CGST Rules relates to statutory audit under GST.

"Audit" has been defined in Section 2(13) of the CGST Act, 2017 and it means the examination of records, returns and other documents maintained or furnished by the registered person under GST Act or the rules made there under or under any other law for the time being in force.

In audit, examination is done to verify the correctness of

(1) Turnover declared

(2) Taxes paid

(3) Refund claimed and

(4) Input Tax credit availed.

As per Section 35(5), every registered person whose turnover during a financial year exceeds the prescribed limit (i.e. ₹ 2 crores) shall get his accounts audited by a chartered accountant or a cost accountant and shall submit a copy of the audited annual accounts, the reconciliation statement in FORM GSTR-9C (Rule 80(3)) under section 44 (2) and such other documents in such form and manner as may be prescribed. However, Section 35(5), which provides for mandatory audit by CA/CMA, has been omitted by Finance Act, 2021 w.e.f. 1st August 2021.

The Finance Act, 2021, has omitted Section 35(5) and substituted Section 44 w.e.f. 1st April 2021 so as to remove the mandatory requirement of furnishing a Reconciliation Statement (GSTR-9C) duly audited by a Practicing Chartered Accountants or Cost Accountants and to provide for filing of the Annual Return (GSTR-9) on *self-certification basis* with a reconciliation statement. (Ref. Notification Nos. 29 to 31 of 2021-Central Tax dated 30th July 2021)

Books of Accounts of Central/State Govt or local authority are not subject to GST Audit by Chartered/Cost Accountant [Notification No. 03/2019-Central Tax dated 29.01.2019]

Any department of the Central Government or a State Government or a local authority, whose books of account are subject to audit by the Comptroller and Auditor General of India or an auditor appointed for auditing the accounts of local authorities under any law for the time being in force shall be exempted by this provision of audit.

13.4 PERIOD OF RETENTION OF ACCOUNTS [SECTION 36]

All accounts maintained together with all invoices, bills of supply, credit and debit notes, and delivery challans relating to stocks, deliveries, inward supply and outward supply shall be preserved for seventy two months (72 months) from the due date of furnishing of annual return for the year pertaining to such accounts & records.

However, a registered person, who is a party to an appeal or revision or any other proceedings before any Appellate Authority or Revisional Authority or Appellate Tribunal or court, whether filed by him or by the Commissioner, or is under investigation for an offence under Chapter XIX, shall retain the books of account and other records pertaining to the subject matter of such appeal or revision or proceedings or investigation for a period of one year after final disposal of such appeal or revision or proceedings or investigation, or for the period specified above, whichever is later.

13.5 ELECTRONIC WAY BILL (E-WAY BILL) [RULE 138]

Introduction of E-way Bill in India has been effected for inter-State movement of goods across the country from 1st April 2018 and on notified dates by respective State Government for intra-state movements. E-way bill is a permit sort of things in electronic form or electronic generated document, required to be generated for the movement of goods over a prescribed threshold limit, from one place to another place with detailed information of goods being transported. Every registered person who causes movement of goods in relation to supply, or for reason other than supply such as sale of goods on approval basis, job worker, etc., or due to inward supply from an unregistered person excluding exempted goods are required to generate E-Way bill. This document is required to be carried by a person in charge of the conveyance. E-Way bill **(EWB) is a twelve-digit (12) number.**

An e-way bill generated in any state is valid throughout the country [Rule 138 (13)].

Though the E-way bill rules for inter-state supply & intra-state supply is same, the threshold limit for inter-state movement of goods is ₹ 50,000 (including GST). The threshold limit for intra-state supply is different from state to state (Delhi/Tamil Nadu/West Bengal has fixed ₹ 1 lakh, while Bihar has fixed ₹ 2 lakh) as notified by respective State Government. As per Govt. of Sikkim Notification No. 01/SGST/2018 dated 29th March 2018, e-way bill is not required to be generated in case of intra-state movement of any goods, of any value, within the area covered under the State of Sikkim.

The generation of E-way bill has been barred if a supplier or recipient does not file GST returns for two or more consecutive tax periods. This is applicable with effect from 15.08.2021.

In this section, E-way bill rules for inter-State movement of goods have been discussed.

Purpose of E-Way Bill

The basic objective of E-way bill is to track movement of goods and check tax evasion. Taxpayers who will not file GST returns (GSTR-3B) for two or more consecutive tax periods shall be restricted from generating e-way bills. Blocking of EWB generation in terms of Rule 138E (a) & (b) of CGST Rules, 2017 has been implemented from 15th August 2021.

Pre-requisite for generation of E-Way Bill

(1) The person who generates e-way bill should be a registered person on GST portal and he should also register in the e-way bill portal. If the transporter is not a registered person under GST, it is mandatory for him/her to get enrolled on e-waybill portal (https://ewaybillgst.gov.in) before generation of the e-way bill.

(2) Tax invoice or bill of supply or delivery challan and Transporter's ID, who is transporting the goods with transporter document number or the vehicle number in which the goods are transported, must be available.

(3) HSN code of goods.

(4) If GSTIN of consignee/recipient of goods is not available, then address, State & PIN code is required.

13.5.1 Statutory Provision

Section 68 of the Central Goods and Services Tax Act, 2017 read with **Rule 138** of CGST Rules, 2017 deals with the provision relating to E-Way Bill.

E-Way Bill Rules

Rules	Remarks
138 (1) to 138 (14)	Provisions relating to EWB
138 (1)	FORM GST EWB-01 (Single EWB)
138(6) & (7)	FORM GST EWB-02 (Consolidated EWB)
138A	Documents and devices to be carried by a person-in-charge of a conveyance
138B	Verification of documents and conveyances
138C	Verification Report (FORM GST EWB-03) (Inspection and verification of goods in transit)
138D	Report of Detention (FORM GST EWB-04)
138E	Restriction on furnishing of information in PART A of FORM GST EWB-01 (Blocking of EWB)

E-Way Bill FORM

FORM	RULE	REMARKS
FORM GST EWB-01	138 (1)	EWB
FORM GST EWB-02	138 (6) & 138(7)	Consolidated EWB
FORM GST EWB-03	138C	Verification Report
FORM GST EWB-04	138D	Report of Detention

Date of implementation: Vide Notification No. 15/2018-Central Tax dated 23rd March 2018, Central Government has notified 1st day of April 2018 as the appointed day for implementation of Nationwide EWB for Interstate movement of goods.

13.5.2 E-Way Bill Portal (Common portal)

Notification No. 9/2018-Central Tax dated 23rd January 2018: The Central Government has notified www.ewaybillgst.gov.in as the Common Goods and Services Tax Electronic Portal for furnishing electronic way bill. NIC manages this portal.

Registration on E-Way Bill Portal: Registration on www.ewaybill.nic.in is not to be understood as registration under section 22 of CGST Act, 2017 because persons who are already registered under section 22 are also required to register on this portal. Registration on the portal merely refers to creation of user login for use of the features on this portal.

Registration by Person having GSTIN: All the registered persons under GST shall also register on the portal of e-way bill namely: http://ewaybill.nic.in using his GSTIN. Once GSTIN is entered, the system sends the OTP to his registered mobile number and after authenticating the same, the system enables him to generate his/her username and password for the e-way bill system. After generation of username and password of his choice, he/she may proceed to make entries to generate EWB.

Registration by Transporter: There may be some transporters, who are not registered under the Goods and Services Tax Act and if such transporters causes the movement of goods for their clients, they are required to generate the e-way bill on behalf of their clients or update the vehicle number for EWB. Hence, they need to enroll on the EWB portal and generate the 15 digits Unique Transporter ID (TRANSIN):

- Public conveyance has also been included as a mode of transport and the responsibility of generating e-way bill in case of movement of goods by public transport would be that of the consignor or consignee.
- Railways has been exempted from generation and carrying of e-way bill with the condition that without the production of e-way bill, railways will not deliver the goods to the recipient. However, railways are required to carry invoice or delivery challan, etc.

Sub-User in E-Way Bill Portal: Some business may have multiple branches within a state. Under these circumstances, the main user can create sub-users and assign the roles to them. He can assign generation of EWB or rejection or report generation activities based on requirements.

For every principal/additional place of business, user can create maximum of ten (10) sub-users.

13.5.3 Mode of Generation of E-Way Bill

The facility of generation, cancellation, updation and assignment of EWB shall be made available through SMS to the supplier, recipient and the transporter, as the case may be.

For each invoice, one EWB has to be generated, irrespective of same or different consignors or consignees are involved.

13.5.4 When Required

E-way bill is required only in the case of movement of goods: Transactions involving goods are sometimes treated as a supply of services. The e-way bill is required not only when the supply is treated as a supply of goods but even when the supply is treated as a supply of services but involves "movement of goods" such as **lease of goods, supply of food/drinks, etc.**

It may be kept in mind that EWB is required in all cases where goods—inventory, capital goods or inputs for job work or any other business assets are involved in movement. There is no difference whether the movement is pursuant to a supply arrangement or an innocent relocation of goods within the State itself.

When EWB to be generated: E-way bill is required to be generated prior to commencement of movement of goods by the person who causes movement of goods of consignment value exceeding ₹ 50,000 (including GST) by road, by own conveyance, a hired one, or a public conveyance:

- In relation to a 'supply'
- For reasons other than a 'supply' (says, return of goods, goods sent for replacement under warranty, branch transfer, etc.)
- Due to inward 'supply' from an un-registered person.

Multiple invoices cannot be clubbed together to generate one EWB, whether same or different consignors or consignee are involved. Separate EWB to be generated for each invoice. Each invoice is considered as one consignment for the purpose of generating EWB.

For this purpose, a supply may be either of the following:

- A supply made for a consideration (payment) in the course of business
- A supply made for a consideration (payment) which may not be in the course of business
- A supply without consideration (without payment). In simpler terms, the term 'supply' usually means a:
  1. Sale—sale of goods and payment made
  2. Transfer—branch transfers for instance
  3. Barter/Exchange-where the consideration in the form of goods instead of in money.

Therefore, EWBs must be generated on the common portal (www.ewaybillgst.gov.in) for all these types of movements by the person who causes movement of such goods.

As per Rule 138(1), in respect of above supply, every registered person shall, before commencement of such movement, furnish information relating to the said goods as specified in Part A of FORM GST EWB-01. Notification No. 12/2018-Central Tax dated 7th March 2018.

(a) **Consignment value:** The consignment value of goods shall be the value, determined in accordance with the provisions of Section 15, declared in an invoice, a bill of supply or a delivery challan, as the case may be, issued in respect of the said consignment and also includes the GST, if any, charged in the said document **but shall exclude the value of exempt supply of goods** where the invoice is issued in respect of both exempt and taxable supply of goods.

(b) **Exception to before movement of goods:** In case of transportation by Railway/Air/Vessel, Sub-rule 2A has been inserted to provide that, **where the goods are transported by railways or by air or vessel, the EWB shall be generated by the registered person, being the supplier or the recipient,** who shall, either before or after the commencement of movement, furnish, on the common portal, the information in Part B of FORM GST EWB-01:

Provided that where the goods are transported by railways, the railways shall not deliver the goods unless the e-way bill is produced at the time of delivery.

(c) **Mandatory E-way bill even if consignment value of goods less than ₹ 50,000:** As per third and fourth proviso to Rule 138(1), for interstate movement of certain specified goods, the EWB need to be generated mandatorily **even if the value of the consignment of goods is less than ₹ 50,000.**

1. Inter-State movement of goods by the Principal to the Job-worker, by Principal/registered Job-worker,
2. Inter-State Transport of Handicraft goods by a dealer exempted from GST registration u/s 24 (i) and (ii)

Note: The expression "handicraft goods" has the meaning as assigned to it in the Government of India, Ministry of Finance, Notification No. 32/2017-Central Tax dated 15th September 2017.

(d) **Import and export of goods:** Since imports and exports have been considered as inter-State supplies under the GST act, the EWB is required to be issued for these transactions as well. In case of import of goods, the importer will generate the e-way bill. The exporter is liable to generate the e-way bill for export supplies.

Voluntary Compliances

As per first proviso to Rule 138(3) the registered person or, the transporter, may, at his option, generate and carry the EWB even if the value of the consignment is less than fifty thousand rupees.

Modification in E-Way Bill

The EWB once generated cannot be edited or modified. Only Part B can be updated. However, if EWB is generated with wrong information, it can be cancelled and generated afresh. The cancellation is required to be done within twenty-four hours from the time of generation.

Consolidated E-Way Bill

Consolidated EWB is a document containing the multiple EWBs for multiple consignments being carried in one conveyance (goods vehicle). That is, the transporter, carrying multiple consignments of various consignors and consignees in one vehicle can generate and carry one consolidated EWB instead of carrying multiple EWBs for those consignments.

Consolidated EWB is like a trip sheet, it contains details of different EWBs in respect of various consignments being transported in one vehicle, and these EWBs will have different validity periods.

Hence, Consolidated EWB does not have any independent validity period. However, individual consignment specified in the Consolidated EWB should reach the destination as per the validity period of the individual EWB.

As per proviso to Rule 138(5), where the goods are transported for a distance of up to fifty kilometers within the State or Union territory from the place of business of the transporter finally to the place of business of the consignee, the details of the conveyance may not be updated in the EWB.

Rule 138(6): After EWB has been generated in accordance with the provisions of Rule 138(1), where multiple consignments are intended to be transported in one conveyance, the transporter may indicate the serial number of EWBs generated in respect of each such consignment electronically on the common portal and a consolidated EWB in **FORMGST EWB-02** maybe generated by him on the said common portal prior to the movement of goods.

Rule 138(7): Where the consignor or the consignee has not generated the EWB in **FORM GST EWB-01** and the aggregate of the consignment value of goods carried in the conveyance is more than fifty thousand rupees, the transporter, except in case of transportation of goods by railways, air and vessel, shall, in respect of inter-State supply, generate the EWB in **FORM GSTEWB-01** on the basis of invoice or bill of supply or delivery challan, as the case may be, and may also generate a consolidated EWB in **FORM GST EWB-02** on the common portal prior to the movement of goods.

13.5.5 When E-Way Bill is not Required (Excluded Goods)

(a) where the goods being transported are specified in Annexure [Rule 138(14)];

(b) where the goods are being transported by a **non-motorized conveyance;**

(c) where the goods are being transported from the customs port, airport, air cargo complex and land customs station to an inland container depot or a container freight station for clearance by Customs;

(d) in respect of movement of goods within such areas as are notified under Rule 138(14) (d) of the State or Union territory Goods and Services Tax Rules in that particular State or Union territory;

(e) where the goods, other than de-oiled cake, being transported, are specified in the Schedule appended to notification No. 2/2017-Central tax (Rate) dated the 28th June 2017 (149 items—Exempt/Nil rated) as amended by Notification No. Central Tax (Rate). 28/2017 dated 22-09-2017; and 35/2017 dated 13-10-2017;

(f) where the goods being transported are **alcoholic liquor for human consumption, petroleum crude, high-speed diesel, motor spirit (commonly known as petrol), natural gas or aviation turbine fuel;**

(g) where the supply of goods being transported is treated as no supply under Schedule III of the Act;

(h) where the goods are being transported—

   (i) under customs bond from an inland container depot or a container freight station to a customs port, airport, air cargo complex and land customs station, or from one customs station or customs port to another customs station or customs port, or

   (ii) under customs supervision or under customs seal;

(i) where the goods being transported are transit cargo from or to Nepal or Bhutan;

(j) Supply of goods by CSD to unit run canteen **Notification No. 7/2017-Central Tax (Rate), dated 28th June** and supply of heavy water and nuclear fuel Notification No. 26/2017-Central Tax (Rate), dated the 21st September 2017;

(k) any **movement of goods caused by defence formation under Ministry of defence** as a consignor or consignee;

(l) where the consignor of goods is the Central Government, Government of any State or a local authority for transport of goods by rail;

(m) where empty **cargo containers are being transported;**

(n) where the goods are being transported up to a distance of 20 kilometers from the place of the business of the consignor to a weighbridge for weighment or from the weighbridge back to the place of the business of the said consignor subject to the condition that the movement of goods is accompanied by a delivery challan issued in accordance with Rule 55; and

(o) Empty cylinders for packing of liquefied petroleum gas are being moved for reasons other than supply.

Note: Part B of EWB shall not be required to be filled where the distance between the consigner or consignee and the transporter is less than 50 kms and transport is within the same state [proviso to Rule 138(5)].

13.5.6 Who should Generate an E-Way Bill?

- **Registered Person**–E-way bill must be generated when there is a movement of goods of more than ₹ 50,000 (including GST) in value, to or from a Registered Person. A Registered person or the transporter may choose to generate and carry EWB even if the value of goods is less than ₹ 50,000.
- **Transporter**–Transporters carrying goods by road, air, rail, etc. also need to generate EWB if the supplier has not generated an EWB.
- **Unregistered Persons**–Unregistered persons are also required to generate EWB. However, where a supply is made by an unregistered person to a registered person, the receiver will have to ensure that all the compliances are met as if, they were the supplier [Rule 138(3)–**Explanation 1**].

Supply by Unregistered to Unregistered: Public conveyance has also been included as a mode of transport and the responsibility of generating e-way bill in case of movement of goods by public transport would be that of the consignor or consignee.

Where an unregistered party is involved in a transaction, the onus of generation of the EWB is shifted to the Taxable Person. However, when none of the parties to the transaction is registered, then either of the parties needs to register with GSTN or the transporter needs to generate the EWB.

An unregistered supplier can generate the e-way bill through "Enrolment for Citizen" option on the E-Way Bill Portal.

Cancellation of EWB [RULE 138(9)]: Temporary number generated after filing PART-A shall be valid for 15 days for updation in PART B.

E Way bill may be cancelled electronically on the common portal/through SMS within 24 hours of generation, provided it has not been verified in accordance with Rule 138B.

13.5.7 Validity of EWB, Rule 138(10)

Validity of the e-way bill or consolidated e-way bill depends upon the distance the goods have to be transported. EWBs follow a time-distance-acceptance based formula.

Validity of e-Way Bill

Distance	Validity of EWB
Up to 200 kms	1 day
For every additional 200 kms or part thereof thereafter	Additional 1 day
Up to 20 km	One day in case of Over Dimensional Cargo or multimodal shipment in which at least one leg involves transport by ship.
For every 20 km or part thereof thereafter	One additional day in case of Over Dimensional Cargo or multimodal shipment in which at least one leg involves transport by ship.

Note: The validity of the EWB may be extended within eight hours from the time of its expiry.

Acceptance of E-Way Bill [Rule 138(11)]

The details of the e-way bill generated shall be made available to the:

(a) supplier, if registered, where the information in Part A of FORM GST EWB-01 has been furnished by the recipient or the transporter; or

(b) recipient, if registered, where the information in Part A of FORM GST EWB-01 has been furnished by the supplier or the transporter, on the common portal, and the supplier or the recipient, as the case may be, shall communicate his acceptance or rejection of the consignment covered by the e-way bill

Time period for Acceptance of E-Way Bill [Rule 138(12)]

If the person to whom the information under Rule 138(11) has been made available does not communicate his acceptance or rejection within **seventy-two hours** of the details being made available to him on the common portal, or the time of delivery of goods whichever is earlier, it shall be deemed that he has accepted the said details.

Nationwide validity [Rule 138(13)]

The e-way bill generated under rule 138 in any State or Union territory shall be valid in every State and Union territory.

Where E-Way Bill not required [Rule 138(14)]

This sub-rule list out the supply/movements of goods, where generation of E-Way bill is not required.

ANNEXURE

[(See rule 138 (14)]

Sl. No.	Description of Goods
(1)	(2)
1.	Liquefied petroleum gas for supply to household and non-domestic exempted category (NDEC) customers
2.	Kerosene oil sold under PDS
3.	Postal baggage transported by Department of Posts
4.	Natural or cultured pearls and precious or semi-precious stones; precious metals and metals clad with precious metal (Chapter 71)
5.	Jewellery, goldsmiths' and silversmiths' wares and other articles (Chapter 71)
6.	Currency
7.	Used personal and household effect
8.	Coral, unworked (0508) and worked coral (9601)

13.5.8 Penalty for Contravention of E-Way Bill Rules

As per Section 122(1) (xiv) of CGST Act, 2017 a person who transport any taxable goods without cover of E-Way bill shall be liable to a penalty of ₹ 10,000 or tax sought to be evaded whichever is greater.

13.5.9 E-Way Bill Under "Bill to Ship to" Model of Supplies

In a typical "Bill To Ship To" model of supply, there are three persons involved in a transaction, namely:

- "A" is the person who has ordered "B" to send goods directly to "C".
- "B" is the person who is sending goods directly to "C" on behalf of "A".
- "C" is the recipient of goods.

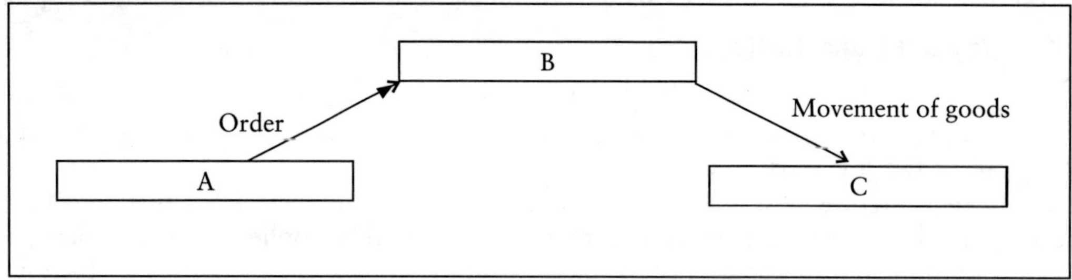

Note: "A" is the person who has ordered "B" to send goods directly to "C".

1. In this complete scenario, two supplies are involved and accordingly two tax invoices are required to be issued:
   - **Invoice 1,** which would be issued by "B" to "A".
   - **Invoice 2** which would be issued by "A" to "C".

2. Who would generate the EWB for the movement of goods, which is taking place from "B" to "C" on behalf of "A".

As per the CGST Rules, 2017 either "A" or "B" can generate the EWB but it may be noted that only one EWB is required to be generated as per the following procedure:

Case 1: Where EWB is generated by "B", the following fields shall be filled in Part A of GST FORM EWB-01:

1.	Bill from	In this field details of "B" are supposed to be filled.
2.	Dispatch From	This is the place from where goods are actually dispatched. It may be the principal or additional place of business of "B".
3.	Bill To	In this field details of "A" are supposed to be filled.
4.	Ship To	In this field address of "C" is supposed to be filled.
5.	Invoice details	Details of Invoice 1 are supposed to be filled.

Case 2: Where EWB is generated by "A", the following fields shall be filled in Part A of GST FORM EWB-01:

1.	Bill from	In this field details of "A" are supposed to be filled.
2.	Dispatch From	This is the place from where goods are actually dispatched. It may be the principal or additional place of business of "B".
3.	Bill To	In this field details of "C" are supposed to be filled.
4	Ship To	In this field address of "C" is supposed to be filled.
5	Invoice details	Details of Invoice 2 are supposed to be filled.

13.5.10 Blocking of E-Way Bill [Rule 138E]

Blocking of e-way bill generation facility means disabling taxpayer from generating E-Way Bill. The GSTINs of such blocked taxpayers cannot be used to generate the e-way bills for outward supply.

No person (including a consignor, consignee, transporter, an e-commerce operator or a courier agency) shall be allowed to furnish the information in PART A of FORM GST EWB-01 in respect of any outward movement of goods of a registered person, who,

(a) being a person paying tax under section 10 or availing the benefit of Notification of the Government of India, Ministry of Finance, Department of Revenue No. 02/2019-Central Tax (Rate), dated 7th March 2019, published in the Gazette of India, Extraordinary, Part II, Section 3, sub-section (i) vide number G.S.R. 189, dated 7th March 2019, has Not furnished the statement in FORM GST CMP-08 for two consecutive quarters; or

(b) being a person other than a person specified in clause (a), has not furnished the returns for a consecutive period of two tax periods; or

(c) being a person other than a person specified in clause (a), has not furnished the statement of outward supplies for any two months or quarters, as the case may be; or

(d) being a person, whose registration has been suspended under the provisions of sub-rule (1) or sub-rule (2) or sub-rule (2A) of rule 21A:

Provided that the Commissioner may, on receipt of an application from a registered person in FORM GST EWB-05, on sufficient cause being shown and for reasons to be recorded in writing, by order, in FORM GST EWB-06, allow furnishing of the said information in PART A of FORM GST EWB-01, subject to such conditions and restrictions as may be specified by him:

Provided further that no order rejecting the request of such person to furnish the information in PART A of FORM GST EWB-01 under the first proviso shall be passed without affording the said person a reasonable opportunity of being heard:

Provided also that the permission granted or rejected by the Commissioner of State tax or Commissioner of Union territory tax shall be deemed to be granted or, as the case may be, rejected by the Commissioner.

Provided also that the said restriction shall not apply during the period from the 20th day of March 2020 till the 15th day of October 2020 in case where the return in FORM GSTR-3B or the statement of outward supplies in FORM GSTR-1 or the statement in FORM GST CMP-08, as the case may be, has not been furnished for the period February 2020 to August 2020:

Provided also that the said restriction shall not apply during the period from the 1st day of May 2021 till the 18th day of August 2021, in case where there turn in FORM GSTR-3B or the statement of outward supplies in FORM GSTR-1 or the statement in FORM GST CMP-08, as the case may be, has not been furnished for the period March 2021 to May 2021.

Non-filing of Return 3B at GST Portal will lead to blocking of EWB generation facility on EWB Portal.

Blocking was proposed w.e.f. 21-06-2019 (Notification No. 22/2019-CT dt. 23-04-2019) but extended to 21-8-2019 (Notification No. 25/2019-CT dt. 21-06-2019) and further extended to 21-11-2019 (Notification No. 36/2019-CT dt. 20-08-2019).

However, blocking of E-Way bill has been made effective from 15-08-2021 on the common portal.

Chapter 14

Returns

14.1 RETURN FRAMEWORK

A registered person under GST is required to file return showing details of inward & outward supply, tax paid and such other information as may be prescribed. There are separate returns for a Normal taxpayer, Composition scheme dealer, non-resident taxpayer, taxpayer registered as an Input Service Distributor, a person liable to deduct or collect the tax (TDS/TCS) and a person granted Unique Identification Number.

The basic features of the returns mechanism in GST include electronic filing of returns, uploading of invoice level information and auto-population of information relating to Input Tax Credit (ITC) from returns of supplier to that of recipient, invoice-level information matching and auto reversal of Input Tax Credit in case of mismatch. Even after completion of more than five years of GST implementation, the return filing mechanism has not been streamlined & still in the making. The complexity of return mechanism and the technical glitches resulted in roll back of invoice-matching, rendering the system prone to ITC frauds. The invoice-matching system has not yet been made operational & filing of GSTR-2 (return of inward supply) & GSTR-3 (monthly return) has been kept in abeyance since implementation of GST. Section 38 and Section 39 of CGST Act, 2017 has been substituted w.e.f. 1st October 2022 vide Notification No. 18/2022-CT dated 28.09.2022 by Section 104 of The Finance Act, 2022 so as to remove the requirement of filing GSTR-2 and GSTR3 return.

Returns can be filed using any of the following mode:

1. Online entry on GSTN portal (www.gst.gov.in)
2. Offline utilities provided by GSTN
3. Third Party Application Software through GST Suvidha Providers (GSPs)

Through Short Messaging Service (SMS): All returns under goods and services tax are to be filed by logging on to www.gst.gov.in. However, newly introduced Rule 67A of the CGST Rules, effective from 1st July 2020, states that if the registered person wants to file a NIL return, it will be considered as being submitted, provided a Short Messaging Service (SMS) is sent from the registered mobile number and further validating the transaction through a One-time password.

The provision relating to filing of returns is contained in Sections 37 to 48 (Chapter IX) of CGST Act, 2017.

Section	Description
Section 37	Furnishing details of outward supplies
Section 38	Furnishing details of inward supplies
Section 39	Furnishing of returns
Section 40	First return
Section 41	Claim of input tax credit and provisional acceptance thereof
Section 42	Matching, reversal and re-claim of input tax credit
Section 43	Matching, reversal and re-claim of reduction in output tax liability
Section 44	Annual Return
Section 45	Final Return
Section 46	Notice to return defaulters
Section 47	Levy of late fee
Section 48	Goods and Services tax practitioners

14.1.1 The GST return framework, which was originally mandated by the Act

Original framework: Step 1: Supplier to enter details of outward supplies in FORM GSTR-1.

Step 2: The outward supplies of the supplier being the inward supplies of the recipient, gets auto-populated in recipient's FORM GSTR-2A.

Step 3: The recipient has an option to add, modify, and delete the values pertaining to his taxes paid on inputs reflecting in his FORM GSTR-2A.

Step 4: The revised values being added/modified/deleted by the recipient gets reflected in supplier's FORM GSTR-1A.

Step 5: If the value reflected in FORM GSTR-1A is the same as appearing in GSTR-1, the supplier/recipient need not take any further action on GSTR-1. In case of difference, the following steps (i) to (iv) are to be adopted, otherwise proceed to Step 6.

(i) In case of difference between GSTR-1A and GSTR-1 of the supplier and if the values found in GSTR-1A is acceptable to supplier, suitable changes to GSTR-1 needs to be made by the supplier.
(ii) If there is a dispute, a mismatch report will be generated. Such report shall be made available to the recipient electronically in Form GST MIS-1 and to the supplier electronically in GST MIS-2.
(iii) After necessary discussions between the parties, if there is a correction required to be made by the supplier, the statement of outward supplies should be rectified, in the month in which such mismatch report has been made available. If there is a correction required to be made by the recipient, the statement of inward supplies should be rectified, in the month in which such a mismatch report has been made available.
(iv) If the rectification has not been made as per Step (iii), the amount of mismatch will be added to the output tax liability of the recipient while filing GSTR-3, in the month succeeding the month in which such discrepancy is made available.

Step 6: Values pertaining to the supplier's inward supplies will have to be compared with his supplier's outward supplies. Upon agreement, values are already correctly populated in his GSTR-2. In case of mismatch, the steps specified in 5(i) to 5(iv) will have to be followed by both the supplier and recipient of the transaction.

Step 7: Part A of GSTR-3 is electronically generated based on the information furnished through GSTR-1, GSTR-2 and other liabilities of preceding tax periods.

Step 8: Supplier, shall discharge his liability towards tax, interest, penalty, fees or any other amount payable under the Act by debiting the electronic cash ledger/electronic credit ledger and include such details in Part B of GSTR-3.

In case, the supplier is eligible for a refund, the information filed in Part B of GSTR-3 will be deemed as a proper refund application under Section 54 of the Act.

Missing invoices and amendments, if any, could only be made in the return of the following tax period latest by 30th September following the end of the financial year.

In a nutshell, registered persons, normally, are required to file FORM GSTR-1 (Return of outward supplies) as per section 37, FORM GSTR-2 (Return of inward supplies) as per section 38 and FORM GSTR-3 (Consolidated/ Summary Return) as per section 39 of the CGST Act, 2017.

14.1.2 Revised/Existing GST Return Framework

(1) FORM GSTR-1A, GSTR-2 and GSTR-3 omitted due to omission of Sections 42, 43 and 43A of CGST Act. (Notification No. 19/2022-Central Tax dated 28.09.2022)
(2) The details of outward supplies of goods or services or both effected during a tax period by a registered person shall be filed in FORM GSTR-1, on or before the tenth day of the month succeeding the said tax period.
(3) A registered person shall not be allowed to furnish the details of outward supplies for a tax period, if the details of outward supplies for any of the previous tax periods has not been furnished by him.
(4) The details of outward supplies furnished by the supplier in FORM GSTR-1 or using the IFF shall be made available electronically to the concerned registered persons (recipients) in Part A of FORM GSTR-2A, in FORM GSTR-4A and in FORM GSTR-6A through the common portal, as the case may be.
(5) The details of tax deducted at source (TDS) furnished by the deductor in FORM GSTR-7 shall be made available to the deductee in Part C of FORM GSTR-2A electronically through the common portal.
(6) The details of tax collected at source (TCS) furnished by an e-commerce operator under section 52 in FORM GSTR-8 shall be made available to the concerned person in Part C of FORM GSTR-2A electronically through the common portal.

(7) An auto-generated statement containing the details of input tax credit shall be made available to the registered person in FORM GSTR-2B, for every month, electronically through the common portal.

(8) A registered person (except OIDAR, ISD, NRTP, Composition scheme dealers, TDS/TCS deductor) shall discharge his liability towards tax, interest, penalty, fees or any other amount payable under the Act by debiting the electronic cash ledger or electronic credit ledger and include the details in the return GSTR-3B on or before the twentieth day of the month succeeding such month.

(9) Editing facilities in GSTR-3B available since December 2020.

(10) Missing invoices and amendments, if any, could only be made in the return of the following tax period latest by 30th November following the end of the financial year.

(11) The CGST Amendment Act, 2022, effective from 1st October 2022, has amended section 16 (eligibility & conditions of availing ITC). ITC is allowed only if the details of input tax credit in respect of the said supply communicated to the recipient under section 38 has not been restricted.

14.1.3 Invoice Furnishing Facility (IFF)

The Invoice Furnishing Facility (IFF) is a facility where quarterly GSTR-1 filers can choose to upload their Business-to-business (B2B) invoices every month, currently under the QRMP scheme only. It is governed by Rule 59(2) of the CGST Rules, available to regular taxpayers having an annual aggregate turnover of up to ₹ 5 crore. One should keep the following points in mind before utilising the IFF:

- The IFF is an optional facility. Non-usage will not attract any late fee.
- The invoices relating to the last month of a quarter are to be uploaded in the GSTR-1 return only.
- There is no requirement to upload invoices in GSTR-1 if the same has been uploaded in the IFF.
- The total value of invoices that can be uploaded per month is restricted to ₹ 50 lakh.
- The details submitted in "IFF" will be reflected in the GSTR-2A and GSTR-2B of the recipients.
- The Invoice Furnishing Facility has been made effective from 01.01.2021 and the first cut-off date was 13th February 2021 for January 2021 (being the first month for the January-March 2021 quarter).

14.2 FURNISHING DETAILS OF OUTWARD SUPPLY [SECTION 37]

GSTR-1 is a statement containing the details of outward supplies; which is to be filed electronically by the following class of registered persons:

(1) Persons whose aggregate turnover during the financial year exceeds the threshold limit (except those registered under section 10 of the Act).

(2) Casual Taxable Persons.

Section 37(3): A registered person, who has furnished the details outward supply in GSTR-1, shall, upon discovery of any error or omission therein, rectify such error or omission in such manner as may be prescribed, and shall pay the tax and interest, if any, in the return to be furnished for such tax period:

Provided that no rectification of error or omission in respect of the details furnished under section 37(1) shall be allowed after the thirtieth day of November following the end of the financial year to which such details pertain, or furnishing of the relevant annual return, whichever is earlier.

Section 37(4): A registered person shall not be allowed to furnish the details of outward supplies under section 37(1) for a tax period, if the details of outward supplies for any of the previous tax periods has not been furnished by him.

Section 37(5): Maximum time allowed for filing GSTR-1 restricted to three years from the due date [Amendment made by Finance Act 2023].

Note: The expression "details of outward supplies" shall include details of invoices, debit notes, credit notes and revised invoices issued in relation to outward supplies made during any tax period.

GSTR-1 Not Applicable: In terms of Section 37(1) read with rule 59(1) of CGST Rules 2017, the details of outward supplies of both goods and services are not required to be furnished by following categories of registered person:

- input service distributor (ISD)
- non-resident taxable person
- person paying tax under composition scheme
- person deducting tax at source
- person collecting tax at source i.e., e-commerce operator (ECO), not being an agent
- a supplier of online information and database access or retrieval services (OIDAR)

Due Date of Filing GSTR-1

(Refer Notification No. 83/2020 dated 10.11.2020)

Sl No.	Description of Persons	Due Date	Remarks
1.	Every registered person (whose Aggregate turnover exceeds ₹ 1.5 crores)	11th of the following month	
2.	Casual taxable persons	11th of the following month	'Casual Taxable Person' (CTP) is defined under Section 2(20) of the Act
3.	Every registered person (whose Aggregate turnover does not exceed ₹ 1.5 crores)	13th of the month succeeding the quarter	The GST portal gives an option of quarterly filing for every registered person whose aggregate turnover does not exceed ₹ 1.5 crores

Notes:

(1) A registered person shall not be allowed to furnish the details of outward supplies during the period from the eleventh day to the fifteenth day of the month succeeding the tax period.

(2) The expression details of outward supplies shall include details of invoices, debit notes, credit notes and revised invoices issued in relation to outward supplies made during any tax period.

Extension of time limit for furnishing the returns: The Commissioner may, for reasons to be recorded in writing, by notification, extend the time limit for furnishing the returns for any class of registered persons.

Extension of time limit notified by the State/UT Commissioner shall be deemed to be notified by CGST Commission.

A taxpayer cannot file GSTR-1 before the end of the current tax period.
However, following are the exceptions to this rule:
(1) Casual taxpayers, after the closure of their business
(2) Cancellation of GSTIN of a normal taxpayer
A taxpayer who has applied for cancellation of registration will be allowed to file GSTR-1 after confirming receipt of the application.

INFORMATION REQUIRED TO BE FURNISHED IN GSTR-1

(As per explanation to section 37 read with rule 59(2) of CGST Rules)

The details of outward supplies are required to be furnished, electronically, in **FORM GSTR-1.**

The registered person is required to furnish details of invoices and revised invoices issued in relation to supplies made by him to registered and unregistered persons during a month and debit notes and credit notes in GSTR-1 in the following manner:

Sl. No.	Invoice wise details of ALL	Consolidated details of ALL	Debit and Credit Notes
1.	Inter-State and Intra-State supplies made to registered persons	Intra-State supplies made to unregistered persons for each rate of tax	Issued during the month for invoices issued previously
2.	Inter-State supplies made to unregistered persons with invoice value exceeding ₹ 2,50,000	Inter-State supplies made to unregistered persons with invoice value up to ₹ 2,50,000 for each rate of tax separately for each State	

From the above table, it can be seen that uploading of invoices depends on whether the supply is Business-to-Business (B2B) or Business-to-Customer (B2C) and whether the supply is intra-State or inter-State.

For B2B supplies, all invoices will have to be uploaded irrespective of whether they are intra-State or inter-State supplies. This is so because the recipient will take ITC and thus, invoice matching is required to be done.

For B2C supplies, uploading in general may not be required, as the buyer will not be taking ITC. However, still in order to implement the destination based principle, invoices of value more than ₹ 2.5 lakh in inter-State B2C supplies will have to be uploaded. For inter-State invoices below ₹ 2.5 lakh, State wise summary will be sufficient and for all intra-State invoices, only consolidated details will have to be given.

Invoices can be uploaded at any time during the tax period and not just at the time of filing.

> Scanned copies of invoices need not to be uploaded. Only certain prescribed fields of information from invoices need to be uploaded e.g., invoice no., date, value, taxable value, rate of tax, amount of tax, etc.
> In case there is no consideration, but the activity is a supply by virtue of Schedule 1 of CGST Act, the taxable value will have to be worked out as prescribed and uploaded.
> Description of each item in the invoice will not be uploaded. Only HSN code in respect of supply of goods and Service accounting code (SAC) in respect of supply of services will have to be fed.

Communication of details of GSTR-1 to the recipient of supply

(Section 37(2) read with sub-rules (3) and (4) of rule 59)

The details of outward supplies for a month furnished by the supplier in FORM GSTR-1 or using the IFF (Invoice Furnishing Facility) shall be made available electronically (auto populated) to the respective recipient(s) in Part A of Form GSTR-2A/Form GSTR-4A (in case of registered person opting for composition levy)/GSTR 6A (for ISD).

The details of tax deducted at source furnished by the deductor under section 39(3) in FORM GSTR-7 shall be made available to the deductee in Part C of FORM GSTR-2A electronically through the common portal.

The details of tax collected at source furnished by an e-commerce operator under Section 52 in FORM GSTR-8 shall be made available to the concerned person in Part C of FORM GSTR-2A electronically through the common portal.

The recipient has the option to add, correct or delete such details and after confirmation, it will be updated in GSTR-1A of supplier in common portal. If the supplier, confirm the same, GSTR-2 will be auto populated.

CONTENTS OF GSTR-1

Basic and Other Details	Details of Outward Supplies
• GSTIN • Legal name and Trade name • Aggregate turnover in previous year • Tax period • HSN-wise summary of outward supplies • Details of documents issued • Advances received/advances	• B2B • B2C • Zero-rated and Deemed exports • Debit/Credit notes issued • Nil rated/Exempted/Non GST • Amendments for prior period

INFORMATION TO BE PROVIDED IN TABLES OF GSTR-1

Table Reference	Description
TABLE 1	GSTIN of Registered person
TABLE 2	Legal name & Trade name of registered person
TABLE 3	Aggregate Turnover in the proceeding financial year
TABLE 4	Invoice-wise details of taxable outward supplies made to registered persons excluding supplies covered by Table 6
TABLE 5	Invoice-wise details of taxable outward inter-State supplies to unregistered persons where the invoice value is more than ₹ 2.5 lakh
TABLE 6	Invoice-wise details of zero-rated supplies and deemed exports
TABLE 7	Consolidated details of taxable supplies (intra-state supplies and inter-state supplies of invoice value up to ₹ 2.5 lakh, net of Debit notes and Credit notes) to unregistered persons
TABLE 8	Nil rated, exempted and non-GST outward supplies
TABLE 9	Amendments to taxable outward supply details furnished in returns for earlier tax periods in Tables 4, 5 & 6
TABLE 10	Amendments to taxable outward supply to unregistered persons furnished in returns for earlier tax periods in Table 7

Table Reference	Description
TABLE 11	Consolidated statement of advances received/advance adjusted in the current tax period/ Amendments of information furnished in earlier tax period. In cases, where assessee has received advance in one tax period and invoice is issued in subsequent tax period, the liability on account of such advances and adjustment thereof against subsequent tax period is required to be shown separately in the return.
TABLE 12	HSN/SAC wise summary of outward supplies The HSN requirement for transactions w.e.f. 1st July 2017 till 31st March 2020 is provided as per Central Tax Notification No. 12/2017 dated 28th June 2017. As per Central Tax Notification No. 78/2020 dated 15th October 2020, number of digits of HSN to be mentioned depending on the Aggregate Turnover during the preceding Financial Year has been notified. It is applicable w.e.f. 1st April 2021
TABLE 13	Documents issued during the tax period Serial no. of invoices for outward supply and inward supply from unregistered persons, revised invoices, debit and credit notes, receipt, payment and refund vouchers, delivery challans for job work, supply on approval, etc. issued during the period including the cancelled ones need to be given under this point.

Interoperability of Electronic way bill (e-way bill) portal with Goods and Services Tax Portal

Since EWB portal allows interoperability with the Goods and Services Tax Portal, following details declared in the EWB portal can be imported into GTR-1 by clicking "Import EWB data" in the respective tiles:

(1) Tables 4A, 4B, 4C
(2) Tables 5A, 5B
(3) Tables 6A, 6B, 6C
(4) Table 12

CORRECTIONS/AMENDMENT IN DETAILS OF OUTWARD SUPPLY OF PRIOR PERIODS

Tables 9, 10 and 11(II) provide for amendments in details of taxable outward supplies furnished in earlier periods (hereinafter referred to as "Amendment Table"). The supplier can make amendments in the particulars furnished in GSTR-1 filed by him **for the prior periods** if he agrees to the mismatch report communicated to him by the system every month, after the processing of the return.

The details of original debit notes/credit notes/refund vouchers issued by the tax-payer in the current tax period as also the revision in the debit notes/credit notes/refund vouchers issued in the earlier tax periods are required to be shown in Table 9 of the GSTR-1.

In the Amendment Table, the suppler is normally required to give details of original invoice (No. and Date), the particulars of which have been wrongly entered in GSTR-1 of the earlier months and are now sought to be amended.

However, it may happen that, a supplier altogether forgets to include the entire original invoice while furnishing the GSTR-1 for a particular month.

In such cases also, he would be required to show the details of the said missing invoice which was issued in earlier month in the Amendment Table only, as such type of errors would also be regarded as data entry error.

TIME LIMIT FOR RECTIFICATION OF ERRORS/OMMISSIONS

A supplier can make corrections of mistakes in subsequent returns of earlier periods but the maximum time limit within which such amendments are permissible is earlier of the following dates:

(1) The thirtieth day of November following the end of the financial year to which such details pertain or
(2) Date of filing of the relevant annual return.

HSN-wise summary of outward supplies: As per Central Tax Notification No. 78/2020 dated 15th October 2020, number of HSN digits to be mention by a registered person in tax invoice has been notified. It is applicable w.e.f. 1st April 2021.

Sl No.	Aggregate Turnover during the preceding financial year	Number of digits of HSN Code
1.	< ₹ 5 crores	4 (optional for B2C supply)
2.	> ₹ 5 crores	6

Note: The HSN requirement for transactions w.e.f. 1st July 2017 till 31st March 2020 is provided as per Central Tax Notification No. 12/2017 dated 28th June 2017, which is as follows.

Sl No.	Aggregate turnover during the preceding financial year	Number of digits of HSN Code
1.	< ₹ 1.5 crores	Nil
2.	> ₹ 1.5 crores but < ₹ 5 Crores	2
3.	> ₹ 5 crores	4

14.3 COMMUNICATION OF DETAILS OF INWARD SUPPLIES AND INPUT TAX CREDIT [SECTION 38]

(1) The details of outward supplies furnished by the registered persons under section 37(1) and of such other supplies as may be prescribed, and an auto-generated statement containing the details of input tax credit shall be made available electronically to the recipients of such supplies in such form and manner, within such time, and subject to such conditions and restrictions as may be prescribed.

(2) The auto-generated statement shall consist of:

(a) details of inward supplies in respect of which credit of input tax may be available to the recipient; and

(b) details of supplies in respect of which such credit cannot be availed, whether wholly or partly, by the recipient,

(i) by any registered person within such period of taking registration as may be prescribed; or

(ii) by any registered person, who has defaulted in payment of tax and where such default has continued for such period as may be prescribed; or

(iii) by any registered person, the output tax payable by whom in accordance with the statement of outward supplies furnished by him under the said sub-section during such period, as may be prescribed, exceeds the output tax paid by him during the said period by such limit as may be prescribed; or

(iv) by any registered person who, during such period as may be prescribed, has availed credit of input tax of an amount that exceeds the credit that can be availed by him in accordance with clause (a), by such limit as may be prescribed; or

(v) by any registered person, who has defaulted in discharging his tax liability in accordance with the provisions of section 49 (12) subject to such conditions and restrictions as may be prescribed; or

(vi) by such other class of persons as may be prescribed.

The registered persons who file details of outward supplies are also required to file the details of inward supplies.

As per the decision taken in 23rd GST Council meeting held at Guwahati on 10th Nov 2017, Central Government vide Notification No. 58/2017-Central Tax dated 15th November 2017 has suspended filing of GSTR-2 and GSTR-3 till indefinite period.

Form and manner of ascertaining details of inward supplies [Rule 60]

[w.e.f. 01.10.2022 vide Notification No. 19/2022-CT dated 28.09.2022]

(1) The details of outward supplies furnished by the supplier in FORM GSTR-1 or using the IFF shall be made available electronically to the concerned registered persons (recipients) in Part A of FORM GSTR-2A, in FORM GSTR-4A and in FORM GSTR-6A through the common portal, as the case may be.

(2) The details of invoices furnished by a non-resident taxable person in his return in FORM GSTR-5 under rule 63 shall be made available to the recipient of credit in Part A of FORM GSTR-2A electronically through the common portal.

(3) The details of invoices furnished by an Input Service Distributor in his return in FORM GSTR-6 under rule 65 shall be made available to the recipient of credit in Part B of FORM GSTR-2A electronically through the common portal.

(4) The details of tax deducted at source furnished by the deductor under section 39(3) in FORM GSTR-7 shall be made available to the deductee in Part C of FORM GSTR-2A electronically through the common portal.

(5) The details of tax collected at source furnished by an e-commerce operator under section 52 in FORM GSTR-8 shall be made available to the concerned person in Part C of FORM GSTR-2A electronically through the common portal.

(6) The details of the integrated tax paid on the import of goods or goods brought in domestic Tariff Area from Special Economic Zone unit or a Special Economic Zone developer on a bill of entry shall be made available in Part D of FORM GSTR-2A electronically through the common portal.

(7) An auto-generated statement containing the details of input tax credit shall be made available to the registered person in FORM GSTR-2B, for every month, electronically through the common portal, and shall consist of:

- (i) the details of outward supplies furnished by his supplier, other than a supplier required to furnish return for every quarter under proviso to section 39 (1), in FORM GSTR-1, between the day immediately after the due date of furnishing of FORM GSTR-1 for the previous month to the due date of furnishing of FORM GSTR-1 for the month;
- (ii) the details of invoices furnished by a non-resident taxable person in FORM GSTR-5 and details of invoices furnished by an Input Service Distributor in his return in FORM GSTR-6 and details of outward supplies furnished by his supplier, required to furnish return for every quarter under proviso to section 39 (1), in FORM GSTR-1 or using the IFF, as the case may be,—
  - (a) for the first month of the quarter, between the day immediately after the due date of furnishing of FORM GSTR-1 for the preceding quarter to the due date of furnishing details using the IFF for the first month of the quarter;
  - (b) for the second month of the quarter, between the day immediately after the due date of furnishing details using the IFF for the first month of the quarter to the due date of furnishing details using the IFF for the second month of the quarter;
  - (c) for the third month of the quarter, between the day immediately after the due date of furnishing of details using the IFF for the second month of the quarter to the due date of furnishing of FORM GSTR-1 for the quarter;
- (iii) the details of the integrated tax paid on the import of goods or goods brought in the domestic Tariff Area from Special Economic Zone unit or a Special Economic Zone developer on a bill of entry in the month.

(8) The Statement in FORM GSTR-2B for every month shall be made available to the registered person,—

- (i) for the first and second month of a quarter, a day after the due date of furnishing of details of outward supplies for the said month, in the IFF by a registered person required to furnish return for every quarter under proviso to section 39 (1), or in FORM GSTR-1 by a registered person, other than those required to furnish return for every quarter under proviso to section 39 (1), whichever is later.
- (ii) in the third month of the quarter, a day after the due date of furnishing of details of outward supplies for the said month, in FORM GSTR-1 by a registered person required to furnish return for every quarter under proviso to section 39 (1).

Details of inward supplies of persons having Unique Identity Number (UIN)

(1) Every person, who has been issued a Unique Identity Number and claims refund of the taxes paid on his inward supplies, shall furnish the details of such supplies of taxable goods or services or both in **FORM GSTR-11** along with application for such refund claim either directly or through a Facilitation Centre, notified by the Commissioner.

(2) Every person, who has been issued a Unique Identity Number for purposes other than refund of the taxes paid, shall furnish the details of inward supplies of taxable goods or services or both as may be required by the proper officer in **FORM GSTR-11.**

14.3.1 Auto Drafted ITC Statement-GSTR 2B [Rule 60(7)]

Notification No. 82/2020-Central Tax dated 10th November 2020 effective from 1st January 2021

Notification No. 19/2022-Central Tax dated 28th Sept 2020 effective from 1st October 2022

Rule 60(7) of CGST Rules, 2017 prescribes for generation of auto-drafted statement containing the details of input tax credit in FORM GSTR-2B for counter-party recipients.

GSTR-2B is an auto-drafted Input Tax Credit (ITC) statement, introduced by GSTN from August 2020 tax period to simplify Input Tax Credit Claim for taxpayers. It is available to the recipient after 12th of a month for the previous month. GSTR-2B provides eligible and ineligible Input Tax Credit (ITC) for each month, similar to GSTR-2A but remains constant or unchanged (static) for a period.

The contents of GSTR-2B are as under:

- GSTR-2B provides details eligible and ineligible Input Tax Credit (ITC) for each month.
- GSTR-2B reflected Invoice wise detail of ITC.
- Document wise details such as invoices, credit notes, debit notes, etc. to view and download.
- It provides supplier wise summary and input tax summary.
- It provides summary statement showing ITC available and non-available for every section.
- Advisory for every section that clarifies the kind of action those taxpayers must take.
- Import of goods and import from SEZ units.

14.3.2 Advance Paid/Adjusted

As per sections 12 and 13, in case of supplies taxable under reverse charge, if the date on which the recipient makes the payment precedes the date of actual receipt of goods or as the case may be 30 days (in case of goods)/60 days (in case of services) from the date of issue of invoice by the supplier, the time of supply is the date of payment.

In such cases, even if the invoice is not received, the recipient is required to pay tax. The details of tax paid on such advance payments are required to be entered in Table 10A.

When the invoice for inward supplies against such advance payments is received in subsequent tax period, the same is shown in Table 10B of GSTR-2 of that tax period. The tax paid on advance in earlier tax period is adjusted with tax on supplies made in current tax period and shown in Table 12.

> The Central Govt vide Notification No. 66/2017-Central Tax dated 15th November 2017, has notify that, in case of supply of **"goods"** by a registered person (other than composition scheme dealer), tax shall be paid on supply of goods and not at the time of receipt of advance payment in respect of supply of such goods.

14.4 FURNISHING OF RETURN [SECTION 39]

(1) Every registered person, other than an Input Service Distributor or a non-resident taxable person or a person paying tax under the provisions of section 10 or section 51 or section 52 shall, for every calendar month or part thereof, furnish, a return, electronically, of inward and outward supplies of goods or services or both, input tax credit availed, tax payable, tax paid and such other particulars, in such form and manner, and within such time, as may be prescribed:

Provided that the Government may notify certain class of registered persons who shall furnish a return for every quarter or part thereof, subject to such conditions and restrictions as may be specified therein.

(2) A person opting composition scheme u/s 10, shall furnish a statement, every quarter or, as the case may be, part thereof, containing the details of payment of self-assessed tax in FORM GST CMP-08, till the 18th day of the month succeeding such quarter and furnish a return for every financial year or as the case may be part thereof in FORM GSTR-4 till the thirtieth day of April following the end of such financial year.

(3) Every registered person required to deduct tax at source under section 51 shall furnish a return in FORM GSTR-7 electronically through the common portal.

(4) Every Input Service Distributor shall, on the basis of details contained in FORM GSTR-6A, and where required, after adding, correcting or deleting the details, furnish electronically the return in FORM GSTR-6, containing the details of tax invoices on which credit has been received and those issued under section 20, through the common portal.

(5) Every registered non-resident taxable person shall furnish a return in FORM GSTR-5 electronically through the common portal, including therein the details of outward supplies and inward supplies and shall pay the tax, interest, penalty, fees or any other amount payable under the Act within twenty days after the end of a tax period or within seven days after the last day of the validity period of registration, whichever is earlier.

(6) The commissioner is empower to extend time limit of furnishing of return by notification for such class of registered persons as may be specified therein.

(7) Every registered person who is required to furnish a return under sub-section (1), other than the person referred to in the proviso thereto, or sub-section (3) or sub-section (5), shall pay to the Government the tax due as per such return not later than the last date on which he is required to furnish such return.

(8) Every registered person who is required to furnish a return under sub-section (1) or sub-section (2) shall furnish a return for every tax period whether or not any supplies of goods or services or both have been made during such tax period.

(9) Where any registered person after furnishing a return under sub-section (1) or sub-section (2) or sub-section (3) or sub-section (4) or sub-section (5) discovers any omission or incorrect particulars therein, other than as a result of scrutiny, audit, inspection or enforcement activity by the tax authorities, he shall rectify such omission or incorrect particulars in the return to be furnished for the month or quarter during which such omission or incorrect particulars in such form and manner as may be prescribed, subject to payment of interest under this Act:

Provided that no such rectification of any omission or incorrect particulars shall be allowed after the thirtieth day of November following the end of the financial year to which such details pertain, or the actual date of furnishing of relevant annual return, whichever is earlier.

(10) A registered person shall not be allowed to furnish a return for a tax period if the return for any of the previous tax periods or the details of outward supplies under sub-section (1) of section 37 for the said tax period has not been furnished by him.

(11) The maximum time limit to furnish said return is three years from the due date of its filing [Amendment made by Finance Act 2023].

14.5 FORM GSTR-3B [SECTION 39, RULE 61(1) AND 61A OF CGST RULES)]

The GSTR-2 and GSTR-3 return has not been made operational. As a stop-gap arrangement, to ensure that the Government's tax collections are not disrupted & to make the transition phase smooth & help the registered person in "ease of compliance", a simple GST return, i.e. FORM GSTR-3B was introduced vide Notification No. 21/2017-Central Tax dated 08.08.2017 by the commissioner, on the recommendation of the GST council.

The GSTR-3B is a consolidated summary return of inward and outward supplies in lieu of GSTR-3. The tax liability of a registered person is discharge by filing GSTR-3B. FORM GSTR-3B can be file on a monthly or quarterly basis, as applicable. For those filing their GST returns monthly, the due date of filing GSTR-3B is 20th day of the month following the month for which the return should be file. For those filing their GST return quarterly, the due date of filing GSTR-3B is 22nd and 24th day of the month depending upon place of registration, following the quarter for which the returns should be filed. **FORM GSTR-3B** must be file and submitted even if a registered person does not have any transactions.

Form GSTR 3B—Not Applicable
(1) Input Service Distributors
(2) Composition scheme dealers
(3) Suppliers of online information and database access or retrieval services (OIDAR)
(4) Non-resident taxable person
(5) TDS/TCS deductor (who is otherwise not liable to pay tax on outward supply)

There are several Tables in FORM GSTR-3B to enter relevant details, for the relevant tax period.

3.1 Tax on outward and reverse charge inward supplies: To provide summary details of outward supplies and inward supplies liable to reverse charge and tax liability thereon.

3.2 Inter-state supplies: To provide details of inter-state supplies made to unregistered persons, composition taxable persons and UIN holders and tax thereon.

4. Eligible ITC: To provide summary details of Eligible ITC claimed, ITC Reversals and Ineligible ITC.

5. Exempt, Nil and Non-GST inward supplies: To provide summary details of exempt, nil and Non-GST inward supplies.

5.1 Interest and Late Fee: To provide summary details of Interest and Late fee payable.

6. Payment of Tax: To provide details of payment of taxes, interest and late fee.

In Table 3.1(a, b, c, e) the details are auto-drafted from FORM GSTR-1 in FORM GSTR-3B. Whereas in Table 3.1(d) the details are auto-drafted from FORM GSTR-2B. One can also add/modify the details in Table 3.1(a, b, c, d, e) if required.

In Table 3.2 Inter-State supplies, the details are auto-drafted from FORM GSTR-1. One can add/modify the auto-drafted details if required. In case the edited details are in downward variance, then such fields will be highlighted in red color.

The details of ITC claimed/ITC reversed in Table 4A (1, 3, 4, 5) and 4B (2) are auto-drafted from relevant entries of FORM GSTR-2B. Other reversals would be required to be done by the taxpayer on his own. Modification in auto-drafted details allowed.

14.6 REVERSAL OF INELIGIBLE ITC

14.6.1 Reporting of ITC availment, reversal and ineligible/blocked ITC in Table 4 of GSTR-3B

Notification No. 14/2022-Central Tax dated 05th July 2022

Circular No. 170/02/2022-GST dated 06th July 2022

CBIC has notified few changes in Table 4 of FORM GSTR-3B for enabling taxpayers to correctly report information regarding ITC availed, ITC reversal and ineligible ITC in Table 4 of GSTR-3B. This change is applicable from 01-09-2022.

Table	Particulars
4A. ITC Available (whether in full of Part)	Total ITC (eligible as well as ineligible) is being auto-populated from GSTR-2B. (Except ineligible ITC due to time barred and POS of intra-state supply is different from the recipient state.)
4B.(1) ITC Reversed	ITC which are absolute in nature and are not reclaimable (Note: 1)
4B.(2) ITC Reversed	ITC, which are not permanent in nature and can be reclaimed in future. (Note: 2)
4C. Net ITC Available	4C=4A-(4B(1)+4B(2))
4D.(1) Ineligible ITC	ITC, which was reversed in 4B (2) and now reclaiming the same, shall also report here.
4D.(2) Ineligible ITC	Ineligible ITC due to time barred and POS of intra state supply is different from the recipient state.

Note 1: ITC, which are absolute in nature and not reclaimable, are such as Rule 38 (reversal of credit by banking company), Rule 42 (reversal of ITC on input and input services on account of exempt supply), Rule 43 (reversal of ITC on capital goods on account of exempt supply) and reversal of ineligible ITC under Section 17(5).

Note 2: ITC which are not permanent in nature and can be reclaimable in future are such as rule 37 (reversal of credit due to non-payment within 180 days), reversal due to invoice received earlier but goods and service received later on account of Section 16(2)(b) and (c).

Total ITC (eligible as well as ineligible) of the taxpayer will be auto-populated from statement in FORM GSTR-2B in different fields of Table 4A of FORM GSTR-3B.

The taxpayer shall not deduct the amount of ineligible input tax credit directly by editing the total amount of input tax credit auto populated in Table 4A of FORM GSTR-3B.

Out of the amounts available in Table 4A of FORM GSTR-3B, if the taxpayer have any ineligible input tax credit which is to be reversed on account of Rule 38 (reversal of credit by a banking company or a financial institution) or Rule 42 (reversal of credit on inputs and input services if the same is used for non-business purpose or used for the outward supply of exempted goods or services) or Rule 43 (reversal of credit on capital goods if the same is used for non-business purpose or used for the outward supply of exempted goods or services) of the CGST Rules, 2017, as the case may be, the same shall be declared in Table 4 (B) (1) of FORM GSTR-3B. In addition to that, if the taxpayer has any input tax credit, which is, blocked as per Section 17(5) of the CGST Act, 2017 the same shall also be declared in Table 4 (B) (1) of FORM GSTR-3B.

The taxpayer shall report reversal of ITC which are not permanent in nature and can be reclaimed in future subject to fulfilment of specific conditions, such as on account of Rule 37 (non-payment of consideration to supplier within 180 days) of CGST Rules, 2017, Section 16(2)(b) (non receipt of goods or services or both in the same tax period in which the invoice has been received) and Section 16(2)(c) (nonpayment of tax by the supplier) of the CGST Act, 2017 in Table 4 (B) (2) of FORM GSTR-3B.

Such input tax credit may be reclaimed in the appropriate table in Table 4 (A) of FORM GSTR-3B on fulfilment of necessary conditions. Further, all such reclaimed input tax credit shall also be shown in Table 4 (D) (1) of FORM GSTR-3B. Table 4 (B) (2) of FORM GSTR-3B may also be used by the taxpayer for reversal of any input tax credit availed in Table 4(A) of FORM GSTR-3B wrongly in any previous tax periods due to any inadvertent/clerical mistakes.

Accordingly, the "Net ITC Available" in Table 4 (C) of FORM GSTR-3B will be as per the formula (4A-[4B (1) + 4B (2)]) and the same will be credited to the electronic credit ledger of the taxpayer and also in Table 6 of FORM GSTR-3B to set-off the out put tax dues, if any.

Input tax credit not available, on account of limitation of time period as specified in Section 16 (4) of the CGST Act, 2017 or where the recipient of an intra-State supply is located in a different State/UT than that of place of supply, may be reported by the taxpayer in Table 4 D (2) of FORM GSTR-3B. Such details are available in Table 4 of FORM GSTR-2B.

If any taxpayer has availed ineligible or blocked credits and in cases where the time limit prescribed under Section 39(9) of the Act for rectification by filing FORM GSTR-3B is over, they may reverse such input tax credit on his own ascertainment by filing FORM GST DRC-03, electronically on the common portal, in accordance with prevailing Acts and Rules, to avoid further litigations and proceedings such as Show Cause Notices demanding tax, interest, imposition of penalty, etc.

In a Nutshell:

(1) All non-reclaimable reversal of ITC needs to be reported in Table 4(B)(1).

(2) All reclaimable ITC reversals may be reported in Table 4(B) (2). It should be noted that ITC reversed under 4(B)(2) can be reclaimed in Table 4(A)(5) at appropriate time and the break-up detail of such reclaimed ITC should be provided in 4(D)(1) in the same return.

(3) The ITC not-available mentioned in GSTR-2B of the taxpayer has to be reported in 4(D) (2) of Table 4.

(4) Any ITC availed inadvertently in Table 4(A) in previous tax periods due to clerical mistakes or some other inadvertent mistake maybe reversed in Table 4(B) (2).

14.6.2 Due date of filing GSTR-3B for persons filing quarterly return

According to Rule 61 (effective from 1st January 2021) of CGST Rules, 2017, the due date of filing GSTR-3B in case of quarterly return filers are as follows:

Sl No.	Class of Registered Person	Due Date
1.	Registered persons whose principal place of business is in the States of Chhattisgarh, Madhya Pradesh, Gujarat, Maharashtra, Karnataka, Goa, Kerala, Tamil Nadu, Telangana, Andhra Pradesh, the Union territories of Daman and Diu and Dadra and Nagar Haveli, Puducherry, Andaman and Nicobar Islands or Lakshadweep.	22nd of the month succeeding such quarter
2.	Registered persons whose principal place of business is in the States of Himachal Pradesh, Punjab, Uttarakhand, Haryana, Rajasthan, Uttar Pradesh, Bihar, Sikkim, Arunachal Pradesh, Nagaland, Manipur, Mizoram, Tripura, Meghalaya, Assam, West Bengal, Jharkhand or Odisha, the Union territories of Jammu and Kashmir, Ladakh, Chandigarh or Delhi.	24th of the month succeeding such quarter

14.6.3 Form and manner of furnishing of GSTR-3B return [Rule 60]

(1) Every registered person (except OIDAR, ISD, NRTP, Composition scheme dealers, TDS/TCS deductor) shall furnish a return u/s 39(1) in FORM GSTR-3B electronically through the common portal for each month, or part thereof, on or before the twentieth day of the month succeeding such month.

(2) A registered person shall discharge his liability towards tax, interest, penalty, fees or any other amount payable under the Act by debiting the electronic cash ledger or electronic credit ledger and include the details in the return GSTR-3B.

(3) A registered person, who is required to furnish GSTR-3B on quarterly basis, shall pay the tax dues for the first two months of the quarter, by depositing the said amount in FORM GST PMT-06, by the twenty-fifth day of the month succeeding such month.

(4) The amount deposited by the registered persons under sub-rule (3) above, shall be debited while filing the return for the said quarter in FORM GSTR-3B, and any claim of refund of such amount lying in balance in the electronic cash ledger, if any, out of the amount so deposited shall be permitted only after the return in FORM GSTR-3B for the said quarter has been filed.

14.6.4 Manner of opting for furnishing quarterly return [Rule 61A]

(1) Every registered person intending to furnish return on a quarterly basis under proviso to section 39 (1) shall in accordance with the conditions and restrictions notified in this regard, indicate his preference for furnishing of return on a quarterly basis, electronically, on the common portal, from the 1st day of the second month of the preceding quarter till the last day of the first month of the quarter for which the option is being exercised:

Provided that where such option has been exercised once, the said registered person shall continue to furnish the return on a quarterly basis for future tax periods, unless the said registered person:

(a) becomes ineligible for furnishing the return on a quarterly basis as per the conditions and restrictions notified in this regard; or

(b) opts for furnishing of return on a monthly basis, electronically, on the common portal:

Provided further that a registered person shall not be eligible to opt for furnishing quarterly return in case the last return due on the date of exercising such option has not been furnished.

(2) A registered person, whose aggregate turnover exceeds 5 crore rupees during the current financial year, shall opt for furnishing of return on a monthly basis, electronically, on the common portal, from the first month of the quarter, succeeding the quarter during which his aggregate turnover exceeds 5 crore rupees.

14.7 SUMMARY OF GST RETURN & THEIR DUE DATES

Return Form	Description	By Whom?	Date of filing
FORM GSTR-1	Outward Supplies	For Monthly Return Filers	11th of the next month Central Tax Notification No. 83/2020 dated 10.11.2020
		For registered persons required to furnish return for every quarter under proviso to section 39(1)	13th of the month succeeding the quarter
FORM GSTR-1A	Details of outward supplies as added, corrected or deleted by the recipient	Auto populated	17th of the next month
FORM GSTR-2	Inward supplies	Auto populated	15th of the next month (Not yet operational)
FORM GSTR-2A	Details of inward supplies made available to the recipient on the basis of FORM GSTR-1 furnished by the supplier. Recipient has the opportunity to accept, reject, amend or delete, which will be reflected in GSTR 1A	Normal/Regular Tax payer	Before 15th of next month
FORM GSTR-3	Monthly return on the basis of finalization of details of outward supplies and inward supplies along with the payment of amount of tax	Auto populated	20th of the next month (Not yet operational)
FORM GSTR-3A	Notice to a registered person who fails to furnish return under section 39 or section 44 or section 45 or section 52	This is not a return, Notice issued by Department to return defaulter	It is a notice issued u/s 46 to taxpayers who have not filed their GST returns

FORM GSTR-3B	Summary of Monthly Return (In lieu of GSTR 3)	Normal/Regular Tax payer	20th of the next month
		Quarterly return filer	22nd & 24th of the month succeeding such quarter
FORM GSTR-4	Quarterly return for compounding taxable person covered under Sec 10	Composition Supplier	18th of the month next to the quarter From FY 2019-20, the quarterly requirement has been changed to annual. The due date is 30th April following the end of the financial year
FORM GSTR-4A	Details of inward supplies made available to the recipient registered under composition scheme on the basis of FORM GSTR-1 furnished by the supplier	Auto populated, recipient has the opportunity to accept, reject, amend or delete, which will be reflected in GSTR 1	15th of the month next to the quarter
FORM GSTR-5	Return for Non-Resident foreign taxable person	Non-Resident Taxable Person	20th of the next month or within seven days after expiry of registration, whichever is earlier
FORM GSTR-6	Return for Input Service Distributor	Input Service Distributor (ISD)	13th of the next month
FORM GSTR-6A	Details of inward supplies made available to the ISD recipient on the basis of FORM GSTR-1 furnished by the supplier	Auto populated, recipient has the opportunity to accept, reject, amend or delete, which will be reflected in GSTR 1	
FORM GSTR-7	Monthly Return of TDS	Tax Deductor u/s 51	10th of the next month
FORM GSTR-7A	TDS Certificate	Tax Deductor	15th of the next month
FORM GSTR-8	Monthly Return of TCS	E-commerce Operator/Tax Collector	10th of the next month
FORM GSTR-9	Annual Return	Normal Tax payer (other than CTP)	31st December of next financial year
FORM GSTR-9A	Simplified Annual return by Compounding taxable persons	Composition Supplier	31st December of next financial year
FORM GSTR-9B	Annual Return by E-Commerce operator	E-Commerce operator	31st December of next financial year
FORM GSTR-9C	Annual Return along with the copy of audited accounts and a reconciliation statement	Normal Tax payer having turnover more than ₹ 2 crores	31st December of next financial year
FORM GSTR-10	Final Return	Every registered person who is required to furnish return u/s 39(1) & whose registration has been surrendered or cancelled	Within three months of the date of cancellation or date of cancellation order, whichever is later
FORM GSTR-11	Details of inward supplies to be furnished by a person having UIN	Person having UIN and claiming refund	No due date. UIN holder can file the form any time after the end of the relevant quarter

Note: A register person whose aggregate annual turnover is less than ₹ 1.5 crores is required to file GSTR-1 on quarterly basis & also to deposit tax through GSTR-3B on quarterly basis. But as per Rule 59(2), such supplier are permitted to upload invoices in Invoice Furnishing Facility (IFF) in order to enable the recipients of supplies to avail Input Tax Credit.

Further, Section 39(7) provides that those tax payers who are eligible to file the return on quarterly basis, shall pay their tax dues on monthly basis, in the manner to be prescribed. Now, vide Notification 81/2020-Central Tax dated 10.11.2020, the above amendment has come into effect from 10.11.2020. Central Tax Notification No. 84/2020 dated 10.11.2020 provides that taxable persons having aggregate turnover of up to ₹ 5 crore in the preceding financial year, are notified as persons who shall be entitled to file GSTR-3B on quarterly basis from January 2021.

Section 39(7) lays down that the taxpayers who opt to file their GSTR-3B returns on quarterly basis shall pay the tax on monthly basis, in the manner prescribed in Notification 85/2020-Central Tax dated 10.11.2020.

14.7.1 Mandatory Filing of Return

Every registered person covered under section 39(1) & 39(2) shall furnish a return for every tax period whether or not any supplies of goods and/or services have been effected during such tax period.

In other words, the registered person covered under Section 39(1) and 39(2) are obliged to file "NIL RETURN" even when there is no transaction effected by them in any tax period.

As per Section 39(10), a registered person shall not be allowed to furnish a return for a tax period if the return for any of the previous tax periods has not been furnished by him.

14.8 FIRST RETURN [SEC 40]

When a person becomes liable to registration after his turnover crossing the threshold limit of ₹ 20 lakhs (₹ 10 lakhs in case of Special Category States), he may apply for registration within 30 days of so becoming liable. Thus, there might be a time lag between a person becoming liable to registration and grant of registration certificate.

During the intervening period, such person might have made the outward supplies, i.e. after becoming liable to registration but before grant of the certificate of registration. After receive of certificate of registration, the registered person would have to issue or raise a revised invoice, to give effect for the taxes liable to be paid under GST laws.

As per **Section 40**, every registered person who has made outward supplies in the period between the date on which he became liable to registration till the date on which registration has been granted shall declare the same in the first return furnished by him after grant of registration.

Input tax credit on purchases prior to the date of registration

As per the provisions of Section 18(1), person making an application for new registration shall be entitled to claim credit of input tax held in inputs as such, inputs contained in semi-finished goods or finished goods held in stock by such person on the day immediately preceding the date from which such person is liable to obtain registration i.e., the supplies made thirty days before the date of registration if the application for registration is made on thirtieth day, from the date on which he became liable to get registered OR the date on which he made an application for registration, if application for registration is made immediately he became liable for registration.

Note: Input tax credit in relation to capital goods held as a fixed asset as on the above date, which will be used or is intended to be used in making taxable supply will not be available, as there is no specific provision in this regard. In such cases, person making an application for registration could effect purchases of such capital goods (if he is intending to purchase any) after receiving the said registration certificate.

14.8.1 Availment of input tax credit [Section 41]

(1) Every registered person shall, subject to such conditions and restrictions as may be prescribed, be entitled to avail the credit of eligible input tax, as self-assessed, in his return and such amount shall be credited to his electronic credit ledger.

(2) The credit of input tax availed by a registered person under sub-section (1) in respect of such supplies of goods or services or both, the tax payable whereon has not been paid by the supplier, shall be reversed along with applicable interest, by the said person in such manner as may be prescribed:

Provided that where the said supplier makes payment of the tax payable in respect of the aforesaid supplies, the said registered person may re-avail the amount of credit reversed by him in such manner as may be prescribed.

> Notification No. 18/2022-Central Tax dated 28.09.2022.
> Section 41 has been amended thereby removing the concept of claiming eligible ITC on provisional basis and Sections 42, 43 and 43A of CGST Act, 2017 has been omitted, thus, doing away with two-way communication process in return filing by Finance Act, 2022 effective from 1st October 2022.

14.8.2 Matching, Reversal and Reclaim of Input Tax Credit [Section 42]

(Omitted w.e.f. 1st October, 2022 vide Notification No. 18/2022-CT dated 28.09.2022 by Section 107 of The Finance Act 2022)

The process of ITC Matching begins after the due date for filing of the return. Matching process is carried out by GSTN. Since filing of GSTR-2 and GSTR-3 has still not been made operational, the matching of input tax credit and verification of output tax liability would still be done on the basis of GSTR 1 furnished for outward supplies and amount of credit availed by recipient apart from values as made available to him in his Form GSTR 2A.

Notification No. 49/2019-CT dated 09.10.2019 inserted new sub-rule (4) to rule 36 of the CGST Rules, 2017; whereby restricting taking of input-tax credit in respect of invoices or debit notes, the details of which have not been uploaded by the suppliers under sub-section (1) of section 37 of the CGST Act, 2017. Accordingly, the Input-tax credit was restricted to 10% of the eligible credit available in respect of invoices or debit notes the details of which have been uploaded by the suppliers.

Details to be matched: The invoices for ITC claims will be matched for duplicates, with the tax paid on the invoices of corresponding outward supplies and with the IGST paid in respect of goods imported by him. For the purpose of matching, GSTIN of supplier and GSTIN of recipient, invoice number, invoice date and tax amount are matched.

Reclaim of reversal: Once claim of ITC on an invoice has been reversed, the recipient cannot claim it again unless the supplier uploads details of that invoice in his return after reversal at any stage, but before the due date of filing of the return for the month of September of the succeeding financial year or the actual filing of the relevant annual return, whichever is earlier.

Once the supplier uploads the details of invoice for corresponding outward supply, the invoice shall automatically appear in the return of the recipient and the recipient shall be eligible to claim ITC on that invoice.

The interest paid by the recipient on reversal shall also be credited back to his cash ledger. However, if any taxpayer claims ITC on an invoice that has been auto reversed in the past without the corresponding supplier uploading details of that invoice, such ITC shall be auto-reversed in the next month itself and a higher interest shall be payable on such auto-reversal.

14.8.3 Duplication of ITC Claims

[Section 42(4) and (6) read with Rule 72]

(1) **Claim of ITC on the same invoice more than once and communication thereof**

[Section 42(4) read with Rule 72]

The recipient might have wrongly claimed ITC more than once on the same invoice. The duplication of ITC claims in the details of inward supplies shall be communicated to the recipient in FORM GST MIS-1 electronically through the common portal.

(2) **Addition of excess ITC claimed on account of duplication of ITC claims**

[Section 42(6)]

The amount claimed as ITC that is found to be in excess on account of duplication of claims shall be added to the output tax liability of the recipient in his return for the month in which the duplication is communicated.

Example: The recipient of supply has filed his return for the month of July 2020 on 20th of August 2020. There is mismatch in the amount of input tax credit availed and amount of tax paid by the supplier on the particular tax invoice, the discrepancy will be made available to recipient in Form GST MIS-1 and to the supplier in Form GST MIS-2 by 31st day of August 2020 through the common portal.

In this case, one has to understand who has committed the error and who should rectify whether the supplier shall make rectification in their GSTR-1 to be submitted for the month of August 2020 OR the recipient shall make rectification in Form GSTR-2 to be submitted for the said month i.e., August 2020. In such a situation, if the supplier has committed the error and corrects it in his GSTR-1 to the said extent there will be increase in his output tax, along with applicable interest. Similarly, if the error has been committed by the recipient and he corrects it in Form GSTR-2, then to the said extent there will be reduction in the amount of input tax credit available for payment of taxes.

However, if neither the supplier nor the recipient rectifies the discrepancy, then the difference amount will get added to the output tax liability of the recipient of supply in his return in FORM GSTR-3/GSTR-3B as the case may be for the month of September 2020. The said differential amount shall be payable by recipient along with applicable interest.

However, if the supplier declares the invoice or debit note in any subsequent month but before the time limit prescribed, say in the month January 2021, the recipient of supply can reduce the relevant tax amount from the output tax liability for the month of January 2021. Further, recipient will also be eligible for refund of interest paid earlier and the said amount will get credited to electronic cash ledger under the head of interest and can be utilized for any payment towards interest in future.

14.8.4 Matching, Reversal and Reclaim of Reduction in Output Tax Liability [Section 43]

(Omitted w.e.f. 1st October, 2022 vide Notification No. 18/2022-CT dated 28.09.2022 by section 107 of The Finance Act 2022)

Where a tax invoice has been issued for supply of any goods and/or services and the taxable value/tax charged in that tax invoice is found to exceed the taxable value/tax payable in respect of such supply, or where the goods supplied are returned by the recipient, or where goods or services or both supplied are found to be deficient, supplier may issue to the recipient a credit note. The output tax liability of the supplier would reduce due to issuance of credit notes.

Supplier issuing a credit note shall declare the details of such credit note in the return for the month during which such credit note has been issued, but not later than September following the end of the financial year in which such supply was made, or the date of furnishing of the relevant annual return, whichever is earlier, and the tax liability shall be adjusted.

However, no reduction in output tax liability of the supplier shall be permitted, if the incidence of tax and interest on such supply has been passed on to any other person.

Procedure for furnishing return and availing input tax credit [Section 43A]: (Omitted w.e.f. 1st October 2022 vide Notification No. 18/2022-CT dated 28.09.2022 by section 107 of The Finance Act, 2022)

14.9 ANNUAL RETURN [SECTION 44]

[Brought into force w.e.f. 01.08.2021 vide Notification no. 29/2021-Central Tax dated 30.07.2021]

Every registered person shall furnish an annual return in **FORM GSTR-9 (FORM GSTR-9A** in case of person opted to pay tax under composition scheme under section 10 & **FORM GSTR-9B,** in case of E-Commerce operator) which may include a self-certified reconciliation statement (**FORM GSTR-9C**), reconciling the value of supplies declared in the return furnished for the financial year, with the audited annual financial statement for every financial year electronically, within such time and in such manner as may be prescribed:

The Commissioner may, on the recommendations of the Council, by notification, exempt any class of registered persons from filing annual return under this section.

The provision of this section shall not apply to any department of the Central Government or a State Government or a local authority, whose books of account are subject to audit by the Comptroller and Auditor-General of India or an auditor appointed for auditing the accounts of local authorities under any law for the time being in force.

The maximum time limit for filing Annual return is three years [Amendment made by Finance Act, 2023]

Types of Annual Return

Following types of Annual Return have been prescribed in Rule 80.

Annual Return	Applicability
FORM GSTR-9	All regular tax payers who file GSTR-1 and GSTR-3B
FORM GSTR-9A	Composition scheme dealer (Not applicable w.e.f. FY 2019-20 due to introduction of FORM GSTR-4)
FORM GSTR-9B	E-Commerce operator
FORM GSTR 9C	Annual Reconciliation statement (self-certified) (By registered person whose aggregate Annual Turnover exceeds ₹ 5 crores)

Due date of filing Annual Return: Every registered person liable to file Annual Return shall file the same on or before the 31st December following the end of the financial year.

Levy of late fee: As per Section 47(2) of CGST Act, 2017, any registered person who fails to furnish Annual Return by the due date shall be liable to pay a late fee of ₹ 100 per day subject to maximum of 0.25% of his turnover in the State or Union Territory. Similar provision exist in respective SGST Acts, also. Therefore, effectively the late fee for delay in filing Annual Return by the due date is ₹ 200 per day subject to a maximum of an amount calculated at 0.50% of his turnover in the State or Union Territory.

The GST Council in its 49th meeting held on 18th Feb 2023 has recommended capping late fee for delayed filing of Annual Return in FORM GSTR-9 for FY 2022-23 onwards for registered persons having aggregate turnover in a financial year up to ₹ 20 crore, as below:

Turnover	Maximum late fee
Registered persons having an aggregate turnover of up to ₹ 5 crores in the said financial year	₹ 50 per day (₹ 25 CGST + ₹ 25 SGST), subject to a maximum of an amount calculated at 0.04 per cent. of his turnover in the State or Union territory (0.02% CGST + 0.02% SGST)
Registered persons having an aggregate turnover of more than ₹ 5 crores and up to ₹ 20 crores in the said financial year	₹ 100 per day (₹ 50 CGST + ₹ 50 SGST), subject to a maximum of an amount calculated at 0.04 per cent. of his turnover in the State or Union territory (0.02% CGST + 0.02% SGST)

Annual Return—Not Applicable

Filing of Annual Return u/s 44 shall not apply to:

- Input Service Distributor
- A person paying tax under Section 51 (TDS)
- A person paying tax under Section 52 (TCS)
- A Casual Taxable person
- Non-resident taxable person

Notification No. 47/2019-Central Tax dated 9th October 2019

Filing of annual return under section 44 of CGST Act for FY 2017-18 and 2018-19 have been made optional for small taxpayers whose aggregate turnover is less than ₹ 2 crores and who had not filed the said return before the due date.

Notification No. 77/2020-Central Tax dated 15th October 2020

Filing of Annual return under Section 44 of CGST Act for FY 2019-20 have been made optional for those registered persons whose aggregate turnover is less than ₹ 2 crores.

Notification No. 10/2022-Central Tax dated 5th July 2022

Taxpayers having annual aggregate turnover up to ₹ 2 crores have been exempted from filing annual return in FORM GSTR 9/9A for the FY 2021-22.

Notification No. 32/2023–CT dated 31-07-2023

Registered person whose aggregate turnover during the FY 2022-23 was upto ₹ 2 Crores is exempted from filing Annual Return in FORM GSTR-9/9A for said financial year.

Audit of accounts by CA/CMA [Section 35(5)]

(Omitted w.e.f. 01.08.2021 vide Notification no. 29/2021-C.T. dated 30th July 2021)

As per Section 35(5) of CGST Act, 2017, every registered person (whether compulsory or voluntarily registered) & whose aggregate turnover (i.e. the turnover of all the registrations having the same Permanent Account Number) during a financial year exceeds two crores rupees, shall get his accounts audited by a CA/CMA and shall furnish following documents electronically.

- A copy of audited annual accounts and
- Reconciliation statement duly certified in FORM GSTR-9C [Rule 80(3)] reconciling the value of supplies as per annual return (FORM GSTR-9) and as per audited financial statement.

Reconciliation Statement (GSTR-9C) will reconcile the value of supplies declared in the return furnished for the financial year with the audited annual financial statement and such other particulars, as may be prescribed.

For the financial year 2018-19 and 2019-20, every registered person whose aggregate turnover exceeds five crore rupees shall get his accounts audited as specified under section 35(5) and he shall furnish a copy of audited annual accounts and a reconciliation statement, duly certified, in FORM GSTR-9C for the said financial year, electronically through the common portal either directly or through a Facilitation Centre notified by the Commissioner. [Vide Notification No. 79/2020-Central Tax dated 15th October 2020]

The Central Government Vide Notification No. 74/2018-Central Tax dated 31st December 2018 has notified GST Annual Return Format (GSTR-9) and Audit Report format (FORM GSTR-9C). The GST Audit Report format comprises of two parts, i.e. PART A-Reconciliation Statement and PART B-Certification, which has to be self-certified.

The due date of filing of GST Annual return & Reconciliation Statement (GSTR-9C) is on or before 31st December following the end of the financial year. However, FY 2017-18 being the first year of implementation of GST, considering the difficulties faced by the businessmen & professional, the Govt had extended the due date of filing of GST Annual return and GST Audit Report for the FY 2017-18 up to 31st January 2020, Vide Removal of Difficulty Order No. 10/2019-Central Tax dated 26th December 2019. The last date of filing Annual return under section 44 read with rule 80 for the FY 2019-20 was extended up to 28.02.2021. [Vide Notification No. 95/2020-Central Tax dated 30th December 2020]

14.9.1 Annual Return by Composition Dealer and Tax Payers Paying Tax Under Notification No. 02/2019-Central Tax (Rate) dated 07.03.2019. [w.e.f. 1st April 2019]

A composition scheme dealer shall furnish a Return (GSTR 4) for every financial year (or part of the financial year) on or before 30th day of April following the end of such financial year. [Notification No. 21/2019-Central Tax dated 23.04.2019]

14.9.2 Changes in Annual Return & Reconciliation Statement Filings

(Amendment to Sections 35 and 44 of CGST Act, 2017; Notification Nos. 29 to 31 of 2021-Central Tax dated 30th July 2021)

Central Board of Indirect Taxes & Customs [CBIC] has notified section 110 and section 111 of Finance Act, 2021 with effect from 1st August 2021. Section 110 of Finance Act 2021, has omitted Section 35 (5) of Central Goods & Service Tax Act, 2017, thus omitting requirement of audit by CA/CMA.

(1) Notification No. 29/2021-Central Tax dated 30th July 2021: In section 35 of the CGST Act, sub-section (5) omitted w.e.f. 1st August 2021. Compliance obligation of mandatory requirement of getting annual accounts audited and submitting reconciliation statement (GSTR-9C) by specified professional removed to allow self-certification.

(2) Notification No. 29/2021-Central Tax dated 30th July 2021

Section 44 has been amended as under: Every registered person, other than an Input Service Distributor, a person paying tax under section 51 or section 52, a casual taxable person and a non-resident taxable person shall furnish an annual return which may include a self-certified reconciliation statement, reconciling the value of supplies declared in the return furnished for the financial year, with the audited annual financial statement for every financial year electronically, within such time and in such form and in such manner as may be prescribed:

Provided that the Commissioner may, on the recommendations of the Council, by notification, exempt any class of registered persons from filing annual return under this section:

Provided further that nothing contained in this section shall apply to any department of the Central Government or a State Government or a local authority, whose books of account are subject to audit by the Comptroller and Auditor-General of India or an auditor appointed for auditing the accounts of local authorities under any law for the time being in force.

(3) Notification No. 30/2021-Central Tax dated 30th July 2021: Ecommerce operator required to collect tax at source under section 52 shall furnish annual statement in FORM GSTR-9B. Every registered person, other than those referred to in the second proviso to section 44, an Input Service Distributor, a person paying tax under section 51 or section 52, a casual taxable person and a non-resident taxable person, whose aggregate turnover during a financial year exceeds five crore rupees, shall also furnish a self-certified reconciliation statement as specified under section 44 in FORM GSTR-9C along with the annual return, on or before 31st December following the end of such FY, electronically through the common portal either directly or through a Facilitation Centre notified by the Commissioner.

(4) Notification No. 31/2021-Central Tax dated 30th July 2021: Registered person whose aggregate turnover in the FY 2020-21 is up to ₹ 2 crores, exempted from filing Annual Return for the said FY.

14.10 FINAL RETURN [SECTION 45]

As per Section 45, read with Rule 81, every registered person who is required to furnish return u/s 39(1) and whose registration has been surrendered/cancelled shall file final return in **FORM GSTR-10** through common portal within:

(a) three months from the date of cancellation (voluntary cancellation) or
(b) date of order of cancellation (forceful cancellation by authority),

whichever is later.

14.11 NOTICE TO RETURN DEFAULTER [SECTION 46]

As per Section 46, notice in **FORM GSTR-3A** shall be issued electronically to a registered person who have failed to file return under Section 39 (monthly return) and under Section 44 (annual return) requiring him to file a return within 15 days in such form and manner as may be prescribed.

It is important to note that, a registered person who has failed to furnish return(s) as prescribed under section 39 including annual return under section 44, read with relevant rules thereto even after serving of notice as specified supra, the proper officer in such cases, can proceed with making a best judgement assessment on the basis of information available with him or gathered by him, anytime within five years from the due date prescribed for filing annual return under section 44 of CGST Act, 2017 for that particular year, and issue an assessment order to that effect (reference to Rule 100(1) of CGST Rules, 2017 can be made.

However, where the return(s) is (are) furnished by a person on whom such order is served, within 30 days from the date of serving of order, the order issued will stand withdrawn but the liability to pay interest for delay in payment and late fee for delay in furnishing returns would continue.

14.12 LEVY OF LATE FEE [SECTION 47]

Any registered person who fails to furnish the details of outward supplies required under section 37 or returns required under section 39 or section 45 or section 52 by the due date shall pay a late fee under CGST Act as under:

Defaulted Return	Late fee under CGST & SGST/UTGST Law	Revised Late fee under CGST & SGST/UTGST Law as per notification (from Oct 2017 to May 2021)
Details of Outward Supplies-GSTR-1 (Section 37)	₹ 100 per day of delay Maximum ₹ 5,000	₹ 25 per day of delay ₹ 10 per day of delay (NIL Return) Maximum ₹ 5,000
Details of Inward Supplies-GSTR-2 (Section 38)	-Same as above-	Omitted (w.e.f. 1st October, 2022 vide Notification No. 18/2022-CT dated 28.09.2022) by sec. 108 of The Finance Act 2022 (No. 6 of 2022)
Monthly Return-GSTR-3/3B (Sec 39)	-Same as above-	₹ 25 per day of delay ₹ 10 per day of delay (NIL Return) Maximum ₹ 5,000
Details of Supplies made by Composition dealers [Section 39(2)]	-Same as above-	₹ 25 per day of delay ₹ 10 per day of delay (NIL Return) Maximum ₹ 5,000
Final Return in case of cancellation of registration (Section 45)	-Same as above-	No revision
Annual Return (Section 44)	₹ 100 per day of delay Maximum = 0.25% on his turnover in the State or Union Territory.	Revised from FY 2022-23 onwards for registered persons having aggregate turnover in a financial year up to ₹ 20 crore as per the recommendation of 49th GST council meeting held on 18th Feb 2023

Notes:

(1) "turnover in State" or "turnover in Union territory" means the aggregate value of all taxable supplies (excluding the value of inward supplies on which tax is payable by a person on reverse charge basis) and exempt supplies made within a State or Union territory by a taxable person, exports of goods or services or both and inter-State supplies of goods or services or both made from the State or Union territory by the said taxable person but excludes central tax, State tax, Union territory tax, integrated tax and cess.

(2) Late fee has been reduced for all taxpayers in case of FORM GSTR-1, FORM GSTR-3B & FORM GSTR-4 from ₹ 100day to ₹ 25/day under CGST Vide Notification No. 64/2017-Central Tax, dt. 15-11-2017 (GSTR-3B) and Notification No. 04/2018-Central Tax, dated 23rd January 2018 (GSTR-1).

(3) Late fee has been completely waived for all taxpayers in case of FORM GSTR-1, FORM GSTR-3B & FORM GSTR-4 for the months/quarters July 2017 to September 2018 are furnished after 22.12.2018 but on or before 31.03.2019 Vide Notification Nos. 75/2018, 76/2018, 77/2018-Central Tax, dt. 31-12-2018.

Cap on Maximum Late Fee for Late Filing of GST Return [Section 47]

Return	Notification
GSTR-3B	Notification No. 19/2021-Central Tax dated 1st June 2021
GSTR-1	Notification No. 20/2021-Central Tax dated 1st June 2021
GSTR-4	Notification No. 21/2021-Central Tax dated 1st June 2021
GSTR-4	Notification No. 22/2021-Central Tax dated 1st June 2021

The maximum late fee payable for late filing of GSTR-1, GSTR-3B and GSTR-4 shall be as under:

Class of Registered person	Nil Tax liability Max Penalty (CGST+ SGST)	Other than Nil Tax liability Max Penalty (CGST+ SGST)
LATE FILING OF GSTR-1/GSTR-3B		
If Aggregate turnover of up to ₹ 1.5 crores in the preceding financial year	₹ 500	₹ 2,000
If Aggregate turnover of more than ₹ 1.5 crores and up to ₹ 5 crores in the preceding financial year	₹ 500	₹ 5,000
If Aggregate turnover more than ₹ 5 crores in the preceding financial year	₹ 500	₹ 10,000
LATE FILING OF GSTR-4		
Composition Tax payer (FY 2021-22 onwards)	₹ 500	₹ 2,000

Cap on Maximum Late Fee—For Late Filing of GSTR-7 [Section 47]

Ref Notification No. 22/2021-Central Tax dated 1st June 2021

(Applicable from June 2021 onwards): The total amount of late fee payable under section 47 by a registered person for failure to furnish the return in FORM GSTR-7 (TDS Return) for the month of June 2021 onwards, by the due date is ₹ 1000.

14.13 GOODS & SERVICES TAX PRACTITIONER [SECTION 48]

Statutory Provision: As per Section 2(55) of CGST Act, 2017 "goods and services tax practitioner" means any person who has been approved under Section 48 to act as such practitioner.

Section 48 of CGST Act, 2017 deals with provision relating to

- Eligibility criteria for enrolment
- Appointment & Removal and
- Duties & obligation of a GST Practitioner

Section 48(2): A registered person may authorize an approved goods and services tax practitioner to furnish the details of outward supplies under section 37 and the return under section 39 or section 44 or section 45 and to perform such other functions in such manner as may be prescribed.

Eligibility Criteria for enrolment as a GST Practitioner: As per Rule 83, an application in FORM GST PCT-01 may be made electronically through the common portal (www.gst.gov.in) either directly or through a Facilitation Centre notified by the Commissioner for enrolment as goods and services tax practitioner by any person who fulfils following conditions:

(1) Basic condition

(i) is a citizen of India
(ii) is a person of sound mind
(iii) is not adjudicated as insolvent
(iv) has not been convicted by a competent court

(2) Education and Work Experience

One should satisfies any of the following conditions, namely:

(a) A retired officer of the Commercial Tax Department of any State Government or of the Central Board of Indirect Taxes and Customs, having worked in a post not lower in rank than that of a Group-B gazetted officer, for a period of not less than two years, OR
(b) A Tax Return Preparer or a Sales Tax Practitioner registered for a period of not less than five years, OR
(c) Passed a graduate or postgraduate degree or its equivalent examination, having a degree in Commerce, Law, Banking including Higher Auditing, or Business Administration or Business Management from any Indian University established by any law for the time being in force, or from a recognises Foreign University, OR has passed final examination of the CA/CMA/CS Institute.

Note: As per Rule 83(3), no person enrolled as a goods and services tax practitioner, by virtue of being enrolled as a Sales Tax Practitioner or Tax return preparer under the earlier Indirect Tax laws, shall be eligible to remain enrolled, unless he passes the GST Practitioner examination conducted by NACIN or by such authority as may be notified by the Commissioner on the recommendations of the Council within a period of 30 months from the appointed date [Notification No. 03/2019-Central Tax dated 29.01.2019].

Appointment & Removal of GST Practitioner: A list of Goods and Services Tax Practitioner enrolled shall be maintained on the Common Portal in **FORM GST PCT-5.**

Any registered person who wants to avail the services of goods and service tax practitioner may, at his option, authorize a GST practitioner on the Common Portal in **FORM GST PCT-6** to carry out certain activities on his behalf.

Similarly, registered person at any time can disengage the GST practitioner through common portal by withdrawing such authorization in **FORM GST PCT-7.**

Forms Used for GST Practitioner

Form	Description
FORM GST PCT-01	Application for Enrolment as GST practitioner
FORM GST PCT-02	Certificate of enrolment as a GST practitioner, issued by an authorised officer
FORM GST PCT-03	Notice seeking additional information on application for enrolment or show cause notice
FORM GST PCT-04	Order of rejection of application for enrolment or disqualification of a GST practitioner found guilty of misconduct
FORM GST PCT-05	Authorisation/withdrawal of authorisation to engage a GST practitioner by a taxable person

Functions of GST Practitioner [Rule 83(8)]: A GST practitioner can undertake any or all of the following activities on behalf of a registered person, if so authorized by him to:

(a) furnish the details of outward and inward supplies;
(b) furnish monthly, quarterly, annual or final return;
(c) make deposit for credit into the electronic cash ledger;
(d) file a claim for refund;
(e) file an application for amendment or cancellation of registration;
(f) furnish information for generation of EWB;
(g) furnish details of challan in FORM GST ITC-04;

(h) file an application for amendment or cancellation of enrolment under rule 58; and

(i) file an intimation to pay tax under the composition scheme or withdraw from the said scheme:

Provided that where any application relating to a claim for refund or an application for amendment or cancellation of registration has been submitted by the goods and services tax practitioner authorized by the registered person, a confirmation shall be sought from the registered person and the application.

The GST practitioner shall:

(a) prepare the statements with due diligence; and

(b) affix his digital signature on the statements prepared by him or electronically verify using his credentials.

In all cases, registered person shall remain to be liable for the correctness of the return filed through GST practitioner.

As per Rule 84, no person shall be eligible to attend before any authority as a goods and services tax practitioner in connection with any proceedings under the Act on behalf of any registered or un-registered person unless he has been enrolled under rule 83.

A single registration is sufficient to practice on all India basis.

Examination for GST Practitioners: The National Academy of Customs, Indirect Taxes & Narcotics (NACIN), Faridabad has been authorized to conduct an examination for confirmation of enrolment of Goods and Service Tax Practitioners (GSTP) in terms of sub-rule (3) of rule 83 of the Central Goods and Service Tax Rules, 2017, vide **Notification No. 24/2018-Central Tax dated 28.5.2018.**

It will be a Computer-Based examination and shall be conducted twice in a year. The registration for the exam can be done by the eligible GSTPs on a registration portal, link of which will be provided on NACIN and CBIC websites. The applicants are required to make online payment of examination fee of ₹ 500 at the time of registration for this exam.

Chapter 15

Payment of Tax

15.1 STATUTORY PROVISION

In GST regime, a taxable person is required to pay Central Tax (CGST), State GST/Union Territory GST (SGST/UTGST) & Integrated tax (IGST). In addition, certain categories of registered persons are required to pay to the government account Tax Deducted at Source (TDS) u/s 51 and Tax Collected at Source (TCS) u/s 52 of CGST Act, 2017. Further, interest, penalty, fees and any other payment will also be required to be paid wherever applicable,

The provisions relating to payment of tax are dealt with in sections 49 to 53 (Chapter X) of CGST Act, 2017 & in Rules 85 to 88 (Chapter IX) of CGST Rules, 2017.

Sections	Description	Rules	Description
49	Payment of tax, interest, penalty and other amounts	85	Electronic Liability Register
49A	Utilization of IGST Credit first	86	Electronic Credit Ledger
49B	Order of utilization of ITC	87	Electronic Cash Ledger
50	Interest on delayed payment of tax	88	Identification number for each transaction
51	Tax deduction at source		
52	Collection of tax at source		
53	Transfer of input tax credit		
77	Tax wrongly collected & paid to Govt account/Deposit of tax under wrong head		

15.2 TYPE OF TAX REGISTER/LEDGER [SECTION 49]

Payments under GST can be made either through electronic cash ledger or through electronic credit ledger as per the provisions of section 49 of CGST Act, 2017 and rules framed thereunder.

Where any payment is made through electronic cash or credit ledger or where any other amount is debited or credited in the said ledgers, a Unique Identification Number (UIN) shall be generated. The UIN relating to discharge of any liability shall be indicated in the corresponding entry in the electronic liability register.

Types of Tax Register/Ledger maintained on GST Portal

On the GST common portal, each registered taxpayer will have three kinds of register/ledgers:

(a) Electronic Liability Register
(b) Electronic Credit Ledger (ITC Ledger)
(c) Electronic Cash Ledger

(a) Electronic Liability Register: The electronic tax liability register specified under section 49(7) shall be maintained in FORM GST PMT-01 for each person liable to pay tax, interest, penalty, late fee or any other amount on the Common Portal and all amounts payable by him shall be debited to the said register.

This register will be maintained separately in two parts for Central Tax, State/UT Tax, Integrated Tax and Cess.

Part I: will show return related liabilities

Part II: will show other than return related liabilities

Debit to this register (liability is created by debiting) will be for following tax liability

Debit in Electronic liability register	
Part I (Return related)	**Part II (Other than return related)**
Tax, interest, fees or other amount payable, including liabilities due to: (1) Opt in for composition or (2) Cancellation of registration	All liabilities other than return related: (1) Reduction or enhancement due to decision of Appeal, rectification, revision, review, etc. (2) Refund of pre-deposit (3) Payments made against SCN or any other voluntary payments

Note: It is pertinent to note that if any liability is payable under Part II then it will not have any effect on return filing. However, if tax is payable under Part I then return will be treated as invalid.

Electronic liability register shall be credited for the following payments (liability is discharged by crediting)

Credit in electronic liability register
(a) Payment of every liability by a registered person (corresponding debit will appear in Electronic Cash ledger/Credit ledger)
(b) Tax Deducted at Source u/s 51
(c) Tax Collected at Source u/s 52
(d) Tax on Reverse Charge on supply of goods or services under Section 9(3) of CGST/SGST Act, Section 5(3) of IGST Act and Section 7(3) of UTGST Act
(e) Tax on supplies from unregistered suppliers under Section 9(4) of CGST/SGST Act, Section 5(4) of IGST Act and Section 7(4) of UTGST Act and composition levy under Section 10 of CGST Act.
(f) Amount paid u/s 10
(g) Interest, penalty, fee or other amount

Order of discharge of tax and other dues: Section 49(8) prescribes the following chronological order in which the liability of a taxable person has to be discharged:

(a) self-assessed tax, and other dues related to returns of previous tax periods;
(b) self-assessed tax, and other dues related to the return of the current tax period;
(c) any other amount payable under this Act or the rules made there under including the demand determined under section 73 or section 74.

(b) Electronic Credit Ledger (ITC Ledger): In terms of provisions of section 49(2) of the CGST Act, 2017 read with Rule 86 of Payment of Tax Rules, the Input Tax Credit (ITC) as self-assessed in the return of a registered person shall be credited to his electronic credit ledger in accordance with sec 41 to be maintained in FORM GST PMT-02.

The Electronic credit ledger shall be debited/credited with following:

Entries Debited	Entries Credited
Utilization towards output tax shown in GSTR-3B return	Self-assessed ITC in GSTR-3B return (ITC on inward supplies from registered tax payers/ISD/ Tax paid under RCM)
Utilization towards liability related to demand	ITC on account of merger
Refund claimed	Transitional credit
	Credit on account of pre-registration inputs of Stock held/ semi-finished goods or finished goods (provided registration applied within 30 days from the date of his liability)
	Credit on opt out from composition scheme to regular tax scheme

The refund of tax wrongly paid or paid in excess for which debit has been made from the electronic credit ledger can be claimed by filing FORM GST PMT-03. If admissible, the said amount will be recredited to electronic credit ledger [Rule 86(4A)].

The electronic credit ledger shall be debited to the extent of discharge of any liability in accordance with the provisions of section 49 [or section 49A or section 49B].

Sequence and restriction for the utilization of Input Tax Credit (ITC):

Input Tax	Can be utilized against	Output Tax
CGST	CGST & IGST	CGST
		IGST
SGST	SGST & IGST	SGST
		IGST
UTGST	UTGST & IGST	UTGST
		IGST
IGST	IGST, CGST, SGST/ UTGST	IGST
		CGST
		SGST/UTGST

Note: Cross utilization of SGST/UTGST & CGST is not permissible.

As per Section 49(4) of the CGST Act, 2017, input tax credit cannot be used for payment of interest penalty. As per Section 2(82), Input tax credit cannot be used for payment of tax under reverse charge basis.

Discharge of tax and other dues [Section 49(8)]

Every taxable person shall discharge his tax and other dues under this Act or the rules made thereunder in the following order, namely:

(a) self-assessed tax, and other dues related to returns of previous tax periods;
(b) self-assessed tax, and other dues related to the return of the current tax period;
(c) any other amount payable under this Act or the rules made thereunder including the demand determined under section 73 or section 74.

Transfer of balance in Electronic Cash Ledger [Section 49 (10)]: A registered person may, on the common portal, transfer any amount of tax, interest, penalty, fee or any other amount available in the electronic cash ledger under this Act, to the electronic cash ledger of:

(a) integrated tax, central tax, State tax, Union territory tax or cess; or
(b) integrated tax or central tax of a distinct person as specified in section 25(4) or 25(5), in such form and manner and subject to such conditions and restrictions as may be prescribed and such transfer shall be deemed to be a refund from the electronic cash ledger under this Act:

Provided that no such transfer under clause (b) shall be allowed if the said registered person has any unpaid liability in his electronic liability register.

GST PMT-09 allows transfer of amount available in the electronic cash ledger (ECL) of one GSTIN to ECL of another GSTIN of the entity having same PAN.

Amendment has been made in CGST Act, 2017 by Finance Act, 2022 notified vide Notification No. 09/2022-Central Tax dated 05.07.2022 to provide for transfer of balance in electronic cash ledger of a registered person to electronic cash ledger of CGST and IGST of a distinct person. CGST Rules, 2017 have also been amended vide Notification No. 14/2022-Central Tax dated 05.07.2022 accordingly.

Section 49A: Utilization of input tax credit subject to certain conditions: The input tax credit on account of central tax, State tax or Union territory tax shall be utilized towards payment of integrated tax, central tax, State tax or Union territory tax, as the case may be, only after the input tax credit available on account of integrated tax has first been utilized fully towards such payment.

Section 49B: Order of utilization of input tax credit: The Government to prescribe any specific order of utilization of input tax credit of any of the taxes for the payment of any tax.

Section 49 A and Section 49 B inserted vide CGST Amendment Act, 2018 provides for utilization of ITC and order of utilization of ITC as follows (w.e.f. 1st Feb 2019):

Credit of	To Be Utilised First For	May Be Utilised Further For Payment of
IGST	IGST	CGST, then SGST/UTGST
CGST	CGST	IGST
SGST/UTGST	SGST/UTGST	IGST

(c) Electronic Cash Ledger [RULE 87]

(1) The electronic cash ledger under section 49(1) of the CGST Act, 2017 read with Rule 87 of Payment of Tax Rules shall be maintained in FORM GST PMT-05 for each person, liable to pay tax, interest, penalty, late fee or any other amount, on the Common Portal for crediting the amount deposited and debiting the payment there from towards tax, interest, penalty, fee or any other amount.

(2) Any person, or a person on his behalf, shall generate a challan in FORM GST PMT-06 on the Common Portal and enter the details of the amount to be deposited by him towards tax, interest, penalty, fees or any other amount.

Challan in FORM GST PMT-06 generated at the Common Portal shall be valid for a period of fifteen days.

(3) Mode of Deposit in electronic cash ledger

Deposit of Tax, interest, penalty, fee or any other amount by a taxable person can be made by the following modes:

(1) Internet Banking
(2) Credit/Debit cards
(3) National Electronic Fund Transfer (NEFT)
(4) Real Time Gross Settlement (RTGS)
(5) Unified payment interface (UPI) or Immediate Payment Services (IMPS) from any bank
(6) Over the Counter payment (OTC) through authorized banks for deposits up to ten thousand rupees per challan per tax period, by cash/cheque/demand draft.

The restriction of ₹ 10,000 per challan per tax period shall not be applicable in following cases:

(a) Government departments or any other deposit to be made by persons as may be notified by the Commissioner in this behalf.
(b) Proper officer or any other officer authorized to recover outstanding dues from any person, whether registered or not, including recovery made through attachment or sale of movable or immovable properties.
(c) Proper officer or any other officer authorized for the amounts collected by way of cash, cheque or demand draft during any investigation or enforcement activity or any ad hoc deposit:

Provided further that a person supplying online information and database access or retrieval services from a place outside India to a non-taxable online recipient referred to in section 14 of the Integrated Goods and Services Tax Act, 2017 may also make the deposit through international money transfer through Society for Worldwide Interbank Financial Telecommunication payment network.

Explanation

(1) For making payment of any amount indicated in the challan, the commission, if any, payable in respect of such payment shall be borne by the person making such payment.

(2) the date of credit to the account of the Government in the authorized bank shall be deemed to be the date of deposit in the electronic cash ledger.

(4) Payment by un-registered person

Any payment required to be made by a person who is not registered under the Act, shall be made on the basis of a temporary identification number generated through the common portal.

[Rule 87(14)] Transfer of tax between distinct persons

Notification No. 09/2022-Central Tax dated 05.07.2022

A registered person may, on the common portal, transfer any amount of tax, interest, penalty, fee or any other amount available in the electronic cash ledger under the Act to the electronic cash ledger for central tax or integrated tax of a distinct person as specified in sub-section (4) or, as the case may be, sub-section (5) of section 25, in FORM GST PMT-09:

Provided that no such transfer shall be allowed if the said registered person has any unpaid liability in his electronic liability register.

Debit/credit entries in Electronic cash ledger in FORM GST PMT-05

Following transactions shall have an effect on the electronic cash ledger and shall be debited/credited accordingly:

(1) Self-payment shall be credited to the ledger;
(2) TDS or TCS to be credited to electronic cash ledger of the person from whom the amount was deducted or collected;
(3) Payment towards tax, interest, penalty, fee or any other amount shall be debited to the ledger;
(4) Balance in Electronic cash ledger after payment of tax and other dues can be claimed as refund. Amount claimed as refund to be debited to the ledger. If refund is rejected, ledger to be re-credited by proper officer by order in Form GST PMT-03.

Note: TDS, TCS, tax under RCM, IGST on import and tax in case of composition levy can be made by debiting electronic cash ledger only.

Discrepancy in Electronic credit/cash ledger and liability register
A registered person shall, upon noticing any discrepancy in his electronic liability register/credit ledger/cash ledger, communicate the same to the officer exercising jurisdiction in the matter, through the Common Portal in FORM GST PMT-04.

15.3 PAYMENT OF TAX IN RESPECT OF SUPPLY COVERED UNDER REVERSE CHARGE [SECTION 9(3) & 9(4)]

The terms "reverse charge" means liability to pay tax by the recipient instead of the supplier of goods or services or both. Reverse charge applies to both goods & services.

Generally, the person effecting taxable supplies is liable to pay taxes. However, in case of imports & supply of certain goods or services as may be notified by the Government on the recommendations of the GST Council, the tax shall be paid by the recipient, which is called payment under reverse charge.

It is thus mandatory to obtain registration under GST for the persons who are liable to pay tax under reverse charge mechanism (RCM), irrespective of turnover & whether supplying taxable goods or service or not.

Discharge of RCM tax liability: Reverse charge tax liability is to be paid by cash by debiting electronic cash ledger & cannot be discharge by using input tax credit.

15.4 PROCEDURE OF PAYMENT OF TAX

(1) Manual or physical challans are not allowed under the GST regime. It is mandatory to generate challans online on the GST Portal.
(2) There is single challan prescribed for all taxes, fees, penalty, interest and other payments to be made under the GST regime.
(3) Challan to be generated in FORM GST PMT-06 for the tax, interest, etc. to be deposited (valid for 15 days).
(4) Payment by non-registered person shall be made on the basis of temporary identification number.
(5) Mandate form (Applicable in case of NEFT and RTGS).
(6) Where the payment is made by way of NEFT or RTGS mode, the mandate form shall be generated along with the challan on the Common Portal and the same shall be submitted to the bank from where the payment is to be made (the said mandate form will be valid for 15 days from the date of generation of challan).
(7) On successful payment, a Challan Identification Number (CIN) will be generated and the same shall be indicated in the challan. On receipt of CIN from the authorized bank, the said amount shall be credited to the electronic cash ledger. However, if CIN is not generated or not communicated, person may represent in FORM GST PMT-07, an application for intimating discrepancy relating to payment to bank/electronic gateway.

15.4.1 Manner of utilization of amount reflected in Electronic Cash Ledger [Section 49(3)]

The amount reflected in the electronic cash ledger may be used for making any payment towards tax, interest, penalty, fee, or any other amount under the relevant tax head in the prescribed manner.

In the ledger, information is kept minor head-wise for each major head. The ledger is displayed major head-wise i.e., IGST, CGST, SGST/UTGST, and CESS. Each major head is divided into five minor heads: Tax, Interest, Penalty, Fee and Others.

Major Heads	Minor Heads
IGST	Tax
CGST	Interest
SGST/UTGST	Penalty
Cess	Fee
	Others

Identification number for each transaction [Rule 88]

(1) A unique identification number shall be generated at the common portal for each debit or credit to the electronic cash or credit ledger, as the case may be.

(2) The unique identification number relating to discharge of any liability shall be indicated in the corresponding entry in the electronic liability register.

(3) A unique identification number shall be generated at the common portal for each credit in the electronic liability register for reasons other than those covered under sub-rule (2).

Summary of FORM under Payment provisions

Sr. No.	Particulars	FORM
1.	Electronic Liability Register	GST PMT-01
2.	Electronic Credit Ledger	GST PMT-02
3.	Electronic Credit or Cash Ledger to be re-credited by proper officer by order if refund is rejected	GST PMT-03
4.	Communication of discrepancy in Electronic Credit Ledger/Cash Ledger/Liability Register	GST PMT-04
5.	Electronic Cash Ledger	GST PMT-05
6.	Challan for deposit of GST	GST PMT-06
7.	Representation if CIN is not generated or communicated	GST PMT-07
8.	Intra-head or inter-head transfer of amount as available in Electronic Cash Ledger	GST PMT-09

15.5 INTEREST ON DELAYED PAYMENT OF TAX [SECTION 50]

Section 50 of CGST Act makes it mandatory for a taxpayer to pay interest on belated payment of tax, i.e. when he fails to pay tax (or part of tax) to the Government's account within the due date.

Interest on delayed payment of Tax [Section 50]: Where payment under GST is not made within the prescribed time, registered taxable person shall pay interest for such delay as under:

Section	Description	Rate of Interest
Section 50(1)	Delay in payment of tax, in full or in part	Max 18%
Section 50(3)	Undue or excess claim of input tax credit under section 42 (10)	Max 24%
Section 50(3)	Undue or excess reduction in output tax liability under section 43 (10)	Max 24%

Note: It may be noted that:

(a) Section 42 (10) CGST/SGST Act deals with contravention of provisions for matching of claims for input tax credit by a recipient.

(b) Section 43 (10) CGST/SGST Act deals with contravention of provisions for matching of claims for reduction in output tax liability by a supplier.

(c) Interest should be charged only on the net tax liability of the taxpayer, after taking into account the admissible input tax credit, i.e. interest shall be levied on that portion of the tax that is paid by debiting the electronic cash ledger [Notification No. 16/2021-Central Tax dated 01.06.2021].

(d) Section 50(2) provides that, interest shall be calculated from the day succeeding the day on which such tax was due to be paid.

Sec 50 (1) of CGST Act has been amended vide Section 112 of Finance Act 2021 Notification No. 16/2021-Central Tax dated 1st June 2021.

In Section 50 of the Central Goods and Services Tax Act, in sub-section (1), for the proviso, the following proviso shall be substituted and shall be deemed to have been substituted with effect from the 1st day of July 2017, namely:

"Provided that the interest on tax payable in respect of supplies made during a tax period and declared in the return for the said period furnished after the due date in accordance with the provisions of Section 39, except where such return is furnished after commencement of any proceedings under Section 73 or Section 74 in respect of the said period, shall be payable on that portion of the tax which is paid by debiting the electronic cash ledger."

Example: M/s X Ltd. reduced the amount of ₹ 2,00,000 from the output tax liability in contravention of provision of Sec 42(10) of the CGST Act for the month of April 2019, which is ineligible credit. The tax department issued a Show Cause Notice (SCN) to pay tax along with interest. M/s X Ltd. paid the tax & interest on 31st July 2019. Calculate interest liability.

Answer. As per Section 42(10), the amount reduced from the output tax liability by undue or excess claim of input tax credit shall be added to the output tax liability of the recipient in his return for the month in which such contravention takes place and such recipient shall be liable to pay interest on the amount so added @24% per annum u/s 50 of CGST Act. The period of interest will be from the date following the due date of payment to the actual date of payment of tax.

Due date of payment	20th May 2019
Period for which interest is due	21st May 2019 to 31st July 2019
No. of days	72 days
Interest liability	₹ 3 lakhs × 24% × 72/365
Interest amount	₹ 14, 203

15.5.1 Rate of Interest

The rate of interest notified by the Government vides Notification no. 13/2017-Central tax dated 28th June 2017 are as follows:

Section	Description	Rate of Interest
50 (1)	Failure to pay tax or part thereof to the Government within period prescribed	18%
50(3)	For undue or excess claim of ITC or reduction of output tax liability	24%
54(12)	Interest on withheld refund	6%
56	Interest on delayed refunds	6%
Proviso to 56	Interest on refund arising from order passed by Adjudicating Authority/ Appellate Authority/Tribunal/Court and not refunded within 60 days	9%

15.5.2 Manner of Computation of interest [Section 50(2)]

(a) The period of interest shall be from the date following the due date of payment to the actual date of payment of tax.

(b) Where the ***tax admitted*** by the taxable person in his return has not been deposited along with the returns, interest is leviable immediately on the payment of the admitted tax.

(c) It may be noted that, Section 39 (7) lays down the last date for remittance as the last date on which the taxable person is required to furnish such return. In addition, Section 2 (117) lays down that a return shall be considered valid only if the tax payable as per the return is paid in full.

(d) Section 73 (5) & 73 (6) provides that if the tax along with interest has been paid, the adjudicating authority shall not serve any show cause notice.

15.6 TDS PROVISION UNDER GST [SECTION 51]

TDS is one of the mode/method to collect tax, under which, certain percentage of amount is deducted by a recipient at the time of making payment to the supplier of taxable goods or services. It acts as a powerful instrument to prevent tax evasion and expands the tax net, as it provides for the creation of an audit trail. The purpose of TDS mechanism is just to enable the Government to have a trail of transactions and to monitor and verify the compliances.

Section 51 of the CGST Act, 2017 read with Rule 66 prescribes the authority and procedure for 'Tax Deduction at Source' under GST.

TDS provision has been made operative with effect from 01.10.2018 Vide Notification No. 50/2018-Central Tax dated 13.09.2018.

When applicable

(i) When the value of taxable supply under a single contract exceeds more than ₹ 2,50,000 (excluding GST).
(ii) GST-TDS applicable on supply of both goods & services.
(iii) At the time of making payment or credit to the supplier by specified entity such as Central/State Govt, Govt authority, Govt department, local authority, PSU, Societies established by Govt or local authority
(iv) The rate of TDS under GST is 2%. In case of inter-state supply, it is 2% under IGST and in case of intra-state supply it is 1% under CGST & 1% under SGST Act.

Who is required to deduct TDS [Section 51(1)]: The following classes of persons shall be required to deduct tax at source.

(a) A Department or establishment of Central Government or State Govt (Except authorities under Ministry of Defence) or

(b) Local authority or

(c) Government Agencies or

(d) Category of persons notified by Govt vide N.No. 50/2018-Central Tax dated 13.09.2018.

(a) An Authority or a Board or any other body
  (i) Set up by Act of Parliament or a State legislature or
  (ii) Establishment by any Government, with 51% or more participation by way of equity or control, to carry out any functions,
(b) Society established by the Central Government or the State Government or a Local Authority under the Societies Registration Act, 1860 (21 of 1860);
(c) Public Sector undertakings (in case of Supply by one PSU to another PSU, TDS provision will not attract, Ref *Notification No. 61/2018-Central Tax dated 5^tht Nov 2018*).

Notification no. 73/2018-Central Tax dated 31st Dec 2018
"Provided also that nothing in this notification shall apply to the supply of goods or services or both which takes place between one person to another person specified under clauses (a), (b), (c) and (d) of sub-section (1) of section 51 of the said Act."

Registration of TDS deductor: A person liable to deduct TDS u/s 51 shall compulsorily register without any threshold limit u/s 24(vi) of the CGST Act. The deductor has a privilege of obtaining registration under GST as a Tax deductor, either by using PAN or TAN issued under the Income-tax Act, 1961. Registration as Tax deductor under GST is separate from registration obtained as normal taxpayer u/s 22 of CGST Act.

Every Government office shall mandatorily registered as tax deductor under GST.

Deposit of TDS with the Government: The amount deducted towards TDS shall be paid to the Central Government within ten days after the end of the month in which such deductions are made.

Time line for filing TDS Return: The deductor is required to file TDS return in FORM GSTR-7 within 10 days from the end of the month.

TDS Certificate: A TDS certificate is required to be issued by deductor (the person who is deducting tax) in FORM GSTR-7A to the deductee (the supplier from whose payment TDS is deducted), within five days of crediting the amount to the Government, failing which the deductor would be liable to pay a late fee of ₹ 100 per day (Max ₹ 5000 under CGST & SGST Act separately) from the expiry of the 5th day till the certificate is issued.

The deductor shall furnish a TDS certificate in FORM GSTR-7A to the deductee.

Example 1: M/s BHEL has awarded three separate contracts for supply of taxable goods to M/s ABC and the value of taxable supply is below ₹ 2.5 lakh in case of each contract but their combined value is more than ₹ 5 lakh. In such a case, deduction of TDS under GST shall not be required, since value of taxable supply in neither of the contract exceeds ₹ 2.5 lakh.

Example 2: M/s Shyam Trading House, Kolkata is a composition scheme dealer under GST registered in West Bengal, received a supply order from Kolkata Municipal corporation (KMC) for supply of stationery items of ₹ 2, 55,000 in April 2022. The Bill was paid in full in October 2022. What will be the GST (TDS) implications on said transaction?

Here, the supplier of goods is a composition scheme dealer & recipient KMC is a local authority. A composition scheme dealer cannot charge GST from buyer. Hence, the value of supply is excluding GST & exceeds ₹ 2.5 lakhs. Hence, GST (TDS) provision will attract.

Example 3: A supply order was placed to a contractor for ₹ 4 lakhs, but payment was made in two installments of ₹ 2.3 lakhs & ₹ 1.7 lakhs each. GST (TDS) shall be required to be deducted from both the payment since law mandate that TDS provision u/s 51 shall be attracted if the contract value exceed ₹ 2.5 lakhs. The value of supply shall be taken as the amount excluding the central tax, State tax, Union territory tax, integrated tax and cess indicated in the invoice.

Example 4: M/s XYZ Ltd. (a PSU) had awarded a R&M contract to M/s ABC, a registered person under GST for ₹ 2,36,000 (including GST @ 18%) during the FY 2021-22. The 1st RA bill was paid on 31st March 2022 for ₹ 1,77,000. Subsequently, the contract value was revised to ₹ 3,54,000 (including GST) due to deviation. The final bill was paid in Oct 2022. What will be the GST (TDS) implications?

Here, the original contract value was below ₹ 2.5 lakhs, but subsequently the same has been revised to ₹ 3,54,000. The contract value excluding GST comes to ₹ 3,00,000 which is more than threshold limit of ₹ 2.5 lakhs. Since it is a taxable supply & recipient is a PSU, GST (TDS) shall be applicable on entire amount of ₹ 3 lakhs.

Example 5: M/s BHEL bags order worth ₹ 900 crores from NTPC Ltd. during FY 2022-23 for supply of emission control equipment including GST @18%. The first lot was supplied in October 2022 against Invoice date of 21st October 2022 for ₹ 350 crores. Payment was released by NTPC Ltd. on 3rd December 2022. Compute the amount of TDS deductible on said supply u/s 51 of CGST Act.

Answer. BHEL and NTPC both are PSUs. As per Notification No. 61/2018-Central Tax dated 05-11-2018 (effective from 1st Oct 2018), supply made by one PSU to another will not attract TDS provision under GST. As such, TDS u/s 51 of CGST Act shall not be deducted in the instant case.

Consequences of non-compliance of TDS provisions:

Sl No.	Event	Consequence
1.	TDS not deducted	Interest to be paid along with the TDS amount; else the amount shall be determined and recovered as per the law
2.	TDS certificate not issued or delayed beyond the prescribed period of five days	Late fee of ₹ 100 per day subject to a maximum of ₹ 5000 (under CGST & SGST separately)
3.	TDS deducted but not paid to the Government or paid later than 10th of the succeeding month	Interest to be paid along with the TDS amount; else the amount shall be determined and recovered as per the law
4.	Late filing of TDS returns	Late fee of ₹ 100 for every day during which such failure continues, subject to a maximum amount of ₹ 5000. (under CGST & SGST separately) As per Notification No. 22/2021-Central Tax dated 1st June 2021, w.e.f. June 2021, the maximum late fee payable for late filing of GSTR-7 has been restricted to ₹ 1000 under CGST Act

When Tax deduction (TDS) is not required under GST: Tax deduction is not required in following situations:

(a) Total value of taxable supply ≤ ₹ 2.5 lakh under a single contract.

(b) Contract value > ₹ 2.5 lakh for both taxable supply and exempted supply, but the value of taxable supply under the said contract ≤ ₹ 2.5 lakh.

(c) Receipt of services which are exempted vide Notification No. 12/2017-Central Tax dated 28.06.2017, as amended from time to time.
(d) Receipt of goods which are exempted. For example goods exempted under notification No. 2/2017-Central Tax (Rate) dated 28.06.2017 as amended from time to time.
(e) Goods on which GST is not leviable. For example petrol, diesel, petroleum crude, natural gas, aviation turbine fuel (ATF) and alcohol for human consumption.
(f) Where the location of the supplier and place of supply is in a State(s)/UT(s), which is different from the State/UT where the deductor is registered.
(g) All activities or transactions specified in Schedule III of the CGST/SGST Acts 2017, irrespective of the value.
(h) Where the payment relates to a tax invoice that has been issued before 01.10.2018.
(i) Where any amount was paid in advance prior to 01.10.2018 and the tax invoice has been issued on or after 01.10.18, to the extent of advance payment made before 01.10.2018.
(j) Where the tax is to be paid on reverse charge by the recipient.
(k) Where the payment is made to an unregistered supplier.
(l) Where the payment relates to "Cess" component.
(m) In case of supply made by Government/PSU to another Government/PSU, irrespective of value of contract/supply.

GST need not to be deducted at sources, where the value of taxable supply under a single contract does not exceed ₹ 2.5 lakh (excluding GST).

Example 6: Govt. of Odisha engages a Contractor of Delhi for construction of Utkal Bhawan at Delhi. The supply would be intra-State supply and Central tax and State tax would be levied. In such case, transfer of TDS (Central tax + State tax of Odisha) to the cash ledger of the supplier (Central tax + State tax of Delhi) would be difficult. So in such a case, GST (TDS) shall not be deducted.

Example 7: Electricity Department of Govt of Sikkim entered into a contract with a registered person of Siliguri, WB for hiring of office space in Siliguri on a monthly rent of ₹ 50,000 (excluding GST) for a period of two years from 1st April 2022. The rent is payable on monthly basis. What will be the TDS implications under GST?

Here, the place of supply & location of supplier is in Siliguri (WB). The recipient/deductor is located in Sikkim. Where the location of the supplier and place of supply is in a State(s)/UT(s), which is different from the State/UT where the deductor is registered, GST (TDS) shall not be deducted.

15.7 TAX COLLECTION AT SOURCE (TCS) [SECTION 52]

TCS refers to the tax which is collected by the electronic commerce operator when a supplier supplies some goods or services through its portal and the payment for that supply is collected by the electronic commerce operator.

Power to collect tax at sources: Section 52 of the CGST Act, 2017 provides for Tax Collection at Source, by e-Commerce Operator in respect of the taxable supplies made through it by other suppliers, where the consideration in respect of such supplies is collected by him e-Commerce Operator.

TCS provision has been made operative with effect from 01.10.2018 vide Notification No. 51/2018-Central Tax dated 13.09.2018.

TCS is to be collected once supply has been made through the e-commerce operator and where the business model is that the consideration is to be collected by the e-commerce operator irrespective of the actual collection of the consideration. For example, if the supply has taken place through the ecommerce operator on 30th October 2018 but the consideration for the same has been collected in the month of November 2018, then TCS for such supply has to be collected and reported in the statement for the month of October, 2018.

Who is an E-commerce operator?

As per Section 2(45) of the CGST Act, 2017, electronic commerce operator means any person who owns, operates or manages digital or electronic facility or platform for electronic commerce.

There are many e-commerce operators [hereinafter referred to as an operator], like Amazon, Flipkart, Jabong, etc. operating in India. These operators display on their portal products as well as services, which are actually supplied by some other person to the consumer. The goods or services belonging to other suppliers are displayed on the portals of the operators and consumers buy such goods/services through these portals. On placing the order for a particular product/service, the actual supplier supplies the selected product/service to the consumer. The price/consideration for the product/service is collected by the e-commerce operator from the consumer and passed on to the actual supplier after the deduction of commission by the Operator.

Rate of TCS: The Government has placed the responsibility on the e-commerce operator to collect the 'tax' at a rate of 1% (0.5% CGST+ 0.5% SGST) from the registered supplier on "net value of taxable supplies".

Notifications No. 52/2018-Central Tax and Notification No. 02/2018-Integrated Tax both dated 20.09.2018 has been issued in this regard.

> The "net value of taxable supplies" means the aggregate value of taxable supplies of goods or services or both, other than the services on which entire tax is payable by the e-commerce operator, made during any month by a registered supplier through such operator reduced by the aggregate value of taxable supplies returned to such supplier during the said month. The value of net taxable supplies is calculated at GSTIN level.

When Tax not to be collected at source

TCS under GST is not required to be collected in following cases:

(a) On exempt supplies
(b) Supplies on which the recipient is required to pay tax on reverse charge basis
(c) Supplies made by the composition taxpayer (since cannot make supplies through e-commerce operator)
(d) On import of goods or services.

Exceptions to the TCS provisions

Here are few exceptions to the TCS provisions for the services provided by an e-commerce platform:

(a) Hotel accommodation/clubs (unregistered suppliers)
(b) Transportation of passengers—radio taxi, motor cab or motorcycle
(c) Housekeeping services like plumbing, carpentry etc. (unregistered suppliers)

Registration by E-commerce operator for TCS: E-commerce operator has to obtain separate registration for TCS irrespective of the fact whether e-Commerce operator is already registered under GST as a supplier or otherwise and has GSTIN.

Registration for TCS by E-commerce operator would be required in each State/UT as the obligation for collecting TCS would be there for every intra-State or inter-State supply. In order to facilitate the obtaining of registration in each State/UT, the e-commerce operator may declare the Head Office as its place of business for obtaining registration in that State/UT where it does not have physical presence.

Foreign e-commerce operator supplying goods or services to a customer in India would be liable to collect TCS on such supply and would be required to obtain registration in each State/UT. If the foreign e-commerce operator does not have physical presence in a particular State/UT, he may appoint an agent on his behalf.

Deposit of TCS with the Government: The amount of tax collected by the Operator is required to be deposited by the 10th of the following month, during which such collection is made. Payment of TCS is not allowed through Input Tax Credit of e-commerce operator.

Credit of tax collected: The amount of TCS deposited by the operator with the appropriate Government will be reflected in the electronic cash ledger of the actual registered supplier (on whose account such collection has been made) on the basis of the statement filed by the operator in FORM GSTR-8 in terms of Rule 67 of the CGST Rules, 2017. The tax collected by the operator shall be credited to the cash ledger of the supplier who has supplied the goods/services through the operator. The supplier can claim credit of the tax collected and reflected in the return by the operator in his [supplier's] electronic cash ledger.

TCS Statement & Return: The e-commerce operator is also required to furnish a monthly statement in FORM GSTR-8 by the 10th of the following month. Section 52 (5) of CGST Act requires filing of Annual Statement by e-commerce operator on or before 31st December following the year end (31st March of relevant year).

Rectification of error or omission [Section 52(6)]

(w.e.f. 1st October, 2022 vide Notification No. 18/2022-CT dated 28.09.2022)

The e-commerce operator can rectify errors or omission in the statements filed, if any, latest by 30th day of November following the end of the financial year or the actual date of furnishing of the relevant annual statement, whichever is earlier.

Consequences of non-compliance of TCS provisions [Section 52(14)]: In case the e-commerce operator fails to collect to tax under section 52 (1) or collects an amount which is less than the amount required to be collected under said sub-section or where he fails to pay to the government the amount collected as tax under section 52(3), he shall be liable to penalty under section 122 (1) (vi) of the Act, i.e. ₹ 10,000 or the amount of TCS involved, whichever is higher.

15.8 TRANSFER OF INPUT TAX CREDIT [SECTION 53]

As per Section 49 (5) (b), (c) and (d) of the Act, SGST/CGST/UTGST credits can be utilize by a tax payer on priority basis to respective SGST/CGST/UTGST dues first. Then, in case of CGST, balance, if any, can be used pay towards IGST. Upon utilization of central tax credit for payment of integrated taxes, the amount collected as central tax will stand reduced to that extent and the Central Government will transfer an amount equal to the credit from the central tax account to the integrated tax account in such manner and within such time as may be prescribed. Such treatment shall be ensured by the Central Government for UTGST and SGST also in respective cases.

Transfer of credit on obtaining separate registration for multiple places of business within a State or Union territory [Rule 41A]

(1) A registered person who has obtained separate registration for multiple places of business in accordance with the provisions of rule 11 and who intends to transfer, either wholly or partly, the unutilised input tax credit lying in his electronic credit ledger to any or all of the newly registered place of business, shall furnish within a period of thirty days from obtaining such separate registrations, the details in FORM GST ITC-02A electronically on the common portal, either directly or through a Facilitation Centre notified in this behalf by the Commissioner:

Provided that the input tax credit shall be transferred to the newly registered entities in the ratio of the value of assets held by them at the time of registration.

Explanation: For the purposes of this sub-rule, it is hereby clarified that the 'value of assets' means the value of the entire assets of the business whether or not input tax credit has been availed thereon.

(2) The newly registered person (transferee) shall, on the common portal, accept the details so furnished by the registered person (transferor) and, upon such acceptance, the unutilised input tax credit specified in FORM GST ITC-02A shall be credited to his electronic credit ledger.

Transfer of certain amounts [Section 53A]: Where any amount has been transferred from the electronic cash ledger under CGST Act to the electronic cash ledger under the State Goods and Services Tax Act or the Union territory Goods and Services Tax Act, the Government shall, transfer to the State tax account or the Union territory tax account, an amount equal to the amount transferred from the electronic cash ledger, in such manner and within such time as may be prescribed.

15.9 TAX WRONGLY COLLECTED & PAID TO CENTRAL GOVERNMENT OR STATE GOVERNMENT [SECTION 77]

Payment of tax based on erroneous determination of 'nature of supply' i.e. a transaction considered as intra-State supply but which is subsequently held to be inter-State supply, is not permitted to be adjusted.

Section 77 of the CGST Act, 2017 provides a remedy for such erroneous payment. In such cases, the taxable person is required to first discharge tax liability under correct head and then claim refund of tax deposited under wrong head. As per Section 77(2), the registered person shall not be required to pay any interest while depositing tax under correct head.

CGST Rules has been amended vide Notification No. 35/2021-Central Tax dated 24.09.2021, and Rule 89(1A) has been inserted in CGST Rules to provide:

(i) Procedure for filing such refund claims;

(ii) Such refund claims can be filed before the expiry of two years from the date of payment of tax under the correct head, or two years from the date of insertion of sub-rule (1A) to Rule 89 in past cases.

For refund of tax wrongly paid, the taxable person has to file an application electronically in FORM GST RFD-01 through the common portal.

Correction of tax wrongly paid: Rule 87(13) provides for inter-transfer of balances available in electronic cash ledger through FORM GST PMT-09 on the common portal. This enables a taxpayer to transfer any amount of tax, interest, penalty, etc. which was wrongly paid in such head in the electronic cash ledger to the correct tax or cess head under IGST, CGST and SGST in the electronic cash ledger. This will reduce the unnecessary hassle of payment of tax again and claiming refund of wrongly paid tax.

15.10 PAYMENT OF TAX AND OTHER AMOUNT IN INSTALLMENTS [SECTION 80]

A taxable person is permitted to make payment of tax and other amount due, on installment basis, other than the amount due as per self-assessed return.

(i) The Commissioner is empower to grant permission only to the taxable person to make payment of any amount due on installment basis, on an application filed electronically in FORM GST DRC-20, (refer Rule 158).

The Commissioner after considering the request by the taxable person (in FORM GST DRC-20) and report of the jurisdictional office, may issue an order in FORM GST DRC-21, allowing the taxable person either extend the time or allow payment of any amount due under the Act on installment basis.

(ii) Applicable for tax amount amounts due other than the self-assessed liability shown in any return.

(iii) The installment period shall not exceed 24 months.

(iv) The taxable person shall also be liable to pay prescribed interest on the amount due from the first day such tax was due to be payable till the date tax is paid.

(v) If default occurs in payment of any one installment the taxable person would be required to pay the whole outstanding balance payable on such date of default itself without further notice.

Chapter 16

Refund Mechanism Under GST

16.1 STATUTORY PROVISION

The provisions pertaining to refund contained in Sections 54 to 58 (Chapter XI) of the CGST Act, 2017 read with Rules 89 to 97A (Chapter X) of the CGST Rules, 2017 aim to streamline and standardise the refund procedures under GST regime. The GST law envisages a simplified, time-bound and technology-driven procedure with minimal human interface between the taxpayer and tax authorities.

As per the explanation to Section 54 of the CGST Act, 2017, the term "refund" includes refund of tax and interest paid on:

1. Zero-rated supplies of goods or services or both; or
2. Inputs or input services used in the effecting such zero-rated supplies of goods or services or both; or
3. Supply of goods regarded as deemed exports; or
4. Refund of unutilized input tax credit at the end of any tax period in case the rate of output tax is less than the rate of input tax (inverted duty structure).

Section	Descriptions
54	Refund of Tax
55	Refund in certain cases
56	Interest on delayed refunds
57	Consumer welfare fund
58	Utilization of fund

Summary of Refund Provision

Descriptions	Provision
Section	54 to 58 of CGST Act, 2017
Rules	Rule 89 to 97A of CGST Rules, 2017
Procedural Circular	Circular No. 17/17/2017-GST dt 15.11.2017 Circular No. 24/24/2017-GST dt 21.12.2017 Circular No. 36/10/2018-GST dt 13.03.2018 (UN entities) Circular No. 43/17/2018-GST dt 13.04.2018 (UN entities) Circular No. 37/11/2018-GST dt 15.03.2018 Circular No. 45/19/2018-GST dt 30.05.2018
Periodicity	For any tax period (monthly/quarterly)
Time limit	Before expiry of two years from the relevant date
Minimum refund to be claimed	₹ 1000

16.2 TYPES OF REFUND UNDER GST

(1) Goods or services or both exported or supplied to an SEZ on payment of IGST
(2) Refund of un-utilized ITC on
  (a) Zero-rated supplies
  (b) Accumulated ITC on inverted duty structure, other than outputs not being Nil rated or fully exempted supply
(3) Tax paid on supply of goods regarded as deemed export [Section 147 of CGST Act]
(4) Refund of balance in electronic cash ledger
(5) Refund on account of issuance of refund voucher for taxes paid on advance, but goods or services are not supplied
(6) Refund of tax deposited with Govt under wrong head due to wrong interpretation of place of supply (IGST paid in lieu of CGST+SGST or vice versa) (Section 77)
(7) Refunds to international tourists of GST paid on goods in India and carried abroad at the time of their departure from India
(8) Tax refundable on account of judgment/decree or order/direction of Appellate authority/tribunal/court
(9) Tax refundable on finalization of provisional assessment
(10) Refund of tax on purchases made by UN bodies or Embassies
(11) Transfer of balance in electronic cash ledger to other GSTIN of same legal entity (i.e. distinct person u/s 25) as provided in Section 49(10).

16.3 REFUND IN CASE OF DEEMED EXPORTS

As per Section 2(39) of CGST Act, 2017, "deemed exports" means such supplies of goods as may be notified under section 147. It is to be noted that only supply of goods and not supply of services can be classified as Deemed Exports.

The Central Government vide Notification No. 48/2017-Central Tax dated 18.10.2017 has notified the following items as "Deemed Exports".

Sl No.	Description of Supply
1.	Supply of goods by a registered person against "Advance Authorization"
2.	Supply of capital goods by a registered person against Export Promotion Capital Goods Authorization
3.	Supply of goods by a registered person to Export-oriented unit
4.	Supply of gold by a bank or Public Sector Undertaking specified in the notification No. 50/2017-Customs, dated the 30th June 2017 (as amended) against Advance Authorization

Deemed exports are the supplies that do not leave India. The payment for such supplies is received either in Indian rupees or convertible foreign exchange. All supplies notified as supply for deemed export will be subject to levy of taxes, i.e. such supplies can be made only by payment of tax.

However, the refund of tax paid on the supply regarded as deemed export is admissible to either the supplier or the recipient. The deemed exporters can either:

(a) levy GST on supply and collect it from the recipient. In this case, the recipient shall apply for a refund.
(b) levy GST on supply and to not collect it from the recipient. In this case, the supplier shall apply for a refund through GST RFD-01. In this case, a declaration is also required from the recipient to the effect that he does not avail any input tax credit of the same.

Note: As per Notification No. 01/2019-Central Tax dated 15.01.2019, "Advance Authorization" means an authorization issued by the "Director General of Foreign Trade" under Chapter 4 of the Foreign Trade Policy 2015-20 for import or domestic procurement of inputs for physical exports.

16.4 REFUND OF UN-UTILISED INPUT TAX CREDIT (ITC)

As per Section 54(3) of the CGST Act, 2017, a registered person may claim refund of un-utilized input tax credit at the end of any tax period, where the credit has accumulated on account of rate of tax on inputs being higher than the rate of tax on output supplies. A tax period is the period for which return is required to be furnished.

GST Law permits refund of un-utilized ITC in two scenarios, if such credit accumulation is

(a) on account of zero-rated supplies, where the registered person has supplied under Bond/LUT or by payment of IGST.

(b) on account of inverted duty structure, where the credit has accumulated on account of rate of tax on inputs being higher than the rate of tax on output supplies (other than nil rated or fully exempt supplies), except supplies of goods or services or both as may be notified by the Government, the same can be claimed as refund.

Recovery of refund of unutilized input tax credit or integrated tax paid on export of goods where export proceeds not realized [Rule 96B]

[Notification No. 16/2020-CT dated 23.03.2020]

(1) Where any refund of unutilized input tax credit on account of export of goods or of integrated tax paid on export of goods has been paid to an applicant but the sale proceeds in respect of such export goods have not been realized, in full or in part, in India within the period allowed under the Foreign Exchange Management Act, 1999 (42 of 1999), including any extension of such period, the person to whom the refund has been made shall deposit the amount so refunded, to the extent of non-realization of sale proceeds, along with applicable interest within thirty days of the expiry of the said period or, as the case may be, the extended period, failing which the amount refunded shall be recovered in accordance with the provisions of section 73 or 74 of the Act, as the case may be, as is applicable for recovery of erroneous refund, along with interest under section 50:

Provided that where sale proceeds, or any part thereof, in respect of such export goods are not realized by the applicant within the period allowed under the Foreign Exchange Management Act, 1999 (42 of 1999), but the Reserve Bank of India writes off the requirement of realization of sale proceeds on merits, the refund paid to the applicant shall not be recovered.

(2) Where the sale proceeds are realized by the applicant, in full or part, after the amount of refund has been recovered from him under sub-rule (1) and the applicant produces evidence about such realization within a period of three months from the date of realization of sale proceeds, the amount so recovered shall be refunded by the proper officer, to the applicant to the extent of realization of sale proceeds, provided the sale proceeds have been realized within such extended period as permitted by the Reserve Bank of India.

Refund of un-utilized ITC not available in following cases:

(a) where the goods exported out of India are subjected to export duty

(b) if the supplier of goods or services or both avails of drawback in respect of central tax or claims refund of the integrated tax paid on such supplies.

Section 54(3) of the CGST Act specifies that refund of un-utilized input tax credit shall be allowed in case of zero-rated supplies effected without payment of tax unless such export are subjected to export duty. Thus, refund of un-utilised ITC on export of exempted/non-taxable goods may be sought by the registered person as per Rule 89 of CGST Rules, 2017.

In case of refund claim arising due to inverted duty structure, the prescribed statements—Statement 1 and Statement 1A of FORM GST RFD-01A have to be filled.

As per Rule 89(3), where the application relates to refund of input tax credit, the electronic credit ledger shall be debited by the applicant by an amount equal to the refund so claimed.

[Circular No. 139/09/2020-GST dated 10th June 2020]: The refund of accumulated ITC shall be restricted to the ITC as per those invoices, the details of which are uploaded by the supplier in FORM GSTR-1 and are reflected in the FORM GSTR-2A of the applicant.

> Amendment in CGST Rules, 2017 has been made vide Notification No. 14/2022-Central Tax dated 05.07.2022 to provide for refund of unutilized Input Tax Credit on account of Export of Electricity. This would facilitate the exporters of electricity in claiming refund of unutilized ITC on zero-rated supplies.

Goods & services on which refund of un-utilized ITC not permitted: In exercise of the powers conferred by section 54(3) of the Central Goods and Services Tax Act, 2017, the Central Government, on the recommendations of the Council has notifies following goods & services on which no refund of un-utilized input tax credit (ITC) shall be allowed.

Supply	Notification	Items
Goods	Notification No. 5/2017-Central Tax (Rate) dated 28th June 2017	Woven fabrics of silk, wool, cotton, Rail locomotives, Self-propelled railway or tramway coaches, vans and trucks, Railway or tramway maintenance or service vehicles, Railway or tramway passenger coaches
Services	Notification No. 15/2017-Central Tax (Rate) dated 28th June 2017	Item 5(b) of Schedule II of CGST Act i.e. Construction services

As per Circular No. 79/53/2018 dated 31.12.2018, refund of tax paid on input services & capital goods is not available for refund on account of inverted duty structure, because as per Section 2(59) of the CGST Act, the term inputs does not include "services" or "capital goods".

Filing for Refund by Unregistered Persons

Circular No. 188/20/2022-GST dated 27.12.2022

Section 54(1) of the CGST Act provides that any person can claim refund of any tax and interest, if any, paid on such tax or any other amount paid by him, by making an application before the expiry of two years from the relevant date in such form and manner as may be prescribed. Further, in terms of section 54 (8)(e) of the CGST Act, in cases where the unregistered person has borne the incidence of tax and not passed on the same to any other person, the said refund shall be paid to him instead of being credited to Consumer Welfare Fund (CWF).

Refund application may be filed by an unregistered persons in cases where the contract/agreement for supply of services of construction of flat/building has been cancelled due to non-completion or delay in construction activity in time or any other reasons or where long-term insurance policy has been terminated prematurely, etc.

The unregistered person shall obtain a temporary registration on the common portal using his Permanent Account Number (PAN). While doing so, the unregistered person shall select the same State/UT where his/her supplier, in respect of whose invoice refund is to be claimed, is registered. Thereafter, the unregistered person would be required to undergo Aadhar authentication.

The application for refund shall be filed in FORM GST RFD-01 on the common portal under the category 'Refund for unregistered person'. The applicant shall upload statement 8 (in pdf format) and all the requisite documents as per the provisions of rule 89 (2) of the CGST Rules. The refund amount claimed shall not exceed the total amount of tax declared on the invoices in respect of which refund is being claimed. Further, the applicant shall also upload the certificate issued by the supplier in terms of rule 89(2) (kb) of the CGST Rules along with the refund application.

As per Section 54(14), no refund shall be granted if the amount is less than one thousand rupees. In cases where the amount paid back by the supplier to the unregistered person on cancellation/termination of agreement/contract for supply of services is less than amount paid by such unregistered person to the supplier, only the proportionate amount of tax involved in such amount paid back shall be refunded to the unregistered person.

16.5 CLAIM OF GST DEPOSITED ON ADVANCE RECEIVED BUT SUBSEQUENTLY REFUNDED TO THE BUYER DUE TO CANCELLATION OF CONTRACT OR NON-SUPPLY OF GOODS OR SERVICES

Refer Circular no. 137/07/2020-GST dated 13 April 2020

Nature of supply	Transaction	Document issued	Event	Treatment under GST
Services	Advance received & GST deposited thereon	Tax invoice issued before supply of services	Contract cancelled before supply of services	(a) Credit note to be issued under section 34 of CGST Act, 2017 for reduction of tax liability. (b) Details of such credit notes shall be declared in the return for the month during which such credit note has been issued. There is no need to file a separate refund claim. (c) Where there is no output liability against which a credit note can be adjusted, refund claim allowable under 'Excess payment of tax, if any' through FORM GST RFD-01.

Services	Advance received & GST deposited thereon	Receipt voucher	Contract cancelled before supply of services	Issue a "refund voucher" in terms of section 31 (3) (e) of the CGST Act read with rule 51 of the CGST Rules. The taxpayer can apply for refund of GST paid on such advances by filing FORM GST RFD-01 under the category "Refund of excess payment of tax".
Goods	Goods supplied & GST deposited thereon	Tax invoice	Goods returned	(a) Credit note to be issued under section 34 of CGST Act, 2017 for reduction of tax liability. (b) Details of such credit notes shall be declared in the return for the month during which such credit note has been issued. There is no need to file a separate refund claim. (c) Where there is no output liability against which a credit note can be adjusted, refund claim allowable under 'Excess payment of tax, if any' through FORM GST RFD-01.

GST amount paid on advance amount, which is refunded subsequently, can be adjusted through Table 9B of GSTR-1.

Note: According to Section 54 of CGST Act, an application for claiming refund of any tax and interest can be made before the expiry of two years.

16.6 WHEN REFUND NOT AVAILABLE

(a) If the goods exported out of India are subject to export duty.
(b) If supplier claims refund of output tax paid under IGST Act.
(c) If the supplier avails duty drawback or refund of IGST on such supplies.

In a case where the refund is claimed on account of supply of goods or services made to SEZ developer/unit, the supplier is required to furnish a declaration that tax has not been collected from SEZ unit/SEZ developer. [Notification No. 03/2019-Central Tax dated 29.01.2019]

16.7 TIME LIMIT FOR FILING REFUND CLAIM

(1) Refund in respect of zero-rated supply and accumulated ITC of inverted duty structure, can be claimed at the end of any tax period.
(2) Refund in respect of purchases made by UN bodies or Embassies to be claimed within six months from the end of quarter in which purchases made.
(3) In all other cases, refund can be claimed within two years of relevant date.

Application for Refund: Rule 89(1) facilitates a taxable person to claim refund in following manner under various circumstances.

Sl No.	Category of Refund	Process of filing
1.	Refund of IGST paid on export of goods	No separate application is required as shipping bill itself will be treated as application for refund.
2.	Refund of IGST paid on export of services/ zero-rated supplies to SEZ units or SEZ developers	Printout of FORM GST RFD-01 needs to be filed online in the common portal along with relevant documentary evidences, wherever applicable.
3.	Refund of unutilized input tax credit due to the accumulation of credit of tax paid on inputs or input services used in making zero-rated supplies of goods or services or both	FORM GST RFD-01 needs to be filed online in the common portal along with necessary documentary evidences, wherever applicable. The amount of credit claimed as refund would be debited in the electronic credit ledger.
4.	Refund relating to balance in the electronic cash ledger in accordance with the provisions of section 49(6)	FORM GST RFD-01 needs to be filed online in the common portal. The amount of claimed as refund would be debited in the electronic cash ledger. Acknowledgement in Form RFD-02 will be auto generated by the system.

The refund due to the applicant can be adjusted towards tax, interest, penalty or any other amount, which the applicant is liable to pay but which remains unpaid under the Act or under any earlier law.

The following types of refunds shall also be made available through FORM GST RFD-01A:

(a) Refund on account of assessment/Provisional Assessment/Appeal/Any Other Order;
(b) Tax paid on an intra-State supply, which is subsequently held to be inter-State supply and vice-versa;
(c) Excess payment of Tax; and
(d) Any other refund.

16.8 WHERE TO FILE THE REFUND CLAIMS

The registered person needs to file the refund claim with the jurisdictional tax authority to which the taxpayer has been assigned as per the administrative order issued in this regard by the Chief Commissioner of Central Tax and the Commissioner of State Tax. In case such an order has not been issued in the State, the registered person is at liberty to apply for refund before the Central Tax Authority or State Tax Authority till the administrative mechanism for assigning of taxpayers to respective authority is implemented.

However, in the latter case, an undertaking is required to be submitted stating that the claim for sanction of refund has been made to only one of the authorities. It is reiterated that the Central Tax officers shall facilitate the processing of the refund claims of all registered persons whether or not such person was registered with the Central Government in the earlier regime. Section 54(8A) provides that, Central Tax Authorities may refund SGST/UTGST also.

Minimum amount of Refund: No refund, if the amount of refund claimed is less than ₹ 1000.

16.9 DOCUMENTS REQUIRED TO BE ENCLOSED ALONG WITH THE REFUND APPLICATION

1. Documentary evidence to establish that a refund is due to the applicant (prescribed under Rule 89(2) of the CGST Rules, 2017).

2. Documentary evidence to prove that incidence of tax and interest had not been passed on to any other person.

3. For above purposes a certificate from a Chartered Accountant/Cost Accountant will suffice the purpose.

Such evidence is not required where refund is being claimed on account of zero-rated supplies, inverted duty structure, etc.

However, if the refund claimed were less than 2 lakh rupees, then documentary evidence would not be required. A self-declaration by the applicant to the effect that incidence of tax has not been pass on to any other person, will suffice the purpose.

Order sanctioning refund [Rule 92]: Where, upon examination of the application, the proper officer is satisfied that a refund under section 54(5) is due and payable to the applicant, he shall make an order in FORM GST RFD-06 sanctioning the amount of refund to which the applicant is entitled, mentioning therein the amount, if any, refunded to him on a provisional basis under section 54(6), amount adjusted against any outstanding demand under the Act or under any existing law and the balance amount refundable.

Refund in Certain Cases [Section 55]

The Government may, on the recommendations of the Council, by notification, specify any specialized agency of the United Nations Organization or any Multilateral Financial Institution and Organization notified under the United Nations (Privileges and Immunities) Act, 1947 (46 of 1947), Consulate or Embassy of foreign countries and any other person or class of persons as may be specified in this behalf, who shall, subject to such conditions and restrictions as may be prescribed, be entitled to claim a refund of taxes paid on the notified supplies of goods or services or both received by them.

Any person eligible to claim refund of tax paid by him on his inward supplies as per notification issued under section 55 shall apply for refund in FORM GST RFD-10 once in every quarter, electronically on the common portal or otherwise, either directly or through a Facilitation Centre notified by the Commissioner, along with a statement of the inward supplies of goods or services or both in FORM GSTR-11.

16.10 INTEREST ON DELAYED REFUND [SECTION 56]

If any tax ordered to be refunded under section 54(5) to any applicant is not refunded within 60 days from the date of receipt of application under section 50(1), interest at such rate not exceeding 6% as may be specified in the notification issued by the Government shall be payable in respect of such refund for the period of delay beyond sixty days from the date of receipt of such application till the date of refund of such tax, to be computed in such manner and subject to such conditions and restrictions as may be prescribed.

Government vide Notification No. 13/2017-Central Tax dated 28-6-2017 has prescribed the rate of interest @ 6% on refund:

Provided that where any claim of refund arises from an order passed by an adjudicating authority or Appellate Authority or Appellate Tribunal or court which has attained finality and the same is not refunded within sixty days from the date of receipt of application filed consequent to such order, interest at such rate not exceeding 9% as may be notified by the Government on the recommendations of the Council shall be payable in respect of such refund from the date immediately after the expiry of 60 days from the date of receipt of application till the date of refund.

Where any interest is due and payable to the applicant under section 56, the proper officer shall make an order along with a payment order in FORM GST RFD-05, specifying therein the amount of refund which is delayed, the period of delay for which interest is payable and the amount of interest payable, and such amount of interest shall be electronically credited to any of the bank accounts of the applicant mentioned in his registration particulars and as specified in the application for refund.

16.11 CONSUMER WELFARE FUND [SECTIONS 57 AND 58]

The Government shall constitute a Fund, to be called the Consumer Welfare Fund

(1) All amounts of duty/central tax/integrated tax/Union territory tax/cess and income from investment along with other monies specified in Section 12C (2) of the Central Excise Act, 1944 (1 of 1944), section 57 of the CGST Act, 2017 read with Section 20 of the IGST Act, 2017, section 21 of the UTGST Act, 2017 and section 12 of the GST (Compensation to States) Act, 2017 shall be credited to the Fund.

An amount equivalent to 50% of the amount of integrated tax determined under section 54(5) of the CGST Act, 2017, read with section 20 of the IGST Act, 2017, shall be deposited in the Fund.

(2) Where any amount, having been credited to the Fund, is ordered or directed to be paid to any claimant by the proper officer, appellate authority or court, the same shall be paid from the Fund.

(3) Accounts of the Fund maintained by the Central Government shall be subject to audit by the Comptroller and Auditor General of India.

Utilization of fund [Section 58]

(1) All sums credited to the Fund shall be authorize by the Government for the welfare of the consumers in such manner as may be prescribed.

(2) The Government or the authority specified by it shall maintain proper and separate account and other relevant records in relation to the Fund and prepare an annual statement of accounts in such form as may be prescribed in consultation with the Comptroller and Auditor-General of India.

Chapter 17

Assessment

17.1 MEANING AND TYPE OF ASSESSMENT

In terms of Section 2(11) of the Act, "assessment" means determination of tax liability under this Act and includes self-assessment, re-assessment, provisional assessment, summary assessment and best judgment assessment.

The CGST Act contemplates following types of Assessments

Section	Nature of assessment
Section 59	Self-assessment
Section 60	Provisional Assessment
Section 61	Scrutiny of returns filed by registered taxable persons
Section 62	Assessment of non-filers of returns
Section 63	Assessment of unregistered persons
Section 64	Summary Assessment in certain special cases

17.2 SELF ASSESSMENT [SECTION 59]

Self-assessment refers to the assessment made by registered person himself/itself while all other assessments are undertaken by tax authorities.

The registered person is required to compute his output tax liability, take the available input tax credit and pay the balance amount and file the returns in the prescribed forms as specified under section 39. Prima facie the department shall accept such self-assessed returns and declarations, subject to scrutiny and other modes of assessment in the selected cases and in the prescribed manner.

The GST Law permit a registered person to rectify any incorrect particulars furnished in the returns. In terms of Section 39(9), if a registered person discovers any omission or incorrect particulars furnished in a return, he is required to rectify such omission or incorrect particulars in the return to be furnished for the tax period during which such omission or incorrect particulars are noticed (along with interest), before 30th November following the end of the financial year, or the actual date of furnishing of relevant annual return, whichever is earlier.

17.3 PROVISIONAL ASSESSMENT [SECTION 60]

(1) In case a taxable person is unable to determine his tax liability due to difficulties in ascertaining transaction value or rate of tax, he may file application in **FORM GST ASMT-01** electronically along with the documents in support of paying the tax on provisional basis. The proper officer shall pass an order, within a period not later than ninety days from the date of receipt of such request, allowing payment of tax on provisional basis at such rate or on such value as may be specified by him.

(2) The payment of tax on provisional basis may be allowed, if the taxable person executes a bond in such form as may be prescribed, and with such surety or security as the proper officer may deem fit, binding the taxable person for payment of the difference between the amount of tax as may be finally assessed and the amount of tax provisionally assessed.

(3) The proper officer shall, within a period not exceeding six months from the date of the communication of the order issued under Section 60(*1*), pass the final assessment order after taking into account such information as may be required for finalizing the assessment:

Provided that the period specified in this sub-section may, on sufficient cause being shown and for reasons to be recorded in writing, be extended by the Joint Commissioner or Additional Commissioner for a further period not exceeding six months and by the Commissioner for such further period not exceeding four years.

(4) The registered person shall be liable to pay interest on any tax payable on the supply of goods or services or both under provisional assessment but not paid on the due date specified under Section 39 (7) or the rules made there under, at the rate specified under Section 50(1), from the first day after the due date of payment of tax in respect of the said supply of goods or services or both till the date of actual payment, whether such amount is paid before or after the issuance of order for final assessment.

(5) Where the registered person is entitled to a refund consequent to the order of final assessment under Section 60(*3*), subject to the provisions of Section 54(*8*), interest shall be paid on such refund as provided in section 56.

17.4 SCRUTINY OF RETURNS (SECTION 61)

(1) The proper officer may scrutinize the return and related particulars furnished by the registered person to verify the correctness of the return and inform him of the discrepancies noticed, if any, in such manner as may be prescribed and seek his explanation thereto.

(2) In case the explanation is found acceptable, the registered person shall be informed accordingly and no further action shall be taken in this regard.

(3) In case no satisfactory explanation is furnished within a period of thirty days of being informed by the proper officer or such further period as may be permitted by him or where the registered person, after accepting the discrepancies, fails to take the corrective measure in his return for the month in which the discrepancy is accepted, the proper officer may initiate appropriate action including those under section 65 or section 66 or section 67, or proceed to determine the tax and other dues under section 73 or section 74.

17.5 ASSESSMENT OF NON-FILERS OF RETURNS (SECTION 62)

According to Section 62(1), where a registered person fails to furnish the return under section 39 or section 45, even after the service of a notice under section 46, the proper officer may proceed to assess the tax liability of the said person to the best of his judgment taking into account all the relevant material which is available or which he has gathered and issue an assessment order within a period of five years from the date specified under section 44 for furnishing of the annual return for the financial year to which the tax not paid relates.

Where the registered person furnishes a valid return within sixty days (extendable by another 60 days subject to certain conditions) of the service of the assessment order under Section 60(*1*), the said assessment order shall be deemed to have been withdrawn but the liability for payment of interest under Section 50(1) or for payment of late fee under Section 47 shall continue.

The order of assessment made under section 62(1) shall be issued in FORM GST ASMT-13 and a summary thereof shall be uploaded electronically in FORM GST DRC-07.

17.6 ASSESSMENT OF UN-REGISTERED PERSONS (SECTION 63)

This section is applicable to unregistered persons i.e., persons who are liable to obtain registration under Section 22 and have failed to obtain registration will come within scope of operation of this section.

The proper officer may pass the best judgment assessment within a period of five years from the date specified under section 44 for furnishing of the annual return for the financial year to which the tax not paid relates in following situations:

(1) where a taxable person fails to obtain registration even though liable to do so.

(2) a person whose registration has been cancelled by proper officer u/s 29(2) but who is liable to pay tax.

Steps involved in Assessment of unregistered persons:

Steps	Actions by proper officer
Step No. 1	Issue of Notice (GST ASMT-14)
Step No. 2	Allow 15 days' time for reply
Step No. 3	Pass the Order (GST ASMT-15)

17.7 SUMMARY ASSESSMENT IN CERTAIN SPECIAL CASES (SECTION 64)

(1) The proper officer may, on any evidence showing a tax liability of a person coming to his notice, with the previous permission of Additional Commissioner or Joint Commissioner, proceed to assess the tax liability of such person to protect the interest of revenue and issue an assessment order, if he has sufficient grounds to believe that any delay in doing so may adversely affect the interest of revenue:

Provided that where the taxable person to whom the liability pertains is not ascertainable and such liability pertains to supply of goods, the person in charge of such goods shall be deemed to be the taxable person liable to be assessed and liable to pay tax and any other amount due under this section.

(2) On an application made by the taxable person within thirty days from the date of receipt of order passed under sub-section (1) or on his own motion, if the Additional Commissioner or Joint Commissioner considers that such order is erroneous, he may withdraw such order and follow the procedure laid down in section 73 or section 74.

The order of assessment under section 64(1) shall be issued in FORM GST ASMT-16 and a summary of the order shall be uploaded electronically in FORM GST DRC-07.

Summary of various assessment orders to be uploaded on portal

As per Notification No. 16/2019-Central Tax dated 29.03.2019, summary of various orders under Sections 62, 63 & 64 of the CGST Act is required to be uploaded electronically in prescribed forms.

Chapter 18

Audit Under GST

18.1 MEANING AND OBJECTIVE OF GST AUDIT

As per Section 2(13) of the CGST Act, 2017 "Audit" means the examination of records, returns and other documents maintained or furnished by the registered person under GST Act or the rules made there under or under any other law for the time being in force to verify:

- the correctness of turnover declared,
- taxes paid,
- refund claimed,
- input tax credit availed, and
- to assess his compliance with the provisions of this Act or the rules made there under.

Objective of Audit

The objective of GST audit is "to verify" i.e. to prove the accuracy/correctness of whether registered person has correctly:

(1) declared his turnover
(2) assessed his liability & paid taxes thereon
(3) claimed eligible Input Tax Credit
(4) claimed the refund, if any
(5) maintained accounts and records/documents
(6) filed his return as per the provisions of the law
(7) complied with all the provisions of the law, rules and notifications

18.2 STATUTORY AUDIT UNDER GST

As per Section 35(5) of CGST Act, 2017, every registered person (whether compulsory or voluntarily registered), whose aggregate turnover during a financial year exceeds <u>two crores</u> rupees get his accounts audited by a CA/ CMA and shall furnish a copy of audited annual accounts and a reconciliation statement, duly certified in FORM GSTR-9C [Rule 80(3)], before 31st December following the end of the FY.

> The Finance Act, 2021, has omitted Section 35(5) and substituted Section 44 w.e.f. 1st April 2021 so as to remove the mandatory requirement of furnishing a Reconciliation Statement (GSTR-9C) duly audited by a Practicing Chartered Accountants or Cost Accountants and to provide for filing of the Annual Return (GSTR-9) on *self-certification basis* with a reconciliation statement.
> (Ref Notification No. 29 to 31 of 2021-Central Tax dated 30th July 2021)

18.3 LEGAL PROVISION OF GST AUDIT

GST being in the nature of a self-assessment tax, audit procedures have been introduced for error correction and ensuring proper compliance. GST audit is not only for reconciliation of tax liability and payment thereof but it also encompasses the verification of compliance of the provisions of the GST Acts, laws etc. by a registered person.

Section 35 of the CGST Act, deals with the maintenance of books of accounts, documents and records. Section 35(5) read with Section 44(2) of the CGST Act and the corresponding Rule 80(3) of the CGST Rules mandate Statutory audit under GST.

The provision relating to Audit by tax authority & Special audit under GST is covered under Chapter XI (Rules 101 and 102) of CGST Rules, 2017.

Sections	Nature of audit	Remarks
35(5)	Statutory Audit by CA/ CMA	If "aggregate turnover" exceeds ₹ 2 crores in a FY *Section 35(5) which provides for mandatory audit by CA/CMA has been omitted by Finance Act, 2021 w.e.f. 1st August 2021. (Ref. Notification No. 29 to 31 of 2021-Central Tax dated 30th July 2021)*
65	Audit by Tax authority	It could be for a FY or multiples thereof (to ascertain correctness of the turnover, exemptions and deductions claimed, the rate of tax applied in respect of the supply of goods or services or both, the input tax credit availed and utilized, refund claimed, etc.)
66	Special Audit by CA/CMA (with the approval of Commissioner, in the interest of revenue)	If at any stage of scrutiny, enquiry, investigation or any other proceedings, the proper officer is of the opinion that the value has not been correctly declared or the credit availed is not within the normal limits, the commissioner may order Special Audit of a registered person through CA/CMA.

Notes:

(1) "Aggregate turnover" to be computed on all India basis against a single PAN.

(2) Any department of the Central Government or a State Government or a local authority, whose books of account are subject to audit by the Comptroller and Auditor General of India (C&AG) or an auditor appointed for auditing the accounts of local authorities under any law for the time being in force shall be exempted from audit u/s 35(5).

(3) The council of the ICAI in its 378th meeting stated that an Internal auditor of an entity cannot undertake GST Audit of the same entity, since GST Audit is a statutory audit.

18.4 TYPES OF AUDIT

GST envisages three types of Audit.

(1) **Audit by taxable person [Section 35(5)]:** To be done by Chartered Accountant/Cost Accountant, where turnover exceeds certain threshold specified in Rule 80(3), i.e. ₹ 2 crores. *(This provision has been omitted by Finance Act, 2021 w.e.f. 1st August 2021, Ref Notification No. 29 to 31 of 2021-Central Tax dated 30th July 2021.)*

(2) **Audit by tax authorities [Section 65]:** To be done by the commissioner or any officer authorized by him in terms of Section 65 of the CGST Act, 2017 read with Section 20(xiv) of the IGST Act, 2017 and Section 21(xv) of UTGST Act, 2017.

(3) **Special Audit [Section 66]:** To be done by a CA/CMA appointed by commissioner in the interest of revenue to determine tax liabilities in complex cases.

The provision relating to Audit under GST is covered in Chapter XI (Rules 101 & 102) of CGST Rules, 2017.

(1) Audit by Taxable person [Section 35(5)]

[Omitted by Finance Act, 2021 w.e.f. 01.08.2021 vide Notification no. 29/2021-C.T. dated 30th July 2021]

- every registered person (whether compulsory or voluntarily registered)
- whose aggregate turnover during a financial year exceeds two crores rupees
- get his accounts audited by a CA/CMA and
- shall furnish a copy of audited annual accounts and a reconciliation statement, duly certified in FORM GSTR-9C (Rule 80(3)).

The Central Government vide Notification No. 74/2018-Central Tax dated 31st December 2018 has notified FORM GSTR-9C comprising Reconciliation Statement and Certification, which has to be certified by a GST auditor, i.e. CA/CMA.

Sec 35(5) read with Section 44(2) of the CGST Act provides that the registered person upon conclusion of the Audit shall furnish the following documents electronically through the common portal either directly or through a facilitation centre notified by the commissioner.

(a) Annual Return
(b) Copy of Audited annual accounts
(c) Reconciliation statement, reconciling the value of supplies declared in the return (GST Annual Return) furnished for the financial year with the audited annual financial statement in FORM GSTR 9C, duly certified
(d) such other particulars, as may be prescribed.

While Rule 80(3) of the CGST Rules speaks of the prescribed threshold limit at ₹ 2 crore which is attributed to the 'aggregate turnover', Section 35(5) speaks of the turnover in the State/turnover attributable to a GSTIN. Therefore, if a registered person is liable to get his accounts audited under Section 35(5), all the registrations obtained under the same PAN will also be liable for such audit, regardless of the turnover in each State in which the other registrations have been obtained.

For example, if the aggregate turnover (PAN based) is at ₹ 4 crores and the registered person is carrying on business in two different States having a turnover of ₹ 2.75 crores (in Delhi) and ₹ 1.25 crores respectively, the law mandates that audit is required to be carried out in both the States.

Central Board of Indirect Taxes & Customs [CBIC] has notified section 110 and section 111 of Finance Act 2021 with effect from 1st August 2021. Section 110 of Finance Act 2021, has omitted Section 35 of Central Goods & Service Tax Act, 2017, thus omitting GST Audit.

(2) Audit by tax authorities (Section 65): The Commissioner or any officer authorized by him, by way of a general or a specific order, may undertake audit of any registered person for such period, at such frequency and in such manner as may be prescribed.

- Period of audit can be for a financial year or part thereof or multiples thereof. (Notification No. 74/2018-Central Tax, dated 31.12.2018)
- Notice for audit shall be issued in FORM GST ADT-01 at least 15 days prior to the date of commencement of audit.
- Following shall be verified during audit by the proper officer and team assigned:
  (a) Documents relied upon for updating books of accounts and returns and statements furnished under the Act and rules made there under
  (b) Correctness of the turnover
  (c) Exemptions and deductions claimed
  (d) Rate of tax applied in respect of supply of goods or services or both
  (e) Input tax credit availed and utilized
  (f) Refund claimed
  (g) Other relevant issues.
- The registered person is obliged to provide all necessary details, documents and information required for completion of an audit.
- Officer shall record the observations in his audit notes and inform the discrepancies to the auditee.
- The auditee can submit his reply to the observations.
- Audit findings shall be informed in FORM GST ADT-02 once the audit is concluded.
- The audit under Section 65 shall be completed within a period of three months from the date of commencement of the audit but a further extension for a period of six months may be provided by the Commissioner.
- Where the Commissioner is satisfied that audit in respect of such registered person cannot be completed within three months, he may, for the reasons to be recorded in writing, extend the period by a further period not exceeding six months.
- On conclusion of audit, the proper officer shall, within thirty days, inform the registered person, whose records are audited, about the findings, his rights and obligations and the reasons for such findings.

- Where the audit conducted under section 65(1) results in detection of tax not paid or short paid or erroneously refunded, or input tax credit wrongly availed or utilized, the proper officer may initiate action under section 73 or section 74.

(3) **Special Audit (Section 66):** As per Sec 66(1) if, during scrutiny, inquiry, investigation or any other proceedings, in the interest of revenue, if it is observed that a registered person has not declared the value correctly/ ITC wrongly availed:

- any officer not below the rank of Assistant Commissioner,
- with the prior approval of the Commissioner,
- direct such registered person by a communication in writing to get his records audited,
- by a CA/CMA as may be nominated by the Commissioner.

(a) The CA/CMA so nominated shall submit Audit report, **within the period of ninety days** (which may be extended for a further period of 90 days on special ground)

(b) Special audit shall be conducted in addition to audit conducted under this law or any other law

(c) Expenses of audit & remuneration of CA/CMA so appointed, shall be determined and paid by the Commissioner

(d) If tax not paid/short paid/erroneously refunded/ITC wrongly availed or utilized detected action shall be initiated under section 73 or section 74.

Special audit provides a lawful and legal way for the GST officers to take the assistance of a CA/CMA to determine tax liabilities in complex cases. The professional expertise of a CA/CMA will be of great significance in ensuring that the interest of revenue is safeguarded at all times.

Note: A Special Audit cannot be conducted for an unregistered taxable person, but can be ordered in respect of the non-filer.

GST AUDIT FORM

Sl. No.	FORM NAME	PURPOSE
1.	FORM GST ADT-01	Notice for Conducting Audit u/s 65(3)
2.	FORM GST ADT-02	Audit Report u/s 65(6)
3.	FORM GST ADT-03	Communication to the registered person for conduct of Special Audit by CA/CMA u/s 66
4.	FORM GST ADT-04	Audit Report u/s 66

18.5 DUE DATE OF FILING GST ANNUAL RETURN

The due date of filing of GST Annual return & GST Audit Report is 31st December following the end of the financial year. However, FY 2017-18 being the first year of implementation of GST, considering the difficulties faced by the businessmen, in exercise of the powers conferred by Section 172 of CGST Act, the Central Govt on the recommendation of the GST Council Vide Removal of Difficulty Order No. 10/2019-Central Tax dated 26th December 2019 has extended the due date of filing of GST Annual return and GST Audit Report for the FY 2017-18 up to 31st January 2020 and Vide Notification No. 80/2020-Central Tax dated 28th Oct 2020 for the FY 2018-19 up to 31st December 2020.

The Finance Act, 2021, has omitted Section 35(5) and substituted Section 44 w.e.f. 1st April 2021. Hence, Annual return (GSTR-9) shall be filed by registered person along with self-certified reconciliation statement. No need to get the accounts audited by a CA/CMA under GST irrespective of turnover. (Ref Notification No. 29 to 31 of 2021-Central Tax dated 30th July 2021)

18.6 CONSEQUENCE OF NON-FILING OF GST ANNUAL RETURN/FAILURE TO GET ACCOUNTS AUDITED AS PER GST LAW

Sec 47(2) provides that in case of failure to submit the GST annual Return within the specified time, a late fee shall be leviable @ ₹ 100/day during which such failure continues subject to a maximum of 0.25% of the turnover in the State/UT.

There is no specific penalty prescribed in the GST law for not getting the accounts audited by a CA/CMA u/s 35(5). Therefore, in terms of Section 125 of the CGST Act, general penalty of up to ₹ 25,000 shall be leviable.

Chapter 19

Inspection, Search, Seizure and Arrest

19.1 STATUTORY PROVISION

The options of Inspection, Search, Seizure and Arrest are exercised, only in exceptional circumstances and as a last resort, to protect the Government Revenue. Therefore, to ensure that these provisions are used properly, effectively and the rights of taxpayers are also protected, it is stipulated that Inspection, Search or Seizure can only be carried out when an officer, of the rank of Joint Commissioner or above, has reasons to believe the existence of such exceptional circumstances. In such cases, the Joint Commissioner may authorize, in writing, any other officer to cause inspection, search and seizure.

However, in case of arrests the same can be carried out only where the person is accused of offences specified for this purpose and the tax amount involved is more than specified limit. Further, provisions for arrests are used in exceptional circumstance and only with prior authorization from the Commissioner.

Chapter XIV [Sections 67 to 72] of the CGST Act stipulates the provisions relating to Inspection, Search, Seizure and Arrest.

Section	Description
67	Power of inspection, search and seizure
68	Inspection of goods in movement
69	Power to arrest
70	Power to summon persons to give evidence and produce documents
71	Access to business premises
72	Officers to assist proper officers

19.2 POWER OF INSPECTION, SEARCH AND SEIZURE (SECTION 67)

'Inspection' is a softer provision than search which enables officers to access any place of business or of a person engaged in transporting goods or who is an owner or an operator of a warehouse or godown.

According to Section 67(1), where the proper officer, not below the rank of Joint Commissioner, has "reasons to believe" that:

(a) the taxable person

(i) Suppressed any transaction of supply of goods or services
(ii) Suppressed stock of goods in hand
(iii) Claimed excess input tax credit
(iv) Contravened any provisions of the Act to evade tax

(b) any person engaged in the business of transporting goods or an owner or operator of a warehouse or a godown or any other place:

(i) is keeping goods which have escaped payment of tax; or
(ii) has kept his accounts or goods in such a manner as is likely to cause evasion of tax payable under the GST law,

he may authorize in writing any other officer of central tax **to inspect** any places of business of the taxable person or the persons engaged in the business of transporting goods or the owner or the operator of warehouse or godown or any other place.

What is the meaning of the phrase 'reason to believe'?

A person is said to have "reason to believe" a thing, if he has sufficient cause to believe that thing but not otherwise.

As per the Indian Penal Code, 1860, "A person is said to have 'reason to believe' a thing, if he has sufficient cause to believe that thing but not otherwise."

Reason to believe is a determination based on intelligent examination and evaluation. It is different from a purely subjective consideration, i.e., an opinion. It is based on facts rather than an interpretation of facts.

GST Law does not mention recording of the "reasons to believe". In fact, Finance Act, 2017 has amended Sec 132(1) & (1A) of Income Tax Act retrospectively stating, that reason to believe, shall not be disclosed to any person or any authority or the Appellate Tribunal.

Other mode of Inspection, Section 67(12): The Commissioner or an officer authorized by him may cause purchase of any goods or services or both by any person authorized by him from the business premises of any taxable person, to check the issue of tax invoices or bills of supply by such taxable person, and on return of goods so purchased by such officer, such taxable person or any person in charge of the business premises shall refund the amount so paid towards the goods after cancelling any tax invoice or bill of supply issued earlier.

Search and Seizure, Section 67(2): The term 'search', in simple language, denotes an action of a Government machinery to go, look through, or examine carefully a place, area, person, object, etc. in order to find something concealed or for the purpose of discovering evidence of a crime. The search of a person or vehicle or premises, etc. can only be done under proper & valid authority of law.

'Seizure' is not defined in GST Act, but as per "Lexicon Dictionary", it is the act of taking possession of property by an officer under legal process.

Pursuant to an inspection carried out under section 67(1) or otherwise, where the proper officer, not below the rank of Joint Commissioner has reasons to believe that:

(a) There are goods, which are liable for confiscation (as per Section 130 of CGST Act)
(b) Any documents or books or other things which will be useful during proceedings and are hidden somewhere,

he can, on his own or through an authorized officer, search and seize the goods and documents:

Provided that where it is not practicable to seize any such goods, the proper officer, or any officer authorized by him, may serve on the owner or the custodian of the goods an order that he shall not remove, part with, or otherwise deal with the goods except with the prior permission of such officer.

The officer will keep the books and documents as long as it is necessary for examination and inquiry. Other books, which are not relevant to the issue of notice, will be returned within 30 days from the date of notice.

The officer authorized under section 67(2) shall have the power to seal or break open the door of any premises or to break open any *almirah*, electronic devices, box, receptacle in which any goods, accounts, registers or documents of the person are suspected to be concealed, where access to such premises, *almirah*, electronic devices, box or receptacle is denied.

What happens after seizure?

Certain safeguards are provided in Section 67 of the CGST Act in respect of the power of search & seizure. These are as follows:

1. The person, whose documents are seized, can make copies only in the presence of an officer of CGST/SGST.
2. The seized goods will be released, on a provisional basis, on a bond and furnishing of a security. Applicable tax, interest and penalty will also have to be paid.
3. If notice is not issued within six months (extendable by six more months) of the seizing the goods, they will be returned.
4. If the goods are hazardous or perishable or there is lack of storage space then the Central or a State Government will notify the officer to dispose of the goods.

   The CBIC, vide its Notification No. 27/2018-Central Tax dated 13.06.2018 has specified 17 categories of goods/class of goods which shall, be disposed of by the proper officer after its seizure having regard to the perishable or hazardous nature, depreciation in value with the passage of time, constraints of storage space or any other relevant considerations of the said goods. For instance, salt, petroleum products, newspapers & periodicals, menthol, campher, saffron, petroleum products, cells, batteries, fireworks, etc.

5. Such goods which are to be disposed of will be listed properly by the officer.

As per Section 67(10), the provisions of the Code of Criminal Procedure, 1973, relating to search and seizure, shall, so far as may be, apply to search and seizure under this section subject to the modification that section 165(5) of the said Code shall have effect as if for the word "Magistrate", wherever it occurs, the word "Commissioner" were substituted.

19.3 INSPECTION OF GOODS IN MOVEMENT (SECTION 68)

Inspection can also be done of the conveyance, carrying a consignment of value exceeding specified limit.

(a) Any consignment, value of which, is exceeding ₹ 50,000, may be stopped at any place for verification of the documents/devices prescribed for movement of such consignments. E Way bill has been prescribed for said purposes.

(b) If on verification of the consignment, during transit, it is found that the goods were removed without prescribed document or the same are being supplied in contravention of any provisions of the Act then the same can be detained or seized and may be subjected to penalties as prescribed.

(c) To ensure transparency and minimize hardships to the trade, the law provides that if during verification, in transit, a consignment is held up beyond 30 minutes the transporter can feed details on the portal. This will ensure accountability and transparency for all such verifications. Moreover, for verification during movement of consignment will also be done through a digital interface and therefore the physical intervention will be minimum and as has already been mentioned that in case of a delay beyond 30 minutes the transporter can feed the details on the portal.

19.4 POWER TO ARREST (SECTION 69)

In the administration of taxation, the provisions for arrests are created to tackle the situations created by some unscrupulous tax evaders. The provisions for arrests under GST Law have sufficient inbuilt safeguards to ensure that these are used only under authorization from the Commissioner.

The term 'arrest' has not been defined in the CGST Act. As per judicial pronouncements, it denotes 'the taking into custody of a person under some lawful command or authority'. The GST Law stipulates that 'arrest' can be made only in those cases where the person is involved in offences specified for the purposes of arrest and the tax amount involved in such offence is more than the specified limit.

Provisions for arrests are used in exceptional circumstance and only with prior authorization from the Commissioner. The Commissioner can authorize an officer to arrest a person, if he has reasons to believe that the person has committed an offence attracting a punishment prescribed under Section 132(1) (a)/(b)/(c)/(d) or section 132(2) of the CGST Act. Power to arrest has to be exercised after careful consideration of the facts on case-to-case basis considering various factors, such as, nature & gravity of offence, quantum of duty evaded, nature & quality of evidence, etc.

Offences specified in Section 132(1) (a), (b), (c) and (d):

(a) Supplies any goods or services or both without issue of any invoice, in violation of the provisions of this Act or the rules made thereunder, with the intention to evade tax;

(b) Issues any invoice or bill without supply of goods or services or both in violation of the provisions of this Act, or the rules made thereunder leading to wrongful availment or utilization of input tax credit or refund of tax;

(c) Avails input tax credit using such invoice or bill referred to in clause (b);

(d) Collects any amount as tax but fails to pay the same to the Government beyond a period of three months from the date on which such payment becomes due.

Arrest can be done in cases where the amount of tax evaded or the amount of input tax credit wrongly availed or utilize or the amount of refund wrongly taken exceeds ₹ 100 lakhs.

Amount of tax evaded/input tax credit wrongly availed or utilized/refund wrongly taken	Prosecution
above ₹ 100 lakhs but does not exceed ₹ 200 lakhs	up to 1 year and fine
above ₹ 200 lakhs but does not exceed ₹ 500 lakhs	up to 3 years and fine
above ₹ 500 lakhs	up to 5 years and fine

A second/subsequent conviction on account of any of the offences specified under Section 132 shall be punishable with imprisonment for a term up to five years and fine.

In case of arrests for specified offences where the tax amount involved is more than ₹ 500 lakhs, the offence is classified as cognizable and non-bailable and in such cases the bail can be considered by a Judicial Magistrate only.

Cognizable offence means serious category of offences in respect of which a police officer has the authority to make an arrest without a warrant and to start an investigation with or without the permission of a court.

19.5 POWER TO SUMMON (SECTION 70)

During the course of any enquiry under GST Act, the proper office may summon any person, to appear before him and give evidence or produce documents. Summons are to be issued as a last resort where assesses are not co-operating and the attendance of the person is considered necessary.

(1) The proper officer under this Act shall have power to summon any person whose attendance he considers necessary either to give evidence or to produce a document or any other thing in any inquiry in the same manner, as provided in the case of a civil court under the provisions of Section 5 of the Code of Civil Procedure, 1908.

(2) Every such inquiry referred to in section 70(*1*) shall be deemed to be a "judicial proceedings" within the meaning of section 193 and section 228 of the Indian Penal Code.

19.6 ACCESS TO BUSINESS PREMISES (SECTION 71)

During the course of any enquiry under this Act, the duly empowered officer can have access to any business premises, which may be required for such purposes.

(1) Any officer under this Act, authorized by the proper officer not below the rank of Joint Commissioner, shall have access to any place of business of a registered person to inspect books of account, documents, computers, computer programs, computer software whether installed in a computer or otherwise and such other things as he may require and which may be available at such place, for the purposes of carrying out any audit, scrutiny, verification and checks as may be necessary to safeguard the interest of revenue.

(2) Every person in charge of place referred to in section 71(*1*) shall, on demand, make available to the officer authorized under section 71(*1*) or the audit party deputed by the proper officer or a cost accountant or chartered accountant nominated under section 66:

(i) such records as prepared or maintained by the registered person and declared to the proper officer in such manner as may be prescribed;
(ii) trial balance or its equivalent;
(iii) statements of annual financial accounts, duly audited, wherever required;
(iv) cost audit report, if any, under section 148 of the Companies Act, 2013;
(v) the income-tax audit report, if any, under section 44AB of the Income-tax Act, 1961; and
(vi) any other relevant record,

for the scrutiny by the officer or audit party or the chartered accountant or cost accountant within a period not exceeding fifteen working days from the day when such demand is made, or such further period as may be allowed by the said officer or the audit party or the chartered accountant or cost accountant.

19.7 OFFICERS TO ASSIST PROPER OFFICERS (SECTION 72)

Under Section 132(1) (a)/(b)/(c)/(d) 72 of CGST Act, the following officers have been empowered and are required to assist GST officers, when called upon:

(1) An Officers of
(a) Police,
(b) Railway
(c) Customs
(d) Land revenue
(e) Village officers,
(f) Officers of State tax and officers of Union territory tax

(2) The Government may, by notification, empower and require any other class of officers to assist the proper officers in the implementation of this Act when called upon to do so by the Commissioner.

Chapter 20

Demand and Recoveries

20.1 STATUTORY PROVISION

The GST Act contains elaborate provisions for the recovery of tax under various situations, which can be broadly classified into the following two categories:

(i) Tax short paid or erroneously refunded or Input Tax Credit wrongly availed; and

(ii) Non-payment of self-assessed tax or amount collected as representing the Tax.

The incidence of short payment of tax or erroneous refund or wrong availment of Input Tax Credit (ITC) may be because of an inadvertent bonafide mistake (Normal Cases) or it may be a deliberate attempt (Fraud Cases) to evade the tax. Since the nature of offence is totally different in both the incidences, hence, separate provisions for recovery of the tax and the amount of penalty have been made to deal with such type of cases. Besides these, there are provisions to encourage voluntary compliance such as no penalty or lesser penalty if the tax dues along with interest, are paid within the specified time limit/incidence.

In order to adhere to the principle of natural justice, before raising any tax demand a notice has to be issued (generally referred to as show cause notice), asking the person chargeable with tax to show cause as to why the specified amount of tax should not be demanded from him.

Chapter XV of the CGST Act, 2017 [Sections 73 to 84] and Chapter XVIII of CGST Rules, 2017 [Rules 142 to 161] contains provisions relating to demands & recovery.

Section 73 of the CGST Act, 2017 provides for determination of tax not paid or short paid or erroneously refunded or input tax credit wrongly availed or utilized for any reason other than fraud or any willful mis-statement or suppression of facts (Normal cases i.e. other than fraud).

Various provisions of Section 73 are tabled below:

Section 73 (1)	Issuance of Show Cause Notice (SCN).
Section 73 (2)	Time limit for issue of the SCN.
Section 73 (3)	Service of a statement for subsequent period.
Section 73 (4)	Statement issued deemed to be notice if ground relied upon are the same.
Section 73 (5)	Payment of amounts before service of SCN.
Section 73 (6)	No service of notice, if tax or penalty paid.
Section 73 (7)	Notice can be issued, if amount settled is less of payable.
Section 73 (8)	No penalty, if tax and interest paid within 30 days of SCN.
Section 73 (9)	Determination of tax, interest and penalty equivalent to 10% of tax or ₹ 10,000 whichever is higher.
Section 73 (10)	Issue of order within three years.
Section 73 (11)	Penalty levied, if self-assessed tax not paid with 30 days of due day of payment of such tax.

Serving of Show cause notice (SCN): As per Section 73 (1), where it appears to the proper officer that:

- any tax has not been paid or short paid (TAX)
- or erroneously refunded (REFUND)
- or where input tax credit has been wrongly availed or utilized (ITC)

For any reason, other than the reason of fraud or any willful-misstatement or suppression of facts to evade tax, The Proper Officer shall **serve notice** on the person chargeable with

- tax which has not been so paid or which has been so short paid or (TAX)
- to whom the refund has erroneously been made (REFUND)
- or who has wrongly availed or utilized input tax credit (ITC)

requiring him to show cause as to why he should not pay the amount specified in the notice along with interest payable thereon under section 50 and a penalty leviable.

Section 74 of the CGST Act, 2017 provides for determination of tax not paid or short paid or erroneously refunded or input tax credit wrongly availed or utilized by reasons of fraud or any willful misstatement or suppression of facts.

This section applies to cases of tax evasion involving:

- fraud
- willful misstatement
- suppression of facts

Which has resulted in

- unpaid/short paid tax or,
- wrong refunds or,
- wrongly availed/utilized input tax credit

Various provisions of Section 74 are tabled below:

Section 74 (1)	Issuance of Show Cause Notice (SCN).
Section 74 (2)	Time limit for issue of the SCN, i.e. six months before order.
Section 74 (3)	Service of a statement for subsequent period.
Section 74 (4)	Statement issued deemed to be notice if ground relied upon are the same.
Section 74 (5)	Payment of tax, interest and 15% of tax as penalty, before service of SCN.
Section 74 (6)	No service of Notice, if tax, interest and penalty paid.
Section 74 (7)	Notice still can be issued, if amount settled is less of payable.
Section 74 (8)	Only penalty of 25% of tax is payable, if tax and interest, reduced penalty paid within 30 days of SCN.
Section 74 (9)	Determination of tax, interest and penalty due from such person and issue an order.
Section 74 (10)	Issue of order within five years relevant date
Section 74 (10)	If tax, interest & penalty equivalent to 50% of tax paid within 30 days of communication of the order, all proceedings shall be concluded.

20.2 SITUATIONS LEADING TO RAISING OF DEMAND

Other than by reason of Fraud or Willful misstatement or Suppression of facts to evade tax—Section 73 (1)	By reason of Fraud or Willful misstatement or Suppression of facts to evade tax—Section 74 (1)
1.Taxes Not Paid 2. Taxes Short Paid 3. Erroneous Refund 4. Input Tax Credit wrongly availed 5. Input Tax Credit wrongly utilized	

20.3 TIME LIMIT FOR ISSUANCE OF SHOW CAUSE NOTICE (SCN)

"Proper officer" is defined under Sec 2(91) of the Act and assigned vide Circular No. 31/2018 dated 09.02.2018 to exercise powers under Sections 73 and 74 for issue of notices and orders.

Other than by reason of Fraud or Willful misstatement or Suppression of facts to evade tax—Section 73 (2)	By reason of Fraud or Willful misstatement or Suppression of facts to evade tax—Section 74 (2)
At least three months prior to the time limit specified under Section 73(10) for issuance of an order.	At least six months prior to the time limit specified under Section 74(10) for issuance of order.

20.4 TIME LIMIT FOR PASSING ASSESSMENT ORDER

Other than by reason of Fraud or Willful misstatement or Suppression of facts to evade tax—Section 73 (2)	By reason of Fraud or Willful misstatement or Suppression of facts to evade tax—Section 74 (2)
Within three years from the due date for furnishing annual return for the financial year to which the tax not paid or short paid or input tax credit wrongly availed or utilized relates to or 3 years from the date of erroneous refund.	Within five years from the due date for furnishing of annual, return for the financial year to which the tax not paid or short paid or input tax credit wrongly availed or utilized relates to or five years from the date of erroneous refund.

20.5 MONETARY LIMIT OF PO FOR ISSUE OF SCN

The monetary limit of different rank of Proper Officer (PO) in relation to issue of show cause notices and orders under Sections 73 and 74 (Circular No. 31/5/2018-GST dated 09.02.2018) are as under:

Designation of Officer	Monetary limit of the amount of CGST (including Cess)	Monetary limit of the amount of IGST (including Cess)	Monetary limit of the amount of CGST and IGST (including Cess)
Superintendent	Up to ₹ 10 lakhs	Up to ₹ 20 lakhs	Up to ₹ 20 lakhs
Deputy or Assistant Commissioner	Above ₹ 10 lakhs up to ₹ 1 crore	Above ₹ 20 lakhs up to ₹ 2 crore	Above ₹ 20 lakhs up to ₹ 2 crore
Additional or Joint Commissioner	Above ₹ 1 crore	Above ₹ 2 crore	Above ₹ 2 crore

20.6 PENAL PROVISION FOR VOLUNTARY PAYMENT OF TAX WITH INTEREST

Action by Tax Payer	Amount of Penalty payable—Normal cases	Amount of Penalty payable—Fraud cases
Tax amount, along with the interest, paid before issuance of Notice.	No Penalty and no Notice shall be issued.	15% of the Tax amount and no Notice shall be issued.
Tax amount, along with the interest, paid within 30 days after issuance of Notice.	Tax plus interest to be paid in full and complete waiver of penalty. All Proceedings deemed to be concluded.	Tax and interest to be paid in full plus penalty @ 25% of tax. All proceedings deemed to be concluded.
Tax amount, along with the interest, paid within 30 days of communication of order.	Tax plus interest to be paid plus 10% of the tax or ₹ 10,000 whichever is higher payable as penalty.	Tax and interest to be paid plus 50% of the tax amount payable as penalty.
Tax amount, along with the interest, paid after 30 days of communication of order.	-do-	100% of the tax amount payable as penalty.

Notes:

(1) The expression "All Proceedings deemed to be concluded" shall not include proceedings under section 132.

(2) Section 132 provides for a list of offences, which shall be punishable with gradation of fine and imprisonment depending on the amount of tax evaded or the amount of input tax credit wrongly availed or utilised or the amount of refund wrongly taken.

20.7 TIMELINE FOR ISSUANCE OF NOTICE & ORDER

Nature of Case	Time for issuance of Notice	Time for issuance of Order
Normal Cases	Within two years and nine months from the due date of filing Annual Return for the Financial Year to which the demand pertains or from the date of erroneous refund.	Within three years from the due date of filing of Annual Return for the Financial Year to which the demand pertains or from the date of erroneous refund.
Fraud Cases	Within four years and six months from the due date of filing of Annual Return for the Financial Year to which the demand pertains or from the date of erroneous refund.	Within five years from the due date of filing of Annual Return for the Financial Year to which the demand pertains or from the date of erroneous refund.

Nature of Case	Time for issuance of Notice	Time for issuance of Order
Any amount collected as tax but not paid	No time limit.	Within one year from the date of issue of notice.
Non-payment of self-assessed Tax	No need to issue a show cause notice.	Recovery proceedings can be started directly.

20.8 GENERAL PROVISIONS RELATING TO DETERMINATION OF TAX [SECTION 75]

This section provides that the period of stay, if any, would be excluded while calculating the time period for issuance of show cause notice or passing of order. This section further provides that the time period during which appeal is pending in any appellate fora would be excluded while calculating the time period for issuance of such notice or passing of order.

1. If an order of court or Appellate Tribunal stays the service of notice or issuance of order then, the period of such stay will get excluded from the period of issuance of order, i.e. three years or five years as the case may be.

2. When a notice has been issued considering the case to be for fraud or for wilful representation or for suppression of facts, and whereas the charges of fraud, suppression and misstatement of facts were not sustainable or not established by an order of Appellate Authority or Appellate Tribunal, then in such case the officer shall determine the tax as if the notice is issued for the normal period of three years.

3. An order required to be issued in pursuance of the direction of the Tribunal or a Court shall be issued within two years from the date of communication of the said direction.

4. As per Section 75(10), proceedings are conclusive, if the order not issued within statutory limit of three or five years u/s 73 or u/s 74 respectively.

What amounts to "suppression"?

As per Explanation 2 provided under Section 75, the term "suppression" shall mean:

"non-declaration of facts or information which a taxable person is required to declare in the return, statement, report or any other document furnished under this Act or the rules made thereunder, or failure to furnish any information on being asked for, in writing, by the proper officer".

20.9 TAX COLLECTED BUT NOT PAID TO THE GOVERNMENT [SECTION 76]

Any amount collected as tax shall be paid to the government irrespective of the fact that said supply is taxable or not.

The Proper Officer (PO) shall resort to issue of SCN in FORM GST DRC-01 in terms of section 76 and not in terms of section 73/74. The person is permitted to make representation in FORM GST DRC-06, against the notice served on to him. After considering such representation made by the person, the Proper Officer shall determine the amount due from the person and pass an order within one year from the date of issue of notice

20.10 TAX WRONGFULLY COLLECTED AND PAID TO CENTRAL OR STATE GOVERNMENT [SECTION 77]

(1) A registered person who has paid the Central tax and State tax or, as the case may be, the Central tax and the Union territory tax on a transaction considered by him to be an intra-State supply, but which is subsequently held to be an inter-State supply, shall be refunded the amount of taxes so paid in such manner and subject to such conditions as may be prescribed.

(2) A registered person who has paid integrated tax on a transaction considered by him to be an inter-State supply, but which is subsequently held to be an intra-State supply, shall not be required to pay any interest on the amount of central tax and State tax or, as the case may be, the Central tax and the Union territory tax payable.

20.11 INITIATION OF RECOVERY PROCEEDINGS [SECTION 78]

Any amount payable in pursuance of an order shall be paid by such person within a period of three months, except in certain specified cases, from the date of service of order failing which recovery proceedings shall be initiated u/s 79. Commissioner can initiate recovery proceedings earlier than the time specified under Section 78 which is three months from the date of service of order.

20.12 MODE OF RECOVERY OF TAX [SECTION 79]

Section 79 provides for various modes of recovery by PO, of amount payable under the CGST Act, 2017 from a person (such person). The modes of recovery, inter alia, includes:

RULES	Power of Proper Officer
143	Recovery by deduction from any money owed
144	Recovery by sale of goods under control of proper officer (DC/AC)
145	Recovery from third parties from whom money is due to such person by issuing notice
146	Recovery through execution of a decree of a civil court (FORM DRC-15)
147	Recovery by sale of movable and immovable property
151	Attachment of debt and shares
152	Attachment of property in custody of public officers or court
153	Attachment of interest in partnership
155	Recovery through land revenue authority
156	Recovery through courts, as if it were a fine imposed under the Code of Criminal Procedure, 1973
157	Recovery from surety
158	Recovery from company in liquidation

Question: Whether recovery of taxes can be made from distinct persons located in different state?

Answer. As per explanation to Section 79, the word person shall include "distinct person" as referred to in Section 25(4)/25(5). Thus, recovery of taxes under GST law can be made from distinct person located in different states/UT also.

20.13 PAYMENT OF TAX AND OTHER AMOUNT IN INSTALMENTS [SECTION 80]

On an application filed by a taxable person, the Commissioner may, for reasons to be recorded in writing, extend the time for payment or allow payment of any amount due under this Act, other than the amount due as per the liability self-assessed in any return, by such person in monthly instalments not exceeding twenty four, subject to payment of interest under section 50 and subject to such conditions and limitations as may be prescribed:

Provided that where there is default in payment of any one instalment on its due date, the whole outstanding balance payable on such date shall become due and payable forthwith and shall, without any further notice being served on the person, be liable for recovery.

20.14 TRANSFER OF PROPERTY TO BE VOID IN CERTAIN CASES [SECTION 81]

Where a person, after any amount has become due from him, creates a charge on or parts with the property belonging to him or in his possession by way of sale, mortgage, exchange, or any other mode of transfer whatsoever of any of his properties in favour of any other person with the intention of defrauding the Government revenue, such charge or transfer shall be void as against any claim in respect of any tax or any other sum payable by the said person.

The transfer will be void, when it is or was with an intention of defrauding the Government revenue.

20.15 TAX TO BE FIRST CHARGE ON PROPERTY [SECTION 82]

Other than as provided under Insolvency and Bankruptcy Code, 2016, this provision shall have an overriding effect over the other provisions contained in any law for the time being in force. This provision provides that if any dues are payable by a taxable person or any other person to the Government, then it would have first charge on the property of such taxable or other person.

20.16 PROVISIONAL ATTACHMENT TO PROTECT REVENUE IN CERTAIN CASES [SECTION 83]

Where during the pendency of any proceedings under section 62 or section 63 or section 64 or section 67 or section 73 or section 74, the Commissioner is of the opinion that for the purpose of protecting the interest of the Government revenue, it is necessary so to do, he may, by order in writing attach provisionally any property, including bank account, belonging to the taxable person in such manner as may be prescribed.

Section 62	Assessment of non-filers
Section 63	Assessment of unregistered persons
Section 64	Summary assessment in special
Section 67	Inspection, search and seizure

The order passed for provisional attachment is valid for one year.

20.17 CONTINUATION AND VALIDATION OF CERTAIN RECOVERY PROCEEDINGS [SECTION 84]

Where any government dues are enhanced as a result of any appeal, revision or other proceedings, it shall not be necessary for the commissioner to serve fresh notice and notice given earlier be continued from the stage at which such proceedings stood immediately before such disposal.

Where any government dues are reduced as a result of any appeal, it shall not be necessary for the Commissioner to serve upon the taxable person a fresh notice of demand.

Chapter 21

Liability to Pay in Certain Cases

21.1 STATUTORY PROVISION

Under the GST regime, tax is payable by the taxable person on the supply of goods and/or services. Liability to pay tax arises when the taxable person crosses the threshold turnover limit.

In general, the supplier of goods or services is liable to pay GST. However, in specified cases like imports and other notified supplies, the liability may be cast on the recipient under the reverse charge mechanism. Further, in some notified cases of intra-state supply of services, the liability to pay GST may be cast on e-commerce operators through which such services are supplied.

Besides above, there are certain specified transactions like liquidation, business transfer, partition of HUF, amalgamation, merger of companies etc. where it becomes difficult to determine the liability to pay outstanding tax, interest & penalty.

Chapter XVI—Liability to pay in certain cases [Sections 85 to 94] of the CGST Act has laid down the provision to determine the person liable to pay tax on such specified transaction.

Section	Description
85	Liability in case of transfer of business
86	Liability of agent and principal
87	Liability in case of amalgamation or merger of companies
88	Liability in case of company in liquidation
89	Liability of directors of private company
90	Liability of partners of a firm to pay tax
91	Liability of guardians, trustees, etc.
92	Liability of court of Wards, etc.
93	Special provisions regarding liability to pay tax, interest or penalty in certain cases
94	Liability in other cases

21.2 LIABILITY IN CASE OF TRANSFER OF BUSINESS [SECTION 85]

(1) Where a taxable person, liable to pay tax under this Act, transfers his business in whole or in part, by sale, gift, lease, leave and license, hire or in any other manner whatsoever, the taxable person and the person to whom the business is so transferred shall, jointly and severally, be liable wholly or to the extent of such transfer, to pay the tax, interest or any penalty due from the taxable person up to the time of such transfer, whether such tax, interest or penalty has been determined before such transfer, but has remained unpaid or is determined thereafter.

(2) Where the transferee of a business referred to in sub-section (1) carries on such business either in his own name or in some other name, he shall be liable to pay tax on the supply of goods or services or both effected by him with effect from the date of such transfer and shall, if he is a registered person under this Act, apply within the prescribed time for amendment of his certificate of registration.

Going Concern Transfer: Sale of business as a 'going concern' [commonly called, lock-stock-barrel basis] is not taxable as per paragraph 4(c), schedule II of the CGST Act read with entry #2 to exemption notification No. 12/2017-Central Tax (Rate) dated 28th June 2017.

21.3 LIABILITY OF AGENT AND PRINCIPAL [SECTION 86]

Where an agent supplies or receives any taxable goods on behalf of his principal, such agent and his principal shall, jointly and severally, be liable to pay the tax payable on such goods under this Act.

Under the GST law, in cases where:

(a) Taxable Goods are supplied by agent on behalf of principal; or

(b) Taxable Goods are procured by agent on behalf of principal;

the agent is primarily liable for tax. However, by virtue of this provision, both agent and principal will be jointly and severally made liable to pay for tax payable on such supplies.

21.4 LIABILITY IN CASE OF AMALGAMATION OR MERGER OF COMPANIES [SECTION 87]

This section deals with the tax liability on certain transactions between the effective date and date of order of Tribunal/Court in case of amalgamation or merger of companies.

(1) When two or more companies are amalgamated or merged in pursuance of an order of court or of Tribunal or otherwise and the order is to take effect from a date earlier to the date of the order and any two or more of such companies have supplied or received any goods or services or both to or from each other during the period commencing on the date from which the order takes effect till the date of the order, then such transactions of supply and receipt shall be included in the turnover of supply or receipt of the respective companies and they shall be liable to tax accordingly.

(2) Notwithstanding anything contained in the said order, for all purposes of this Act, the said two or more companies shall be treated as distinct companies for the period up to the date of the said order and the registration certificates of the said companies shall be cancelled, with effect from the date of the said order.

21.5 LIABILITY IN CASE OF COMPANY IN LIQUIDATION [SECTION 88]

This section deals with the tax and other dues of a company in case it is wound up or liquidated. This section should be read with Rule 160 of CGST Rules, 2017.

(1) When any company is being wound up whether under the orders of a Court or Tribunal or otherwise, every person appointed as receiver of any assets of a company (hereinafter referred to as the "liquidator"), shall, within thirty days after his appointment, give intimation of his appointment to the Commissioner.

(2) The Commissioner shall, after making such inquiry or calling for such information as he may deem fit, notify the liquidator within three months from the date on which he receives intimation of the appointment of the liquidator, the amount which in the opinion of the Commissioner would be sufficient to provide for any tax, interest or penalty which is then, or is likely thereafter to become, payable by the company.

(3) When any private company is wound up and any tax, interest or penalty determined under this Act on the company for any period, whether before or in the course of or after its liquidation, cannot be recovered, then every person who was a director of such company at any time during the period for which the tax was due shall, jointly and severally, be liable for the payment of such tax, interest or penalty, unless he proves to the satisfaction of the Commissioner that such non-recovery cannot be attributed to any gross neglect, misfeasance or breach of duty on his part in relation to the affairs of the company.

21.6 LIABILITY OF DIRECTORS OF PRIVATE COMPANY [SECTION 89]

This section deals with recovery of tax dues, interest or penalty from the directors of a private company, where the private company has not discharged any of its tax, penalty or interest liability towards the supply of goods or services or both.

(1) Notwithstanding anything contained in the Companies Act, 2013 (18 of 2013), where any tax, interest or penalty due from a private company in respect of any supply of goods or services or both for any period cannot be recovered, then, every person who was a director of the private company during such period shall, jointly and severally, be liable for the payment of such tax, interest or penalty unless he proves that the non-recovery cannot be attributed to any gross neglect, misfeasance or breach of duty on his part in relation to the affairs of the company.

(2) Where a private company is converted into a public company and the tax, interest or penalty in respect of any supply of goods or services or both for any period during which such company was a private company cannot be recovered before such conversion, then, nothing contained in sub-section (1) shall apply to any person who was a director of such private company in relation to any tax, interest or penalty in respect of such supply of goods or services or both of such private company:

Provided that nothing contained in this sub-section shall apply to any personal penalty imposed on such director.

21.7 LIABILITY OF PARTNERS OF A FIRM TO PAY TAX [SECTION 90]

This section deals with the liability of a partner of a firm to pay any tax, interest or penalty that was otherwise payable by the firm.

- (i) Where a partnership firm is liable to pay any tax, interest or penalty, all the partners of such firm will be jointly and severally liable to pay such amounts.
- (ii) If any of the partners retire, then such partner or the firm shall intimate the Commissioner by a notice in writing within one month from the date of retirement. In such cases, the retiring partner shall be liable to pay tax, interest and penalty, if any, up to the date of his retirement (whether determined or not prior to retirement).
- (iii) However, where no such intimation is given by the partner to the Commissioner within one month from retirement date, the liability of such retired partner will continue till the date on which the intimation is received by the Commissioner.
- (iv) The provision will be equally applicable for LLPs.

21.8 LIABILITY OF GUARDIANS, TRUSTEES, ETC. [SECTION 91]

This section enables collection of tax, interest or penalty from the guardians, trustees or agents of a minor or any other incapacitated person in respect of the business carried on for them.

Where the business in respect of which any tax, interest or penalty is payable under this Act is carried on by any guardian, trustee or agent of a minor or other incapacitated person on behalf of and for the benefit of such minor or other incapacitated person, the tax, interest or penalty shall be levied upon and recoverable from such guardian, trustee or agent in like manner and to the same extent as it would be determined and recoverable from any such minor or other incapacitated person, as if he were a major or capacitated person and as if he were conducting the business himself, and all the provisions of this Act or the rules made thereunder shall apply accordingly.

The expression 'incapacitated person' is not defined in the Act. It should refer only to a person who is a person of unsound mind or one who is terminally ill.

21.9 LIABILITY OF COURT OF WARDS, ETC. [SECTION 92]

This section empowers collection of tax, interest or penalty from Administrator General, Official Trustee or any receiver or manager, who controls the estate or any portion thereof in respect of the taxable person who owns a business and whose estate is being controlled.

Where the estate or any portion of the estate of a taxable person owning a business in respect of which any tax, interest or penalty is payable under this Act is under the control of the Court of Wards, the Administrator General, the Official Trustee or any receiver or manager (including any person, whatever be his designation, who in fact manages the business) appointed by or under any order of a court, the tax, interest or penalty shall be levied upon and be recoverable from such Court of Wards, Administrator General, Official Trustee, receiver or manager, in like manner and to the same extent as it would be determined and be recoverable from the taxable person as if he were conducting the business himself, and all the provisions of this Act or the rules made thereunder shall apply accordingly.

21.10 SPECIAL PROVISIONS REGARDING LIABILITY TO PAY TAX, INTEREST OR PENALTY IN CERTAIN CASES [SECTION 93]

Section 93 of GST Act is subject to Insolvency and Bankruptcy Code, 2016. The objects clause of Insolvency and Bankruptcy Code inter-alia is to provide that it has been enacted amongst other things to 'alter the order of priority of payment of Government dues'.

Section 53 of Insolvency and Bankruptcy Code, 2016 which provides for distribution of assets of a company starts with a non-obstante clause against 'any law' enacted by Central or State Government. As per Section 53, the Government dues stand fifth in the order of priority.

As per Section 74 of CGST Act, 2017, tax, interest, penalty can be demanded for a period of five years from the relevant date. However, Section 82 of CGST Act, 2017 states that any amount payable by a taxable person or any other person on account of tax, interest or penalty shall be a first charge on the property of such taxable person or other person, subject to Insolvency and Bankruptcy Code, 2016.

Special provisions regarding liability to pay tax, interest or penalty in certain cases have been discussed as under:

(1) Death of person (individual)

(a) In case of continuation of business after death:
The legal representative or the any other person who carries on the business after his death is liable to pay tax, interest, penalty or any other due which is due from the deceased person; or

(b) In case of discontinuation of business before or after his death.

The legal representative is liable to pay the tax, interest, penalty or any other dues to the Government, from and to the extent of the estate of the deceased.

The legal representative or any other person as the case may be is liable to pay the tax, interest or penalty whether:

(a) It has been determined before his death but has remained unpaid or

(b) It has been determined after his death.

(2) Partition of HUF or AOP

(i) In case of a HUF or AOP property is partitioned between the member or group of members then the liability to pay tax, interest or penalty is on each member or group of members (jointly and severally) who got a portion in that property.

(ii) The member or the group of members is/are liable only up to the time of partition whether such tax, interest and penalty has been determined before partition but has remained unpaid or is determined after such partition.

(3) Dissolution of firm

(i) In case the firm is dissolved every person who was a partner up to the time of dissolution is jointly and severally liable to pay the tax, interest or penalty.

(ii) The person who was a partner is liable to pay tax even if it is determined before dissolution but not paid or determined after dissolution.

(iii) The provision applicable for partnership firm would equally apply for LLP as well.

(4) Termination of Guardianship or Trusteeship

(i) In case the guardian is carrying on the business on behalf of a ward or the trustee who carries the business under the trust on behalf of beneficiary, then on the termination of guardianship or trusteeship,

(a) The ward or the beneficiary is liable to pay tax, interest or penalty up to the time of such termination.

(b) The ward or the beneficiary is liable to pay tax, interest or penalty determined before the termination of guardianship or trusteeship but not paid or determined after such termination.

(ii) he above provisions are applicable to extent that there is no contrary provision in Insolvency and Bankruptcy Code, 2016.

21.11 LIABILITY IN OTHER CASES [SECTION 94]

This section discusses the liability of partners of firm or members of AOP or HUF on discontinuation of business.

(i) In case of discontinuance of business, the firm or AOP or HUF, the liability of the firm/AOP/HUF shall be determined (up to the date of discontinuance) as if no such discontinuance had taken place.

(ii) Every partner of such firm or member of such AOP or HUF at the time of discontinuance shall be jointly and severally liable for payment of tax, interest and penalty imposed.

(iii) In case of change in the constitution of the firm or association, the partners and members who existed before reconstitution shall be liable jointly and severally to pay tax, interest or penalty for any period up to the date of reconstitution. This will operate even if the retirement was intimated to the Commissioner in terms of Section 90.

(iv) Discontinuance includes dissolution of firm or association and partition in case of HUF.

(v) This provision, the way it applies to a partnership firm will apply to an LLP as well.

Chapter 22

Advance Rulings Under GST

22.1 STATUTORY PROVISION

The provision relating to **Advance Ruling** has been laid in Sections 95 to 106 (Chapter XVII) of the Central Goods and Service Tax Act, 2017 [identical provisions are there in the State Goods & Services Tax Laws] & Rules 103 to 107A of the CGST Rules, 2017.

Section	Description
95	Definitions
96	Authority for advance ruling
97	Application for advance ruling
98	Procedure on receipt of application
99	Appellate Authority for Advance Ruling
100	Appeal to Appellate Authority
101	Orders of Appellate Authority
102	Rectification of advance ruling
103	Applicability of advance ruling
104	Advance ruling to be void in certain circumstances
105	Powers of Authority and Appellate Authority
106	Procedure of Authority and Appellate Authority

22.2 MEANING & OBJECTIVES OF ADVANCE RULING

Meaning: The term "Advance ruling" has been defined in Section 95(a) as under:

"Advance ruling" means a decision provided by the Authority or the Appellate Authority to an applicant on matters or on questions specified in section 97(2) or section 100(1) of the CGST Act, 2017, in relation to the supply of goods or services or both being undertaken or proposed to be undertaken by the applicant.

Applicant means any person registered or desirous to be registered under GST for supply of goods or services. A recipient/proposed recipient of goods or services cannot avail Advance Ruling (AAR—Tamil Nadu—11th Sept 2018).

Objectives: The aim of Advance Ruling is to provide certainty to the taxpayer with respect to his obligations under the GST Act and an expeditious ruling, so that the relationship between the taxpayer and administration is smooth and transparent and helps to avoid unnecessary litigation.

(a) Provide certainty in tax liability in advance in relation to an activity proposed to be undertaken by the applicant
(b) Attract Foreign Direct Investment (FDI)
(c) Reduce litigation
(d) Pronounce ruling expeditiously in a transparent and inexpensive manner.

21.3 CONSTITUTION OF ADVANCE RULING AUTHORITY (SECTION 96)

The AAR shall be located in each State/Union Territory constituted under the provisions of State Goods and Services Tax Act and Union Territory Goods and Services tax Act. The ruling given by the AAR and AAAR will be applicable only within the jurisdiction of the concerned state or union territory.

It would consist of one member from amongst the officers of the Central Tax and one member from amongst the officers of the State Tax, not below the rank of Joint Commissioner which shall be appointed by the Central and State Governments respectively.

As per Section 96 of the State GST Acts, the State Government may, on the recommendation of the Council, notify any AAR located in another State to act as the Authority for Advance Ruling for the State.

22.4 MATTERS/QUESTIONS WHICH CAN BE REFERRED FOR ADVANCE RULING [SECTION 97(2)]

Following categories of questions can be asked from the Authority for Advance Ruling by making an application in the prescribed form, along with requisite fee;

(a) classification of any goods or services or both;
(b) applicability of a notification issued under the provisions of this Act;
(c) determination of time and value of supply of goods or services or both;
(d) admissibility of input tax credit of tax paid or deemed to have been paid;
(e) determination of the liability to pay tax on any goods or services or both;
(f) whether applicant is required to be registered;
(g) whether any particular thing done by the applicant with respect to any goods or services or both amounts to or results in a supply of goods or services or both, within the meaning of that term.

The above list is inclusive and therefore the Authority will not admit questions or matters, which fall outside the purview of the issues stated above.

> Determination of place of supply is not covered under any of the clauses (a) to (g) of Section 97(2) of the CGST Act, 2017. Further, the use of term 'shall', is an imperative command restricting the scope of advance ruling only to the questions enumerated in the said sub-section. Thus, question relating to determination of place of supply, is beyond the scope of advance ruling.

22.5 MATTERS WHICH CANNOT BE REFERRED TO ADVANCE RULING

Matters other than those mentioned in clauses (a) to (g) of Section 97 (2) of the CGST Act, cannot be raised with the AAR or AAAR.

For example:

(1) Questions pertaining determination of place of supply
(2) Transactions already undertaken in the past
(3) Questions involving Transitional Credits
(4) Matter relating to E Way Bill
(5) Anti-Profiteering issues, etc.

Additionally, if the matter on which advance ruling is sought is already pending or decided in any proceedings in the applicant's case under any of the provisions of the Act, then the AAR shall not admit such application.

> A recipient/proposed recipient of goods or services cannot sought Advance ruling, unless he is liable to pay tax under Reverse charge [ORDER NO. GST-ARA-82/2018-19/Bombay-12 dated 23.01.2019].

22.6 PROCEDURE FOR OBTAINING ADVANCE RULING

Rule 104 of CGST Rules, 2017 prescribes the FORM and manner of making application to the Authority for Advance Ruling. An application for obtaining an advance ruling under section 97(1) shall be made on the GST common portal in FORM GST ARA-01 and shall be accompanied by a fee of ₹ 5000 along with all the relevant documents duly verified.

Procedure on receipt of application (Section 98): Section 98 provides for the procedure to be adopted by the advance ruling authority on receipt of an application seeking advances ruling. On receipt of such application, the authority shall send a copy of it to the officer concerned and call upon him to furnish the relevant records.

The authority then will examine the application and such records and hear the applicant and the concerned officer through their authorized representative or in person. An order will then be passed either admitting or rejecting the application. No such application shall be admitted, which has a question similar to any previously pending question or any matter previously decided in relation to the applicant, in any proceedings under any other provisions of the GST Act. If the authority wishes to reject an application, it can do so only after providing an opportunity of being heard to the applicant and also the order thus made should provide the reason for rejections. A copy of above order shall be sent to the applicant and concerned officer.

The time limit for disposal of application is within 90 days of receipt of application.

Manual filing and processing: As the GST common portal could not be made functional to accept applications online for obtaining Advance Ruling, a new Rule 107A inserted, and Circular No. 25/25/2017-GST was issued to allow manual filing and processing for the same. So now for the time being an application for obtaining advance ruling can be made manually, in quadruplicate, in FORM GST ARA-01.

22.7 APPELLATE AUTHORITY FOR ADVANCE RULING (SECTION 99)

Any Appellate Authority constituted under any State or Union Territory GST Act shall be deemed to have jurisdiction over that State or UT only. It would consist of the Chief Commissioner of Central Tax as designated by the Board and the Commissioner of State Tax having jurisdiction over the applicant.

22.8 APPEAL TO THE APPELLATE AUTHORITY (SECTION 100)

The concerned officer, the jurisdictional officer or an applicant aggrieved by any advance ruling pronounced under section 98(4), may appeal to the Appellate Authority.

This period may be extended by another 30 days if sufficient cause is disclosed by the appellant before the authority

Time limit	30 days from the date of receipt of the ruling
Condonation of delay	Up to 30 days, if sufficient cause shown
Fee	₹ 10,000 by Applicant No fee payable in case of Appeal by Concerned officer/jurisdictional officer
Who can prefer Appeal	Applicant, Concerned officer, Jurisdictional officer
FORM	FORM GST ARA-02 (Applicant)
FORM	FORM GST ARA-03 (Concerned officer/jurisdictional officer)

Orders of Appellate Authority [Section 101]: An appellate authority shall pass such order as it may deem fit either confirming or modifying the ruling of the advance ruling authority made u/s 98(6) or reference u/s 98(5).

Rectification of Advance Ruling [Section 102]: The Authority or the Appellate Authority may amend any order passed by it under section 98 or section 101, so as to rectify any error apparent on the face of the record, if such error/mistake:

(a) is noticed by the AAR or the Appellate Authority on its own accord, or
(b) is brought to its notice by the concerned officer, the jurisdictional officer, the applicant or the appellant within a period of six months from the date of the order:

Provided that no rectification which has the effect of enhancing the tax liability or reducing the amount of admissible input tax credit shall be made unless the applicant or the appellant has been given an opportunity of being heard.

22.9 APPLICABILITY OF ADVANCE RULING [SECTION 103 (1)]

An advance ruling pronounced by AAR or AAAR shall be binding only on

(1) The applicant and
(2) The concerned officer or the jurisdictional officer in respect of the applicant.

The applicability of advance ruling limited to the person who has applied for an advance ruling.

Time period for applicability of Advance Ruling [Section 103(2)]: GST Law does not provide for a fixed time period for which the ruling shall be valid. It holds good so long as the law, facts or circumstances supporting the original advance ruling remain same/have not changed.

Advance ruling to be void [Section 104]: Where the Authority or the Appellate Authority finds that advance ruling pronounced by it under section 98(4) or section 101(1) has been obtained by the applicant or the appellant by fraud or suppression of material facts or misrepresentation of facts, it may, by order, declare such ruling to be void ab-initio and there upon all the provisions of this Act or the rules made there under shall apply to the applicant or the appellant as if such advance ruling had never been made.

22.10 POWERS OF AUTHORITY AND APPELLATE AUTHORITY [SECTION 105]

The Authority or the Appellate Authority shall, for the purpose of exercising its powers regarding:

(a) discovery and inspection;
(b) enforcing the attendance of any person and examining him on oath;
(c) issuing commissions and compelling production of books of account and other records shall be deemed to be a civil court under the Code of Civil Procedure, 1908.

Procedure of Authority and Appellate Authority [Section 106]: The Authority or the Appellate Authority shall, subject to the provisions of this chapter, have power to regulate its own procedure.

Chapter 23

Appeals and Revision

23.1 STATUTORY PROVISION

A person who is aggrieved by a decision or order passed against him by an adjudicating authority, can file an appeal to the Appellate Authority (AA). It is important to note that it is only the aggrieved person who can file the appeal. Also, the appeal must be against a decision or order passed under the Act.

The time limit for the party to file an appeal before the AA is three months from the date of communication of the impugned order. However, the AA may condone a delay of up to one month, if he is satisfied that there was sufficient cause for such delay.

Section 107 of the CGST Act, 2017 read with Rules 108 and 109 of the CGST Rules, 2017, provides provisions for preferring an appeal against the order of the Adjudicating Authority to the Appellate Authority.

Such appeals are broadly of two kinds:

(a) tax-related and
(b) procedure-related.

Tax law recognizes that on any given set of facts and laws, there can be different opinions or viewpoints. Hence, it is likely that the taxpayer may not agree with the "adjudication order" so passed by the tax officer. It is equally possible that the department may itself not be in agreement with the adjudication order in some cases. It is for this reason that the statute provides further channels of appeal, to both sides.

Appeals level	Order passing authority	Appeal before	Section
1st	Adjudicating Authority	First Appellate Authority	107
2nd	First Appellate Authority	Appellate Tribunal	109-110
3rd	Appellate Tribunal	High Court	111-116
4th	High Court	Supreme court	117-118

23.2 ADJUDICATING AUTHORITY

Section 2(4) of the CGST Act, 2017 defines adjudicating authority to mean any authority, appointed or authorized to pass any order or decision under this Act. However, following are not covered under the ambit of adjudicating authority:

(a) Central Board of Indirect Taxes and Customs
(b) Revisional Authority
(c) Authority for Advance Ruling
(d) Appellate Authority for Advance Ruling
(e) The Appellate Authority
(f) The Appellate Tribunal
(g) The Authority referred to in section 171(2) (i.e. NAPA)

23.3 APPEALS TO APPELLATE AUTHORITY [SECTION 107]

Appellate Authority shall be:

(a) the Commissioner (Appeals) where such decision or order is passed by the Additional or Joint Commissioner;

(b) the Additional Commissioner (Appeals) where such decision or order is passed by the Deputy or Assistant Commissioner or Superintendent.

A person who is aggrieved by a decision or order passed against him by an adjudicating authority, can file an appeal to the Appellate Authority (AA, for short).

> It is important to note that it is only the aggrieved person who can file the appeal. Also, the appeal must be against a decision or order passed under the Act. The time limit for the party to file an appeal before the AA is three months from the date of communication of the impugned order. But the AA may condone a delay of up to one month, if he is satisfied that there was sufficient cause for such delay.

The AA has to follow the principles of natural justice—such as hearing the appellant, allowing reasonable adjournments (not more than three), permitting additional grounds (if found reasonable), etc. The AA can also make such further inquiry as may be necessary.

The Order-in-appeal has to be a "speaking order" i.e. it should state the points for determination, the decision thereon and the reasons for the decision.

23.4 REVISIONAL AUTHORITY [SECTION 108]

In terms of Section 2(99) of the CGST Act, "Revisional Authority" means an authority appointed or authorized for revision of decision or orders as referred to in Section 108.

Section 108(1) of the CGST Act provides that subject to the provision of Section 121, the Revisional Authority may:

(a) either on his own motion or

(b) based on the information received by him or

(c) based on the request of the Commissioner of State Tax or Commissioner of Union Territory tax,

call for and examine the record of any proceeding, and if he considers that any decision or order passed under the CGST Act, or SGST Act or UTGST Act, by any officer subordinate to him is:

(a) erroneous in so far as it is prejudicial to the interest of the revenue and is illegal or improper or has not taken into account certain material facts, whether available at the time of issuance of the said order or not or

(b) in consequence of an observation by the Comptroller and Auditor General of India.

The revisional authority may, if necessary, stay the operation of such decision or order for such period as he deems fit and after giving the person concerned an opportunity of being heard and after making such further inquiry as may be necessary, pass such order, as he thinks just and proper, including enhancing or modifying or annulling the said decision or order.

Who can approach the GST revisional authority?

The Revisional Authority may decide whether to act or not on any matter. The Commissioner of State tax or Union Territory tax may only request the Revisional Authority to exercise its powers. The taxpayer cannot approach the GST Revisional Authority but will only be given an opportunity of being heard in case an order is to be passed against him.

Non-Applicability: Section 108(2) of the Act provides that the Revisional Authority shall not exercise any power, if the order has been subject to:

(a) an appeal under:

- Section 107 (appeal to appellate authority) or
- Section 112 (appeal to appellate Tribunal) or
- Section 117 (appeal to High court) or
- Section 118 (appeal to Supreme Court) or

(b) the period specified under section 107(2) has not yet expired or more than three years have expired after the passing of the decision or order sought to be revised; or

(c) the order has already been taken for revision under this section at an earlier stage; or

(d) the order has been passed in exercise of the powers under Section 108 (1).

Time limit to approach the GST Revisional Authority: The Revisional Authority cannot take up any matter where more than three years have passed since the date of the order/decision. Further, where the Revisional Authority seeks to pass an order in respect to any point not raised and subject to an appeal before the Appellate Authority, Appellate Tribunal, High Court or Supreme Court, the time limit for the Revisional Authority is one year from the date of such order. Hence, the Revisional Authority needs to be approached within this time limit.

Appointment of Revisional Authority: The Central Government vide Notification No. 05/2020-Central Tax, dated 13th January 2020 authorizes the following as the Revisional Authority:

Sl No.	Revisional Authority	For Orders Passed by
1.	The Principal Commissioner or Commissioner of Central Tax	for decisions or orders passed by the Additional or Joint Commissioner of Central Tax
2.	The Additional or Joint Commissioner of Central Tax	for decisions or orders passed by the Deputy Commissioner or Assistant Commissioner or Superintendent of Central Tax.

23.5 CONSTITUTION OF GST APPELLATE TRIBUNAL AND BENCHES THEREOF [SECTION 109]

(1) Based on the recommendation of the Council and by Notification, the Central Government shall constitute Goods & Service Tax Appellate Tribunal (GSTAT) for hearing appeals against the orders passed by the Appellate Authority or Revisional Authority.

(2) The powers of the Appellate Tribunal shall be exercisable by the National Bench or Regional Benches, State Bench and Area Benches.

(3) National Bench shall be situated at New Delhi, which shall be presided over by President, one Technical Member (Centre) and one Technical Member (State).

(4) The Regional Benches, State bench and Area Bench shall consist of a Judicial Member, one Technical Member (Centre) and one Technical Member (State).

(5) The National Bench or Regional Benches shall hear the appeals only where one of the issues involved relates to the place of supply.

(6) The State Bench or Area Benches shall hear the appeals involving matters other than matters covering place of supply.

(7) The President and the State President shall by general or special order distribute the business or transfer cases among Regional Benches or Area Benches in a State.

(8) Any matter (other than matter involving question of law) involving tax, input tax credit, fine, fee or penalty determined in any order appealed against, not exceeding ₹ 5 lakhs may be heard by single member bench.

(9) No act or proceedings of the Appellate Tribunal shall be questioned or shall be invalid merely only on the ground of the existence of any vacancy or defect in the constitution of Appellate Tribunal.

(10) Vide Notification having S.O. 3009 (E), dated August 21, 2019, the Central Govt. has notified the locations of State Benches and Area Benches of the Goods and Services Tax Appellate Tribunal (GSTAT).

23.6 PRESIDENT AND MEMBERS OF APPELLATE TRIBUNAL, THEIR QUALIFICATION, APPOINTMENT, CONDITIONS OF SERVICE, ETC. [SECTION 110]

(1) A person shall not be qualified for appointment as:

(a) the President, unless he has been a Judge of the Supreme Court or is or has been the Chief Justice of a High Court, or is or has been a Judge of a High Court for a period not less than five years;

(b) a Judicial Member, unless he (i) has been a Judge of the High Court; or (ii) is or has been a District Judge qualified to be appointed as a Judge of a High Court; or (iii) is or has been a Member of Indian Legal Service and has held a post not less than Additional Secretary for three years;

(c) a Technical Member (Centre) unless he is or has been a member of Indian Revenue (Customs and Central Excise) Service, Group A, and has completed at least fifteen years of service in Group A;

(d) a Technical Member (State) unless he is or has been an officer of the State Government not below the rank of Additional Commissioner of Value Added Tax or the State goods and services tax or such rank as may be notified by the concerned State Government on the recommendations of the Council with at least three years of experience in the administration of an erstwhile law or the State Goods and Services Tax Act or in the field of finance and taxation.

(2) The President and the Judicial Members of the National Bench and the Regional Benches shall be appointed by the Government after consultation with the Chief Justice of India or his nominee.

(3) The Technical Member (Centre) and Technical Member (State) of the National Bench and Regional Benches shall be appointed by the Government on the recommendations of a Selection Committee consisting of such persons and in such manner as may be prescribed.

(4) The Judicial Member of the State Bench or Area Benches shall be appointed by the State Government after consultation with the Chief Justice of the High Court of the State or his nominee.

(5) The Technical Member (Centre) of the State Bench or Area Benches shall be appointed by the Central Government and Technical Member (State) of the State Bench or Area Benches shall be appointed by the State Government in such manner as may be prescribed.

(6) No appointment of the Members of the Appellate Tribunal shall be invalid merely by the reason of any vacancy or defect in the constitution of the Selection Committee.

(7) Before appointing any person as the President or Members of the Appellate Tribunal, the Central Government or, as the case may be, the State Government, shall satisfy itself that such person does not have any financial or other interests which are likely to prejudicially affect his functions as such President or Member.

23.7 PROCEDURE BEFORE APPELLATE TRIBUNAL [SECTION 111]

(1) The Appellate Tribunal shall not, while disposing of any proceedings before it or an appeal before it, be bound by the procedure laid down in the Code of Civil Procedure, 1908, but shall be guided by the principles of natural justice and subject to the other provisions of this Act and the rules made thereunder, the Appellate Tribunal shall have power to regulate its own procedure.

(2) The Appellate Tribunal shall, for the purposes of discharging its functions under this Act, have the same powers as are vested in a civil court under the Code of Civil Procedure, 1908 while trying a suit in respect of the following matters, namely:

(a) summoning and enforcing the attendance of any person and examining him on oath;
(b) requiring the discovery and production of documents;
(c) receiving evidence on affidavits;
(d) subject to the provisions of sections 123 and 124 of the Indian Evidence Act, 1872, requisitioning any public record or document or a copy of such record or document from any office;
(e) issuing commissions for the examination of witnesses or documents;
(f) dismissing a representation for default or deciding it ex parte;
(g) setting aside any order of dismissal of any representation for default or any order passed by it ex parte; and
(h) any other matter, which may be prescribed.

(3) Any order made by the Appellate Tribunal may be enforced by it in the same manner as if it were a decree made by a court in a suit pending therein, and it shall be lawful for the Appellate Tribunal to send for execution of its orders to the court within the local limits of whose jurisdiction:

(a) in the case of an order against a company, the registered office of the company is situated; or
(b) in the case of an order against any other person, the person concerned voluntarily resides or carries on business or personally works for gain.

(4) All proceedings before the Appellate Tribunal shall be deemed to be judicial proceedings within the meaning of sections 193 and 228, and for the purposes of section 196 of the Indian Penal Code, and the Appellate Tribunal shall be deemed to be civil court for the purposes of section 195 and Chapter XXVI of the Code of Criminal Procedure, 1973.

23.8 AMOUNT PAYABLE FOR FILING OF APPEAL

The right to appeal is a statutory right which operates within the limitations placed on it by the law. Tax laws mandate some "pre-deposit" so as to discourage frivolous appeals and also safeguard some bonafied interest of both the taxpayer & the revenue.

For filing of appeal, following amounts shall have to be remitted as "pre-deposit".

Nature of Appeal	Appeal before Appellate Authority [Section 107(6)]	Appeal before Appellate Tribunal (GSTAT) [Section 112(8)]
Demand which are not contested	Entire amount of demand (tax, interest, fine, penalty)	Entire amount of demand (tax, interest, fine, penalty)
Demand which are contested	A sum equal to 10% of amount in dispute subject to a maximum of ₹ 25 crores (w.e.f. 01.02.2019)	A sum equal to 20% of amount in dispute subject to a maximum of ₹ 50 crores (w.e.f. 01.02.2019)

Notes:

(1) No appeal shall be filed with the appellate authority, unless the applicant has paid in full tax, interest, fine, fee & penalty arising from the impugned order as admitted by him and pre-deposit mentioned above.

(2) There shall be no fee for application made before the Appellate Tribunal for rectification of errors. No pre-deposit shall be payable in case of appeal filed by the tax authorities.

(3) Under the IGST Act, for all the inter-state transactions, the maximum cap for the pre-deposit amounts is ₹ 50 crores and ₹ 100 crores before first appellate authority and appellate tribunal, respectively.

23.9 APPEALS TO APPELLATE TRIBUNAL (SECTION 112)

The Tribunal is the second level of appeal. Appeal to the Tribunal by the aggrieved person is to be filed within three months from the communication of the order under appeal. Further, Tribunal has the power to condone delay (of up to three months in case of appeals or 45 days in case of cross objections, beyond the mandatory period) on being satisfied that there is sufficient cause for the delay. The Tribunal has the discretion of not admitting any appeal involving an amount of ₹ 50,000 or less.

Appeals by the department (CGST/SGST) before the AA/Tribunal: The Department itself, if not in agreement with the decision or order passed by the (initial) adjudicating authority or the appellate authority can appeal before the AA/Tribunal. The GST Law provides that in such cases, the department can file what is commonly known as a "review application/appeal".

23.10 ORDERS OF APPELLATE TRIBUNAL (SECTION 113)

(i) The Appellate Tribunal to pass the order confirming, modifying or annulling the decision or order appealed against.

(ii) The Appellate Tribunal also has power to remand the case back to the appellate authority or the Revisional authority or the original adjudicating authority.

(iii) Maximum three adjournments shall be granted to a party on showing reasonable cause to be recorded in writing.

(iv) The Appellate Tribunal is empowered to amend its order to rectify any mistake apparent from record. However, tribunal may rectify its order if the mistake is brought to its notice by Commissioner or other party to appeal within period of three months of date of such order. Opportunity of being heard to be granted in case such rectification results into enhancing an assessment or reducing a refund or input tax credit or otherwise increasing the liability.

(v) The Appellate Tribunal to hear and decide the appeal, as far as possible, within a period of one year from the date of filing.

(vi) The Appellate Tribunal to communicate the copy of order to appellate authority/Revisional authority/ original adjudicating authority, the appellant, the jurisdictional Commissioner, Commissioner of State Tax or Union Territory Tax.

(vii) The jurisdictional officer shall issue a statement in FORM GST APL-04 clearly indicating the final amount of demand confirmed by the Appellate Tribunal.

23.11 FINANCIAL AND ADMINISTRATIVE POWERS OF PRESIDENT (SECTION 114)

The President shall exercise such financial and administrative powers over the National Bench and Regional Benches of the Appellate Tribunal as may be prescribed. The President shall have the authority to delegate such of his financial and administrative powers as he may think fit to any other Member or any officer of the National

Bench and Regional Benches, subject to the condition that such Member or officer shall, while exercising such delegated powers, continue to act under the direction, control and supervision of the President.

23.12 INTEREST ON REFUND OF AMOUNT PAID FOR ADMISSION OF APPEAL (SECTION 115)

Where an amount paid by the appellant under section 107(6) or section 112(8) is required to be refunded consequent to any order of the Appellate Authority or of the Appellate Tribunal, interest at the rate specified under section 56 (i.e. 6%) shall be payable in respect of such refund from the date of payment of the amount till the date of refund of such amount.

23.13 APPEARANCE BY AUTHORIZED REPRESENTATIVE (SECTION 116)

Any person required to appear before a Proper Officer/First Appellate Authority/Appellate Tribunal can assign an authorized representative to appear on his behalf, unless he is required by the Act to appear personally.

An authorized representative can be:

1. a relative
2. a regular employee
3. a lawyer practicing in any court in India
4. any chartered accountant/cost accountant/company secretary, with a valid certificate of practice
5. a retired officer of the Tax Department of any State Government or of the Excise Dept. whose rank was minimum Group-B gazetted officer
6. any tax return preparer.

Retired officers cannot appear in place of the concerned person within one year from the date of their retirement.

23.14 APPEAL TO THE HIGH COURT (SECTION 117)

The law provides that either side (department or party), if *aggrieved* by any order passed by the State Bench or Area Bench of the Tribunal, may file an appeal to the High Court and the High Court may admit such appeal if it is satisfied that the case involves *a substantial question of law*. It is to be noted that on facts, the tribunal is the final authority.

Appeals to the High Court are to be filed within 180 days in FORM GST APL-08, but the HC has the power to condone delay on being satisfied of sufficient cause for the same. No appeal shall lie before a High Court if such order is passed by National Bench or Regional Benches.

On being satisfied that a substantial question of law is involved, the High Court shall formulate that question, and the appeal shall be heard only on the question so formulated. However, the High Court has the power to hear the appeal on any other substantial question of law, if it is satisfied that the case involves such question. The High Court shall decide the questions of law so formulated and deliver such judgment thereon containing the grounds on which such decision is founded and may award such cost as it deems fit. The High Court may determine any issue, which has not been determined by the Tribunal or has been wrongly determined by the Tribunal, by reason of a decision on such questions of law. Appeal to be heard by a Bench of not less than two Judges of High Court.

23.15 APPEAL TO SUPREME COURT (SECTION 118)

An appeal shall lie to the Supreme Court:

(a) from any order passed by the National Bench or Regional Benches of the Appellate Tribunal; or

(b) from any judgment or order passed by the High Court in an appeal made under section 117 in any case which, on its own motion or on an application made by or on behalf of the party aggrieved, immediately after passing of the judgment or order, the High Court certifies to be a fit one for appeal to the Supreme Court.

A (direct) appeal shall also lie to the Supreme Court from any orders passed by the National/Regional Bench of the Tribunal. It may be noted that the National/Regional Bench of the Tribunal has jurisdiction to entertain appeal if the dispute or one of the issues in dispute involves place of supply.

23.16 SUMS DUE TO BE PAID NOTWITHSTANDING APPEAL, ETC. [SECTION 119]

Notwithstanding that an appeal has been preferred to the High Court or the Supreme Court, sums due to the Government as a result of an order passed by the National or Regional Benches of the Appellate Tribunal under section 113 (1) or an order passed by the State Bench or Area Benches of the Appellate Tribunal under section 113 (1) or an order passed by the High Court under section 117, as the case may be, shall be payable in accordance with the order so passed.

23.17 APPEAL NOT TO BE FILED IN CERTAIN CASES [SECTION 120]

This section provides for non-filing of appeal by the tax authorities in certain cases.

(i) On recommendation of Council, the Board may issue order or instructions or directions fixing monetary limits for the purpose of regulating the filing of appeal or application by Officer of central tax.

(ii) In case the Officer has not filed an appeal/application against any decision/order in view of such order/ instruction/directions, it shall not preclude him from filing appeal/application in any other cases involving same/similar issue or question of law.

(iii) No party in appeal/application shall contend that the Officer has acquiesced (agreed/consented) in the decision on the disputed issue by not filing an appeal/application.

(iv) The Appellate Tribunal or court hearing such appeal/application shall have regard to the circumstances under which appeal/application was not filed by the Officer in pursuance of such order/instructions/ directions.

23.18 NON-APPEALABLE DECISIONS AND ORDERS [SECTION 121]

No appeals whatsoever can be filed against the following orders:

(a) an order of the Commissioner or other authority empowered to direct transfer of proceedings from one officer to another officer;

(b) an order pertaining to the seizure or retention of books of account, register and other documents; or

(c) an order sanctioning prosecution under the Act; or

(d) an order passed under section 80 (payment of tax in installments).

Chapter 24

Offences and Penalties

24.1 STATUTORY PROVISION

Punitive provisions in GST Law hve been made for effective implementation of GST to take strict action against offenders and to do justice to tax abiding citizen.

Offences under GST system are broadly divided into two categories:

(1) Offences attracting fiscal penalties
  (a) Revenue issues
  (b) Procedural issues

(2) Offences attracting prosecution

The provisions relating to offences & penalties are covered in Sections 122 to 138 (Chapter XIX) read with Rule 162 of the CGST Rules, 2017.

Section	Description
122	Penalty for certain offences
123	Penalty for failure to furnish information return
124	Fine for failure to furnish statistics
125	General penalty
128	Power to waive penalty or fee or both
129	Detention, seizure and release of goods and conveyances in transit
130	Confiscation of goods or conveyances and levy of penalty
132	Punishment for certain offences
138	Compounding of offences

24.2 PENALTIES UNDER GST [SECTION 122]

The word "penalty" has not been defined in the GST Law but judicial pronouncements and principles of jurisprudence have laid down the nature of a penalty as:

(i) a temporary punishment or a sum of money imposed by statute, to be paid as punishment for the commission of a certain offence;

(ii) a punishment imposed by law or contract for doing or failing to do something that was the duty of a party to do.

Section 122 is divided into three sub-sections:

(1) Prescribes 21 types of offences, any one of which, if committed, can attract penalty of ₹ 10,000 or equal to the amount of tax involved, whichever is higher.

(2) Offences committed are <u>not due to</u> either fraud or willful misstatement or suppression of facts. Penalty will get reduced to 10% of tax involved, subject to a minimum ₹ 10,000

(3) Person is not directly involved in any evasion but may aid or abet or may be a party to evasion or if he does not attend summons or produce documents. Penalty in such a cases would be up to ₹ 25,000.

(a) Section 122(1): An offender has to pay a penalty amount, which will be highest of following:-

- ₹ 10,000
- An amount equivalent to the tax evaded
- The tax not deducted under section 51 or short deducted
- Tax not collected under section 52 or short collected or collected but not paid
- Input tax credit availed of or passed on or distributed irregularly
- Refund claimed fraudulently.

(b) Section 122(1A): Any person who retains the benefit of a transaction covered under clauses (i), (ii), (vii) or (ix) of section 122(1) and at whose instance such transaction is conducted, shall be liable to a penalty of an amount equivalent to the tax evaded or input tax credit availed of or passed on.

(c) Section 122(1B): Inserted by Amendment through Finance Act, 2023

Any electronics commerce operator who:

(i) allows supply of goods & services by un-registered person (except allowed by notification)

(ii) allows inter-state supply of goods & services by in-eligible person

(iii) fails to furnish correct details of outwards supply in GSTR-8

shall be liable to pay ₹ 10,000 or amount of tax evaded whichever is higher.

(d) Section 122(2): Any registered person who supplies any goods or services or both on which any tax has not been paid or short-paid or erroneously refunded, or where the input tax credit has been wrongly availed or utilized, penalty shall be paid as under:

Fraud	100% of tax evaded subject to a minimum of ₹ 10,000
Other than fraud	Penalty of ten thousand rupees or 10% of the tax due from such person, whichever is higher

(e) Section 122(3): Not only the taxable person but **any person** who:

- Helps any person to commit fraud under GST
- Acquires/receives any goods/services with full knowledge that it is in violation of GST Rules
- Fails to appear before the tax authority on receiving a summons
- Fails to issue an invoice according to GST Rules
- Fails to account/vouch any invoice appearing in the books

shall be liable to a penalty which may extend to ₹ 25,000.

24.3 LIST OF OFFENCES UNDER GST

The CGST Act, 2017 has lists 21 offences in section 122(1), apart from the penalty prescribed under section 10 for availing composition scheme by a taxable person who is not eligible for it.

The said offences are as follows:

(i) supplies any goods or services or both without issue of any invoice or issues an incorrect or false invoice with regard to any such supply;

(ii) issues any invoice or bill without supply of goods or services or both in violation of the provisions of this Act or the rules made there under;

(iii) collects any amount as tax but fails to pay the same to the Government beyond a period of three months from the date on which such payment becomes due;

(iv) collects any tax in contravention of the provisions of this Act but fails to pay the same to the Government beyond a period of three months from the date on which such payment becomes due;

(v) fails to deduct the tax in accordance with the provisions of section 51(1), or deducts an amount which is less than the amount required to be deducted under the said sub-section, or where he fails to pay to the Government under section 51(2) thereof, the amount deducted as tax;

(vi) fails to collect tax in accordance with the provisions of section 52(1), or collects an amount which is less than the amount required to be collected under the said sub-section or where he fails to pay to the Government the amount collected as tax under section 52(3);

(vii) takes or utilizes input tax credit without actual receipt of goods or services or both either fully or partially, in contravention of the provisions of this Act or the rules made there under;

(viii) fraudulently obtains refund of tax under this Act;
(ix) takes or distributes input tax credit in contravention of section 20, or the rules made there under;
(x) falsifies or substitutes financial records or produces fake accounts or documents or furnishes any false information or return with an intention to evade payment of tax due under this Act;
(xi) is liable to be registered under this Act but fails to obtain registration;
(xii) furnishes any false information with regard to registration particulars, either at the time of applying for registration, or subsequently;
(xiii) obstructs or prevents any officer in discharge of his duties under this Act;
(xiv) transports any taxable goods without the cover of documents as may be specified in this behalf;
(xv) suppresses his turnover leading to evasion of tax under this Act;
(xvi) fails to keep, maintain or retain books of account and other documents in accordance with the provisions of this Act or the rules made there under;
(xvii) fails to furnish information or documents called for by an officer in accordance with the provisions of this Act or the rules made there under or furnishes false information or documents during any proceedings under this Act;
(xviii) supplies, transports or stores any goods which he has reasons to believe are liable to confiscation under this Act;
(xix) issues any invoice or document by using the registration number of another registered person;
(xx) tampers with, or destroys any material evidence or document;
(xxi) disposes of or tampers with any goods that have been detained, seized, or attached under this Act,

Offences under GST by Companies, LLPs, HUFs and Others: For any offence committed by a company, both the officer in charge (such as director, manager, secretary) as well as the company will be held liable.

For LLPs, HUFs & Trust, the partner/karta/managing trustee will be held liable.

24.4 PENALTY FOR FAILURE TO FURNISH INFORMATION RETURN (SECTION 123)

If a person who is required to furnish an information return under section 150 fails to do so within the period specified in the notice issued under sub-section (3) thereof, the proper officer may direct that such person shall be liable to pay a penalty of ₹ 100 day subject to a maximum of ₹ 5000, for the period during which the failure to furnish such return continues.

24.5 FINE FOR FAILURE TO FURNISH STATISTICS (SECTION 124)

If any person required to furnish any information or return under section 151:

- fails to furnish such information or return without reasonable cause or
- willfully furnishes false information or return,

he shall be punishable with a fine which may extend to ₹ 10,000.

In case of a continuing offence to a further fine which may extend to ₹ 100 for each day after the first day during which the offence continues subject to a maximum limit of ₹ 25,000.

24.6 GENERAL PENALTY (SECTION 125)

Any offense under GST for which penalty is not specifically mentioned will be liable to a penalty, which may extend ₹ 25,000.

24.7 GENERAL PRINCIPLE REGARDING IMPOSING PENALTY (SECTION 126)

The officer under this Act shall while imposing penalty in an order for a breach of any law, regulation or procedural requirement, specify the nature of the breach and the applicable law, regulation or procedure under which the amount of penalty for the breach has been specified.

(a) No penalty shall be imposed on any person without giving him an opportunity of being heard.
(b) The penalty imposed under this Act shall depend on the facts and circumstances of each case and shall be commensurate with the degree and severity of the breach.
(c) There will be NO penalty for "minor breaches" of tax regulations or procedural requirements.
Minor breaches means:
- Amount of tax involved less than ₹ 5000
- Omission or mistake is easily rectifiable.

(d) When a person voluntarily discloses to an officer under this Act the circumstances of a breach of the tax law, regulation or procedural requirement prior to the discovery of the breach by the officer under this Act, the proper officer may consider this fact as a mitigating factor when quantifying a penalty for that person.

24.8 POWER TO IMPOSE PENALTY IN CERTAIN CASES (SECTION 127)

Where the proper officer is of the view that a person is liable to a penalty and the same is not covered under any proceedings under section 62/63/64/73/74/129 or section 130, he may issue an order levying such penalty after giving a reasonable opportunity of being heard to such person.

24.9 POWER TO WAIVE PENALTY OR FEE OR BOTH (SECTION 128)

The Government may, by notification, waive in part or full, any penalty referred to in section 122/123/125 or any late fee referred to in section 47 for such class of taxpayers and under such mitigating circumstances as may be specified therein on the recommendations of the GST Council.

24.10 DETENTION, SEIZURE AND RELEASE OF GOODS AND CONVEYANCES IN TRANSIT (SECTION 129)

Detention means not allowing access to the "owner of the goods" by a legal order/notice. However, the ownership of goods still lies with the owner.

Seizure is taking over of actual possession of the goods by the department. Seizure can be made only after inquiry/investigation that the goods are liable to confiscation.

Where any person transports any goods or stores any goods while they are in transit in contravention of the provisions of this Act or the rules made there under, all such goods and conveyance used as a means of transport for carrying the said goods and documents relating to such goods and conveyance shall be liable to detention or seizure.

However, no such goods or conveyance shall be detained or seized without serving an order of detention or seizure on the person transporting the goods.

After detention or seizure, such goods and conveyance shall be released in following manner:

- **If the owner of the goods come forward:** On payment of 100% of tax applicable on such goods & in case of exempted goods, on payment of 2% of value of goods or ₹ 25,000 whichever is less.
- **If the owner of the goods does not come forward:** On payment of 50% of value of goods (excluding tax) & in case of exempted goods, on payment of 5% of value of goods or ₹ 25,000 whichever is less.
- Upon furnishing a security equivalent to the amount payable above in such form and manner as may be prescribed.

No tax/interest/penalty shall be determined under section 129(3) without giving the person concerned an opportunity of being heard.

Where the person transporting any goods or the owner of the goods fails to pay the amount of tax and penalty as provided above in section 129(1) within 14 days of such detention or seizure, further proceedings shall be initiated in accordance with the provisions of section 130.

Question: Who will be considered as owner of the goods for the purpose of Section 129(1) of the CGST Act?

Answer. The CBIC vide Circular No. 76/50/2018 dated 31.12.2018 has clarified as under:

If the invoice or any other specified documents is accompanying the consignment of goods, then either the consignor or the consignee should be deemed to be the owner.

If the invoice or any other specified documents is not accompanying the consignment of goods, then in such cases, the proper officer should determine who should be declared as the owner of the goods.

24.11 CONFISCATION OF GOODS OR CONVEYANCES AND LEVY OF PENALTY (SECTION 130)

Confiscation means the action of taking or seizing someone's property with authority.

Confiscation of the goods is the ultimate act after proper adjudication. Once confiscation takes place, the ownership as well as the possession goes out of the hands of the original owner and into the hands of the Government Authority.

The goods and the conveyance will be confiscated if, any person:

(i) supplies or receives any goods in contravention of any of the provisions of this Act or the rules made thereunder with intent to evade payment of tax; or
(ii) does not account for any goods on which he is liable to pay tax under this Act; or
(iii) supplies any goods liable to tax under this Act without having applied for registration; or
(iv) contravenes any of the provisions of this Act or the rules made there under with intent to evade payment of tax; or
(v) uses any conveyance as a means of transport for carriage of goods in contravention of the provisions of this Act or the rules made thereunder unless the owner of the conveyance proves that it was so used without the knowledge or connivance of the owner himself, his agent, if any, and the person in charge of the conveyance,

then, all such goods or conveyances shall be liable to confiscation and the person shall be liable to penalty under section 122.

Whenever confiscation of any goods or conveyance is authorized by this Act, the officer adjudging it shall give to the owner of the goods an option to pay fine, in lieu of confiscation, as the said officer thinks fit, subject to a maximum of market value of the goods confiscated, less the tax chargeable thereon.

> Provided also that where any such conveyance is used for the carriage of the goods or passengers for hire, the owner of the conveyance shall be given an option to pay in lieu of the confiscation of the conveyance a fine equal to the tax payable on the goods being transported thereon.

Once confiscated, the goods will become the property of the government. Three months' time will be given for payment of the confiscation fine after which the goods will be sold.

Confiscation or penalty not to interfere with other punishments (Section 131)

Confiscation will not affect other punishments under the provisions of GST, i.e., all penalties and prosecutions will still be applicable.

24.12 PUNISHMENT FOR CERTAIN OFFENCES (SECTION 132)

Section 132 of the Act can be directly resorted, wherever offence is committed and it is not necessary to follow the procedure of assessment, demand and recovery or penalty proceedings. In the scheme of the Act, Section 132 stands independently and the moment a competent officer on inspection and search, finds any offence committed under Section 132 of the Act, prosecution can be directly launched.

Whoever commit any of the following offences as prescribed u/s 132(1) shall be punishable with imprisonment and fine:

(a) Making a supply without issue of an invoice or grossly mis-declaring the description of the supply on invoice, in contravention of this Act, to intentionally evade tax;
(b) Issues any invoice or bill without supply in violation of the provisions of this Act/rules made thereunder leading to wrongful availment of credit or refund of tax;
(c) Avails input tax credit using such invoice or bill referred to above;
(d) Collects any amount as tax but fails to pay the same to the credit of the Government beyond a period of three months from the date on which such payment becomes due;
(e) Evades tax, fraudulently avails input tax credit or fraudulently obtains refund and where such offence is not covered under instances (1) to (4) above;
(f) Falsification or substitution of financial records or producing fake accounts, documents or furnishes any false information with an intention to evade payment of tax;
(g) Obstructs or prevents any officer in the discharge of his duties;
(h) Acquires possession of or transporting, removing, depositing, keeping, concealing, supplying, or purchasing or dealing in any other manner with any goods which he knows or has reason to believe that such goods are liable to confiscation under this Act or the rules made thereunder;
(i) Receives or deals with any supply of services which he knows or has reason to believe are in contravention of any provisions of this Act or the rules made thereunder;
(j) Tampers with or destroys any material evidence or documents;

(k) Fails to supply any information which he is required to supply under this Act or the rules made thereunder or (unless with a reasonable belief, the burden of proving which shall be upon him, that the information supplied by him is true) supplies false information;

(l) Attempts to commit or abets the commission of any of the offences mentioned above.

The scheme of punishment provided in section 132(1) is as follows:

Offences	Punishment (Imprisonment & Fine)
(1) Tax evaded/ITC credit wrongly availed/Refund wrongly taken	
(a) If the amount involve exceed ₹ 5 crores	Up to five years *Plus* fine
(b) If the amount involve is between ₹ 2 crs & ₹ 5 crores	Up to three years *Plus* fine
(c) If the amount involve is between ₹ 1 crs and ₹ 2 crores (Only for offence u/s 132(1)(b)	Up to one year *Plus* fine
(2) Commit offences such as falsify record/prevent or obstruct officer/tamper or destroy evidence	Six months/fine or both
(3) Repeated offences	Up to five years *Plus* fine

The offences specified in clause (*a*) or clause (*b*) or clause (*c*) or clause (*d*) of section 132 (1) shall be cognizable and non-bailable. (Cognizable *means arrest without a warrant*)

As per Section 132(6), a person shall not be prosecuted for any offence under this section except with the previous sanction of the Commissioner.

Notes: Recommendation in 48th GST Council meeting

(1) Minimum period of imprisonment shall be six months

(2) Minimum threshold limit of tax amount for lunching prosecution raised to ₹ 2 crores from ₹ 1 crores (Amendment made by Finance Act, 2023)

(3) Decriminalize certain offences specified under clause (g), (j) and (k) of section 132(1) of CGST Act, 2017, viz.

(a) obstruction or preventing any officer in discharge of his duties;

(b) deliberate tempering of material evidence;

(c) failure to supply the information.

24.13 LIABILITY OF OFFICERS [SECTION 133]

If any officer, who are engaged in collection of statistical information, compilation, computerization or in GST common portal, willfully disclose any information otherwise than required under Act, shall be punishable with imprisonment up to six months or fine of ₹ 25,000 or both.

Persons liable for prosecution	Nature of offence	Prosecution
Person engaged in connection with the collection of statistics under Section 151	Willfully discloses any information or the contents of any return furnished under this Act or rules made thereunder otherwise than in execution of his duties under the said sections or for the purposes of prosecution for an offence under this Act or under any other Act for the time being in force	The guilty person shall be punishable with imprisonment for a term which may extend to six months or with fine which may extend to twenty-five thousand rupees, or with both
Person engaged in compilation or computerization thereof or if any officer of central tax having access to information specified under sub-Section (1) of section 150		
If any person engaged in connection with the provision of service on the common portal or the agent of common portal		

Cognizance of Offences & Presumption of Culpable Mental State [Sections 134-136]

No court shall take cognizance of any offence punishable under this Act or the rules made thereunder except with the previous sanction of the Commissioner, and no court inferior to that of a Magistrate of the First Class, shall try any such offence.

For prosecution, presumption of culpable mental state is necessary. The accused person has to prove the fact that he had no such mental state with respect to the act charged as an offence in that prosecution.

Culpable mental state includes: (a) Intention, (b) Motive, (c) Knowledge of the fact, (d) Belief in or reason to believe a fact.

24.14 OFFENCES BY COMPANIES AND CERTAIN OTHER PERSONS [Section 137]

If offences are committed by companies and certain other persons wherein the offence has been committed with the consent of any director, manager, secretary or other officers of the company, then such director, manager, secretary or other officers of the company shall also be deemed to be guilty of that offence and shall be liable to be proceeded against and punished accordingly.

If offences are committed by taxable person being a partnership firm or a LLP or HUF or a trust, the partner or Karta or managing trustee respectively shall deemed to be guilty of offence and shall be liable to be proceeded against and punished accordingly.

24.15 COMPOUNDING OF OFFENCES [SECTION 138]

Any offence under this Act may, either before or after the institution of prosecution, be compounded by the Commissioner on payment, by the person accused of the offence, to the Central Government or the State Government, as the case be, of such compounding amount in such manner as may be prescribed.

Compounding shall be allowed only after making payment of tax, interest and penalty involved in such offences.

A person who has been allowed to compound once in respect of any offence under the Act in respect of supplies of value exceeding one crore rupees, further compounding shall not be allowed.

The amount for compounding of offences is:

	Old provision	New Provision (Amendment made by Finance Act, 2023)
Minimum	₹ 10,000 or 50% of tax involved (whichever is higher)	25% of tax involved
Maximum	₹ 30,000 or 150% of tax involved (whichever is higher)	100% of tax involved

On payment of such compounding amount, no further proceedings shall be initiated under this Act against the accused person in respect of the same offence and any criminal proceedings, if already initiated in respect of the said offence, shall stand abated.

Amendment made by Finance Act, 2023

(a) Irrespective of the amount, if a person deals with goods liable for confiscation or services in contravention of the provisions, he can apply for compounding.

(b) The limit of ₹ 1 crore applicable earlier to apply for compounding of certain offences has been removed.

(c) Earlier, a person accused of committing an offence under any other law could not apply for compounding. This restriction has now been removed.

(d) A person who is accused of issuing fake invoices without an actual supply of goods or services would not be allowed to apply for compounding now.

Offences, Arrests & Prosecution

Section	Provision
Section 69(1)	Power to authorize arrest for offences under Section 132 (1)
Section 132(6)	No person can be prosecuted without prior approval of Commissioner
Section 134	No court shall take cognizance of any offence punishable under the CGST Act without prior sanction of the Commissioner
Section 138	Commissioner is empowered to compound the offences under this Act

Chapter 25

Transitional Provisions

25.1 STATUTORY PROVISION

Chapter XX [Sections 139 to 142] of the CGST Act read with CGST Rules 117 to 121, stipulates the provisions relating to transition from the erstwhile excise/VAT/service tax etc. regime to the GST regime, due to implementation of GST law w.e.f. 1st July 2017.

Section	Description
139	Migration of existing taxpayers
140	Transitional arrangements for input tax credit
141	Transitional provisions relating to job work
142	Miscellaneous transitional provisions

25.2 MIGRATION OF EXISTING TAX PAYERS [SECTION 139]

(1) On and from the appointed day, every person registered under any of the existing laws (*other than a person deducting tax or an Input Service Distributor (ISD)* who were registered under various earlier Indirect Tax Laws) and having a valid Permanent Account Number (PAN) shall be issued a certificate of registration on provisional basis, in FORM GST REG-25 incorporating GSTIN, subject to such conditions and in such form and manner as may be prescribed, which unless replaced by a final certificate of registration under section 139(2), shall be liable to be cancelled if the conditions so prescribed are not complied with.

A taxable person who was granted multiple registrations under the pre-GST law on the basis of a single Permanent Account Number (PAN) shall be granted only one provisional registration under the GST Act.

(2) The final certificate of registration shall be granted in FORM GST REG-06 subject to fulfillment of such other conditions as laid down in CGST Rules for registration.

(3) The certificate of registration issued to a person under section 139(1) shall be deemed to have not been issued, if the said registration is cancelled in pursuance of an application filed by such person that he was not liable to registration under section 22 or section 24.

25.3 TRANSITIONAL ARRANGEMENTS OF INPUT TAX CREDIT [SECTION 140]

As per CGST Rule 117, every registered person entitled to take credit of input tax under section 140 shall, submit a declaration electronically in **FORM GST TRAN-1**, duly signed, on the common portal specifying therein, separately, the amount of input tax credit of eligible duties and taxes, as defined in Explanation 2 to section 140, to which he is entitled under the provisions of the said section within 31st December 2019 [Vide Notification No. 49/2019-CT dt. 09.10.2019].

The amount of credit allowed shall be credited to the electronic credit ledger of the applicant maintained in FORM GST PMT-2 on the common portal.

(1) A registered person, other than a person opting to pay tax under section 10 (composition scheme dealer), shall be entitled to take, in his electronic credit ledger, the amount of CENVAT credit carried forward in the return relating to the period ending with the day immediately preceding the appointed day, furnished by him under the pre-GST law in such manner as may be prescribed:

Provided that the registered person shall not be allowed to take credit in the following circumstances, namely:

(i) where the said amount of credit is not admissible as input tax credit under GST Act; or

(ii) where he has not furnished all the returns required under the pre-GST law for the period of six months immediately preceding the appointed date; or

(iii) where the said amount of credit relates to goods manufactured and cleared under such exemption notifications as are notified by the Government.

(2) A registered person, other than a person opting to pay tax under section 10, shall be entitled to carry forward of unavailed tax credit in relation to capital goods:

Provided that the registered person shall not be allowed to take credit unless the said credit was admissible as CENVAT credit under the pre-GST law and is also admissible as input tax credit under GST Act.

(3) A registered person, who was not liable to be registered under the pre-GST law, or who was engaged in the manufacture of exempted goods or provision of exempted services, shall be entitled to take, in his electronic credit ledger, credit of eligible duties in respect of inputs held in stock and inputs contained in semi-finished or finished goods held in stock on the appointed day subject to the following conditions, namely:

(i) such inputs or goods are used or intended to be used for making taxable supplies under this Act;

(ii) the said registered person is eligible for input tax credit on such inputs under this Act;

(iii) the said registered person is in possession of invoice or other prescribed documents evidencing payment of duty under the existing law in respect of such inputs;

(iv) such invoices or other prescribed documents were issued not earlier than twelve months immediately preceding the appointed day; and

(v) the supplier of services is not eligible for any abatement under this Act:

Provided that where a registered person, other than a manufacturer or a supplier of services, is not in possession of an invoice or any other documents evidencing payment of duty in respect of inputs, then, such registered person shall be allowed @ 60% on such goods which attract central tax @ 9% or more and @40% for other goods of the central tax applicable on supply of such goods after the appointed date and shall be credited after the central tax payable on such supply has been paid. Where integrated tax is paid on such goods, the amount of credit shall be allowed @30% and 20% respectively of the said tax.

(4) A registered person, who was engaged in the manufacture of taxable as well as exempted goods or provision of taxable as well as exempted services under pre-GST law, but which are liable to tax under GST Act, shall be entitled to carry forward the credit of input tax held in stock and inputs contained in semi-finished or finished goods.

(5) Tax credit in respect of inputs or input services received on or after the appointed day but the duty or tax in respect of which has been paid by the supplier under the erstwhile law within a period of thirty days from the appointed day or within such further period as extended by the commissioner.

(6) A registered person, who was either paying tax at a fixed rate or paying a fixed amount in lieu of the tax payable under the existing law shall be entitled to take, in his electronic credit ledger, credit of eligible duties in respect of inputs held in stock and inputs contained in semi-finished or finished goods held in stock on the appointed day subject to the following conditions, namely:

(i) such inputs or goods are used or intended to be used for making taxable supplies under this Act;

(ii) the said registered person is not paying tax under section 10;

(iii) the said registered person is eligible for input tax credit on such inputs under this Act;

(iv) the said registered person is in possession of invoice or other prescribed documents evidencing payment of duty under the existing law in respect of inputs; and

(v) such invoices or other prescribed documents were issued not earlier than twelve months immediately preceding the appointed day.

(7) The input tax credit on account of any services received prior to the appointed day by an Input Service Distributor shall be eligible for distribution as credit under this Act even if the invoices relating to such services are received on or after the appointed day.

(8) Where a registered person having centralized registration under the existing law has obtained a registration under this Act, such person shall be allowed to take, in his electronic credit ledger, credit of the amount of CENVAT

credit carried forward in a return, furnished under the existing law by him, in respect of the period ending with the day immediately preceding the appointed day in such manner as may be prescribed:

Provided that if the registered person furnishes his return for the period ending with the day immediately preceding the appointed day within three months of the appointed day, such credit shall be allowed subject to the condition that the said return is either an original return or a revised return where the credit has been reduced from that claimed earlier.

(9) Where any CENVAT credit availed for the input services provided under the existing law has been reversed due to non-payment of the consideration within a period of three months, such credit can be reclaimed subject to the condition that the registered person has made the payment of the consideration for that supply of services within a period of three months from the appointed day.

(10) The amount of credit under sub-sections (3), (4) and (6) shall be calculated in such manner as may be prescribed.

25.4 TRANSITIONAL PROVISIONS RELATING TO JOB WORK [SECTION 141]

141(1) Inputs removed for job work and returned on or after the appointed day: In case inputs removed by a Principal to a Job Worker's premises that are returned to the Principal within six months (or within an extended period of further two months), no tax shall be payable. However, if the inputs are not returned within six months or such extended period of two months, then the input tax credit availed by the Principal shall be recovered as arrears of tax under CGST Law and no input tax credit of such tax paid shall be allowed under the CGST Law.

141(2) Semi-finished goods removed for job work and returned on or after the appointed day: In case semi-finished goods removed by a Principal to a Job Worker's premises that are returned to the Principal within six months (or within an extended period of further two months), no tax shall be payable. However, if the semi-finished goods are not returned within six months or such extended period of an additional two months then the input tax credit availed by the Principal shall stand reversed under the erstwhile law or recovered as arrears under the CGST Law.

- Rule 119 prescribes that every principal and the job worker shall file a declaration in FORM GST TRAN-1 specifying the stock held at job worker's premises. The time limit for furnishing the above declaration in TRAN-1 has been prescribed in Rule 117.
- The manufacturer may, instead of bringing the said goods back to his place of business, transfer the said goods to the premises of any registered person for the purpose of supplying there from to places within India or for exports.

141(3) Finished goods removed for carrying out certain processes and returned on or after the appointed day: Excisable goods are manufactured and removed from the place of business without payment of duty for carrying out tests or any other process (not amounting to manufacture), to any other premises, whether registered or not, in terms of the earlier law prior to the appointed day.

Subsequently such goods, are returned to the said place of business on or after the appointed day, then no tax shall be payable if the said goods, after undergoing the process, are returned to the said place within six months from the appointed day.

(i) The period of six months may be extended by the Commissioner for a further period not exceeding two months.

(ii) If the said goods are not returned within six months or extended period, from the appointed day, the input tax credit shall be liable to be recovered under the erstwhile law. If the input tax credit is not recovered under the erstwhile law, it will be recovered as an arrear under the CGST Act.

(iii) The manufacturer may, in terms of the provisions of the earlier law, transfer the said goods from the premises of the job worker on payment of tax if the supplies are made within India or without payment of tax for exports.

141(4) Declaration of stock held by a principal and job-worker: Every person to whom the provisions of section 141 apply shall, within a period of 90 days from appointed date, submit a declaration electronically in FORM GST TRAN-1, specifying therein, the stock of the inputs, semi-finished goods or finished goods, as applicable, held by him on the appointed day.

25.5 MISCELLANEOUS TRANSITIONAL PROVISION [SECTION 142]

Section	Analysis
142(1)	Duty paid goods returned to the place of business on or after the appointed day. This transitional provision provides for refund of duties paid on goods under erstwhile law when returned to the place of business. The person receiving the said goods back under the GST regime would be eligible to refund of the duty paid under the erstwhile law at the time of removal of goods.
142(2)(a)	Issue of supplementary invoices, debit or credit notes where price is revised in pursuance of a contract. The price of any goods or services or both is revised upwards on or after the appointed day, shall be deemed to be an outward supply made under this Act.
142(2)(b)	The price of any goods or services or both is revised downwards on or after the appointed day, shall be deemed to be in respect of outward supply made under this Act.
142(3)	The section provides that where any person has made an application for refund of CENVAT credit, duty, tax or interest paid, the same would have to be processed in terms of the provisions contained in the respective erstwhile laws. The provisions of GST law would have no bearing on the same.
142(4)	Every claim for refund filed after the appointed day for refund of any duty or tax paid under pre-GST law in respect of the goods or services exported before or after the appointed day shall be disposed of in accordance with the provisions of pre-GST law.
142(5)	Every claim of refund of tax filed after the appointed date paid under the pre-GST law in respect of services not provided shall be disposed of in accordance with the provisions of the erstwhile law and any amount eventually accruing to him shall be paid in cash.
142(6)(a)	Every proceeding of appeal, review or reference relating to a CLAIM for CENVAT credit initiated whether before, on or after the appointed day under the pre-GST law. If the input credit are finally allowed: A refund would accrue to the claimant in cash.
142(6)(b)	Every proceeding of appeal, review or reference relating to RECOVERY for CENVAT credit initiated whether before, on or after the appointed day under the pre-GST law. If the input credit is disallowed: It would become recoverable as an arrear of tax under the CGST.
142(7)(a)	Every proceeding of appeal, review or reference relating to any output duty or tax liability initiated whether before, on or after the appointed day under the existing law and if any amount becomes recoverable from the claimant.
142(7)(b)	Every proceeding of appeal, review or reference relating to any output duty or tax liability initiated whether before, on or after the appointed day under the existing law, and any amount found to be admissible to the claimant.
142(8)(a)	In pursuance of an assessment or adjudication proceedings instituted, whether before, on or after the appointed day, under the existing law, any amount of tax, interest, fine or penalty becomes RECOVERABLE from the person, should be recovered as an arrear of tax under CGST Act in terms of Circular No. 42/16/2018-GST dated 13/04/2018. Such liability is to be paid through the utilization of amounts available in the electronic credit ledger or electronic cash ledger of the registered person, and the same shall be recorded in Part II of the Electronic Liability Register (FORM GST PMT-01). The amount so recovered would not be allowed as input tax credit under the CGST laws.
142(8)(b)	In pursuance of an assessment or adjudication proceedings instituted, whether before, on or after the appointed day, under the pre-GST law, any amount of tax, interest, fine or penalty becomes REFUNDABLE to the taxable person, It would accrue to the claimant as refund in cash under the erstwhile law.
142(9)(a)	Where any return, furnished under the existing law, is revised after the appointed day and if, pursuant to such revision, any amount is found to be recoverable or any amount of CENVAT credit is found to be inadmissible. If any amount is recoverable: It should be recovered as an arrear of tax under the CGST Act. The amount so recovered would not be allowed as input tax credit.
142(9)(b)	Where any return, furnished under the existing law, is revised after the appointed day but within the time limit specified for such revision under the existing law and if, pursuant to such revision, any amount is found to be refundable or CENVAT credit is found to be admissible. If the amount is allowable as refund: It would accrue to the claimant as cash refund under the erstwhile law.

Section	Analysis
142(10)	Goods or services or both supplied (in pursuance of a contract entered into prior to the appointed day) i.e., ongoing contracts on or after the appointed day shall be liable to tax under GST. It provides that in respect of a contract entered into prior to GST regime, the goods or services or both which are supplied on or after the introduction of GST would be liable to tax under the GST Act to the extent the supply takes place after introduction of GST. Even if the construction contract or works contract is entered into prior to the date of introduction of GST, the contracts would be taxable under the GST Act. **Example:** A contract for construction of a Office building was entered on 12th May 2017. However, the work was actually executed between 5th July 2017 to 31st October 2017. The said supply will be taxable under GST law. However, the contract price will undergo changes since the indirect taxes such as ED/VAT/services, etc. applicable under pre-GST law have been subsumed into GST.
142(11)(a)	No tax shall be payable on goods under this Act to the extent the tax was leviable on the said goods under the Value Added Tax Act of the State. Goods, to the extent tax was leviable under the Value Added Tax Act of the state; considering the non-obstante clause, it is provided that even though any of the ingredients of supply prescribed in Section 12 occur after the appointed date, if VAT was lawfully levied (even if not yet paid), VAT alone will be leviable and not GST.
142(11)(b)	No tax shall be payable on services under this Act to the extent the tax was leviable on the said services under Chapter V of the Finance Act, 1994. Service, to the extent Service Tax was leviable on the said service. In short, GST shall not be levied on a supply to the extent Value Added Tax or Service Tax, as the case may be, was leviable on the said supply. **Example:** Advance of ₹ 1,00,000 was received on 10th June 2017 for service to be rendered in July 2017. The invoice for the service was raised for ₹ 1,50,000 on 31st July 2017. GST shall be levied only on ₹ 50,000.
142(11)(c)	Where tax was paid on any supply both under the Value Added Tax and under Chapter V of the Finance Act, 1994, tax shall be leviable under this Act to the extent of supplies made after the appointed day i.e., supply of goods or services or both supplied after the appointed day. This transition provision deals with transactions which have suffered tax (Value Added Tax or Service Tax) because consideration was received under the earlier law, whereas the supply is made after the date of introduction of GST. **Example:** A contract for construction of factory building was entered in April 2017 for ₹ 1 crores. Advance received till 30th June 2017 amounts to ₹ 10 lakhs. Value Added Tax of ₹ 40,000 and Service Tax of ₹ 60,000 have been paid on the said advance. The entire work has been executed after 1st July 2017. GST shall be levied on ₹ 1 crore as per Section 13 (time of supply of Service) of the CGST Act. The value added tax and service tax paid shall be allowed as credit under the erstwhile law in the manner as may be prescribed.
142(12)	Any goods sent on approval basis, not earlier than six months before the appointed day, are rejected and returned to the seller on or after the appointed day, Tax treatment shall be as follows: (1) Where the goods are returned to the seller within six months or further extended period up to two months from the appointed date, no tax shall be payable on such goods (2) If the goods are taxable under GST and (a) Returned to the seller after six months/further extended period up to two months from the appointed day, tax shall be payable by the "person returning the goods". (b) Not returned to the seller within six months/further extended period up to two months from the appointed day, tax shall be payable by the "person sending the goods on approval basis".
142(13)	No deduction of tax at source under section 51 of CGST Act shall be made by the deductor on sale made under existing law which is subject to TDS and has also issued an invoice before the appointed day i.e. prior to 1st July 2017.

Example 1: A supplier has raised Tax invoice in pre-GST regime but goods have been supplied as well as payment is made in GST regime. Whether there is any tax implication for the payment made in the GST regime?

Answer. As per Section 142(11) (a) of the CGST Act, no GST is payable on goods, if tax was levied on said goods under VAT Act of the State. Since 100% tax liability has been discharged in the pre-GST period, there will not be any tax implication under GST when payment is made.

Example 2: In case a debit note is to be issued under Section 142(2)(a) of the CGST Act or a credit note under Section 142(2)(b) of the CGST Act, what will be the tax rate applicable—the rate in the pre-GST regime or the rate applicable under GST?

Answer. (1) As per the provisions of section 142(2) of the CGST Act, in case of revision of prices of any goods or services or both on or after the appointed day (i.e., 01.07.2017), a supplementary invoice or debit/credit note may be issued which shall be deemed to have been issued in respect of an outward supply made under the CGST Act.

(2) Therefore, in case of revision of prices, after the appointed date, of any goods or services supplied before the appointed day thereby requiring issuance of any supplementary invoice, debit note or credit note, the rate as per the provisions of the GST Acts (both CGST and SGST or IGST) would be applicable.

Chapter 26

Miscellaneous Provision

Chapter XXI of the CGST Act, 2017 deals with miscellaneous provision. It covers section 143 to section 174.

Section	Provisions
143	Job work procedure
144	Presumption as to documents in certain cases
145	Admissibility of micro films, facsimile copies of documents and computer printouts as documents and as evidence
146	Common portal
147	Deemed exports
148	Special procedure for certain processes
149	Goods and services tax compliance rating
150	Obligation to furnish information return
151	Power to collect statistics
152	Bar on disclosure of information
153	Taking assistance from an expert
154	Power to take samples
155	Burden of proof
156	Persons deemed to be public servants
157	Protection of action taken under this Act
158	Disclosure of information by a public servant
159	Publication of information in respect of persons in certain cases
160	Assessment proceedings, etc., not to be invalid on certain ground
161	Rectification of errors apparent on the face of record
162	Bar on jurisdiction of civil courts
163	Levy of fee
164	Power of Government to make rules
165	Power to make regulations
166	Laying of rules, regulations and notifications
167	Delegation of powers
168	Power to issue instructions or directions
169	Service of notice in certain circumstances
170	Rounding off of tax, etc.
171	Anti-profiteering measure
172	Removal of difficulties
173	Amendment of Act 32 of 1994
174	Repeal and saving

Section 143: Job work Procedure: The term "job work" has been defined in Section 2(68) of the CGST Act, 2017. It means any treatment or process undertaken by a person on goods belonging to another registered person. In any job work there are at least two parties involved, i.e. the principal and the job worker. The principal must be a registered person under GST. In job work, the principal send inputs or capital goods to the job worker to carry out the process to make a usable product. Neither the principal nor the job worker provide 100% materials.

As per Rule 55, the goods sent for job work can be without an invoice, but a proper delivery challan containing specific details must be issued while sending goods to the job worker.

For detailed discussion, please refer chapter "Job work Procedure under GST".

Section 144: Presumption as to documents in certain cases: Presumptions means inferences drawn from known sources, unless there is contrary evidence.

Where any document:

(i) is produced by any person under this Act or any other law for the time being in force; or

(ii) has been seized from the custody or control of any person under this Act or any other law for the time being in force; or

(iii) has been received from any place outside India in the course of any proceedings under this Act or any other law for the time being in force, such document shall be treated as valid evidence, unless prove to the contrary.

Section 145: Admissibility of micro films, facsimile copies of documents and computer printouts as documents and as evidence: The term 'document' has been defined under Section 2(41) so as to include written or printed record of any sort and electronic record as defined in the Information Technology Act, 2000. Any information stored electronically or any hard copies made thereof is treated as document.

Section 146: Common Portal: The Government may, on the recommendations of the Council, notify the Common Goods and Services Tax Electronic Portal for facilitating registration, payment of tax, furnishing of returns, computation and settlement of integrated tax, electronic way bill and for carrying out such other functions and for such purposes as may be prescribed.

The Central Government vide Notification No. 4/2017-Central Tax dated 19-06-2017 has notified www.gst.gov.in as the GST Electronic portal for facilitating registration, payment of tax, furnishing of returns etc. and www.ewaybillgst.gov.in as the GST Electronic Portal for furnishing electronic way bill (EWB) vide Notification No. 09/2018-Central Tax dated 23-01-2017.

Section 147: Deemed exports: The Government may, on the recommendations of the Council, notify certain supplies of goods as deemed exports. The notified goods would be deemed to be exported, if such goods are manufactured in India although they do not leave India and payments are received in Indian rupees or convertible foreign exchange.

The Central Government vide Notification No. 48/2017 dated 18-10-2017 has notified following classes of "Supply of Goods" as deemed export:

Sl No.	Description of Supply
1.	Supply of goods by a registered person against Advance Authorization
2.	Supply of capital goods by a registered person against Export Promotion Capital Goods Authorization
3.	Supply of goods by a registered person to Export Oriented Unit
4.	Supply of gold by a bank or Public Sector Undertaking specified in the notification No. 50/2017-Customs, dated the 30th June 2017 (as amended) against Advance Authorization

Explanation:

For the purposes of this notification:

1. "Advance Authorization" means an authorization issued by the Director General of Foreign Trade under Chapter 4 of the Foreign Trade Policy 2015-20 for import or domestic procurement of inputs on pre-import basis for physical exports.

2. Export Promotion Capital Goods Authorization means an authorization issued by the Director General of Foreign Trade under Chapter 5 of the Foreign Trade Policy 2015-20 for import of capital goods for physical exports.

3. "Export Oriented Unit" means an Export Oriented Unit or Electronic Hardware Technology Park Unit or Software Technology Park Unit or Bio-Technology Park Unit approved in accordance with the provisions of Chapter 6 of the Foreign Trade Policy 2015-20.

Deemed exports supplies cannot be made under bond/LUT and tax to be paid at the time of supply. Further, refund of tax paid on such supplies can be claimed either by a recipient or a supplier.

Section 148: Special procedure for certain processes: The Government may, on the recommendations of the Council, and subject to such conditions and safeguards as may be prescribed, notify certain classes of registered persons, and the special procedures to be followed by such persons including those with regard to registration, furnishing of return, payment of tax and administration of such persons.

In exercise of the power conferred by Section 148 of CGST Act, the Government have issued several notifications. Following are few example.

Notification	Description
43/2018-CT, dt 10.09.2018	Extends the due date for filing of Form GSTR-1 for taxpayers having aggregate turnover up to ₹ 1.5 crores for the specified periods.
21/2009-CT, dt. 23.04.2019	Notifies procedure for quarterly tax payment and annual filing of return for taxpayers availing the benefit of Notification No. 02/2019-CT (Rate), dt. 07.03.2019.
60/2019-CT, dt. 26.11.2019	Extends the due date for furnishing of return in Form GSTR-3B for registered persons in Jammu and Kashmir for the months of July, 2019 to September 2019.
64/2020-CT, dt. 31.08.2020	Extends the due date for filing Form GSTR-4 for financial year 2019-2020 to 31.10.2020.
77/2020-CT, dt. 15.10.2020	Filing of annual return under Section 44(1) of CGST Act for FY 2019-20 optional for small taxpayers whose aggregate turnover is less than ₹ 2 crores and who have not filed the said return before the due date.

Section 149: Goods and services tax compliance rating: GST compliance rating is a method of performance rating of all registered taxable person with regard to how compliant they are with respect to GST provisions. A score will be assigned based on their performance. The tax compliance rating, will be on the lines of credit rating of companies. It will be done automatically and displayed on the web portal of the Goods and Services Tax Network (GSTN). This will not only discipline errant traders, but will also lead to greater customer awareness and with the ratings available for everyone to see, making a choice would be extremely easy. With a system like this, accountability will find precedence as non-compliance could prove costly.

Basis of Compliance Rating

The rating will be assigned to a registered taxable person, based on following parameters:

(1) Timely payment of taxes
(2) Timely filing of returns
(3) Timely reconciliations
(4) Compliance of various provision under GST within prescribed time limit, such as issue of invoice, e-way bill, correct claim of ITC
(5) Cooperation with the GST authorities

Need of compliance rating: The idea behind this concept of tax administration is to compel dealers to be fully GST compliant and on time with uploading of invoices and other necessary documents. Under GST regime, input tax credit is available to a registered taxable person only upon Invoice Matching. A person can claim input tax credit in GSTR-2 (inward supplies, i.e. purchase details for the month) only when the seller has also filed his GSTR-1 (outward supply, i.e. monthly sales details), and the details on both these forms match or reconcile with each other.

Benefits of Compliance Rating

Following benefits will accrue to a registered dealer for better compliance rating:

- Better goodwill
- Chance of getting tax refund timely

- Will attract more business
- Lesser chance of audit by tax authority

How to maintain better compliance rating:

(1) File GST Returns on time
(2) Pay tax dues before filing Return, otherwise it will be treated as invalid return as per Section 2(117)
(3) Avoid wrong availment of ITC
(4) Submit Annual Return (GSTR-9) within due dates
(5) Avoid mismatch of invoice issued & return filed
(6) Issue proper invoice

Section 150: Obligation to furnish information return: Any person, who is responsible for maintaining record of registration or statement of accounts or any periodic return or document containing details of payment of tax and other details of transaction of goods or services or both or transactions related to a bank account or consumption of electricity or transaction of purchase, sale or exchange of goods or property or right or interest in a property under any law for the time being in force, shall furnish an information return of the same in respect of such periods, within such time, in such form and manner and to such authority or agency as may be prescribed.

A person who fails to furnish information return shall be liable to pay penalty of ₹ 100 day subject to a maximum of ₹ 5000 u/s 123 of CGST Act, 2017.

The person can be a taxable person, local authority, banking company, electricity board, stock exchange, central excise & custom authority, income tax authority, RBI, ROC, etc.

Section 151: Power to collect statistics: This section authorizes the Commissioner or officers authorizes by him, to collect any statistics relating to any matter that may be required.

As per section 124 of CGST Act, 2017, if any person required to furnish any information or return under section 151:

- Fails to furnish such information or return without reasonable cause or
- Willfully furnishes false information or return,

he shall be punishable with a fine which may extend to ₹ 10,000.

In case of a continuing offence to a further fine which may extend to ₹ 100 for each day after the first day during which the offence continues subject to a maximum limit of ₹ 25,000.

Section 152: Bar on disclosure of information: Any information obtained shall not be published so as to enable any particulars to be identified as referring to a particular taxpayer, without the prior written consent of the taxpayer or his authorized representative.

Any person who is engaged in connection with collection of statistics under Section 151 or compilation or computerization willfully discloses any information or contents of any return under this Section, or otherwise in execution of his duties shall be punished with Imprisonment for a term which may extend to six months or fine which may extend to ₹ 25000 or with both in terms of section 133.

Section 153: Taking assistance from an expert: Any officer not below the rank of Assistant Commissioner may, having regard to the nature and complexity of the case and the interest of revenue, take assistance of any expert (e.g. IT professional, lawyer, engineer, CA, etc.) at any stage of scrutiny, inquiry, investigation or any other proceedings before him.

Section 154: Power to take samples: The Commissioner or an officer author authorized by him may take samples of goods from the possession of any taxable person, where he considers it necessary, and provide a receipt for any samples so taken.

Sec 155: Burden of proof: The onus of proving that the taxable person is right in his claims would vest with him, where the taxable person has claimed any input tax credit under Chapter V (Input Tax Credit) of CGST Act, 2017.

Section 156: Persons deemed to be public servants: All persons discharging functions under this Act shall be deemed to be public servants within the meaning of section 21 of the Indian Penal Code.

As the persons discharging official functions are deemed to be public servants, any offences against such persons and offences by such persons would be dealt with in accordance with Section 21 of IPC.

Section 157: Protection of action taken under this Act: Immunity from any legal or departmental proceedings is provided to the GST officers and officers of the Tribunal u/s 157, for the acts done in good faith under the provisions of CGST Act.

Section 158: Disclosure of information by a public servant: Any information obtained during the course of any proceeding shall be kept confidential and should not be disclosed.

Exceptions:

Information may disclosed in following circumstance:

(1) Required under any other laws
(2) For audit purpose
(3) For service of notice/demand
(4) Information sought by Government
(5) To data entry agency appointed by department for updation of data base.

Section 159: Publication of information in respect of persons in certain cases

(1) If the Commissioner, or any other officer authorized by him in this behalf, is of the opinion that it is necessary or expedient in the public interest to publish the name of any person and any other particulars relating to any proceedings or prosecution under this Act in respect of such person, it may cause to be published such name and particulars in such manner as it thinks fit.

(2) No publication under this section shall be made in relation to any penalty imposed under this Act until the time for presenting an appeal to the Appellate Authority under section 107 has expired without an appeal having been presented or the appeal, if presented, has been disposed of.

Explanation: *In the case of firm, company or other association of persons, the names of the partners of the firm, directors, managing agents, secretaries and treasurers or managers of the company, or the members of the association, as the case may be, may also be published if, in the opinion of the Commissioner, or any other officer authorized by him in this behalf, circumstances of the case justify it.*

Section 160: Assessment proceedings, etc., not to be invalid on certain ground: Assessment, re-assessment and other proceedings that are listed in this section will be valid even though there may be:

(a) **Mistake,** (b) **Defect** or (c) **Omission:** Provided they be in 'substance' and 'effect' in conformity with the intents, purposes and requirements of the Act.

Section 161: Rectification of errors apparent on the face of record: Any authority, who has passed or issued any decision or order or notice or certificate or any other document, may rectify any error which is apparent on the face of record in such decision or order or notice or certificate or any other document, either on its own motion or where such error is brought to its notice by any officer appointed under GST Act or by the affected person.

The time limit to request the rectification is three months. However, the officer who has passed the decision/order can make the rectification suo-motu till six months from the date of issue of such decision or order.

There is no time limit for rectification of error, which is purely clerical or arithmetical nature.

Section 162: Bar on jurisdiction of civil court: Tax being a civil liability, its levy, imposition and collection can be challenged before the Civil Court.

GST law expressly barred civil court jurisdiction unless a dispute involve substantial question of law.

Section 163: Levy of fee: This provision empowers the Central Government to collect fees for supplying copies of the orders/documents.

Wherever a copy of any order or document is to be provided to any person on an application made by him for that purpose, there shall be paid such fee as may be prescribed.

Section 164: Power of Government to make rules: The Government may, on the recommendations of the Council, by notification, make rules for carrying out the provisions of this Act.

The power to make rules conferred by this section shall include the power to give retrospective effect to the rules or any of them from a date not earlier than the date on which the provisions of this Act come into force.

Section 165: Power to make regulations: The Board may, by notification, make regulations consistent with this Act and the rules made thereunder to carry out the provisions of this Act.

Recommendation of the GST Council is not called for in this case.

Section 166: Laying of rules, regulations and notifications: Every rule made by the Government, every regulation made by the Board and every notification issued by the Government under this Act, shall be laid, as soon as may be after it is made or issued, before each House of Parliament, while it is in session, for a total period of thirty days which may be comprised in one session or in two or more successive sessions, and if, before the expiry of the session immediately following the session or the successive sessions aforesaid, both Houses agree in making any modification in the rule or regulation or in the notification, as the case may be, or both Houses agree that the rule or regulation or the notification should not be made, the rule or regulation or notification, as the case may be, shall thereafter have effect only in such modified form or be of no effect, as the case may be; so, however, that any such modification or annulment shall be without prejudice to the validity of anything previously done under that rule or regulation or notification, as the case may be.

Section 167: Delegation of Powers: The Commissioner may, by notification, direct that subject to such conditions, if any, as may be specified in the notification, any power exercisable by any authority or officer under this Act may be exercisable also by another authority or officer as may be specified in such notification.

Section 168: Power to issue instructions or directions: It is the Competent Authority who is empowered to issue the orders, instruction or directions. The purpose is to bring in uniformity in the implementation of the Act; and it is binding on all GST officers.

Sub-section (2) of section 168 designates the Commissioner or Joint Secretary posted in the Board for exercising certain powers conferred under specific provisions. Such powers would be exercised with the approval of the Board.

Section 168A: Power of Government to extend time limit in special circumstances: This section was inserted to empower vide Taxation and Other Laws (Relaxation of Certain Provisions) Ordinance, 2020 to empower the Government to extend the time limit, in respect of actions which could not be completed due to force majeure, namely, war, epidemic, flood, drought, etc. or any other calamity caused by nature affecting the implementations of provisions of CGST Act, 2017.

Section 169: Service of notice in certain circumstances: Any decision, order, summons, notice or other communication under the Act or the rules, must be communicated to the intended notice receiver by way of 'service of notice'.

The mode of communication can be through physical delivery, regd. post/speed post or courier with acknowledgement, electronic means or publication in a newspaper.

Section 170: Rounding off of tax, etc.: The amount of tax, interest, penalty, fine or any other sum payable, and the amount of refund or any other sum due, under the provisions of this Act shall be rounded off to the nearest rupee and, for this purpose, where such amount contains a part of a rupee consisting of paise, then, if such part is fifty paise or more, it shall be increased to one rupee and if such part is less than fifty paise it shall be ignored.

Section 171: Anti-profiteering measure: The National Anti-profiteering Authority (NAA) was set up in November 2017 under Section 171 of the CGST Act to check unfair profiteering activities by registered suppliers.

The National Anti-profiteering Authority (NAA) is the statutory mechanism under GST Law to check the unfair profiteering activities by the registered suppliers under GST Law. The Authority's core function is to ensure that the commensurate benefits of the reduction in GST rates on goods and services done by the GST Council and of the Input tax credit are passed on to the recipients by way of commensurate reduction in the prices by the suppliers.

Initially, NAA was set up for two years until 2019, but it was later extended until November 2021. The GST Council, in its 45th meeting in September 2021, gave another one-year extension until November 30, 2022, to NAA and also decided to shift the work to CCI after that.

The CBIC vide Notification No. 23/2022-Central Tax dated 23rd Nov 2022 has empower the Competition Commission of India (CCI) to handle anti-profiteering cases under CGST Act, 2017 with effect from December 1, 2022.

Section 172: Removal of difficulties: The responsibility to implement the legislations is that of the appropriate Government.

The Government has powers to issue a general or special order in consistent with the provisions of the Act to remove difficulty in implementation of any provision of the Act.

The maximum time limit for passing such order shall be five years from the date of implementation of the CGST Act.

Section 173: Amendment of Act 32 of 1994: Save as otherwise provided in this Act, Chapter V of the Finance Act, 1994 shall be omitted.

Section 174: Repeal and saving: Whenever an enactment is repealed or substituted by a new enactment, the new enactment should provide for a clause relating to repeal or saving of certain provisions under the old law.

This would ensure that the rights, powers, liabilities, duties, privileges, obligations, etc. created under the old laws are intact and are not affected by the enactment of new law by repealing the old laws.

Repeal means not omission, rather restricted application. It shall apply to the extent applicable. For example, VAT/CST laws and Central Excise Act, 1944 and Central Excise Tariff Act, 1985 would continue to operate in respect of Certain petroleum products (i.e. HSD, petrol, ATF, crude oil) & tobacco products which are outside the ambit of GST.

Saving of erstwhile law means assessment & proceedings initiated under earlier laws shall continue.

Chapter 27

Job Work Provision

27.1 Statutory provision

Section 143 of the CGST Act, 2017 deals with job work procedure. The principal may under intimation send any inputs, semi-finished goods or capital goods, without payment of tax, to a job worker for job work and from there subsequently send to another job worker and likewise.

The principal is required to file Form GST ITC-04 by the 25th day of the month succeeding the quarter. The said form will serve as intimation as envisaged under section 143 of the CGST Act, 2017.

As per third proviso to Rule 138 of the CGST Rules, 2017 it is compulsory where principal and job worker are situated inter-state, then in case of job work transactions, e-way bill must be generated for inter-state movement of goods without any monetary limit.

As per Section 19(2) and 19(5) of CGST Act, 2017, the principal can also send goods directly to the place of job worker without receiving the said goods in his premises first and Input Tax Credit can also be availed in such cases though the principal has not received the goods.

Definition: As per Section 2(68) of CGST Act, 2017, "job work" means any treatment or process undertaken by a person on goods belonging to another registered person and the expression "job worker" shall be construed accordingly.

Analysis of Definition: Following can be interpreted from the definition:

(a) there must be at least two persons;
(b) The goods should belong to another registered person;
(c) Treatment or process to be undertaken on the said goods shall be by the job worker, whether registered or not.

Therefore, if some treatment or process is undertaken by a job worker on goods belonging to an unregistered person, it will not be considered as job work under GST and it shall be merely treated as work.

What is treatment or process?

The treatment or process involves various operations on goods belonging to others.

(1) Processing of inputs to make final product (contract manufacturing)
(2) Packing, labelling, testing & inspection of goods of another person
(3) Repair & maintenance work, tailoring, milling, bus body building, jewelry making, etc.
(4) Food processing, chemical processing, etc.
(5) Processing of hides, skins and leather, etc.

27.2 NATURE OF SUPPLY

As per Entry 3 to Schedule II, any treatment or process which is applied to another person's goods is a supply of services. So, job work is a "service".

As per explanation (ii) to section 22 of CGST Act, 2017 the value of the goods supplied by the principal shall not be included in the aggregate turnover of the registered job worker. So, to determine the value of job work charges, value of goods sent by the principal shall not be included.

Sending goods for job work is not a supply as such, but it acquires the character of supply only when the inputs/capital goods sent for job work are neither received back by the principal nor supplied further by the principal from the place of business/premises of the job worker within the stipulated period of being sent out.

Supply of goods by the principal from the place of business/premises of the job worker will be regarded as supply by the principal and not by the job worker.

27.3 SCOPE/AMBIT OF JOB WORK

The job worker is expected to work on the goods sent by the principal only. In addition to the goods received from the principal, the job worker can use his own goods for providing the services of job work.

After completion of the job work, the job worker shall return the said goods to the principal's premises under delivery challan and prepare his invoice for job work charges. In case where inputs, semi-finished goods and capital goods are not returned to the principal within prescribed time limit, the same will be treated as supply of the principal. (Refer Circular No. 38/12/2018-Central Tax dated 26th March 2018).

Goods can be supplied directly to the customer from the place of job worker, only if the job worker is a registered person or the place of job work is declared as "additional place of business" by the principal in his certificate of registration.

27.4 REGISTRATION

A job worker is required to obtain registration under GST where his aggregate turnover, to be computed on all India basis, in a financial year exceeds the threshold limit regardless of whether the principal and the job worker are located in the same State or in different States.

As per explanation (ii) to section 22 of CGST Act, 2017 for computing aggregate turnover of the job worker, the value of goods supplied by the principal shall not be included.

Responsibility of keeping proper accounts of the inputs and capital goods sent for job work lies with the principal.

27.5 DOCUMENTS REQUIRED FOR SENDING GOODS TO JOB WORKER

(i) By principal to the job worker: The principal shall prepare Delivery Challan in triplicate, two copies of which may be sent to the job worker along with goods. The job worker should send one copy of the said challan along with the goods, while returning them to the principal.

(ii) From one job worker to another job worker: Goods may move under the cover of a challan issued either by the principal or the job worker. Alternatively, the challan issued by the principal may be endorsed by the job worker indicating the quantity and description of goods being sent.

(iii) From the job worker back to the principal: The job worker should send one copy of the challan received by him from the principal.

(iv) In piecemeal by the job worker: The challan issued originally by the principal cannot be endorsed and a fresh challan is required to be issued by the job worker.

As per third proviso to Rule 138 of the CGST Rules, 2017 it is compulsory to generate e-way bill for inter-state movement of goods without any monetary limit, where the principal and job worker are situated in two different states.

27.6 PLACE OF SUPPLY

Place of supply for job work charges shall be govern by section 12 (2) of IGST Act, 2017.

(i) If the principal (supplier of the goods) and recipient (buyer of the goods) are in the same State, then

SGST and CGST shall be levied, though the job worker is in different State.

(ii) If the principal and recipient are in different States, then IGST shall be levied, even though the recipient is in the State where the job worker is situated.

27.7 CLARIFICATION ISSUED BY CENTRAL GOVERNMENT ON JOB WORK

The Central Government *vide Circular No. 38/12/2018-Central Tax dated 26th March 2018* has clarified various issues related to job work, which are as follows:

(1) The registered principal may, without payment of tax, send inputs or capital goods to a job worker for job work and on completion of the job work, the principal shall either bring back the goods to his place of business or supply (including export) the same directly from the place of business/premises of the job worker within one year in case of inputs or within three years in case of capital goods. In case of moulds, dies, jigs and fixtures or tools, no time limit prescribed for return of the same.

As per CGST Amendment Act, 2018, w.e.f. 1st Feb 2019, the commissioner has been empowered to extend the time limit of one year to additional one year (for inputs) & additional period of two years (for capital goods).

(2) Movement of goods from the principal to the job worker and the documents and intimation required therefor:

The following is clarified with respect to the issuance of challan, furnishing of intimation and other documentary requirements in this regard:

(i) Where goods are sent by principal to only one job worker: The principal shall prepare in triplicate, the challan in terms of rules 45 and 55 of the CGST Rules, for sending the goods to a job worker. Two copies of the challan may be sent to the job worker along with the goods. The job worker should send one copy of the said challan along with the goods, while returning them to the principal. The FORM GST ITC-04 will serve as the intimation as envisaged under section 143 of the CGST Act, 2017.

(ii) Where goods are sent from one job worker to another job worker: In such cases, the goods may move under the cover of a challan issued either by the principal or the job worker. In the alternative, the challan issued by the principal may be endorsed by the job worker sending the goods to another job worker, indicating therein the quantity and description of goods being sent. The same process may be repeated for subsequent movement of the goods to other job workers.

(iii) Where the goods are returned to the principal by the job worker: The job worker should send one copy of the challan received by him from the principal while returning the goods to the principal after carrying out the job work.

(iv) Where the goods are sent directly by the supplier to the job worker: In this case, the goods may move from the place of business of the supplier to the place of business/premises of the job worker with a copy of the invoice issued by the supplier in the name of the buyer (i.e. the principal) wherein the job worker's name and address should also be mentioned as the consignee, in terms of Rule 46(o) of the CGST Rules. The buyer (i.e., the principal) shall issue the challan under rule 45 of the CGST Rules and send the same to the job worker directly in terms of para (i) above. In case of import of goods by the principal which are then supplied directly from the customs station of import, the goods may move from the customs station of import to the place of business/ premises of the job worker with a copy of the Bill of Entry and the principal shall issue the challan under rule 45 of the CGST Rules and send the same to the job worker directly.

(v) Where goods are returned in piecemeal by the job worker: In case the goods after carrying out the job work, are sent in piecemeal quantities by a job worker to another job worker or to the principal, the challan issued originally by the principal cannot be endorsed and a fresh challan is required to be issued by the job worker.

(vi) Submission of intimation: Rule 45(3) of the CGST Rules provides that the principal is required to furnish the details of challans in respect of goods sent to a job worker or received from a job worker or sent from one job worker to another job worker during a quarter in FORM GST ITC-04 by the 25th day of the month succeeding the quarter or within such period as may be extended by the Commissioner. It is clarified that it is the responsibility of the principal to include the details of all the challans relating to goods sent by him to one or more job worker or from one job worker to another and its return therefrom. The FORM GST ITC-04 will serve as the intimation as envisaged under section 143 of the CGST Act.

(3) Issue of invoice, determination of place of supply and payment of GST:

Following is clarified with respect to the issuance of an invoice, time of supply and value of supply:

(i) Supply of job work services: The job worker, as a supplier of services, is liable to pay GST on the value of supply of such service, if he is liable to be registered. The value of moulds and dies, jigs and fixtures or tools may not be included in the value of job work services provided its value have been factored in the price for the supply of such services by the job worker.

Comment: *The reference here to section 15(2)(b) implies that only if the job-workers was required to provide the moulds but provided by the Principal, then the value of moulds should be included in the value of job-work charges. But, if almost all cases, the Principal provides the moulds not as an option but as an obligation to ensure that the job-worker is not burdened with the responsibility of making the moulds. Providing the mould is not* *a 'liability of job-worker met by Principal'. As such, GST is applicable on the 'transaction value'. Inclusion of value of capital goods or inputs provided as 'free issue' material to the job-work does not requires to be included the value of job-work charges. Please see previous comment about 'sending moulds not being supply'. When it is not a supply, it cannot be included in the value.*

(ii) Supply of goods by the principal from the place of business/premises of job worker: Section 143 of the CGST Act provides that the principal may supply, from the place of business/premises of a job worker after completion of job work or otherwise. Since the supply is being made by the principal, it is clarified that the time, value and place of supply would have to be determined in the hands of the principal irrespective of the location of the job worker's place of business/premises. Further, the invoice would have to be issued by the principal. It is also clarified that in case of exports directly from the job worker's place of business/premises, the LUT or bond, as the case may be, shall be executed by the principal.

Illustration: The principal is located in State A, the job worker in State B and the recipient in State C. In case the supply is made from the job worker's place of business/premises, the invoice will be issued by the supplier (principal) located in State A to the recipient located in State C. The said transaction will be an inter-State supply. In case the recipient is also located in State A, it will be an intra-State supply.

Comment: *In the above illustration, it does not clearly mention that the Principal who desires to make direct supplies from the premises of job worker (State B) will be required to register in State B to be compliant with proviso to section 143(1). Care should to taken that each State is a distinct jurisdiction for purposes of section 22 of CGST Act regarding registration.*

(iii) Supply of waste and scrap generated during the job work: Section 143(5) of the CGST Act provides that the waste and scrap generated during the job work may be supplied by the registered job worker directly from his place of business or by the principal in case the job worker is not registered. The principles enunciated in Para (ii) above would apply mutatis mutandis in this case.

(4) **Violation of conditions laid down in section 143:** If the inputs or capital goods are neither returned nor supplied from the job worker's place of business/premises within the specified time period, the principal would issue an invoice for the same and declare such supplies in his return for that particular month in which the time period of one year/three years has expired. The date of supply shall be the date on which such inputs or capital goods were initially sent to the job worker and interest for the intervening period shall also be payable on the tax. If such goods are returned by the job worker after the stipulated time period, the same would be treated as a supply by the job worker to the principal and the job worker would be liable to pay GST if he is liable for registration in accordance with the provisions contained in the CGST 11 Act read with the rules made thereunder.

(5) **Availability of input tax credit to the principal and job worker:** According to Section 19(2) of CGST Act, input tax credit would be available to the principal, irrespective of the fact whether the inputs or capital goods are received by the principal and then sent to the job worker for processing, etc. or whether they are directly received at the job worker's place of business/premises, without being brought to the premises of the principal. The job worker is also eligible to avail ITC on inputs, etc. used by him in supplying the job work services if he is registered.

(6) Transitional provisions relating to job work: According to Section 141 of CGST Act, if any inputs/semi-finished goods/excisable goods sent for job work prior to 01/07/2017 for the purpose of further processing, testing and reconditioning, etc., no tax shall be payable if goods returned within six months from 01/07/2017. The period may be extended by two months by the commissioner, if further sufficient cause may be shown.

If not returned with in the period specified, the ITC can be recovered in accordance with section 142(8) (a) of CGST Act, which is as follows:

(i) ITC recovered through assessments/proceedings under earlier law (pre-GST) (e.g.: Excise)
(ii) Where not recovered under (i), ITC would be recovered as arrears under GST Law.

According to Section 141(4) of CGST Act, the principal and job worker should submit a declaration electronically in form TRAN-01 specifying the goods held in stock at job worker premises.

27.8 RATES OF GST ON JOB WORK

CGST rates for job work is as follows:

(i) CGST @2.5% in case of services by way of job work relating to:

(a) Printing of newspapers
(b) Textiles and textile products falling under Chapters 50 to 63 in the First Schedule to the Customs Tariff Act, 1975 (51of 1975)

(c) All products falling under Chapter 71 in the First Schedule to the Customs Tariff Act, 1975
(d) Printing of books (including braille books), journals and periodicals
(e) Printing of all goods falling under Chapter 48 or 49, which attract CGST @2.5% or nil
(f) Processing of hides, skins and leather falling under Chapter 41 in the First Schedule to the Customs Tariff Act, 1975
(g) manufacture of leather goods or foot wear falling under Chapter 42 or 64 in the First Schedule to the Customs Tariff Act, 1975 (51of 1975) respectively
(h) All food and food products falling under Chapters 1 to 22 in the First Schedule to the Customs Tariff Act, 1975
(i) All products falling under Chapter 23 in the First Schedule to the Customs Tariff Act, 1975 except dog and cat food put up for retail sale falling under tariff item 23091000 of the said Chapter
(j) Manufacture of clay bricks falling under tariff item 69010010 in the First Schedule to the Customs Tariff Act, 1975 (51of 1975)
(k) Tailoring services.

(ii) CGST @6% in case Services by way of job work in relation to:
(a) manufacture of umbrella;
(b) printing of all goods falling under Chapter 48 or 49, which attract CGST @6%.

(iii) CGST @ 0.75% in case of services by way of job work in relation to diamonds falling under chapter 71 in the First Schedule to the Customs Tariff Act, 1975 (51of 1975)

(iv) CGST @ 9% on contract Manufacturing services to brand owners for manufacture of alcoholic liquor for human consumption [Circular 164/20/2021 dated 06-10-2021]

(v) CGST @ 9% on contract Manufacturing services on physical inputs (goods) owned by others, other than above.

Notifications Issued Under CGST
(1) Notification No. 11/2017-Central Tax (Rate) dated June 28, 2017;
(2) Notification No. 20/2017-Central Tax (Rate) dated August 22, 2017;
(3) Notification No. 31/2017-Central Tax (Rate) dated October 13, 2017;
(4) Notification No. 46/2017-Central Tax (Rate) dated November 14, 2017;
(5) Notification No. 1/2018-Central Tax (Rate) dated January 25, 2018;
(6) Notification No. 20/2019-Central Tax (Rate) dated 30.09.2019;
(7) Notification No. 26/2019-Central Tax (Rate) dt. 22.11.2019.

Chapter 28

Works Contract Provision

28.1 INTRODUCTION

A works contract is basically a "composite supply" involving supply of both goods & services in the execution of a contract entered into between parties. A contract of works, may relate to both movable and immovable properties. For example, construction of road, bridge, tunnel, building and supply & installation of Plant & Machineries when affixed permanently on earth is a works contract in relation to immovable property. Similarly, repair & maintenance of P&M, vehicles, office equipment, fabrication, supply & installation of equipment, etc. which involves element of both goods & services is a works contracts in relation to immovable properties.

Under GST Law, the definition of "works contract" has been restricted to any work undertaken for an "immovable property" only. Turnkey or other contracts for supply & installation of Plant & Machinery, supply of pre-fabricated building, etc. which do not result in creation of immovable property would plausibly be treated as "composite supplies" but not works contract and depending on the principal supply, tax liability would be determine as per Section 8(a) of the CGST Act, either as a supply of goods or services. Composite supply relating to immovable property only treated as "works contract" under GST Law. As per Para 6(a) of Schedule II to the CGST Act, 2017, works contract as defined in section 2(119) of the CGST Act, 2017 shall be treated as supply of service. Therefore, any composite supply which is movable in nature is not covered under "works contract" in GST regime.

The GST law specifically provides that 'works contract' as well as 'construction of a complex or a building', civil structure or a part thereof shall be treated as supply of services as per Schedule II of the CGST Act. Under the previous indirect tax dispensation, there were issues in tax treatment of works contract. Both the Central Government (on the services component of a works contract) & the State Governments (on the sale of goods portion involved in the execution of a works contract) used to levy taxes. Thus, the same work was subject to taxation by both Central and State Government. GST aims to put at rest the controversy by defining what will constitute a works contract & by stating that a works contract will be treated as a supply of service and specifying a uniform rate of tax on same nature of "works contract" across India. Further, there is no concept of partial reverse charge on "works contract" in GST regime.

It is pertinent to mention that; all "works contracts" are composite supply but all composite supplies are not "works contract".

Example 1: Mr. X contracted a carpenter to make a dining set, consisting of one table and four chairs. The carpenter supplied goods like teak wood, ply, nails, fevicol, color and labor services too and made the dining set. Is it "works contracts" or "composite supply"?

Answer. The final product is dining set (furniture), which is a movable property. Therefore, it will be considered as a "composite supply" rather than a works contract.

Example 2: Kolkata Municipal Corporation (KMC) awarded a contract to Mr. Shyam, for repair & maintenance of a road for ₹ 25 lakhs. The work involves preparation of surface, sand filling & bitumen carpeting through deployment of labour. Is it "works contracts" or "composite supply"?

Answer. The repair & maintenance of road involves materials & labour. Therefore, it is a "composite supply". Since the composite supply is relate to construction/repair & maintenance of immovable property, i.e. road, it is "works contract" and squarely covered within the scope of Section 2(119) of CGST Act. Further, as per Para 6(a) of Schedule II to the CGST Act, 2017 all "works contract" are services. Therefore, a supply to qualify as works contract, it must be a "composite supply".

Example 3: M/s ABC Ltd. awarded a contract to M/s OTIS Elevator for supply & installation of a lift in its administrative building. The contract has four components namely, Supply of lift, installation, testing & commissioning. Is it "works contracts" or "composite supply"?

Answer. The subject work is a composite supply of goods & services involving supply of lift, installation, testing & commissioning. Since lift is affixed permanently on earth/building, it is immovable in nature. Therefore, it will cover within the definition of "works contract".

28.2 DEFINITION/STATUTORY PROVISION

Under GST Laws, the definition of "Works Contract" has been restricted to any composite supply made for an "Immovable Property" unlike the erstwhile VAT and Service Tax regime where composite supply for movable properties were also treated as "works contract".

As per Section 2(119) of the CGST Act, 2017 "works contract" means a contract for:

- building, construction,
- fabrication,
- completion, erection, installation,
- fitting out,
- improvement, modification,
- repair, maintenance, renovation,
- alteration or commissioning

of any immovable property wherein transfer of property in goods (whether as goods or in some other form) is involved in the execution of such contract.

Thus, from the above it can be seen that the term works contract has been restricted to contract for building, construction, fabrication, repair, maintenance, renovation, alteration or commissioning, etc. of any immovable property only. Any such composite supply undertaken on goods say for example a fabrication or paint job done in automotive body shop will not fall within the definition of term works contract per se under GST. Such contracts would continue to remain composite supplies, but will not be treated as a Works Contract for the purposes of GST.

As per Para 6 (a) of Schedule II to the CGST Act, 2017, works contracts as defined in section 2(119) of the CGST Act, 2017 shall be treated as a supply of services. Thus, there is a clear demarcation of a works contract as a supply of service under GST.

Difference between works contract & composite supply under GST

Ground of difference	Works contract	Composite supply
Nature of Supply	Immovable	Movable
Type of Supply	Services	Goods/Services
Definition	Defined in Section 2(119) of CGST Act	Defined in Section 2(30) of CGST Act
Rate of GST	Specific rate of GST applies to whole transaction value	GST rate of principle supply apply to whole transaction value
Maximum Rate of GST	18%	28%
Availability of ITC	Restriction applies. Available on plant & machineries, repair & maintenance of immovable properties (if the same not capitalised) and further supply of works contract service.	Available in all cases, except when depreciation claimed on GST component of Capital goods and subject to restriction u/s 17(5) of CGST Act.
Maintenance of accounts/records	Mandatory, as per Rule 56 (14) of the CGST Rules, 2017	Not mandatory in all cases
Time of Supply	Governed by Section 13 of CGST Act	Governed by either Section 12 or 13 of CGST Act, 2017 depending upon nature of supply.
Place of Supply	Generally, where the immovable property is located	Depends upon location of buyer & seller

28.3 VALUATION OF WORKS CONTRACT SERVICE

In terms of Section 15(1) of the CGST Act, value of taxable supply shall be the transaction value (which is the price paid or payable by the recipient) provided the supplier and recipient are not related parties and price is the sole consideration for the supply.

Therefore, transaction value agreed between the parties is only relevant for valuation purposes under GST. However, in terms of Section 15(2) (b) of the Act, if any amount which the supplier is liable to pay but the same has been incurred by the receiver of the supply, then the said amount has to be added while determining the transaction value.

Valuation of the services provided by a works contractor is the total consideration charged. In a case where the works contract includes the transfer of property in land or undivided share of land, as the case may be, the transaction value shall be calculated as follows:

Value of works contract = Total amount charged for such supply-(minus) value of land or undivided share of land.

Where:

(a) The total amount charged means sum of consideration charged for aforesaid service and amount charged for transfer of land or undivided share of land, as the case may be (total amount charged)

(b) value of land/undivided share of land is 1/3rd of the total amount charged for such supply.

Explanation: For the above purpose, "total amount" means the sum total of:

(a) consideration charged for aforesaid service; and

(b) amount charged for transfer of land or undivided share of land, as the case may be

Note 2 given under Notification 11/17-Central Tax (Rate) dated 28th June 2017 provides deduction of 33.33% towards cost of land.

28.4 TAXABILITY OF FREE OF COST (FOC) ISSUE OF MATERIALS BY CUSTOMER TO CONTRACTOR (SERVICE PROVIDER)

The supply of goods or services to an unrelated person without consideration, is not a supply as per Section 7 of CGST Act & consequently, GST shall not be applicable on such FOC (free of cost) issue of materials by customer to contractor. However, as per Section 15(2)(b), if supply was the obligation of supplier, but recipient has supply for whatever reason, even though it is supplied free of cost (FOC), it will be included in the value of supply & form part of transaction value for the purpose of levy of GST. So, commercial arrangement between the supplier and recipient of supply is the guiding factor to determine, whether free of cost (FOC) issue of materials by customer to contractor (service provider) for execution of works contract service will form part of transaction value or not. If a works contract is awarded for a price say, ₹ 20 crores and it is stated in the contract agreement that the price is excluding value of certain materials which is to be supplied by the customer and not within the scope of contractor, in such cases value of materials supplied free of cost (FOC) by the customer to the contractor for execution of said works contract will not form part of transaction value.

Example 1: M/s ABC Ltd. has awarded a contract to M/s Pave infrastructure for construction of a boundary wall. As per terms of contract, all materials required for said construction, such as cement, brick, sand, bricks, steel, etc. shall be supplied by M/s ABC Ltd. free of cost but labour, mason and tools & tackles etc. shall be supplied by M/s Pave infrastructure for execution of said contract. The contract price is ₹ 20 lakhs, which excludes cost of materials (₹ 8 lakhs) to be supplied by M/s ABC Ltd. Determine transaction value as per Section 15, for the purpose of levy of GST.

Answer. The subject work is a works contract service as it relates to construction of immovable property. The scope of supply between customer & service provider is clearly demarcated. The supply of material is not the obligation of M/s Pave infrastructure (contractor), so there is no requirement to add the value of such materials to contract price for determination of transaction value. The transaction value in the instant case shall be ₹ 20 lakhs. Materials supplied by M/s ABC Ltd. to M/s Pave Infra free of cost (FOC) shall not attract GST, since there is no consideration & they are not related parties.

Example 2: Whether supply of materials to contractor free of cost (FOC) for execution of works contract is part of taxable value/transaction value for the purpose of levy of GST?

Answer. As per Section 7(1), (c) read with Para 2 of Schedule I of the CGST Act, supplies between related persons or distinct persons in the course or furtherance of business is a supply even if made without consideration. However, free supplies between unrelated persons are not "supplies".

In terms of Section 15(2)(b), any amount that the supplier is liable to pay in relation to such supply but which has been incurred by the recipient of the supply and not included in the price actually paid or payable for the goods or services or both, it will be included with the value of supply.

Therefore, it depends upon commercial terms of contract as to whether cost of such materials supplied free of cost (FOC) to the contractor will form part of transaction value or not. If supply of materials was within the scope of contractor & contract price has been determined accordingly but for ease of execution of contract, the customer (contractee) has procured the materials & supplied free of cost to the contractor, the cost of such materials shall form part of transaction value for the purpose of levy of GST. The intention of the legislature is to include such amounts which are to be borne or agreed to be borne by the supplier and form a part of the consideration to be received by the supplier.

Suppose, as per terms of contract, supply of material was within the scope of contractee and the contract price agreed upon between the parties excludes cost of materials to be supplied by the contractee (customer). In such case, it will not form part of transaction value. Since contractor & contractee (recipient/customer) are unrelated person, supply of materials to contractor free of cost (FOC) for execution of works contract will not form part of taxable value/transaction value.

Example 3: M/s XYZ Ltd. (contractee) has awarded a contract for construction of a tunnel to M/s Starcon Infraprojects Ltd. (contractor) for ₹ 20 crores (excluding GST). As per terms of contract, the contractee shall supplies Cement to the contractor for execution of the works and the cost of cement so supplied shall be recovered from the bill of the contractor. The total value of cement supplied to the contractor for the said work is ₹ 4.5 crores excluding GST. Compute transaction value for the purpose of levy of GST?

Answer. Construction of a tunnel is a works contract service, since it relates to immovable property. As per terms of contract, M/s XYZ Ltd. (contractee) will recover the cost of material supplied to the contractor from bill payable to them for execution of works contract. Therefore, consideration is involved & it is a taxable supply. Supply of cement by contractee to the contractor is a separate trading transaction. M/s XYZ Ltd. will raise tax invoice on M/s Starcon Infraprojects Ltd. for cement supplied, for which transaction value shall be ₹ 4.5 crore and will attract GST @ 28% (i.e. rate of GST applicable on cement). M/s Starcon Infraprojects Ltd. (contractor) will raise tax invoice on M/s XYZ Ltd. (contractee) for works contract service provided, for which transaction value is ₹ 20 crore and charged GST @ 18% (i.e. rate of GST applicable on works contract service).

28.5 AVAILABILITY OF INPUT TAX CREDIT (ITC) ON WORKS CONTRACT SERVICE

Input tax credit means claiming the credit of GST paid on purchase of goods & services, which are used in providing outward supply in the course of or for furtherance of business. The works contractor shall be entitled to claim input tax credit under section 16 on all input and input services used in supply of works contract services. The only prohibition given is by way of block credits under section 17(5) (c) and (d) of CGST Act, which reads as follows:

(c) The works contract services when supplied for construction of an immovable property (other than plant and machinery) except where it is an input service for further supply of works contract service (e.g., a contractor receiving works contract services from sub-contractor, which is to be further supplied to client, i.e., contractee is eligible for ITC).

(d) Goods or services or both received by a taxable person for construction of an immovable property (other than plant and machinery) on his own account including when such goods or services or both are used in the course of furtherance of business.

Note: Restriction is there on input services and not on input.

As per Section 2(59), "input" means any goods other than capital goods used or intended to be used by a supplier in the course or furtherance of business.

As per Section 2(60), "input service" means any service used or intended to be used by a supplier in the course or furtherance of business.

The explanation under these clauses states that for the purpose of clauses (c) and (d) the expression 'construction' includes reconstruction, renovation, addition or alteration or repairs to the extent of capitalisation to the said immovable property.

As per section 17(5) (c) of the CGST Act, 2017, input tax credit shall be available in respect of "works contract" services in following two situations:

(1) Where works contract relates to plant and machinery, or

(2) Where such work contract is an input service for further supply of works contract service [main contractor can availed ITC of services received from sub-contractor in similar line of business].

Thus, ITC for works contract can be availed only by a registered person, who is in the same line of business and is using such services received for further supply of works contract service. For example, a building developer may sublet the whole work or engage a sub-contractor for certain portion of the work. The sub-contractor will charge GST in the tax invoice raised on the main contractor. The main contractor will be entitled to take ITC on the tax invoice raised by his subcontractor, as his output is works contract service. However, if the main contractor provides works contract service to a company, say in the manufacturing business, then ITC of GST paid on the invoice raised by the works contractor shall not be available to the manufacturing company. It is pertinent to mention that credit of GST paid on works contract services would be allowed only if the output supply is also works contract services However, this restriction does not apply to works contract service pertaining to supply & installation of plant and machinery.

As per section 17(5) (d) of the CGST Act, 2017, goods or services or both received by a taxable person for construction of an immovable property (other than plant or machinery) on his own account including when such goods or services or both are used in the course or furtherance of business. Inward supply of services from real estate agent, architect, interior decorators and contractors are all blocked as these are involved in the establishment of the immovable property for own use.

The expression 'plant and machinery' has been defined through explanation in Sec 17 of Chapter V of the CGST Act to mean apparatus, equipment, and machinery fixed to earth by foundation or structural support that are used for making outward supply of goods or services or both and includes such foundation and structural supports but excludes:

(i) Land, building or any other civil structures;
(ii) Telecommunication towers; and
(iii) Pipelines laid outside the factory premises

Plant and Machinery in certain cases when affixed permanently to the earth by foundation or structural support would constitute immovable property. When a works contract is for the construction of plant and machinery, the credit of GST paid to the works contractor would be available to the recipient, whatever is the business of the recipient, subject to the condition that depreciation is not claimed on GST amount capitalised with the cost of P&M in the books. This is because works contract in respect of plant and machinery comes within the exclusion clause of the negative list and ITC would be available when used in the course of or for furtherance of business.

As per explanation to Section 17(5) (d) of CGST Act, the expression "construction" includes re-construction, renovation, additions or alterations or repairs, to the extent of capitalization, to the said immovable property.

From above explanation, it can be infer that if any "construction work" is not capitalised in the books & charged to revenue/expenses, ITC will be available to recipient of such works contract service.

Example 1: M/s XYZ Ltd. is in the business of generation of Hydro-electricity. The company purchased cement, steels and other material for use in the construction of a dam for generation of electricity. Whether the company can claim ITC of GST paid on procurement of such construction materials?

Answer. Though the dam (immovable property) is used in the course or in furtherance of business, as per Section 17(5) (d) GST paid on inward supply of goods or services for 'own use' would not be eligible for input tax credit. Since dam is constructed for own use, though it is for furtherance of business, ITC not available.

Example 2: M/s ABC Ltd. purchased cement and steel for construction of pillars to prepare platform for installation of a DG Set in its office premises. Is ITC available on GST paid for procurement of such materials?

Answer. Yes, ITC available. Structural support for plant and machinery is included in the definition of plant and machinery.

Example 3: A company purchased building materials such as cement, steels, paints, etc. for repair & maintenance of its office building. Whether ITC available for GST paid on building materials?

Answer. Repair and maintenance of building is a works contract service. However, if the repair & maintenance work is treated as revenue expenditure & charged to P&L account, ITC available. If, capitalized in the books, ITC not available.

Example 4: M/s XYZ & Associates, a registered person under GST has awarded a contract for renovation & painting of its office building to a contractor for ₹ 6 lakhs with a completion schedule of two months. The work also involves partition of the building into different cabins & provisions of making new toilets for their staff. The contractor raised bill for ₹ 7.08 lakhs including GST & used SAC of works contract service in its invoice. Is M/s XYZ & Associates, eligible to claim ITC of ₹ 1.08 lakhs paid as GST on inward supply?

Answer. The term works contract as defined in Section 2(119) of CGST Act, 2017 covers improvement, modification, repair, maintenance & renovation of a building. Therefore, repairs and maintenance of immovable property is a works contract service. As per explanation to Section 17(5) (c), ITC on works contract is disallowed only when the works contract is capitalized in the books of recipient (other than P&M). Repair & maintenance of an immovable property is a "works contract" service but if the same is not capitalised in the books of recipient & charged to P&L A/c, ITC available.

Example 5: M/s NBCC Ltd. awarded a contract to M/s Ashoka Buildcon (contractor) for construction of a building for ₹ 80 crores in May 2022. For the purpose of execution of said work, the contractor purchased cement, steel, sand, aggregates, etc. The contractor also availed services of architect, interior designer, legal advices, etc. and paid fees to all of them against tax invoice. M/s Ashoka Buildcon (contractor) wants to know whether they are eligible to claim ITC on inwards supplies.

Answer. M/s Ashoka Buildcon (contractor) has purchased input & input services for construction of building. ITC can be claimed on GST paid on procurement of input (cement, steel, sand, aggregates, etc.) & input services (i.e. services of architect, interior designer, legal service) which are used for further supply of services to client.

28.6 CONDITIONS FOR CLAIMING ITC

A registered person shall be entitled to claim input tax credit only upon fulfilment of the following conditions [Section 16(2) of CGST Act].

(1) He is in possession of tax invoice/debit note issued by a registered supplier or any other tax paying documents.

(2) He has received the goods and/or services or both. In case of supply of goods in lots/instalments, the credit would be available in full on the receipt of the last lot/instalment.

(3) The tax charged on such supply is paid to the Government by the supplier (by way of cash or by utilizing input tax credit).

(4) He has furnished a valid return.

(5) He paid the Invoice amount to the supplier within 180 days from the date of issue of invoice.

28.7 REFUND OF UN-UTILISED ITC

Accumulation of Input Tax Credit happens when the tax paid on inputs is more than the output tax liability. As per Section 54(3) of the CGST Act, 2017, a registered person may claim refund of unutilised input tax credit at the end of any tax period.

Where the credit has accumulated on account of rate of tax on inputs being higher than the rate of tax on output supplies (other than nil rated or fully exempt supplies), except supplies of goods or services or both as may be notified by the Government on the recommendations of the Council, it is called inverted duty structure. In such cases also, refund can be applied under Section 54 of the CGST Act, 2017 read with Rule 89 of the CGST Rules, 2017.

The input & input services used in the execution of works contract such cement, steel, marble, tiles, misc. construction materials, construction equipment & inward services attract either 28% or 18% GST. However, the maximum rate of GST on works contract service is 18% and in some cases, it is 5% or 12%. This will lead to accumulation of ITC because of inverted duty structure. Though ITC on account of inverted duty structure on input is available for refund, there is no refund u/s 54(3) of any input tax credit accumulated due to inverted duty structure, in case of supply of construction services specified under item 5(b) of Schedule II of CGST Act. [Ref: Notification no. 15/2017-Central Tax (Rate) dated 28th June 2017].

28.8 TIME OF SUPPLY OF "WORKS CONTRACT"

There is no separate provision in GST laws for determination of time of supply (point of taxation) of "works contract". As per Para 6 (a) of Schedule II to the CGST Act, 2017, works contracts as defined in section 2(119) of the CGST Act, 2017 shall be treated as a supply of services. Therefore, time of supply provision of services shall be made applicable to "works contract" services.

Section 13 of CGST Act, 2017 stipulate the provisions relating to determination of time of supply of services. As per Section 13(2), Supply of services on which supplier is liable to pay GST, time of supply of services depends upon whether invoice is issued within prescribed time or not.

Situations	Time of Supply of Service
Invoice is issued within prescribed time	Time of supply of service is earlier of (a) Date of Invoice (b) Date of receipt of payment
Invoice is not issued within prescribed time	Time of supply of service is earlier of (a) Date of providing service (b) Date of receipt of payment
Other cases (where invoice not to be issued)	Time of supply is Date of receipt of service in the books of account of recipient

Where the execution of the works contract goes beyond three months with periodic payment obligation for the recipient, it will be treated as continuous supply of service [Section 2(33)] and invoicing will have to be done as per Section 31(5) of CGST Act, 2017.

Due date of payment	Date of invoice
Ascertainable from the contract	On or before the due date of payment (as per the contract terms)
Not ascertainable from the contract	Before or at the time of receipt of the payment
Linked to completion of an event	On or before the date of completion of that event

Further, as per section 31(6) of the CGST Act, 2017, in case where the supply of services ceases under a contract before the completion of the supply, the invoice shall be issued at the time when the supply ceases and such invoice shall be issued to the extent of the supply made before such cessation.

28.9 PLACE OF SUPPLY IN RESPECT OF "WORKS CONTRACT"

The place of supply provisions determines the place, i.e., taxable jurisdiction where the tax should reach. Under the GST Law, the place of supply of services in relation to immovable property is location of the immovable property. Works Contract under GST would necessarily involve immovable property. In view of the same, the place of supply would be governed by Section 12(3) of the IGST Act, 2017. Where both the supplier and recipient are located in India, the place of supply would be where the immovable property is located.

In case the immovable property is located outside India, and the supplier as well as recipient both are located in India, the place of supply would be the location of recipient as per proviso to Section 12(3) of the IGST Act, 2017.

As per Section 13(4) of the IGST Act, 2017, in cases where either the Supplier or the Recipient are located outside India, the place of supply shall be the place where the immovable property is located or intended to be located.

In some cases, the immovable property may be located in more than one State, e.g. highway construction services, railway track laying project, etc. Such a contract may involve execution of work across multiple states. In such cases, the place of supply would be each such State where the immovable property is located and hence, there may be a requirement for the vendor to raise separate invoices for the same project.

Example 1: M/s IVRCL Infrastructure Ltd. registered in Andhra Pradesh was awarded works contract by Kolkata Municipal Corporation (West Bengal) for construction of Bridge near Howrah situated in Kolkata. The place of supply of services is Kolkata (West Bengal) and M/s IVRCL Infrastructure Ltd. need to get GST registration in West Bengal.

Example 2: M/s Sunflag Iron & Steel Ltd. (Odisha) asks M/s Everest Constructions registered in West Bengal to build a blast furnace in their Odisha steel plant

Place of supply: Odisha,

GST Payable: CGST & SGST

Although M/s Everest construction is located & registered in West Bengal, the goods/P&M (blast furnace) is being installed at site in Odisha, which will be the place of supply. This is a works contract service covered u/s 2(119) of CGST Act.

Note: M/s Everest Constructions will have to be registered in Odisha to take up this contract, if they have any office/establishment in the State of Odisha. They can opt to register as a casual taxable person, which will be valid for 90 days (extendable by 90 days more, based on a reasonable cause).

28.10 MAINTENANCE OF ACCOUNTS/RECORDS

As per Rule 56 (14) of the CGST Rules, 2017, every registered person executing works contract shall keep separate accounts for works contract showing:

(a) the names and addresses of the persons on whose behalf the works contract is executed;
(b) description, value and quantity (wherever applicable) of goods or services received for the execution of works contract;
(c) description, value and quantity (wherever applicable) of goods or services utilized in the execution of works contract;
(d) the details of payment received in respect of each works contract; and
(e) the names and addresses of suppliers from whom he received goods or services.

28.11 TAXABILITY OF LIQUIDATED DAMAGES/PENALTY LEVIED FOR NON-PERFORMANCE OF WORKS CONTRACT

As per Para 5(d) of Schedule II to the CGST Act, 2017 the activity of 'agreeing to the obligation to refrain from an act, or to tolerate an act or a situation, or to do an act' as a supply of service. Liquidated damages/penalty payable to Government for tolerating non-performance of contract is exempted from GST, as per Entry No. 62 of Notification No. 12/2017-Central Tax (Rate) dated 28.06.2017.

In other cases, i.e. liquidated damages/penalty levied by non-Government entity, unless there is no agreement, express or implied, by the aggrieved party receiving the liquidated damages, to refrain from or tolerate an act or to do anything for the party paying the liquidated damages for tolerating non-performance of contract, it is not taxable.

The CBIC has clarified that amount received in lieu of liquidated damages/penalty for breach of contract is not a consideration for supply of any goods or services, unless there is a separate agreement between the parties to receive/pay consideration to refrain from or tolerate an act for breach of contract. It is a mere flow of money from the party who causes breach of the contract to the party who suffers loss or damage due to such non-performance of contract. Such payments do not constitute consideration for a supply and are not taxable.

[Circular No. 178/10/2022-GST dated 3rd August 2022]

28.12 REGISTRATION REQUIREMENT FOR PROVIDING WORKS CONTRACT

The registration under GST is PAN based and State specific. Every taxable person (subject to threshold limit) is required to obtain a PAN-based registration in each of such State or Union territory from where he effects taxable supply. In GST registration, the supplier is allotted a unique 15-digit alphanumeric number called "GSTIN" (GST Identification Number) begin with state code. Without registration, a person can neither collect tax from his customers nor claim any input Tax Credit of tax paid by him.

As per Section 22(1), every supplier shall be liable to be registered under GST, "in" the State or Union territory, from where he makes taxable supply of goods or services or both, if his aggregate turnover in a FY exceeds threshold limit. In case of inter-state supply of goods (except handicraft goods/goods sent for job work), registration is mandatory irrespective of threshold limit, whereas in case of inter-state supply of services, registration is mandatory if the turnover in a FY exceeds ₹ 20 lakhs (₹ 10 lakhs in case of special category states). It is pertinent to mention that registration under GST is required 'in' the State 'from which' taxable supplies are made.

Therefore, for the purposes of obtaining registration, it is important to identify the 'origin' of supply even though GST is a 'destination' based tax. Tax goes to the destination State but registration is required in the origin-State. In case of "works contract" service which is immovable in nature, place of supply is where the immovable property is located. Place of supply (as determined from IGST Act) provides the 'destination' and this is not relevant for registration. The location of supplier is relevant for registration.

Therefore, a taxable person who is providing works contract service shall be required to obtain registration in the state from where he is providing services.

As per Section 2(71) "location of the supplier of services" means,

(a) where a supply is made from a place of business for which the registration has been obtained, the location of such place of business;
(b) where a supply is made from a place other than the place of business for which registration has been obtained (a fixed establishment elsewhere), the location of such fixed establishment;
(c) where a supply is made from more than one establishment, whether the place of business or fixed establishment, the location of the establishment most directly concerned with the provisions of the supply; and
(d) in absence of such places, the location of the usual place of residence of the supplier.

As per Section 2(50), "fixed establishment" means a place (other than the registered place of business) which is characterized by a sufficient degree of permanence and suitable structure in terms of human and technical resources to supply services, or to receive and use services for its own needs.

Example 1: A service provider in the business of renting of immovable property has its registered office at Delhi (place of business). The property for rent along with an office is located in Mumbai (place of supply). In this case, the registered office will be the principal place of business but the property in Mumbai will NOT be regarded as a fixed establishment of the service provider as the degree of permanence required in representing the interests of the supplier does not exist in Mumbai. Registration under GST is required in Delhi & not in Maharashtra.

Example 2: A contract is for supply, installation, testing & commissioning of firefighting system where the duration of installation work at the site is (say) three months, at Chamba, HP. The fabrication of equipment is undertaken at the factory at Kolkata and the material is transported to the site (Chamba, HP) and engineers and technical teams are deputed for installation, testing & commissioning. For the limited duration of three months, the installation team will be present at the site office, i.e. Chamba, HP. In this case, the factory will be the principal place of business (Kolkata) but the site (Chamba, HP) will NOT be regarded as a fixed establishment of the supplier. Registration under GST is required in West Bengal and not in Himachal Pradesh.

Example 3: M/s GE Electricals Ltd., a company registered in Mumbai is engaged in the business of Supply, installation, testing and commissioning of Switch yard equipment for power station across the country, is registered under GST in the State of Maharashtra. The company was awarded a contract of ₹ 20 crores by M/s NHPC Ltd. for construction of Switch yard systems for one of its power plants located in the state of Himachal Pradesh. The company (GE Electrical) supply the materials/equipment from their Mumbai factory & depute their technical staff and engineers to HP for a period of six months, for installation, testing & commissioning of the work. Is M/s GE Electricals Ltd. is required to obtained registration under GST in the state of Himachal Pradesh.

Answer. The activity of Supply, installation, testing & commissioning of Switch yard equipment is a composite supply. Since the switch yard equipment are affixed permanently on earth, it is a works contract in relation to immovable property and squarely covered under Section 2(119) of CGST Act. Further, as per Para 6(a) of Schedule II to the CGST Act, 2017, works contract as defined in Section 2(119) of the CGST Act, 2017 are treated as supply of service. In case of supply of service related to immovable property, location of supply is where immovable property is located. As per Sec 22(1), registration is required in the state from which taxable supply is made. Since the company is making supply of works contract service from Mumbai, registration in Maharashtra is required. Further, since M/s GE Electricals Ltd. does not have fixed place of business/establishment in the state of Himachal Pradesh (HP), registration under GST in the state of HP is not required. This view has also been upheld by Authority of Advance Ruling (AAR, Rajasthan) in their Order No. Raj/AAR/2018-19/07 dated 01-07-2018 in the matter of M/s Jaimin Engineering Pvt. Ltd.

Example 4: Mr X, a registered person who is engaged in renting of commercial property is having principal place of business in Kolkata but few commercial properties are also located in Delhi, which is let out. Is Mr X required to obtain registration under GST in Delhi.

Answer. Since the principal place of business is located in Kolkata from where service is provided, registration under GST is required in Kolkata (West Bengal). Registration under GST in Delhi shall be required, if Mr X has any fixed establishment/place of business in Delhi. Mere location of the property in Delhi shall not be treated as fixed place of business, though place of supply of service is Delhi being immovable property.

Example 5: M/s Lanco Infratech Ltd. (contractee), having its corporate office in Mumbai awarded a contract to M/s Gammon Infra Ltd. Hyderabad (contractor) for construction of a dam in the state of Sikkim. M/s Gammon Infra Ltd. is registered under GST in the state of Telangana. The duration of the contract is for three years. Is M/s Gammon Infra Ltd. (contractor) required to obtain registration under GST in the state of Sikkim?

Answer. As per Section 22(1) of CGST Act, registration under GST is required 'in' the State 'from which' taxable supplies are made. Construction of dam is a "works contract" service being immovable in nature and place of supply is Sikkim where the immovable property is located. For the purpose of construction of dam, huge quantity of steel, cement, sand, aggregates, other construction materials & engineer, technician, labour are required. The nature of supply & duration of contract is such that, it cannot be supplied from Hyderabad, Telangana. Therefore, a fixed establishment is required in the State of Sikkim, where the work is being carried out. Therefore, registration under GST is mandatory for M/s Gammon Infra Ltd. in the state of Sikkim.

28.13 RATE OF GST ON WORKS CONTRACT SERVICE

Works contract services are taxable @1.5%, 5%, 7.5%, 12% or 18% depending upon the nature of works contract.

Detailed guideline regarding applicability of GST on Real Estate Project (REP) has been provided in Notification No. 03/2019-Central Tax (Rate) dated 29.03.2019.

The rate of GST for works Contract service have been prescribed in Sl. No. 3 of Notification No. 11/2017-Central Tax (Rate) dated 28.06.2017 as amended from time to time through various notifications mentioned here under.

(1) Notification No. 20/2017-Central Tax (Rate) dated 22.08.2017
(2) Notification No. 24/2017-Central Tax (Rate) dated 21.09.2017
(3) Notification No. 31/2017-Central Tax (Rate) dated 13.10.2017
(4) Notification No. 46/2017-Central Tax (Rate) dated 14.11.2017
(5) Notification No. 01/2018-Central Tax (Rate) dated 25.01.2018
(6) Notification No. 03/2019-Central Tax (Rate) dated 29.03.2019
(7) Notification No. 06/2021-Central Tax (Rate) dated 30.09.2021
(8) Notification No. 22/2021-Central Tax (Rate) dated 31.12.2021
(9) Notification No. 03/2022-Central Tax (Rate) dated 13.07.2022

Sl No.	Description of Services	Rate of GST (CGST+SGST)	Remarks
(i)	Construction of affordable residential apartments by a promoter in a Residential Real Estate Project (herein after referred to as RREP) which commences on or after 1st April 2019 or in an ongoing RREP in respect of which the promoter has not exercised option to pay central tax on construction of apartments at the rates as specified for item (ie) or (if) below, as the case may be, in the manner prescribed therein, intended for sale to a buyer, wholly or partly, except where the entire consideration has been received after issuance of completion certificate, where required, by the competent authority or after its first occupation, whichever is earlier.	1.5%	Amended Vide Notification No. 03/2019-Central Tax (Rate) dated 29.03.2019 (Provisions of paragraph 2 of this notification shall apply for valuation of this service)
(ia)	Construction of residential apartments other than affordable residential apartments by a promoter in an RREP which commences on or after 1st April 2019 or in an ongoing RREP in respect of which the promoter has not exercised option to pay central tax on construction of apartments at the rates as specified for item (ie) or (if) below, as the case may be, in the manner prescribed therein, intended for sale to a buyer, wholly or partly, except where the entire consideration has been received after issuance of completion certificate, where required, by the competent authority or after its first occupation, whichever is earlier.	7.5%	-do-

(ib)	Construction of commercial apartments (shops, offices, godowns, etc.) by a promoter in an RREP which commences on or after 1st April 2019 or in an ongoing RREP in respect of which the promoter has not exercised option to pay central tax on construction of apartments at the rates as specified for item (ie) or (if) below, as the case may be, in the manner prescribed therein, intended for sale to a buyer, wholly or partly, except where the entire consideration has been received after issuance of completion certificate, where required, by the competent authority or after its first occupation, whichever is earlier.	7.5%	-do-
(ic)	Construction of affordable residential apartments by a promoter in a Real Estate Project (herein after referred to as REP) other than RREP, which commences on or 0.75 three after 1st April 2019 or in an ongoing REP other than RREP in respect of which the promoter has not exercised option to pay central tax on construction of apartments at the rates as specified for item (ie) or (if) below, as the case may be, in the manner prescribed therein, intended for sale to a buyer, wholly or partly, except where the entire consideration has been received after issuance of completion certificate, where required, by the competent authority or after its first occupation, whichever is earlier.	1.5%	-do-
(id)	Construction of residential apartments other than affordable residential apartments by a promoter in a REP other than a RREP which commences on or after 1st April 2019 or in an ongoing REP other than RREP in respect of which the promoter has not exercised option to pay central tax on construction of apartments at the rates as specified for item (ie) or (if) below, as the case may be, in the manner prescribed therein, intended for sale to a buyer, wholly or partly, except where the entire consideration has been received after issuance of completion certificate, where required, by the competent authority or after its first occupation, whichever is earlier.	7.5%	-do-
(ie)	Construction of an apartment in an ongoing project under any of the schemes specified in sub-item (b), sub-item (c), sub item (d), sub-item (da) and sub-item (db) of item (iv); sub-item (b), sub-item (c), sub-item (d) and sub-item (da) of item (v); and sub-item (c) of item (vi), against serial number 3 of the Table, in respect of which the promoter has exercised option to pay central tax on construction of apartments at the rates as specified for this item.	12%	-do-
(if)	Construction of a complex, building, civil structure or a part thereof, including, (i) commercial apartments (shops, offices, godowns, etc.) by a promoter in a REP other than RREP, (ii) residential apartments in an ongoing project, other than affordable residential apartments, in respect of which the promoter has exercised option to pay central tax on construction of apartments at the rates as specified for this item in the manner prescribed herein, but excluding supply by way of services specified at items (i), (ia), (ib), (ic), (id) and (ie) above intended for sale to a buyer, wholly or partly, except where the entire consideration has been received after issuance of completion certificate, where required, by the competent authority or after its first occupation, whichever is earlier.	18%	-do-
(ii)	~~Composite supply of works contract as defined in clause 119 of section 2 of Central Goods and Services Tax Act, 2017~~	~~18%~~	This entry omitted Vide N.No. 03/2019-CT(R) dt. 29-03-2019 w.e.f. 1st April 2019

(iii)	~~Composite supply of works contract as defined in clause (119) of section 2 of the Central Goods and Services Tax Act, 2017, supplied to Central Government, State Government, Union territory, a local authority by way of construction, erection, commissioning, installation, completion, fitting out, repair, maintenance, renovation, or alteration of,-~~ ~~(a) a historical monument, archaeological site or remains of national importance, archaeological excavation, or antiquity specified under the Ancient Monuments and Archaeological Sites and Remains Act, 1958 (24 of 1958);~~ ~~(b) canal, dam or other irrigation works;~~ ~~(c) pipeline, conduit or plant for (i) water supply (ii) water treatment, or (iii) sewerage treatment or disposal~~	~~12%~~	This entry omitted Vide N.No. 03/2022-CT(R) dt. 13-07-2022 w.e.f. 18th July 2022
(iv)	~~Composite supply of works contract as defined in clause (119) of section 2 of the Central Goods and Services Tax Act, 2017, supplied by way of construction, erection, commissioning, installation, completion, fitting out, repair, maintenance, renovation, or alteration of,-~~ ~~(a) a road, bridge, tunnel, or terminal for road transportation for use by general public;~~ ~~(b) a civil structure or any other original works pertaining to a scheme under Jawaharlal Nehru National Urban Renewal Mission or Rajiv Awaas Yojana;~~ ~~(c) a civil structure or any other original works pertaining to the "In-situ redevelopment of existing slums using land as a resource, under the Housing for All (Urban) Mission/Pradhan Mantri Awas Yojana (Urban);~~ ~~(d) a civil structure or any other original works pertaining to the "Beneficiary led individual house construction/enhancement" under the Housing for All (Urban) Mission/Pradhan Mantri Awas Yojana;~~ ~~(da) a civil structure or any other original works pertaining to the "Economically Weaker Section (EWS) houses" constructed under the Affordable Housing in partnership by State or Union territory or local authority or urban development authority under the Housing for All (Urban) Mission/Pradhan Mantri Awas Yojana (Urban);~~ ~~(db) a civil structure or any other original works pertaining to the "houses constructed or acquired under the Credit Linked Subsidy Scheme for Economically Weaker Section (EWS)/Lower Income Group (LIG)/Middle Income Group-1 (MIG-1)/Middle Income Group-2 (MIG-2)" under the~~ ~~Housing for All (Urban) Mission/Pradhan Mantri Awas Yojana (Urban);'~~ ~~(e) a pollution control or effluent treatment plant, except located as a part of a factory; or~~ ~~(f) a structure meant for funeral, burial or cremation of deceased~~ ~~(g) a building owned by an entity registered under section 12AA or 12AB of the Income Tax Act, 1961 (43 of 1961), which is used for carrying out the activities of providing, centralised cooking or distribution, for mid-day meals under the mid-day meal scheme sponsored by the Central Government, State Government, Union territory or local authorities~~	~~12%~~	This entry omitted Vide N.No. 03/2022-CT(R) dt. 13-07-2022 w.e.f. 18th July 2022

(v)	~~Composite supply of works contract as defined in clause (119) of section 2 of the Central Goods and Services Tax Act, 2017, supplied by way of construction, erection, commissioning, or installation of original works pertaining to,-~~ ~~(a) railways, including monorail and metro;~~ ~~(b) a single residential unit otherwise than as a part of a residential complex;~~ ~~(c) low-cost houses up to a carpet area of 60 square metres per house in a housing project approved by competent authority empowered under the 'Scheme of Affordable Housing in Partnership' framed by the Ministry of Housing and Urban Poverty Alleviation, Government of India;~~ ~~(d) low cost houses up to a carpet area of 60 square metres per house in a housing project approved by the competent authority under-(1) the "Affordable Housing in Partnership" component of the Housing for All (Urban) Mission/Pradhan Mantri Awas Yojana; (2) any housing scheme of a State Government;~~ ~~(da) low-cost houses up to a carpet area of 60 square metres per house in an affordable housing project which has been given infrastructure status vide notification of Government of India, in Ministry of Finance, Department of Economic Affairs vide F. No. 13/6/2009-INF, dated the 30th March,2017.~~ ~~(e) post-harvest storage infrastructure for agricultural produce including a cold storage for such purposes; or~~ ~~(f) mechanized food grain handling system, machinery or equipment for units processing agricultural produce as food stuff excluding alcoholic beverages~~	~~12%~~	This entry omitted Vide N.No. 03/2022-CT(R) dt. 13-07-2022 w.e.f. 18th July 2022
(va)	~~Composite supply of works contract as defined in clause (119) of section 2 of the Central Goods and Services Tax Act, 2017, other than that covered by items (i), (ia), (ib), (ic), (id), (ie) and (if) above, supplied by way of construction, erection, commissioning, installation, completion, fitting out, repair, maintenance, renovation, or alteration of affordable residential apartments covered by sub-clause (a) of clause (xvi) of paragraph 4 below, in a project which commences on or after 1st April, 2019, or in an ongoing project in respect of which the promoter has not exercised option to pay central tax on construction of apartments at the rates as specified for item (ie) or (if), as the case may be, in the manner prescribed therein~~	~~12%~~	This entry omitted Vide N.No. 03/2022-CT(R) dt. 13-07-2022 w.e.f. 18th July 2022
(vi)	~~Composite supply of works contract as defined in clause (119) of section 2 of the Central Goods and Services Tax Act, 2017 provided to the Central Government, State Government, Union Territory or a local authority by way of construction, erection, commissioning, installation, completion, fitting out, repair, maintenance, renovation, or alteration of –~~ ~~(a) a civil structure or any other original works meant predominantly for use other than for commerce, industry, or any other business or profession;~~ ~~(b) a structure meant predominantly for use as (i) an educational, (ii) a clinical, or(iii) an art or cultural establishment; or~~ ~~(c) a residential complex predominantly meant for self-use or the use of their employees or other persons specified in paragraph 3 of the Schedule III of the Central Goods and Services Tax Act, 2017~~	~~12%~~	This entry omitted Vide N.No. 03/2022-CT(R) dt. 13-07-2022 w.e.f. 18th July 2022

(vii)	Composite supply of works contract as defined in clause (119) of section 2 of the Central Goods and Services Tax Act, 2017, involving predominantly earth work (that is, constituting more than 75% of the value of the works contract) provided to the Central Government, State Government, Union territory, local authority, a Governmental Authority or a Government Entity.	5%	Provided that where the services are supplied to a Government Entity, they should have been procured by the said entity in relation to a work entrusted to it by the Central Government, State Government, Union territory or local authority, as the case may be.
(viii)	Composite supply of works contract as defined in clause (119) of section 2 of the Central Goods and Services Tax Act, 2017 and associated services, in respect of offshore works contract relating to oil and gas exploration and production (E&P) in the offshore area beyond 12 nautical miles from the nearest point of the appropriate base line.	12%	
(ix)	~~Composite supply of works contract as defined in clause (119) of section 2 of the Central Goods and Services Tax Act, 2017 provided by a sub-contractor to the main contractor providing services specified in item (iii) or item (vi) above to the Central Government, State Government, Union territory or a local authority.~~	~~12%~~	This entry omitted Vide N.No. 03/2022-CT(R) dt. 13-07-2022 w.e.f. 18th July 2022
(x)	Composite supply of works contract as defined in clause (119) of section 2 of the Central Goods and Services Tax Act, 2017 provided by a sub-contractor to the main contractor providing services specified in item (vii) above to the Central Government, State Government, Union territory or a local authority.	12% (Increased from 5% to 12% Vide N.No. 03/2022-CT(R) dt. 13-07-2022 w.e.f. 18th July 2022)	Provided that where the services are supplied to a Government Entity, they should have been procured by the said entity in relation to a work entrusted to it by the Central Government, State Government, Union territory or local authority, as the case may be.
(xi)	Services by way of housekeeping, such as plumbing, carpentering, etc. where the person supplying such service through electronic commerce operator is not liable for registration under sub-section (1) of section 22 of the Central Goods and Services Tax Act, 2017.	5%	Provided that credit of input tax charged on goods and services has not been taken.
(xii)	Construction services other than (iii), (iv), (v),(va) (vi),(vii), (viii) and (ix) above.	18%	Amended Vide N.No. 03/2022-CT(R) dt. 13-07-2022 w.e.f. 18th July 2022

Chapter 29

Government Services

INTRODUCTION

Central Government, State Governments & local authorities provides a large number of services to its citizen & business entity which includes law and justice, defence, education & training, health care, registration & licencing, travel & tourism, financial services, transport services, IT & communication, corporate affair, external affairs, consumer affairs, environment & forest, etc. At the same time, Government & local authorities also procure goods & services from individual & business entity.

As per Section 2(17)(i) of CGST Act, 2017, the term business includes "any activity or transaction undertaken by the Central Government, a State Government or any local authority in which they are engaged as public authorities".

It is clearly evident from above definition that, for the purposes of GST any activity or transaction undertaken by the Central or State Government or any local authority, in which they are engaged as public authorities, shall be deemed to be business.

Except a few, most of the services provided by the Government are liable to be taxed under reverse charge i.e. recipient is required to pay tax on the same instead of Government paying to itself. Further, in case of supply made to Governments and local authorities, TDS u/s 51 of CGST Act shall be deducted @2% (CGST+SGST) while making payment to the supplier.

However, certain exemption has been provided in regard to supplies made to Government and supplies made by Government.

Section 11(1) of the CGST Act, 2017 empowers the Government to issue notifications on the recommendations of the council to exempt, by notification, goods or services or both from the whole or part of the tax leviable thereon. By exercising the said powers, the Government had issued Notification no. 12/2017-Central Tax (rate) dated 28th June 2017 and several amendment has been made through subsequent notifications.

List of Government Services exempted from GST

[Notification no. 12/2017-Central Tax (rate) dated 28th June 2017]

4	Services by Central Government, State Government, Union territory, local authority or governmental authority by way of any activity in relation to any function entrusted to a municipality under article 243 W of the Constitution.
5	Services by a Central Government, State Government, Union territory, local authority or Governmental Authority by way of any activity in relation to any function entrusted to a Panchayat under Article 243G of the Constitution.
7	Services provided by the Central Government, State Government, Union territory or local authority to a business entity with an aggregate turnover of up to such amount in the preceding financial year as makes it eligible for exemption from registration under the Central Goods and Services Tax Act, 2017 (12 of 2017). (Except services by department of post, transportation of goods or passengers and renting immovable property)

8	Services provided by the Central Government, State Government, Union territory or local authority to another Central Government, State Government, Union territory or local authority.
9	Services provided by Central Government, State Government, Union territory or a local authority where the consideration for such services does not exceed five thousand rupees. (Except services by department of post, transportation of goods or passengers)
9C	Supply of service by a Government Entity to Central Government, State Government, Union territory, local authority or any person specified by Central Government, State Government, Union territory or local authority against consideration received from Central Government, State Government, Union territory or local authority, in the form of grants.
24C	Services by the Department of Posts by way of post card, inland letter, book post and ordinary post (envelopes weighing less than 10 grams).
34A	Services supplied by Central Government, State Government, Union territory to their undertakings or Public Sector Undertakings (PSUs) by way of guaranteeing the loans taken by such undertakings or PSUs from the banking companies & financial institutions
61	Services provided by the Central Government, State Government, Union territory or local authority by way of issuance of passport, visa, driving licence, birth certificate or death certificate.
62	Services provided by the Central Government, State Government, Union territory or local authority by way of tolerating non-performance of a contract for which consideration in the form of fines or liquidated damages is payable to the Central Government, State Government, Union territory or local authority under such contract.
63	Services provided by the Central Government, State Government, Union territory or local authority by way of assignment of right to use natural resources to an individual farmer for cultivation of plants and rearing of all life forms of animals, except the rearing of horses, for food, fibre, fuel, raw material or other similar products.
65	Services provided by the Central Government, State Government, Union territory by way of deputing officers after office hours or on holidays for inspection or container stuffing or such other duties in relation to import export cargo on payment of Merchant Overtime charges.
65A	Services by way of providing information under the Right to Information Act, 2005 (22 of 2005).
69	Any services provided by the National Skill Development Corporation set up by the Government of India.

FAQ ON GOVERNMENT SERVICES

Question 1: What is the meaning of 'Government'?

Answer: As per section 2(53) of the CGST Act, 2017, 'Government' means the Central Government. As per clause (23) of section 3 of the General Clauses Act, 1897 the 'Government' includes both the Central Government and any State Government. As per clause (8) of section 3 of the said Act, the 'Central Government', in relation to anything done or to be done after the commencement of the Constitution, means the President. As per Article 53 of the Constitution, the executive power of the Union shall be vested in the President and shall be exercised by him either directly or indirectly through officers subordinate to him in accordance with the Constitution. Further, in terms of Article 77 of the Constitution, all executive actions of the Government of India shall be expressed to be taken in the name of the President. Therefore, the Central Government means the President and the officers subordinate to him while exercising the executive powers of the Union vested in the President and in the name of the President. Similarly, as per clause (60) of section 3 of the General Clauses Act, 1897, the 'State Government', as respects anything done after the commencement of the Constitution, shall be in a State the Governor, and in an Union Territory the Central Government. As per Article 154 of the Constitution, the executive power of the State shall be vested in the Governor and shall be exercised by him either directly or indirectly through officers subordinate to him in accordance with the Constitution. Further, as per Article 166 of the Constitution, all executive actions of the Government of State shall be expressed to be taken in the name of Governor. Therefore, State Government means the Governor or the officers subordinate to him who exercise the executive powers of the State vested in the Governor and in the name of the Governor.

Question 2: Are various corporations formed under the Central Acts or State Acts or various government companies registered under the Companies Act, 1956/2013 or autonomous institutions set up by special Acts covered under the definition of 'Government'?

Answer: No. The corporations formed under the Central or a State Act or various companies registered under the Companies Act, 1956/2013 or autonomous institutions set up by the State Acts will not be covered under the definition of 'Government' and therefore, services provided by them will be taxable unless exempted by a notification.

Question 3: Are various regulatory bodies formed by the Government covered under the definition of 'Government'?

Answer: No. A regulatory body, also called regulatory agency, is a public authority or a governmental body, which exercises functions, assigned to them in a regulatory or supervisory capacity. These bodies do not fall under the definition of Government.

Examples of regulatory bodies are—Competition Commission of India, Press Council of India, Directorate General of Civil Aviation, Forward Market Commission, Inland Water Supply Authority of India, Central Pollution Control Board, Securities and Exchange Board of India.

Question 4: Would a statutory body, corporation or an authority constituted under an Act passed by the Parliament or any of the State Legislatures be regarded as 'Government' or "local authority" for the purposes of the GST Acts?

Answer: A statutory body, corporation or an authority created by the Parliament or a State Legislature is neither 'Government' nor a 'local authority'. Such statutory bodies, corporations or authorities are normally created by the Parliament or a State Legislature in exercise of the powers conferred under Article 53(3)(b) and Article 154(2)(b) of the Constitution respectively.

It is a settled position of law (*Agarwal* vs. *Hindustan Steel*, AIR 1970 Supreme Court 1150) that the manpower of such statutory authorities or bodies do not become officers subordinate to the President under Article 53(1) of the Constitution and similarly to the Governor under Article 154(1). Such a statutory body, corporation or an authority as a juridical entity is separate from the State and cannot be regarded as the Central or a State Government and also do not fall in the definition of 'local authority'. Thus, regulatory bodies and other autonomous entities would not be regarded as the government or local authorities for the purposes of the GST Acts.

Question 5: Are all local bodies constituted by a State or Central Law regarded as local authorities for the purposes of the GST Acts?

Answer: No. The definition of 'local authority' is very specific and means only those bodies which are mentioned as 'local authorities' in clause (69) of section 2 of the CGST Act, 2017. It would not include other bodies, which are merely described as a 'local body' by virtue of a local law.

For example, State Governments have setup local developmental authorities to undertake developmental works like infrastructure, housing, residential and commercial development, construction of houses, etc. The Governments setup these authorities under the Town and Planning Act. Examples of such developmental authorities are Delhi Development Authority, Ahmedabad Development Authority, Bangalore Development Authority, Chennai Metropolitan Development Authority, Bihar Industrial Area Development Authority, etc. Such developmental authorities formed under the Town and Planning Act are not qualified as local authorities for the purposes of the GST Acts.

Question 6: Who is a local authority?

Answer: Local authority is defined in clause (69) of section 2 of the CGST Act, 2017 and means the following:

(i) a "Panchayat" as defined in clause (d) of Article 243 of the Constitution;

(ii) a "Municipality" as defined in clause (e) of Article 243P of the Constitution;

(iii) a Municipal Committee, a Zila Parishad, a District Board, and any other authority legally entitled to, or entrusted by the Central Government or any State Government with the control or management of a municipal or local fund;

(iv) a Cantonment Board as defined in section 3 of the Cantonments Act, 2006;

(v) a Regional Council or a District Council constituted under the Sixth Schedule to the Constitution;

(vi) a Development Board constituted under Article 371 of the Constitution; or

(vii) a Regional Council constituted under Article 371A of the Constitution.

Question 7: Are Government or local authority or governmental authority liable to pay tax?

Answer: Yes. The Government or a local authority or a governmental authority is liable to pay tax on supply of services other than the services notified as exempt or notified as neither a supply of goods nor a supply of services under clause (b) of sub-section (2) of section 7 of the CGST Act, 2017. In respect of services other than:

(i) renting of immovable property;
(ii) services by the Department of Posts; and
(iii) services in relation to an aircraft or a vessel, inside or outside the precincts of an airport or a port, the service recipients are required to pay the tax under reverse charge mechanism.

Question 8: Are all services provided by the Government or local authority exempted from payment of tax?

Answer: No, all services provided by the Government or a local authority are not exempt from tax. As for instance, services, namely,

(i) services by the Department of Posts;
(ii) services in relation to an aircraft or a vessel, inside or outside the precincts of an airport or a port;
(iii) transport of goods or passengers; or
(iv) any service, other than services covered under (i) to (iii) above, provided to business entities are not exempt and that these services are liable to tax.

That said, most of the services provided by the Central Government, State Government, Union Territory or local authority are exempt from tax. These include services provided by government or a local authority or governmental authority by way of any activity in relation to any function entrusted to a municipality under Article 243W of the Constitution and services by a governmental authority by way of any activity in relation to any function entrusted to a Panchayat under Article 243G of the Constitution.

Question 9: Would services provided by one department of the Government to another department of the Government be taxable?

Answer: Services provided by one department of the Central Government/State Government to another department of the Central Government/State Government are exempt under notification No. 12/2017 Central Tax (Rate), dated 28.06.2017 [S. No 8 of the Table].

However, this exemption is not applicable to:

(a) services provided by the Department of Posts;
(b) services in relation to a vessel or an aircraft inside or outside the precincts of a port or an airport;
(c) services of transport of goods and/or passengers.

Question 10: What is the scope of 'pure services' mentioned in the exemption notification No. 12/2017-Central Tax (Rate), dated 28.06.2017?

Answer: In the context of the language used in the notification, supply of services without involving any supply of goods would be treated as supply of 'pure services'. For example, supply of manpower for cleanliness of roads, public places, architect services, consulting engineer services, advisory services, and like services provided by business entities not involving any supply of goods would be treated as supply of pure services. On the other hand, let us take the example of a governmental authority awarding the work of maintenance of streetlights in a municipal area to an agency, which involves apart from maintenance, replacement of defunct lights and other spares. In this case, the scope of the service involves maintenance work and supply of goods, which falls under the works contract services. The exemption is provided to services involves only supply of services and not for works contract services.

Question 11: What are the transport services provided by the Government or local authorities exempt from tax?

Answer: Transport services provided by the Government to passengers by:

(i) railways in a class other than:
  (a) first class; or
  (b) an air-conditioned coach;
(ii) metro, monorail or tramway;
(iii) inland waterways;
(iv) public transport, other than predominantly for tourism purpose, in a vessel between places located in India; and
(v) metered cabs or auto rickshaws (including E-rickshaws) are exempt from tax.

Question 12: Whether an amount in the form of royalty or any other form paid/payable to the Government for assigning the rights to use of natural resources is taxable?

Answer: The Government provides license to various companies including Public Sector Undertakings for exploration of natural resources like oil, hydrocarbons, iron ore, manganese, etc. For having assigned the rights to use the natural resources, the licensee companies are required to pay consideration in the form of annual license fee, lease charges, royalty, etc. to the Government. The activity of assignment of rights to use natural resources is treated as supply of services and the licensee is required to pay tax on the amount of consideration paid in the form of royalty or any other form under reverse charge mechanism.

Question 13: Would services in relation to supply of motor vehicles to Government be taxable?

Answer: Supply of a motor vehicle meant to carry more than twelve passengers by way of giving on hire to a state transport undertaking is exempted from tax. The exemption is applicable to services provided to state transport undertaking and not to other departments of Government or local authority. Generally, such State transport undertakings/corporations are established by law with a view to providing public transport facility to the commuters. In some cases, transport undertakings hire the buses on lease basis from private persons on payment of consideration. The services by way of supply of motor vehicles to such state transport undertaking are exempt from payment of tax. However, supplies of motor vehicles to Government Departments other than the state transport undertakings are taxable.

Question 14: Whether a Government Department, required to deduct tax at source, is liable to take registration as a normal taxpayer?

Answer: The Government Department is required to take registration as a normal taxpayer only if it makes a taxable supply of goods and/or services and in such cases, the registration shall be obtained on the basis of PAN but bank account is not mandatory. However, if it is not making any taxable supply of goods and/or services, it is required to register only as a deductor of tax at source for deduction of TDS u/s 51 on the basis of TAN/PAN.

Question 15: What is the significance of services provided by Government or a local authority by way of tolerating non-performance of a contract for which consideration in the form of fines or liquidated damages is payable to the Government or the local authority?

Answer: Non-performance of a contract or breach of contract is one of the conditions normally stipulated in the Government contracts for supply of goods or services.

Non-performance of contract by the supplier of service in case of supplies to Government is covered under the exemption from payment of tax vide Entry 62 of notification No. 12/2017-Central Tax (Rate) dated 28th June, 2017. Thus, any consideration received by the Government from any person or supplier for non-performance of contract is exempted from tax.

Question 16: What is the GST implications on Coaching services supplied by coaching institutions and NGOs under the central sector scheme?

Answer: Entry 72 of notification No. 12/2017-Central Tax (Rate) dated 28th June 2017, exempts services provided to the Central Government, State Government, Union territory administration under any training programme for which total expenditure is borne by the Central Government, State Government, Union territory administration.

Question 17: What is the GST implications on Ambulance services provided by Private service provider (PSP) to Government?

Answer: Function of "health & sanitation" is entrusted to Panchayat under Article 243G of Constitution of India and function of public health is entrusted to Municipality under Article 243W of 12th Schedule to the Constitution of India.

Services provided by the Private service provider (PSP) to Govt by way of transportation of patient against consideration in the form of fee or otherwise charged from the govt is exempted under Entry 3 of notification No. 12/2017-Central Tax (Rate) dated 28th June, 2017.

Question 18: Will the services provided by Police or security agencies of Government to PSUs or corporate entities or sports events held by private entities be taxable?

Answer: Yes. Services provided by Police or security agencies of Government to PSU/private business entities are not exempt from GST. Such services are taxable supplies and the recipients are required to pay the tax under reverse charge mechanism on the amount of consideration paid to Government for such supply of services.

Question 19: Whether services in the nature of change of land use, commercial building approval, utility services provided by a governmental authority are taxable?

Answer: Regulation of land-use, construction of buildings and other services listed in the Twelfth Schedule to the Constitution which have been entrusted to Municipalities under Article 243W of the Constitution, when provided by governmental authority are exempt from payment of tax.

Chapter 30

Place of Supply

30.1 INTRODUCTION

The place of supply provisions determines the place, i.e. taxable jurisdiction where the tax should reach. The place of supply and the location of the supplier are the two determinants to ascertain the nature of supply, i.e. whether a supply is intra-State or inter-State.

Places of supply provisions have been framed for goods and services, keeping in mind the destination/consumption principle. In other words, the place of supply is based on the place of consumption of goods or services. As goods are tangible, the determination of their place of supply, based on the consumption principle, is not difficult. Generally, the place of delivery of goods becomes the place of supply. However, the services being intangible in nature, it is not easy to determine the exact place where services are acquired, enjoyed and consumed. In respect of certain categories of services, the place of supply is determined with reference to a proxy.

> As per Section 2(86) "place of supply" means the place of supply as referred to in Chapter V of the Integrated Goods and Services Tax Act.

30.2 STATUTORY PROVISIONS

For a supply to attract GST, the place of supply should be in India. The place of supply of any goods or services is determined based on Sections 10, 11, 12 and 13 of IGST Act, 2017.

Separate provisions for the supply of goods and services have been made for the determination of their place of supply. Separate provisions for the determination of the place of supply in respect of domestic supplies and cross border supplies have been framed.

PLACE OF SUPPLY PROVISION UNDER IGST ACT, 2017

Sections Reference	Provision
Section 10	Place of supply of goods other than import and export
Section 11	Place of supply of goods in case of Import & Export
Section 12	Place of supply of services in case of Domestic Supplies
Section 13	Place of supply of services in case of cross-border supplies

The provision relating to place of supply of goods can be broadly covered in four categories:

(1) Movement of goods

(2) No movement of goods

(3) Goods supplied in a vessel or conveyance

(4) Import & export of goods

(1) Movement of goods

Place of Supply of Goods where movement involves

Supply	Place of supply
Involves movement of goods, whether by the supplier or recipient or by any other person	Location of the goods where movement of goods terminate for delivery to the recipient
Goods are delivered by the seller to the recipient on the direction of a third person, before or during the movement of goods, by way of transfer of documents of title to the goods or some other way (Section 10(1)(b)).	It will assumed that the third person has received the goods and the place of supply of such goods will be the principal place of business of 3rd person.

(2) No movement of goods

Place of Supply where movement of goods is not involved

Supply	Place of supply
No movement of goods either by supplier or recipient	Location of such goods at the time of delivery to the recipient
The goods are assemble or installed at site	Place of such installation or assembly

(3) Goods supplied in a vessel or conveyance

Supply	Place of supply
Goods are supplied on board a conveyance, including a vessel, an aircraft, a train or a motor vehicle	Location at which such goods are taken on board. **Example:** If an aircraft departs from New Delhi to Kolkata after taking on board goods for consumption at New Delhi, the place of supply will be New Delhi.

(4) Import & Export of Goods

Supply	Place of supply	Type of GST
Goods imported into India	Location of the importer in India	Always IGST on import
Exported from India	Location of exporter in India	Zero-rated Supply/Export can be made either on payment of IGST/through bond/LUT
Supply to SEZ (SEZ are outside Customs Territory of India, it is treated as Export)	Location of exporter in India	Zero-rated Supply/IGST

Section 7 of the Integrated Goods and Services Tax Act, 2017 provides that all the supplies of goods and services to SEZ would be treated as inter-State supplies and accordingly the same will be liable to IGST based on Section 5(1) of the IGST Act, 2017.

Section 7(2) of the IGST Act, 2017 provides that supply of goods imported into the territory of India till they cross the customs frontiers of India shall be treated as Inter State Supply. Further, proviso to Section 5(1) provides that integrated tax on goods imported into India shall be levied under Customs Law.

30.3 PLACE OF SUPPLY OF GOODS OTHER THAN IMPORT AND EXPORT (SECTION 10)

Sl No.	Nature of Supply	Place of Supply
1.	Where the supply involves the movement of goods, whether by the supplier or the recipient or by any other person	Location of the goods at the time at which, the movement of goods terminates for delivery to the recipient.
2.0	Where the goods are delivered to the recipient, or any person on the direction of the third person by way of transfer of title or otherwise, it shall be deemed that the third person has received the goods	The principal place of business of such person.

Sl No.	Nature of Supply	Place of Supply
3.	Where there is no movement of goods either by supplier or recipient	Location of such goods at the time of delivery to the recipient.
4.	Where goods are assembled or installed at site	The place where the goods are assembled or installed.
5.	Where the goods are supplied on-board a conveyance like a vessel, aircraft, train or motor vehicle	The place where such goods are taken onboard the conveyance.
6.	Where the place of supply of goods cannot be determined in terms of sub-sections (2), (3), (4) and (5)	It shall be determined in such manner as may be Prescribed.

30.4 PLACE OF SUPPLY OF GOODS IN CASE OF IMPORT AND EXPORT (SECTION 11)

Sl No.	Nature of Supply	Place of Supply
1.	Import	Location of Importer
2.	Export	Location of Exporter

(a) Ms. Shalini (registered in Mumbai) imports school bags from China for her shop.

Place of supply: Mumbai, GST Payable: IGST

(b) Ms. Ankita (registered in Kolkata) exports Indian perfumes to UK.

Place of supply: Kolkata, GST Payable: Exempted (Zero-rated supply)

30.5 PLACE OF SUPPLY OF SERVICES IN CASE OF DOMESTIC SUPPLIES (SECTION 12)

(Where the location of supplier of services and the location of the recipient of services is in India)

(i) In respect of the following 12 categories of services, the place of supply is determined with reference to a proxy. Rest of the services are governed by a default provision.

Sl No.	Nature of Supply	Place of Supply
1.	Immovable property related to services, including hotel accommodation	Location at which the immovable property or boat or vessel is located or intended to be located. If located outside India: Location of the recipient.
2.	Restaurant and catering services, personal grooming, fitness, beauty treatment and health service	Location where the services are actually performed.
3.	Training and performance appraisal	B2B: Location of such Registered person. B2C: Location where the services are actually performed.
4.	Admission to an event or amusement park	Place where the event is actually held or where the park or the other place is located.
5.	Organizing an event	B2B: Location of such Registered person. B2C: Location where the event is actually held. If the event is held outside India, location of the recipient.
6.	Transportation of goods, including mails	B2B: Location of such Registered Person. B2C: Location at which such goods are handed over for their transportation.
7.	Passenger transportation	B2B: Location of such registered person. B2C: Place where the passenger embarks on the conveyance for a continuous journey.
8.	Services on board a conveyance	Location of the first scheduled point of departure of that conveyance for the journey.

9.	Banking and other financial services	Location of the recipient of services on the records of the supplier. Location of the supplier of services if the location of the recipient of services is not available.
10.	Insurance services	B2B: Location of such registered person. B2C: Location of the recipient of services on the records of the supplier.
11.	Advertisement services to the Government	The place of supply shall be taken as located in each of such States proportionate value in case of multiple States.
12.	Telecommunication service	Services involving fixed line, circuits, dish etc., and place of supply is the location of such fixed equipment. In case of mobile/internet post-paid services, it is the location of billing address of the recipient. In case of sale of pre-paid voucher, the place of supply is the place of sale of such vouchers. In other cases, it is the address of the recipient in records.

As per proviso to Section 12(3) of IGST Act, if an immovable property is located or intended to be located outside India, the place of supply shall be the location of the recipient.

Example: Ministry of External affairs (MEA), Govt of India, New Delhi awarded a contract to M/s Mannu Lal & Sons of Delhi for Development of Integrated Check Post at Biratnagar, Nepal along Indo-Nepal border.

Here the nature of service is "works contract" service since the supply is in relation to immovable property. The immovable property is located outside India. The location of the recipient, i.e. MEA is in New Delhi. Therefore, the place of supply shall be New Delhi as per proviso to Section 12(3) of IGST Act.

Section 12(3) of IGST Act reproduced here under....

> The place of supply of services:
> (a) directly in relation to an immovable property, including services provided by architects, interior decorators, surveyors, engineers and other related experts or estate agents, any service provided by way of grant of rights to use immovable property or for carrying out or co-ordination of construction work; or
> (b) by way of lodging accommodation by a hotel, inn, guest house, home stay, club or campsite, by whatever name called, and including a house boat or any other vessel; or
> (c) by way of accommodation in any immovable property for organizing any marriage or reception or matters related thereto, official, social, cultural, religious or business function including services provided in relation to such function at such property; or
> (d) any services ancillary to the services referred to in clauses (*a*), (*b*) and (*c*), shall be the location at which the immovable property or boat or vessel, as the case may be, is located or intended to be located:
> ***Provided that if the location of the immovable property or boat or vessel is located or intended to be located outside India, the place of supply shall be the location of the recipient.***

(ii) For the rest of the services other than those specified above, a default provision has been prescribed as under:

DEFAULT RULE FOR SERVICES OTHER THAN 12 SPECIFIED SERVICES

Sl No.	Description of Supply	Place of Supply
1.	B2B	Location of such registered person
2.	B2C	(i) Location of the recipient where the address on record exists, and (ii) Location of the supplier of services in other cases

30.6 PLACE OF SUPPLY OF SERVICES IN CASE OF CROSS BORDER SUPPLIES (SEC 13)

(Where the location of the supplier of services or the location of the recipient of services is outside India)

(i) *In respect of the following categories of services, the place of supply is determined with reference to a proxy. Rest of the services are governed by a default provision*

Sl No.	Nature of Supply	Place of Supply
1.	Services supplied for goods that are required to be made physically available from a remote location by way of electronic means (Not applicable in case of goods that are temporarily imported into India for repairs and exported)	The location where the services are actually performed. The location where the goods are situated.
2.	Services supplied to an individual and requiring the physical presence of the receiver	The location where the services are actually performed.
3.	Immovable property-related services, including hotel accommodation	Location at which the immovable property is located.
4.	Admission to an event or amusement park	The place where the event is actually held.
5.	If the said three services are supplied at more than one locations. i.e., (i) Goods & individual related (ii) Immovable property-related (iii) Event related	
5.1	At more than one location, including a location in the taxable territory	Its place of supply shall be the location in the taxable territory where the greatest proportion of the service is provided.
5.2	In more than one State	Its place of supply shall be each such State in proportion to the value of services provided in each State.
5.3	Banking, financial institutions, NBFC Intermediary services, hiring of vehicles' services, etc.	Location of the supplier of Service.
6.	Transportation of goods	The place of destination of the goods.
7.	Passenger transportation	Place where the passenger embarks on the conveyance for a continuous journey.
8.	Services on-board a conveyance	The first scheduled point of departure of that conveyance for the journey.
9.	Online information and database access or retrieval services	The location of recipient of service.

(ii) For the rest of the services other than those specified above, a default provision has been prescribed as under:

Default Rule for the cross-border supply of services other than nine specified services		
Sl No.	**Description of Supply**	**Place of Supply**
1.	Any	Location of the recipient of service. If not available in the ordinary course of business: The location of the supplier of service.

Export/Import Services

A supply would be treated as import or export, if certain conditions are satisfied. These conditions are as under:

Export of Services	Import of Services
Means the supply of any service, where (a) the supplier of service is located in India, (b) the recipient of service is located outside India, (c) the place of supply of service is outside India, (d) the payment for such service has been received by the supplier of service in convertible foreign exchange, and (e) the supplier of service and the recipient of service are not merely establishments of a distinct person in accordance with explanation 1 of section 8	Means the supply of any service, where (a) the supplier of service is located outside India, (b) the recipient of service is located in India, and (c) the place of supply of service is in India.

Important Points

(1) Section 2(10) of the IGST Act, 2017 defines import of goods to mean bringing goods into India from a place outside India.

(2) Section 12. Place of supply of services where location of supplier and recipient is in India

Section 12(3): Place of Supply of immovable property in following cases shall be the location at which the immovable property is located or intended to be located:

(a) directly in relation to an immovable property, including services provided by architects, interior decorators, surveyors, engineers and other related experts or estate agents, any service provided by way of grant of rights to use immovable property or for carrying out or co-ordination of construction work; or

(b) by way of lodging accommodation by a hotel, inn, guest house, home stay, club or campsite, by whatever name called, and including a house boat or any other vessel; or

(c) by way of accommodation in any immovable property for organising any marriage or reception or matters related thereto, official, social, cultural, religious or business function including services provided in relation to such function at such property; or

(d) any services ancillary to the services referred to in clauses (a), (b) and (c).

Section 12(4): The place of supply of restaurant and catering services, personal grooming, fitness, beauty treatment, health service including cosmetic and plastic surgery shall be the location where the services are actually performed.

Section 12(5): The place of supply of services in relation to training and performance appraisal to:

(a) a registered person, shall be the location of such person;

(b) a person other than a registered person, shall be the location where the service are actually performed.

Section 12(6): The place of supply of services provided by way of admission to a cultural, artistic, sporting, scientific, educational, entertainment event or amusement park or any other place and services ancillary thereto, shall be the place where the event is actually held or where the park or such other place is located.

Section 12(7): The place of supply of services provided by way of:

(a) organisation of a cultural, artistic, sporting, scientific, educational or entertainment event including supply of services in relation to a conference, fair, exhibition, celebration or similar events; or

(b) services ancillary to organisation of any of the events or services referred to in clause (a), or assigning of sponsorship to such events:

(i) to a registered person, shall be the location of such person;

(ii) to a person other than a registered person, shall be the place where the event is actually held and if the event is held outside India, the place of supply shall be the location of the recipient.

Section 12 (8): The place of supply of services by way of transportation of goods, including by mail or courier to:

(a) a registered person, shall be the location of such person;

(b) a person other than a registered person, shall be the location at which such goods are handed over for their transportation:

Provided that where the transportation of goods is to a place outside India, the place of supply shall be the place of destination of such goods.

Section 12(9): The place of supply of passenger transportation service to:

(a) a registered person, shall be the location of such person;

(b) a person other than a registered person, shall be the place where the passenger embarks on the conveyance for a continuous journey:

Provided that where the right to passage is given for future use and the point of embarkation is not known at the time of issue of right to passage, the place of supply of such service shall be determined in accordance with the provisions of Section 12(2).

Section 12(10): The place of supply of services on board a conveyance, including a vessel, an aircraft, a train or a motor vehicle, shall be the location of the first scheduled point of departure of that conveyance for the journey.

Section 12 (11): The place of supply of telecommunication services including data transfer, broadcasting, cable and direct to home television services to any person shall:

(a) in case of services by way of fixed telecommunication line, leased circuits, internet-leased circuit, cable or dish antenna, be the location where the telecommunication line, leased circuit or cable connection or dish antenna is installed for receipt of services;

(b) in case of mobile connection for telecommunication and internet services provided on post-paid basis, be the location of billing address of the recipient of services on the record of the supplier of services;

(c) in cases where mobile connection for telecommunication, internet service and direct to home television services are provided on pre-payment basis through a voucher or any other means:

(i) through a selling agent or a re-seller or a distributor of subscriber identity module card or re-charge voucher, be the address of the selling agent or re-seller or distributor as per the record of the supplier at the time of supply; or

(ii) by any person to the final subscriber, be the location where such prepayment is received or such vouchers are sold;

(d) in other cases, be the address of the recipient as per the records of the supplier of services and where such address is not available, the place of supply shall be location of the supplier of services:

Provided that where the address of the recipient as per the records of the supplier of services is not available, the place of supply shall be location of the supplier of services:

Section 12 (12): The place of supply of banking and other financial services, including stock broking services to any person shall be the location of the recipient of services on the records of the supplier of services:

Provided that if the location of recipient of services is not on the records of the supplier, the place of supply shall be the location of the supplier of services.

Section 12(13): The place of supply of insurance services shall:

(a) to a registered person, be the location of such person;

(b) to a person other than a registered person, be the location of the recipient of services on the records of the supplier of services.

Section 12(14): The place of supply of advertisement services to the Central Government, a State Government, a statutory body or a local authority meant for the States or Union territories identified in the contract or agreement shall be taken as being in each of such States or Union territories and the value of such supplies specific to each State or Union territory shall be in proportion to the amount attributable to services provided by way of dissemination in the respective States or Union territories as may be determined in terms of the contract or agreement entered into in this regard or, in the absence of such contract or agreement, on such other basis as may be prescribed.

Section 13. Place of supply of services where location of supplier or location of recipient is outside India

As per Section 13(3)(a) of the IGST Act, 2017 the place of supply of service in respect of goods that are required to be made physically available by the recipient of service to the supplier of service shall be the location where the services are actually performed.

As per proviso to Section 13(3)(a) of the IGST Act, 2017 where services are provided in respect of goods from a remote location by electronic means, the place of supply shall be the location where the goods are actually located.

Section 13(4): The place of supply of service in relation to an immovable property, including services supplied in this regard by experts and estate agents, supply of hotel accommodation by a hotel, inn, guest house, club or campsite, by whatever name called, grant of rights to use immovable property, services for carrying out or co-ordination of construction work, including architects or interior decorators, shall be the place where the immovable property is located or intended to be located.

Section 13(5): The place of supply of services supplied by way of admission to, or organization of, a cultural, artistic, sporting, scientific, educational, or entertainment event, or a celebration, conference, fair, exhibition, or similar events, and of services ancillary to such admission will be the place where the event is actually held.

Part-II

The Goods & Services Tax (Compensation to States) Act, 2017

INDEX OF SECTIONS

Section	Description
1.	Short title, extent and commencement
2.	Definitions
3.	Projected growth rate
4.	Base year
5.	Base year revenue
6.	Projected revenue for any year
7.	Calculation and release of compensation
8.	Levy & collection of Cess
9.	Returns, payments and refunds
10.	Crediting proceeds of Cess to Fund
11.	Other provisions relating to Cess
12.	Power to make rules
13.	Laying of rules before Parliament
14.	Power to remove difficulties
8(2).	Compensation Cess Rate Schedule

INTRODUCTION

The GST Compensation Cess is imposed as a levy in addition to the regular GST taxes. The cess is imposed on the supply of certain luxurious and demerit goods and services that attract 28% GST. The cess rate usually ranges from 1% to 25% and is levied over and above the GST rate.

The GST (Compensation to States) Act, 2017 is an Act to provide for compensation to the States for the loss of revenue arising on account of implementation of the goods and services tax in pursuance of the provisions of the Constitution (One Hundred and First Amendment) Act, 2016.

This Act, inter-alia provides:

(a) That the revenue proposed to be compensated would consist of revenues from all taxes that stands subsumed into the GST law, as audited by the CAG;

(b) For reckoning the growth rate of revenue subsumed for a State at 14% per annum;

(c) That the compensation will be released bi-monthly based on the provisional numbers furnished by the Central Accounting Authorities and the final adjustment to be done after the accounts are subjected to audit by CAG; That the revenue of States directly devolved to Mandi/Municipalities would be considered as revenue subsumed;

(d) Levy of a cess over and above the GST on certain notified goods to compensate States for five years on account of revenue loss suffered by them;

(e) That the proceeds of the cess will be utilised to compensate States that warrant payment of compensation;

(f) That 50% of the amount remaining un-utilised in the fund at the end of the fifth year will be transferred to the Centre and the balance 50% would be distributed amongst the State and Union Territories in the ratio of total revenues from SGST/UTGST of the fifth year;

(g) The Cess would not be leviable on supplies made by a person who has opted for composition levy;

(h) The cess levied under this Act would be payable over and above the CGST, SGST/UTGST and IGST tax leviable. Cess would be levied on whole value exclusive of GST, i.e. for transaction value as per Section 15 is ₹ 100 and GST Rate is 18% then Cess would be levied on ₹ 100.

Calculation would be ₹ 100+18% GST+ % Compensation Cess (as specified).

(i) Exporter will be eligible to claim refund of Cess paid under the Act on export of goods on the similar lines as refund of IGST paid on exports.

1. Short title, extent and commencement.

(1) This Act may be called the Goods and Services Tax (Compensation to States) Act, 2017.

(2) It extends to the whole of India.

(3) It shall come into force on such date as the Central Government may, by notification in the Official Gazette, appoint.

2. Definitions.

(1) In this Act, unless the context otherwise requires:

(a) "central tax" means the central goods and services tax levied and collected under the Central Goods and Services Tax Act;

(b) "Central Goods and Services Tax Act" means the Central Goods and Services Tax Act, 2017;

(c) "cess" means the goods and services tax compensation cess levied under section 8;

(d) "compensation" means an amount, in the form of goods and services tax compensation, as determined under section 7;

(e) "Council" means the Goods and Services Tax Council constituted under the provisions of Article 279A of the Constitution;

(f) "Fund" means the Goods and Services Tax Compensation Fund referred to in section 10;

(g) "input tax" in relation to a taxable person, means:

(i) cess charged on any supply of goods or services or both made to him;

(ii) cess charged on import of goods and includes the cess payable on reverse charge basis;

(h) "Integrated Goods and Services Tax Act" means the Integrated Goods and Services Tax Act, 2017;

(i) "integrated tax" means the integrated goods and services tax levied and collected under the Integrated Goods and Services Tax Act;

(j) "prescribed" means prescribed by rules made, on the recommendations of the Council, under this Act;

(k) "projected growth rate" means the rate of growth projected for the transition period as per section 3;

(l) "Schedule" means the Schedule appended to this Act;

(m) "State" means:

(i) for the purposes of sections 3, 4, 5, 6 and 7 the States as defined under the Central Goods and Services Tax Act; and

(ii) for the purposes of Sections 8, 9, 10, 11, 12, 13 and 14 the States as defined under the Central Goods and Services Tax Act and the Union territories as defined under the Union Territories Goods and Services Tax Act;

(n) "State tax" means the State goods and services tax levied and collected under the respective State Goods and Services Tax Act;

(o) "State Goods and Services Tax Act" means the law to be made by the State Legislature for levy and collection of tax by the concerned State on supply of goods or services or both;

(p) "taxable supply" means a supply of goods or services or both which is chargeable to the cess under this Act;

(q) "transition date" shall mean, in respect of any State, the date on which the State Goods and Services Tax Act of the concerned State comes into force;
(r) "transition period" means a period of five years from the transition date; and
(s) "Union Territories Goods and Services Tax Act" means the Union Territories Goods and Services Tax Act, 2017.

(2) The words and expressions used and not defined in this Act but defined in the Central Goods and Services Tax Act and the Integrated Goods and Services Tax Act shall have the meanings respectively assigned to them in those Acts.

3. Projected growth rate.

The projected nominal growth rate of revenue subsumed for a State during the transition period shall be fourteen per cent (14%) per annum.

4. Base year.

For the purpose of calculating the compensation amount payable in any financial year during the transition period, the financial year ending 31st March 2016, shall be taken as the base year.

5. Base year revenue.

(1) Subject to the provision of sub-sections (2), (3), (4), (5) and (6), the base year revenue for a State shall be the sum of the revenue collected by the State and the local bodies during the base year, on account of the taxes levied by the respective State or Union and net of refunds, with respect to the following taxes, imposed by the respective State or Union, which are subsumed into goods and services tax.

(2) In respect of the State of Jammu and Kashmir, the base year revenue shall include the amount of tax collected on sale of services by the said State Government during the base year.

(3) In respect of the States mentioned in sub-clause (g) of clause (4) of Article 279A of the Constitution, the amount of revenue foregone on account of exemptions or remission given by the said State Governments to promote industrial investment in the State, with respect to such specific taxes referred to in sub-section (1), shall be included in the total base year revenue of the State, subject to such conditions as may be prescribed.

(4) The Acts of the Central Government and State Governments under which the specific taxes are being subsumed into the goods and services tax shall be such as may be notified.

(5) The base year revenue shall be calculated as per sub-sections (1), (2), (3) and (4) on the basis of the figures of revenue collected and net of refunds given in that year, as audited by the Comptroller and Auditor-General of India.

(6) In respect of any State, if any part of revenues mentioned in sub-sections (1), (2), (3) and (4) are not credited in the Consolidated Fund of the respective State, the same shall be included in the total base year.

6. Projected revenue for any year.

The projected revenue for any year in a State shall be calculated by applying the projected growth rate over the base year revenue of that State.

Illustration: If the base year revenue for 2015-16 for a concerned State, calculated as per section 5 is one hundred rupees, then the projected revenue for financial year 2018-19 shall be as follows:

Projected Revenue for 2018-19=100 (1+14/100)3 revenue of the State, subject to such conditions as may be prescribed.

7. Calculation and release of compensation.

(1) The compensation under this Act shall be payable to any State during the transition period.

(2) The compensation payable to a State shall be provisionally calculated and released at the end of every two months period, and shall be finally calculated for every financial year after the receipt of final revenue figures, as audited by the Comptroller and Auditor-General of India.

(3) The total compensation payable for any financial year during the transition period to any State shall be calculated in the following manner, namely:

(a) the projected revenue for any financial year during the transition period, which could have accrued to a State in the absence of the goods and services tax, shall be calculated as per section 6;
(b) the actual revenue collected by a State in any financial year during the transition period shall be:

(i) the actual revenue from State tax collected by the State, net of refunds given by the said State under Chapters XI and XX of the State Goods and Services Tax Act;

(ii) the integrated goods and services tax apportioned to that State; and

(iii) any collection of taxes on account of the taxes levied by the respective State under the Acts specified in sub-section (4) of section 5, net of refund of such taxes,

(c) as certified by the Comptroller and Auditor-General of India;

(d) the total compensation payable in any financial year shall be the difference between the projected revenue for any financial year and the actual revenue collected by a State referred to in clause (b).

(4) The loss of revenue at the end of every two months period in any year for a State during the transition period shall be calculated, at the end of the said period, in the following manner, namely:

(a) the projected revenue that could have been earned by the State in absence of the goods and services tax till the end of the relevant two months period of the respective financial year shall be calculated on a pro-rata basis as a percentage of the total projected revenue for any financial year during the transition period, calculated in accordance with section 6.

Illustration: If the projected revenue for any year calculated in accordance with section 6 is one hundred rupees, for calculating the projected revenue that could be earned till the end of the period of ten months for the purpose of this sub-section shall be 100 × (5/6)=₹ 83.33;

(b) the actual revenue collected by a State till the end of relevant two months period in any financial year during the transition period shall be—

(i) the actual revenue from State tax collected by the State, net of refunds given by the State under Chapters XI and XX of the State Goods and Services Tax Act;

(ii) the integrated goods and services tax apportioned to that State, as certified by the Principal Chief Controller of Accounts of the Central Board of Excise and Customs; and

(iii) any collection of taxes levied by the said State, under the Acts specified in sub-section (4) of section 5, net of refund of such taxes;

(c) the provisional compensation payable to any State at the end of the relevant two months period in any financial year shall be the difference between the projected revenue till the end of the relevant period in accordance with clause (a) and the actual revenue collected by a State in the said period as referred to in clause (b), reduced by the provisional compensation paid to a State till the end of the previous two months period in the said financial year during the transition period.

(5) In case of any difference between the final compensation amount payable to a State calculated in accordance with the provisions of sub-section (3) upon receipt of the audited revenue figures from the Comptroller and Auditor-General of India, and the total provisional compensation amount released to a State in the said financial year in accordance with the provisions of sub-section (4), the same shall be adjusted against release of compensation to the State in the subsequent financial year.

(6) Where no compensation is due to be released in any financial year, and in case any excess amount has been released to a State in the previous year, this amount shall be refunded by the State to the Central Government and such amount shall be credited to the Fund in such manner as may be prescribed.

8. Levy and collection of cess.

(1) There shall be levied a cess on such intra-State supplies of goods or services or both, as provided for in section 9 of the Central Goods and Services Tax Act, and such inter-State supplies of goods or services or both as provided for in section 5 of the Integrated Goods and Services Tax Act, and collected in such manner as may be prescribed, on the recommendations of the Council, for the purposes of providing compensation to the States for loss of revenue arising on account of implementation of the goods and services tax with effect from the date from which the provisions of the Central Goods and Services Tax Act is brought into force, for a period of five years or for such period as may be prescribed on the recommendations of the Council.

The period for levy and collection of cess under section 8(1) of the Goods and Services Tax (Compensation to States) Act, 2017 has been extended upto the 31st March, 2026 vide Notification No.01/2022-Compensation Cess dated 24-06-2022.

Provided that no such cess shall be leviable on supplies made by a taxable person who has decided to opt for composition levy under section 10 of the Central Goods and Services Tax Act.

(2) The cess shall be levied on such supplies of goods and services as are specified in column (2) of the Schedule, on the basis of value, quantity or on such basis at such rate not exceeding the rate set forth in the corresponding entry in column (4) of the Schedule, as the Central Government may, on the recommendations of the Council, by notification in the Official Gazette, specify:

Provided that where the cess is chargeable on any supply of goods or services or both with reference to their value, for each such supply the value shall be determined under section 15 of the Central Goods and Services Tax Act for all intra-State and inter-State supplies of goods or services or both:
Provided further that the cess on goods imported into India shall be levied and collected in accordance with the provisions of section 3 of the Customs Tariff Act, 1975, at the point when duties of customs are levied on the said goods under section 12 of the Customs Act, 1962, on a value determined under the Customs Tariff Act, 1975.

9. Returns, payments and refunds.

(1) Every taxable person, making a taxable supply of goods or services or both, shall:

(a) pay the amount of cess as payable under this Act in such manner;

(b) furnish such returns in such forms, along with the returns to be filed under the Central Goods and Services Tax Act; and

(c) apply for refunds of such cess paid in such form, as may be prescribed.

(2) For all purposes of furnishing of returns and claiming refunds, except for the form to be filed, the provisions of the Central Goods and Services Tax Act and the rules made thereunder, shall, as far as may be, apply in relation to the levy and collection of the cess leviable under section 8 on all taxable supplies of goods or services or both, as they apply in relation to the levy and collection of central tax on such supplies under the said Act or the rules made thereunder.

10. Crediting proceeds of cess to Fund.

(1) The proceeds of the cess leviable under section 8 and such other amounts as may be recommended by the Council, shall be credited to a non-lapsable Fund known as the Goods and Services Tax Compensation Fund, which shall form part of the public account of India and shall be utilized for purposes specified in the said section.

(2) All amounts payable to the States under section 7 shall be paid out of the Fund.

(3) Fifty per cent of the amount remaining unutilized in the Fund at the end of the transition period shall be transferred to the Consolidated Fund of India as the share of Centre, and the balance fifty per cent shall be distributed amongst the States in the ratio of their total revenues from the State tax or the Union territory goods and services tax, as the case may be, in the last year of the transition period.

(4) The accounts relating to Fund shall be audited by the Comptroller and Auditor General of India or any person appointed by him at such intervals as may be specified by him and any expenditure in connection with such audit shall be payable by the Central Government to the Comptroller and Auditor-General of India.

(5) The accounts of the Fund, as certified by the Comptroller and Auditor-General of India or any other person appointed by him in this behalf together with the audit report thereon shall be laid before each House of Parliament.

11. Other provisions relating to cess.

(1) The provisions of the Central Goods and Services Tax Act, and the rules made thereunder, including those relating to assessment, input tax credit, non-levy, short-levy, interest, appeals, offences and penalties, shall, as far as may be, mutatis mutandis, apply, in relation to the levy and collection of the cess leviable under section 8 on the intra-State supply of goods and services, as they apply in relation to the levy and collection of central tax on such intra-State supplies under the said Act or the rules made thereunder.

(2) The provisions of the Integrated Goods and Services Tax Act, and the rules made thereunder, including those relating to assessment, input tax credit, non-levy, short-levy, interest, appeals, offences and penalties, shall, mutatis mutandis, apply in relation to the levy and collection of the cess leviable under section 8 on the inter-State supply of goods and services, as they apply in relation to the levy and collection of integrated tax on such inter-State supplies under the said Act or the rules made thereunder:

Provided that the input tax credit in respect of cess on supply of goods and services leviable under section 8, shall be utilised only towards payment of said cess on supply of goods and services leviable under the said section.

12. Power to make rules.

(1) The Central Government shall, on the recommendations of the Council, by notification in the Official Gazette, make rules for carrying out the provisions of this Act.

(2) In particular, and without prejudice to the generality of the foregoing power, such rules may provide for all or any of the following matters, namely:

(a) the conditions which were included in the total base year revenue of the States, referred to in sub-clause (g) of clause (4) of Article 279A of the Constitution, under sub-section (3) of section 5;

(b) the conditions subject to which any part of revenues not credited in the Consolidated Fund of the respective State shall be included in the total base year revenue of the State, under sub-section (6) of section 5;

(c) the manner of refund of compensation by the States to the Central Government under sub-section (6) of section 7;

(d) the manner of levy and collection of cess and the period of its imposition under sub-section (1) of section 8;

(e) the manner and forms for payment of cess, furnishing of returns and refund of cess under sub-section (1) of section 9; and

(f) any other matter which is to be, or may be, prescribed, or in respect of which provision is to be made, by rules.

13. Laying of rules before Parliament.

Every rule made under this Act by the Central Government shall be laid, as soon as may be after it is made, before each House of Parliament, while it is in session, for a total period of thirty days which may be comprised in one session or in two or more successive sessions, and if, before the expiry of the session immediately following the session or the successive sessions aforesaid, both Houses agree in making any modification in the rule or both Houses agree that the rule should not be made, the rule shall thereafter have effect only in such modified form or be of no effect, as the case may be; so, however, that any such modification or annulment shall be without prejudice to the validity of anything previously done under that rule.

14. Power to remove difficulties.

(1) If any difficulty arises in giving effect to the provisions of this Act, the Central Government may, on the recommendations of the Council, by order published in the Official Gazette, make such provisions, not inconsistent with the provisions of this Act, as appear to it to be necessary or expedient for removing the difficulty:

Provided that no order shall be made under this section after the expiry of five years from the commencement of this Act.

(2) Every order made under this section shall, as soon as may be after it is made, be laid before each House of Parliament.

GST COMPENSATION CESS (RATE) NOTIFICATIONS

Notification No. & Date of issue	Subject
01/2017-Compensation Cess (Rate), dt. 28-06-2017	Rates of GST Compensation Cess on supply of specified goods
02/2017-Compensation Cess (Rate), dt. 28-06-2017	Rates of compensation cess on supply of specified services
03/2017-Compensation Cess (Rate), dt. 18-07-2017	Increase in Compensation Cess rates on cigarettes
04/2017-Compensation Cess (Rate), dt. 20-07-2017	Exemption of Cess on buying & selling of second hand goods
05/2017-Compensation Cess (Rate), dt. 11-09-2017	Amendment in rate of Compensation Cess on various motor vehicles

06/2017-Compensation Cess (Rate), dt. 13-10-2017	Reduction in cess rates for leasing of motor vehicles purchased and leased prior to 01.07.2017
01/2018-Compensation Cess (Rate), dt. 25-01-2018	NIL Compensation Cess on old & used motor vehicles
02/2018-Compensation Cess (Rate), dt. 26-07-2018	NIL Compensation Cess on Fuel Cell motor vehicles
01/2019-Compensation Cess (Rate), dt. 29-06-2019	NIL Compensation Cess on supply of goods by a retail outlet established in the departure area of an international airport, beyond the immigration counters, to an outgoing international tourist
03/2019-Compensation Cess (Rate), dt. 30-09-2019	Disallow the refund of compensation cess in case of inverted duty structure for tobacco and manufactured tobacco substitutes
01/2021-Compensation Cess (Rate), dt. 30-09-2021	Entry 4B—Chapter heading 2202, i.e. Carbonated Beverages of Fruit Drink or Carbonated Beverages with Fruit Juice will attract Cess @12%
02/2021-Compensation Cess (Rate), dt. 28-12-2021	Substitution of new Chapter heading. Amendment to N.No. 1/2017-Compensation Cess (Rate), dated the 28th June 2017
01/2023-Compensation Cess (Rate), dt. 28-02-2023	Substitution of new entry against Sl. No. 41A. Amendment to N.No. 1/2017-Compensation Cess (Rate), dated the 28th June 2017
02/2023-Compensation Cess (Rate), dt. 31-03-2023	Compensation Cess rate of tobacco, gutkha, pan masala linked with retail sale price. Amendment to N.No. 1/2017-Compensation Cess (Rate), dated the 28th June 2017
03/2023-Compensation Cess (Rate), dt. 26-07-2023	Compensation Cess rate of tobacco, gutkha, pan masala without declaredretail sale price. Amendment to N.No. 1/2017-Compensation Cess (Rate), dated the 28th June 2017

COMPENSATION CESS RATE SCHEDULE-GOODS

[See Sec 8(2)]

Ref Notification No. 01/2017-Compensation Cess (Rate), dt. 28-06-2017

S. No.	Chapter/Heading/Sub-heading/Tariff item	Description of Goods	Rate of goods and services tax compensation cess
(1)	(2)	(3)	(4)
1.	2106 90 20	Pan-masala with declared retail price	0.32R per unit
1A.	2106 90 20	Pan Masala, other than goods covered under S. No. 1 above	60%
2.	2202 10 10	Aerated waters	12%
3.	2202 10 20	Lemonade	12%
4.	2202 10 90	Others	12%
4A.	2202 99 90	Caffeinated Beverages	12%
4B.	2202	Carbonated Beverages of Fruit Drink or Carbonated Beverages with Fruit Juice	12%
5.	2401	Unmanufactured tobacco (without lime tube) bearing a brand name	0.36R per unit
5A.	2401	Unmanufactured tobacco (with lime tube)–bearing a brand name, other than goods covered under S. No.6 above	65%
6.	2401	Unmanufactured tobacco (with lime tube) – bearing a brand name with declared retail price	0.36R per unit
7.	2401 30 00	Tobacco refuse, bearing a brand name with declared retail price	0.32R per unit

S. No.	Chapter/Heading/Sub-heading/Tariff item	Description of Goods	Rate of goods and services tax compensation cess
7A.	2401 30 00	Tobacco refuse, bearing a brand name, other than goods covered under S. No. 7 above	61%
8.	2402 10 10	Cigar and cheroots	21% or ₹ 4170 per thousand, whichever is higher
9.	2402 10 20	Cigarillos	21% or ₹ 4170 per thousand, whichever is higher
10.	2402 20 10	Cigarettes containing tobacco other than filter cigarettes, of length not exceeding 65 millimetres	5% + ₹ 2076 per thousand
11.	2402 20 20	Cigarettes containing tobacco other than filter cigarettes, of length exceeding 65 millimetres but not exceeding 75 millimetres	5% + ₹ 3668 per thousand
12.	2402 20 30	Filter cigarettes of length (including the length of the filter, the length of filter being 11 millimetres or its actual length, whichever is more) not exceeding 65 millimetres	5% + ₹ 2076 per thousand
13.	2402 20 40	Filter cigarettes of length (including the length of the filter, the length of filter being 11 millimetres or its actual length, whichever is more) exceeding 65 millimetres but not exceeding 70 millimetres	5% + ₹ 2747 per thousand
14.	2402 20 50	Filter cigarettes of length (including the length of the filter, the length of filter being 11 millimetres or its actual length, whichever is more) exceeding 70 millimetres but not exceeding 75 millimetres	5% + ₹ 3668 per thousand
15.	2402 20 90	Other cigarettes containing tobacco	36% + ₹ 4170 per thousand
16.	2402 90 10	Cigarettes of tobacco substitutes	₹ 4006 per thousand
17.	2402 90 20	Cigarillos of tobacco substitutes	12.5% or ₹ 4,006 per thousand whichever is higher
18.	2402 90 90	Other	12.5% or ₹ 4,006 per thousand whichever is higher
19.	2403 11 10	'Hookah' or 'gudaku' tobacco bearing a brand name with declared retail sale price	0.36R per unit
19A.	2403 11 10	'Hookah' or 'gudaku' tobacco, bearing a brand name, other than goods covered under S. No. 19 above	72%
20.	2403 11 10	Tobacco used for smoking 'hookah' or 'chilam' commonly known as 'hookah' tobacco or 'gudaku' not bearing a brand name with declared retail sale price	0.12R per unit
20A.	2403 11 10	Tobacco used for smoking 'hookah' or 'chilam' commonly known as 'hookah' tobacco or 'gudaku', not bearing a brand name, other than goods covered under S. No. 20 above	17%
21.	2403 11 90	Other water pipe smoking tobacco not bearing a brand name with declared retail sale price	0.08R per unit

S. No.	Chapter/Heading/Sub-heading/Tariff item	Description of Goods	Rate of goods and services tax compensation cess
21A.	2403 11 90	Other water pipe smoking tobacco, not bearing a brand name, other than goods covered under S. No. 21 above	11%
22.	2403 19 10	Smoking mixtures for pipes and cigarettes with declared retail sale price	0.69R per unit
22A.	2403 19 10	Smoking mixtures for pipes and cigarettes, other than goods covered under S. No. 22 above	290%
23.	2403 19 90	Other smoking tobacco bearing a brand name with declared retail sale price	0.28R per unit
23A.	2403 19 90	Other smoking tobacco bearing a brand name, other than goods covered under S. No. 23 above	49%
24.	2403 19 90	Other smoking tobacco not bearing a brand name with declared retail sale price	0.08R per unit
24A.	2403 19 90	Other smoking tobacco, not bearing a brand name, other than goods covered under S. No. 24 above	11%
24B.	2403 91 00	"Homogenised" or "reconstituted" tobacco, bearing a brand name with declared retail sale price	0.36R per unit
24C.	2403 91 00	"Homogenised" or "reconstituted" tobacco, bearing a brand name, other goods covered under S. No. 24 B above	72%
25.	2404 11 00	"Homogenised" or "reconstituted" tobacco, bearing a brand name	72%
26.	2403 99 10	Chewing tobacco (without lime tube) with declared retail sale price	0.56R per unit
26A.	2403 99 10	Chewing tobacco (without lime tube), other than goods covered under S. No. 26 above	160%
27.	2403 99 10	Chewing tobacco (with lime tube) with declared retail sale price	0.56R per unit
27A.	2403 99 10	Chewing tobacco (with lime tube), other than goods covered under S. No. 27 above	142%
28.	2403 99 10	Filter khaini with declared retail sale price	0.56R per unit
28A.	2403 99 10	Filter khaini, other than goods covered under S. No. 28 above	160%
29.	2403 99 20	Preparations containing chewing tobacco with declared retail sale price	0.36R per unit
29A.	2403 99 20	Preparations containing chewing tobacco, other than goods covered under S. No. 29 above	72%
30.	2403 99 30	Jarda scented tobacco with declared retail sale price	0.56R per unit
30A.	2403 99 30	Jarda scented tobacco, other than goods covered under S. No. 30 above	160%
31.	2403 99 40	Snuff with declared retail sale price	0.36R per unit
31A.	2403 99 40	Snuff, other than goods covered under S. No. 31 above	72%
32.	2403 99 50	Preparations containing snuff with declared retail sale price	0.36R per unit
32A.	2403 99 50	Preparations containing snuff, other than goods covered under S. No. 32 above	72%

S. No.	Chapter/Heading/Sub-heading/Tariff item	Description of Goods	Rate of goods and services tax compensation cess
33.	2403 99 60	Tobacco extracts and essence bearing a brand name with declared retail sale price	0.36R per unit
33A.	2403 99 60	Tobacco extracts and essence, bearing a brand name, other than good covered under S. No. 33 above	72%
34.	2403 99 60	Tobacco extracts and essence not bearing a brand Name with declared retail sale price	0.36R per unit
34A.	2403 99 60	Tobacco extracts and essence, not bearing a brand name, other than goods covered under S. No. 34 above	65%
35.	2403 99 70	Cut tobacco with declared retail sale price	0.14R per unit
35A.	2403 99 70	Cut tobacco, other than goods covered under S. No. 35 above	20%
36.	2403 99 90	Pan masala containing tobacco 'Gutkha' with declared retail sale price	0.61R per unit
36A.	2403 99 90	Pan masala containing tobacco 'Gutkha', other than goods covered under S. No. 36 above	204%
36B.	2403 99 90	All goods, other than pan masala containing tobacco 'gutkha', bearing a brand name, with declared retail sale price	0.43R per unit
36C.	2403 99 90	All goods, other than pan masala containing tobacco 'gutkha', bearing a brand name, other than good covered under S.No.36B above	96%
36D.	2403 99 90	All goods, other than pan masala containing tobacco 'gutkha', not bearing a brand name, with declared retail sale price	0.43R per unit
36E.	2403 99 90	All goods, other than pan masala containing tobacco 'gutkha', not bearing a brand name, other than goods covered under S. No. 36D above	89%
37.	2404 11 00 or 2404 19 00	All goods, other than pan masala containing tobacco 'gutkha', bearing a brand name	96%
38.	2404 11 00 or 2404 19 00	All goods, other than pan masala containing tobacco 'gutkha', not bearing a brand name	89%
39.	2701	Coal; briquettes, ovoids and similar solid fuels manufactured from coal	₹ 400 per tonne
40.	2702	Lignite, whether or not agglomerated, excluding jet	₹ 400 per tonne
41.	2703	Peat (including peat litter), whether or not agglomerated	₹ 400 per tonne
41A.	27	Coal rejects supplied by a coal washery, arising out of coal on which compensation cess has been paid and no input tax credit thereof has not been availed by any person	NIL
42.	8702 10	Motor vehicles for the transport of not more than thirteen persons, including the driver	15%
42A.	87	All old and used motor vehicles	NIL
42B.	87	Fuel Cell Motor Vehicles	NIL
43.	8702 or 8703	Motor vehicles cleared as ambulances duly fitted with all the fitments, furniture and accessories necessary for an ambulance from the factory manufacturing such motor vehicles	NIL

S. No.	Chapter/Heading/Sub-heading/Tariff item	Description of Goods	Rate of goods and services tax compensation cess
44.	8703 10 10, 8703 80	Electrically operated vehicles, including three wheeled electric motor vehicles	NIL
45.	8703	Three-wheeled vehicles	NIL
46.	8703	Following motor vehicles of length not exceeding 4000mm, namely: (a) Petrol, Liquefied petroleum gases (LPG) or compressed natural gas (CNG) driven vehicles of engine capacity not exceeding 1200cc; and (b) Diesel driven vehicle of engine capacity not exceeding 1500cc for persons with orthopedic physical disability subject to the condition that an officer not below the rank of deputy secretary to the Government of India in the department of heavy industries certifies that the said goods shall be used by the person with orthopedic physical disability in accordance with the guidelines issued by the said department.	NIL
47.	8703 40, 8703 50,	Following vehicles, with both spark-ignition internal combustion reciprocating piston engine and electric motor as motors for propulsion: (a) Motor vehicles cleared as ambulances duly fitted with all the fitments, furniture and accessories necessary for an ambulance from the factory manufacturing such motor vehicles (b) Three-wheeled vehicles (c) Motor vehicles of engine capacity not exceeding 1200 cc and of length not exceeding 4000 mm (d) Motor vehicles other than those mentioned at (a), (b) and (c) above. **Explanation:** For the purposes of this entry, the specification of the motor vehicle shall be determined as per the Motor Vehicles Act, 1988 (59 of 1988) and the rules made there under	 NIL NIL NIL 15%
48.	8703 60, 8703 70	Following vehicles, with both compression-ignition internal combustion piston engine (diesel or semi-diesel) and electric motor as motors for propulsion: (a) Motor vehicles cleared as ambulances duly fitted with all the fitments, furniture and accessories necessary for an ambulance from the factory manufacturing such motor vehicles (b) Three-wheeled vehicles (c) Motor vehicles of engine capacity not exceeding 1500 cc and of length not exceeding 4000 mm (d) Motor vehicles other than those mentioned at (a), (b) and (c) above. **Explanation:** For the purposes of this entry, the specification of the motor vehicle shall be determined as per the Motor Vehicles Act, 1988 (59 of 1988) and the rules made there under.	 NIL NIL NIL NIL

S. No.	Chapter/Heading/Sub-heading/Tariff item	Description of Goods	Rate of goods and services tax compensation cess
49.	8703	Hydrogen vehicles based on fuel cell tech and of length not exceeding 4000 mm. **Explanation.** For the purposes of this entry, the specification of the motor vehicle shall be determined as per the Motor Vehicles Act, 1988 (59 of 1988) and the rules made thereunder.	NIL
50.	8703 21 or 8703 22	Petrol, liquefied petroleum gases (LPG) or compressed natural gas (CNG) driven motor vehicles of engine capacity not exceeding 1200 cc and of length not exceeding 4000 mm. **Explanation.** For the purposes of this entry, the specification of the motor vehicle shall be determined as per the Motor Vehicles Act, 1988 (59 of 1988) and the rules made thereunder.	1%
51.	8702, 8703 31	Diesel driven motor vehicles of engine capacity not exceeding 1500 cc and of length not exceeding 4000 mm. **Explanation:** For the purposes of this entry, the specification of the motor vehicle shall be determined as per the Motor Vehicles Act, 1988 (59 of 1988) and the rules made thereunder.	3%
52.	8703	Motor vehicles of engine capacity not exceeding 1500 cc	17%
52A.	8703	Motor vehicles of engine capacity exceeding 1500 cc other than motor vehicles specified against entry at S. No 52B	20%
52B.	8703	Motor vehicles known as Utility Vehicles, by whatever name called including Sports Utility Vehicles (SUV), Multi Utility Vehicles (MUV), Multi-purpose vehicles (MPV) or Cross-Over Utility Vehicles(XUV), with engine capacity exceeding 1500cc; Length exceeding 4000 mm and Ground Clearance of 170 mm and above	22%
53.	8711	Motorcycles of engine capacity exceeding 350 cc.	3%
54.	8802 or 8806	Other aircraft (for example, helicopters, aeroplanes), for personal use.	3%
55.	8903	Yacht and other vessels for pleasure or sports	3%

Note: "R" appearing in column (4) means "retail sale price" as provided in the Schedule to the Goods and Services Tax (Compensation to States) Act, 2017 (15 of 2017)

Illustration: Calculation of goods and services tax compensation cess on Pan Masala (S. No. 1 in the Schedule above):

Rate of goods and services tax compensation cess = 0.32R per unit;

If retail sale price of unit (pouch) of Pan Masala = ₹ 10;

Goods and services tax compensation cess leviable = 0.32R = 0.32*10 = ₹ 3.2 per unit (pouch).

COMPENSATION CESS RATE SCHEDULE-SERVICES

[See Sec 8(2)]

Ref Notification No. 02/2017-Compensation Cess (Rate), dt. 28-06-2017

Sl No.	Description of supply of services	Chapter, section, heading or group as the case may be	The maximum rate (%) at which goods & services tax compensation cess may be collected
(1)	(2)	(3)	(4)
1	Transfer of the right to use any goods for any purpose (whether or not for a specified period) for cash, deferred payment or other valuable consideration	Chapter 99	Same rate of cess as applicable on supply of similar goods involving transfer of title in goods
2	Transfer of right in goods or of undivided share in goods without the transfer of title thereof	Chapter 99	Same rate of cess as applicable on supply of similar goods involving transfer of title in goods
3	Any other supply of services	Chapter 99	NIL

Part-III

Articles of Constitutions of India

Article No.	Description
1(1)	India is Union of States
148	C&AG Audit
243G	Functions entrusted to Panchayat
243W	Functions entrusted to Municipality
245	Bifurcation of Power between Union and States
246A	Concurrent power to Union and States to levy GST
248	Residual powers with Parliament
265	Taxation Powers-Limitations under Constitution
268 to 271	Distribution of Revenue between Union and States
269A	IGST for inter-state supply
269A(1)	Apportionment of IGST between Union and States
269A(2)	Powers to determine place of supply and interstate supply
279A	Council of GST
286	Restriction on power of taxation
301 to 303	Inter-state Trade and commerce—No restrictions
366(12)	Definitions of "goods"
366(12A)	Definitions of "GST"
366(26A)	Definitions of "service"
366(29A)	Deemed sale of goods under Constitution

Article 1(1): India is Union of states: Article 1(1) in the Constitution states that India, that is Bharat, shall be a Union of States.

Article 148: C&AG Audit: The Comptroller and Auditor General of India (CAG) is the Constitutional Authority in India, established under Article 148 of the Constitution of India. The prime responsibility of this authority is to audit the receipts and expenditures of the state governments and the union government in India including those of the entities and corporations financed by the government. The reports generated by the CAG are crucially important for the Public Accounts Committees (PACs) and Committees on Public Undertakings (COPUs), which are part of the state and Central Governments. The CAG of India only performed the role of an Auditor General and not of a Comptroller. It means audit by this office is not an administrative but a financial audit.

Article 243G: Functions entrusted to Panchayat: The functions entrusted to a Panchayat under the Eleventh Schedule to Article 243G of the Constitution are as under:

(i) Agriculture, including agricultural extension.
(ii) Land improvement, implementation of land reforms, land consolidation and soil conservation.
(iii) Minor irrigation, water management and watershed development.

(iv) Animal husbandry, dairying and poultry.
(v) Fisheries.
(vi) Social forestry and farm forestry.
(vii) Minor forest produce.
(viii) Small scale industries, including food processing industries.
(ix) Khadi, village and cottage industries.
(x) Rural housing.
(xi) Drinking water.
(xii) Fuel and fodder.
(xiii) Roads, culverts, bridges, ferries, waterways and other means of communication.
(xiv) Rural electrification, including distribution of electricity.
(xv) Non-conventional energy sources.
(xvi) Poverty alleviation programme.
(xvii) Education, including primary and secondary schools.
(xviii) Technical training and vocational education.
(xix) Adult and non-formal education.
(xx) Libraries.
(xxi) Cultural activities.
(xxii) Markets and fairs.
(xxiii) Health and sanitation, including hospitals, primary health centres and dispensaries.
(xxiv) Family welfare.
(xxv) Women and child development.
(xxvi) Social welfare, including welfare of the handicapped and mentally retarded.
(xxvii) Welfare of the weaker sections, and in particular, of the Scheduled Castes and the Scheduled Tribes.
(xxviii) Public distribution system.
(xxix) Maintenance of community assets.

Article 243W: Functions entrusted to Municipality: The functions entrusted to a municipality under the Twelfth Schedule to Article 243W of the Constitution are as under:

(a) Urban planning including town planning. (b) Regulation of land-use and construction of buildings. (c) Planning for economic and social development. (d) Roads and bridges. (e) Water supply for domestic, industrial and commercial purposes. (f) Public health, sanitation conservancy and solid waste management. (g) Fire services. (h) Urban forestry, protection of the environment and promotion of ecological aspects. (i) Safeguarding the interests of weaker sections of society, including the handicapped and mentally retarded. (j) Slum improvement and upgradation. (k) Urban poverty alleviation. (l) Provision of urban amenities and facilities such as parks, gardens, playgrounds. (m) Promotion of cultural, educational and aesthetic aspects. (n) Burials and burial grounds; cremations, cremation grounds; and electric crematoriums. (o) Cattle pounds; prevention of cruelty to animals. (p) Vital statistics including registration of births and deaths. (q) Public amenities including street lighting, parking lots, bus stops and public conveniences. (r) Regulation of slaughter houses and tanneries.

Article 245: Bifurcation of Power between Union & States: India, in the Constitution, has been described as a federation of States. Indian Constitution provides for three lists for distribution of legislative and executive power between the Center and the States; i.e.

1. the Union (Central) List,
2. the State List, and
3. the Concurrent List (subjects within the ambit of the Union Government and the State Governments).

Articles 268 to 293 deal with the provisions of financial relation between Centre and states. The Constitution divides the taxing powers between the Centre and the states. The Parliament has exclusive power to levy taxes on subjects enumerated in the Union list, the state legislature has exclusive power to levy taxes on subjects enumerated in the State list, both can levy taxes on subjects enumerated in the concurrent list, whereas residuary power of taxation lies with parliament only.

Article 246A: Concurrent power to Union and States to levy GST: The Constitution (101st Amendment) Act, 2016 which came to operation w.e.f. 16th September 2016 inserted new Article 246A which makes enabling provisions for the Union and States with respect to the GST legislation. It further specifies that Parliament has exclusive power to make laws with respect to GST on inter State supplies.

Article 248: Residual powers with Parliament: (1) Subject to Article 246A, Parliament has exclusive power to make any law with respect to any matter not enumerated in the Concurrent List or State List.

(2) Such power shall include the power of making any law imposing a tax not mentioned in either of those Lists.

Article 265: Taxation Powers—Limitations under Constitution: Taxes not to be imposed save by authority of law. No tax shall be levied or collected except by authority of law.

The schemes of allocation of taxing powers between the Centre and the States is based on the broad principle that the taxes of a local nature have been allotted to the States while taxes which having a tax base extending over more than one State, or which should be levied on a uniform basis throughout the country and not vary from State to State, or which can be collected more conveniently by the Centre rather than the States have been allotted to the entre.

Articles 268-271: Distribution of Revenue between Union & States: There are few Articles in the Indian Constitution which specifically focuses on distribution of revenues.

(a) Article 268: Duties levied by the Union but collected and appropriated by the States
(b) Article 269: Taxes levied and collected by the Union but assigned to the States
(c) Article 270: Taxes levied and distributed between Union and States
(d) Article 271: Surcharge on certain duties and taxes for purposes of the Union

Article 268 refers to stamp duties. The proceeds of any such duty leviable within any State in any financial year shall not form part of the consolidated Fund of India but shall be assigned to that State.

Article 268A provided that tax on services shall be apportioned between Union and States. [Omitted w.e.f. 16-9-2016 due to introduction of GST]

Article 269: Taxes levied and collected by the Union but assigned to the States.

Taxes which shall be levied and collected by the Government of India which are included in this Article:

(a) the consignment of goods which takes place in the course of inter-state trade or commerce,
(b) sale or purchase of goods, which takes place in the course of inter-state trade or commerce.

Article 269A: IGST on inter-state supply

[Inserted vide The Constitution (101st Amendment) Act, 2016 w.e.f. 16-9-2016]

Centre to levy & collect IGST on supplies in the course of inter-State trade or commerce including imports.

(1) Goods and services tax on supplies in the course of inter-State trade or commerce shall be levied and collected by the Government of India and such tax shall be apportioned between the Union and the States in the manner as may be provided by Parliament by law on the recommendations of the Goods and Services Tax Council.

Explanation: For the purposes of this clause, supply of goods, or of services, or both in the course of import into the territory of India shall be deemed to be supply of goods, or of services, or both in the course of inter-State trade or commerce.

(2) The amount apportioned to a State under clause (1) shall not form part of the Consolidated Fund of India.

(3) Where an amount collected as tax levied under clause (1) has been used for payment of the tax levied by a State under Article 246A, such amount shall not form part of the Consolidated Fund of India.

(4) Where an amount collected as tax levied by a State under Article 246A has been used for payment of the tax levied under clause (1), such amount shall not form part of the Consolidated Fund of the State.

(5) Parliament may, by law, formulate the principles for determining the place of supply, and when a supply of goods, or of services, or both takes place in the course of inter-State trade or commerce.

Article 279A: Council of GST: Article 279A of the Constitution empowers the president to constitute a joint forum of the central and states namely, Goods and Services Tax Council. Goods and Services Tax Council is a constitutional body for making recommendations to the Union and State Government on issues related to Goods and Service Tax. The provisions relating to GST council came into force on 12th September 2016 and President constituted GST council on 15th September 2016.

(A) Constitution of GST Council:

The GST council shall consist of the following members, namely:

(a) The Union Finance Minister is the Chairperson

(b) The Union Ministers of state in charge of Revenue of Finance is the Member

(c) The Minister in charge of Finance or Taxation or any other Minister nominated by each State Government are the Members

(B) Powers and Duties of the GST Council:

The following points describe the work responsibilities and powers of the members of the GST Council

(1) The GST Council shall make recommendations to the Union and the States on

(a) The taxes, cesses and surcharges levied by the Union, the states and the local bodies, which may be subsumed in the Goods and Services tax;

(b) The goods and services that may be subjected to, or exempted from the GST;

(c) Model GST Laws, principles of levy, apportionment of Goods and Services tax levied on supplies in the course of inter-state trade or commerce under Article 269A and the principles that govern the place of supply;

(d) The threshold limit of turnover below which goods and services may be exempted from GST;

(e) The rates including floor rates for specified period, to raise additional resources during any natural calamities or disaster;

(f) Special provision with respect to Special Category States;

(g) Any other matter relating to the goods and services tax, as the council may decide.

(2) GST Council shall recommend the date on which the goods and services tax be levied on petroleum crude, high speed diesel, motor spirit, natural gas and aviation turbine fuel.

(3) The Goods and Services tax council shall establish a mechanism to adjudicate any dispute:

(a) Between the Government of India and one or more States; or

(b) Between the Government of India and any State or States on one side and one or more other States on the other side; or

(c) Between two or more States, arising out of the recommendation of the council or implementation thereof.

(4) While discharging the functions conferred by the article, the GST Council shall be guided by the need for a harmonized structure of goods and services tax and for the development of a harmonized national market for goods and services.

(5) The GST Council shall determine the procedure in the performance of its functions.

(C) Quorum for the GST Council Meetings:

One-half of the total number of the members of the GST Council shall constitute the quorum at its meeting.

(D) Voting Powers of the GST Council Meetings:

Every decision of the GST Council shall be taken at a meeting, by a majority of not less than three-fourths of the weighted votes of the members present and voting, in accordance with the following principles, namely:-

(a) The votes of Central Government shall have a weightage of one-third of total votes cast, and

(b) The votes of all State Governments taken together shall have a weightage of two-thirds of the total votes cast, in that meeting.

Article 286: Restriction on power of taxation: The State has like the Union, power to levy tax on supply of goods or services or both other than of newspapers. Article 286 however imposes the following restrictions on the State's power to impose tax on goods or services.

(a) Article 286 (1) (a) prohibits a state to impose a tax on the supply of goods or services or both which take place outside the State i.e. inter-state supply of goods or services or both.

(b) Article 286(1) (b) prohibits State to impose tax in the course of import of goods and services or export of goods and services out of the territory of India.

Articles 301-303: Inter-state Trade & commerce—No restrictions: Article 301 talks about the freedom of trade, commerce, and intercourse throughout the country. It states that subject to other provisions under Part XIII, the freedom to carry on these activities shall be free. Freedom here means the right to freedom of movement of persons, property, things that may be tangible or intangible, unobstructed by barriers within the state (intra-state) or across the states (inter-state).

Article 302 gives power to the Parliament to impose restrictions on the freedom of trade, commerce or intercourse carried on within a state or across states anywhere in the territory of India. These restrictions can solely be imposed taking into due consideration the interests of the public. The power to decide whether something is in the interest of the public or not is solely given to the Parliament.

Article 303(1) states that the Parliament does not have the power to make any law, which will keep one State at a more preferable position than the other State, by virtue of any entry in trade and commerce in any one of the lists in 7th Schedule. However, clause (2) states that the Parliament can do so if it is proclaimed by law that it is essential to make such provisions or regulations, as there is indeed a scarcity of goods in some parts of the country. The power to decide whether there is a scarcity of goods in some parts of the territory or not is vested in the hands of the Parliament.

Article 366(12): Definitions of "goods": "Goods" includes all materials, commodities, and articles.

Article 366(12A): Definitions of "GST": "Goods and services tax" to mean any tax on supply of goods or services or both except taxes on the supply of the alcoholic liquor for human consumption."

Article 366(26A): Definitions of "services": The Constitution (101 Amendment) Act, 2016 inserted in clause 366(26A) the definition of "services" to mean anything other than goods.

Section 2(102) of CGST Act, 2017 define "services" means anything other than goods, money and securities but includes activities relating to the use of money or its conversion by cash or by any other mode, from one form, currency or denomination, to another form, currency or denomination for which a separate consideration is charged.

Explanation: For the removal of doubts, it is hereby clarified that the expression "services" includes facilitating or arranging transactions in securities.

Article 366(29A): Deemed sale of goods under Constitution: 'Sale' includes a delivery of goods on hire-purchase or any system of payment by instalments. This is 'deemed sale' and is taxable.

Schedule II of the CGST Act, 2017 classifies certain supplies as 'goods' or 'services'. Out of the matters listed in clause (29A) of Article 366, which deems certain transactions as sale of goods, GST Law treats (i) works contract, (ii) transfer of right to use goods and, (iii) supply of goods, being food etc. as part of any service, as service. Paragraph 5(f) dealing with transfer of right to use goods and paragraph 6 (b) dealing with supply of goods, being food, etc. as part of any service, the words used in the clause are almost identical to the words contained in clause (29A) which is apparent from use of words "for cash, deferred payment or other valuable consideration".

GST REVENUE COLLECTION

(₹ in Crores)

Month	2022-23	2021-22	2020-21	2019-20
April	167540	139708	32294	113865
May	140885	97821	62009	100289
June	144616	92800	90917	99938
July	148995	116393	87422	102083
August	143612	112020	86449	98203
September	147686	117010	95480	91917
October	151718	130127	105155	95380
November	145867	131526	104963	103491
December	149507	129780	115174	103184
January	157554	140986	119875	110818
February	149577	133026	113143	105366
March	160122	142095	123902	97597
Annual average	**149722**	**123608**	**94731.91**	**101844**

Acronyms

Acronym	Full Form
ARN	Application Reference Number
ASP	Application Service Provider
AA	Appellate Authority
AAR	Authority for Advance Ruling
B2B	Business to Business
B2C	Business to Customer
CBIC	Central Board of Indirect Taxes & Customs
CGST	Central Goods & Services Tax
CTP	Casual Taxable Person
CPIN	Common Portal Identification Number (14 digit)
CIN	Challan Identification Number (17 digit)
CKD	Completely knocked Down
DCA	Del-Credere Agent
DSA	Direct Selling Agents
DTA	Domestic Tariff Area
EBN	E-Way Bill Number
ECL	Electronic Cash Ledger
ELR	Electronic Liability Register
E-TIN	E Commerce Operator TIN
EGM	Export General Manifest
E-FPB	Electronic Focal Point Branch
FAA	First Appellate Authority
FORM RFD	Refund Form
FC	Facilitation Centre
FSI	Floor Space Index
GSP	GST Suvida Provider
GST	Goods & Services Tax
GSTAT	GST Appellate Tribunal
GSTR	Goods & Services Tax Return
GSTN	Goods & Services Tax Network
GSTIN	Goods & Services Taxpayers Identification Number (15 Digits)
HSN	Harmonized System of Nomenclature
ICEGATE	Indian Customs Electronic Gateway
IFF	Invoice Furnishing Facility
IGST	Integrated Goods & Services Tax

IMPS	Immediate Payment services
IRP	Invoice Registration Portal
IRN	Invoice Reference Number
ISD	Input Service Distributors
ITC	Input Tax Credit
MSP	Managed Service Provider
NAPA	National Anti-profiteering Authority
NAAAR	National Appellate Authority for Advance Ruling
NRTP	Non-Resident Taxable Person
NIU	National Information Utility
OCPB	Over the Counter Payment in Branches
ODC	Over Dimensional Cargo
OIDAR	Online Information & Data base Access and Retrieval Services
PO	Proper Officer
POS	Place of Supply (of Goods or Services)
PLC	Prime Location Charges
PSLC	Priority Sector Lending Certificate
QRMP	Quarterly Return Monthly Payment
RCM	Reverse Charge Mechanism
REP	Real Estate Project
RREP	Residential Real Estate Project
RFID	Radio Frequency Identification Device
RNR	Revenue Neutral Rate
RWA	Resident Welfare Association
SAC	Services Accounting Code (Six digits)
SCN	Show Cause Notice
SEZ	Special Economic Zone
SGST	State Goods & Services Tax
SKD	Semi Knocked Down
TDR	Transferable Development Rights
TDF	Transit Declaration Form
TRU	Tax Research Unit
UTGST	Union Territory Goods & Services Tax
UID	Unique Identification
UIN	Unique Identity Number (For foreign Embassy or Agencies)
UPI	Unified Payment System
UQC	Unit Quantity Code (Unit of Measurement)
WCO	World Customs Organisation

Index

L

M

N

O

P

R

S

T

V

W